HINSHAW'S
Historical Index
of
WINCHESTER INDIANA
Newspapers
1857–1984

Gregory P. Hinshaw

HERITAGE BOOKS
2009

HERITAGE BOOKS
AN IMPRINT OF HERITAGE BOOKS, INC.

Books, CDs, and more—Worldwide

For our listing of thousands of titles see our website
at
www.HeritageBooks.com

Published 2009 by
HERITAGE BOOKS, INC.
Publishing Division
100 Railroad Ave. #104
Westminster, Maryland 21157

Copyright © 2009 Gregory P. Hinshaw

All rights reserved. No part of this book may be reproduced or transmitted in any form or by any means, electronic or mechanical, including photocopying, recording or by any information storage and retrieval system without written permission from the author, except for the inclusion of brief quotations in a review.

International Standard Book Numbers
Paperbound: 978-0-7884-5013-6
Clothbound: 978-0-7884-8211-3

Foreword

Several years ago, when doing genealogy, I discovered that a wealth of information existed in the newspapers of Randolph County, Indiana. Later, when I was writing a history of my local congregation, I used the newspapers to substitute for the records of the congregation that had been lost. While researching for the sesquicentennial history of Farmland, Indiana, I read all of the available Farmland newspapers. When I wrote my doctoral dissertation on Randolph County as the model rural school system of the nation in the early years of the twentieth century, I again turned to newspapers to assist in my research. In order to tell the story completely, I decided to try to read every surviving Winchester newspaper. In retrospect, it was a heady undertaking, taking about five years to complete. It also meant reading about 20,000 issues of more than a half dozen different papers across nearly 130 years. At some point, I decided to make systematic notes of my findings. Monisa Wisener, former county historian and curator of the Randolph County Historical Museum, suggested that I make my findings available to more people, so I decided to enter them in a systematic fashion into a spreadsheet, allowing them to be sorted by category. It took an additional year (writing a dissertation in the process) to enter and revise the final product. Undoubtedly, in this work of more than 10,000 entries, there are some errors. I have diligently tried to correct all of them, but I apologize for those that I certainly must have missed.

I do apologize in advance for the violations of the historian's dedication to objectivity. The user will find this index heavily slanted toward Quakers and Republicans, categories to which I belong and in which I am interested. This is not a genealogical index, for including every genealogical reference would likely have increased its length many times over. There are other sources available that can help researchers in that area.

Among those who must be mentioned for their courtesy in helping to make this project a reality are Monisa Wisener, Lana Wolfe, former Randolph County Recorder, and Jane Grove, present Randolph County Recorder.

I am reminded of the words of Woodrow Wilson, then a professor of history, in 1895: "What is the history of a nation except the history of its villages written large?" as well as the words of Willard Heiss, well-known Indiana genealogist, who was a native of Randolph County and said of his home that it was "where the grass is a little greener and the sky is a little bluer." I hope that those who use this index will see the larger stories of American history woven through the local tales of this place in East Central Indiana.

Gregory P. Hinshaw

Organization of the Index

Each entry is categorized by subject. A summary of the entry is also included. For ease of use, the index is alphabetical first by subject, then by summary. Subject categories are:

Buildings, including information relating to notable buildings and structures in the county. Of interest are entries relating to county buildings and structures on the Courthouse Square in Winchester.

Businesses, including information relating to nearly every type of commercial enterprise in the county. Generally, the summaries are alphabetized by city or town.

Cemeteries

Churches, alphabetized first by denomination then by congregation.

Clubs/Organizations, including everything from the Red Cross to the 4-H clubs and everything in between.

Klan, an organization of short duration but of wide modern interest in historical scholarship, thus leading to its separate categorization.

Libraries

Lodges, generally alphabetized by the name of the order, then the location of the local lodge. This category includes dozens of different types of organizations.

Miscellaneous

Newspapers, the press generally commented on the rise and fall of rival newspapers in Winchester and the surrounding towns.

People, including information about activities of notable individuals in the county, as well as prominent people with local connections.

Politics, including information relating to elections, office-holding, and partisan political organization.

Post Offices
Schools
Transportation, including information about roads and highways, bridges, and railroads, electric railroads, and airports.
World War I
World War II

Newspaper Sources

Winchester Democrat, at least five different incarnations of the *Democrat* have existed. The only surviving issues are from the fourth incarnation, established in 1885 and folding in 1894, and the fifth, established in 1894. The last series continued as a weekly until 1935, when it merged with the *Winchester News* to form the *News-Democrat*, which was soon after renamed the *Winchester News*. In 1926 and 1927 a daily edition, called the ***Winchester Daily News***, was published.
Availability: Indiana State Library (Microfilm, 1885-1891, 1900-1935)

Winchester Herald, this paper, established in 1875, was a Republican weekly. It combined with the *Winchester Journal* in 1920 to form the *Winchester Journal-Herald*. Most issues since late 1885 have survived.
Availability: Indiana State Library (Microfilm, 1885-1920)
Randolph County Recorder's Office (Microfilm, 1885-1920)

Winchester Journal, this paper, established in 1843 as the *Winchester Patriot*, was the county's leading Whig, then Republican, paper. It was a weekly and was combined with the *Winchester Herald* in 1920 to form the *Winchester Journal-Herald*. Most issues of the newspaper since late 1857 have survived
Availability: Indiana State Library (Microfilm, 1857-1920)
Randolph County Historical Museum (Microfilm, 1857-1899)
Winchester Community Public Library (Microfilm, 1886-1920)
Randolph County Recorder's Office (Microfilm, 1886-1920)

Winchester Journal-Herald, this Republican paper was formed as a merger of the *Herald* and the *Journal* in 1920. It was a weekly until 1933, when it became bi-weekly. It became a daily in 1937 and continued as such until 1943, when it became a tri-weekly, being printed on Tuesday, Thursday, and Saturday. In 1968 it became the rural daily for the *News-Gazette*, continuing until 1969, when it was combined with the *News-Gazette*.

    Availability: Indiana State Library (Microfilm, 1920-1969)
                           Randolph County Historical Museum
                           (Originals, 1939-1969)
                           Winchester Community Public Library
                           (Microfilm, 1920-1968)
                           Randolph County Recorder's Office
                           (Microfilm, 1920-1968)

Winchester News, this Democratic paper was formed in 1934 as the *Winchester Daily News*. It absorbed the *Winchester Democrat* in 1935 and was known as the *Winchester News-Democrat* for a short time. It 1943 the publication was reduced to three times weekly: Monday, Wednesday, and Friday, to alternate with the *Winchester Journal-Herald*. The publication merged with the *Union City Times-Gazette* in 1968 to form the *News-Gazette*.

    Availability: Indiana State Library (Microfilm, 1936-1968)
                           Randolph County Historical Museum
                           (Originals, 1939-1968)
                           Winchester Community Public Library
                           (Microfilm, 1943-1968)
                           Randolph County Recorder's Office
                           (Microfilm, 1943-1968)

[Winchester] News-Gazette, this paper was formed from the combination of the *Winchester News* and the *Union City Times-Gazette* in 1968. It has been printed daily since that time. The *Winchester Journal-Herald* was absorbed in 1969.

The paper printed both Union City and Winchester editions for many years, and, until about 1991, offices were maintained in both cities.

Availability: Indiana State Library (Microfilm, 1968-present)
Randolph County Historical Museum (Originals, 1968-1983)
Winchester Community Public Library (Microfilm, 1968-present)
Randolph County Recorder's Office (Microfilm, 1968-present)

Date	Newspaper	Category	Summary/Subject
10/14/1891	Journal	Buildings	Bartonia, store burned
9/23/1908	Journal	Buildings	Bundy's Mill will be moved away
2/11/1920	Herald	Buildings	Carlos City, elevator burns
6/18/1884	Journal	Buildings	County Asylum, additional building to be built
7/30/1884	Journal	Buildings	County Asylum, contract for will be let tomorrow
12/17/1884	Journal	Buildings	County Asylum, improvements are nearly complete
1/22/1972	News-Gazette	Buildings	County Home, history of
9/19/1900	Herald	Buildings	County Home, new infirmary
3/1/1899	Herald	Buildings	County Home, plans for new infirmary
2/20/1970	News-Gazette	Buildings	County Hospital, addition complete
5/24/1911	Journal	Buildings	County Hospital, advocacy for
4/19/1951	Journal-Herald	Buildings	County Hospital, aerial photo of new Randolph County Hospital wing
4/9/1919	Journal	Buildings	County Hospital, already transferred to county
3/6/1919	Democrat	Buildings	County Hospital, board organized; D. E. Cox is president; Philip Kabel is secretary-treasurer; other members are John A. Shockney and G. W. Hiatt; hospital will use Voris Home
6/18/1919	Journal	Buildings	County Hospital, commissioners approve remodeling Hetty Vorhis Home into
9/16/1920	Democrat	Buildings	County Hospital, contracts awarded
2/13/1918	Herald	Buildings	County Hospital, County Hospital may be built with J. D. Miller donation
5/22/1918	Herald	Buildings	County Hospital, erection postponed
6/18/1919	Herald	Buildings	County Hospital, Hetty Vorhis Home to be converted into
11/25/1953	News	Buildings	County Hospital, new wing of Randolph County Hospital is completed
8/21/1936	News-Democrat	Buildings	County Hospital, photos and history
8/13/1919	Herald	Buildings	County Hospital, plan to remodel Hetty Vorhis home into
12/8/1969	News-Gazette	Buildings	County Hospital, Winchester, hospital, history of [UC Edition]
1/30/1969	Journal-Herald	Buildings	County Hospital, Winchester, hospital, new wing
2/7/1969	Journal-Herald	Buildings	County Hospital, Winchester, hospital, new wing
11/1/1968	Journal-Herald	Buildings	County Hospital, Winchester, hospital, plans for addition
6/12/1970	News-Gazette	Buildings	County Hospital, Winchester, hospital, will be dedicated on June 14
5/24/1899	Journal	Buildings	County Infirmary, bids for
4/5/1899	Journal	Buildings	County Infirmary, bids to build

Date	Source	Category	Description
6/7/1871	Journal	Buildings	County Office Building, roof repaired
4/2/1983	News-Gazette	Buildings	Courthouse featured in Saturday Extra
9/26/1877	Journal	Buildings	Courthouse has no heat
5/9/1877	Journal	Buildings	Courthouse is being "rodded"
6/6/1883	Journal	Buildings	Courthouse is being repainted
7/11/1877	Journal	Buildings	Courthouse issues: hitch racks, stoves, gilt-edged pumpkins
12/13/1871	Journal	Buildings	Courthouse opposed; county owned interest in City Hall
5/16/1883	Journal	Buildings	Courthouse to be repainted
5/1/1939	Journal-Herald	Buildings	Courthouse tower
5/2/1939	Journal-Herald	Buildings	Courthouse tower
5/3/1939	Journal-Herald	Buildings	Courthouse tower
9/27/1941	Journal-Herald	Buildings	Courthouse tower poem
1/16/1901	Herald	Buildings	Courthouse tower should be removed
2/16/1939	Journal-Herald	Buildings	Courthouse tower will be removed during remodeling
7/18/1939	Journal-Herald	Buildings	Courthouse tower, is it an idol?
4/11/1877	Journal	Buildings	Courthouse was not accepted from contractor on March 28
3/28/1877	Journal	Buildings	Courthouse will be accepted from contractor today
1/16/1889	Journal	Buildings	Courthouse will be heated by natural gas
7/25/1877	Journal	Buildings	Courthouse will be occupied on the first proximate [August 1, 1877]
8/9/1939	Journal-Herald	Buildings	Courthouse will not be remodeled by WPA
6/12/1954	Journal-Herald	Buildings	Courthouse, "Twon't be long now!"
11/28/1877	Journal	Buildings	Courthouse, 24-light chandelier in courtroom; and steam heat
10/27/1880	Journal	Buildings	Courthouse, 3000 pound bell was carried in Sesquicentennial parade in Baltimore
6/18/1884	Journal	Buildings	Courthouse, auditor, new safe for office
1/13/1892	Journal	Buildings	Courthouse, auditor's office, new safe has arrived
3/12/1936	News-Democrat	Buildings	Courthouse, automatic clock winder received
1/5/1881	Journal	Buildings	Courthouse, bell is not loud
1/20/1916	Democrat	Buildings	Courthouse, bell rang in windstorm; first ringing since 1914; Republicans said it was a sign that Providence was pleased with their return to power
11/13/1918	Journal	Buildings	Courthouse, bell was rung to celebrate the armistice
1/12/1980	News-Gazette	Buildings	Courthouse, bell, history of

Date	Source	Category	Description
4/29/1874	Journal	Buildings	Courthouse, bell, old iron bell that hung on four posts on Courthouse Square has been taken to Cincinnati for repairs
7/29/1954	Journal-Herald	Buildings	Courthouse, bell, photo of
6/23/1875	Journal	Buildings	Courthouse, bids for; described as 76 x 111 with 156 foot tower
10/24/1877	Journal	Buildings	Courthouse, boilers placed in
8/8/1877	Journal	Buildings	Courthouse, building on north side of Courthouse should be torn down
10/25/1911	Journal	Buildings	Courthouse, cannon to be mounted on the Square
5/28/1884	Journal	Buildings	Courthouse, cannons, J. K. Martin moved cannons from Square to cemetery
9/27/1975	News-Gazette	Buildings	Courthouse, centennial of cornerstone
7/20/1865	Journal	Buildings	Courthouse, Chain put up around Public Square
1/13/1915	Journal	Buildings	Courthouse, chandelier in courtroom is removed after forty years of use
2/7/1883	Journal	Buildings	Courthouse, changes in court room
8/14/1912	Journal	Buildings	Courthouse, Charles Puckett replaces George Ennis as custodian
6/13/1877	Journal	Buildings	Courthouse, Charley Horn is superintendent of brick work
9/2/1979	News-Gazette	Buildings	Courthouse, Civil War Monument
9/23/1980	News-Gazette	Buildings	Courthouse, Civil War Monument, new sword
1/26/1961	Journal-Herald	Buildings	Courthouse, clerk's office moves to third floor
7/2/1954	News	Buildings	Courthouse, clock
11/19/1890	Herald	Buildings	Courthouse, clock changed back to sun time
10/15/1890	Herald	Buildings	Courthouse, clock changed from sun to standard time
10/31/1883	Journal	Buildings	Courthouse, clock for tower is being placed in position
7/24/1901	Journal	Buildings	Courthouse, clock has stopped
12/20/1893	Journal	Buildings	Courthouse, clock is not running
1/27/1915	Journal	Buildings	Courthouse, clock is running occasionally; no chimes
11/7/1883	Journal	Buildings	Courthouse, clock is working, has a ninety pound hammer
6/24/1954	Journal-Herald	Buildings	Courthouse, clock last struck at 10 a.m. on June 24, 1954
8/18/1886	Journal	Buildings	Courthouse, clock stopped
11/26/1890	Journal	Buildings	Courthouse, clock taken off standard time
10/9/1942	Journal-Herald	Buildings	Courthouse, clock weights go to scrap drive
10/3/1883	Journal	Buildings	Courthouse, clock will be placed in position in a few days

Date	Source	Category	Description
8/29/1883	Journal	Buildings	Courthouse, clock, bids for will be received next week
9/12/1883	Journal	Buildings	Courthouse, clock, F. M. Herron of Indianapolis will supply a No. 18 Seth Thomas clock for the Courthouse for $1300
9/26/1883	Journal	Buildings	Courthouse, clock, platform for is being made ready
3/26/1936	News-Democrat	Buildings	Courthouse, clock, work on begins
5/7/1919	Journal	Buildings	Courthouse, commissioners approve plan to remove courthouse tower and to accept hospital
3/20/1889	Journal	Buildings	Courthouse, commissioners approved building Soldiers' Monument
12/15/1880	Journal	Buildings	Courthouse, commissioners are considering closing north and south entrances to the Courthouse and putting in vaults
12/14/1865	Journal	Buildings	Courthouse, Commissioners ordered sale of old courthouse and brick privy to highest bidder in January
6/6/1888	Journal	Buildings	Courthouse, commissioners' room is altered
12/3/1902	Herald	Buildings	Courthouse, complaints about town clock not working
9/29/1875	Journal	Buildings	Courthouse, cornerstone laying
9/22/1875	Journal	Buildings	Courthouse, cornerstone laying program
9/8/1875	Journal	Buildings	Courthouse, cornerstone laying, Colonel R. W. Thompson will speak
9/15/1875	Journal	Buildings	Courthouse, cornerstone will be laid on September 28, 1875
7/18/1917	Journal	Buildings	Courthouse, county agent will get half of surveyor's room; partition will be put in
6/16/1927	Democrat	Buildings	Courthouse, county auditor has plans to remove the courthouse tower and add a third story with a flat roof; the "steeple" rocks in the wind and is a firetrap
9/13/1871	Journal	Buildings	Courthouse, County Commissioners have meeting to discuss plans
9/27/1871	Journal	Buildings	Courthouse, County Commissioners visit Covington, Ohio to see Courthouse
4/2/1919	Journal	Buildings	Courthouse, county council made appropriation to remove courthouse tower
12/24/1873	Journal	Buildings	Courthouse, County Office Building, lettering on the side said "IOOF"
11/22/1882	Journal	Buildings	Courthouse, County Superintendent Lesley and Surveyor Russell have moved into the old Sheriff's Office

Date	Source	Category	Description
6/12/1878	Journal	Buildings	Courthouse, county superintendent's office has been removed to Grand Jury Room; old office will be occupied by records and papers of the treasurer
1/13/1915	Journal	Buildings	Courthouse, courtroom ordered to be altered by Judge Shockney; newspaper says that the tower should be removed
2/7/1882	Journal	Buildings	Courthouse, courtroom renovated
10/25/1928	Democrat	Buildings	Courthouse, dedication of war memorial planned
5/4/1954	Journal-Herald	Buildings	Courthouse, drawing of remodeled courthouse
8/16/1882	Journal	Buildings	Courthouse, driven well being installed
6/28/1952	Journal-Herald	Buildings	Courthouse, editorial calls tower a "firetrap"
11/18/1874	Journal	Buildings	Courthouse, editorial favors building a new courthouse
2/5/1944	Journal-Herald	Buildings	Courthouse, editorial favors new courthouse
6/14/1916	Journal	Buildings	Courthouse, effort to put the courthouse clock back in order; many are homesick to hear the bell
7/5/1916	Journal	Buildings	Courthouse, flagpole, thirty feet high with seven by fourteen flag on tower
8/25/1875	Journal	Buildings	Courthouse, foundation is progressing
10/1/1913	Journal	Buildings	Courthouse, foundation laid to set cannon on southeast [sic] corner of Square
8/20/1902	Journal	Buildings	Courthouse, fountain is on east side of Square
7/27/1898	Herald	Buildings	Courthouse, fountains
9/26/1894	Herald	Buildings	Courthouse, fountains on courthouse lawn
8/20/1902	Journal	Buildings	Courthouse, four fountains put around the Square for the use of man and beast
7/3/1954	Journal-Herald	Buildings	Courthouse, freedom light built on lawn
6/28/1882	Journal	Buildings	Courthouse, galvanized work needs repainting
4/25/1877	Journal	Buildings	Courthouse, George Ennis is custodian
2/18/1914	Journal	Buildings	Courthouse, Grand Jury calls the courthouse inadequate; J. E. Hinshaw, foreman
2/19/1914	Democrat	Buildings	Courthouse, Grand Jury condemned courthouse tower as a dangerous firetrap; also said that courthouse was crowded
12/7/1881	Journal	Buildings	Courthouse, Grand Jury condemned old jail
2/27/1884	Journal	Buildings	Courthouse, Holmes County, Ohio will build a courthouse like ours

5

Date	Source	Category	Description
2/2/1974	News-Gazette	Buildings	Courthouse, honor roll on lawn fell during windstorm
8/18/1984	News-Gazette	Buildings	Courthouse, honor roll, World War II, photograph
5/10/1871	Journal	Buildings	Courthouse, horses are being pastured on public square [doubtful]
6/7/1871	Journal	Buildings	Courthouse, horses never pastured on public square
10/29/1977	News-Gazette	Buildings	Courthouse, interior repainted
11/13/1907	Herald	Buildings	Courthouse, iron fence being built around Soldiers Monument
8/30/1905	Journal	Buildings	Courthouse, iron fence planned around soldiers' monument
6/27/1877	Journal	Buildings	Courthouse, is still not occupied
5/9/1883	Journal	Buildings	Courthouse, jail and office building are being removed
8/22/1953	Journal-Herald	Buildings	Courthouse, Joe Hamilton's "Musings of Courthouse Tower"
8/29/1953	Journal-Herald	Buildings	Courthouse, Joe Hamilton's "Musings of Courthouse Tower"
7/26/1882	Journal	Buildings	Courthouse, Journal advocates tearing down old jail and office building
6/28/1916	Journal	Buildings	Courthouse, Judge Shockney ordered a flag placed on the courthouse tower to remain until soldiers returned from the Mexican Conflict
6/28/1916	Herald	Buildings	Courthouse, Judge Shockney orders flag put on top
1/17/1872	Journal	Buildings	Courthouse, letter advocating courthouse someplace other than the Public Square
2/3/1936	News-Democrat	Buildings	Courthouse, letter to the editor says courthouse is not fireproof
4/19/1928	Journal-Herald	Buildings	Courthouse, Lincoln Plaque
4/19/1928	Democrat	Buildings	Courthouse, Lincoln Tablet is installed
3/29/1928	Democrat	Buildings	Courthouse, Lincoln Tablet will be unveiled on April 6, 1928
5/2/1877	Journal	Buildings	Courthouse, Marshal Ward set out trees on Courthouse Square
9/23/1954	Journal-Herald	Buildings	Courthouse, Monks, Merritt critical of removal of courthouse tower
7/27/1892	Herald	Buildings	Courthouse, monument unveiled
7/13/1892	Journal	Buildings	Courthouse, monument will be unveiled on July 21, 1892
5/15/1889	Journal	Buildings	Courthouse, monument, A. A. McCain's plan adopted
5/29/1889	Journal	Buildings	Courthouse, monument, bids awarded for foundation
3/20/1889	Journal	Buildings	Courthouse, monument, committee appointed
7/24/1889	Journal	Buildings	Courthouse, monument, contracts for awarded
8/21/1889	Herald	Buildings	Courthouse, monument, cornerstone laid

Date	Source	Category	Description
8/21/1889	Journal	Buildings	Courthouse, monument, cornerstone laying
7/31/1889	Journal	Buildings	Courthouse, monument, cornerstone will be laid on August 15, 1889
4/11/1917	Herald	Buildings	Courthouse, monument, flag placed on top
7/20/1892	Journal	Buildings	Courthouse, monument, history of
10/10/1907	Democrat	Buildings	Courthouse, monument, iron fence planned
8/6/1890	Journal	Buildings	Courthouse, monument, last of stone work installed
12/2/1891	Journal	Buildings	Courthouse, monument, much discontent over monument
9/14/1984	News-Gazette	Buildings	Courthouse, monument, original plan to finance monument described
3/13/1889	Herald	Buildings	Courthouse, monument, petition for
10/21/1891	Journal	Buildings	Courthouse, monument, problems with bronze
8/6/1890	Herald	Buildings	Courthouse, monument, top stone put on
7/27/1892	Journal	Buildings	Courthouse, monument, unveiling
6/18/1890	Journal	Buildings	Courthouse, monument, work began on last Monday
3/16/1892	Journal	Buildings	Courthouse, monument, work resumed
4/6/1904	Herald	Buildings	Courthouse, Muncie Star of April 1, 1904 printed photo of Randolph County Courthouse taken in 1861; the picture shows the pointed cupola on the top; the picture is owned by Charles C. Smith of Winchester
12/29/1977	News-Gazette	Buildings	Courthouse, mural
4/22/1978	News-Gazette	Buildings	Courthouse, mural
4/20/1978	News-Gazette	Buildings	Courthouse, mural in place
1/26/1983	News-Gazette	Buildings	Courthouse, mural of courthouse in place in courthouse
3/7/1877	Journal	Buildings	Courthouse, nearly completed
11/10/1880	Journal	Buildings	Courthouse, new bell
12/22/1880	Journal	Buildings	Courthouse, new bell cost $250
9/5/1877	Journal	Buildings	Courthouse, new bell has a fine tone
11/10/1880	Journal	Buildings	Courthouse, new bell has been placed into position
2/25/1880	Journal	Buildings	Courthouse, new cannon to be kept in the basement
6/24/1924	Journal-Herald	Buildings	Courthouse, new flagpole
8/7/1924	Democrat	Buildings	Courthouse, new flagpole; four sections; six inches at base in a five foot block of cement; has a bronze eagle on top
6/8/1916	Democrat	Buildings	Courthouse, new rope on courthouse bell; clock is dead

Date	Source	Category	Description
7/14/1880	Journal	Buildings	Courthouse, new walk is planned around Public Square
11/13/1901	Journal	Buildings	Courthouse, north and south entrances were closed many months ago; sidewalks were removed last week
7/14/1915	Journal	Buildings	Courthouse, O. E. Way to remodel courtroom
11/8/1911	Journal	Buildings	Courthouse, Old 44 [cannon] plans to put in cement on Square
9/10/1913	Journal	Buildings	Courthouse, Old 44 [cannon] put in cement on Square
10/8/1913	Herald	Buildings	Courthouse, Old 44 cannon is mounted on Courthouse Square
10/6/1942	Journal-Herald	Buildings	Courthouse, Old 44 cannon will not go to scrap, gun on southeast corner will
9/17/1913	Herald	Buildings	Courthouse, Old 44 cannon, plans to mount on Square
3/17/1859	Journal	Buildings	Courthouse, old market house on Public Square sold for $5
6/27/1877	Journal	Buildings	Courthouse, old stoves put in
3/7/1877	Journal	Buildings	Courthouse, P. H. Dean has taken a photo of the new courthouse
6/4/1983	News-Gazette	Buildings	Courthouse, photo of artillery piece on courthouse lawn given to scrap drive during World War II
7/17/1967	News	Buildings	Courthouse, photo of dinner in hallway c1914-15
7/15/1968	Journal-Herald	Buildings	Courthouse, photo of military honor roll on lawn, began in 1960
5/12/1915	Journal	Buildings	Courthouse, photo of old courthouse
6/21/1905	Herald	Buildings	Courthouse, photo of old courthouse in Charley Pierce's window; bricks from the building were used for building the building at northeast corner of Main and Franklin
7/1/1954	Journal-Herald	Buildings	Courthouse, photos
7/3/1954	Journal-Herald	Buildings	Courthouse, photos
4/25/1957	Journal-Herald	Buildings	Courthouse, photos
9/6/1882	Journal	Buildings	Courthouse, picture of old courthouse will be in new county history; it is of Miss Amelia Brice presenting the flag to Co. E, 8th IVI; the picture belongs to General Browne
1/3/1872	Journal	Buildings	Courthouse, plans for
12/12/1877	Journal	Buildings	Courthouse, plans for will be kept by auditor
8/3/1938	Journal-Herald	Buildings	Courthouse, plans to remodel, alludes to plan "many years ago" to remove the tower
9/23/1942	Journal-Herald	Buildings	Courthouse, plans to scrap Old 44 cannon

Date	Source	Category	Description
8/30/1876	Journal	Buildings	Courthouse, plastering starts
1/21/1880	Journal	Buildings	Courthouse, portico is out of order
2/4/1936	Journal-Herald	Buildings	Courthouse, power winder put on clock
8/20/1871	Journal	Buildings	Courthouse, Randolph County Commissioners are visiting courthouses in other places
2/7/1872	Journal	Buildings	Courthouse, referendum, plans for
9/8/1915	Journal	Buildings	Courthouse, remodeling of courtroom by O. E. Way is nearly done; custodian will have a sleeping room
11/21/1888	Journal	Buildings	Courthouse, safe purchased for Clerk's office
11/21/1906	Herald	Buildings	Courthouse, Sayers, W. J. letter about courthouse square
12/23/1885	Journal	Buildings	Courthouse, sheriff's office moved from jail to back room of Treasurer's office
3/16/1898	Journal	Buildings	Courthouse, sheriff's office moved to room adjoining the courtroom on the east; former room is now a part of the treasurer's office
8/13/1902	Herald	Buildings	Courthouse, sheriff's office to be made into a ladies restroom; sheriff moved to northwest corner of second floor, across the hall from the surveyor and county superintendent
8/13/1902	Journal	Buildings	Courthouse, Sheriff's office will become ladies toilet; Sheriff will move to the northwest corner upstairs, where the office was when the courthouse was first built
10/8/1957	Journal-Herald	Buildings	Courthouse, Sherman tank approved to be placed on lawn
12/24/1957	Journal-Herald	Buildings	Courthouse, Sherman tank arrives
10/17/1929	Democrat	Buildings	Courthouse, sidewalk is completed around the Doughboy
4/6/1892	Journal	Buildings	Courthouse, sidewalks planned to all four entrances
8/23/1876	Journal	Buildings	Courthouse, slating is progressing
9/10/1913	Journal	Buildings	Courthouse, Sons of Veterans to put cannon on the Square
10/15/1914	Democrat	Buildings	Courthouse, south door to be replaced by a window
4/5/1876	Journal	Buildings	Courthouse, stone work is in progress
6/7/1876	Journal	Buildings	Courthouse, stonecutters on strike
4/29/1908	Herald	Buildings	Courthouse, storm put courthouse clock out of commission; hurled Tobin District School [in Darke County, Ohio] into yard
2/11/1961	Journal-Herald	Buildings	Courthouse, story of tin boxes in clerk's [now recorder's] office

Date	Source	Category	Description
11/22/1882	Journal	Buildings	Courthouse, street lamps ordered for courthouse and jail
10/30/1935	News-Democrat	Buildings	Courthouse, T. Clark Gray, 83, of Montana, helped to build the courthouse; may be the only one still living
2/11/1880	Journal	Buildings	Courthouse, telephone installed
3/13/1889	Journal	Buildings	Courthouse, the northwest room in the second story has been divided into two rooms
4/25/1883	Journal	Buildings	Courthouse, the old county officers' building is a thing of the past
4/4/1883	Journal	Buildings	Courthouse, the work of tearing down the old public buildings is under progress
8/6/1953	Journal-Herald	Buildings	Courthouse, tower "looks like it must go"
5/15/1919	Democrat	Buildings	Courthouse, tower to be removed [planned but did not occur for 35 years]
1/22/1919	Journal	Buildings	Courthouse, tower will probably be removed at some point; an addition will be built
4/25/1912	Democrat	Buildings	Courthouse, town clock is undependable when the wind blows
6/21/1916	Journal	Buildings	Courthouse, town clock is working but is striking too much
8/27/1919	Herald	Buildings	Courthouse, town clock to be repaired; has not functioned in several years
12/12/1883	Journal	Buildings	Courthouse, treasurer's office, new safe
9/6/1928	Democrat	Buildings	Courthouse, trench gun is placed on Square by American Legion
8/2/1876	Journal	Buildings	Courthouse, walls are nearly up
11/15/1928	Democrat	Buildings	Courthouse, war memorial [doughboy] was dedicated; statue was a gift of the Goodrich Family; Hoffman donated the stone at cost
10/3/1877	Journal	Buildings	Courthouse, water tank doesn't function
5/27/1871	Journal	Buildings	Courthouse, Winchester Journal supports the building of a new Courthouse
5/15/1912	Journal	Buildings	Courthouse, wooden benches have been removed from lawn; iron benches remain
2/6/1878	Journal	Buildings	Courthouse, woodwork is warping
7/7/1875	Journal	Buildings	Courthouse, work commenced on foundation
10/28/1914	Herald	Buildings	Courthouse, work of putting a window where door was on south side of the Courthouse is almost done
10/25/1876	Journal	Buildings	Courthouse, work of putting windows in; iron work on tower will start

Date	Source	Category	Description
5/9/1883	Journal	Buildings	Courthouse, work of tearing down the old buildings on the Square
8/20/1919	Journal	Buildings	Courthouse, work started on Monday to brace the courthouse tower due to sentiment that wanted to keep it
9/4/1946	News	Buildings	Courthouse, World War II honor roll on lawn dismantled
9/10/1935	Journal-Herald	Buildings	Courthouse, WPA suggests the building of a new courthouse
2/9/1928	Journal-Herald	Buildings	Courthouse, WRC placed Lincoln plaque inside
9/12/1907	Democrat	Buildings	Deerfield, flour mill razed
8/28/1907	Journal	Buildings	Deerfield, mill being razed
4/6/1887	Journal	Buildings	Deerfield, old tavern building blown down
5/16/1953	Journal-Herald	Buildings	Fairgrounds, Dick Hinshaw built two new buildings
12/18/1863	Journal	Buildings	Farmland "we have no church house in town"
4/18/1867	Journal	Buildings	Farmland fire
4/25/1867	Journal	Buildings	Farmland fire
7/2/1977	News-Gazette	Buildings	Farmland Opera House
4/15/1978	News-Gazette	Buildings	Farmland Opera House
8/18/1875	Journal	Buildings	Farmland, "new brick block"
1/23/1908	Democrat	Buildings	Farmland, big fire
12/1/1897	Journal	Buildings	Farmland, big fire
6/26/1889	Journal	Buildings	Farmland, Bly and Thornburg's new block is commenced
6/14/1928	Democrat	Buildings	Farmland, Bosh Bakery and Brown Studio damaged by fire
7/6/1881	Journal	Buildings	Farmland, brick building north of Dennis Thornburg's will soon be done
3/2/1881	Journal	Buildings	Farmland, building planned north of Dennis Thornburg's Block
12/31/1890	Journal	Buildings	Farmland, calaboose is ready
2/28/1918	Democrat	Buildings	Farmland, church on Main Street, owned by Sina Morris, is made into theatre
6/27/1867	Journal	Buildings	Farmland, D. Thornburg will erected business room on his corner lot
7/28/1875	Journal	Buildings	Farmland, Davis, Shaw, Watson Brick Block under construction
3/13/1889	Herald	Buildings	Farmland, Dennis Thornburg Block mentioned
3/31/1909	Herald	Buildings	Farmland, Dennis Thornburg Block sold; built 32 years ago
3/3/1880	Journal	Buildings	Farmland, Dennis Thornburg has moved into his new house
5/5/1880	Journal	Buildings	Farmland, Dennis Thornburg has moved into his new residence
12/28/1887	Journal	Buildings	Farmland, Dennis Thornburg has moved to new building

Date	Source	Category	Description
11/12/1879	Journal	Buildings	Farmland, Dennis Thornburg is erecting new residence
7/30/1879	Journal	Buildings	Farmland, Dennis Thornburg is preparing to build a new house on his farm south of town
7/30/1879	Journal	Buildings	Farmland, Dennis Thornburg is preparing to build a residence on his house south of Farmland
5/5/1880	Journal	Buildings	Farmland, Dennis Thornburg moved into new residence
3/9/1898	Journal	Buildings	Farmland, Emma Burres has begun work on a new building
12/7/1887	Journal	Buildings	Farmland, explosion at
12/7/1887	Herald	Buildings	Farmland, explosion ruined new bank and opera house and two buildings of N. E. Gray to the west
3/27/1895	Journal	Buildings	Farmland, fire
4/18/1867	Journal	Buildings	Farmland, fire at IOOF Hall
4/25/1867	Journal	Buildings	Farmland, fire at IOOF Hall was arson
3/10/1875	Journal	Buildings	Farmland, fire burned G. B. Watson and J. S. Davis Buildings
3/10/1875	Journal	Buildings	Farmland, fire destroyed G. B. Watson's building and James S. Davis's building
6/22/1922	Democrat	Buildings	Farmland, fire in Fast Grocery and K of P Hall
6/21/1922	Journal-Herald	Buildings	Farmland, fire on June 19 damaged Fast's Grocery and K of P Hall in Taylor Building
4/16/1902	Journal	Buildings	Farmland, fire west of the Opera House
6/19/1913	Democrat	Buildings	Farmland, Foster's Shoe Store and Clayton Millinery burned Wednesday
6/18/1913	Journal	Buildings	Farmland, Foster's Shoe Store burned last Thursday
4/2/1879	Journal	Buildings	Farmland, Gable Building built
4/29/1908	Journal	Buildings	Farmland, George B. Watson to erect a brick building on W. Henry, 52 x 80
4/23/1919	Herald	Buildings	Farmland, Goodrich Brothers plan new $44,000 elevator
4/23/1913	Herald	Buildings	Farmland, Hay Bailer [sic] Building and 1856 Grain Elevator razed for replacement by brick
12/1/1886	Herald	Buildings	Farmland, Hewitt Building purchased by James and Ira Branson, who will raze it to make room for a bank
6/27/1867	Journal	Buildings	Farmland, IOOF plans building 60 x 22
9/21/1972	News-Gazette	Buildings	Farmland, IORM Building damaged by fire
8/31/1881	Journal	Buildings	Farmland, J. B. Branson's new brick room
2/19/1890	Journal	Buildings	Farmland, J. J. Clayton will erect new livery barn, north of railroad

Date	Source	Category	Description
11/22/1866	Journal	Buildings	Farmland, Jethro Macy is building a two-story building for a tin shop and a hall
11/22/1866	Journal	Buildings	Farmland, Jethro Macy's Hall built
7/20/1881	Journal	Buildings	Farmland, Joseph Branson's block, foundation laid
9/5/1894	Journal	Buildings	Farmland, Kramer Building planned
12/1/1897	Herald	Buildings	Farmland, large fire
7/30/1919	Herald	Buildings	Farmland, livery barn, build in 1852, razed to be replaced by brick block on North Main
4/26/1916	Herald	Buildings	Farmland, Lula C. Jaqua sold Clayton Block to J. H. Lumpkin
7/30/1919	Journal	Buildings	Farmland, Luther Thornburg has torn down old livery barn; a new building is to be built
7/14/1875	Journal	Buildings	Farmland, Masonic and Odd Fellows blocks are under construction
10/27/1880	Journal	Buildings	Farmland, N. E. Gray's new building mentioned
5/1/1895	Journal	Buildings	Farmland, new cement watering trough
9/6/1961	News	Buildings	Farmland, new Foster Shoe Store building
4/24/1919	Democrat	Buildings	Farmland, new grain elevator is being erected
5/14/1890	Herald	Buildings	Farmland, new livery barn
9/25/1919	Democrat	Buildings	Farmland, old elevator, built by Macy, Shaw, and Thornburg in 1854, razed; new elevator is 130 feet high
7/30/1919	Journal	Buildings	Farmland, old livery barn torn down
9/4/1919	Democrat	Buildings	Farmland, plans for a new city building to be built north of Weiler and Lumpkin [never built]
6/28/1876	Journal	Buildings	Farmland, plans for calaboose
4/22/1908	Herald	Buildings	Farmland, plans to build city building [not built]
3/5/1890	Journal	Buildings	Farmland, Sherman House built in 1869 by Matthew Reeves
3/5/1890	Journal	Buildings	Farmland, Sherman House burned
4/16/1902	Herald	Buildings	Farmland, small fire
9/22/1880	Journal	Buildings	Farmland, Stanley and Harbour's new building mentioned
4/18/1883	Journal	Buildings	Farmland, W. J. Davisson is building a new residence
2/8/1899	Journal	Buildings	Fountain City [Wayne County], old Levi Coffin Homestead sold
9/9/1896	Journal	Buildings	Huntsville, "old school house" "new IOOF Hall"
4/6/1881	Journal	Buildings	Jail, A. G. Campfield will build jail
7/27/1881	Journal	Buildings	Jail, brick work commenced
10/1/1879	Journal	Buildings	Jail, commissioners have decided to build a new jail

Date	Source	Category	Description
3/30/1881	Journal	Buildings	Jail, contract for jail will be let on Monday
1/19/1881	Journal	Buildings	Jail, E. J. Hodgson of Indianapolis is architect of new jail
2/7/1882	Journal	Buildings	Jail, heat does not work properly
1/21/1978	News-Gazette	Buildings	Jail, history of
9/18/1984	News-Gazette	Buildings	Jail, lawsuit over conditions
3/4/1914	Journal	Buildings	Jail, Lee L. Driver is seeking a picture of the old jail for his history book
2/7/1883	Journal	Buildings	Jail, Masonic Order should sell interest in old jail
9/24/1879	Journal	Buildings	Jail, new jail is likely
4/22/1858	Journal	Buildings	Jail, new jail is nearing completion
1/12/1881	Journal	Buildings	Jail, new jail to be erected
4/15/1914	Herald	Buildings	Jail, old iron fence from jail is taken to County Infirmary
6/6/1883	Journal	Buildings	Jail, old jail is being torn down
7/8/1891	Journal	Buildings	Jail, old jail story by Farquhar
3/21/1883	Journal	Buildings	Jail, old jail will be razed this year
3/14/1883	Journal	Buildings	Jail, old jail will be torn down after May 15, 1883
4/4/1883	Journal	Buildings	Jail, old jail, Cal Diggs and John Carter have purchased the old jail building and commenced the work of tearing it down
5/19/1886	Journal	Buildings	Jail, old jail, George Smith has a cane made from a log of old jail
6/20/1883	Journal	Buildings	Jail, old jail, iron shipped to Cincinnati; weighed 50,000 pounds
4/18/1883	Journal	Buildings	Jail, old jail, last meeting of F & A. M. in old lodge room next Saturday
7/5/1882	Journal	Buildings	Jail, order to occupy
5/17/1882	Journal	Buildings	Jail, problems with
8/2/1882	Journal	Buildings	Jail, rooms are rented out in old jail
10/25/1882	Journal	Buildings	Jail, Sheriff's office moved to new jail building
2/2/1881	Journal	Buildings	Jail, work will begin on new jail about April 1, 1881
4/5/1911	Journal	Buildings	Liber College [Jay County], building destroyed by fire
9/13/1876	Journal	Buildings	Liberty Hall exists near Jericho
10/4/1882	Journal	Buildings	Liberty Hall is near Jericho
9/30/1970	News-Gazette	Buildings	Lickskillet, log cabin burned
5/15/1895	Journal	Buildings	Lickskillet, Ludwick Store burned
1/25/1899	Journal	Buildings	Losantville, fire
1/1/1908	Herald	Buildings	Losantville, new calaboose
5/24/1899	Journal	Buildings	Losantville, Opera House will be built
5/23/1964	Journal-Herald	Buildings	Lynn, building razed
5/11/1904	Journal	Buildings	Lynn, C. R. Carter and bank are building a cement block building

Date	Source	Category	Description
12/27/1982	News-Gazette	Buildings	Lynn, depot
11/29/1882	Journal	Buildings	Lynn, Dr. Hamilton's Building is nearly done
3/24/1897	Journal	Buildings	Lynn, E. J. and Will Hinshaw are planning a business block
5/13/1903	Herald	Buildings	Lynn, fire
10/14/1969	Journal-Herald	Buildings	Lynn, groundbreaking for new city building
7/7/1897	Journal	Buildings	Lynn, Hinshaw Block is nearly completed
10/19/1870	Journal	Buildings	Lynn, IOOF Hall and schoolhouse erected this season
2/8/1888	Journal	Buildings	Lynn, Old Masonic Block and Eckerlie's [sic] Block removed and replaced by three-story block
2/6/1969	Journal-Herald	Buildings	Lynn, plans for new city building
2/7/1969	Journal-Herald	Buildings	Lynn, plans for new city building
9/7/1892	Journal	Buildings	Lynn, Platt and Horner are building new building
7/14/1979	News-Gazette	Buildings	Lynn, southwest corner of Main and Church, buildings razed
1/27/1897	Journal	Buildings	Lynn, W. E. and Elkanah Hinshaw contemplate building a business block on South Main Street
5/15/1912	Herald	Buildings	Maxville Mill being moved away
7/3/1971	News-Gazette	Buildings	Maxville Swimming Pool to be reopened by Tim McGuire
3/13/1971	News-Gazette	Buildings	Modoc Mill burned; closed earlier in the year
12/17/1935	News-Democrat	Buildings	Modoc, clipping of 1891 fire
8/9/1916	Herald	Buildings	Modoc, fire
8/10/1916	Democrat	Buildings	Modoc, fire
3/22/1916	Herald	Buildings	New Dayton, Ray-Roe Homestead razed
12/15/1875	Journal	Buildings	Olive Branch, fire destroyed Addington's Store
7/11/1981	News-Gazette	Buildings	Orphans Home
12/18/1972	News-Gazette	Buildings	Orphans Home being razed
5/2/1888	Journal	Buildings	Orphan's Home established
7/3/1968	Journal-Herald	Buildings	Orphans Home sold
7/18/1888	Journal	Buildings	Orphan's Home, A. J. Favorite awarded bids for main addition
10/25/1893	Journal	Buildings	Orphans' Home, barn will be like that of Zimri Hinshaw
1/13/1916	Democrat	Buildings	Orphans Home, history
7/30/1936	News-Democrat	Buildings	Orphans Home, history and photos
3/22/1899	Journal	Buildings	Orphans Home, James Moorman Orphans Home completed
1/11/1899	Journal	Buildings	Orphans Home, new Orphans Home is rapidly approaching completion

Date	Source	Category	Description
2/11/1920	Herald	Buildings	Orphan's Home, O. V. Cuppy replaces Thomas Brown as superintendent; Brown served four years after Allen Hiatt; children attend Winchester Friends Church
2/6/1889	Journal	Buildings	Orphan's Home, officers of
5/11/1898	Herald	Buildings	Orphans Home, plan to build new home 1/4 mile south of old one
6/19/1889	Journal	Buildings	Orphan's Home, temporarily taken over by county
4/16/1919	Journal	Buildings	Parker City, former Vaught Furniture Buildings sold
9/14/1971	News-Gazette	Buildings	Parker Mill razed
1/18/1893	Journal	Buildings	Parker, 100 new houses will be erected
10/11/1882	Journal	Buildings	Parker, Dragoo-Gunckle Block nearly complete
8/23/1871	Journal	Buildings	Parker, fire at Parker, formerly Morristown
2/28/1877	Journal	Buildings	Parker, Grange Building will be remodeled
5/9/1894	Journal	Buildings	Parker, new calaboose
6/20/1968	Journal-Herald	Buildings	Parker, new fire station
9/12/1983	News-Gazette	Buildings	Parker, old fire bell installed
5/20/1891	Journal	Buildings	Parker, old Grange Building will be remodeled
5/6/1891	Journal	Buildings	Parker, rooms being built north of the IOOF Block
4/2/1919	Journal	Buildings	Ridgeville will erect new town building, library, firehouse
9/20/1882	Journal	Buildings	Ridgeville, bank and D. C. Braden are building new buildings
7/12/1916	Journal	Buildings	Ridgeville, big fire
7/12/1916	Herald	Buildings	Ridgeville, big fire
12/9/1903	Herald	Buildings	Ridgeville, big fire on December 5, 1903
9/2/1896	Journal	Buildings	Ridgeville, Braden Building burned
8/13/1919	Herald	Buildings	Ridgeville, city building, contract let
1/12/1916	Herald	Buildings	Ridgeville, elevator burned
7/13/1916	Democrat	Buildings	Ridgeville, fire
6/30/1909	Journal	Buildings	Ridgeville, First National Bank and Ames Building will be built
8/28/1975	News-Gazette	Buildings	Ridgeville, Hiatt Building being razed
10/4/1882	Journal	Buildings	Ridgeville, M. R. Hiatt's new block
6/13/1961	Journal-Herald	Buildings	Ridgeville, new post office to be built
12/30/1920	Democrat	Buildings	Ridgeville, new town hall is completed at a cost of $14,000
3/29/1882	Journal	Buildings	Ridgeville, W. R. Hiatt will build a new building on Walnut Street
3/27/1895	Journal	Buildings	Rural, fire
8/2/1916	Herald	Buildings	Saratoga Canning Factory burns

5/12/1967	News	Buildings	Saratoga, elevator razed; another elevator remained in town
10/24/1906	Journal	Buildings	Saratoga, mill, new mill built
10/16/1963	News	Buildings	Saratoga, new fire department building
4/5/1923	Democrat	Buildings	Stone Station Store burned; owned by Ed Harmon
6/12/1919	Democrat	Buildings	Stone Station, new elevator
8/31/1922	Democrat	Buildings	Stone Station, old elevator is being razed
10/9/1979	News-Gazette	Buildings	Union City Depot purchased by city
6/14/1962	Journal-Herald	Buildings	Union City Elevator burns
5/18/1950	Journal-Herald	Buildings	Union City Hospital to be dedicated on May 24
4/25/1972	News-Gazette	Buildings	Union City Labor Temple dedication
8/25/1970	News-Gazette	Buildings	Union City, Branham Hotel to be razed
5/9/1883	Journal	Buildings	Union City, fire
8/27/1914	Democrat	Buildings	Union City, hospital planned
7/23/1952	News	Buildings	Union City, old Big Four Depot razed
5/20/1896	Journal	Buildings	Union City, row of wooden buildings burned
1/29/1936	News-Democrat	Buildings	Union City, Tibbetts Building, fire
9/6/1871	Journal	Buildings	Washington Hall is near Jericho Meetinghouse
2/24/1973	News-Gazette	Buildings	Winchester Elevator, built 1896; central tower built in 1913; addition in 1929
3/7/1972	News-Gazette	Buildings	Winchester Elevator, old part to be razed; built in 1876; history of
12/30/1978	News-Gazette	Buildings	Winchester K. of P. Building is falling in
2/1/1944	Journal-Herald	Buildings	Winchester Masonic Block burned
6/23/1983	News-Gazette	Buildings	Winchester to build new city building
11/15/1947	Journal-Herald	Buildings	Winchester, 416 S. Meridian described [now Randolph County Historical Museum]
4/19/1899	Journal	Buildings	Winchester, Adam Hirsch, Sr. is building a two-story brick block, 41 x 65 on E. Washington St.
6/1/1949	News	Buildings	Winchester, Armory site selected
11/10/1950	News	Buildings	Winchester, Armory to be dedicated on November 12
6/24/1885	Journal	Buildings	Winchester, Ashton Building is being moved for a new building
4/5/1893	Journal	Buildings	Winchester, bank building and corner building will be razed
5/4/1939	Journal-Herald	Buildings	Winchester, Beeson Clubhouse completed
6/5/1982	News-Gazette	Buildings	Winchester, bell from old City Building (installed in 1910) removed
5/19/1897	Journal	Buildings	Winchester, Best Building on W. Franklin Street will soon be replaced

Date	Source	Category	Description
5/27/1903	Herald	Buildings	Winchester, bids on new hotel
3/27/1895	Journal	Buildings	Winchester, brick work on electric light station
5/24/1899	Journal	Buildings	Winchester, Bud Irvin will build two brick business rooms on the south side of the Square
5/22/1912	Journal	Buildings	Winchester, building at rear of McNees Hotel is being demolished; it was built by the father of Eli Haworth and once served as the Irvin Hotel
4/29/1896	Journal	Buildings	Winchester, building west of Hiatt's Livery Barn is getting a new front
5/18/1910	Journal	Buildings	Winchester, Canada Block is being modernized inside and out
8/10/1910	Journal	Buildings	Winchester, Canada Block is being stuccoed
10/12/1910	Herald	Buildings	Winchester, Canada Block on west side of Square to be rebuilt; three business rooms with concrete veneer
3/9/1865	Journal	Buildings	Winchester, Carters to build brick building on southwest corner of Public Square
12/5/1900	Herald	Buildings	Winchester, Charley Favorite's Building built
5/16/1883	Journal	Buildings	Winchester, Charley Magee plans iron front on his business room
11/20/1918	Herald	Buildings	Winchester, Citizens Bank Building is being stuccoed
5/30/1888	Journal	Buildings	Winchester, City Building completed
8/19/1982	News-Gazette	Buildings	Winchester, City Building photo
8/21/1984	News-Gazette	Buildings	Winchester, City Building under construction
10/14/1903	Herald	Buildings	Winchester, City Building was accepted last Saturday; started on November 28, 1902; cost $2000
8/18/1982	News-Gazette	Buildings	Winchester, City Building was built in 1902; city council then consisted of W. Y. Puckett, J. M. Segraves, B. S. Hunt, R. B. Puckett, and H. E. McNees
4/17/1984	News-Gazette	Buildings	Winchester, City Building, bids on
9/3/1902	Herald	Buildings	Winchester, City Building, Hampton Gettinger is planning new city building
5/16/1888	Journal	Buildings	Winchester, City Building, new city building, at rear of Journal Block, is being enclosed
10/29/1902	Journal	Buildings	Winchester, city hall, ground is broken for
11/20/1984	News-Gazette	Buildings	Winchester, city will purchase and raze Cooper Building, located on the east side of N. Main between Washington and North
6/8/1881	Journal	Buildings	Winchester, Cranor Block, brick work is being completed

Date	Source	Category	Description
7/26/1899	Journal	Buildings	Winchester, D. F. Irvin will build a new three-story business block adjoining the W. E. Miller Block on the east; 40 x 100; it will be occupied by the IORM
3/4/1896	Journal	Buildings	Winchester, Dan Hoffman is erected a building south of the Square
7/23/1936	News-Democrat	Buildings	Winchester, DAR cabin, history and photos
8/10/1910	Journal	Buildings	Winchester, David Haworth frame house; Newton Haworth has photo
8/30/1928	Democrat	Buildings	Winchester, Davis Block, data and photo
8/26/1891	Herald	Buildings	Winchester, Davis Brothers Block planned for east side of Square
6/22/1926	Daily News	Buildings	Winchester, Davis Building is nearly done
7/7/1926	Daily News	Buildings	Winchester, Davis Building is ready for occupancy
4/25/1912	Democrat	Buildings	Winchester, Davis Building planned for South Main
2/18/1926	Democrat	Buildings	Winchester, Davis Building to be built on S. Main Street
3/29/1917	Democrat	Buildings	Winchester, Davis Building to be expanded
2/19/1973	News-Gazette	Buildings	Winchester, demolition of elevator
6/2/1886	Journal	Buildings	Winchester, Dennis Kelley Block, ground broken
5/19/1886	Journal	Buildings	Winchester, Dennis Kelley closed contract with Mr. Gettinger for a business block on the old tombstone corner
1/23/1895	Journal	Buildings	Winchester, Dennis Kelley plans a building between his block and the Journal Building
10/13/1886	Journal	Buildings	Winchester, Dennis Kelley will move into new room next week
8/11/1886	Herald	Buildings	Winchester, Dennis Kelley's block nearly done
7/3/1895	Journal	Buildings	Winchester, Dennis Kelley's new block, brick work completed
5/19/1886	Journal	Buildings	Winchester, Dennis Kelley's new block, work on
9/9/1903	Herald	Buildings	Winchester, Dr. Hunt's new office, Washington and East Streets
10/3/1894	Journal	Buildings	Winchester, drawing of Dennis Kelley's Block
10/3/1894	Journal	Buildings	Winchester, drawing of W. E. Miller's Buildings
10/12/1892	Journal	Buildings	Winchester, Dud Davis will build a residence and blacksmith shop south of the Old Franklin House
7/26/1972	News-Gazette	Buildings	Winchester, East Side Grain Elevator razed
1/16/1918	Herald	Buildings	Winchester, Engle Block, corner Main and Franklin, sold to Citizens Banking Company
4/26/1899	Herald	Buildings	Winchester, excavation for Hirsch Building and W. E. Miller Building

Date	Source	Category	Description
4/11/1877	Journal	Buildings	Winchester, F. A. Engle is building a business block on southeast corner of Square
11/29/1876	Journal	Buildings	Winchester, F. A. Engle will build three story brick block on southeast corner of Public Square
4/23/1879	Journal	Buildings	Winchester, F. A. Engle's new block
12/27/1965	News	Buildings	Winchester, fire on North Meridian
4/5/1893	Journal	Buildings	Winchester, Fletcher, Sheriff is building a residence at Main and South Streets; Martin Reeder's old house to be moved next to the jail
6/5/1912	Journal	Buildings	Winchester, frame buildings on the east side of the Square are being razed
10/16/1918	Journal	Buildings	Winchester, frame buildings on the west side of the Square are being razed; Peoples Loan and Trust will build there
4/11/1877	Journal	Buildings	Winchester, frame saloon building on East Washington Street is removed
6/2/1927	Democrat	Buildings	Winchester, Franklin House is being razed
10/12/1892	Journal	Buildings	Winchester, Franklin House, barn of is being razed
1/15/1902	Herald	Buildings	Winchester, Franklin House, history of
9/26/1906	Herald	Buildings	Winchester, Gaddis Livery Barn slipped from foundation; was Gordon's Rink; used for McKinley Campaign
1/30/1878	Journal	Buildings	Winchester, General Stone will build new residence in south part of town
2/27/1878	Journal	Buildings	Winchester, General Stone will move old residence to South Main Street to make way for new
3/20/1878	Journal	Buildings	Winchester, General Stone's house will cost $12,000
5/1/1878	Journal	Buildings	Winchester, General Stone's old house settled on Main Street
11/13/1878	Journal	Buildings	Winchester, General Stone's residence is nearly complete
3/8/1893	Journal	Buildings	Winchester, George Keller and Frank Moorman plan a new building between Farmers and Merchants Bank and Masonic Block; Dennis Kelley plans a new building south of the Journal Building; and Alfred Rice plans a new building on north
6/29/1865	Journal	Buildings	Winchester, George McAdams will erect brick building at Meridian and Franklin Streets
6/18/1908	Democrat	Buildings	Winchester, Goodrich Elevator will be the largest in the state
4/29/1914	Herald	Buildings	Winchester, Goodrich Elevator, work started on it

Date	Source	Category	Description
7/3/1912	Herald	Buildings	Winchester, Goodrich Home being completed
5/29/1912	Herald	Buildings	Winchester, Goodrich home started; Hiatt and Hirsch Blocks being built; only three frame buildings are left on the Square
10/16/1976	News-Gazette	Buildings	Winchester, Goodrich Mansion sold
11/1/1976	News-Gazette	Buildings	Winchester, Goodrich Mansion to be razed
9/15/1932	Democrat	Buildings	Winchester, Goodrich Park, log cabin given to park
11/28/1913	Herald	Buildings	Winchester, Goodrich's new elevator will be 109 feet tall
2/18/1903	Journal	Buildings	Winchester, Hampton Gettinger designed Hotel and Presbyterian Church
9/25/1878	Journal	Buildings	Winchester, Harrison House burned
12/24/1966	Journal-Herald	Buildings	Winchester, Herald Newspaper office razed
12/29/1915	Herald	Buildings	Winchester, Hetty Vorhis Home for Old Women nearly done
1/20/1915	Journal	Buildings	Winchester, Hetty Vorhis Home is being planned
2/23/1916	Herald	Buildings	Winchester, Hetty Vorhis Home opened Monday
3/3/1915	Journal	Buildings	Winchester, Hetty Vorhis Home purchased lots
2/23/1916	Journal	Buildings	Winchester, Hetty Vorhis Home was formally opened Monday
6/23/1915	Journal	Buildings	Winchester, Hetty Vorhis Home, bids awarded
5/26/1915	Journal	Buildings	Winchester, Hetty Vorhis Home, contract for
1/19/1916	Journal	Buildings	Winchester, Hetty Vorhis Home, photos
6/23/1915	Herald	Buildings	Winchester, Hetty Vorhis Old Ladies Home, contract awarded
9/9/1914	Herald	Buildings	Winchester, Hetty Vorhis plans old ladies home
7/3/1912	Herald	Buildings	Winchester, Hiatt and Hirsch Blocks being built
12/25/1912	Journal	Buildings	Winchester, Hirsch and Hiatt Blocks are complete
6/1/1910	Herald	Buildings	Winchester, Hirsch Brothers building new "flat building" on E. Washington Street
5/25/1910	Journal	Buildings	Winchester, Hirsch Building on East Washington Street to be replaced by flats
5/15/1912	Journal	Buildings	Winchester, Hirsch Estate Building and Clyde Hiatt Building; bids for
12/31/1926	Daily News	Buildings	Winchester, Hoffman Monument Works builds new building on Franklin Street
7/18/1912	Democrat	Buildings	Winchester, Hoke Building planned, south of Hiatt and Hirsch Blocks on Main Street

Date	Source	Category	Description
8/18/1915	Herald	Buildings	Winchester, Hoosier Automobile Company will build garage on Franklin Street
4/10/1901	Journal	Buildings	Winchester, IORM and T. F. Moorman to build new building
10/18/1917	Democrat	Buildings	Winchester, Irvin Theatre has been converted into a factory
5/15/1912	Herald	Buildings	Winchester, J. A. Long's new building is brick and opposite G. R. & I. depot (photo)
6/20/1917	Journal	Buildings	Winchester, J. E. Hinshaw moves to Stone Mansion
4/21/1909	Herald	Buildings	Winchester, J. T. Moorman building new structure behind People's Loan and Trust
3/20/1878	Journal	Buildings	Winchester, James Moorman will soon build brick blocks on North Front
5/25/1892	Journal	Buildings	Winchester, Jay Goodrich will build elevator
4/17/1895	Journal	Buildings	Winchester, John Richardson is building an addition to his residence
6/26/1878	Journal	Buildings	Winchester, John Richardson put up fence at residence
2/19/1890	Journal	Buildings	Winchester, John Richardson will erect a two-story brick building on West Franklin Street
7/25/1877	Journal	Buildings	Winchester, John Richardson will put third floor on his business block
4/27/1887	Journal	Buildings	Winchester, John Richardson, new fence at residence
11/23/1881	Journal	Buildings	Winchester, Journal Building, Nathan Reed purchased
12/17/1966	Journal-Herald	Buildings	Winchester, K of P Building photo
8/22/1964	Journal-Herald	Buildings	Winchester, K of P Building photos, built in 1893
12/18/1976	News-Gazette	Buildings	Winchester, K of P Building, third floor is dangerous
4/26/1893	Journal	Buildings	Winchester, K of P may put third story on new block
12/7/1892	Herald	Buildings	Winchester, Kelley Block is seven years old
1/14/1903	Journal	Buildings	Winchester, Kelley Block, picture, built in 1886; expanded north in 1895
9/16/1926	Daily News	Buildings	Winchester, Kizer Block, addition to rear
9/26/1894	Herald	Buildings	Winchester, Kizer Block, built as post office
8/29/1894	Herald	Buildings	Winchester, Kizer, W. D. plans two buildings south of the IOOF Building
9/5/1894	Journal	Buildings	Winchester, Kizer's Block, ground broken for
10/3/1936	Daily News	Buildings	Winchester, Labor Temple was formerly the Red Men's Hall
3/8/1882	Journal	Buildings	Winchester, livery stable on Main Street is being torn down to be replaced by a new one
9/4/1912	Journal	Buildings	Winchester, Long Produce Building is being completed

Date	Source	Category	Description
3/28/1969	Journal-Herald	Buildings	Winchester, lumber yard razed
11/22/1911	Herald	Buildings	Winchester, M. L. Mills Building will be done in two weeks
6/28/1911	Journal	Buildings	Winchester, M. L. Mills Building, excavation for
3/22/1911	Herald	Buildings	Winchester, M. L. Mills will build at southeast corner of Meridian and Franklin
6/13/1883	Journal	Buildings	Winchester, Magee putting new front on his building
6/5/1936	News-Democrat	Buildings	Winchester, many storefronts being remodeled
6/12/1878	Journal	Buildings	Winchester, Martin made brick for General Stone's residence; courthouse is pressed brick
7/22/1874	Journal	Buildings	Winchester, Meridian and Washington, southeast corner, two new buildings, each 21 feet on Meridian and back 80 feet; corner will be Journal Building; other will be post office and Good Templars Hall upstairs
12/27/1965	News	Buildings	Winchester, Meridian Street, frame building between By-Lo (Kelley Block) and old Newspaper office destroyed by fire
6/13/1883	Journal	Buildings	Winchester, Miller and Fudge's New Block, ground broken for
6/14/1899	Journal	Buildings	Winchester, Miller Block and Hirsch Block are under construction
5/24/1899	Journal	Buildings	Winchester, Miller Block, foundation in
6/4/1902	Journal	Buildings	Winchester, Miller Building and Kabel Building under construction
11/9/1911	Democrat	Buildings	Winchester, Mills Building is nearly complete
8/27/1919	Herald	Buildings	Winchester, Monks Home purchased by Browne for use by Poland China Company
11/27/1907	Journal	Buildings	Winchester, Moorman Building, photo
6/7/1893	Herald	Buildings	Winchester, Moorman Buildings, northeast corner of Square, being razed
6/20/1883	Journal	Buildings	Winchester, Moorman Way and Lewis plan building on north side of Square
7/3/1878	Journal	Buildings	Winchester, Moorman Way will erect brick building on North Front
7/26/1980	News-Gazette	Buildings	Winchester, Moorman-Ault House
3/28/1929	Democrat	Buildings	Winchester, Morris Block is started on South Main Street
1/17/1877	Journal	Buildings	Winchester, National Bank, J. C. Johnson will remodel National Bank Building with iron front
6/3/1874	Journal	Buildings	Winchester, Neff and Bowen Building awaits brick

Date	Source	Category	Description
8/5/1874	Journal	Buildings	Winchester, Neff and Bowen's new building is about complete
8/26/1874	Journal	Buildings	Winchester, Neff, A. J., new business house on south side of Square
9/10/1873	Journal	Buildings	Winchester, Neff, H. H. is building house on Meridian Street
5/1/1963	News	Buildings	Winchester, new armory
6/6/1963	Journal-Herald	Buildings	Winchester, new armory
7/13/1964	News	Buildings	Winchester, new armory to be dedicated on July 18 by Governor Matthew Welsh
8/15/1894	Journal	Buildings	Winchester, new bank building described
7/11/1894	Journal	Buildings	Winchester, new bank room is done
10/1/1926	Daily News	Buildings	Winchester, new building is being built between the City Building and the hotel
1/10/1894	Herald	Buildings	Winchester, new building on north side of Square
3/27/1912	Herald	Buildings	Winchester, new buildings (Hiatt and Hirsch) to be built on east side of Square
10/15/1903	Democrat	Buildings	Winchester, new city building accepted
9/4/1902	Democrat	Buildings	Winchester, new city building is planned
5/12/1981	News-Gazette	Buildings	Winchester, new city building is planned
4/24/1895	Journal	Buildings	Winchester, new electric light plan on North West Street
4/9/1971	News-Gazette	Buildings	Winchester, new Marsym Building and new Burger Chef
4/3/1912	Journal	Buildings	Winchester, O. E. Davis is building a new garage on South Main Street
8/13/1913	Journal	Buildings	Winchester, old brewery on W. North Street being razed
6/27/1883	Journal	Buildings	Winchester, old building on north side of Square was built about 1826; torn down
4/26/1893	Journal	Buildings	Winchester, old buildings pulled down on North Front
7/10/1878	Journal	Buildings	Winchester, Old Corner Building to be rebuilt by James Moorman and Moorman Way; excavation for additions
6/20/1883	Journal	Buildings	Winchester, old house on north side of the Square is being razed; sixty years old; no sawed lumber in it
12/3/1971	News-Gazette	Buildings	Winchester, Old Journal Building Photograph
12/10/1971	News-Gazette	Buildings	Winchester, Old Journal Building Photograph [article says it was Engle Building, built in 1866 from old Courthouse]
12/19/1906	Journal	Buildings	Winchester, Old Journal Building will be modernized by Jet Moorman

Date	Source	Category	Description
12/24/1966	Journal-Herald	Buildings	Winchester, old newspaper building in 100 block of N. Meridian, built in 1903, is razed
6/1/1984	News-Gazette	Buildings	Winchester, old service station/police station on East Washington Street razed
7/27/1910	Herald	Buildings	Winchester, Old Woolen Mill, built in 1880, being razed; mill had previously used the old Seminary Building
10/29/1969	Journal-Herald	Buildings	Winchester, People's Loan and Trust building demolition; photo
11/27/1907	Herald	Buildings	Winchester, photo of Moorman Building
10/16/1956	Journal-Herald	Buildings	Winchester, photo of Old Woolen Mill on Carl Street
2/7/1912	Herald	Buildings	Winchester, plans for new buildings
8/4/1983	News-Gazette	Buildings	Winchester, plans for new city building
4/18/1956	News	Buildings	Winchester, police station at Main and Washington removed
10/27/1897	Herald	Buildings	Winchester, Pretlow Block is nearly completed
10/16/1895	Journal	Buildings	Winchester, Pretlow Block will be built
5/6/1908	Journal	Buildings	Winchester, Pretlow Block, drawing of
7/14/1897	Journal	Buildings	Winchester, Pretlow Block, work on
6/23/1897	Herald	Buildings	Winchester, Pretlow, J. J. bought lot to build block on Meridian Street
4/23/1984	News-Gazette	Buildings	Winchester, Pythian (Sanzo) Building, work; bricks from Farmland School used to close front windows on third floor
2/7/1894	Herald	Buildings	Winchester, Pythian Block nearing completion
6/7/1978	News-Gazette	Buildings	Winchester, Pythian Building
8/14/1978	News-Gazette	Buildings	Winchester, Pythian Building sold
9/10/1979	News-Gazette	Buildings	Winchester, Pythian Building work nearly complete
4/30/1979	News-Gazette	Buildings	Winchester, Pythian Building, east part of 3rd floor removed
11/29/1978	News-Gazette	Buildings	Winchester, Pythian Building, leased in late 1973 and early 1974 by Local Council JOUAM to others
3/25/1978	News-Gazette	Buildings	Winchester, Pythian Building, no tax exemption was filed after 1974
3/24/1978	News-Gazette	Buildings	Winchester, Pythian Building, title is held by State JOUAM
4/13/1979	News-Gazette	Buildings	Winchester, Pythian Building; roof collapses
6/19/1972	News-Gazette	Buildings	Winchester, Randolph County Bank razed building to east
12/20/1971	News-Gazette	Buildings	Winchester, Randolph Hotel became Beachler Apartments
6/15/1904	Journal	Buildings	Winchester, Randolph Hotel opened Saturday
8/21/1907	Journal	Buildings	Winchester, Randolph Hotel, photo

Date	Source	Category	Description
6/29/1898	Journal	Buildings	Winchester, Red Men will build north of Journal Block
6/7/1899	Herald	Buildings	Winchester, Red Men will put third story on D. F. Irvin's new block on south side of Square
8/19/1908	Herald	Buildings	Winchester, Rice's Mill being razed
8/8/1877	Journal	Buildings	Winchester, Richardson's third floor is nearly complete
12/11/1913	Democrat	Buildings	Winchester, Smith Building, corner of Main and North Streets, is occupied for first time
8/6/1913	Herald	Buildings	Winchester, Smith Building, corner of Main and North Streets, started
8/13/1919	Journal	Buildings	Winchester, Snedeker Block is being razed
5/22/1907	Herald	Buildings	Winchester, Snedeker Building being razed to be replaced by Goodrich Brothers with a brick block
8/21/1919	Democrat	Buildings	Winchester, Snedeker Building is being razed; it was built after the Civil War
8/6/1919	Herald	Buildings	Winchester, Snedeker Building to be razed and replaced
10/4/1876	Journal	Buildings	Winchester, Snedeker is erecting a large business room on North Main Street
8/21/1878	Journal	Buildings	Winchester, Snedeker plans large hall over his business rooms on North Main Street
11/13/1878	Journal	Buildings	Winchester, Snedeker's Hall is nearly complete
1/27/1979	News-Gazette	Buildings	Winchester, Stone Mansion
9/15/1915	Herald	Buildings	Winchester, Stone Mansion traded
6/14/1917	Democrat	Buildings	Winchester, Stone Mansion, J. E. Hinshaw and family are moving to W. E. Miller Property
6/20/1917	Journal	Buildings	Winchester, Stone Mansion, J. E. Hinshaw is moving into the house, which has been modernized
12/16/1916	Herald	Buildings	Winchester, Stone Mansion, J. E. Hinshaw purchased it and will move there in the spring
9/27/1916	Journal	Buildings	Winchester, Stone Mansion, J. E. Hinshaw will become owner
4/10/1901	Herald	Buildings	Winchester, T. F. Moorman and Red Men to build on North Main Street
4/22/1885	Journal	Buildings	Winchester, Temperance Hall Block is located on the west side of the Square
5/12/1911	Democrat	Buildings	Winchester, Thomas Ward House moved from south side of Square to West South Street; house is 50 years hold
1/20/1875	Journal	Buildings	Winchester, Thomas Ward will build east of the City Hall this season

Date	Source	Category	Description
4/19/1911	Journal	Buildings	Winchester, three story brick on the south side of the Square, occupied by T. J. Ashton and the GAR, is for sale
2/7/1883	Journal	Buildings	Winchester, two new buildings are planned for south side of Square
6/14/1899	Journal	Buildings	Winchester, W. D. Clark's new house and barn are progressing
8/29/1894	Herald	Buildings	Winchester, W. D. Kizer Building is planned
9/4/1912	Journal	Buildings	Winchester, W. E. Miller Building, brick placed for new third floor
8/1/1912	Democrat	Buildings	Winchester, W. E. Miller Company to add third floor
1/13/1897	Journal	Buildings	Winchester, W. E. Miller has purchased General Stone Property
7/31/1912	Herald	Buildings	Winchester, W. E. Miller to add third story to building
4/17/1889	Journal	Buildings	Winchester, W. E. Miller will erect three story building on old Cottom Property on south side of Square
2/20/1889	Journal	Buildings	Winchester, W. E. Miller will expand his business house to the east 22 1/2 feet
3/19/1902	Herald	Buildings	Winchester, W. E. Miller, Adam Kabel, Sr., and Adam Kabel, Jr. to build three new buildings on the south side of the Square
7/24/1889	Journal	Buildings	Winchester, W. E. Miller's new store described
10/14/1978	News-Gazette	Buildings	Winchester, Ward House photo
5/10/1911	Herald	Buildings	Winchester, Ward House to be moved to West South Street
3/15/1911	Journal	Buildings	Winchester, Ward House, on the Square, will be sold
10/14/1874	Journal	Buildings	Winchester, Way, F. M., new building, post office, south of Journal Building
2/25/1903	Herald	Buildings	Winchester, Winchester Herald, new building on North Meridian Street
1/4/1893	Journal	Buildings	Winchester, Winchester Journal moves to new building on North Meridian Street, 20 x 53
8/17/1892	Journal	Buildings	Winchester, Winchester Journal will build a building, 20 x 80, two-stories, on North Meridian Street
10/19/1892	Journal	Buildings	Winchester, Winchester Journal, brick work completed on new building
9/21/1892	Journal	Buildings	Winchester, Winchester Journal, first brick laid on new office
6/14/1893	Journal	Buildings	Winchester, work of tearing down the old bank began yesterday
2/7/1883	Journal	Buildings	Winchester, Yunker Property on Main Street will be covered with a business block
11/20/1878	Journal	Buildings	Windsor, fire

Date	Source	Category	Description
10/11/1923	Democrat	Buildings	Windsor, fire burns IORM Hall, barber shop, and grocery
9/29/1897	Herald	Buildings	Windsor, KGE is building a two-story business block and hall
6/2/1965	News	Buildings	Wysong Home on Hogback Road
3/20/1971	News-Gazette	Buildings	Wysong Home sold
7/22/1858	Journal	Business	Mills exist at Lynnville, Union City, Deerfield, Farmland
8/3/1968	Journal-Herald	Businesses	Acme-Goodrich Corporation dissolved
7/25/1946	Journal-Herald	Businesses	Advance Telephone Company, serving rural Winchester, purchased by Eastern Indiana Telephone Company
11/22/1899	Herald	Businesses	Arba, Crete, Bartonia featured
2/25/1961	Journal-Herald	Businesses	Banks, Carlos Bank building sold to church; to be razed
1/12/1933	Journal-Herald	Businesses	Banks, Carlos Bank closed Saturday
10/30/1919	Democrat	Businesses	Banks, Carlos City exists
6/17/1915	Democrat	Businesses	Banks, Carlos City, new bank
6/30/1920	Journal-Herald	Businesses	Banks, Carlos, Farmers Banking Company exists
6/23/1915	Herald	Businesses	Banks, Carlos, organized and building being built
6/9/1915	Journal	Businesses	Banks, Carlos, work is progressing on bank building
2/3/1915	Journal	Businesses	Banks, Carlos, work to establish
7/9/1938	Journal-Herald	Businesses	Banks, Citizens Bank of Ridgeville exists; S. C. Williams is a director
1/10/1924	Journal-Herald	Businesses	Banks, Citizens National Bank exists in Winchester
2/16/1933	Journal-Herald	Businesses	Banks, Citizens National Bank recently sold to People's Loan and Trust
7/9/1937	Journal-Herald	Businesses	Banks, Citizens State Bank of Ridgeville exists
3/6/1930	Journal-Herald	Businesses	Banks, Commercial National Bank and Atlas State Bank of Union City merged as Commercial Bank and Trust Company
7/21/1933	Journal-Herald	Businesses	Banks, Farmers and Merchants Bank may sell
12/11/1930	Journal-Herald	Businesses	Banks, Farmers and Merchants Bank of Winchester closed Monday
1/22/1931	Journal-Herald	Businesses	Banks, Farmers and Merchants Bank of Winchester reopened
9/24/1902	Herald	Businesses	Banks, Farmland First National Bank organized
10/6/1939	Journal-Herald	Businesses	Banks, Farmland People's Loan and Trust robbed on Wednesday, October 4; $2521.55 taken
8/6/1931	Democrat	Businesses	Banks, Farmland State Bank is purchased by People's Loan and Trust Company

Date	Source	Category	Description
8/6/1931	Journal-Herald	Businesses	Banks, Farmland State Bank taken over by People's Loan and Trust Company
5/4/1887	Journal	Businesses	Banks, Farmland, Farmers and Citizens Bank organized
12/28/1887	Journal	Businesses	Banks, Farmland, Farmers and Citizens Bank, history
1/23/1919	Democrat	Businesses	Banks, Farmland, First National Bank of Farmland to move into stone and brick new building by February 15, 1919
9/17/1902	Journal	Businesses	Banks, Farmland, First National Bank organized
1/28/1936	News-Democrat	Businesses	Banks, Farmland, First National Bank sold Saturday
5/8/1919	Democrat	Businesses	Banks, Farmland, National Bank moved to old Wright-Meeks Building, which has been remodeled
5/4/1887	Herald	Businesses	Banks, Farmland, new bank organized
4/30/1975	News-Gazette	Businesses	Banks, Farmland's new People's Loan and Trust building opens
12/21/1887	Herald	Businesses	Banks, Farmland's state bank opened
1/26/1933	Journal-Herald	Businesses	Banks, fraud at Citizens National Bank of Winchester
5/25/1910	Journal	Businesses	Banks, Greensfork Township State Bank established
3/13/1965	Journal-Herald	Businesses	Banks, Greensfork Township, new building
3/17/1954	News	Businesses	Banks, history of Saratoga State Bank
7/24/1952	Journal-Herald	Businesses	Banks, Losantville Bank history
7/23/1977	News-Gazette	Businesses	Banks, Losantville, 75th anniversary
9/10/1913	Herald	Businesses	Banks, Losantville, bank will soon be complete and ready for occupancy
10/4/1928	Democrat	Businesses	Banks, Losantville, Farmers Bank robbed
7/24/1902	Democrat	Businesses	Banks, Losantville, new bank
7/30/1902	Journal	Businesses	Banks, Losantville, new bank opened
5/22/1901	Herald	Businesses	Banks, Losantville, plans to organize
8/14/1889	Herald	Businesses	Banks, Lynn Bank organized
4/5/1954	News	Businesses	Banks, Lynn Deposit Bank (later Citizen's Bank) organized in 1892
9/25/1907	Journal	Businesses	Banks, Lynn, Citizens Bank is being reorganized as a state bank
9/25/1907	Herald	Businesses	Banks, Lynn, Citizens Bank reorganized as state bank
5/2/1900	Herald	Businesses	Banks, Lynn, Citizens Banking Company organized; took over private Lynn Deposit Bank
5/2/1900	Journal	Businesses	Banks, Lynn, new bank organized
5/7/1964	Journal-Herald	Businesses	Banks, Lynn, new building

Date	Source	Category	Description
3/10/1965	News	Businesses	Banks, Lynn, new building
4/20/1904	Herald	Businesses	Banks, Lynn, new building to be of cement blocks
1/5/1931	Democrat	Businesses	Banks, Modoc Bank robbed
10/26/1933	Democrat	Businesses	Banks, Modoc Bank robbed
3/1/1960	Journal-Herald	Businesses	Banks, Modoc People's Loan and Trust robbed
1/21/1903	Journal	Businesses	Banks, Modoc, new bank organized
1/14/1974	News-Gazette	Businesses	Banks, Mutual Home Federal Savings and Loan to build on N. Main in Winchester; first bank from outside county
5/27/1975	News-Gazette	Businesses	Banks, Mutual Home opens on June 1
1/13/1972	News-Gazette	Businesses	Banks, Parker Banking Company is sold to Hernley Family
9/27/1899	Herald	Businesses	Banks, Parker Banking Company organized
9/27/1899	Journal	Businesses	Banks, Parker, bank organized
10/6/1899	Democrat	Businesses	Banks, Parker, new bank
7/28/1977	News-Gazette	Businesses	Banks, Parker, new bank building
6/24/1976	News-Gazette	Businesses	Banks, Parking Banking Company plans to build branch on State Road 32; main building was built in 1959
8/6/1931	Journal-Herald	Businesses	Banks, Peoples Loan and Trust bought Farmland State Bank
4/10/1901	Herald	Businesses	Banks, People's Loan and Trust Company organization
10/13/1982	News-Gazette	Businesses	Banks, People's Loan and Trust East branch expanding
2/27/1968	Journal-Herald	Businesses	Banks, People's Loan and Trust eastside branch built
5/9/1968	Journal-Herald	Businesses	Banks, People's Loan and Trust eastside branch will open on May 13
2/18/1970	News-Gazette	Businesses	Banks, People's Loan and Trust new Winchester building to be done in 1970
10/7/1970	News-Gazette	Businesses	Banks, People's Loan and Trust occupies new Winchester building
12/9/1967	Journal-Herald	Businesses	Banks, People's Loan and Trust plans eastside branch
8/30/1969	Journal-Herald	Businesses	Banks, People's Loan and Trust plans new building in Winchester
2/15/1984	News-Gazette	Businesses	Banks, People's Loan and Trust sold
10/4/1969	Journal-Herald	Businesses	Banks, People's Loan and Trust vacated building in Winchester to raze it; built in 1899; home of People's Loan and Trust since 1907 [actually built as the old Journal Building long before]
12/14/1982	News-Gazette	Businesses	Banks, People's Loan and Trust, East branch reopening is December 18
6/18/1925	Journal-Herald	Businesses	Banks, Philip Kabel is president of Farmers and Merchants Bank

Date	Source	Category	Description
6/12/1984	News-Gazette	Businesses	Banks, proposal to change bank laws to allow cross county banking
11/21/1894	Herald	Businesses	Banks, Randolph County Bank, A. C. Beeson elected president
12/5/1900	Herald	Businesses	Banks, Randolph County Bank, history of
5/15/1965	Journal-Herald	Businesses	Banks, Randolph County Bank, history of
11/16/1956	News	Businesses	Banks, Randolph County Bank, new building
10/25/1899	Herald	Businesses	Banks, Randolph County Bank, new quarters
10/23/1957	News	Businesses	Banks, Randolph County Bank, opening of new building
11/29/1893	Herald	Businesses	Banks, Ridgeville Bank liquidated on November 20, 1893
12/19/1939	Journal-Herald	Businesses	Banks, Ridgeville Citizens Bank sold to People's Loan and Trust; had been formed on December 31, 1929 from First National Bank and Ridgeville State Bank in State Bank Building
10/4/1938	Journal-Herald	Businesses	Banks, Ridgeville National Bank liquidated on December 21, 1929
4/3/1901	Herald	Businesses	Banks, Ridgeville State Bank established; L. L. Williams was director
5/10/1911	Herald	Businesses	Banks, Ridgeville State Bank remodeled with new façade; GAR uses second floor
10/17/1905	Herald	Businesses	Banks, Ridgeville State Bank robbed
4/17/1901	Herald	Businesses	Banks, Ridgeville State Bank, organization of described
6/14/1906	Democrat	Businesses	Banks, Ridgeville to get a national bank
10/25/1905	Journal	Businesses	Banks, Ridgeville, bank robbery
6/30/1880	Journal	Businesses	Banks, Ridgeville, new bank opens tomorrow
1/9/1901	Journal	Businesses	Banks, Ridgeville, state bank incorporated
10/29/1975	News-Gazette	Businesses	Banks, Rural Loan and Savings Company, grand opening at 200 W. Oak, Union City
2/7/1975	News-Gazette	Businesses	Banks, Rural Loan and Savings of Hartford City plans Union City branch at Oak and Union Streets
8/27/1975	News-Gazette	Businesses	Banks, Rural Loan and Savings of Hartford City will open in Union City
3/9/1904	Herald	Businesses	Banks, Saratoga Bank opened
11/19/1903	Democrat	Businesses	Banks, Saratoga has new bank
12/3/1971	News-Gazette	Businesses	Banks, Saratoga robbed
10/28/1903	Journal	Businesses	Banks, Saratoga, bank organized
3/9/1910	Herald	Businesses	Banks, Spartanburg, new bank will open
8/15/1964	Journal-Herald	Businesses	Banks, Spartanburg, new building

Date	Source	Category	Description
12/5/1877	Journal	Businesses	Banks, Union City National Bank becomes Commercial Bank
3/14/1907	Democrat	Businesses	Banks, Union City National Bank organized
8/11/1932	Democrat	Businesses	Banks, Union City, Commercial Bank and Trust robbed
10/27/1897	Journal	Businesses	Banks, Union City, Commercial National Bank organized
3/18/1909	Democrat	Businesses	Banks, Union City, Union Trust Company organized
12/18/1930	Journal-Herald	Businesses	Banks, Union Loan and Trust Company of Union City closed last Saturday
10/12/1984	News-Gazette	Businesses	Banks, Winchester Bancorporation acquires People's Loan and Trust
5/10/1923	Journal-Herald	Businesses	Banks, Winchester has four banks
1/5/1927	Journal-Herald	Businesses	Banks, Winchester Home and Savings Association exists
12/21/1974	News-Gazette	Businesses	Banks, Winchester Home and Savings Association merged into Mutual Federal Savings Bank on January 1, 1974
8/8/1933	Journal-Herald	Businesses	Banks, Winchester Home and Savings Association moves to old Randolph County Bank Building
3/13/1889	Journal	Businesses	Banks, Winchester Home and Savings Association organized
4/9/1955	Journal-Herald	Businesses	Banks, Winchester Home and Savings Association to build on North Main; had been at Washington and Meridian for 21 years
3/31/1909	Herald	Businesses	Banks, Winchester Home and Savings Association, 20th anniversary
3/25/1964	News	Businesses	Banks, Winchester Home and Savings Association, history
2/8/1888	Journal	Businesses	Banks, Winchester, Bank of C. L. Lewis and Company opened last week
7/1/1874	Journal	Businesses	Banks, Winchester, Building and Loan Association started
10/16/1918	Herald	Businesses	Banks, Winchester, Citizens Bank moves to Main and Franklin
8/9/1917	Democrat	Businesses	Banks, Winchester, Citizens Bank opens on the south side of the Square
3/20/1878	Journal	Businesses	Banks, Winchester, Citizens Bank will be successor to Winchester Bank
4/21/1915	Journal	Businesses	Banks, Winchester, Citizens Loan and Investment Company established
1/5/1933	Democrat	Businesses	Banks, Winchester, Citizens National Bank merges with Peoples Loan and Trust Company
1/16/1918	Journal	Businesses	Banks, Winchester, Citizens National Bank purchased Engle Block

Date	Source	Category	Description
3/27/1918	Journal	Businesses	Banks, Winchester, Citizens National Bank purchased Engle Block
5/10/1917	Democrat	Businesses	Banks, Winchester, Citizens National Bank will open in the Kabel Block on the south side of the Square
4/10/1878	Journal	Businesses	Banks, Winchester, Farmers and Merchants Bank commenced [as successor to Winchester Bank]
8/3/1933	Democrat	Businesses	Banks, Winchester, Farmers and Merchants Bank consolidates with Randolph County Bank
1/5/1898	Journal	Businesses	Banks, Winchester, Farmers and Merchants Bank, history of
9/22/1859	Journal	Businesses	Banks, Winchester, James Moorman and Moorman Way are building a bank building
3/5/1890	Journal	Businesses	Banks, Winchester, Lewis Bank closed at Winchester and Lynn
3/12/1890	Journal	Businesses	Banks, Winchester, Lewis Bank failure (also at Lynn)
1/6/1865	Journal	Businesses	Banks, Winchester, National Bank is being organized
4/10/1901	Journal	Businesses	Banks, Winchester, Peoples Loan and Trust Company organized
11/28/1907	Democrat	Businesses	Banks, Winchester, People's Loan and Trust moves from Engle Block to Moorman Block
10/8/1913	Herald	Businesses	Banks, Winchester, Randolph County Bank gets new electric clock
1/18/1899	Journal	Businesses	Banks, Winchester, Randolph County Bank will be modernized
12/19/1907	Democrat	Businesses	Banks, Winchester, Savings Loan and Trust Co. organized
12/18/1907	Herald	Businesses	Banks, Winchester, Savings Loan and Trust Company is established today
11/13/1907	Herald	Businesses	Banks, Winchester, Savings Loan and Trust Company to be organized in old People's Loan and Trust Building
5/5/1875	Journal	Businesses	Banks, Winchester, second Building and Loan Association organized
8/22/1860	Journal	Businesses	Banks, Winchester, Way and Moorman's bank building is almost complete
11/30/1898	Herald	Businesses	Bear Creek Natural Gas and Oil Company organized
10/12/1870	Journal	Businesses	Bloomingport described
8/23/1905	Herald	Businesses	Bundy Saw Mill, three miles south of Winchester is reopened
3/28/1883	Journal	Businesses	Carlos, described
2/1/1969	Journal-Herald	Businesses	Carlos, Old West River Casket Corporation sold to become Carlos Casket Shell
11/20/1963	News	Businesses	Carlos, Tharp Doll Hospital

Date	Source	Category	Description
9/15/1948	News	Businesses	Citizens Heat, Light, and Power sold to American Gas and Electric (I and M); covered Farmland, Ridgeville, Fountain City, Carlos, Modoc, Saratoga, Deerfield, Lynn, Spartanburg, and Losantville
9/10/1890	Journal	Businesses	Crete, Joseph Bright has moved his goods from Lickskillet to Crete
5/11/1910	Herald	Businesses	Deerfield Elevator burns
11/27/1942	Journal-Herald	Businesses	Deerfield Grocery closing
4/11/1964	Journal-Herald	Businesses	Deerfield, history of store
2/17/1859	Journal	Businesses	Deerfield, Whipple's Mill sold to James G. Roberts
5/21/1963	Journal-Herald	Businesses	Eastern Indiana Telephone Company is sold to GT & E
2/8/1906	Democrat	Businesses	Eastern Indiana Telephone Company obtained Saratoga exchange
4/21/1909	Herald	Businesses	Eastern Indiana Telephone Company takes over Saratoga Exchange
5/6/1966	News	Businesses	Eastern Indiana Telephone Company, General Telephone, and Sullivan Telephone merge as General Telephone of Indiana
7/22/1903	Herald	Businesses	Eastern Indiana Telephone Company, Ridgeville Telephone Company, Farmland Telephone Company, Parker, Union City, Central Union, all exist in Randolph County
3/20/1984	News-Gazette	Businesses	Farmland
7/21/1886	Herald	Businesses	Farmland as it is
2/22/1882	Journal	Businesses	Farmland businesses described
1/19/1865	Journal	Businesses	Farmland businesses listed
1/19/1865	Journal	Businesses	Farmland described
9/22/1880	Journal	Businesses	Farmland is has the second highest volume of grain shipped between Union City and Indianapolis
8/7/1901	Journal	Businesses	Farmland Telephone Company extended to 1.5 miles east of Olive Branch
6/14/1900	Democrat	Businesses	Farmland Telephone Company recently organized
5/2/1911	Herald	Businesses	Farmland to get electric lights
3/17/1880	Journal	Businesses	Farmland, A. C. Black is attorney
8/26/1976	News-Gazette	Businesses	Farmland, Advanced Drainage Systems to open on West Henry St.
12/4/1984	News-Gazette	Businesses	Farmland, Alan Brown recently purchased Norman's Recreation Center
3/27/1895	Herald	Businesses	Farmland, Barker and Mills Harness Shop burned
8/20/1952	News	Businesses	Farmland, Bill Keever Studio opened at S. Plum and E. Henry

Date	Source	Category	Description
5/22/1980	News-Gazette	Businesses	Farmland, Billman's Meat Market existed from 1925-1931
4/24/1953	News	Businesses	Farmland, Charles Vannatter establishes Farmland Dry Cleaners
7/14/1932	Democrat	Businesses	Farmland, Claude Lykins buys meat market
10/18/1860	Journal	Businesses	Farmland, David Macy and Sons establish wagon shop in Farmland
11/29/1882	Journal	Businesses	Farmland, David Macy is the in the stove business again
9/24/1903	Democrat	Businesses	Farmland, described
9/23/1978	News-Gazette	Businesses	Farmland, disco
6/7/1983	News-Gazette	Businesses	Farmland, Dr. Charles Skidmore opens medical practice
6/21/1969	Journal-Herald	Businesses	Farmland, Dr. Harold Parker starts practice in Nixon Building; Dr. Nixon retired about 1965; Dr. Raleigh Miller had been there weekly
1/9/1984	News-Gazette	Businesses	Farmland, Dr. Skidmore opens his practice
12/8/1948	News	Businesses	Farmland, Duart Beauty Shop sold by H. Henderson to Mrs. Luther Thornburg
4/5/1952	Journal-Herald	Businesses	Farmland, E. L. Steiner opened Christina's Drapery Shop
3/26/1890	Herald	Businesses	Farmland, Erther's Store and IORM in "old Thornburg Block"
8/10/1970	News-Gazette	Businesses	Farmland, Farmland Locker Plant moved to new location
7/12/1916	Herald	Businesses	Farmland, Farmland Lumber Yard sold by Mills to Peter Kuntz
1/24/1894	Herald	Businesses	Farmland, first licensed saloon in twenty years
6/18/1913	Journal	Businesses	Farmland, Foster's Shoe Store damaged by fire
6/18/1913	Herald	Businesses	Farmland, Foster's Shoe Store was damaged by fire
5/14/1983	News-Gazette	Businesses	Farmland, Foster's Shoe Store, centennial
12/19/1952	News	Businesses	Farmland, Gene Hiatt Watch Shop opened on West Henry
6/7/1899	Herald	Businesses	Farmland, Goodrich Brothers purchased Farmland Elevator from Dennis Thornburg
3/5/1952	News	Businesses	Farmland, Groves Café sold to Mulls
4/14/1948	News	Businesses	Farmland, Groves Café sold to Paul Cook
1/30/1889	Herald	Businesses	Farmland, H. F. Wood purchased Watson's Grocery
1/15/1913	Journal	Businesses	Farmland, Ham McFarland sold his hardware store to Noah Wright
9/4/1964	News	Businesses	Farmland, Hensley's Café is sold to Don Hoover
12/21/1973	News-Gazette	Businesses	Farmland, Hiatt House restaurant opens in Kramer Building; Gene and Betty Hiatt, owners
1/14/1966	News	Businesses	Farmland, HPC Apartments

Date	Source	Category	Description
1/9/1918	Herald	Businesses	Farmland, Hubbard Garage burned
1/10/1918	Democrat	Businesses	Farmland, Hubbard Garage burned
8/24/1922	Democrat	Businesses	Farmland, J. H. McFarland Furniture Store is sold to George I. Bosh
5/16/1861	Journal	Businesses	Farmland, J. S. Addington has general store
6/30/1953	Journal-Herald	Businesses	Farmland, Kenneth Shaw purchased Roscoe Pursley Feed Mill
4/26/1877	Journal	Businesses	Farmland, L. C. DeVoss and David Wasson are attorneys who moved to town
7/14/1972	News-Gazette	Businesses	Farmland, liquor store discussion; Rev. Barney Jester, Rev. David Phillips, and Rev. Orville Fisher led opposition
8/25/1972	News-Gazette	Businesses	Farmland, liquor store is approved
6/17/1960	News	Businesses	Farmland, Louis Lumpkin, DVM starts in Farmland
3/5/1964	Journal-Herald	Businesses	Farmland, lumberyard and stockyards closed
10/9/1959	News	Businesses	Farmland, Maple Terrace Flower Shop and Beauty Bar in P. O. Building; owned by Betty Roeger
1/25/1923	Democrat	Businesses	Farmland, McFarland repurchased the furniture store from Bosh
11/17/1967	News	Businesses	Farmland, new Thornburg Funeral Home near Monroe Central School
9/10/1936	Daily News	Businesses	Farmland, new Thornburg Funeral Home to be dedicated
4/10/1918	Herald	Businesses	Farmland, Oswald Mill burned
4/11/1918	Democrat	Businesses	Farmland, Oswald Mill burned; also burned three years ago
12/3/1947	News	Businesses	Farmland, Paul Mendenhall takes over bulk plan after the death of Ernest Bolinger
4/5/1972	News-Gazette	Businesses	Farmland, plans for liquor store
12/27/1905	Herald	Businesses	Farmland, saw mill burned
1/17/1894	Journal	Businesses	Farmland, Shaffer Saloon will open in Farmland, first licensed saloon in 25 years
9/20/1951	Journal-Herald	Businesses	Farmland, Shaw, Glen purchased North End Grocery
7/30/1964	Journal-Herald	Businesses	Farmland, Shockney Seed Service will open in the winter
8/21/1872	Journal	Businesses	Farmland, Simon Barnum sold out to Judge Miller
8/28/1872	Journal	Businesses	Farmland, Simon Barnum sold out to Judge Miller
3/25/1949	News	Businesses	Farmland, Slaughter-Owens Agency formed; history of previous agencies
9/11/1967	News	Businesses	Farmland, Starlight Ballroom opens in Farmland Opera House
5/5/1911	Democrat	Businesses	Farmland, to get electric power plant
8/13/1979	News-Gazette	Businesses	Farmland, Village Pantry to open on August 16

Date	Publication	Category	Description
7/9/1919	Herald	Businesses	Farmland, Weiler and Lumpkin to build annex to store
2/13/1884	Journal	Businesses	Farmland, will get telephone office soon
8/21/1952	Journal-Herald	Businesses	Farmland, William Keever opens photography studio
8/31/1973	News-Gazette	Businesses	Gulf Stations ceased
7/10/1974	News-Gazette	Businesses	Harrisville Grain Company closes
12/5/1942	Journal-Herald	Businesses	Harrisville Grocery closing
2/16/1910	Journal	Businesses	Harrisville, Luther Coats sold out to Frank Rowe
11/15/1947	Journal-Herald	Businesses	Haworth's Mill of pioneer days described
6/28/1980	News-Gazette	Businesses	Hinshaw Ag Copter
4/16/1951	News	Businesses	Hoosier Automobile Company, history of
5/25/1950	Journal-Herald	Businesses	Hubbard Manufacturing article
12/1/1886	Herald	Businesses	Huntsville
3/30/1887	Journal	Businesses	Huntsville
8/10/1887	Herald	Businesses	Huntsville
3/29/1916	Journal	Businesses	Huntsville, George A. Rowe recently moved into town to start in auto and garage business
3/2/1916	Journal	Businesses	Huntsville, George Rowe sells cars
10/26/1964	News	Businesses	Huntsville, grocery still exists
3/29/1949	Journal-Herald	Businesses	Huntsville, Indianapolis Star of March 29 features Gaines Store
12/3/1902	Herald	Businesses	Huntsville, Israel Johnson takes over his brother's store
3/17/1971	News-Gazette	Businesses	Huntsville, junk yards; only 2 adult lifelong residents in the village
1/15/1896	Journal	Businesses	Huntsville, Levi Johnson sold out
5/2/1952	News	Businesses	Huntsville, store for sale (photo)
5/29/1901	Journal	Businesses	Jericho Telephone Company disbanded; another will be organized
5/1/1901	Journal	Businesses	Jericho Telephone Company exists; officers listed
8/26/1981	News-Gazette	Businesses	Jericho Telephone Company, 1901
7/3/1901	Journal	Businesses	Jericho, Advance Telephone Company organized near Jericho
2/20/1974	News-Gazette	Businesses	Landfill planned
2/20/1918	Journal	Businesses	Lewellen, E. F. has had store at Nigger Holler for 25 years; also has one at Mull
2/20/1918	Journal	Businesses	Lewellen, E. F. is "Nigger Holler Merchant"
5/6/1952	Journal-Herald	Businesses	Lickskillet, Gail Meranda died, once owned store at Lickskillet for 15 years
9/10/1890	Journal	Businesses	Lickskillet, Joseph Bright has moved his goods from Lickskillet to Crete

Date	Publication	Category	Description
5/15/1895	Journal	Businesses	Lickskillet, Ludwick's Store and House burned
9/10/1890	Journal	Businesses	Lickskillet, Lum Ludwick takes over Jo [sic] Bright's store
2/23/1887	Journal	Businesses	Losantville
7/24/1952	Journal-Herald	Businesses	Losantville bank history
11/8/1899	Herald	Businesses	Losantville featured
12/21/1973	News-Gazette	Businesses	Losantville, Muncie Tool and Die to build new building here
5/23/1984	News-Gazette	Businesses	Lynn
1/23/1895	Journal	Businesses	Lynn
12/15/1886	Journal	Businesses	Lynn
7/23/1902	Journal	Businesses	Lynn and Fountain City telephone companies merged
11/29/1899	Herald	Businesses	Lynn featured; town named by Nathan Hinshaw, Jesse Johnson, and Paul Beard
6/3/1903	Journal	Businesses	Lynn Telephone Company is erecting temporary building
11/4/1903	Herald	Businesses	Lynn, Citizens Bank will build new building
10/1/1903	Democrat	Businesses	Lynn, described
4/29/1971	News-Gazette	Businesses	Lynn, Meyer Manufacturing Company (caskets) burned
8/14/1895	Journal	Businesses	Lynn, Miles J. Furnas purchased hardware store
6/28/1973	News-Gazette	Businesses	Lynn, Ralph Hinshaw retires as a florist
2/22/1912	Democrat	Businesses	Lynn, to get electricity
10/4/1911	Journal	Businesses	Maxville, Rollie Wright sold the Maxville Mill to Reuben Oren
5/8/1984	News-Gazette	Businesses	Modoc and Losantville
11/15/1899	Herald	Businesses	Modoc featured
6/27/1975	News-Gazette	Businesses	Modoc, liquor store attempted to be established by Tom Fields
1/21/1903	Journal	Businesses	Modoc, new bank
3/9/1887	Journal	Businesses	Modoc/Carlos City featured
3/22/1871	Journal	Businesses	Morristown, Dotson and Macy are refitting the old stand of A. Devoss, occupying the corner of Main and Railroad, north of hotel
9/8/1950	News	Businesses	Mull, Don Hoover sold Mull Grocery to Jordans
10/22/1919	Herald	Businesses	Mull, Gail Meranda has completed new store
5/15/1895	Herald	Businesses	Mull, Lindsay Ludwick's store burned
9/16/1896	Journal	Businesses	Mull, Mack Ludwick starts a store
9/4/1919	Democrat	Businesses	Mull, Meranda's new store is nearly completed
8/14/1940	Journal-Herald	Businesses	Mull, Quality Service Store opened on August 10

Date	Source	Category	Description
12/26/1877	Journal	Businesses	Neff Post Office, Canada's Store and Post Office burned on Tuesday of last week
9/6/1899	Journal	Businesses	Neff, store sold by Mr. Hewitt to Curg [sic] Engle
1/31/1906	Journal	Businesses	Nigger Holler Store exists
4/3/1901	Herald	Businesses	Nigger Holler, E. F. Lewellen started store in 1895
1/15/1896	Journal	Businesses	Nigger Holler, I. H. Armtrout [sic] will build a business room for E. F. Lewellen
3/18/1896	Herald	Businesses	Nigger Hollow, mentioned
12/15/1875	Journal	Businesses	Olive Branch, Addington's Store burned
12/24/1879	Journal	Businesses	Olive Branch, Alonzo Brinkley in old stand under Masonic Hall; Benjamin Morris preached here last Sabbath
12/19/1877	Journal	Businesses	Olive Branch, Byrd's Store mentioned
1/9/1907	Journal	Businesses	Olive Branch, Charles Amburn purchased store
4/4/1877	Journal	Businesses	Olive Branch, G. H. Byrd and Samuel McNees had store
3/29/1876	Journal	Businesses	Olive Branch, James Richwine had store
9/28/1881	Journal	Businesses	Olive Branch, L. Brinkley is storekeeper; Henry Courtner starts third year as teacher
9/28/1881	Journal	Businesses	Olive Branch, L. Brinkley owns store
10/19/1881	Journal	Businesses	Olive Branch, Lon Brinkley sells goods
11/22/1916	Journal	Businesses	Olive Branch, Robert P. Horn died; once in business at Olive Branch
3/16/1887	Journal	Businesses	Olive Branch, S. C. Williams and Daniel Jones will start a wagon shop
3/19/1879	Journal	Businesses	Olive Branch, Samuel Ford has grocery
4/4/1877	Journal	Businesses	Olive Branch, Samuel McNees and Green H. Byrd will have store
4/11/1877	Journal	Businesses	Olive Branch, Samuel McNees moved to Olive Branch
4/25/1877	Journal	Businesses	Olive Branch, Samuel McNees moved to Olive Branch to run store
4/17/1878	Journal	Businesses	Olive Branch, store moved to Fairview; Broods blacksmith; Mullenix Shoes
11/19/1960	Journal-Herald	Businesses	OMCO history
4/3/1984	News-Gazette	Businesses	Parker
11/9/1892	Journal	Businesses	Parker has secured a glass factory
5/3/1893	Journal	Businesses	Parker has secured church furniture factory and buggy factory
7/10/1901	Journal	Businesses	Parker Telephone Company organized
8/3/1904	Herald	Businesses	Parker Telephone Company purchased Losantville Telephone plant

1/20/1915	Journal	Businesses	Parker, Eastern Indiana Telephone Company will erect brick building
11/20/1901	Herald	Businesses	Parker, furniture factory rebuilt
5/8/1965	Journal-Herald	Businesses	Parker, history of Central Manufacturing
9/22/1983	News-Gazette	Businesses	Parker, Thornburg Funeral Home was sold to Joe Davis; had been owned by Guy and Tim Faussett since 1978
5/15/1901	Journal	Businesses	Parker, Vaught Brothers burned
5/15/1901	Herald	Businesses	Parker, Vaught Brothers burns
6/3/1914	Herald	Businesses	Parker, Vaught Brothers Furniture Company sold
8/25/1909	Herald	Businesses	Parker, Vaught Brothers Furniture Company sold at auction
6/22/1904	Journal	Businesses	Parker, Woodbury Glass will move to Winchester
9/13/1965	News	Businesses	People's Loan and Trust, photos of all buildings
12/15/1909	Herald	Businesses	Pinch gets telephone service
10/10/1970	News-Gazette	Businesses	Pinch, Randolph County Hybrid Growers, organized in 1939; moved to Pinch in 1942
6/5/1901	Journal	Businesses	Randolph County has 661 independent telephones and 195 central union telephones
12/16/1936	Daily News	Businesses	Randolph County Rural Electrification (Lee Gaddis on the committee); Nettle Creek, Stoney Creek, and Monroe Townships will be electrified from Muncie; Winchester to electrify Ward Township; West River will be electrified from Wayne County
1/31/1936	News-Democrat	Businesses	Randolph County Rural Electrification Corporation directors were re-elected; Lee Gaddis was one of the five; plans were being made for rural electrification in Randolph County
3/27/1984	News-Gazette	Businesses	Ridgeville
1/23/1895	Journal	Businesses	Ridgeville
1/19/1887	Herald	Businesses	Ridgeville as it is
2/8/1939	Journal-Herald	Businesses	Ridgeville Elevator burned
10/21/1968	Journal-Herald	Businesses	Ridgeville goes to seven digit phone numbers
10/22/1903	Democrat	Businesses	Ridgeville, described
7/17/1901	Herald	Businesses	Ridgeville, Goodrich Elevator completed
8/20/1902	Journal	Businesses	Ridgeville, Jenkinson had first store in Ridgeville, then Newtown, in 1843
11/8/1899	Journal	Businesses	Ridgeville, Kitselman Brothers to move to Muncie
3/8/1905	Herald	Businesses	Ridgeville, Kitselman history

Date	Source	Category	Description
11/14/1900	Herald	Businesses	Ridgeville, Kitselman Steel and Wire moves to Muncie
5/21/1936	News-Democrat	Businesses	Ridgeville, Kraft Cheese Plant to open on May 29, 1936
11/26/1925	Journal-Herald	Businesses	Ridgeville, Lay Broom Factory will move to Portland
4/10/1952	Journal-Herald	Businesses	Ridgeville, Lee Hollowell sold agency to Charles J. Mock
12/12/1935	News-Democrat	Businesses	Ridgeville, National Brush and Broom Factory dissolved; will be sold
9/26/1980	News-Gazette	Businesses	Ridgeville, no doctor in town since 1970
9/9/1909	Democrat	Businesses	Saloon, last saloon in county is closed
4/10/1984	News-Gazette	Businesses	Saratoga and Deerfield
8/4/1886	Herald	Businesses	Saratoga as she was found
4/15/1978	News-Gazette	Businesses	Saratoga Elevator closed
11/1/1899	Herald	Businesses	Saratoga featured
1/26/1976	News-Gazette	Businesses	Saratoga, Campbell's Soup Plant to close; established in 1912; purchased by Campbell's in 1948
7/9/1971	News-Gazette	Businesses	Saratoga, Moyer Chevrolet to be sold
11/27/1918	Herald	Businesses	Saratoga, saw mill ceases
1/8/1902	Journal	Businesses	Saratoga, the Branch Independent Telephone Company organized
5/25/1922	Democrat	Businesses	Shedville Store burned
3/12/1879	Journal	Businesses	Shedville, Alonzo Brinkly [sic] started grocery at Maranda's [sic] Saw Mills, six miles north of Farmland
7/29/1903	Journal	Businesses	Snow Hill, C. R. Carter sold out to Ora Study
5/26/1960	Journal-Herald	Businesses	Speedway, Frank Funk sells
4/11/1953	Journal-Herald	Businesses	Speedway, sold by Frank Funk
6/8/1938	Journal-Herald	Businesses	Stone Station Elevator burned; it previously burned on May 22, 1932
5/26/1932	Democrat	Businesses	Stone Station Elevator burns
2/23/1922	Democrat	Businesses	Stone Station Elevator is sold
10/2/1951	Journal-Herald	Businesses	Stone Station, Grocery sold by Charlie Schubert to William Gulley
6/24/1920	Democrat	Businesses	Stone Station, new elevator completed
12/14/1887	Journal	Businesses	Stone Station, store of Cal R. Hunt burned last Tuesday
9/6/1899	Journal	Businesses	Stone Station, store sold by N. Culberson to Edward Harman, son of Daniel
9/20/1952	Journal-Herald	Businesses	Stone Station, store sold to Rev. Spare
7/25/1975	News-Gazette	Businesses	Telephone companies, Old General Telephone Building at 114 E. Franklin razed; history of telephone companies in Randolph County

Date	Source	Category	Description
6/21/1947	Journal-Herald	Businesses	Telephone Company history
8/8/1917	Herald	Businesses	Twin Bridges, store burned
6/5/1984	News-Gazette	Businesses	Union City
7/17/1901	Journal	Businesses	Union City Automobile Company organized
5/15/1957	News	Businesses	Union City Bottling Company, history
11/15/1969	Journal-Herald	Businesses	Union City Coca-Cola plant sold to Portland plant
3/20/1961	News	Businesses	Union City switched to dial phones
6/16/1926	Daily News	Businesses	Union City Telephone Company is sold to Interstate Telephone Company
9/25/1901	Journal	Businesses	Union City, auto factory, contracts for Lambert's auto factory
11/11/1982	News-Gazette	Businesses	Union City, Burger Chef (established in 1977) becomes Hardees
1/9/1976	News-Gazette	Businesses	Union City, Champion Del-Mar sold to Triangle Pacific
12/5/1981	News-Gazette	Businesses	Union City, Coca-Cola plant moves to Portland
12/6/1978	News-Gazette	Businesses	Union City, Coca-Cola plant to close
7/23/1940	Journal-Herald	Businesses	Union City, Coke Bottling
8/27/1903	Democrat	Businesses	Union City, described
2/3/1976	News-Gazette	Businesses	Union City, Essex International Plant closes
2/5/1976	News-Gazette	Businesses	Union City, Essex International was Backstay Welt, established in 1898; history
8/26/1914	Herald	Businesses	Union City, Ford's Hospital opened
11/22/1980	News-Gazette	Businesses	Union City, Kirshbaum's closed in 1977
12/28/1950	Journal-Herald	Businesses	Union City, new Westinghouse plant
5/17/1951	Journal-Herald	Businesses	Union City, new Westinghouse plant
6/28/1926	Daily News	Businesses	Union City, Union Heat, Light, and Power Company sold to Indiana-Ohio Public Service Company
2/8/1984	News-Gazette	Businesses	Union City, Westinghouse scales back
1/27/1972	News-Gazette	Businesses	Union City, Westinghouse, 20th anniversary
7/31/1984	News-Gazette	Businesses	Winchester
3/28/1973	News-Gazette	Businesses	Winchester A & P closing after 50 years
6/3/1903	Herald	Businesses	Winchester and Eastern Indiana Telephone Companies consolidated
11/10/1932	Journal-Herald	Businesses	Winchester Department Store is going out of business
2/13/1889	Journal	Businesses	Winchester Electric Light Company organized
3/22/1971	News-Gazette	Businesses	Winchester Elevator closed
4/22/1941	Journal-Herald	Businesses	Winchester glass strike ended

Date	Source	Category	Description
5/11/1950	Journal-Herald	Businesses	Winchester goes to automatic dial on May 11
6/17/1958	Journal-Herald	Businesses	Winchester has seven auto dealers
7/15/1961	Journal-Herald	Businesses	Winchester Marsh Store opened
5/26/1960	Journal-Herald	Businesses	Winchester Speedway sold
11/22/1905	Herald	Businesses	Winchester Telephone Company bought Parker exchange and became Eastern Indiana Telephone Company
11/18/1896	Journal	Businesses	Winchester Telephone Exchange established by Fockler Brothers
12/24/1884	Journal	Businesses	Winchester Wagon Works has closed down
10/19/1881	Journal	Businesses	Winchester Wagon Works organized
8/16/1911	Herald	Businesses	Winchester, "phone trouble," battle between phone companies, ends
4/17/1982	News-Gazette	Businesses	Winchester, 3-D (Danners) Grand Opening
1/8/1982	News-Gazette	Businesses	Winchester, 3-D and Marsh being built
6/12/1980	News-Gazette	Businesses	Winchester, Armstrong Flag Pole is 100 feet tall; built by Hinshaw Building Service
3/27/1981	News-Gazette	Businesses	Winchester, Armstrong, Uncle Sam is erected
1/8/1983	News-Gazette	Businesses	Winchester, Boston Store closed
1/15/1983	News-Gazette	Businesses	Winchester, Boston Store is closing
3/23/1898	Journal	Businesses	Winchester, Boston Store opened
8/10/1934	Journal-Herald	Businesses	Winchester, Boston Store will move to site of W. E. Miller Store in Winchester by October 1
12/16/1916	Herald	Businesses	Winchester, Bowers Book Store sold
3/8/1969	Journal-Herald	Businesses	Winchester, Bunsold's Grocery out of business
7/21/1984	News-Gazette	Businesses	Winchester, Bunsold's Grocery, history of
4/13/1973	News-Gazette	Businesses	Winchester, Bunsold's Supermarket exists
9/22/1970	News-Gazette	Businesses	Winchester, Burger Chef planned
11/20/1889	Journal	Businesses	Winchester, businessmen
11/20/1947	Journal-Herald	Businesses	Winchester, By-Lo Furniture sold to a corporation
3/5/1890	Journal	Businesses	Winchester, C. L. Lewis & Co. Bank closed; also one recently at Lynn
9/30/1969	Journal-Herald	Businesses	Winchester, Champion Homes plant complete
6/4/1969	Journal-Herald	Businesses	Winchester, Champion Homes to be built
5/22/1912	Journal	Businesses	Winchester, Charles Favorite School Wagon Factory is located on Railroad Avenue
5/3/1899	Journal	Businesses	Winchester, Chinese laundry opened
7/12/1905	Herald	Businesses	Winchester, Citizens Light Company started

43

Date	Source	Category	Description
4/9/1902	Herald	Businesses	Winchester, Coats and Hinshaw (SD and JE) have elevators at Winchester, Deerfield, and Albany
3/31/1970	News-Gazette	Businesses	Winchester, Colonel Sanders visits
3/31/1897	Journal	Businesses	Winchester, Cooperative Telephone Company organized
11/25/1914	Herald	Businesses	Winchester, Dr. Fletcher Langdon plans to establish a hospital
5/26/1909	Herald	Businesses	Winchester, E. R. Hiatt retires
10/16/1918	Journal	Businesses	Winchester, Eastern Indiana Telephone Company is permitted to expand
10/12/1984	News-Gazette	Businesses	Winchester, Eastern Indiana Telephone Company merged with General Telephone Co. in 1963
11/29/1916	Herald	Businesses	Winchester, Eastern Indiana Telephone Company takes over Farmland Telephone Company; now controls Farmland, Winchester, Parker, Ridgeville, and Saratoga
10/9/1918	Herald	Businesses	Winchester, Eastern Indiana Telephone Company to combine Redkey Telephone Company, Ridgeville Telephone Company, Farmland Telephone Company, and Lynn Telephone Company
6/4/1919	Herald	Businesses	Winchester, Eastern Indiana Telephone Company; Dunkirk Telephone Company is merged
4/6/1910	Herald	Businesses	Winchester, Ed Addington sold grocery
10/12/1984	News-Gazette	Businesses	Winchester, Edgar L. Monks Loan Corporation was formed in 1937
2/22/1905	Journal	Businesses	Winchester, Elsworth Hinshaw to build livery on W. Franklin St.
2/14/1929	Democrat	Businesses	Winchester, Engle's Music Store to move to Hiatt and Payne Building, southeast corner of the Square
9/20/1911	Herald	Businesses	Winchester, Farmer's Telephone Company gets Eastern Indiana country franchise
1/14/1914	Journal	Businesses	Winchester, Farmers' Telephone Company; C. C. Fisher and Ed Heaston are among the directors
2/9/1916	Herald	Businesses	Winchester, Farmer's Telephone Company; officers, C. C. Fisher, treasurer; J. E. Heaston, director, et al
9/14/1968	Journal-Herald	Businesses	Winchester, first cocktail lounge in Randolph County
1/12/1968	News	Businesses	Winchester, first modern hard liquor permits issued
12/28/1949	News	Businesses	Winchester, G & K Glove Factory will move to Farmland on February 1, 1950
10/18/1979	News-Gazette	Businesses	Winchester, G. C. Murphy has existed in Winchester since 1929

Date	Paper	Category	Description
1/11/1899	Herald	Businesses	Winchester, Goodrich Brothers Hay and Grain incorporated
5/15/1913	Democrat	Businesses	Winchester, Goodrich Elevator burned
5/14/1913	Journal	Businesses	Winchester, Goodrich Elevator burns
5/14/1913	Herald	Businesses	Winchester, Goodrich Elevator destroyed by fire
4/30/1914	Democrat	Businesses	Winchester, Goodrich Elevator is ready; tower is 120 feet high
7/12/1905	Herald	Businesses	Winchester, Goodrich Elevator moved from Washington and West Streets to North Main
4/24/1918	Herald	Businesses	Winchester, Goodrich Elevator, addition
10/30/1926	Daily News	Businesses	Winchester, Graft Elevator burns
11/4/1926	Democrat	Businesses	Winchester, Graft Elevator burns
7/17/1936	News-Democrat	Businesses	Winchester, Graft Elevator burns
2/17/1927	Democrat	Businesses	Winchester, Graft's new elevator is under construction
5/2/1906	Herald	Businesses	Winchester, Greer-Wilkinson building lumber yard
7/1/1983	News-Gazette	Businesses	Winchester, GTE Service Center to consolidate with Richmond
4/6/1949	News	Businesses	Winchester, Gulley Studebaker established
5/6/1903	Journal	Businesses	Winchester, H. W. Bowers to move bookstore to K of P Block
1/28/1920	Herald	Businesses	Winchester, Hecker and Doyel occupy new garage on North Main Street
9/1/1973	News-Gazette	Businesses	Winchester, Henizer and Shopman's Grocery closing
9/24/1936	Daily News	Businesses	Winchester, Hiatt and Payne Hardware Store is going out of business; photo
7/9/1957	Journal-Herald	Businesses	Winchester, Hinshaw Building Service
5/19/1951	Journal-Herald	Businesses	Winchester, history of Anchor Hocking
7/13/1963	Journal-Herald	Businesses	Winchester, history of industry
8/2/1928	Democrat	Businesses	Winchester, history of Overmyer, Woodbury, By-Lo
2/3/1915	Herald	Businesses	Winchester, hospital established at 711 W. Franklin Street; photo
10/24/1917	Herald	Businesses	Winchester, Irvin Theatre closed
7/4/1929	Democrat	Businesses	Winchester, J. C. Penney to open in Winchester
7/31/1978	News-Gazette	Businesses	Winchester, J. C. Penney was established in Winchester in 1929
9/5/1929	Journal-Herald	Businesses	Winchester, J. C. Penny established in Winchester in Mills Building
9/7/1904	Journal	Businesses	Winchester, J. F. Wentz purchased 1/2 interest in E. R. Hiatt Studio
1/30/1895	Journal	Businesses	Winchester, John Summers established Quaker Seed Company

Date	Publication	Category	Description
10/12/1887	Journal	Businesses	Winchester, Joseph Lay and Company established in Winchester
12/8/1984	News-Gazette	Businesses	Winchester, Keener's Sports Store, W. Franklin, is closing; oldest blacksmith building in city
12/14/1971	News-Gazette	Businesses	Winchester, Kentucky Fried Chicken opened
9/1/1972	News-Gazette	Businesses	Winchester, Lobdell-Emery begins
10/16/1973	News-Gazette	Businesses	Winchester, Lobdell-Emery begins
9/11/1901	Herald	Businesses	Winchester, lumber yard, new (Wilkinson)
10/2/1924	Democrat	Businesses	Winchester, Lyric Theatre nearly completed
10/13/1983	News-Gazette	Businesses	Winchester, Maul Brothers changed to Maul Technology
1/7/1926	Democrat	Businesses	Winchester, McCamish Factory opens on east end of Franklin Street
11/1/1978	News-Gazette	Businesses	Winchester, McDonalds, groundbreaking
1/18/1905	Journal	Businesses	Winchester, Miller and Furnas Grocery, photo
12/21/1984	News-Gazette	Businesses	Winchester, Mutual Loan and Finance of Winchester is owned by Mutual Security of Portland
11/12/1984	News-Gazette	Businesses	Winchester, NAPA Auto Supply opens
6/15/1949	News	Businesses	Winchester, new A & P Supermarket
2/13/1901	Journal	Businesses	Winchester, new city flouring mill is operational
10/18/1905	Herald	Businesses	Winchester, new elevator being completed
5/12/1897	Journal	Businesses	Winchester, new factory is being built west of town
8/25/1915	Herald	Businesses	Winchester, new Ford Agency in Canada Block
3/23/1904	Herald	Businesses	Winchester, new hotel to be called the "Randolph"
9/8/1909	Herald	Businesses	Winchester, New Irvin Theatre
1/4/1911	Herald	Businesses	Winchester, new telephone company organized in Orphan's Home Church, west of Winchester
7/16/1970	News-Gazette	Businesses	Winchester, no photographer in Winchester
10/24/1984	News-Gazette	Businesses	Winchester, OMCO moves corporate headquarters back to Winchester after five years in Muncie
12/21/1894	Journal	Businesses	Winchester, organ factory burned
11/20/1940	Journal-Herald	Businesses	Winchester, Overmyer Mould established on November 26, 1920
3/23/1936	News-Democrat	Businesses	Winchester, Overmyer, frame "birthplace" of Overmyer Mould to be razed; photo
6/16/1859	Journal	Businesses	Winchester, Page, William, request for a liquor license denied
8/6/1982	News-Gazette	Businesses	Winchester, People's Drug Store opens

46

Date	Source	Category	Description
4/17/1959	News	Businesses	Winchester, photo of People's Loan and Trust Building
6/15/1904	Herald	Businesses	Winchester, Randolph Hotel opened last Saturday
7/31/1969	Journal-Herald	Businesses	Winchester, Randolph Nursing Home groundbreaking
3/26/1968	Journal-Herald	Businesses	Winchester, Randolph Nursing Home planned
9/1/1983	News-Gazette	Businesses	Winchester, Randolph Nursing Home, expansion
7/16/1970	News-Gazette	Businesses	Winchester, Reed's Pharmacy closed
9/18/1930	Democrat	Businesses	Winchester, Rev. Lee Chamness opened a barber shop
7/17/1918	Journal	Businesses	Winchester, Ridgeville Telephone Company, Farmland Telephone Company, Lynn Telephone Company, Local Telephone Company, Redkey Telephone Company to merge with Eastern Indiana Telephone Company
10/31/1900	Herald	Businesses	Winchester, S. D. Coats and J. E. Hinshaw take over J. W. Bishop's elevator; opposite Big 4 Depot
12/18/1907	Journal	Businesses	Winchester, Savings, Loan, and Trust Company organized in Engle Block, southeast corner of Square
8/15/1973	News-Gazette	Businesses	Winchester, Shepherd's Clothing is closing
4/1/1982	News-Gazette	Businesses	Winchester, Silver Towne, new building
1/19/1966	News	Businesses	Winchester, St. John Chevrolet sold to Geyer
10/7/1969	Journal-Herald	Businesses	Winchester, Standard Securities to move; old building will be razed
12/7/1904	Journal	Businesses	Winchester, Thomas G. Gaddis purchased livery barn
12/7/1904	Journal	Businesses	Winchester, Thomas Gaddis Livery Barn on North Meridian Street
12/15/1972	News-Gazette	Businesses	Winchester, VAL Discount Store to open
11/18/1909	Democrat	Businesses	Winchester, W. E. Hiatt and Tully Hinshaw are building a grocery at Union and Short Streets
6/12/1902	Democrat	Businesses	Winchester, W. E. Miller booklet described
8/11/1932	Journal-Herald	Businesses	Winchester, W. E. Miller Store became Winchester Department Store
4/9/1890	Journal	Businesses	Winchester, Wagon Works, General Stone sold
8/10/1892	Journal	Businesses	Winchester, Wagoner-French Organ Company organized; includes T. F. Moorman, J. P. Goodrich, G. Leggett, and others
7/1/1978	News-Gazette	Businesses	Winchester, Waltz Drug Store closes
5/27/1967	Journal-Herald	Businesses	Winchester, West End Grocery closed

Date	Source	Category	Description
11/4/1903	Herald	Businesses	Winchester, Window Glass factory sold to Monarch Gas Company and dismantled
3/21/1967	Journal-Herald	Businesses	Winchester, WIUC has new radio tower
1/26/1979	News-Gazette	Businesses	Winchester, WIUC sold
4/29/1967	Journal-Herald	Businesses	Winchester, WIUC to go on the air
7/19/1917	Democrat	Businesses	Winchester, Woodbury Glass Company burns
7/18/1917	Journal	Businesses	Winchester, Woodbury Glass Factory burned
7/10/1907	Journal	Businesses	Winchester, Woodbury Glass factory to enlarge
7/25/1917	Herald	Businesses	Winchester, Woodbury Glass to rebuild
9/29/1897	Journal	Businesses	Windsor, W. T. Davis Store being built
10/6/1939	Journal-Herald	Businesses	Woodbury Glass organized July 1893 at Parker; moved to Winchester in November 1904; closed in 1920; reopened under Turner Glass of Terre Haute on April 22, 1920; became General Glass in 1930, later Anchor Hocking
8/6/1902	Journal	Cemeteries	Bear Creek Cemetery Association has been organized
7/31/1907	Journal	Cemeteries	Bear Creek Cemetery Association, A. H. Huffman, president
11/22/1916	Journal	Cemeteries	Bear Creek Cemetery Board completed; Asa Addington to collect money
8/16/1916	Journal	Cemeteries	Bear Creek Cemetery to be incorporated
4/19/1940	Journal-Herald	Cemeteries	Bear Creek Cemetery traded part of church lot for more cemetery space
6/10/1908	Herald	Cemeteries	Bear Creek, A. H. Huffman, president; C. T. Addington, secretary
6/6/1907	Democrat	Cemeteries	Bear Creek, A. H. Huffman, president; Calvin Addington, secretary
3/28/1917	Journal	Cemeteries	Bear Creek, A. M. Addington, president
4/4/1917	Journal	Cemeteries	Bear Creek, A. M. Addington, president; G. E. Addington, secretary
3/29/1917	Democrat	Cemeteries	Bear Creek, A. M. Addington, president; G. E. Addington, secretary-treasurer
3/24/1915	Herald	Cemeteries	Bear Creek, B. F. Addington, president; G. E. Addington, secretary
3/24/1915	Journal	Cemeteries	Bear Creek, B. F. Addington, president; George E. Addington, secretary
4/1/1914	Journal	Cemeteries	Bear Creek, B. Frank Addington, president; Calvin Addington, secretary
4/29/1920	Democrat	Cemeteries	Bear Creek, board consists of George Addington, Bill Smith, Will Green, and Alfred Addington

Date	Source	Category	Description
9/6/1916	Journal	Cemeteries	Bear Creek, election for cemetery association will be held on October 31, 1916 at New Dayton
4/5/1916	Journal	Cemeteries	Bear Creek, Grant Wright, president; George E. Addington, secretary
5/30/1888	Journal	Cemeteries	Bear Creek, iron fence is to be put up at New Dayton Cemetery
3/28/1888	Herald	Cemeteries	Bear Creek, iron fence to be erected
8/5/1909	Democrat	Cemeteries	Bear Creek, J. C. Bundy, president, Calvin Addington, secretary
3/23/1910	Herald	Cemeteries	Bear Creek, J. C. Bundy, president; C. T. Addington, secretary
7/22/1903	Journal	Cemeteries	Bear Creek, L. L. Williams president; C. T. Addington, secretary
8/3/1904	Journal	Cemeteries	Bear Creek, L. L. Williams president; C. T. Addington, secretary
4/27/1905	Democrat	Cemeteries	Bear Creek, L. L. Williams president; Calvin Addington, secretary
4/3/1913	Democrat	Cemeteries	Bear Creek, Luther L. Williams, president
7/25/1906	Journal	Cemeteries	Bear Creek, Luther L. Williams, president; Calvin Addington, secretary
4/3/1912	Herald	Cemeteries	Bear Creek, Luther L. Williams, president; T. Calvin Addington, secretary
6/11/1919	Herald	Cemeteries	Bear Creek, New Dayton Cemetery Association appointed a committee to repair the church
7/12/1916	Journal	Cemeteries	Bear Creek, plans for permanent organization of cemetery association; over $1000 subscribed
6/4/1902	Journal	Cemeteries	Bear Creek, plans to organize New Dayton Cemetery Association
4/5/1916	Journal	Cemeteries	Bear Creek, U. G. Wright, president; George E. Addington, secretary
9/4/1907	Herald	Cemeteries	Cherry Grove Cemetery Association organized on August 31, 1907
8/1/1907	Journal	Cemeteries	Cherry Grove Cemetery Association to be organized on August 31
4/27/1898	Journal	Cemeteries	Cherry Grove has 347 unmarked graves and a headstone dated 1817
10/3/1894	Journal	Cemeteries	Cherry Grove, Preparative Meeting's regulations on cemetery
9/23/1914	Democrat	Cemeteries	County Infirmary, cemetery is unmarked and located in the orchard
4/3/1912	Herald	Cemeteries	County Infirmary, death and burial listed
10/25/1899	Journal	Cemeteries	Dunkirk
7/1/1903	Journal	Cemeteries	Dunkirk cleaned last Wednesday
7/8/1903	Journal	Cemeteries	Dunkirk described
10/14/1885	Journal	Cemeteries	Dunkirk, cleanup next Saturday
6/17/1903	Journal	Cemeteries	Dunkirk, cleanup planned

Date	Source	Category	Description
2/18/1984	News-Gazette	Cemeteries	Dunkirk, history of
7/7/1984	News-Gazette	Cemeteries	Dunkirk, restoration of
7/7/1880	Journal	Cemeteries	Fountain Park dedicated
6/9/1880	Journal	Cemeteries	Fountain Park will be dedicated on July 3, 1880
11/29/1882	Journal	Cemeteries	Fountain Park, GAR is getting four cannon for the cemetery
3/17/1880	Journal	Cemeteries	Fountain Park, General Stone donated cemetery
10/29/1879	Journal	Cemeteries	Fountain Park, General Stone will donate new cemetery
11/28/1877	Journal	Cemeteries	Fountain Park, meeting to plan new cemetery in Winchester
11/12/1879	Journal	Cemeteries	Fountain Park, new cemetery will be called
5/18/1910	Journal	Cemeteries	Fountain Park, new vault
9/17/1971	News-Gazette	Cemeteries	Fountain Park, old caretaker's house razed
8/28/1970	News-Gazette	Cemeteries	Fountain Park, plans for new caretaker's house
6/23/1880	Journal	Cemeteries	Fountain Park, program for the dedication
10/24/1883	Journal	Cemeteries	Fountain Park, sexton's house is almost done
12/20/1882	Journal	Cemeteries	Fountain Park, the cannon arrived last week
6/27/1883	Journal	Cemeteries	Fountain Park, vault and gates erected
6/4/1884	Journal	Cemeteries	Hodson, located in Stoney Creek Township?
5/31/1975	News-Gazette	Cemeteries	Hoover, history of
6/2/1975	News-Gazette	Cemeteries	Hoover, history of
8/29/1900	Journal	Cemeteries	Huntsville, cemetery association, first officers listed
5/31/1905	Herald	Cemeteries	Huntsville, improvement and fence
7/25/1900	Journal	Cemeteries	Huntsville, plans for cemetery organization
4/7/1886	Journal	Cemeteries	Maxville Cemetery Association will be organized on April 16, 1886
5/17/1917	Democrat	Cemeteries	Maxville Cemetery has been sold to Woodlawn Cemetery Association
5/27/1920	Democrat	Cemeteries	Maxville, new soldiers monument
5/31/1911	Journal	Cemeteries	Maxville, old cemetery affairs settled
5/16/1917	Journal	Cemeteries	Maxville, old cemetery transferred to Woodlawn Cemetery Association
5/31/1911	Herald	Cemeteries	Maxville, trustees of burying ground appointed by Maxville Church
3/20/1907	Journal	Cemeteries	Mount Zion Cemetery Association organized recently
6/11/1902	Journal	Cemeteries	New Dayton, 1st cemetery board appointed
6/30/1909	Journal	Cemeteries	Parker, plans for a new cemetery on Losantville Pike, southeast of town [never happened]

Date	Source	Topic	Description
1/4/1911	Journal	Cemeteries	Randolph Mount Pleasant Cemetery Association was recently formed in Washington Township
9/11/1901	Journal	Cemeteries	Reitenour Cemetery Association organized
4/23/1902	Journal	Cemeteries	Reitenour Cemetery Association organized
4/10/1902	Democrat	Cemeteries	Reitenour Cemetery Association to be organized
4/24/1902	Democrat	Cemeteries	Reitenour Cemetery Association was organized
4/11/1917	Journal	Cemeteries	Reitenour Cemetery Association was organized in April 1902
5/26/1897	Journal	Cemeteries	Saratoga, IOOF took charge of cemetery
9/18/1889	Journal	Cemeteries	Sparrow Creek, cemetery to be cleaned up
8/19/1891	Journal	Cemeteries	Sparrow Creek, meeting at cemetery; no internments there for 15 years
5/7/1902	Journal	Cemeteries	Stone Station, near, Mr. and Mrs. Henry Kizer were buried there in 1833; cemetery is now abandoned
10/12/1904	Journal	Cemeteries	Union Chapel, Glen Batchelor's hands are buried there
8/1/1894	Herald	Cemeteries	White River Christian, body of Littlebury Diggs moved from White River Cemetery, ten miles west of town, to Fountain Park
5/5/1915	Herald	Cemeteries	White River Friends, Addison Cox appointed sexton
5/5/1915	Journal	Cemeteries	White River, Addison Cox is new secretary
1/29/1919	Journal	Cemeteries	White River, cemetery association recently incorporated: Silas Benson, president; David Cox, treasurer; Harrison Cox, secretary
10/16/1918	Journal	Cemeteries	White River, meeting to elect trustees will be held on October 21, 1918
3/22/1911	Journal	Cemeteries	Whitewater [Wayne County], graves from old Friends Burial ground are being moved to Goshen
6/26/1912	Herald	Cemeteries	Winchester area cemeteries, history
12/15/1886	Journal	Cemeteries	Winchester, bodies removed to new cemetery
7/24/1889	Journal	Cemeteries	Winchester, bodies removed to new cemetery (Wilmore and Ferguson)
9/28/1887	Journal	Cemeteries	Winchester, bodies were moved to Fountain Park
7/22/1891	Journal	Cemeteries	Winchester, body of mother of W. E. Burk removed from old cemetery to Richmond
11/14/1894	Journal	Cemeteries	Winchester, Captain Daly had remains of his father, mother, and brother removed to Fountain Park
6/15/1881	Journal	Cemeteries	Winchester, cemetery sexton is ill from moving bodies from old graveyard

Date	Source	Topic	Description
11/17/1880	Journal	Cemeteries	Winchester, General Stone had some bodies removed to new cemetery
2/3/1892	Journal	Cemeteries	Winchester, Grandmother Pugh buried in old cemetery
12/8/1886	Herald	Cemeteries	Winchester, graves moved from old cemetery to Fountain Park
5/26/1886	Journal	Cemeteries	Winchester, many bodies removed from old cemetery
2/6/1889	Journal	Cemeteries	Winchester, Mary Ann Maunderbach was interred at old cemetery
6/3/1885	Journal	Cemeteries	Winchester, old cemetery is in bad repair
6/6/1883	Journal	Cemeteries	Winchester, old cemetery is in bad repair
8/7/1895	Journal	Cemeteries	Winchester, old cemetery to be cleaned
8/31/1887	Journal	Cemeteries	Winchester, remains of Dol Shaw's child removed from old cemetery
10/10/1888	Journal	Cemeteries	Winchester, remains of George Fletcher were moved from old to new cemetery
5/25/1881	Journal	Cemeteries	Winchester, several bodies moved to new cemetery
8/?/1938	Journal-Herald	Churches	Cherry Grove Camp Meeting, new tabernacle
8/16/1917	Democrat	Churches	Clear Run Church is located 3.5 miles southwest of Lynn
3/11/1874	Journal	Churches	Days Creek Church located two miles west of Ridgeville
2/4/1915	Democrat	Churches	New church of a few years ago not used [probably U. B. Church in Jackson Township]
11/4/1948	Journal-Herald	Churches	New Pittsburg to be dedicated on November 7
6/24/1903	Herald	Churches	New Pittsburg Union Church was dedicated on June 21, 1903; cost $2300
6/11/1903	Democrat	Churches	New Pittsburg, Union Church will be dedicated on June 21, 1903
3/11/1874	Journal	Churches	Olive Branch revival began on Thursday before second Saturday in February; Led by Thomas Addington, Henry Cole, P. S. Stephens (M. E.), W. Cougill (M. E.), Hollingsworth (M. E.), J. H. Bond (Friends), N. Thornburg (Friends), and Whitaker (Friends)
8/29/1888	Herald	Churches	Ridgeville, two new brick churches being built
8/30/1876	Journal	Churches	Stone Station, plans for church 1/4 mile east with Jesse Diggs, J. Kolp, and P. W. Henizer involved
9/1/1909	Herald	Churches	Teachers, 193 of Randolph County's township school teachers are church members; 27 are Quakers
2/23/1910	Herald	Churches	White River Township Sunday Schools, attendance listed for each

Date	Source	Category	Description
11/20/1895	Herald	Churches	Winchester Sunday School attendance: Main Street, 181; Presbyterian, 185; Methodist, 216; Friends 91; Evangelical, 107
3/6/1912	Herald	Churches	Winchester, attorneys and church in Winchester
7/13/1946	Journal-Herald	Churches	Winchester, colored church where Perry Baker hatchery now is; church is now a house west of town
12/20/1976	News-Gazette	Churches	Winchester, history of churches
10/4/1911	Herald	Churches	Winchester, history of denominations; Presbyterian Church was organized in 1881; old building was built in 1887
12/4/1895	Herald	Churches	Winchester, history; M. E. Church organized circa 1832 with buildings in 1835, 1857, 1885; Evangelical Church organized on May 1, 1851 with church built in 1863; Main Street organized in August 1866; Friends about 1873; Catholic Church built in 1875; East Street organized in 1887 and built in 1891; Presbyterian organized in 1842, building in 1853, new building in 1887; Friends Quarterly Meeting is one of the largest in the world
7/28/1880	Journal	Churches-AME	[Bethel] colored people are building frame church on Peter Ladd farm
8/30/1882	Journal	Churches-AME	Bethel, built in 1880
9/28/1881	Journal	Churches-AME	Cabin Creek AME Church dedicated last Sabbath
9/28/1881	Journal	Churches-AME	Cabin Creek, AME Church on Cabin Creek was dedicated last Sabbath by Rev. Crosbey of Richmond
2/26/1908	Herald	Churches-AME	Shiloh, (Rural) Elkanah Benson is moving part of A. Benson's house, it being the old Shilo Church
4/20/1881	Journal	Churches-AME	Shiloh, colored people near Rural plan to repair their church
7/26/1899	Journal	Churches-AME	Snow Hill, AME meeting in Jacob B. Hinshaw's grove
8/13/1884	Journal	Churches-AME	Snow Hill, AME meeting in Jacob B. Hinshaw's grove
11/9/1892	Herald	Churches-AME	Winchester AME services in Snedeker's Hall
7/6/1887	Journal	Churches-AME	Winchester, AME Church is nearly completed
8/3/1887	Journal	Churches-AME	Winchester, AME Church will be dedicated by Rev. Dr. Townsend
7/27/1887	Journal	Churches-AME	Winchester, AME Church will be dedicated on August 7, 1887
8/5/1887	Democrat	Churches-AME	Winchester, AME Church will open next Sunday
3/23/1887	Journal	Churches-AME	Winchester, AME folks bought a lot of Thomas Ward in southwest part of town and will commence erection of a church at once

53

Date	Source	Category	Description
3/23/1892	Journal	Churches-AME	Winchester, AME quarterly meeting held in Snedeker's Hall
5/2/1888	Journal	Churches-AME	Winchester, B. J. Davis is new pastor of "colored church" [AME or ME (Colored)?]
6/29/1887	Herald	Churches-AME	Winchester, church now enclosed
8/10/1887	Herald	Churches-AME	Winchester, church opened
5/26/1886	Journal	Churches-AME	Winchester, congregation of AME Church was organized here Thursday last with 22 members
7/24/1878	Journal	Churches-AME	Winchester, E. M. C. Crosby, former pastor
9/2/1891	Herald	Churches-AME	Winchester, exists
6/22/1887	Journal	Churches-AME	Winchester, new AME Church is now enclosed
11/14/1883	Journal	Churches-AME	Winchester, plans to build church
4/13/1887	Herald	Churches-AME	Winchester, purchased lot of Thomas Ward; have 22 members
7/23/1890	Journal	Churches-AME	Winchester, Rev. Brandon is pastor of colored church here
11/8/1882	Journal	Churches-AME	Winchester, Rev. Coats has organized a class of the AME Church here; no permanent location yet
9/20/1882	Journal	Churches-AME	Winchester, Rev. J. T. Coats is new minister
6/25/1902	Herald	Churches-AME	Winchester, Rev. William Johnson, pastor of AME Church "of this city"
6/20/1888	Journal	Churches-AME	Winchester, Trustees of Second M. E. Church are trying to purchase the AME Church of F. M. Way in the southwest part of town
7/8/1887	Democrat	Churches-AME	Winchester's new AME Church is nearing completion
4/17/1959	News	Churches-Baptist	Arabia Missionary Baptist listed in directory; existed in 1958
7/27/1968	Journal-Herald	Churches-Baptist	Arabia not listed [moved to Farmland in late 1967 or early 1968]
12/8/1976	News-Gazette	Churches-Baptist	Chapelwood exists
12/2/1983	News-Gazette	Churches-Baptist	Chapelwood, new sanctuary will be dedicated on December 4
9/6/1980	News-Gazette	Churches-Baptist	Farmland Faith Baptist, 15th anniversary, John Kastelein present
11/9/1968	Journal-Herald	Churches-Baptist	Farmland, Faith Baptist Church moves to new location
8/12/1975	News-Gazette	Churches-Baptist	Maranatha Baptist Church exists
10/31/1975	News-Gazette	Churches-Baptist	Maranatha Baptist Church moved to house on U. S. 27
8/22/1975	News-Gazette	Churches-Baptist	Maranatha Baptist Church will be formally established on August 31; independent and fundamental
5/13/1977	News-Gazette	Churches-Baptist	Maranatha, history of; established in 1975; met in Winchester, then at pastor's home north of Winchester

Date	Source	Category	Description
4/22/1891	Journal	Churches-Baptist	Mosier Schoolhouse, Colista Smithson obituary, mentions Baptist church at Mosier Schoolhouse
8/21/1872	Journal	Churches-Baptist	Nettle Creek, there are only two Republican members of this church
9/12/1888	Herald	Churches-Baptist	Ridgeville, new building
12/26/1888	Journal	Churches-Baptist	Ridgeville, new church erected at a cost of $3500; will be dedicated on December 24, 1888 by Prof. Sally of Hillsdale College
3/28/1888	Journal	Churches-Baptist	Ridgeville, new church planned
12/12/1888	Herald	Churches-Baptist	Ridgeville, to be dedicated on December 23, 1888
9/14/1984	News-Gazette	Churches-Baptist	Union City, Bible Baptist Church exists at 228 1/2 W. Pearl
6/15/1984	News-Gazette	Churches-Baptist	Union City, Bible Baptist Church moved to 228 1/2 W. Pearl
3/17/1972	News-Gazette	Churches-Baptist	Winchester Central Baptist Church exists at 118 1/2 W. Washington [established in 1971]
4/21/1973	News-Gazette	Churches-Baptist	Winchester Central Baptist Church to build on Old 27; church started over a year ago
7/18/1952	News	Churches-Baptist	Winchester First Missionary Baptist Church exists
2/3/1976	News-Gazette	Churches-Baptist	Winchester First Missionary Baptist Church exists
11/29/1977	News-Gazette	Churches-Baptist	Winchester First Missionary Baptist Church, "contrary to rumors . . . Is still open"
3/17/1972	News-Gazette	Churches-Baptist	Winchester Missionary Baptist Church exists
3/9/1904	Herald	Churches-Brethren	Dunkard Church exists two miles north of Saratoga
10/1/1914	Democrat	Churches-Brethren	Shaver, Levi was baptized in Bear Creek near Quaker Hill by the Dunkards on August 3, 1913
6/9/1966	Journal-Herald	Churches-Catholic	St. Joseph's Parish Hall will be dedicated on June 12
6/10/1978	News-Gazette	Churches-Catholic	St. Joseph's to be dedicated on Sunday, June 11
6/28/1965	News	Churches-Catholic	St. Joseph's, architect's plans for new church [plans never used]
9/6/1975	News-Gazette	Churches-Catholic	St. Joseph's, centennial
4/27/1965	Journal-Herald	Churches-Catholic	St. Joseph's, groundbreaking for new parish hall
9/9/1966	News	Churches-Catholic	St. Joseph's, history of
6/17/1978	News-Gazette	Churches-Catholic	St. Joseph's, history of
1/6/1978	News-Gazette	Churches-Catholic	St. Joseph's, new church under construction
7/8/1891	Journal	Churches-Catholic	Union City, cornerstone will be laid on July 12, 1891
7/26/1893	Herald	Churches-Catholic	Union City, dedicated last Sunday

Date	Source	Category	Description
7/8/1891	Journal	Churches-Catholic	Union City, new Catholic Church
8/2/1876	Journal	Churches-Catholic	Winchester, Catholic Church is nearly enclosed
5/26/1875	Journal	Churches-Catholic	Winchester, Catholics will commence to building on West Washington Street
8/21/1895	Journal	Churches-Catholic	Winchester, church repaired
5/9/1877	Journal	Churches-Catholic	Winchester, new Catholic Church will be dedicated on May 13, 1877 by Bishop Joseph Dewenger
4/14/1875	Journal	Churches-Catholic	Winchester, plans for Catholic Church
10/25/1866	Journal	Churches-Catholic	Winchester, plans to build a Catholic Church
6/19/1863	Journal	Churches-Catholic	Winchester, plans to build a Catholic Church
4/2/1919	Journal	Churches-Catholic	Winchester, plans to remodel Catholic Church
12/8/1897	Herald	Churches-Christian	Addington, Rev. Thomas writes of differences between Christian Church and Disciples of Christ
9/19/1959	Journal-Herald	Churches-Christian	Antioch rejoined United Church of Christ
1/6/1886	Journal	Churches-Christian	Buena Vista Church has new bell
4/23/1947	News	Churches-Christian	Buena Vista Church infested with termites
4/19/1954	News	Churches-Christian	Buena Vista history
7/22/1948	Journal-Herald	Churches-Christian	Buena Vista rededication
1/16/1907	Journal	Churches-Christian	Buena Vista to be rededicated on January 20
12/19/1906	Herald	Churches-Christian	Buena Vista, church remodeling is nearly completed
1/9/1907	Journal	Churches-Christian	Buena Vista, church to be dedicated on January 20, 1907 by N. H. Thornburg
7/12/1906	Democrat	Churches-Christian	Buena Vista, church to be repaired
2/10/1909	Journal	Churches-Christian	Buena Vista, John N. Moore's obituary says that the church was originally organized at Oren's Schoolhouse
12/30/1885	Journal	Churches-Christian	Buena Vista, Lijah Johnson preaches; put bell on church
7/11/1906	Journal	Churches-Christian	Buena Vista, plans to enlarge
7/4/1906	Herald	Churches-Christian	Buena Vista, plans to enlarge church
1/9/1907	Herald	Churches-Christian	Buena Vista, work begun on church
1/12/1910	Journal	Churches-Christian	Capron, Rev. Levi and Emily celebrate 50th anniversary
9/2/1926	Daily News	Churches-Christian	Carlos Christian Church burned by lightning

Date	Source	Category	Description
5/16/1888	Journal	Churches-Christian	Carlos Christian Church dedicated on April 29, 1888
12/27/1916	Journal	Churches-Christian	Carlos City will be rededicated on December 31, 1916 by N. H. Thornburg
1/11/1888	Herald	Churches-Christian	Carlos City, new Christian Church
8/30/1928	Democrat	Churches-Christian	Carlos will be dedicated on September 9, 1928 by J. F. Burnett and Rev. Dennison of Dayton
5/9/1888	Journal	Churches-Christian	Carlos, Christian Church was dedicated last Sabbath
5/16/1888	Journal	Churches-Christian	Carlos, Christian Church was dedicated on April 29, 1888 by Rev. I. V. D. R. Johnson; class was organized by Rev. I. V. D. R. Johnson eighteen months ago; building is 32 x 60
10/6/1927	Democrat	Churches-Christian	Carlos, cornerstone was laid on October 2, 1927
5/9/1888	Herald	Churches-Christian	Carlos, dedication on April 29, 1888
2/17/1886	Journal	Churches-Christian	Carlos, plans to build a church
2/23/1887	Journal	Churches-Christian	Carlos, plans to build a church
10/6/1880	Journal	Churches-Christian	Christian Church has many members who are Democrats
5/1/1930	Democrat	Churches-Christian	Christian Churches are now united with the Congregational Churches
12/16/1908	Journal	Churches-Christian	Clear Creek Church to be rededicated on December 20, 1908 by J. F. Burnett
12/24/1908	Democrat	Churches-Christian	Clear Creek was rededicated
12/17/1908	Democrat	Churches-Christian	Clear Creek will be rededicated on December 20, 1908 by J. F. Burnett
7/4/1883	Journal	Churches-Christian	Clear Creek, Christian Church is erecting new church four miles north of town
3/15/1954	News	Churches-Christian	Clear Creek, history
3/17/1909	Herald	Churches-Christian	Clear Creek, obituary of Elizabeth Spera says she joined the Clear Creek Free Will Baptist Church in 1881 and that the building became the property of the Christian Church [seems unlikely]
10/17/1912	Democrat	Churches-Christian	Clear Creek, photo
3/19/1958	News	Churches-Christian	Congregational Christian Churches in Randolph County withdraw from the United Church of Christ
10/1/1902	Journal	Churches-Christian	Convention of the Christian Church divided, north and south, in 1858 and reunited in 1890 at Marion, Indiana
10/6/1880	Journal	Churches-Christian	Democrats, many members of the Christian Church are Democrats

Date	Source	Category	Description
3/8/1889	Democrat	Churches-Christian	Dunkirk Christian Church existed in 1868 according to obituary of Mary E. Green
3/16/1881	Journal	Churches-Christian	Dunkirk Christian Church mentioned
7/6/1879	Journal	Churches-Christian	Dunkirk Christian Church, Catherine Mosier joined in 1859 under Andy McNees
11/28/1906	Herald	Churches-Christian	Dunkirk, Calvin Puckett joined Christian Church at Dunkirk under the preaching of Rev. Thomas Addington [long before]
8/6/1879	Journal	Churches-Christian	Dunkirk, Catherine Moser obituary says she joined this church in the winter of 1859 under Andrew McNees
9/27/1882	Journal	Churches-Christian	Dunkirk, Hiram Jones's obituary says he was an elder of this church at the time of his death
9/12/1877	Journal	Churches-Christian	Dunkirk, Jonathan Wright is pastor
3/1/1871	Journal	Churches-Christian	Dunkirk, monthly meeting of Christians will be held at Dunkirk next Sabbath
12/12/1906	Herald	Churches-Christian	Dunkirk, Mrs. Clinton Starbuck was member; transferred to Buena Vista in 1866
7/30/1879	Journal	Churches-Christian	Dunkirk, Ora Woolf obituary says he joined this church in December 1876 under Rev. W. Ross
1/2/1901	Herald	Churches-Christian	Eastern Indiana Christian Association plans to buy Ridgeville College
9/21/1910	Journal	Churches-Christian	Eastern Indiana Christian Conference is being held at Farmland
12/28/1898	Journal	Churches-Christian	Farmland Christian Church purchased parsonage
4/13/1905	Democrat	Churches-Christian	Farmland gets college [did not occur]
4/26/1893	Journal	Churches-Christian	Farmland, A. M. Addington replaces Isaac Johnson as pastor
9/5/1888	Journal	Churches-Christian	Farmland, Christian Church will be dedicated next Sabbath, September 9, 1888, by Rev. H. Y. Rush, of West Milton, Ohio
10/27/1967	News	Churches-Christian	Farmland, church is listed as United Church of Christ
9/6/1957	News	Churches-Christian	Farmland, history of Christian Church
8/17/1892	Journal	Churches-Christian	Farmland, I. V. D. R. Johnson is elected pastor
4/26/1893	Journal	Churches-Christian	Farmland, I. V. D. R. Johnson resigned as pastor; A. M. Addington starts as pastor
9/21/1881	Journal	Churches-Christian	Farmland, Isaac Johnson, pastor, 1881-82
4/13/1881	Journal	Churches-Christian	Farmland, Joab Driver elected superintendent

Date	Source	Category	Description
4/9/1890	Journal	Churches-Christian	Farmland, Mr. Warren purchased old Christian Church
5/16/1888	Herald	Churches-Christian	Farmland, new Christian Church built by W. W. Fowler
5/23/1888	Journal	Churches-Christian	Farmland, new church under construction
7/27/1968	Journal-Herald	Churches-Christian	Farmland, not listed as United Church of Christ
8/13/1925	Democrat	Churches-Christian	Farmland, rededication
4/17/1965	Journal-Herald	Churches-Christian	Farmland, Verlin Smith is new pastor
1/16/1968	Journal-Herald	Churches-Christian	Farmland, was United Church of Christ according to obituary of Rev. Blaine Thornburg
4/25/1894	Herald	Churches-Christian	Good Hope will be dedicated on April 29, 1894 by J. K. Cortner
2/15/1900	Democrat	Churches-Christian	Harrisville Christian Church dedicated on February 4
1/24/1900	Journal	Churches-Christian	Harrisville Christian Church to be dedicated in February
5/24/1899	Herald	Churches-Christian	Harrisville, A. C. Peacock given contract to build new church
1/17/1900	Herald	Churches-Christian	Harrisville, church to be dedicated on February 4, 1900 by Rev. Samuels
10/19/1978	News-Gazette	Churches-Christian	Harrisville, groundbreaking
7/1/1965	Journal-Herald	Churches-Christian	Harrisville, history of
3/15/1899	Journal	Churches-Christian	Harrisville, new church planned
6/7/1899	Journal	Churches-Christian	Harrisville, new church started; Hampton Gettinger, architect
1/24/1900	Journal	Churches-Christian	Harrisville, new church to be dedicated on first Sunday in February; history of new building
5/10/1899	Herald	Churches-Christian	Harrisville, plans for new church
2/15/1900	Democrat	Churches-Christian	Harrisville, was dedicated on February 4, 1900
12/5/1883	Journal	Churches-Christian	Losantville will be dedicated in near future
5/28/1884	Journal	Churches-Christian	Losantville, Christian Church will be dedicated on first Sabbath in June
6/11/1884	Journal	Churches-Christian	Losantville, Christian Church will be dedicated on July 1 by Byrket and Bowen
10/31/1883	Journal	Churches-Christian	Losantville, Christian Church will be dedicated on November 4, 1883
4/26/1882	Journal	Churches-Christian	Losantville, church plans to build
6/14/1882	Journal	Churches-Christian	Losantville, contract for new church will be let soon
10/31/1883	Journal	Churches-Christian	Losantville, dedication
11/22/1882	Journal	Churches-Christian	Losantville, foundation of new church is laid
9/12/1894	Herald	Churches-Christian	Middleton Christian Church exists

Date	Source	Category	Description
10/14/1954	Journal-Herald	Churches-Christian	Mississinewa Christian Church to be rededicated on October 17
11/19/1879	Journal	Churches-Christian	Mississinewa, "Christian Friends" [sic] of Green Township are building new meetinghouse
12/31/1879	Journal	Churches-Christian	Mississinewa, church will be dedicated on the fourth Sunday in January by Rev. Burkett
3/19/1879	Journal	Churches-Christian	Mississinewa, New Lights are building a church at Shedville, 100 x 150
8/3/1922	Democrat	Churches-Christian	Mississinewa, Shedville Church dedication Sunday
2/18/1874	Journal	Churches-Christian	Morristown, Christian Church will be dedicated on fourth Sabbath in February by Rev. J. T. Lynn
7/2/1903	Democrat	Churches-Christian	Muncie First [Delaware County], photograph
9/2/1886	Journal	Churches-Christian	New Liberty to be dedicated on September 20
9/2/1896	Journal	Churches-Christian	New Liberty will be dedicated on September 20, 1896
8/26/1896	Journal	Churches-Christian	New Liberty will probably be dedicated on September 6, 1896
9/21/1887	Journal	Churches-Christian	New Liberty, Curtis E. Bales, Marion Morris, Ora Harris, W. O. Bales, and Daken Vanderburg licensed as exhorters in Christian Church; all are members of Liberty
9/2/1896	Herald	Churches-Christian	New Liberty, dedication on third Sunday in October
10/1/1980	News-Gazette	Churches-Christian	New Liberty, dedication to take place on October 19
1/14/1955	News	Churches-Christian	New Liberty, photo
5/23/1912	Democrat	Churches-Christian	New Pittsburg Christian Church exists
6/10/1903	Journal	Churches-Christian	New Pittsburg, Methodist and Christian Church to be dedicated on June 21
8/17/1887	Journal	Churches-Christian	North White River Christian Church dedicated on August 28
8/17/1887	Herald	Churches-Christian	North White River will be dedicated on August 28, 1887
2/9/1887	Journal	Churches-Christian	North White River, building committee consists of Carrier, Dull, Jeffry [sic]
12/8/1886	Journal	Churches-Christian	North White River, church will be built soon
8/17/1887	Journal	Churches-Christian	North White River, church will be dedicated on August 28, 1887
2/13/1919	Democrat	Churches-Christian	North White River, Ed Moser is Sunday School superintendent
7/1/1896	Herald	Churches-Christian	North White River, fight at Children's Meeting
9/18/1919	Democrat	Churches-Christian	North White River, Jessie Oren replaces Nannie Martin as pastor
12/27/1917	Democrat	Churches-Christian	North White River, Joe White, pastor

Date	Source	Category	Description
1/1/1920	Democrat	Churches-Christian	North White River, John Brown, Sunday School superintendent
7/4/1894	Journal	Churches-Christian	North White River, M. E. Mull replaces E. F. Lewellen as superintendent
5/29/1919	Democrat	Churches-Christian	North White River, M. J. Clements resigned as clerk of church after eighteen years of service; Job Jeffrey replaced her; Clements had originally replaced him
5/14/1919	Herald	Churches-Christian	North White River, Mahala Mull, superintendent
7/4/1894	Journal	Churches-Christian	North White River, officers listed
6/16/1921	Democrat	Churches-Christian	North White River, ordinations, Jesse Oren, pastor
4/21/1886	Journal	Churches-Christian	North White River, plans to build church in Lickskillet
8/25/1920	Democrat	Churches-Christian	North White River, Rev. Oren will continue for another year as pastor
2/16/1887	Herald	Churches-Christian	North White River, site purchased
10/22/1919	Herald	Churches-Christian	North White River, there will be a new belfry placed on the church in place of the old one
7/28/1911	Democrat	Churches-Christian	North White River, Will Milburn will be pastor for coming year
7/9/1873	Journal	Churches-Christian	Olive Branch Christian Church raised and will be completed after harvest (Walnut Corner)
12/4/1912	Journal	Churches-Christian	Olive Branch Christian Church to be dedicated on December 15, 1912
10/15/1873	Journal	Churches-Christian	Olive Branch Christian Church to be dedicated on October 26, 1873
10/1/1873	Journal	Churches-Christian	Olive Branch Christian Church, Rev. John Byrkit to dedicate on 4th Sunday in October
8/18/1915	Herald	Churches-Christian	Olive Branch Church is being remodeled; basement is complete
12/17/1902	Journal	Churches-Christian	Olive Branch, church is being repaired
7/9/1873	Journal	Churches-Christian	Olive Branch, church is raised; W. S. Addington will occupy dry goods stand in Olive Branch; bridge planned across Bear Creek near Olive Branch
4/2/1873	Journal	Churches-Christian	Olive Branch, church under construction; village described
11/13/1970	News-Gazette	Churches-Christian	Olive Branch, Dave Peters, pastor
8/26/1909	Democrat	Churches-Christian	Olive Branch, Dek Judy, pastor
1/10/1912	Journal	Churches-Christian	Olive Branch, Eddie Mosier has contracts for new church
7/30/1873	Journal	Churches-Christian	Olive Branch, Eli Hiatt is superintendent of Olive Branch Sabbath School
8/25/1915	Herald	Churches-Christian	Olive Branch, homecoming will be held on August 29, 1915

Date	Source	Category	Description
9/8/1983	News-Gazette	Churches-Christian	Olive Branch, Jerry Keener, superintendent
8/8/1906	Journal	Churches-Christian	Olive Branch, Lonnie Mullen replaces N. H. Thornburg as pastor
12/18/1964	News	Churches-Christian	Olive Branch, Marvin McNees, pastor
10/27/1967	News	Churches-Christian	Olive Branch, Marvin McNees, pastor
10/16/1969	Journal-Herald	Churches-Christian	Olive Branch, Marvin McNees, pastor
8/31/1979	News-Gazette	Churches-Christian	Olive Branch, officers: Lora Blunk, superintendent; Stella Patrick, clerk; Helen Lewellen, treasurer
9/1/1976	News-Gazette	Churches-Christian	Olive Branch, Piner replaces Youngblood as pastor
5/11/1887	Journal	Churches-Christian	Olive Branch, Rachael Brown, superintendent
12/18/1912	Herald	Churches-Christian	Olive Branch, rededicated by J. F. Burnett
12/18/1912	Journal	Churches-Christian	Olive Branch, rededicated last Sunday
12/19/1912	Democrat	Churches-Christian	Olive Branch, rededication
10/1/1873	Journal	Churches-Christian	Olive Branch, Rev. Byrket will dedicate on the fourth Sunday in October.
6/6/1980	News-Gazette	Churches-Christian	Olive Branch, Rev. Lemoine Wright, pastor, died
1/11/1968	Journal-Herald	Churches-Christian	Olive Branch, Taylor Weekley resigned as pastor in 1963
12/4/1912	Herald	Churches-Christian	Olive Branch, to be dedicated on December 15, 1912
8/20/1873	Journal	Churches-Christian	Olive Branch, W. Fowler and J. Elwood of Farmland completed meeting house
10/15/1873	Journal	Churches-Christian	Olive Branch, will be dedicated by Rev. John Byrket on October 26, 1873
12/24/1902	Journal	Churches-Christian	Olive Branch, will be dedicated on December 28, 1902 by J. F. Burnett
9/17/1873	Journal	Churches-Christian	Parker Christian Church is being built
5/10/1899	Journal	Churches-Christian	Parker Christian Church is meeting in Gunkler's Hall
8/28/1880	Journal	Churches-Christian	Parker Christian Church sold to Friends
2/1/1899	Journal	Churches-Christian	Parker, J. R. Cortner organized First Christian Church of Parker last Sunday with forty members; there are 21 Christian Churches in Randolph County
1/11/1899	Herald	Churches-Christian	Parker, plans to organize Christian Church by Rev. Cortner
11/30/1910	Journal	Churches-Christian	Pleasant Grove Christian Church new building
12/7/1910	Herald	Churches-Christian	Pleasant Grove Christian Church was dedicated on December 4, 1910

Date	Source	Category	Description
11/30/1910	Journal	Churches-Christian	Pleasant Grove, new church will be dedicated on December 4, 1910 by Rev. Stovenour
7/16/1982	News-Gazette	Churches-Christian	Pleasant Hill purchased additional land
1/4/1955	Journal-Herald	Churches-Christian	Pleasant Hill will be rededicated on January 9
1/6/1955	Journal-Herald	Churches-Christian	Pleasant Hill, history
4/14/1981	News-Gazette	Churches-Christian	Pleasant Hill, Lloyd Shepherd, pastor
9/27/1957	News	Churches-Christian	Pleasant Hill, parsonage dedication
8/5/1983	News-Gazette	Churches-Christian	Pleasant Hill, plans for addition
2/1/1888	Herald	Churches-Christian	Randolph County has 19 Christian Churches (18 buildings) with 2877 members
4/30/1902	Journal	Churches-Christian	Randolph County has 20 Christian [New Light] Churches
5/4/1898	Journal	Churches-Christian	Randolph County, Christian Church claims to be the largest denomination in county
3/19/1879	Journal	Churches-Christian	Shedville Christian Church built
2/23/1881	Journal	Churches-Christian	Shiloh Christian Church dedicated on February 20, 1881
4/28/1880	Journal	Churches-Christian	Shiloh Christian Church is unsafe; a new one is needed (Pleasant Hill Items)
12/26/1906	Journal	Churches-Christian	Shiloh Christian Church to be rededicated on December 30
8/11/1880	Journal	Churches-Christian	Shiloh Christian Church, new building
6/9/1880	Journal	Churches-Christian	Shiloh Christian Church, old building razed
5/5/1880	Journal	Churches-Christian	Shiloh Christian Church, old building sold
4/28/1880	Journal	Churches-Christian	Shiloh Church is unsafe and will be torn down
5/5/1880	Journal	Churches-Christian	Shiloh, brick church will be sold on May 22, 1880
3/2/1881	Journal	Churches-Christian	Shiloh, church dedicated on February 20, 1881
9/22/1880	Journal	Churches-Christian	Shiloh, church is finished
2/23/1881	Journal	Churches-Christian	Shiloh, church will be dedicated on February 20, 1881 by Isaac Johnson
2/2/1881	Journal	Churches-Christian	Shiloh, church will be dedicated on third Sunday of present month
6/9/1880	Journal	Churches-Christian	Shiloh, new church is under construction; old one was torn down
8/11/1880	Journal	Churches-Christian	Shiloh, new church will be raised this week
10/4/1923	Journal-Herald	Churches-Christian	Sparrow Creek Church mentioned
3/6/1907	Journal	Churches-Christian	Sparrow Creek/Sugar Creek Christian Church organized

Date	Source	Category	Description
10/8/1925	Democrat	Churches-Christian	Sugar Creek Christian Church, commonly known as Sparrow Creek Chapel, was organized 19 years ago by Zelma Mills
10/3/1906	Journal	Churches-Christian	Sugar Creek, church organized at Sparrow Creek
11/23/1949	News	Churches-Christian	Union Chapel Christian Church will be rededicated on November 27
9/3/1902	Herald	Churches-Christian	Union Chapel, new building dedicated on August 24, 1902 at a cost of $1600, replacing 40 year old building; old building is now a farm residence
10/13/1976	News-Gazette	Churches-Christian	Union Chapel, photo
7/23/1913	Journal	Churches-Christian	White River to be remodeled
4/14/1880	Journal	Churches-Christian	White River, Calvin McNees, Superintendent of Sabbath School
3/23/1887	Herald	Churches-Christian	Winchester Christian Church organized Monday with 32 members
11/12/1890	Journal	Churches-Christian	Winchester Christian Church to be dedicated on November 16, 1890
2/8/1939	Journal-Herald	Churches-Christian	Winchester East Street Christian Church being remodeled
3/17/1939	Journal-Herald	Churches-Christian	Winchester East Street Church to be rededicated on March 19
5/24/1911	Journal	Churches-Christian	Winchester East Street, basement excavated
6/18/1980	News-Gazette	Churches-Christian	Winchester to dedicate educational annex on June 22; cost $375,000
6/29/1956	News	Churches-Christian	Winchester, addition
10/13/1956	Journal-Herald	Churches-Christian	Winchester, addition will be dedicated on November 4
12/3/1914	Democrat	Churches-Christian	Winchester, being remodeled
11/19/1890	Journal	Churches-Christian	Winchester, Christian Church dedicated last Sunday; 30 x 60; cost $2,000
10/29/1890	Journal	Churches-Christian	Winchester, Christian Church will be dedicated on third Sabbath in November by Rev. D. A. Long, President of Antioch College
3/30/1887	Journal	Churches-Christian	Winchester, class of Christian Church established in Snedeker's Hall after meetings by John R. Cortner and I. V. D. R. Johnson
4/30/1890	Journal	Churches-Christian	Winchester, cornerstone of new church will be laid on May 1, 1890
12/10/1926	Daily News	Churches-Christian	Winchester, dedication of new Sunday School room and parsonage
11/19/1890	Herald	Churches-Christian	Winchester, East Street Christian Church dedicated
10/7/1896	Journal	Churches-Christian	Winchester, East Street Christian Church has a new bell

Date	Source	Category	Description
9/19/1906	Journal	Churches-Christian	Winchester, First Christian Church to be reopened on Sunday, September 23, 1906
9/19/1906	Herald	Churches-Christian	Winchester, First Christian Church will be rededicated on September 23, 1906
6/25/1979	News-Gazette	Churches-Christian	Winchester, groundbreaking for addition
7/22/1966	News	Churches-Christian	Winchester, history of
4/18/1888	Herald	Churches-Christian	Winchester, history of
4/16/1890	Herald	Churches-Christian	Winchester, lot being cleared to build church
4/9/1890	Journal	Churches-Christian	Winchester, lot being cleared to build East Street Christian Church
10/23/1889	Journal	Churches-Christian	Winchester, plans to build church
12/16/1914	Journal	Churches-Christian	Winchester, rededication on December 2, 1914 by J. F. Burnett
12/17/1914	Democrat	Churches-Christian	Winchester, rededication planned for December 20, 1914; new room was added
10/29/1890	Herald	Churches-Christian	Winchester, will be dedicated on November 16, 1890 by D. A. Long
9/25/1878	Journal	Churches-Christian	Windsor Christian Church, Thomas Addington, pastor
7/14/1875	Journal	Churches-Christian	Windsor, bids for new church
6/18/1873	Journal	Churches-Christian	Windsor, church is getting a bell
9/25/1919	Democrat	Churches-Christian	Windsor, new church to be built
1/26/1887	Herald	Churches-Christian	Windsor, revived one year ago
2/17/1875	Journal	Churches-Christian	Windsor, solicitations for building new church
1/23/1891	Democrat	Churches-Church of God	New Pittsburg, sanctified meetings, "Sankeys"
12/18/1945	Journal-Herald	Churches-Church of God	Praise Chapel burned
12/17/1945	News	Churches-Church of God	Praise Chapel burned on December 6
9/11/1970	News-Gazette	Churches-Church of God	Praise Chapel, groundbreaking for addition on September 13
5/20/1891	Herald	Churches-Church of God	Saints will have a meeting in Dr. Hiatt's grove, east of Winchester
11/1/1948	News	Churches-Church of God	Winchester Church of God (Cleveland, Tenn.) established at 429 N. Walnut St.
10/18/1963	News	Churches-Church of God	Winchester, Church of God on N. Jackson St., exists
10/19/1870	Journal	Churches-Congregational	Winchester, church meets in City Hall
1/13/1870	Journal	Churches-Congregational	Winchester, Congregational Church exists
6/3/1874	Journal	Churches-Congregational	Winchester, Congregational Sabbath School exists

Date	Source	Category	Description
7/7/1870	Journal	Churches-Congregational	Winchester, Rev. Mr. Bell starts as pastor of Congregational Church
2/9/1876	Journal	Churches-Congregational	Winchester, Sabbath School exists
4/7/1875	Journal	Churches-Congregational	Winchester, Sabbath School exists; J. M. Hodson and Evan Thornton are members
4/28/1875	Journal	Churches-Congregational	Winchester, Sabbath School will meet at Winchester Friends Church next Sabbath
5/5/1875	Journal	Churches-Congregational	Winchester, T. F. Moorman, secretary; J. M. Hodson, superintendent
6/27/1888	Journal	Churches-Disciples	Lynn Christian Church dedicated
7/28/1886	Journal	Churches-Disciples	Lynn Christian Church dedicated by Elder Carpenter, 36 x 60
12/2/1914	Journal	Churches-Disciples	Lynn Christian Church dedication; cost $7598
7/14/1886	Journal	Churches-Disciples	Lynn Christian Church will be dedicated on July 25, 1886 by L. L. Carpenter
9/3/1914	Democrat	Churches-Disciples	Lynn Church of Christ repaired
7/28/1886	Herald	Churches-Disciples	Lynn Disciples Church dedicated
6/22/1956	News	Churches-Disciples	Lynn First Church of Christ annex
10/30/1970	News-Gazette	Churches-Disciples	Lynn First Church of Christ will dedicate new building on November 1; work began on November 30, 1969; cost $260,000
2/18/1965	Journal-Herald	Churches-Disciples	Lynn First has built two annexes since 1957
6/19/1957	News	Churches-Disciples	Lynn First, dedication of annex planned on June 23
9/9/1964	News	Churches-Disciples	Lynn North Church of Christ will be dedicated on September 13
7/14/1886	Journal	Churches-Disciples	Lynn, bell for new church arrived; weighs 700 pounds
8/18/1886	Herald	Churches-Disciples	Lynn, Christian Church organized last winter, recently built a $2000 church
3/20/1901	Journal	Churches-Disciples	Lynn, court case over liberals versus radicals
6/27/1888	Journal	Churches-Disciples	Lynn, history of
7/14/1886	Herald	Churches-Disciples	Lynn, new Christian Church to be dedicated on July 25, 1886
4/16/1964	Journal-Herald	Churches-Disciples	Lynn, North Church of Christ starts new building
3/20/1901	Herald	Churches-Disciples	Lynn, suit over musical instruments in the church
3/5/1914	Democrat	Churches-Disciples	Lynn, West Christian Church to be enlarged
7/2/1908	Democrat	Churches-Disciples	Modoc and Parker Disciples Churches exist

Date	Source	Category	Description
6/19/1912	Journal	Churches-Disciples	Mt. Gilead, big storm blew roof off of church; also damaged Crete Elevator
8/4/1954	News	Churches-Disciples	New Lisbon, addition
4/18/1958	News	Churches-Disciples	New Lisbon, educational unit will be dedicated on April 20
10/26/1911	Democrat	Churches-Disciples	New Lisbon, history
4/19/1956	Journal-Herald	Churches-Disciples	New Lisbon, photo
11/28/1936	Daily News	Churches-Disciples	New Lisbon, rededication on Wednesday night; new basement
10/4/1891	Journal	Churches-Disciples	Parker Christian Church dedicated
11/9/1910	Herald	Churches-Disciples	Parker Christian Church remodeled; rededication will take place on November 13, 1910
9/24/1903	Democrat	Churches-Disciples	Parker City has Cambellite Church, but it has no services at present
9/30/1891	Journal	Churches-Disciples	Parker, Christian Church will be dedicated on October 4, 1891 by Elder Harkins of Union City
9/30/1891	Herald	Churches-Disciples	Parker, church to be dedicated on October 4, 1891 by Elder Harkins
5/20/1891	Journal	Churches-Disciples	Parker, old church from Mud Valley [east of Selma in Delaware County] moved to Parker by W. D. Stone
2/15/1900	Democrat	Churches-Disciples	Parker, South Main Street church is purchased by Disciples
3/14/1907	Democrat	Churches-Disciples	Randolph County Christian Co-op organized on June 25, 1905; group has organized Christian Church in Parker and just started another in Modoc
11/27/1912	Journal	Churches-Disciples	Ridgeville Church of Christ exists
4/25/1883	Journal	Churches-Disciples	Salem Christian Church, new church planned
10/17/1883	Journal	Churches-Disciples	South Salem Christian Church will be dedicated on the first Sunday in October
9/13/1928	Democrat	Churches-Disciples	South Salem rededicated on September 9, 1928; memorial windows and balcony have been added
5/18/1956	News	Churches-Disciples	South Salem to build addition
10/31/1883	Journal	Churches-Disciples	South Salem, dedication postponed until the second Sunday in November
6/27/1967	Journal-Herald	Churches-Disciples	South Salem, history of
7/29/1957	News	Churches-Disciples	South Salem, interior of church rededication
2/20/1964	Journal-Herald	Churches-Disciples	South Salem, parsonage dedication
11/14/1883	Journal	Churches-Disciples	South Salem, Salem Church dedicated last Sabbath

8/11/1984	News-Gazette	Churches-Disciples	South Salem, tower hit by lightning
2/26/1903	Democrat	Churches-Disciples	Spartanburg Christian Church will be dedicated on March 1, 1903
2/25/1903	Herald	Churches-Disciples	Spartanburg Christian Church, dedication on March 1, 1903
9/30/1920	Democrat	Churches-Disciples	Spartanburg, dedication of new church took place last Sunday; cost $30,000; organized in 1867
12/12/1917	Herald	Churches-Disciples	Spartanburg, Rev. Richard Motley, former pastor, goes to federal prison
3/18/1920	Democrat	Churches-Disciples	Spartanburg, work started on church
11/5/1913	Journal	Churches-Disciples	Union City Christian Church damaged by fire
9/4/1936	Daily News	Churches-Disciples	Union City Christian Church to be rededicated on September 13, 1936
3/17/1972	News-Gazette	Churches-Disciples	Union City Church of Christ exists on Plum, north of Willow [established in 1971]
8/12/1958	Journal-Herald	Churches-Disciples	Union City First to be remodeled inside
11/6/1913	Democrat	Churches-Disciples	Union City, church damaged by fire
6/28/1876	Journal	Churches-Disciples	Union City, new Christian Church
4/8/1896	Journal	Churches-Disciples	White River, Ed. I. Brown, superintendent
6/7/1876	Journal	Churches-Disciples	Winchester Christian Church dedicated
5/17/1876	Journal	Churches-Disciples	Winchester Christian Church dedicated on May 17
5/17/1876	Journal	Churches-Disciples	Winchester Christian Church will be dedicated on first Sabbath in June by J. C. Tully
7/15/1966	News	Churches-Disciples	Winchester Church of Christ [non-instrumentalist] formed at 113 1/2 North Main
2/23/1967	Journal-Herald	Churches-Disciples	Winchester Church of Christ [non-instrumentalist] meets at 202 N. 6th St.
4/19/1974	News-Gazette	Churches-Disciples	Winchester Church of Christ [non-instrumentalist] will be dedicated on April 21; established on May 15, 1966
6/12/1973	News-Gazette	Churches-Disciples	Winchester Church of Christ [non-instrumentalist], groundbreaking for new building was held on June 10; church was established in 1966
1/19/1898	Journal	Churches-Disciples	Winchester Main Street Christian Church purchased a new communion set
1/6/1904	Journal	Churches-Disciples	Winchester Main Street Christian Church will build a new church this year [did not occur]
4/7/1915	Herald	Churches-Disciples	Winchester Main Street Church of Christ to be dedicated
4/15/1915	Journal	Churches-Disciples	Winchester Main Street Church of Christ was dedicated on April 11, 1915

Date	Source	Category	Description
3/31/1915	Journal	Churches-Disciples	Winchester Main Street Church of Christ will be dedicated on April 11, 1915
4/7/1915	Journal	Churches-Disciples	Winchester Main Street Church of Christ will be dedicated on April 11, 1915
3/31/1915	Herald	Churches-Disciples	Winchester Main Street Church of Christ will be dedicated on April 11, 1915 by George Shively
4/15/1915	Democrat	Churches-Disciples	Winchester Main Street dedication
9/17/1977	News-Gazette	Churches-Disciples	Winchester Main Street will be rededicated on October 2
5/10/1911	Herald	Churches-Disciples	Winchester Main Street, Church of Christ to build a new church this summer to seat 900
2/25/1914	Herald	Churches-Disciples	Winchester Main Street, church to be occupied
4/1/1915	Democrat	Churches-Disciples	Winchester Main Street, church will be dedicated on April 11, 1915
5/16/1912	Democrat	Churches-Disciples	Winchester Main Street, cornerstone laid
5/15/1912	Journal	Churches-Disciples	Winchester Main Street, cornerstone laying
5/22/1912	Journal	Churches-Disciples	Winchester Main Street, cornerstone laying
5/15/1912	Herald	Churches-Disciples	Winchester Main Street, cornerstone to be laid next Sunday
5/24/1911	Herald	Churches-Disciples	Winchester Main Street, groundbreaking for new church
12/27/1911	Herald	Churches-Disciples	Winchester Main Street, history of
8/5/1966	News	Churches-Disciples	Winchester Main Street, history of
8/19/1966	News	Churches-Disciples	Winchester Main Street, history of
5/27/1914	Journal	Churches-Disciples	Winchester Main Street, notice of sale of old church
6/13/1917	Journal	Churches-Disciples	Winchester Main Street, old building sold to Nazarenes
6/7/1911	Herald	Churches-Disciples	Winchester Main Street, picture of new building
3/29/1911	Herald	Churches-Disciples	Winchester Main Street, plans for new church
6/7/1911	Journal	Churches-Disciples	Winchester Main Street, plans for new church
5/12/1911	Democrat	Churches-Disciples	Winchester Main Street, work started on new church
1/5/1887	Journal	Churches-Disciples	Winchester, A. L. Nichols, new superintendent
6/1/1881	Journal	Churches-Disciples	Winchester, D. M. Hueston is moving the old Campbellite Church to his lots near the depot [this was originally a Presbyterian Church]
12/22/1875	Journal	Churches-Disciples	Winchester, Martin Reeder has purchased old Christian Church
6/8/1881	Journal	Churches-Disciples	Winchester, old church has been relocated to the corner of Meridian and Pearl

Date	Source	Category	Description
6/8/1881	Journal	Churches-Disciples	Winchester, old church is being used as a store/warehouse
1/12/1876	Journal	Churches-Disciples	Winchester, spire on new church was considerably damaged by the storm
9/15/1875	Journal	Churches-Disciples	Winchester, work started on new Christian Church
11/27/1940	Journal-Herald	Churches-Evangelical	Emmettsville rededicated
2/5/1879	Journal	Churches-Evangelical	Emmettsville, Evangelical Association is erecting church near
2/5/1879	Journal	Churches-Evangelical	Emmettsville, German Evangelical Church built at
1/16/1889	Herald	Churches-Evangelical	Winchester German Evangelical Church was built in 1863; 30 x 40; has been remodeled; is "like M. E. Church in doctrine"
2/16/1865	Journal	Churches-Evangelical	Winchester, bell purchased for German Church
1/23/1889	Journal	Churches-Evangelical	Winchester, Elias Boltz, superintendent
11/13/1863	Journal	Churches-Evangelical	Winchester, German Evangelical Association is building church on W. Franklin Street, 30 x 40
1/2/1889	Journal	Churches-Free Methodist	Farmland, Free Methodist Church organized
1/23/1895	Journal	Churches-Free Methodist	Farmland, Free Methodists are holding meetings; they have four members
6/15/1962	News	Churches-Friends	"Quaker Parson"
8/4/1981	News-Gazette	Churches-Friends	4-H Royalty [Quakers]
1/12/1916	Herald	Churches-Friends	82% of Friends are rural
6/4/1913	Journal	Churches-Friends	Addington, Luther bought a car; first minister in Randolph County to own one
4/21/1915	Journal	Churches-Friends	Addington, Rev. removed as postal carrier at Ridgeville
7/13/1933	Democrat	Churches-Friends	American Friends Service Committee peace caravan is in Randolph County
2/3/1897	Journal	Churches-Friends	Anderson [Madison County], Miss Mary Nichols of Lynn has accepted the pastorate of the church at Central Avenue and 14th Street
8/9/1922	Journal-Herald	Churches-Friends	Apostolic Friends Yearly Meeting
2/16/1916	Herald	Churches-Friends	Arba has parsonage; Rev. Percy Thomas is pastor
1/14/1914	Herald	Churches-Friends	Arba, addition to be dedicated on January 25, 1914
1/29/1913	Herald	Churches-Friends	Arba, attempt to organize a Christian Endeavor
12/11/1913	Democrat	Churches-Friends	Arba, belfry and vestibule are nearly completed
10/27/1915	Herald	Churches-Friends	Arba, centennial
10/20/1915	Journal	Churches-Friends	Arba, centennial of church
4/13/1892	Journal	Churches-Friends	Arba, Christian Endeavor organized

Date	Source	Category	Description
11/14/1894	Journal	Churches-Friends	Arba, Clark Shawley will preach every two weeks
8/10/1887	Journal	Churches-Friends	Arba, Clarkson Charles is superintendent
1/29/1908	Herald	Churches-Friends	Arba, David Coppock will serve as pastor
12/25/1913	Democrat	Churches-Friends	Arba, David S. Coppock gave farewell sermon
10/23/1965	Journal-Herald	Churches-Friends	Arba, history of
3/18/1908	Herald	Churches-Friends	Arba, horse and buggy stolen at Arba Friends Church
8/1/1888	Journal	Churches-Friends	Arba, J. J. Fulgham, member of the Friends Church and Prohibitionist, will vote for Harrison
9/17/1913	Herald	Churches-Friends	Arba, John Reddick starts as pastor
9/12/1959	Journal-Herald	Churches-Friends	Arba, photo of Pastor Joseph E. Watkins
9/1/1897	Journal	Churches-Friends	Arba, Quaker wedding described
10/30/1907	Herald	Churches-Friends	Arba, Quakers near will not raise tobacco
3/12/1914	Democrat	Churches-Friends	Arba, Rev. John Redic [sic] is pastor
9/18/1895	Journal	Churches-Friends	Arba, Rev. Shawley preached last sermon at this place
6/3/1908	Herald	Churches-Friends	Arba, Rev. Swanders is "minister for this place"
6/29/1904	Herald	Churches-Friends	Arba, will be dedicated on July 17, 1904
5/4/1887	Journal	Churches-Friends	Arba, William C. Brown will probably be engaged to preach at Arba for the coming year
2/20/1895	Journal	Churches-Friends	Archer [Florida], described by Irena Beard
1/23/1918	Herald	Churches-Friends	Army, "Quakers go to make up army" from New York Times
4/19/1923	Democrat	Churches-Friends	Baptism story
3/27/1912	Journal	Churches-Friends	Barr, Sarah wrote a letter on women preaching
2/29/1888	Journal	Churches-Friends	Barrett, Isaac M., is an Ohio State Senator from Greene County and Chairman of the Evangelistic Committee of Indiana Yearly Meeting
6/15/1983	News-Gazette	Churches-Friends	Bear Creek broadcasts "The Joy of Living" on WZZY
12/1/1975	News-Gazette	Churches-Friends	Bear Creek to dedicate new annex
9/7/1934	Journal-Herald	Churches-Friends	Bear Creek, Adam Flatter will start as pastor
8/1/1894	Herald	Churches-Friends	Bear Creek, all day meeting at Quaker Hill, seven miles northwest of here
10/17/1929	Democrat	Churches-Friends	Bear Creek, annual rally
2/11/1880	Journal	Churches-Friends	Bear Creek, B. F. Morris is holding meeting at Olive Branch Friends Church

Date	Source	Category	Description
8/13/1913	Journal	Churches-Friends	Bear Creek, baptism took place in the creek under another denomination
7/26/1911	Herald	Churches-Friends	Bear Creek, basket meeting in Addington's Grove
7/26/1911	Journal	Churches-Friends	Bear Creek, basket meeting in Addington's Grove
7/28/1911	Democrat	Churches-Friends	Bear Creek, basket meeting in Addington's Grove, Luther E. Addington, pastor
7/1/1891	Journal	Churches-Friends	Bear Creek, Calvin Johnson has regular appointment
6/26/1982	News-Gazette	Churches-Friends	Bear Creek, centennial
7/16/1982	News-Gazette	Churches-Friends	Bear Creek, centennial; Lila Hersberger donated painting of Christ
11/20/1924	Journal-Herald	Churches-Friends	Bear Creek, Charley Hiatt preached at Quaker Hill, Sunday morning and evening"
5/24/1899	Herald	Churches-Friends	Bear Creek, Christian Endeavor, new officers: John Potter, president; Dora Brinkley, secretary
11/29/1905	Journal	Churches-Friends	Bear Creek, church was rededicated
11/22/1905	Journal	Churches-Friends	Bear Creek, church will be rededicated
8/31/1904	Journal	Churches-Friends	Bear Creek, Claude Adams's horse was stolen at Quaker Hill
12/20/1911	Herald	Churches-Friends	Bear Creek, fight occurred; George Chalfant, et al
1/25/1882	Journal	Churches-Friends	Bear Creek, Friends talk of a series of meetings at Olive Branch
1/2/1952	News	Churches-Friends	Bear Creek, Huffman, Gerald military funeral at Bear Creek
10/1/1884	Journal	Churches-Friends	Bear Creek, I. P. Watts will give a Republican political speech there on October 10, 1884
3/5/1914	Democrat	Churches-Friends	Bear Creek, Judge Engle Saturday assessed a fine of $5 and costs against Charles Allender, a young man of near Olive Branch, northwest of this city, against whom a recent jury returned a verdict of guilty for disturbing church services at the Quaker Hill church.
9/29/1927	Journal-Herald	Churches-Friends	Bear Creek, Judge Hinshaw of New Castle will make address
5/25/1898	Herald	Churches-Friends	Bear Creek, Junior Christian Endeavor held; organized a few months before
2/12/1925	Democrat	Churches-Friends	Bear Creek, Laura Fetters, pastor
3/22/1917	Democrat	Churches-Friends	Bear Creek, Logan Hunt is pastor
4/10/1919	Democrat	Churches-Friends	Bear Creek, Logan Hunt is pastor
1/20/1909	Journal	Churches-Friends	Bear Creek, Luther Addington and Mrs. Barr are conducting revival
1/2/1907	Journal	Churches-Friends	Bear Creek, Luther Addington is conducting revival

Date	Source	Category	Description
9/30/1911	Democrat	Churches-Friends	Bear Creek, Luther E. Addington resigns as pastor after 5 years
11/1/1944	News	Churches-Friends	Bear Creek, memorial services for soldier, Ernest E. Huffman, at Bear Creek
8/10/1946	Journal-Herald	Churches-Friends	Bear Creek, new basement is being constructed; services held at New Dayton
11/4/1896	Herald	Churches-Friends	Bear Creek, new Christian Endeavor officers listed
4/12/1923	Democrat	Churches-Friends	Bear Creek, next Sunday and Sunday evening will be Rev. Logan Hunt's regular preaching here; Everybody invited
4/24/1924	Democrat	Churches-Friends	Bear Creek, Ola Johnson had regular appointment
11/29/1923	Democrat	Churches-Friends	Bear Creek, Ola Johnson, next Sunday is her regular appointment
5/18/1904	Journal	Churches-Friends	Bear Creek, Phariba Stephens will be at Bear Creek Friends Church next Sabbath evening
11/22/1905	Herald	Churches-Friends	Bear Creek, rededication
7/25/1947	News	Churches-Friends	Bear Creek, rededication planned
11/22/1916	Herald	Churches-Friends	Bear Creek, Rev. Logan Hunt filled his regular appointment
9/27/1911	Journal	Churches-Friends	Bear Creek, Rev. Luther E. Addington will resign as pastor after five years
5/10/1911	Herald	Churches-Friends	Bear Creek, Rev. Potter filled Rev. Addington's pulpit at Quaker Hill Sunday morning and evening
2/11/1891	Journal	Churches-Friends	Bear Creek, Rev. S. S. Hinshaw has closed a revival with thirty conversions at Bear Creek
2/11/1891	Journal	Churches-Friends	Bear Creek, Rev. S. S. Hinshaw has closed a very successful revival meeting at Bear Creek; there were over thirty conversions
1/14/1926	Journal-Herald	Churches-Friends	Bear Creek, revival meeting begins tonight (Sunday) at Bear Creek, one mile west of Huffman's Corner
2/16/1939	Journal-Herald	Churches-Friends	Bear Creek, revival services are continuing under Rev. Holliday and Rev. Collins
2/3/1942	Journal-Herald	Churches-Friends	Bear Creek, revival under Mildred Allen
7/25/1929	Democrat	Churches-Friends	Bear Creek, road "tarred" in front of and east of Bear Creek Friends Church; people had to go around to get there
12/20/1950	News	Churches-Friends	Bear Creek, sends packages to Rex Hunt and Gerald Huffman in the army
4/25/1883	Journal	Churches-Friends	Bear Creek, Society of Friends at Olive Branch contemplates building a new church this summer
7/4/1929	Democrat	Churches-Friends	Bear Creek, storm damaged Quaker Hill Church

Date	Source	Category	Description
9/22/1927	Democrat	Churches-Friends	Bear Creek, Sunday School and church were held in the Huffman school house as they are redecorating the inside of the church
4/1/1896	Herald	Churches-Friends	Bear Creek, Sunday School reorganized, S. C. Williams, superintendent
9/22/1927	Journal-Herald	Churches-Friends	Bear Creek, The Bear Creek Sunday School and church have been holding their meetings at Huffman's Corner schoolhouse for two Sundays due to redecorating
2/26/1914	Democrat	Churches-Friends	Bear Creek, the jury in the case of Charles Allender, charged with disturbing a meeting at Quaker Hill church, northwest of this city, found the defendant guilty after being out from 5 p.m. Thursday until 8:30 Friday. Thirty ballots were taken. His companions pleaded guilty and were fined $5 and costs
9/11/1913	Democrat	Churches-Friends	Bear Creek, the members of the Bear Creek Friends Church held an all day meeting in the B. F. Addington grove north of the church, Sunday, September 7
1/28/1891	Herald	Churches-Friends	Bear Creek, the Quaker Hill Church, north New Dayton, is having quite a revival now, stirring up the entire neighborhood
2/5/1925	Journal-Herald	Churches-Friends	Bear Creek, The revival at Bear Creek has been largely attended the past week with several conversions under the pastor, Laura Fetters, assisted by Rev. Frank Long of Farmland
9/13/1923	Democrat	Churches-Friends	Bear Creek, they are going to straighten Bear Creek north of the church house
11/2/1892	Journal	Churches-Friends	Beard, Elkanah resigns as pastor of Portland Friends Church
8/22/1894	Journal	Churches-Friends	Blackford County, Winchester Quarterly Meeting established two indulged meetings in
10/20/1915	Journal	Churches-Friends	Bloomingport being remodeled
1/19/1916	Journal	Churches-Friends	Bloomingport rededication Sunday
12/15/1915	Journal	Churches-Friends	Bloomingport remodeled
12/15/1915	Journal	Churches-Friends	Bloomingport remodeling complete
1/12/1916	Herald	Churches-Friends	Bloomingport to be dedicated on January 16, 1916 by Rev. Kenworthy
8/14/1907	Herald	Churches-Friends	Bloomingport, Allie Benbow has regular appointment
7/16/1919	Herald	Churches-Friends	Bloomingport, church purchases Delco light plant
1/12/1898	Journal	Churches-Friends	Bloomingport, dedication of church postponed

Date	Source	Category	Description
5/4/1898	Journal	Churches-Friends	Bloomingport, dedication postponed until May 22 by Esther Cook and Samuel Mills
8/26/1903	Journal	Churches-Friends	Bloomingport, disorder
9/1/1915	Journal	Churches-Friends	Bloomingport, Ed Howell preaches
10/8/1913	Herald	Churches-Friends	Bloomingport, Edward Tenney to preach
5/7/1913	Herald	Churches-Friends	Bloomingport, Edwin Eenney [sic], regular appointment
11/6/1918	Journal	Churches-Friends	Bloomingport, Frank Edwards had regular appointment
10/8/1919	Herald	Churches-Friends	Bloomingport, Frank Edwards has regular appointment
12/31/1913	Herald	Churches-Friends	Bloomingport, James L. Newman reelected Sunday School superintendent
5/29/1912	Herald	Churches-Friends	Bloomingport, John Hardwick has regular appointment
12/31/1919	Herald	Churches-Friends	Bloomingport, list of officers of Sunday School
4/9/1919	Herald	Churches-Friends	Bloomingport, Rev. Frank Edwards as appointment
12/3/1919	Herald	Churches-Friends	Bloomingport, Rev. Frank Edwards has regular appointment
7/9/1919	Herald	Churches-Friends	Bloomingport, Rev. Frank Edwards of Greenfield is "our pastor"
1/21/1920	Herald	Churches-Friends	Bloomingport, Rev. Frank Edwards preaches
2/23/1910	Herald	Churches-Friends	Bloomingport, Rev. J. M. Binford, regular appointment
12/28/1910	Herald	Churches-Friends	Bloomingport, Rev. J. M. Binford, regular appointment
10/6/1909	Herald	Churches-Friends	Bloomingport, Rev. John Binford has regular appointment
11/22/1905	Herald	Churches-Friends	Bloomingport, Rev. Willis Cook is a former pastor
3/7/1906	Herald	Churches-Friends	Bloomingport, revival
9/17/1919	Herald	Churches-Friends	Bloomingport, Rufus King, noted minister, preached
1/5/1898	Journal	Churches-Friends	Bloomingport, Society of Friends purchased U. B. Church; will be dedicated next Sunday by Allen Jay
1/3/1912	Herald	Churches-Friends	Bloomingport, Sunday School officers listed
1/1/1913	Herald	Churches-Friends	Bloomingport, Sunday School officers listed
7/1/1903	Journal	Churches-Friends	Bloomingport, Sunday School officers listed; Logan Hunt was a teacher
3/25/1874	Journal	Churches-Friends	Bloomingport, talk of building Friends Church in town
5/11/898	Herald	Churches-Friends	Bloomingport, to be dedicated on May 22, 1898 by Rev. S. C. Mills; did not occur in January
1/12/1898	Herald	Churches-Friends	Bloomingport, U. B. Church rededicated by Friends last Sunday by Rev. Allen [did not occur]

Date	Source	Category	Description
8/19/1908	Journal	Churches-Friends	Bloomingport, Walter Malone will be at Friends Church starting on September 6
6/3/1908	Herald	Churches-Friends	Bloomingport, William Smith preached
4/5/1916	Journal	Churches-Friends	Bluff Point [Jay County], Chris Hinshaw has appointment
5/24/1916	Journal	Churches-Friends	Bluff Point [Jay County], Chris Hinshaw has appointment
8/21/1924	Journal-Herald	Churches-Friends	Bluff Point [Jay County], Frank Edwards has appointment
6/28/1905	Journal	Churches-Friends	Brown Schoolhouse, Rev. Levi Cox preached at
5/13/1908	Journal	Churches-Friends	Brown Schoolhouse, Sunday School organized
3/6/1878	Journal	Churches-Friends	Buena Vista, Elijah Johnson, colored minister of the Friends Church, moved near
9/19/1877	Journal	Churches-Friends	Buena Vista, Friends have a nice church
12/30/1885	Journal	Churches-Friends	Buena Vista, Lijah Johnson preached; new bell
5/23/1877	Journal	Churches-Friends	Buena Vista, Samuel Wright has contract for building Quaker Church at Buena Vista
7/19/1900	Democrat	Churches-Friends	Cabin Creek, Andrew McNees debated Quakers on baptism at Cabin Creek in the 1850s
10/13/1909	Herald	Churches-Friends	Carmel [Hamilton County], pastor criticized wearing of feathers in ladies' hats
10/5/1933	Democrat	Churches-Friends	Carter, F. E. is named superintendent of Indiana Yearly Meeting but will continue as pastor at Winchester Friends Church
8/8/1888	Journal	Churches-Friends	Carthage, Rev. Elwood Scott, minister of Friends Church and Prohibitionist, announces for Republicans
1/22/1919	Journal	Churches-Friends	Cedar was rededicated last Sunday
5/14/1913	Herald	Churches-Friends	Cedar, C. O. Wright has regular appointment
6/20/1894	Journal	Churches-Friends	Cedar, Christian Endeavor exists
1/22/1919	Journal	Churches-Friends	Cedar, church was rededicated last Sunday
2/17/1892	Journal	Churches-Friends	Cedar, Emily Bond, obituary; head of meeting
8/3/1881	Journal	Churches-Friends	Cedar, Friends Church getting ready for dedication
7/6/1881	Journal	Churches-Friends	Cedar, Friends Church is being rapidly erected
8/9/1911	Herald	Churches-Friends	Cedar, John Hardwick has regular appointment
10/18/1911	Herald	Churches-Friends	Cedar, John Hardwick has regular appointment
12/4/1912	Herald	Churches-Friends	Cedar, John Hardwick has regular appointment

Date	Source	Category	Description
11/23/1910	Herald	Churches-Friends	Cedar, Logan Hunt has a regular appointment to preach
8/23/1911	Herald	Churches-Friends	Cedar, Logan Hunt has regular appointment
4/24/1912	Herald	Churches-Friends	Cedar, Logan Hunt is present pastor
12/21/1910	Herald	Churches-Friends	Cedar, Logan Hunt preached
9/11/1912	Herald	Churches-Friends	Cedar, Logan Hunt preaches farewell sermon
3/11/1896	Journal	Churches-Friends	Cedar, Mrs. Marion Morris will conduct revival
4/4/1917	Journal	Churches-Friends	Cedar, Olive Harris filled regular monthly appointment
4/4/1917	Journal	Churches-Friends	Cedar, Olive Harris has regular appointment
5/10/1911	Herald	Churches-Friends	Cedar, Rev. John Hardwick preaches
4/7/1886	Herald	Churches-Friends	Center [Wayne County], building described
9/2/1926	Journal-Herald	Churches-Friends	Center [Wayne County], meetings held there, first in two years
9/12/1883	Journal	Churches-Friends	Center [Wayne County], Union Church to be dedicated next Sunday, September 16, 1883
9/12/1883	Journal	Churches-Friends	Center Union [Wayne County], church three miles north of Williamsburg will be dedicated on September 16, 1883
8/15/1906	Journal	Churches-Friends	Charlottesville [Rush County], Rev. Frank Edwards preaches every Sunday
6/27/1949	News	Churches-Friends	Cherry Grove Church is being removed; schoolhouse is now Pegg workshop
5/12/1921	Democrat	Churches-Friends	Cherry Grove is building new church
11/15/1941	Journal-Herald	Churches-Friends	Cherry Grove no longer listed in church listing
3/31/1875	Journal	Churches-Friends	Cherry Grove, Brice visited to obtain subscriptions for his newspaper
3/30/1892	Journal	Churches-Friends	Cherry Grove, Christian Endeavor organized
8/30/1893	Journal	Churches-Friends	Cherry Grove, church is being repaired
6/7/1893	Journal	Churches-Friends	Cherry Grove, church will be repaired
3/1/1893	Journal	Churches-Friends	Cherry Grove, discussion of a new building for Cherry Grove and Bloomingport Friends Churches one mile east of Bloomingport at crossroads
1/11/1893	Journal	Churches-Friends	Cherry Grove, I. H. Furnas, superintendent
11/17/1897	Journal	Churches-Friends	Cherry Grove, John and Louella Turner will go as missionaries to Mexico
11/17/1897	Herald	Churches-Friends	Cherry Grove, John and Luella Turner go to Mexico as missionaries

Date	Source	Category	Description
8/27/1890	Journal	Churches-Friends	Cherry Grove, John Carter and Will Mills joined the FMBA
6/30/1897	Journal	Churches-Friends	Cherry Grove, John Carter elected superintendent
1/2/1895	Journal	Churches-Friends	Cherry Grove, John Carter selected as superintendent
2/2/1898	Journal	Churches-Friends	Cherry Grove, letter from John Turner, Quaker missionary in Mexico
4/18/1894	Journal	Churches-Friends	Cherry Grove, new benches received
2/17/1927	Journal-Herald	Churches-Friends	Cherry Grove, Olive Harris, pastor
9/12/1940	Journal-Herald	Churches-Friends	Cherry Grove, reopened under Herbert Surface
1/24/1918	Democrat	Churches-Friends	Cherry Grove, Rev. Howell of Modoc is regular preacher
3/10/1915	Journal	Churches-Friends	Cherry Grove, Roe Amburn, pastor
3/10/1915	Journal	Churches-Friends	Cherry Grove, Roe Amburn, pastor
10/20/1921	Democrat	Churches-Friends	Cherry Grove, skeleton of Indian viewed at dedication of church; found when basement was excavated
10/6/1921	Democrat	Churches-Friends	Cherry Grove, to be dedicated on October 16, 1921 by Rev. Truman C. Kenworthy
6/28/1893	Journal	Churches-Friends	Cherry Grove, Winnie Hinshaw, elected superintendent
8/25/1861	Journal	Churches-Friends	Civil War, story of Richmond Quaker and horse for war effort
12/7/1922	Journal-Herald	Churches-Friends	Clemenceau visited Timothy Nicholson in Richmond; Sarah Copeland gave him a bouquet
10/2/1889	Journal	Churches-Friends	Coats, Columbus, Quaker minister, filed for divorce
5/4/1889	Democrat	Churches-Friends	Coats, Columbus, Quaker minister, has marital problems
11/1/1876	Journal	Churches-Friends	Coffin, Charles F. [leading Indiana Quaker of Richmond] voted straight Republican ticket
9/12/1980	News-Gazette	Churches-Friends	Cole, Kara, General Secretary of Friends United Meeting, photo
7/26/1911	Journal	Churches-Friends	Concord [Wayne County], Christopher Hinshaw, pastor
5/11/1898	Journal	Churches-Friends	Concord [Wayne County], William C. Brown has a regular appointment
3/9/1942	Journal-Herald	Churches-Friends	Conscientious objectors from Randolph County
9/26/1862	Journal	Churches-Friends	Conscientious objectors, 125 reported in Randolph County by enrolling officer
10/10/1862	Journal	Churches-Friends	Conscientious objectors, list of
9/18/1918	Herald	Churches-Friends	Cowan [Delaware County], Viola Johnson has appointment
12/27/1893	Journal	Churches-Friends	Cox, Levi F. starts as pastor of Carmel Friends Church [Randolph County native]
7/8/1920	Democrat	Churches-Friends	Dayton [Ohio], Charles E. Hiatt of Winchester is pastor

Date	Source	Category	Description
7/7/1920	Journal-Herald	Churches-Friends	Dayton Friends visited C. E. Hiatt at Long View Farm
10/11/1928	Journal-Herald	Churches-Friends	Delaware Union [Delaware County] to buy or build a church, Frank Bird, pastor
3/29/1969	Journal-Herald	Churches-Friends	Dennis, Congressman David is visited by Young Friends
5/31/1917	Democrat	Churches-Friends	Draft, many county draft officials are Quakers
9/20/1917	Democrat	Churches-Friends	Draft, young Quakers meet in Richmond to discuss
1/26/1887	Journal	Churches-Friends	Dunkirk items
3/2/1887	Journal	Churches-Friends	Dunkirk, "the Friends at old Dunkirk has [sic] organized a class"
7/21/1880	Journal	Churches-Friends	Dunkirk, meeting to be held [by Friends or others?]
8/16/1882	Journal	Churches-Friends	Dunkirk, meetinghouse built about 1828
10/26/1870	Journal	Churches-Friends	Dunkirk, meetings held there and Winchester
7/1/1903	Herald	Churches-Friends	Dunkirk, old Dunkirk, "only a part of the old church . . . still stands"
1/26/1887	Journal	Churches-Friends	Dunkirk, pranks at protracted meeting
9/29/1952	News	Churches-Friends	Earlham College invited Senator Richard Nixon to speak
4/7/1921	Democrat	Churches-Friends	Earlham College-Indiana Yearly Meeting relations are described
10/18/1916	Herald	Churches-Friends	Economy [Wayne County], dedication of Friends Church will take place on October 22, 1916
8/6/1925	Democrat	Churches-Friends	Edwards, David [M]. said the Bible was not infallible
9/19/1917	Journal	Churches-Friends	Edwards, Frank is pastoring in Blackford County
5/21/1913	Journal	Churches-Friends	Entiat [Washington State], obituary of Pastor Lee Thornburg, native of Randolph County
3/4/1903	Herald	Churches-Friends	Farmland Friends Church burned
3/5/1903	Democrat	Churches-Friends	Farmland Friends Church burned; built in 1889
11/27/1889	Journal	Churches-Friends	Farmland Friends Church, 34 x 50, 18 feet to ceiling
5/17/1882	Journal	Churches-Friends	Farmland Monthly Meeting was organized last Saturday
3/30/1881	Journal	Churches-Friends	Farmland Quaker church dedicated last Sunday by Rev. Scott
3/2/1881	Journal	Churches-Friends	Farmland Quakers are putting new seats in meeting house
10/7/1903	Journal	Churches-Friends	Farmland will be dedicated next Sabbath
3/4/1983	News-Gazette	Churches-Friends	Farmland, annex will be dedicated on March 6
1/28/1880	Journal	Churches-Friends	Farmland, B. F. Morris described as "pastor"
10/5/1881	Journal	Churches-Friends	Farmland, B. F. Morris will move to Martinsville, Ohio

Date	Source	Category	Description
10/12/1881	Journal	Churches-Friends	Farmland, B. F. Morris, farewell sermon
1/28/1880	Journal	Churches-Friends	Farmland, B. F. Morris, pastor
12/31/1879	Journal	Churches-Friends	Farmland, B. F. Morris, pastor
10/15/1879	Journal	Churches-Friends	Farmland, B. F. Morris, to move to town
6/1/1881	Journal	Churches-Friends	Farmland, Ben Morris, pastor
8/11/1886	Herald	Churches-Friends	Farmland, Benjamin Morris, pastor
10/15/1879	Journal	Churches-Friends	Farmland, Benjamin Morris, Quaker preacher, will move to Farmland as soon as he can rent a house
10/29/1919	Herald	Churches-Friends	Farmland, Charles Sweet is retained as pastor
5/4/1892	Journal	Churches-Friends	Farmland, Christian Endeavor exists
12/31/1879	Journal	Churches-Friends	Farmland, David Macy built stairway to get Friends to room over tin store
2/7/1882	Journal	Churches-Friends	Farmland, David Wasson is Superintendent of Sabbath School
11/20/1889	Herald	Churches-Friends	Farmland, description of new church (Martindale Items)
7/27/1881	Journal	Churches-Friends	Farmland, Elder Johnson, colored preacher, preached
9/9/1903	Journal	Churches-Friends	Farmland, Fred E. Smith resigns as pastor and at Bear Creek
10/9/1901	Journal	Churches-Friends	Farmland, Fred Smith will go to Cleveland for 3 months [to attend Bible College]
3/20/1878	Journal	Churches-Friends	Farmland, Friends are holding meetings at the Christian Church
3/5/1879	Journal	Churches-Friends	Farmland, Friends are trying to refurbish Macy Hall for church purposes
8/22/1894	Journal	Churches-Friends	Farmland, Friends Church was dedicated last Sunday by C. A. Francisco
1/15/1890	Journal	Churches-Friends	Farmland, Friends Church will have cantata "Jephtha"; rumored that John Flood will lead the choir and play bass drum
2/4/1880	Journal	Churches-Friends	Farmland, Friends have a new bell
2/16/1938	Journal-Herald	Churches-Friends	Farmland, Friends Peace Conference to be held on February 17
1/16/1889	Journal	Churches-Friends	Farmland, Friends will erect church
6/4/1879	Journal	Churches-Friends	Farmland, Friends will soon have Macy Hall ready for meeting
2/26/1960	News	Churches-Friends	Farmland, History of the A C Class
12/31/1890	Journal	Churches-Friends	Farmland, J. B. Branson elected superintendent
7/1/1885	Journal	Churches-Friends	Farmland, James Robbins, Sunday School Superintendent
6/12/1964	News	Churches-Friends	Farmland, Masons have St. John feast at Farmland Friends Church
9/10/1913	Journal	Churches-Friends	Farmland, Milo Hinkle resigns as pastor

7/28/1897	Journal	Churches-Friends	Farmland, new bell at Friends Church
11/27/1889	Journal	Churches-Friends	Farmland, new church described: 34 x 50 with 18 foot ceilings; built by David Wasson
2/20/1889	Journal	Churches-Friends	Farmland, new church is a go
6/5/1889	Herald	Churches-Friends	Farmland, new church is enclosed
6/26/1889	Journal	Churches-Friends	Farmland, new church is nearly complete
8/8/1894	Journal	Churches-Friends	Farmland, new church will be dedicated on August 19, 1894
6/13/1894	Journal	Churches-Friends	Farmland, new seats and paper in Friends Church
2/12/1919	Journal	Churches-Friends	Farmland, Noah V. Wright is with Friends Unit in France
2/1/1882	Journal	Churches-Friends	Farmland, petition to Winchester Quarterly Meeting for the establishment of Farmland Monthly Meeting
10/8/1948	News	Churches-Friends	Farmland, photo of Rev. John Randolph
3/30/1881	Journal	Churches-Friends	Farmland, Quaker Church dedicated last Sunday by Rev. Scott
1/7/1880	Journal	Churches-Friends	Farmland, Quakers had first meetings in room over Macy's Tin Store Sunday night
3/2/1881	Journal	Churches-Friends	Farmland, Quakers have moved seats into new meetinghouse
9/10/1879	Journal	Churches-Friends	Farmland, Quakers have room over Hiatt Store almost ready
10/27/1880	Journal	Churches-Friends	Farmland, Quakers make church of east schoolhouse
10/27/1880	Journal	Churches-Friends	Farmland, Quakers will make a church out of building bought of A. W. Cunningham
7/12/1882	Journal	Churches-Friends	Farmland, Quakers will stop harvesting to go to meeting and take hands with them
10/6/1915	Journal	Churches-Friends	Farmland, rededication Sunday
10/5/1881	Journal	Churches-Friends	Farmland, Rev. B. F. Morris will move to Martinsville, Ohio
3/13/1930	Democrat	Churches-Friends	Farmland, Rev. Clinton O. Reynolds died
4/27/1881	Journal	Churches-Friends	Farmland, several members of the M. E. Church have transferred to the Quaker Church
9/3/1913	Journal	Churches-Friends	Fountain City [Wayne County], Fred Smith resigned as pastor to go to Greensboro, North Carolina
4/18/1917	Herald	Churches-Friends	Friends [Five Years Meeting] define position on war
5/29/1872	Journal	Churches-Friends	Friends and Liberal Republicans
9/25/1872	Journal	Churches-Friends	Friends and politics
10/2/1872	Journal	Churches-Friends	Friends and politics at Indiana Yearly Meeting

5/23/1918	Democrat	Churches-Friends	Friends and the Red Cross work; the Friends are no slackers when it comes to philanthropy
4/14/1915	Herald	Churches-Friends	Friends customs have changed but not attitudes (Whirl of Society)
4/18/1917	Herald	Churches-Friends	Friends define position on war (Indiana Yearly Meeting)
9/6/1900	Democrat	Churches-Friends	Friends denounce imperialism; report of Philanthropic Committee
7/28/1911	Democrat	Churches-Friends	Friends object to "Quaker" as commercial label
8/30/1893	Journal	Churches-Friends	Friends Yearly Meeting Home, house and barn to be built [near Spartanburg]
10/9/1889	Journal	Churches-Friends	GAR, General Report of Indiana Yearly Meeting advises Friends not to join
7/9/1890	Journal	Churches-Friends	Geneva [Adams County], William C. Brown, of Winchester, preaches and at West Grove [Adams County]
12/9/1891	Journal	Churches-Friends	Georgetown [Illinois], A. J. Wooten starts as pastor
2/22/1923	Democrat	Churches-Friends	Grassy Run [Clinton County, Ohio], history; last meetinghouse was built in 1883 of brick
6/26/1912	Journal	Churches-Friends	Green Schoolhouse, basket meeting
12/25/1912	Journal	Churches-Friends	Green Schoolhouse, Sarah Barr and Mrs. David Harris in revival
5/30/1915	Journal	Churches-Friends	Green Schoolhouse; Alva C. Green obituary; member at Green Schoolhouse in 1909; he donated ground for church; funeral by Sarah Barr
9/16/1967	Journal-Herald	Churches-Friends	Greenfield [Hancock County] Church criticizes "pro-Red Quakers"
10/24/1877	Journal	Churches-Friends	Gurneyism, letter against by "H"
10/21/1914	Journal	Churches-Friends	Hardwick, Rev. J. W. has moved to Van Wert, Ohio, where he has accepted the "Christian Church" [sic] there
3/10/1951	Journal-Herald	Churches-Friends	Harvey, Congressman Ralph meets with Marvin H. Thornburg and Virgil E. Peacock, who protest universal military training
4/2/1884	Journal	Churches-Friends	Hinshaw, Enos H. has been nominated by the Democrats for trustee of White River Township to get the "d----d Quaker vote"
5/17/1905	Journal	Churches-Friends	Hinshaw, Meredith is preaching at White Oak [Jay County]
8/30/1893	Journal	Churches-Friends	Home for Aged Ministers near Spartanburg has six rooms, 36 x 48
7/27/1881	Journal	Churches-Friends	Howard, Minnesota has a Quaker Church
12/2/1903	Journal	Churches-Friends	Hubbard, Riley goes to pastor Maxwell Friends Church [Hancock County]

Date	Source	Category	Description
5/13/1918	Herald	Churches-Friends	Huffman, Herb goes to Everett, Washington
11/29/1916	Journal	Churches-Friends	Hunt, Clarence at school at Westfield
7/1/2903	Journal	Churches-Friends	Hunt, Logan is a Sunday School teacher at Bloomingport
11/5/1919	Journal	Churches-Friends	Hunt, Logan is pastor at Mt. Pleasant and Martindale
10/2/1945	Journal-Herald	Churches-Friends	Indiana Friends oppose peacetime draft
10/13/1915	Herald	Churches-Friends	Indiana Yearly Meeting appoints committee for Indiana Centennial
6/2/1909	Journal	Churches-Friends	Indiana Yearly Meeting Farm in Greensfork Township, sale of
9/19/1917	Journal	Churches-Friends	Indiana Yearly Meeting has special meeting about conscription; 2500 members conscripted
7/21/1886	Journal	Churches-Friends	Indiana Yearly Meeting House damaged by storm last week
9/23/1903	Journal	Churches-Friends	Indiana Yearly Meeting is at Marion
10/14/1903	Journal	Churches-Friends	Indiana Yearly Meeting is at Marion
10/11/1882	Journal	Churches-Friends	Indiana Yearly Meeting is not like it once was
8/17/1922	Democrat	Churches-Friends	Indiana Yearly Meeting opposes the Ku Klux Klan
7/1/1926	Democrat	Churches-Friends	Indiana Yearly Meeting will be held in Muncie or Fairmount due to remodeling at Richmond
6/29/1926	Daily News	Churches-Friends	Indiana Yearly Meeting, discussion of where to hold sessions
10/3/1877	Journal	Churches-Friends	Indiana Yearly Meeting, Dr. Hiatt attended the dedication of the Friends Yearly Meetinghouse in 1822 and this session
10/4/1882	Journal	Churches-Friends	Indiana Yearly Meeting, editor of Winchester Journal attended last Saturday
7/20/1904	Journal	Churches-Friends	Indiana Yearly Meeting, Elwood O. Ellis returned home
7/27/1904	Journal	Churches-Friends	Indiana Yearly Meeting, Elwood O. Ellis to sanitarium
7/13/1904	Journal	Churches-Friends	Indiana Yearly Meeting, Elwood O. Ellis, clerk, disappeared
8/30/1893	Journal	Churches-Friends	Indiana Yearly Meeting, house and barn will be built at Friends' Home for Poor and Infirm Women and Ministers near Spartanburg
10/9/1889	Journal	Churches-Friends	Indiana Yearly Meeting, Judge Doan, Quaker of Wilmington, Ohio, reacts to IYM's Peace Committee's comments on GAR
10/3/1877	Journal	Churches-Friends	Indiana Yearly Meeting, Quaker Yearly Meeting Sunday was the largest ever
9/14/1965	Journal-Herald	Churches-Friends	Indiana Yearly Meeting, statement on Vietnam
7/2/1926	Daily News	Churches-Friends	Indiana Yearly Meeting, trustees move sessions to Muncie

Date	Source	Category	Description
4/10/1907	Herald	Churches-Friends	Indiana Yearly Meeting-Western Yearly Meeting joint session
11/26/1879	Journal	Churches-Friends	Jay County, obituary of Elizabeth Keys Smith says she went to Friends Meeting in Jay County in 1848
8/16/1893	Journal	Churches-Friends	Jay, Isaiah absconded
8/9/1893	Herald	Churches-Friends	Jay, Rev. Isaiah, accused of theft
1/28/1874	Journal	Churches-Friends	Jericho correspondence
5/14/1977	News-Gazette	Churches-Friends	Jericho featured in Saturday Extra
11/7/1906	Journal	Churches-Friends	Jericho to be rededicated Sunday at 11 o'clock by Allen Jay
1/29/1896	Journal	Churches-Friends	Jericho, "Quaker College has fine attendance"
4/11/1906	Journal	Churches-Friends	Jericho, $1048 subscribed to build new church
9/12/1958	News	Churches-Friends	Jericho, addition will be dedicated on September 21
4/24/1912	Journal	Churches-Friends	Jericho, births in the neighborhood among Friend Quakers mean President Roosevelt will have more supporters
4/27/1898	Journal	Churches-Friends	Jericho, C. F. Hinshaw bought an organ; there will be Quaker music at our house [at home or church?]
8/22/1906	Journal	Churches-Friends	Jericho, church is being enlarged
2/4/1891	Journal	Churches-Friends	Jericho, church repaired and modernized
4/5/1899	Journal	Churches-Friends	Jericho, David McDowell, superintendent
3/24/1875	Journal	Churches-Friends	Jericho, division continues
4/28/1875	Journal	Churches-Friends	Jericho, division continues
2/14/1877	Journal	Churches-Friends	Jericho, division; John Douglas and Esther Frame will attempt to remedy
10/2/1918	Journal	Churches-Friends	Jericho, Francis Leroy Frazier died in service; funeral at Jericho
1/28/1874	Journal	Churches-Friends	Jericho, Friends oppose Grangers
7/20/1950	Journal-Herald	Churches-Friends	Jericho, history
12/22/1886	Herald	Churches-Friends	Jericho, history of
9/16/1978	News-Gazette	Churches-Friends	Jericho, history of Philimathian Lyceum
4/6/1898	Journal	Churches-Friends	Jericho, John H. Pickett elected superintendent
10/4/1923	Democrat	Churches-Friends	Jericho, John Hinshaw is superintendent; Rachel Brooks preaches on first Sunday; Elvan Thornburg preaches on the second and fourth Sundays; Ira Johnson preaches on the third Sunday
9/13/1905	Journal	Churches-Friends	Jericho, John Hinshaw replaces Ozro Hodgins as Sunday School Superintendent
10/26/1984	News-Gazette	Churches-Friends	Jericho, Kenneth Pohlenz is new pastor
5/5/1875	Journal	Churches-Friends	Jericho, Liberty Hall is nearby

Date	Source	Category	Description
10/2/1918	Journal	Churches-Friends	Jericho, Luke Woodard was pastor 15 years ago
4/17/1971	News-Gazette	Churches-Friends	Jericho, Mark Peacock works with "end war" group
11/7/1906	Herald	Churches-Friends	Jericho, new Friends Church will be dedicated on November 11, 1906
7/14/1920	Journal-Herald	Churches-Friends	Jericho, Ola Johnson, pastor
12/27/1866	Journal	Churches-Friends	Jericho, Peacock Quaker wedding described
3/22/1923	Democrat	Churches-Friends	Jericho, Rev. Ira Johnson has regular appointment
8/4/1915	Herald	Churches-Friends	Jericho, Rev. Mary Cox of Hadley has a regular appointment
3/28/1877	Journal	Churches-Friends	Jericho, separate meetings are being held
5/16/1867	Journal	Churches-Friends	Jericho, Silas Cox, superintendent of Sabbath School
1/11/1882	Journal	Churches-Friends	Jericho, singing at [was it at the school?]
5/24/1968	News	Churches-Friends	Jericho, steeple was struck by lightning
2/4/1903	Journal	Churches-Friends	Jericho, tramp arrested for sleeping in Jericho Church
2/17/1875	Journal	Churches-Friends	Jericho, trouble with some withdrawing
11/8/1906	Democrat	Churches-Friends	Jericho, will be dedicated on November 11, 1906 by Allen Jay
4/6/1898	Journal	Churches-Friends	Jericho, will the Quaker fight? [Spanish-American War]
11/28/1906	Journal	Churches-Friends	Johnson, Calvin filled appointment at Pike [Jay County]
3/8/1922	Journal-Herald	Churches-Friends	Kittrell, John died; C. E. Hiatt had funeral
8/28/1924	Democrat	Churches-Friends	Klan boycotts Indiana Quakers in Anderson/Pendleton area
4/14/1886	Herald	Churches-Friends	Kokomo [Howard County], singing and pastor
10/13/1875	Journal	Churches-Friends	Koll, Daniel, Primitive Friend of Salem, Ohio, preached at City Hall, deplored degeneracy in the Friends Church
8/29/1900	Journal	Churches-Friends	Little Blue River [Rush County], Rev. E. S. Hinshaw has appointment
5/1/1878	Journal	Churches-Friends	Long Lake [Michigan], letter from
7/26/1923	Journal-Herald	Churches-Friends	Losantville Apostolic Friends
9/23/1914	Herald	Churches-Friends	Losantville Apostolic Friends Church organized by Charles D. W. Hiatt, Ola Hiatt, Charles Foultz of Parker, Etta Seagraves of Losantville, and Gretta Newby of Jonesboro
9/23/1914	Journal	Churches-Friends	Losantville Apostolic Friends incorporated
8/28/1924	Journal-Herald	Churches-Friends	Losantville, 11th Annual Meeting of Apostolic Friends will be held on September 4

Date	Source	Category	Description
9/23/1914	Democrat	Churches-Friends	Losantville, Apostolic Friends Church is incorporated with state; members are Charles D. W. Hiatt and Ola of Farmland; Charles Foutz of Parker; Etta Seagraves of Losantville; and Greta Newby of Jonesboro
7/12/1922	Journal-Herald	Churches-Friends	Losantville, Apostolic Friends to have quarterly meeting at Jonesboro; anniversary meeting on September 7 at Losantville
5/14/1913	Herald	Churches-Friends	Losantville, Charles Hiatt preaches in hall
2/19/1879	Journal	Churches-Friends	Losantville, Friends from Farmland will hold meetings
10/5/1892	Journal	Churches-Friends	Losantville, Friends Sunday School opened
9/10/1913	Herald	Churches-Friends	Losantville, Modern Friends expect to finish church in time for Quarterly Meeting in October
12/4/1907	Journal	Churches-Friends	Lynn to be dedicated on December 8, 1907 by Allen Jay
3/12/1940	Journal-Herald	Churches-Friends	Lynn to host regional peace conference
8/11/1886	Journal	Churches-Friends	Lynn, "red hot third party political speech"
6/1/1887	Journal	Churches-Friends	Lynn, Casper Hodson, superintendent
12/4/1907	Herald	Churches-Friends	Lynn, dedication next Sunday by Rev. Allen Jay
10/3/1968	Journal-Herald	Churches-Friends	Lynn, funeral for Westlake, Vietnam death
9/17/1913	Journal	Churches-Friends	Lynn, Henry Pickett resigned as pastor; Milo Hinkle will replace him; Hinkle has been serving at Farmland
10/7/1914	Journal	Churches-Friends	Lynn, Luther Addington accepted pastorate
9/30/1914	Journal	Churches-Friends	Lynn, Milo Hinkle resigns as pastor to go to Richmond
9/10/1913	Journal	Churches-Friends	Lynn, Milo Hinkle to replace Henry Pickett as pastor
6/26/1907	Journal	Churches-Friends	Lynn, new Friends Church
2/13/1913	Democrat	Churches-Friends	Lynn, plans for addition
9/6/1905	Journal	Churches-Friends	Lynn, Quaker band exists
2/20/1889	Journal	Churches-Friends	Lynn, Rev. Henry Pickett is a stalwart Republican
3/6/1895	Journal	Churches-Friends	Lynn, talk of a new Friends Church in Lynn
9/17/1913	Journal	Churches-Friends	Lynn, to be rededicated on September 21, 1913 by Ira C. Johnson and Henry Pickett
2/16/1898	Herald	Churches-Friends	Manton, Michigan, J. W. Vinnedge of near Lynn takes over as pastor
5/21/1919	Journal	Churches-Friends	Martindale Church to be rededicated next Sunday by Ira Johnson
8/10/1904	Journal	Churches-Friends	Martindale has new church bell
1/9/1953	Journal-Herald	Churches-Friends	Martindale history

Date	Source	Category	Description
1/17/1912	Journal	Churches-Friends	Martindale installed hollow wire gasoline lighting
8/25/1886	Journal	Churches-Friends	Martindale Preparative Meeting organized at Jackson Schoolhouse
1/29/1908	Journal	Churches-Friends	Martindale Sunday School bought an organ; Henry Pickett will preach next week
1/2/1901	Journal	Churches-Friends	Martindale, Andrew Edwards will continue as Sunday School Superintendent
12/30/1891	Journal	Churches-Friends	Martindale, Andrew Edwards will continue as superintendent
12/31/1890	Journal	Churches-Friends	Martindale, Andrew Edwards, superintendent
4/6/1898	Journal	Churches-Friends	Martindale, Benjamin Morris, of Wabash, secured for a year as pastor
11/29/1916	Journal	Churches-Friends	Martindale, Charles Wright preaches
9/12/1917	Journal	Churches-Friends	Martindale, Charles Wright preaches last sermon
8/22/1917	Journal	Churches-Friends	Martindale, Charley Wright has appointment to preach
11/23/1887	Journal	Churches-Friends	Martindale, church will be dedicated on December 4, 1887 by Benjamin F. Morris
4/20/1910	Journal	Churches-Friends	Martindale, E. E. Hale preaches on 1st and 3rd Sabbath
9/21/1910	Journal	Churches-Friends	Martindale, E. E. Hale resigns as pastor
7/25/1888	Journal	Churches-Friends	Martindale, Elijah Johnson has a regular appointment to preach
5/12/1949	Journal-Herald	Churches-Friends	Martindale, Future Builders Class exists
1/3/1894	Herald	Churches-Friends	Martindale, G. W. Jarrett, superintendent
7/2/1890	Journal	Churches-Friends	Martindale, G. W. Jarrett, superintendent
10/17/1917	Journal	Churches-Friends	Martindale, George Addington starts as pastor
12/25/1918	Journal	Churches-Friends	Martindale, George E. Addington had regular appointment
10/17/1917	Journal	Churches-Friends	Martindale, George E. Addington starts as pastor
12/22/1915	Journal	Churches-Friends	Martindale, George Lamb elected Superintendent of the Sunday School
6/28/1916	Journal	Churches-Friends	Martindale, George Lamb is Sunday School Superintendent
3/5/1913	Journal	Churches-Friends	Martindale, Golda Hinshaw to preach
3/5/1913	Journal	Churches-Friends	Martindale, Goldie Hinshaw and Charles Wright, pastors
9/27/1916	Journal	Churches-Friends	Martindale, Goldie Hinshaw preached
6/28/1916	Journal	Churches-Friends	Martindale, Goldie Hinshaw preached in place of Wilda Hiatt
1/11/1923	Journal-Herald	Churches-Friends	Martindale, Guy Wolfe, Sunday School superintendent

Date	Source	Category	Description
7/23/1919	Journal	Churches-Friends	Martindale, Henry Pickett filled appointment
7/23/1919	Journal	Churches-Friends	Martindale, Henry Pickett had regular appointment
5/2/1968	Journal-Herald	Churches-Friends	Martindale, history of
12/2/1908	Herald	Churches-Friends	Martindale, hosts Holiness convention
4/10/1889	Journal	Churches-Friends	Martindale, Isaac Frazier reelected superintendent
1/2/1889	Journal	Churches-Friends	Martindale, Isaac Frazier, superintendent
4/22/1891	Journal	Churches-Friends	Martindale, J. E. Edwards, superintendent
6/28/1911	Journal	Churches-Friends	Martindale, J. L. Edwards is reelected Sunday School superintendent
1/5/1910	Journal	Churches-Friends	Martindale, J. L. Edwards re-elected Sunday School Superintendent
1/4/1911	Journal	Churches-Friends	Martindale, J. L. Edwards re-elected Sunday School Superintendent
10/19/1910	Journal	Churches-Friends	Martindale, J. W. Hardwick preaches on 1st and 3rd Sabbath
5/4/1910	Journal	Churches-Friends	Martindale, J. W. Hardwick preaches on second and fourth Sundays; E. E. Hale preaches on first and third Sundays
10/17/1923	Journal-Herald	Churches-Friends	Martindale, John Hardwick preaches
5/4/1910	Journal	Churches-Friends	Martindale, John Hardwick preaches on 2nd and 4th Sabbath
4/20/1892	Journal	Churches-Friends	Martindale, last Sabbath S. S. Hinshaw and Dr. Huddleston of Winchester organized a Christian Endeavor at Martindale with twenty members
1/10/1917	Journal	Churches-Friends	Martindale, Laura Edwards is superintendent of Sunday School
1/10/1917	Journal	Churches-Friends	Martindale, Laura Edwards, Sunday School Superintendent
1/14/1914	Journal	Churches-Friends	Martindale, Laura Fetters starts as Sunday School superintendent
1/14/1914	Journal	Churches-Friends	Martindale, Laura Fetters, Sunday School Superintendent
5/7/1890	Journal	Churches-Friends	Martindale, Levi Cox will preach every fourth Sabbath
10/22/1919	Journal	Churches-Friends	Martindale, Logan Hunt preaches
10/4/1911	Journal	Churches-Friends	Martindale, Logan Hunt preaches on 2nd and 4th Sundays
9/11/1918	Journal	Churches-Friends	Martindale, Logan Hunt replaces George E. Addington as pastor
4/19/1911	Journal	Churches-Friends	Martindale, Logan Hunt starts as pastor; John Hardwick continues
1/28/1920	Journal	Churches-Friends	Martindale, Logan Hunt, pastor
7/14/1909	Journal	Churches-Friends	Martindale, Meredith Hinshaw filled appointment
9/22/1909	Journal	Churches-Friends	Martindale, Meredith Hinshaw has regular appointment

Date	Source	Category	Description
3/9/1887	Herald	Churches-Friends	Martindale, money is being raised to build church
6/21/1916	Journal	Churches-Friends	Martindale, Myrl Hough has regular appointment
3/22/1916	Journal	Churches-Friends	Martindale, Myrl Hough preaches
12/1/1915	Journal	Churches-Friends	Martindale, Myrl Hough starts as pastor in March; Wilda Hiatt will continue as pastor
2/29/1888	Journal	Churches-Friends	Martindale, N. B. Baldwin, superintendent; Uriah Hinshaw, corresponding secretary
7/4/1888	Journal	Churches-Friends	Martindale, N. B. Baldwin, superintendent; Uriah Hinshaw, treasurer
9/21/1888	Herald	Churches-Friends	Martindale, new church is being erected
10/6/1897	Journal	Churches-Friends	Martindale, obituary of Betsy Hodgin Frazier Fisher
1/7/1914	Journal	Churches-Friends	Martindale, Ola Johnson (first Sunday) and Charles Wright are pastors
6/3/1914	Journal	Churches-Friends	Martindale, Ola Johnson preaches next Sabbath
1/7/1914	Journal	Churches-Friends	Martindale, Ola Johnson starts as pastor; Charles Wright continues
1/1/1913	Journal	Churches-Friends	Martindale, Ollie Albertson is reelected Sunday School superintendent; Olive Pursley, secretary
3/6/1918	Journal	Churches-Friends	Martindale, Ollie Albertson is Sunday School Superintendent
6/23/1950	News	Churches-Friends	Martindale, Orval Hinshaw is superintendent
6/24/1939	Journal-Herald	Churches-Friends	Martindale, Orville Hinshaw, superintendent
5/21/1919	Journal	Churches-Friends	Martindale, rededication next Sunday by Ira C. Johnson
1/7/1891	Herald	Churches-Friends	Martindale, reorganization of Sunday School
7/9/1890	Herald	Churches-Friends	Martindale, reorganization of Sunday School
10/31/1888	Journal	Churches-Friends	Martindale, reorganization of Sunday School: Isaac Frazier, superintendent
6/11/1919	Journal	Churches-Friends	Martindale, Rev. Hale was pastor nine years ago
7/31/1924	Journal-Herald	Churches-Friends	Martindale, Rev. Hardwick pastor
10/4/1911	Journal	Churches-Friends	Martindale, Rev. Logan Hunt will preach at on the 2nd and 4th Sundays
1/7/1914	Herald	Churches-Friends	Martindale, Rev. Viola Johnson has regular appointment
12/2/1908	Journal	Churches-Friends	Martindale, Roe Bundy will be pastor next year
12/12/1906	Journal	Churches-Friends	Martindale, Ruby Oren preached
10/24/1906	Journal	Churches-Friends	Martindale, Ruby Oren preaches often

Date	Source	Category	Description
1/11/1923	Journal-Herald	Churches-Friends	Martindale, Sunday School officers listed
1/3/1894	Journal	Churches-Friends	Martindale, Sunday School officers listed
10/31/1888	Journal	Churches-Friends	Martindale, Sunday School officers listed
7/3/1889	Journal	Churches-Friends	Martindale, Sunday School officers listed
12/30/1896	Journal	Churches-Friends	Martindale, Sunday School officers listed; G. W. Jarrett, superintendent
4/7/1886	Herald	Churches-Friends	Martindale, Sunday School officers listed; N. B. Baldwin, superintendent; William Miller, assistant superintendent; Uriah Hinshaw, corresponding secretary; Logan Hunt, chorister
10/7/1896	Journal	Churches-Friends	Martindale, Susan Magner of Portland preaches [often]
11/3/1897	Journal	Churches-Friends	Martindale, Susie Magner has last appointment
2/12/1890	Journal	Churches-Friends	Martindale, Tennis J. [sic] Coffin, superintendent
8/30/1905	Journal	Churches-Friends	Martindale, Viola Miller is Sunday School Superintendent
7/13/1904	Journal	Churches-Friends	Martindale, Viola Miller, superintendent
7/19/1916	Journal	Churches-Friends	Martindale, Wilda Hiatt has regular appointment
3/18/1914	Journal	Churches-Friends	Martindale, Wilda Hiatt has regular appointment to preach
12/1/1915	Journal	Churches-Friends	Martindale, Wilda Hiatt preaches on the second and fourth Sundays; Myrl Hough will preach on the first and third Sundays, starting in March
1/15/1873	Journal	Churches-Friends	Matamoras, Mexico, Quaker mission started
12/2/1903	Journal	Churches-Friends	Maxwell [Hancock County], Riley Hubbard moved there
3/14/1877	Journal	Churches-Friends	Merrill, Henry left Friends for M. E. Church
5/1/1878	Journal	Churches-Friends	Michigan letter tells of Friends services at Long Lake
7/21/1875	Journal	Churches-Friends	Middletown, plans to start Friends Church
6/23/1948	News	Churches-Friends	Miller, Perry of Tecumseh, Michigan is a Quaker and Prohibition candidate for Lt. Governor of Michigan
1/22/1890	Journal	Churches-Friends	Milton [Wayne County], claimed to be first Friends Church to have a bell; Journal points out that this is not true
5/23/1888	Journal	Churches-Friends	Milton [Wayne County], Rev. Isaiah Jay preached at Milton Friends Church, "only place in the country where an organ is used by the Friends"

Date	Source	Category	Description
5/24/1882	Journal	Churches-Friends	Ministry and Oversight of the Friends Church is like the Masonic Lodge [secretive]
7/10/1943	Journal-Herald	Churches-Friends	Morgan Creek [Wayne County] dedicate service flag
6/17/1896	Journal	Churches-Friends	Morgan Creek [Wayne County] to be dedicated next Sunday, June 21
8/21/1895	Journal	Churches-Friends	Morgan Creek [Wayne County], church nearly completed
5/1/1895	Journal	Churches-Friends	Morgan Creek [Wayne County], Friends Sunday School organized at Morgan Creek
3/29/1911	Journal	Churches-Friends	Morgan Creek [Wayne County], John Hardwick and Roe Amburn, pastors
3/1/1911	Journal	Churches-Friends	Morgan Creek [Wayne County], John Hardwick, preaches at
1/30/1895	Journal	Churches-Friends	Morgan Creek [Wayne County], plan to erect a church at Cranor's Schoolhouse, two and a half miles south of Carlos
6/17/1896	Journal	Churches-Friends	Morgan Creek Chapel [Wayne County] will be dedicated next Sunday by Allen Jay
2/13/1895	Journal	Churches-Friends	Morgan Creek, Carlos, work to begin on new Friends Church south of town [Morgan Creek in Wayne County]
4/23/1919	Journal	Churches-Friends	Mount Pleasant Church to rebuild
2/19/1890	Journal	Churches-Friends	Mount Pleasant Friends Church dedicated
2/5/1890	Journal	Churches-Friends	Mount Pleasant Friends Church to be dedicated on February 16 by Levi Cox
5/12/1915	Journal	Churches-Friends	Mount Pleasant gets electricity
5/28/1931	Democrat	Churches-Friends	Mount Pleasant Sunday School, article
10/29/1919	Journal	Churches-Friends	Mount Pleasant to be rededicated on November 9 by Ira C. Johnson; Riley and Mary Hubbard, pastors
10/29/1919	Herald	Churches-Friends	Mount Pleasant to be rededicated on November 9, 1919 by Aaron Napier and Ira C. Johnson
7/24/1889	Journal	Churches-Friends	Mount Pleasant, arrangements are being made to build a new Friends Church near Old Snow Hill
4/8/1896	Journal	Churches-Friends	Mount Pleasant, C. R. Jennings, superintendent
4/9/1919	Journal	Churches-Friends	Mount Pleasant, called meeting held to reorganize, rebuild, or disband church
7/15/1896	Herald	Churches-Friends	Mount Pleasant, children's day
5/9/1936	News-Democrat	Churches-Friends	Mount Pleasant, Community Builders Class will meet with Otis Hinshaw

Date	Source	Category	Description
2/19/1890	Herald	Churches-Friends	Mount Pleasant, dedicated by Levi Cox and Ira Johnson; church was organized by Cal Hinshaw and Amos Hall
2/19/1890	Journal	Churches-Friends	Mount Pleasant, description of dedication
3/12/1890	Herald	Churches-Friends	Mount Pleasant, donors listed; cost $770
3/7/1894	Herald	Churches-Friends	Mount Pleasant, Elwood Hinshaw going home; interesting story
2/5/1890	Journal	Churches-Friends	Mount Pleasant, Friends Church near old Snow Hill will be dedicated on February 16, 1890
6/24/1978	News-Gazette	Churches-Friends	Mount Pleasant, history of and Grace Hinshaw
4/15/1891	Herald	Churches-Friends	Mount Pleasant, J. Calvin Hinshaw, prominent member, died
3/19/1890	Journal	Churches-Friends	Mount Pleasant, list of contributors for building listed
12/18/1919	Herald	Churches-Friends	Mount Pleasant, Logan Hunt preached
11/5/1919	Journal	Churches-Friends	Mount Pleasant, Logan Hunt starts as pastor; he will continue at Martindale
12/11/1889	Herald	Churches-Friends	Mount Pleasant, new church will be completed by Christmas
2/12/1890	Herald	Churches-Friends	Mount Pleasant, new church will be dedicated Sunday
8/14/1889	Herald	Churches-Friends	Mount Pleasant, plans for church
5/20/1908	Journal	Churches-Friends	Mount Pleasant, Roe Bundy has regular appointment
3/28/1900	Journal	Churches-Friends	Mount Pleasant, Silas Cox is pastor this year
2/19/1890	Herald	Churches-Friends	Mount Pleasant, Society of Friends near Old Snow Hill was dedicated last Sunday
9/15/1927	Democrat	Churches-Friends	Mount Pleasant, thieves stole the carpet from the church
4/24/1919	Democrat	Churches-Friends	Mount Pleasant, to be repaired
10/25/1882	Journal	Churches-Friends	Mount Vernon Preparative Meeting established five miles south of Winchester
12/28/1887	Herald	Churches-Friends	Mount Vernon, meetings at
12/27/1916	Journal	Churches-Friends	New Dunkirk, dedication by Truman Kenworthy on December 31, 1916
3/11/1920	Democrat	Churches-Friends	New Dunkirk, Elvin Thornburg is pastor
6/4/1919	Herald	Churches-Friends	New Dunkirk, Green Schoolhouse is being used by Quakers
12/27/1916	Journal	Churches-Friends	New Dunkirk, Green Schoolhouse to be rededicated as Friends Church on December 31 by Rev. Kenworthy, Rev. Johnson, and George Addington
4/26/1911	Herald	Churches-Friends	New Dunkirk, meetings are being held at Green Schoolhouse

Date	Source	Category	Description
11/22/1911	Journal	Churches-Friends	New Garden [Wayne County], centennial of church
7/18/1888	Herald	Churches-Friends	New Hope, Cynthia Mills will preach at New Hope and Shiloh
6/27/1888	Herald	Churches-Friends	New Hope, Cynthia Mills will preach at New Hope at 11 and Shiloh at 3
3/14/1888	Herald	Churches-Friends	New Hope, Friends organized a Sabbath School: Elwood Hinshaw, superintendent; Elza Hinshaw, W. E. Hinshaw, Sarah Oyler, Mrs. Thursia Hinshaw, teachers
4/11/1888	Herald	Churches-Friends	New Hope, Friends Sabbath School "east of Rural"; Elwood Hinshaw
2/27/1889	Herald	Churches-Friends	New Hope, Rev. Wasson preaches at the "brick," east of Snow Hill
5/12/1886	Herald	Churches-Friends	New Hope, William Brown, John W. Pickett, and Julia A. Bond went to New Hope Meeting and secured school house with hope to build by next fall (Church Notes)
1/19/1898	Journal	Churches-Friends	New York Yearly Meeting, report of; Mollie Nichols there
10/28/1908	Herald	Churches-Friends	Nicholson, S. E., leading Indiana Quaker, endorses James E. Watson for governor
4/8/1908	Herald	Churches-Friends	Nicholson, Timothy, Indiana's leading Quaker, endorses James E. Watson for Governor
6/22/1956	News	Churches-Friends	Old Quaker happenings
7/1/1891	Journal	Churches-Friends	Olive Branch [Blackford County], Calvin Johnson filled appointment
2/1/1888	Journal	Churches-Friends	Olive Branch [Blackford County], David Wasson, of Farmland, attended dedication last Sunday
6/2/1941	Journal-Herald	Churches-Friends	Osborn, Richard Allen left for CPS Camp
4/28/1880	Journal	Churches-Friends	Parker Christian Church sold to Friends
9/24/1903	Democrat	Churches-Friends	Parker City, Silas Cox and Harvey Thornburg are preachers
10/17/1894	Herald	Churches-Friends	Parker, disturbance by factory workers
5/10/1882	Journal	Churches-Friends	Parker, first meeting of Parker Preparative Meeting will be held on May 12, 1882
12/17/1879	Journal	Churches-Friends	Parker, Friends are going to purchase church building owned by Alex Fowler
4/3/1889	Journal	Churches-Friends	Parker, Friends Church to be remodeled this spring
4/28/1880	Journal	Churches-Friends	Parker, Friends purchased Christian Church on 26th instant
2/14/1877	Journal	Churches-Friends	Parker, Friends will hold meeting at M. E. Church
9/17/1902	Journal	Churches-Friends	Parker, O. P. Thornburg, pastor
5/10/1882	Journal	Churches-Friends	Parker, Preparative Meeting first held on May 12, 1882
3/9/1956	News	Churches-Friends	Parker, remodeling

Date	Source	Category	Description
2/22/1899	Herald	Churches-Friends	Parker, Rev. Jim Carmon, Rev. Smith, Rev. Addington, pastors
4/1/1896	Herald	Churches-Friends	Parker, S. S. Hinshaw, pastor
2/13/1889	Journal	Churches-Friends	Parker, T. F. Adams, M. E. Class Leader, attended Quaker Meetings at Parker
8/19/1983	News-Gazette	Churches-Friends	Parker, will be rededicated on August 21, 1983
10/23/1971	News-Gazette	Churches-Friends	Peace Pilgrim visits Randolph County, including Jericho and Winchester Friends
11/25/1908	Herald	Churches-Friends	Peaceful Valley, "Greensfork" Friends Church mentioned
11/18/1908	Herald	Churches-Friends	Peaceful Valley, "Greensfork" Friends Church was dedicated Sunday
9/10/1914	Democrat	Churches-Friends	Peaceful Valley, "Ray Amburn" is pastor and will remain "for conference year"
8/26/1971	News-Gazette	Churches-Friends	Peaceful Valley, addition will be dedicated on August 29
7/24/1913	Democrat	Churches-Friends	Peaceful Valley, Calvin Johnson has regular appointment
3/21/1921	Democrat	Churches-Friends	Peaceful Valley, cigarette burns a buggy in the lot
4/19/1917	Democrat	Churches-Friends	Peaceful Valley, Elvin Thornburg preaches
9/17/1914	Democrat	Churches-Friends	Peaceful Valley, Elvin Thornburg to preach
4/4/1917	Herald	Churches-Friends	Peaceful Valley, Elvin Thornburg to preach
2/11/1932	Democrat	Churches-Friends	Peaceful Valley, Goldie Hinshaw has an appointment next Sunday
8/12/1920	Democrat	Churches-Friends	Peaceful Valley, Olive Harris has been pastor for past year
7/5/1969	Journal-Herald	Churches-Friends	Peaceful Valley, parsonage will be dedicated on July 6
1/24/1944	News	Churches-Friends	Peaceful Valley, poem
8/19/1925	Democrat	Churches-Friends	Peaceful Valley, Rachel Brooks replaces Allie Benbow as pastor
5/29/1930	Democrat	Churches-Friends	Peaceful Valley, Rev. Goldie Hinshaw has a regular appointment
4/29/1914	Herald	Churches-Friends	Peaceful Valley, Rev. Hinshaw and wife present fourth Sunday of each month
4/24/1913	Democrat	Churches-Friends	Peaceful Valley, Roe Amburn has regular appointment
9/18/1913	Democrat	Churches-Friends	Peaceful Valley, Roe Amburn preaches
3/2/1922	Democrat	Churches-Friends	Peaceful Valley, Roy Amburn will be the pastor
5/13/1908	Journal	Churches-Friends	Peaceful Valley, Sunday School organized in Brown Schoolhouse
1/6/1909	Herald	Churches-Friends	Peaceful Valley, the Friends Monthly Meeting has purchased the old school building in Greensfork Township; new church has a membership of 24

Date	Source	Category	Description
9/21/1905	Democrat	Churches-Friends	Pike [Jay County], Rev. Elwood Hinshaw has a regular appointment near Bluff Point
3/6/1889	Journal	Churches-Friends	Pleasant Valley [Adams County], Calvin and Ira C. Johnson are there
3/28/1917	Journal	Churches-Friends	Poling [Jay County], Chris Hinshaw, preaches
10/4/1876	Journal	Churches-Friends	Politics, vote on train to Indiana Yearly Meeting shows large majority for Hayes
3/30/1892	Journal	Churches-Friends	Politics, William Horn is not a member of the Friends Church
1/30/1884	Journal	Churches-Friends	Poplar Run Meetinghouse was dedicated on January 20, 1884 by Samuel Pitts and James Mills
1/17/1912	Journal	Churches-Friends	Poplar Run was dedicated by Ira C. Johnson
10/11/1899	Herald	Churches-Friends	Poplar Run, biography of Sylvania Puckett Remmel continued
10/4/1899	Herald	Churches-Friends	Poplar Run, biography of Sylvania Puckett Remmel recalls first song sung at Poplar Run
1/3/1912	Herald	Churches-Friends	Poplar Run, church will be rededicated on January 7, 1912
12/27/1911	Journal	Churches-Friends	Poplar Run, dedication will occur on January 7, 1912
4/6/1950	Journal-Herald	Churches-Friends	Poplar Run, history of
7/5/1945	Journal-Herald	Churches-Friends	Poplar Run, Murray Hubbard, KIA, member at Poplar Run
4/5/1916	Journal	Churches-Friends	Poplar Run, Ola Johnson has appointment
6/9/1949	Journal-Herald	Churches-Friends	Poplar Run, parsonage will be dedicated on June 12
4/12/1916	Herald	Churches-Friends	Poplar Run, Rev. Viola Johnson has regular appointment
1/29/1919	Herald	Churches-Friends	Poplar Run, Sunday School endorses Sheriff Davisson's actions in regard to liquor traffic
2/15/1882	Journal	Churches-Friends	Poplar Run, W. C. Diggs, Superintendent of Sabbath School
7/12/1911	Journal	Churches-Friends	Poplar Run, work will begin on church about August 1, 1911
3/10/1909	Journal	Churches-Friends	Portland [Jay County], dedication of church on March 14, 1909
4/13/1892	Journal	Churches-Friends	Portland [Jay County], Elkanah Beard has accepted pastorate
11/2/1892	Journal	Churches-Friends	Portland [Jay County], Elkanah Beard resigned as pastor
8/8/1883	Journal	Churches-Friends	Portland [Jay County], Friends Church dedicated last Sunday; James Moorman of Winchester gave $700
12/22/1909	Herald	Churches-Friends	Poughkeepsie (New York) newspaper features Friends Church
7/29/1914	Herald	Churches-Friends	Prohibition Party meetings held at Jericho and Arba Friends Churches
6/2/1897	Journal	Churches-Friends	Providence [Darke County, Ohio], Jesse C. Johnson will preach

Date	Source	Category	Description
10/25/1860	Journal	Churches-Friends	Quaker Democrats in Miami County; are very rare
10/19/1904	Journal	Churches-Friends	Quaker Hill, new minister (Mull Items)
8/28/1863	Journal	Churches-Friends	Quakers and the war
3/29/1941	Daily News	Churches-Friends	Quakers on the Randolph County [Draft] Advisory Board: Gilvie Brown, Cecil Owens, and maybe others
7/24/1872	Journal	Churches-Friends	Quakers refused to let G. W. Julian speak in Dublin, Indiana
5/22/1918	Journal	Churches-Friends	Quakers sound no trumpet on war relief
11/10/1897	Herald	Churches-Friends	Quakers, are they vanishing (in Philadelphia)?
5/24/1899	Herald	Churches-Friends	Quarterly Meeting is a poor time for businesses in Winchester
11/26/1890	Journal	Churches-Friends	Ralston, Mrs. J. W., daughter of Joseph B. Branson, of Farmland, who was pastor of Friends Church in Leroy, Iowa, died
6/23/1952	News	Churches-Friends	Randolph County has three residents at Third World Conference of Friends
7/17/1907	Journal	Churches-Friends	Randolph County Quakers now living in California are described
12/24/1925	Democrat	Churches-Friends	Randolph Union will be dedicated next Sunday by Harry Hayes
3/29/1973	News-Gazette	Churches-Friends	Randolph, Rachel Edwards writes letter to editor against ERA
1/23/1918	Herald	Churches-Friends	Red Cross, Friends Red Cross Band at work
7/24/1878	Journal	Churches-Friends	Richmond [Wayne County] School Board purchased old Friends Schoolhouse and part of Yearly Meeting property
6/28/1893	Journal	Churches-Friends	Richmond [Wayne County], offered pastorate to Elwood O. Ellis; he declined
5/23/1929	Democrat	Churches-Friends	Richmond First [Wayne County] is the largest structure of any Friends edifice in the U. S. or Canada; Richmond is the "capital of Quakerism"
10/3/1906	Journal	Churches-Friends	Ridgeville, Friends Sunday School will be next Sabbath at the usual hour
6/25/1903	Democrat	Churches-Friends	Ridgeville, M. R. Hiatt will soon begin the erection of a church in Ridgeville to be given to the Friends or Quakers. Mr. Hiatt will build it without outside assistance which is something unusual in the line of church building in this locality. And should certainly be commended for his liberality
8/30/1900	Democrat	Churches-Friends	Roosevelt, Theodore, opinion of Quakers described

Date	Source	Category	Description
12/4/1901	Herald	Churches-Friends	Rural [then Union Church] will be dedicated on December 8, 1901 by Rev. I. V. D. R. Johnson
12/11/1901	Journal	Churches-Friends	Rural [then Union Church], dedication postponed
6/11/1902	Herald	Churches-Friends	Rural [then Union Church], Hinshaw's statement on William McKinley
7/2/1902	Herald	Churches-Friends	Rural [then Union Church], more on Hinshaw's statement on McKinley
5/27/1903	Herald	Churches-Friends	Rural [then Union Church], new organ
4/8/1903	Journal	Churches-Friends	Rural [then Union Church], officers listed for Sunday School
3/23/1904	Herald	Churches-Friends	Rural [then Union Church], Rev. W. O. Bales and Uriah Hinshaw appointed delegates to County Sunday School Convention
4/24/1901	Journal	Churches-Friends	Rural [then Union Church], Sunday School organized
3/30/1904	Herald	Churches-Friends	Rural [then Union Church], Sunday School reorganized; Uriah Hinshaw, superintendent
1/14/1903	Herald	Churches-Friends	Rural [then Union Church], trustees election
11/27/1901	Journal	Churches-Friends	Rural [then Union Church], will be dedicated on December 8, 1901 by I. V. D. R. Johnson [It was later postponed]
6/5/1901	Journal	Churches-Friends	Rural [then Union Church], William Owens manages Sunday School at Woods Station
3/28/1929	Journal-Herald	Churches-Friends	Rural Friends Church damaged by lightning
3/3/1920	Journal	Churches-Friends	Rural Friends Church dedicated; cost $5860; Elvan Thornburg, pastor
11/14/1952	News	Churches-Friends	Rural Friends Church remodeled
2/11/1920	Journal	Churches-Friends	Rural Friends Church to be dedicated on February 22 by Ira C. Johnson
3/3/1920	Journal	Churches-Friends	Rural was dedicated by Ira C. Johnson on February 22, 1920
10/16/1907	Herald	Churches-Friends	Rural, "Rev. Gray of Farmland was elected pastor of this church"
3/7/1917	Journal	Churches-Friends	Rural, Ad Peacock and Charles Wright preach
8/15/1917	Journal	Churches-Friends	Rural, Ad Peacock and Charley Wright have regular appointment to preach
4/29/1908	Journal	Churches-Friends	Rural, Allie Benbow has regular appointment
3/11/1908	Herald	Churches-Friends	Rural, Allie Benbow, pastor
3/22/1905	Herald	Churches-Friends	Rural, bell placed on church
6/22/1926	Daily News	Churches-Friends	Rural, big wind broke out church windows
7/3/1907	Journal	Churches-Friends	Rural, C. R. Jennings re-elected Sunday School Superintendent

Date	Source	Category	Description
4/27/1904	Journal	Churches-Friends	Rural, Carry Owens and Ona Wilson attended dedication at Rural Sunday (Martindale Items)
11/29/1916	Journal	Churches-Friends	Rural, Charles Wright preaches
5/17/1916	Journal	Churches-Friends	Rural, Charles Wright preaches on 4th Sunday
4/12/1916	Journal	Churches-Friends	Rural, Charley Wright filled appointment
9/12/1917	Journal	Churches-Friends	Rural, Charley Wright gave farewell sermon
4/5/1916	Journal	Churches-Friends	Rural, Charley Wright has appointment
12/5/1917	Journal	Churches-Friends	Rural, Charlie Bundy has appointment
11/5/1919	Journal	Churches-Friends	Rural, church and Sunday school are being held in Noldo Blansett's house during construction
2/13/1953	News	Churches-Friends	Rural, classrooms will be dedicated on February 15 by George E. Addington
2/2/1953	Journal-Herald	Churches-Friends	Rural, dedication of classrooms
2/19/1920	Democrat	Churches-Friends	Rural, dedication of new church
8/27/1977	News-Gazette	Churches-Friends	Rural, Ed and Claudia Thornburg had Quaker wedding
2/10/1886	Journal	Churches-Friends	Rural, Friends have a series of meetings at White River Church [Disciples]
5/13/1885	Journal	Churches-Friends	Rural, Friends have been moved out from meeting in the Rural Schoolhouse
2/10/1886	Journal	Churches-Friends	Rural, Friends held a series of meeting at White River Chapel
3/1/1882	Journal	Churches-Friends	Rural, Friends meeting at the brick every Sabbath
1/4/1888	Herald	Churches-Friends	Rural, Friends Meeting east of [filmed with 1887, but appears to be 1888]
4/8/1885	Journal	Churches-Friends	Rural, Friends purchased house of G. A. Edwards for a meetinghouse
12/15/1886	Journal	Churches-Friends	Rural, Friends still hope to build a church at Rural
3/3/1886	Journal	Churches-Friends	Rural, Friends Sunday School at Rural
3/3/1886	Journal	Churches-Friends	Rural, Friends will hold Sabbath School and church in the hall above Gearhart Store this spring and summer
10/17/1917	Journal	Churches-Friends	Rural, George Addington starts as pastor
5/10/1916	Journal	Churches-Friends	Rural, Goldie Hinshaw filled appointment
8/9/1916	Journal	Churches-Friends	Rural, Goldie Hinshaw preached
9/13/1916	Journal	Churches-Friends	Rural, Goldie Hinshaw preached
5/31/1916	Journal	Churches-Friends	Rural, Goldie Hinshaw will preach
11/30/1922	Democrat	Churches-Friends	Rural, Goldie Hinshaw will preach this week

Date	Source	Category	Description
3/25/1914	Journal	Churches-Friends	Rural, Huff and Pickett preach
12/31/1913	Journal	Churches-Friends	Rural, Isoline Haworth and Emaline Huff preach every 4th Sunday
5/24/1916	Journal	Churches-Friends	Rural, John Shawley filled appointment; Chris Hinshaw preaches at Bluff Point; Charles Wright will preach at Rural next week
4/29/1914	Journal	Churches-Friends	Rural, Logan Hunt preaches
6/21/1916	Journal	Churches-Friends	Rural, Lyle Green has regular appointment
12/21/1910	Journal	Churches-Friends	Rural, Mrs. Barr preaches
2/25/1920	Herald	Churches-Friends	Rural, new church was dedicated by Elvin Thornburg and Ira C. Johnson; cost $6000
2/11/1920	Herald	Churches-Friends	Rural, new church will be dedicated Sunday at 1:30 p.m.
6/28/1916	Journal	Churches-Friends	Rural, next Sunday is Goldie Hinshaw's appointment
11/23/1905	Democrat	Churches-Friends	Rural, O. P. Thornburg preaches
7/29/1908	Journal	Churches-Friends	Rural, Olynthus Cox preached [and several weeks prior]
2/14/1917	Journal	Churches-Friends	Rural, plans to build a new church or rebuild the old one
2/24/1942	Journal-Herald	Churches-Friends	Rural, poem
4/1/1885	Journal	Churches-Friends	Rural, problems over use of schoolhouse by Friends Church
4/8/1885	Journal	Churches-Friends	Rural, problems over use of schoolhouse by Friends Church
1/9/1907	Herald	Churches-Friends	Rural, Rev. O. P. Thornburg, pastor
3/17/1909	Journal	Churches-Friends	Rural, Roe Amburn, pastor
1/9/1907	Journal	Churches-Friends	Rural, Ruby Oren fills regular appointment
3/3/1886	Journal	Churches-Friends	Rural, rumor is that Friends will meet above the store in Rural this summer
11/5/1919	Journal	Churches-Friends	Rural, services are being held in Noldo Blansett's house
3/5/1884	Journal	Churches-Friends	Rural, Silas Hinshaw says Friends will probably build a new church at or near Woods Station this coming season
1/1/1908	Herald	Churches-Friends	Rural, Vern Cox, Sunday School Superintendent
5/13/1885	Journal	Churches-Friends	Rural, vote confirmed the decision of the director to bar Friends from schoolhouse
2/11/1920	Journal	Churches-Friends	Rural, will be dedicated on February 22, 1920 by Ira C. Johnson
7/24/1943	Journal-Herald	Churches-Friends	Rural, will dedicate service flag; lists names of servicemen
12/22/1915	Herald	Churches-Friends	Shawnee Quaker Mission described
12/14/1887	Journal	Churches-Friends	Southland College, Arkansas, burned
12/7/1887	Journal	Churches-Friends	Southland College, Robert E. Pretlow at

Date	Source	Category	Description
5/3/1882	Journal	Churches-Friends	Southland Institute, Arkansas, described by Jesse C. Johnson
9/23/1976	News-Gazette	Churches-Friends	Teen Ambassadors exist
5/2/1970	News-Gazette	Churches-Friends	Teen Ambassadors, history of
7/6/1972	News-Gazette	Churches-Friends	Teen Ambassadors, Jan Crouch named director
11/12/1890	Journal	Churches-Friends	Thornton, Mrs. [Martha B.], organized new church "below Camden" [in Jay County]
10/24/1956	News	Churches-Friends	Trueblood, D. Elton endorses Vice-President Nixon
2/18/1874	Journal	Churches-Friends	Vinegar Hill also called Mount Pleasant (Snow Hill correspondent)
6/5/1895	Journal	Churches-Friends	Walnut Corner [Jay County] dedicated
6/5/1895	Journal	Churches-Friends	Walnut Corner [Jay County], church will be dedicated on June 16, 1895 by Robert W. Douglas
3/29/1882	Journal	Churches-Friends	Washington Township, Society of Friends in Washington Township has witnessed a great many conversions and renewals
1/21/1891	Herald	Churches-Friends	Wasson, David preaching at Brick Schoolhouse near Rural
1/14/1891	Herald	Churches-Friends	Wasson, David preaching at Washington Township School No. 1
3/18/1955	News	Churches-Friends	West River [Wayne County], church bell stolen then returned
3/21/1967	Journal-Herald	Churches-Friends	West River [Wayne County], Rep. Waltz is a member
6/3/1914	Journal	Churches-Friends	White Oak [Jay County], Luther Addington is a former pastor
4/26/1905	Journal	Churches-Friends	White Oak [Jay County], Meredith Hinshaw is pastor
7/14/1920	Journal-Herald	Churches-Friends	White River Friends Church dedicated on July 11, 1920 by Ira C. Johnson
9/8/1875	Journal	Churches-Friends	White River Monthly Meeting now rotates between White River, Jericho, and Winchester
1/11/1893	Journal	Churches-Friends	White River Monthly Meeting will be held only in Winchester in the future
5/10/1882	Journal	Churches-Friends	White River Monthly Meeting, a number of members were received at White River Monthly Meeting, including 41 in Jay County, including the Jay County superintendent, and three from Muncie
6/17/1943	Journal-Herald	Churches-Friends	White River service flag dedicated, 22 stars
7/14/1886	Herald	Churches-Friends	White River, "young men ought not to chew gum at White River Meeting House"
5/29/1878	Journal	Churches-Friends	White River, Berchvillites won't play euchre or checkers, but will play croquet

Date	Source	Category	Description
11/30/1933	Democrat	Churches-Friends	White River, biography of Mary Cox Beard says that White River had a separate log schoolhouse
9/3/1884	Journal	Churches-Friends	White River, Blaine and Logan Club formed
3/16/1892	Journal	Churches-Friends	White River, Christian Endeavor Society organized
12/31/1919	Herald	Churches-Friends	White River, church is being remodeled
6/20/1973	News-Gazette	Churches-Friends	White River, dedication of annex
2/15/1899	Journal	Churches-Friends	White River, donations to Rev. Simpson Hinshaw
6/4/1890	Herald	Churches-Friends	White River, GAR holds memorial exercises at
9/4/1924	Journal-Herald	Churches-Friends	White River, Ira Johnson and James Saylor preach
7/2/1919	Journal	Churches-Friends	White River, James B. Benson returned from relief work overseas
12/18/1924	Journal-Herald	Churches-Friends	White River, James Saylor has appointment
1/27/1892	Journal	Churches-Friends	White River, Job Harris died; he had once been head of White River Meeting
9/8/1926	Daily News	Churches-Friends	White River, Lee Chamness is new pastor; he will serve with Ira C. Johnson
4/8/1914	Journal	Churches-Friends	White River, Logan Hunt has regular appointment to preach
7/16/1913	Journal	Churches-Friends	White River, Logan Hunt preaches
4/8/1914	Journal	Churches-Friends	White River, Logan Hunt preaches
6/4/1913	Journal	Churches-Friends	White River, Logan Hunt preaches on 3rd Sunday
11/12/1919	Journal	Churches-Friends	White River, meeting at McKinley School due to remodeling
6/14/1871	Journal	Churches-Friends	White River, Nathan and Esther Frame will hold services
4/25/1883	Journal	Churches-Friends	White River, new church planned
8/29/1917	Journal	Churches-Friends	White River, next Sunday is Wallace Johnson's appointment
10/21/1896	Herald	Churches-Friends	White River, Republican pole raising at White River Friends Church and Schoolhouse
2/19/1913	Journal	Churches-Friends	White River, revival services
2/14/1924	Journal-Herald	Churches-Friends	White River, Saylor and Douglas preach
6/11/1943	Journal-Herald	Churches-Friends	White River, service flag to be dedicated; [one dedicated at Rural earlier]
11/12/1919	Journal	Churches-Friends	White River, Sunday School and church held at McKinley School due to remodeling
8/29/1917	Journal	Churches-Friends	White River, Wallace Johnson has appointment to preach
9/9/1983	News-Gazette	Churches-Friends	White River, William Haworth is new pastor
8/1/1906	Herald	Churches-Friends	Whitewater [Wayne County], Rev. Oliver Frazer not recalled as pastor

Date	Source	Category	Description
5/17/1876	Journal	Churches-Friends	Wilmington [Ohio], Judge Doane is a member, he commanded a division at Resaca, Georgia during the Civil War
1/18/1905	Journal	Churches-Friends	Wilmington, Ohio has the largest Friends Church (900 members)
9/5/1941	Journal-Herald	Churches-Friends	Wilson, Max to CO Camp at Merom
2/25/1880	Journal	Churches-Friends	Winchester Friends Church has organ for Sabbath School
2/3/1875	Journal	Churches-Friends	Winchester Friends Church, Elkanah Beard left, Henry Merrill started as pastor
7/19/1876	Journal	Churches-Friends	Winchester Friends Church, Rev. Henry Merrill resigned to go to Knightstown
6/29/1904	Journal	Churches-Friends	Winchester Friends pipe organ to be dedicated on July 1
12/8/1915	Herald	Churches-Friends	Winchester Monthly Meeting and the peace testimony
8/23/1916	Herald	Churches-Friends	Winchester Quarterly Meeting
5/20/1896	Journal	Churches-Friends	Winchester Quarterly Meeting appointed building committee
5/25/1887	Journal	Churches-Friends	Winchester Quarterly Meeting approved work under William Watts at Decatur, Indiana
4/26/1882	Journal	Churches-Friends	Winchester Quarterly Meeting granted monthly meeting to Farmland and Parker and one for Jay County; also decided to do away with one of the clerks
8/22/1894	Journal	Churches-Friends	Winchester Quarterly Meeting has two indulged meetings in Blackford County
11/22/1899	Journal	Churches-Friends	Winchester Quarterly Meeting opposes polygamy
7/29/1874	Journal	Churches-Friends	Winchester Quarterly Meeting organized last Saturday
2/3/1875	Journal	Churches-Friends	Winchester Quarterly Meeting thanks city for use of City Hall
10/27/1880	Journal	Churches-Friends	Winchester Quarterly Meeting, Buena Vista and Olive Branch asking to be discontinued
8/19/1896	Journal	Churches-Friends	Winchester Quarterly Meeting, building committee listed
6/16/1897	Journal	Churches-Friends	Winchester Quarterly Meeting, building committee visited Muncie, Rushville, Cambridge City, and Richmond to study buildings
12/10/1873	Journal	Churches-Friends	Winchester Quarterly Meeting, committee came and decided to locate inside the corporation [town limits]
1/7/1874	Journal	Churches-Friends	Winchester Quarterly Meeting, committee selected lot one block east of Public Square
7/22/1874	Journal	Churches-Friends	Winchester Quarterly Meeting, first session will be held in City Hall Saturday

Date	Source	Category	Description
10/8/1873	Journal	Churches-Friends	Winchester Quarterly Meeting, Friends Yearly Meeting divided New Garden Quarterly Meeting; plans to build house
10/13/1897	Journal	Churches-Friends	Winchester Quarterly Meeting, history of; now the largest in the world
12/28/1904	Herald	Churches-Friends	Winchester Quarterly Meeting, Meredith Hinshaw, superintendent
12/10/1873	Journal	Churches-Friends	Winchester Quarterly Meeting, new Quarterly Meeting of Friends at this place has 2000 members
12/6/1899	Journal	Churches-Friends	Winchester Quarterly Meeting, petition against polygamist congressman
7/3/1872	Journal	Churches-Friends	Winchester Quarterly Meeting, plans to establish
11/21/1900	Journal	Churches-Friends	Winchester Quarterly Meeting, plans to print directory
8/21/1895	Journal	Churches-Friends	Winchester Quarterly Meeting; committee proposes new building
1/7/1874	Journal	Churches-Friends	Winchester Quarterly Meetinghouse, subscriptions taken for
7/4/1917	Journal	Churches-Friends	Winchester, "Save the waste and win the war" is sermon topic
1/5/1887	Herald	Churches-Friends	Winchester, "The spirit, work, and life of George Fox will never die. The Friend's Church as a rebuke to ritualism and an advocate of spirituality that has never presented a bolder front than now [sic]"
4/10/1907	Herald	Churches-Friends	Winchester, "Why I am a Quaker" by W. J. Sayers
5/5/1984	News-Gazette	Churches-Friends	Winchester, 1910 Sunday School photo
2/10/1915	Journal	Churches-Friends	Winchester, 35th anniversary of Winchester Friends Christian Endeavor
1/1/1890	Journal	Churches-Friends	Winchester, Abijah Wooten starts as pastor
7/11/1888	Journal	Churches-Friends	Winchester, after six months release, Enos Hiatt reelected superintendent
6/6/1888	Journal	Churches-Friends	Winchester, Amanda Way and Frankie Pier spoke at Memorial Services
8/11/1870	Journal	Churches-Friends	Winchester, Amos Bond, Society of Friends minister, preached at City Hall last Sabbath
5/25/1970	News-Gazette	Churches-Friends	Winchester, annex was dedicated
5/19/1970	News-Gazette	Churches-Friends	Winchester, annex will be dedicated on May 24
7/5/1911	Journal	Churches-Friends	Winchester, Arlie Brown replaces B. F. Marsh as Sunday School superintendent
6/12/1878	Journal	Churches-Friends	Winchester, basement of church is partitioned for use by public schools

Date	Source	Category	Description
9/1/1897	Journal	Churches-Friends	Winchester, bids awarded for new church
9/20/1911	Herald	Churches-Friends	Winchester, biography of Frank Cornell, new pastor
3/21/1968	Journal-Herald	Churches-Friends	Winchester, brick house west of church razed; had been annex for 10 years
8/19/1874	Journal	Churches-Friends	Winchester, brick work on new church will soon be completed
8/26/1874	Journal	Churches-Friends	Winchester, brick work on new Friends Church is nearly completed
9/10/1902	Herald	Churches-Friends	Winchester, C. E. Hiatt resigns as pastor
9/3/1902	Journal	Churches-Friends	Winchester, Charles E. Hiatt resigns as pastor to go to Muncie Friends Church
4/17/1895	Journal	Churches-Friends	Winchester, Charles E. Hiatt starts as pastor
4/10/1895	Herald	Churches-Friends	Winchester, Charles Hiatt will be new pastor; has been pastor at Centerville for three years
1/9/1895	Journal	Churches-Friends	Winchester, Charles Hiatt will start as pastor in April
1/25/1917	Democrat	Churches-Friends	Winchester, Christian Endeavor, 36th anniversary
5/18/1898	Journal	Churches-Friends	Winchester, church dedicated
7/26/1882	Journal	Churches-Friends	Winchester, church is built correctly, entered from side; no one has to turn around to see who comes in
7/7/1897	Journal	Churches-Friends	Winchester, church is meeting at City Hall
4/12/1917	Democrat	Churches-Friends	Winchester, church put flag on top; first in state to do so
10/28/1914	Herald	Churches-Friends	Winchester, church will be reopened next Sunday
5/19/1897	Journal	Churches-Friends	Winchester, church will not be torn down for a few days
4/1/1926	Democrat	Churches-Friends	Winchester, church will reopen on April 4, 1926 (Easter); photo
8/19/1896	Herald	Churches-Friends	Winchester, committee appointed to make arrangements to build new church
8/19/1896	Journal	Churches-Friends	Winchester, committee to build new Friends Church included Joseph Goddard and Joseph Keys and others
10/20/1897	Journal	Churches-Friends	Winchester, cornerstone laid
10/20/1897	Herald	Churches-Friends	Winchester, cornerstone of new church laid on October 19, 1897
3/25/1874	Journal	Churches-Friends	Winchester, dirt removed to commence new Friends Church
6/10/1874	Journal	Churches-Friends	Winchester, dirt to be given away at Friends Church
12/30/1891	Herald	Churches-Friends	Winchester, Dr. Huddleston, Sunday School superintendent
12/31/1902	Herald	Churches-Friends	Winchester, E. M. Woodard is new pastor

Date	Source	Category	Description
1/7/1903	Journal	Churches-Friends	Winchester, Edward M. Woodard starts as pastor
1/31/1877	Journal	Churches-Friends	Winchester, either Robert Knight or Elkanah Beard will occupy the Friends Church pulpit in the future
7/14/1886	Journal	Churches-Friends	Winchester, Elkanah Beard farewell sermon after 13 years to go to Arkansas
4/13/1892	Journal	Churches-Friends	Winchester, Elkanah Beard leaves to pastor Portland Friends Church
1/20/1875	Journal	Churches-Friends	Winchester, Elkanah Beard preaches farewell sermon at Friends Church; succeeded by Henry Merrill of Cincinnati
6/15/1887	Journal	Churches-Friends	Winchester, Enos H. Hiatt replaces Joel H. Williams as superintendent
12/24/1925	Democrat	Churches-Friends	Winchester, fire damages church
4/11/1917	Journal	Churches-Friends	Winchester, flag raised
10/6/1897	Journal	Churches-Friends	Winchester, foundation of new church completed
1/19/1860	Journal	Churches-Friends	Winchester, Francis W. Thomas, Quaker minister, will be at the Courthouse next Sabbath
6/7/1911	Journal	Churches-Friends	Winchester, Frank Cornell will replace George Levering as pastor after Yearly Meeting
4/7/1927	Democrat	Churches-Friends	Winchester, Fred Carter will start as pastor after Yearly Meeting; Frank Cornell resigned last summer
4/2/1873	Journal	Churches-Friends	Winchester, Friends meetings described
12/1/1897	Journal	Churches-Friends	Winchester, Friends move services to old Central School
1/6/1909	Journal	Churches-Friends	Winchester, Friends Quarterly Meeting increased business in Winchester on Saturday
6/11/1873	Journal	Churches-Friends	Winchester, Friends services advertisement
6/21/1871	Journal	Churches-Friends	Winchester, Friends services with Nathan and Esther Frame
10/20/1909	Herald	Churches-Friends	Winchester, George Levering starts as pastor
9/15/1909	Journal	Churches-Friends	Winchester, George Levering, from Galion, Ohio, is new pastor
8/12/1969	Journal-Herald	Churches-Friends	Winchester, groundbreaking for addition
2/10/1904	Herald	Churches-Friends	Winchester, gymnasium constructed in basement
3/14/1877	Journal	Churches-Friends	Winchester, Henry A. Merrill [former pastor] has joined the North Indiana M. E. Conference and is preaching at Greenfield
7/8/1966	News	Churches-Friends	Winchester, history of
3/29/1928	Democrat	Churches-Friends	Winchester, history of Messenger Society; organized in 1905

Date	Source	Category	Description
6/16/1915	Herald	Churches-Friends	Winchester, history; first meeting was attended by thirty people; text was "The Shepherd's Care of the Sheep"
6/12/1907	Journal	Churches-Friends	Winchester, house to south is being remodeled as a parsonage
1/21/1880	Journal	Churches-Friends	Winchester, J. Charles, Superintendent of Sunday School
1/9/1889	Journal	Churches-Friends	Winchester, J. S. Hiatt reelected superintendent
12/1/1886	Journal	Churches-Friends	Winchester, J. W. Pickett, superintendent
6/7/1882	Journal	Churches-Friends	Winchester, James Moorman is giving away houses; one to Mary Moon [a rumor?]
5/11/1945	News	Churches-Friends	Winchester, James S. Mullen, KIA, memorial service at Winchester Friends Church
2/2/1887	Journal	Churches-Friends	Winchester, Joel Williams is superintendent
9/21/1950	Journal-Herald	Churches-Friends	Winchester, John E. Best, KIA on March 31, 1945, funeral at Winchester Friends
12/2/1896	Herald	Churches-Friends	Winchester, John Kittrell to hold revival
8/11/1870	Journal	Churches-Friends	Winchester, Jonathan Hodges [sic] and Mrs. Hollingsworth, Friends' Church, preached on the street in Winchester
6/4/1913	Journal	Churches-Friends	Winchester, Knights of Pythias Meeting held at church
5/19/1897	Herald	Churches-Friends	Winchester, last quarterly meeting held in old building
4/28/1897	Journal	Churches-Friends	Winchester, last social held in the old building will be on May 4
9/1/1897	Herald	Churches-Friends	Winchester, Luther Shetterly given contract to build new building
4/6/1898	Journal	Churches-Friends	Winchester, M. Z. Kirk, agent for the American Friend, there
7/22/1874	Journal	Churches-Friends	Winchester, Martin A. Reeder is pushing new Friends meetinghouse forward
3/30/1887	Journal	Churches-Friends	Winchester, Martin Reeder and wife joined Friends Church
1/6/1875	Journal	Churches-Friends	Winchester, Martin Reeder has successfully completed the largest church in the city
3/26/1873	Journal	Churches-Friends	Winchester, meeting in City Hall
11/29/1943	News	Churches-Friends	Winchester, memorial service for PFC David Denney
5/18/1898	Herald	Churches-Friends	Winchester, new church dedication
2/17/1897	Journal	Churches-Friends	Winchester, new church is planned
12/2/1874	Journal	Churches-Friends	Winchester, new church will be dedicated on December 20, 1874

Date	Source	Category	Description
12/9/1874	Journal	Churches-Friends	Winchester, new church will be dedicated on December 20, 1874 by Robert W. Douglas, David Updegraft, Henry A. Merrill, and Mary H. Rogers
4/29/1874	Journal	Churches-Friends	Winchester, new Friends Church
2/25/1880	Journal	Churches-Friends	Winchester, new organ purchased and placed in Friends Church for use of the Gospel Band
6/6/1907	Democrat	Churches-Friends	Winchester, new parsonage, south of the church, is almost ready
6/25/1919	Herald	Churches-Friends	Winchester, new Sunday School officers listed
5/12/1897	Journal	Churches-Friends	Winchester, next Sabbath will be the last service in the old church
5/21/1914	Democrat	Churches-Friends	Winchester, observes Peace Day
6/30/1897	Journal	Churches-Friends	Winchester, old church is being torn down
4/28/1897	Journal	Churches-Friends	Winchester, old time wedding is last social event in old church
4/28/1897	Herald	Churches-Friends	Winchester, old time wedding was the last social event in the old building
7/4/1877	Herald	Churches-Friends	Winchester, organ in church used in Murphy Meeting
2/25/1880	Journal	Churches-Friends	Winchester, organ placed in Friends Church for use of the Sabbath School
6/6/1888	Journal	Churches-Friends	Winchester, organ used for memorial services at Winchester Friends Church; first time an organ has been used in Friends Church in Randolph County
4/13/1933	Democrat	Churches-Friends	Winchester, peace institute
5/11/1898	Journal	Churches-Friends	Winchester, picture and article
10/2/1981	News-Gazette	Churches-Friends	Winchester, pipe organ remodeled
6/29/1904	Journal	Churches-Friends	Winchester, pipe organ to be dedicated Friday evening
5/25/1904	Journal	Churches-Friends	Winchester, pipe organ, work of erecting begins
5/20/1896	Herald	Churches-Friends	Winchester, plans for new building
6/30/1897	Journal	Churches-Friends	Winchester, plans for new church are accepted
4/29/1874	Journal	Churches-Friends	Winchester, plans for new church described
6/17/1896	Journal	Churches-Friends	Winchester, POSA held meeting there
1/27/1875	Journal	Churches-Friends	Winchester, preparative meeting established; Elkanah Beard preached farewell sermon
6/13/1974	News-Gazette	Churches-Friends	Winchester, Quaker Girls Sunday School Class, 50th anniversary; established in June 1924
9/1/1859	Journal	Churches-Friends	Winchester, Quaker meeting was held in M. E. Church on Tuesday last

Date	Source	Category	Description
7/1/1858	Journal	Churches-Friends	Winchester, Quaker meeting will be held in Presbyterian Church
5/5/1897	Journal	Churches-Friends	Winchester, Quaker Wedding Social described; last social event in old church
8/21/1895	Herald	Churches-Friends	Winchester, Quarterly Meeting committee recommends building of new meetinghouse
2/18/1950	Journal-Herald	Churches-Friends	Winchester, race relations meeting to be held Sunday
2/11/1874	Journal	Churches-Friends	Winchester, Recorder [William C.] Brown attended Friends Meeting
3/2/1939	Journal-Herald	Churches-Friends	Winchester, Regional Peace Conference will be held in Winchester on March 8
10/15/1914	Democrat	Churches-Friends	Winchester, remodeling
1/21/1926	Democrat	Churches-Friends	Winchester, repair after fire and new pipe organ
4/17/1895	Herald	Churches-Friends	Winchester, Rev. Charles Hiatt moved to Dick Kemp property by the new school building
1/9/1895	Journal	Churches-Friends	Winchester, Rev. Charles Hiatt will start as pastor in April 1895
4/10/1918	Journal	Churches-Friends	Winchester, Rev. Cornell preached, "What Friends should do to make the world safe for democracy"
7/15/1926	Daily News	Churches-Friends	Winchester, Rev. Cornell retires to Florida
9/27/1911	Journal	Churches-Friends	Winchester, Rev. Frank Cornell described
4/30/1925	Democrat	Churches-Friends	Winchester, Rev. Frank Cornell resigns as pastor
5/14/1925	Democrat	Churches-Friends	Winchester, Rev. Frank Cornell will stay as pastor after all
12/25/1912	Herald	Churches-Friends	Winchester, Rev. Frank Cornell, photo
2/19/1919	Journal	Churches-Friends	Winchester, Rev. Geo. C. Levering, former pastor, died in North Carolina
7/26/1911	Herald	Churches-Friends	Winchester, Rev. George Levering resigns to go to Spiceland Friends Church
5/19/1875	Journal	Churches-Friends	Winchester, Rev. H. A. Merrill will speak to old soldiers at decoration
5/26/1875	Journal	Churches-Friends	Winchester, Rev. Henry Merrill is a graduate of a college of music
7/19/1876	Journal	Churches-Friends	Winchester, Rev. Henry Merrill moved to Knightstown
9/13/1911	Journal	Churches-Friends	Winchester, Rev. Levering is leaving
7/5/1975	News-Gazette	Churches-Friends	Winchester, Rev. Raymond Breaker dies
10/13/1909	Herald	Churches-Friends	Winchester, Rev. W. J. Sayers farewell sermon and photo
3/4/1909	Democrat	Churches-Friends	Winchester, Rev. W. J. Sayers preached a "strong sermon" against dancing, skating, and card playing

Date	Source	Topic	Description
9/16/1908	Herald	Churches-Friends	Winchester, Rev. W. J. Sayers preached against voting for Thomas Marshall for governor on the liquor issue
7/8/1908	Herald	Churches-Friends	Winchester, Rev. W. J. Sayers resigns
8/5/1908	Herald	Churches-Friends	Winchester, Rev. W. J. Sayers will remain despite resignation
10/5/1898	Journal	Churches-Friends	Winchester, Richmond Item of Monday says that Winchester Friends Church is the finest in the state
9/26/1877	Journal	Churches-Friends	Winchester, Robert Knight, farewell sermon
12/22/1897	Herald	Churches-Friends	Winchester, roof completed on new church
12/15/1897	Journal	Churches-Friends	Winchester, roof is on new church
4/13/1892	Journal	Churches-Friends	Winchester, S. S. Hinshaw secured as pastor
12/13/1893	Journal	Churches-Friends	Winchester, S. S. Hinshaw will continue as pastor
1/10/1877	Journal	Churches-Friends	Winchester, Sabbath School organized; E. C. Thornton, superintendent; B. F. Mullen, secretary; F. M. Way, treasurer
12/23/1874	Journal	Churches-Friends	Winchester, seats put in the new church the wrong way; dedication by David Updegraft, Robert W. Douglas, Mary Rogers, Elkanah Beard, Ruth Johnson, and others
3/28/1918	Democrat	Churches-Friends	Winchester, service flag dedicated
3/27/1918	Journal	Churches-Friends	Winchester, service flag dedicated: Lloyd Farquhar, Floyd Brown, Max Wentz, Garland Thornhill, Jonas Stonerock, Everett Stanley, Harold Ryan, Ernest Bantz, Charles Davis, Ulysses Davis, Ona Parker, Ralph Edwards, Effel Sparrow, Walter Simmons, Verne Simmons, Roger Ludy, Charles Ludy, Don Harbour, Elza Conyers, Guy Boggs, George Pike, John Curtiss, Glen Diggs, Ed Clark, Hobart Cox, Earl J. Shetterly
12/1/1897	Herald	Churches-Friends	Winchester, services moved to Central School
4/13/1892	Journal	Churches-Friends	Winchester, Simpson Hinshaw secured as pastor
10/14/1954	Journal-Herald	Churches-Friends	Winchester, special seminar on peace to be held
6/20/1929	Democrat	Churches-Friends	Winchester, tablet to Thomas Hutchens put in church
6/21/1899	Herald	Churches-Friends	Winchester, Thomas Moorman as head of meeting; discussion of bell and organ
4/11/1917	Journal	Churches-Friends	Winchester, U. S. flag raised
9/9/1983	News-Gazette	Churches-Friends	Winchester, VBS paid for new cross for Goodrich Park

Date	Source	Category	Description
8/15/1941	Journal-Herald	Churches-Friends	Winchester, W. C. Dennis spoke at America First meeting at Winchester Friends Church
7/15/1908	Journal	Churches-Friends	Winchester, W. J. Sayers resigns as pastor
10/6/1909	Journal	Churches-Friends	Winchester, W. J. Sayers resigns as pastor; Rev. Levering will start
8/5/1908	Journal	Churches-Friends	Winchester, W. J. Sayers to remain as pastor
4/6/1933	Democrat	Churches-Friends	Winchester, will host one day peace conference by AFSC; Raymond Wilson, Clarence Pickett, and Richard Cary will be present
12/23/1903	Journal	Churches-Friends	Winchester, William Sayers replaces Edward Woodard as pastor
3/9/1898	Journal	Churches-Friends	Winchester, woodwork will soon be completed
2/23/1887	Journal	Churches-Friends	Wooten, Rev. A. J. says every Friends Church of importance should have a pastor
6/26/1912	Herald	Churches-Friends	Wright, Charles recently started into the ministry
9/22/1984	News-Gazette	Churches-LDS	Mormon Connection in Randolph County
4/26/1963	News	Churches-LDS	Winchester, Latter Day Saints Branch established
1/29/1981	News-Gazette	Churches-LDS	Winchester, Mormon missionaries in
3/13/1863	Journal	Churches-Lutheran	Maxville, patriotic meeting held at Lutheran Church near Maxville
1/23/1960	Journal-Herald	Churches-Lutheran	Our Saviour meets at Beeson Clubhouse
6/15/1967	Journal-Herald	Churches-Lutheran	Our Saviour will be dedicated on June 18, 1967
6/15/1961	Journal-Herald	Churches-Lutheran	Our Saviour, formal organization on June 18
10/12/1966	News	Churches-Lutheran	Our Saviour, groundbreaking will be on October 16
1/7/1966	News	Churches-Lutheran	Our Saviour, moves from 128 1/2 N. Main to Beeson Clubhouse
11/23/1968	Journal-Herald	Churches-Lutheran	Our Saviour, pipe organ to be dedicated on November 27
1/22/1966	Journal-Herald	Churches-Lutheran	Our Saviour, plans for new building
7/26/1860	Journal	Churches-Lutheran	South of Georgetown, T. M. Browne has political appointment at Lutheran Church south of Georgetown
6/20/1981	News-Gazette	Churches-Lutheran	Trinity, history
6/12/1982	News-Gazette	Churches-Lutheran	Trinity, history
11/6/1970	News-Gazette	Churches-Lutheran	Trinity, old church razed; old white 1860 building remains
4/28/1886	Herald	Churches-Lutheran	Union City, new church will be dedicated on May 23, 1886
9/15/1959	Journal-Herald	Churches-Lutheran	Winchester Lutheran Church is established

Date	Source	Category	Description
12/18/1959	News	Churches-Lutheran	Winchester, first Lutheran minister appointed
6/30/1959	Journal-Herald	Churches-Lutheran	Winchester, Lutheran Church to be established through the efforts of George Daly
6/9/1915	Journal	Churches-M. P.	Hopewell M. P. Church will be rededicated next Sunday
8/26/1914	Journal	Churches-M. P.	Hopewell, fire at "Hopewell Christian Church" [sic]
12/4/1918	Herald	Churches-M. P.	New Dayton, church is vacant, Jacob Ullom owns it
4/26/1916	Herald	Churches-M. P.	New Dayton, decision made to be a Methodist Protestant Church
4/26/1916	Herald	Churches-M. P.	New Dayton, meeting held to select trustees
9/27/1917	Democrat	Churches-M. P.	New Dayton, new Bible
4/26/1917	Herald	Churches-M. P.	New Dayton, new Bible, donors listed
8/28/1895	Journal	Churches-Methodist	Barrax Corner, new church [Grace Chapel]
12/3/1925	Journal-Herald	Churches-Methodist	Bartonia M. E. Church reopened/rededicated
12/14/1887	Journal	Churches-Methodist	Bartonia M. E. Church will be dedicated on December 18, 1887 by Rev. J. H. Ford of New Castle
11/26/1958	News	Churches-Methodist	Bartonia, addition will be dedicated on November 30
12/28/1887	Journal	Churches-Methodist	Bartonia, dedication
9/7/1887	Herald	Churches-Methodist	Bartonia, plans for a new church
12/3/1925	Democrat	Churches-Methodist	Bartonia, rededicated last Sunday
12/14/1887	Herald	Churches-Methodist	Bartonia, will be dedicated next Sunday
11/2/1915	Journal	Churches-Methodist	Bethel to be dedicated next Sunday by Rev. Somerville Light, Hugh Morris [who was ill and did not attend], and B. H. Franklin
11/4/1915	Democrat	Churches-Methodist	Bethel, church will be dedicated on November 7, 1915
11/10/1915	Herald	Churches-Methodist	Bethel, dedicated last Sunday by Rev. Somerville Light
11/10/1915	Journal	Churches-Methodist	Bethel, dedication
8/18/1915	Herald	Churches-Methodist	Bethel, dedication of "New Hope" church is delayed
9/22/1915	Herald	Churches-Methodist	Bethel, new church will be called "Bethel" [not New Hope]
6/23/1915	Journal	Churches-Methodist	Bethel, new church will be called "New Hope"
8/11/1915	Herald	Churches-Methodist	Bethel, new church, called "New Hope," will be dedicated Sunday; there are plans to remodel New Dayton Church
6/23/1915	Herald	Churches-Methodist	Bethel, new Methodist Church on Tucker Farm is nearly complete
11/15/1915	Journal	Churches-Methodist	Bethel, will be dedicated next Sunday

Date	Source	Category	Description
4/14/1915	Journal	Churches-Methodist	Bethel, work started by O. E. Way on M. E. Church on Tucker land
9/29/1886	Journal	Churches-Methodist	Concord M. E. Church moved by J. P. Edwards
1/27/1886	Journal	Churches-Methodist	Concord M. E. Church to be moved to Modoc
11/19/1873	Journal	Churches-Methodist	Concord, five miles southeast of Huntsville, will be dedicated on December 7, 1873 by Rev. S. N. Campbell of New Castle
3/15/1911	Journal	Churches-Methodist	Concord, George A. Howell, obituary; was once class leader at Concord
10/27/1886	Journal	Churches-Methodist	Concord, J. P. Edwards is moving church to Modoc
1/9/1954	Journal-Herald	Churches-Methodist	Deerfield history
7/16/1947	News	Churches-Methodist	Deerfield Methodist is building addition
5/25/1887	Journal	Churches-Methodist	Deerfield, cornerstone laid on Saturday of last week
12/7/1887	Herald	Churches-Methodist	Deerfield, dedication by Rev. Seamans of Portland
12/14/1887	Journal	Churches-Methodist	Deerfield, new chandelier
8/10/1887	Herald	Churches-Methodist	Deerfield, new church almost done
3/30/1887	Journal	Churches-Methodist	Deerfield, new church is being built
4/20/1887	Herald	Churches-Methodist	Deerfield, new church under construction
12/1/1886	Herald	Churches-Methodist	Deerfield, plans for new church
10/25/1916	Journal	Churches-Methodist	Deerfield-Saratoga, history of Methodism
9/21/1892	Journal	Churches-Methodist	Epworth Leagues have been organized at Mt. Zion (Vincent), Lynn (John Wesley), and Spartanburg (Bowen)
7/17/1889	Journal	Churches-Methodist	Fairview, bids for church on July 24, 1889
5/19/1932	Democrat	Churches-Methodist	Fairview, historical marker in the cemetery is to be dedicated on May 22, 1932
1/8/1890	Journal	Churches-Methodist	Fairview, M. E. Church will be dedicated on January 12, 1890 by H. N. Merrick of Fort Wayne College
8/20/1964	Journal-Herald	Churches-Methodist	Fairview, new parsonage
8/7/1889	Journal	Churches-Methodist	Fairview, recollections of old M. E. Church; new church will be 48 x 32 and cost $1135; old church was built about 1847
12/14/1922	Democrat	Churches-Methodist	Farmland M E Church was rededicated on December 10, 1922
5/16/1867	Journal	Churches-Methodist	Farmland M. E. Church is being pushed to completion for dedication
12/4/1922	Journal-Herald	Churches-Methodist	Farmland M. E. Church rededication

Date	Source	Category	Description
11/22/1866	Journal	Churches-Methodist	Farmland Meeting House built
6/15/1956	News	Churches-Methodist	Farmland to be dedicated on June 17
9/2/1896	Journal	Churches-Methodist	Farmland, cornerstone was laid yesterday
6/23/1875	Journal	Churches-Methodist	Farmland, M. E. Church bought new parsonage
6/9/1897	Journal	Churches-Methodist	Farmland, M. E. Church dedicated last Sunday by D. H. Moore
8/19/1896	Journal	Churches-Methodist	Farmland, M. E. Church is under construction
1/22/1868	Journal	Churches-Methodist	Farmland, M. E. Church will be dedicated in February 1868
3/10/1897	Journal	Churches-Methodist	Farmland, M. E. Church will be dedicated on March 21, 1897
11/22/1866	Journal	Churches-Methodist	Farmland, meetinghouse is nearly done
2/24/1897	Journal	Churches-Methodist	Farmland, new M. E. Church is nearly done
2/19/1896	Journal	Churches-Methodist	Farmland, new M. E. Church planned
7/26/1899	Journal	Churches-Methodist	Farmland, new parsonage planned
2/4/1915	Democrat	Churches-Methodist	Farmland, pastor resigned [major scandal]
7/22/1896	Journal	Churches-Methodist	Farmland, plans for M. E. Church
10/31/1906	Journal	Churches-Methodist	Grace Chapel is being repaired
2/19/1896	Journal	Churches-Methodist	Grace Chapel to be dedicated on March 1, 1896
7/13/1968	Journal-Herald	Churches-Methodist	Grace Chapel, "former Grace Chapel"
3/11/896	Herald	Churches-Methodist	Grace Chapel, Barrix, new church dedicated by I. C. Reade, President of Taylor University
2/19/1896	Herald	Churches-Methodist	Grace Chapel, church to be dedicated on March 1, 1896
3/4/1896	Journal	Churches-Methodist	Grace Chapel, Goodview, new church dedicated
2/19/1896	Journal	Churches-Methodist	Grace Chapel, Grace Chapel, two miles south of Good View, will be dedicated on March 1, 1896 by Rev. J. J. Reed of Upland College
7/9/1890	Journal	Churches-Methodist	Grace Chapel, M. E. Class exists at Hunt's Schoolhouse (Barrax Corner)
9/4/1895	Journal	Churches-Methodist	Grace Chapel, new M. E. Church planned at Barrix [sic] Corner
10/2/1895	Journal	Churches-Methodist	Grace Chapel, S. A. Clevenger will build the new church at Barrix [sic] Corner
11/27/1953	News	Churches-Methodist	Hopewell, history
3/9/1892	Journal	Churches-Methodist	Hunt, C. S. is M. E. preacher
10/19/1898	Herald	Churches-Methodist	Huntsville (Trenton), parsonage to be enlarged; church to be repaired

Date	Source	Category	Description
2/8/1943	Journal-Herald	Churches-Methodist	Huntsville Methodist Church burned
5/17/1946	News	Churches-Methodist	Huntsville Methodist Church has mortgage burning
10/10/1906	Journal	Churches-Methodist	Huntsville, church is being remodeled
11/2/1898	Journal	Churches-Methodist	Huntsville, church is being repaired
2/6/1907	Journal	Churches-Methodist	Huntsville, church was rededicated Sunday, February 3, by Rev. Mr. Paranogian; congregation raised $946.84 to cover $700 indebtedness on project
12/12/1888	Journal	Churches-Methodist	Huntsville, church will get an organ
1/30/1907	Journal	Churches-Methodist	Huntsville, church will reopen Sunday
10/28/1914	Journal	Churches-Methodist	Huntsville, church windows replaced
1/2/1889	Journal	Churches-Methodist	Huntsville, D. T. Alvin, superintendent
2/28/1953	Journal-Herald	Churches-Methodist	Huntsville, dedication of Community Building
1/8/1896	Journal	Churches-Methodist	Huntsville, E. K. Olwin, superintendent
2/28/1917	Journal	Churches-Methodist	Huntsville, Epworth League organized
8/25/1897	Journal	Churches-Methodist	Huntsville, Epworth League organized
9/23/1952	Journal-Herald	Churches-Methodist	Huntsville, first pioneer party
4/24/1872	Journal	Churches-Methodist	Huntsville, G. W. Jarrett, Sabbath School superintendent
9/10/1943	News	Churches-Methodist	Huntsville, Good Samaritan Sunday School Class organized
9/8/1897	Journal	Churches-Methodist	Huntsville, hill by the church is being cut down
4/6/1984	News-Gazette	Churches-Methodist	Huntsville, history
8/18/1984	News-Gazette	Churches-Methodist	Huntsville, history of; located in cemetery 1830-42; present site purchased in 1839; church built in 1842 with John Harris donating all of the cash needed ($300) and donated labor
5/19/1880	Journal	Churches-Methodist	Huntsville, J. Daugherty is Superintendent of Sabbath School
3/18/1914	Journal	Churches-Methodist	Huntsville, Ladies Aid Society was organized on Thursday
6/22/1887	Journal	Churches-Methodist	Huntsville, M. E. Church repaired at a cost of $150
5/3/1899	Journal	Churches-Methodist	Huntsville, M. E. Church will be reopened on May 7, 1899
5/5/1949	Journal-Herald	Churches-Methodist	Huntsville, men work farm to establish Community Building
4/20/1945	News	Churches-Methodist	Huntsville, new church to be dedicated

Date	Source	Category	Description
5/18/1898	Herald	Churches-Methodist	Huntsville, new Epworth League officers: Zana Sheppard, president; Lina Gaddis, 1st vice-president; Arlie Sheppard, secretary, et al
5/3/1916	Journal	Churches-Methodist	Huntsville, new hitch racks purchased
1/5/1898	Journal	Churches-Methodist	Huntsville, Nicholas Kabel, superintendent; W. Z. Sheppard, second assistant superintendent
12/12/1888	Herald	Churches-Methodist	Huntsville, old parsonage sold
5/17/1871	Journal	Churches-Methodist	Huntsville, plans for ME Parsonage
3/29/1871	Journal	Churches-Methodist	Huntsville, Robert Hunter, Sunday School Superintendent
1/5/1898	Journal	Churches-Methodist	Huntsville, Sunday School officers listed
7/3/1889	Journal	Churches-Methodist	Huntsville, Sunday School officers listed
1/18/1888	Journal	Churches-Methodist	Huntsville, W. T. Farquhar elected superintendent
1/8/1908	Journal	Churches-Methodist	Huntsville, W. Z. Edwards, Sunday School Superintendent
6/24/1914	Journal	Churches-Methodist	Huntsville, wind blew out three stained glass windows on Monday
6/24/1914	Herald	Churches-Methodist	Huntsville, windstorm blew out three art glass windows
10/12/1898	Journal	Churches-Methodist	Huntsville, work on church
7/4/1877	Herald	Churches-Methodist	Huntsville, work on church
1/4/1888	Journal	Churches-Methodist	Huntsville-Unionport Charge mentioned
4/29/1885	Journal	Churches-Methodist	Kizer Chapel will be used for an AME camp meeting
1/10/1872	Journal	Churches-Methodist	Kizer's Chapel exists
8/15/1877	Journal	Churches-Methodist	Kizer's Chapel exists
8/30/1876	Journal	Churches-Methodist	Kizer's Chapel exists
9/30/1874	Journal	Churches-Methodist	Kizer's Chapel exists
6/7/1871	Journal	Churches-Methodist	Kizer's Chapel exists
4/11/1867	Journal	Churches-Methodist	Kizer's Chapel exists one mile north of Winchester
8/2/1882	Journal	Churches-Methodist	Kizer's Chapel, obituary of Richard Smith Hagerman says that Kizer's Chapel had already "went down"
1/17/1877	Journal	Churches-Methodist	Kizer's Chapel, revival held
2/16/1876	Journal	Churches-Methodist	Kizer's Chapel, Tom Kizer has leased the chapel to Rev T. W. Thornburg for a long number of years
11/28/1888	Journal	Churches-Methodist	Lebanon M. E. Church remodeled

Date	Source	Category	Description
8/3/1910	Journal	Churches-Methodist	Lebanon, "old Lebanon Church site" mentioned
7/21/1915	Journal	Churches-Methodist	Lebanon, "trees where old Lebanon used to stand"
10/8/1902	Journal	Churches-Methodist	Lebanon, church to be sold at auction on October 18, 1902
6/7/1871	Journal	Churches-Methodist	Lebanon, Edward M. Barr, Sabbath School Superintendent
9/4/1901	Journal	Churches-Methodist	Lebanon, meeting to move church is held at Clarence Johnson Schoolhouse
1/23/1901	Journal	Churches-Methodist	Lebanon, plan to move church to Bundy Saw Mill as a Union Church
1/16/1895	Journal	Churches-Methodist	Locust Grove M. E., new church at Neff
5/25/1922	Democrat	Churches-Methodist	Locust Grove, five miles southeast of Parker, burned on May 19, 1922; furniture was saved
1/16/1895	Journal	Churches-Methodist	Locust Grove, new church at Neff
1/2/1895	Journal	Churches-Methodist	Locust Grove, new M. E. Church at Neff will be dedicated on January 6, 1895
7/16/1925	Democrat	Churches-Methodist	Locust Grove, reunion of church on grounds; church was not rebuilt after fire
6/25/1890	Herald	Churches-Methodist	Losantville M. E. Church elected trustees at the Christian Church
3/15/1900	Democrat	Churches-Methodist	Losantville M. E. Church will be dedicated on April 1
3/22/1900	Democrat	Churches-Methodist	Losantville M. E. Church will be dedicated on April 1, 1900
5/31/1899	Herald	Churches-Methodist	Losantville, an M. E. Class will be organized here
3/21/1900	Herald	Churches-Methodist	Losantville, church will be dedicated on April 1, 1900 by A. W. Lamport of Richmond
8/17/1892	Journal	Churches-Methodist	Losantville, contention over division of old Trenton M. E. Circuit
12/23/1983	News-Gazette	Churches-Methodist	Losantville, history; revival at Concord, meetings in Wiggins Hall; established in 1876 as M. E. Church with Christian, Christian Scientist, and Quaker use; 1884-Union Church built, called Antioch Union Church; new church dedicated on April 1, 1900; Between 1916 and 1920 Locust Grove and Franklin Churches on the Circuit were abandoned
3/21/1900	Journal	Churches-Methodist	Losantville, new church will be dedicated on April 1, 1900
9/6/1899	Journal	Churches-Methodist	Losantville, new M. E. Church is being built
3/20/1895	Journal	Churches-Methodist	Losantville, talk of establishing an M. E. Church
8/18/1886	Herald	Churches-Methodist	Lynn, at beginning of present pastorate, church had only 16 members

Date	Source	Category	Description
6/25/1879	Journal	Churches-Methodist	Lynn, church is being repaired
10/11/1893	Herald	Churches-Methodist	Lynn, church reopened last Sabbath
9/1/1886	Herald	Churches-Methodist	Lynn, dedication of M. E. Church will take place on second Sabbath in [October], not first Sabbath due to Friends Yearly Meeting
8/25/1886	Herald	Churches-Methodist	Lynn, dedication will take place in October
12/13/1866	Journal	Churches-Methodist	Lynn, M. E. Church is being used as a public school
10/13/1886	Journal	Churches-Methodist	Lynn, M. E. Church will be dedicated
10/6/1886	Journal	Churches-Methodist	Lynn, M. E. Church will be dedicated by Rev. J. H. Ford of New Castle
9/29/1886	Journal	Churches-Methodist	Lynn, M. E. Church will be dedicated on October 9, 1886
6/16/1886	Journal	Churches-Methodist	Lynn, M. E. Church will probably be dedicated on July 4, 1886
4/7/1886	Herald	Churches-Methodist	Lynn, new building planned
9/1/1886	Journal	Churches-Methodist	Lynn, new church will be dedicated on second Sunday in October
7/28/1886	Journal	Churches-Methodist	Lynn, new M. E. Church described
7/7/1875	Journal	Churches-Methodist	Lynn, plans for parsonage
10/13/1886	Herald	Churches-Methodist	Lynn, was dedicated on October 10, 1886
9/8/1875	Journal	Churches-Methodist	Lynn, work on new M. E. parsonage
6/24/1858	Journal	Churches-Methodist	Macksville, church will be dedicated on 29th instant by Rev. J. B. Barr
5/6/1914	Journal	Churches-Methodist	Maxville M. E. Church to be dedicated on June 14, 1914
8/5/1914	Herald	Churches-Methodist	Maxville to be dedicated on August 9, 1914 by Rev. B. S. Hollopeter; history
6/10/1914	Journal	Churches-Methodist	Maxville to be dedicated on July 5, 1914 by W. D. Parr and W. B. Freeland
7/29/1914	Journal	Churches-Methodist	Maxville will be dedicated on August 9, 1914
8/5/1914	Journal	Churches-Methodist	Maxville will be dedicated on August 9, 1914 by W. B. Freeland and B. S. Hollopeter
1/21/1914	Journal	Churches-Methodist	Maxville, brick work on new church is now completed
6/4/1964	Journal-Herald	Churches-Methodist	Maxville, church building is purchased by the Evangelical Christian Church
10/23/1963	News	Churches-Methodist	Maxville, church to be sold by cemetery association
5/27/1914	Journal	Churches-Methodist	Maxville, dedication to be delayed
6/24/1914	Journal	Churches-Methodist	Maxville, dedication to be delayed again

Date	Source	Category	Description
12/17/1925	Democrat	Churches-Methodist	Maxville, fire destroyed the old M. E. Church, being used as a house, on December 10, 1925
8/12/1914	Journal	Churches-Methodist	Maxville, history and dedication
5/26/1909	Journal	Churches-Methodist	Maxville, new church is needed
8/14/1913	Democrat	Churches-Methodist	Maxville, new church planned
4/28/1915	Journal	Churches-Methodist	Maxville, old church moved and made into a house
12/17/1925	Journal-Herald	Churches-Methodist	Maxville, old M. E. Church (then a house) burned
8/13/1913	Journal	Churches-Methodist	Maxville, plans for new church
8/5/1914	Herald	Churches-Methodist	Maxville, someone broke out 60 panes of colored glass at old church
11/18/1908	Herald	Churches-Methodist	Maxville, talk of a new church
5/12/1886	Journal	Churches-Methodist	Maxville, W. Mills, superintendent
8/6/1914	Democrat	Churches-Methodist	Maxville, will be dedicated on August 9, 1914
9/10/1913	Herald	Churches-Methodist	Maxville, work begins on new church
3/5/1947	News	Churches-Methodist	Modoc Methodist Church to be rededicated on March 9; it is Concord M. E. Church, built 1874; moved to Modoc in 1885; addition in 1928; remodeled 1945-47
10/2/1907	Herald	Churches-Methodist	Modoc, church is building belfry
10/30/1889	Herald	Churches-Methodist	Modoc, Concord M. E. Church reopened at Modoc last Sunday
10/16/1889	Journal	Churches-Methodist	Modoc, M. E. Church remodeled; will be rededicated on October 26, 1889
2/18/1874	Journal	Churches-Methodist	Mt. Pleasant Schoolhouse, Meredith Hinshaw is holding protracted meeting
9/21/1892	Journal	Churches-Methodist	Mt. Zion has been remodeled and will reopen on September 25, 1892
4/15/1940	Journal-Herald	Churches-Methodist	Mt. Zion history
2/8/1911	Journal	Churches-Methodist	Mt. Zion rededication
2/8/1911	Journal	Churches-Methodist	Mt. Zion to be rededicated on February 19, 1911 by Rev. T. M. Guild, D. D.
2/22/1911	Journal	Churches-Methodist	Mt. Zion was dedicated on February 19, 1911 by Rev. Williams of Union City
2/8/1911	Herald	Churches-Methodist	Mt. Zion will be dedicated on February 19, 1911 by Rev. Thomas M. Guild
4/26/1882	Journal	Churches-Methodist	Mt. Zion, church to be remodeled and get a bell [is this ME or Christian?]
10/19/1910	Journal	Churches-Methodist	Mt. Zion, plans to enlarge with a basement and bell

Date	Source	Category	Description
3/1/1911	Herald	Churches-Methodist	Mt. Zion, rededication; was remodeled at a cost of $1600
3/1/1911	Journal	Churches-Methodist	Mt. Zion, story of dedication
10/26/1910	Journal	Churches-Methodist	Mt. Zion, work commenced on remodeling
1/22/1908	Journal	Churches-Methodist	Mt. Zion, Zimri Hinshaw, Sunday School Superintendent
4/21/1886	Journal	Churches-Methodist	Mt. Zion, Zimri Hinshaw, superintendent
6/12/1947	Journal-Herald	Churches-Methodist	New Dayton Church being repaired
2/27/1918	Herald	Churches-Methodist	New Dayton Church now unused
3/22/1916	Herald	Churches-Methodist	New Dayton Church, lawsuit over property
12/6/1876	Journal	Churches-Methodist	New Dayton M. E. Church will be dedicated on December 17, 1876 by Rev. E. Holstock, Presiding Elder of Muncie District
2/7/1924	Journal-Herald	Churches-Methodist	New Dayton Sunday School exists
6/23/1927	Journal-Herald	Churches-Methodist	New Dayton Sunday School exists
3/2/1916	Journal	Churches-Methodist	New Dayton, advertisement for sale
7/26/1876	Journal	Churches-Methodist	New Dayton, church at Bear Creek Cemetery will be dedicated around the first of September
11/15/1876	Journal	Churches-Methodist	New Dayton, church at Bear Creek Cemetery will be dedicated on November 19, 1876
3/22/1916	Herald	Churches-Methodist	New Dayton, church sold to Jacob Ullom for $125
3/29/1876	Journal	Churches-Methodist	New Dayton, church will be 30 x 46
3/23/1916	Democrat	Churches-Methodist	New Dayton, disputes over church property
7/12/1923	Journal-Herald	Churches-Methodist	New Dayton, Elvin Thornburg preaching
2/10/1886	Journal	Churches-Methodist	New Dayton, Friends, Christians, and Methodists held revival
7/7/1927	Journal-Herald	Churches-Methodist	New Dayton, Guy Wolfe preaches
9/20/1952	Journal-Herald	Churches-Methodist	New Dayton, Harry Karns put sign on church building
3/24/1915	Herald	Churches-Methodist	New Dayton, meeting to plan remodeling
3/1/1876	Journal	Churches-Methodist	New Dayton, Methodists are building a church at New Dayton, 36 x 40
12/29/1915	Herald	Churches-Methodist	New Dayton, new officers of Sunday School listed
2/24/1916	Democrat	Churches-Methodist	New Dayton, notice of sale
5/14/1919	Journal	Churches-Methodist	New Dayton, Sunday School organized last Sunday; John Olvey, superintendent

Date	Source	Category	Description
1/5/1916	Herald	Churches-Methodist	New Dayton, Sunday School teachers listed
6/24/1903	Journal	Churches-Methodist	New Pittsburg, M. E. Church dedicated last Sunday [Union Church]
6/10/1903	Journal	Churches-Methodist	New Pittsburg, Methodist and Christian Church to be dedicated on June 21
6/30/1870	Journal	Churches-Methodist	Olive Branch, M. E. Quarterly Meeting was held in a grove last Saturday and Sunday
5/7/1919	Journal	Churches-Methodist	Olive Branch, Rebecca Stonestreet Rust's obituary says she joined this church about 1865
11/9/1910	Herald	Churches-Methodist	Parker M. E. Church to be rededicated on December 18, 1910
11/27/1940	Journal-Herald	Churches-Methodist	Parker recently dedicated
4/5/1905	Herald	Churches-Methodist	Parker, C. L. Reed, superintendent of Sunday School
11/2/1898	Herald	Churches-Methodist	Parker, church to be dedicated next Sunday
4/6/1973	News-Gazette	Churches-Methodist	Parker, dedication of carillon
11/9/1898	Journal	Churches-Methodist	Parker, M. E. Church dedicated last week (Diamond Hill Items)
10/30/1889	Journal	Churches-Methodist	Parker, M. E. Church is nearing completion
8/17/1898	Journal	Churches-Methodist	Parker, M. E. Church to be remodeled
12/4/1889	Journal	Churches-Methodist	Parker, M. E. Church will be opened on December, 7, 1889
12/18/1889	Journal	Churches-Methodist	Parker, new M. E. Church was dedicated last Sabbath by Rev. Albright
8/19/1963	News	Churches-Methodist	Parker, new steeple
12/25/1889	Journal	Churches-Methodist	Parker, remodeled M. E. Church was dedicated on December 15, 1889 by P. J. Albright; cost $605.24
7/6/1910	Journal	Churches-Methodist	Parker, to be remodeled
5/12/1949	Journal-Herald	Churches-Methodist	Photo
7/5/1860	Journal	Churches-Methodist	Pleasant Hill, new M. E. Church is being built by Samuel Payton, one and a half miles north of Farmland
8/14/1895	Journal	Churches-Methodist	Randolph County, Dr. John L. Smith described the M. E. Circuit in 1840-41: Winchester, Spartanburg, Economy, Widow Williams near Hopewell, Canada's (Mt. Zion), Huntsville, Newport, Windsor, Grubbs near Modoc, Thornburg's Chapel, Maxville, Sumwalts, Bear Creek, Reitneour Church, Deerfield, and Union Chapel

Date	Source	Category	Description
1/18/1882	Journal	Churches-Methodist	Rehobeth M. E. Church dedicated last Sabbath by R. D. Spellman, assisted by Pastor Rev. Bacon
11/25/1914	Journal	Churches-Methodist	Rehobeth M. E. Church to be rededicated on December 6, 1914
11/30/1881	Journal	Churches-Methodist	Rehobeth, church is complete except the seats
1/11/1882	Journal	Churches-Methodist	Rehobeth, church will be dedicated next Sunday
9/7/1881	Journal	Churches-Methodist	Rehobeth, Fowler and Graham have begun work on a new church
3/4/1908	Herald	Churches-Methodist	Rehobeth, Hamites are using an old log building as a church, four miles northwest of Farmland; led by Ham Pursley and known as the "Holy Rollers"
1/28/1907	Herald	Churches-Methodist	Rehobeth, Hamites/Burning Bush told to stay out of church
2/3/1875	Journal	Churches-Methodist	Rehobeth, Mr. Hulderman accidentally shot himself in the hand at Rehobeth Church
8/10/1881	Journal	Churches-Methodist	Rehobeth, new church planned
1/11/1888	Journal	Churches-Methodist	Rehobeth, plan to get bell for church
8/13/1914	Democrat	Churches-Methodist	Rehobeth, plans for new church
12/21/1904	Herald	Churches-Methodist	Rehobeth, problems with the "Burning Bush" group
2/12/1890	Journal	Churches-Methodist	Reitenour's, James G. Roberts, obituary; class leader at Reitenours from about 1840 until about 1858
1/30/1889	Journal	Churches-Methodist	Ridgeville M. E. Church dedicated last Sabbath
7/25/1918	Democrat	Churches-Methodist	Ridgeville M. E. Church rededicated
7/22/1903	Journal	Churches-Methodist	Ridgeville M. E. Church to be dedicated on August 2, 1903 by Dr. C. C. Cissell
7/22/1903	Herald	Churches-Methodist	Ridgeville M. E. Church to reopen on August 2, 1903
9/11/1959	News	Churches-Methodist	Ridgeville Methodist Church will dedicate addition on September 13
7/23/1903	Democrat	Churches-Methodist	Ridgeville, church will be reopened on August 2, 1903
1/30/1889	Herald	Churches-Methodist	Ridgeville, dedicated on January 27, 1889; cost $3,982
1/30/1889	Journal	Churches-Methodist	Ridgeville, M. E. Church was dedicated last Sunday by Rev. H. N. Herrick
9/12/1888	Herald	Churches-Methodist	Ridgeville, new building
12/26/1888	Journal	Churches-Methodist	Ridgeville, new church erected at a cost of $4000
3/28/1888	Journal	Churches-Methodist	Ridgeville, new church planned
11/26/1873	Journal	Churches-Methodist	Ridgeville, new parsonage

Date	Source	Category	Description
12/16/1874	Journal	Churches-Methodist	Ridgeville, new parsonage
9/26/1888	Journal	Churches-Methodist	Ridgeville, old church will be occupied by Granville Barnes as a wagon shop
2/29/1888	Herald	Churches-Methodist	Ridgeville, plans for new building
1/16/1889	Herald	Churches-Methodist	Ridgeville, will be dedicated on January 27, 1889
4/24/1878	Journal	Churches-Methodist	Rural, talk of establishing an M. E. Church in Rural
5/12/1954	News	Churches-Methodist	Saratoga history
5/14/1903	Democrat	Churches-Methodist	Saratoga M. E. Church will be dedicated on June 7, 1903
5/20/1903	Journal	Churches-Methodist	Saratoga M. E. Church will be dedicated on June 7, 1903
1/4/1968	Journal-Herald	Churches-Methodist	Saratoga Methodist Church and Saratoga EUB Church merged
12/24/1980	News-Gazette	Churches-Methodist	Saratoga to dedicate annex on December 28
8/16/1911	Journal	Churches-Methodist	Saratoga will be rededicated next Sunday
4/19/1969	Journal-Herald	Churches-Methodist	Saratoga, church still had large bell tower
6/25/1902	Herald	Churches-Methodist	Saratoga, cornerstone ready for new church
6/10/1903	Journal	Churches-Methodist	Saratoga, dedicated Sunday by Dr. Parr
6/10/1903	Herald	Churches-Methodist	Saratoga, dedication
6/17/1903	Journal	Churches-Methodist	Saratoga, dedication
6/11/1903	Democrat	Churches-Methodist	Saratoga, Fletcher Warren purchased the old church
5/22/1902	Democrat	Churches-Methodist	Saratoga, new M. E. Church planned
5/8/1878	Journal	Churches-Methodist	Saratoga, new M. E. Church will be dedicated on May 19, 1878 by M. H. Mendenhall
10/12/1905	Democrat	Churches-Methodist	Saratoga, new parsonage
12/16/1903	Herald	Churches-Methodist	Saratoga, old M. E. Church being razed; IOOF will build on the site
12/9/1903	Journal	Churches-Methodist	Saratoga, old M. E. Church is being razed to make room for IOOF Hall
5/21/1902	Herald	Churches-Methodist	Saratoga, plans for new building
8/16/1911	Herald	Churches-Methodist	Saratoga, reopening of church on August 20, 1911 with J. E. Williams, D. D.
5/20/1903	Herald	Churches-Methodist	Saratoga, to be dedicated on June 7, 1903 by W. D. Parr
10/25/1916	Journal	Churches-Methodist	Spartanburg M. E. Church will be dedicated next Sunday
10/26/1916	Democrat	Churches-Methodist	Spartanburg M. E. Church will be dedicated next Sunday, October 29, 1916

Date	Source	Category	Description
2/16/1916	Journal	Churches-Methodist	Spartanburg will build new brick church
11/1/1916	Herald	Churches-Methodist	Spartanburg, church dedication Sunday
11/9/1898	Herald	Churches-Methodist	Spartanburg, church to be rededicated on November 13, 1898
3/2/1892	Journal	Churches-Methodist	Spartanburg, Del Hinshaw, superintendent
3/16/1916	Democrat	Churches-Methodist	Spartanburg, groundbreaking for new church
7/12/1923	Democrat	Churches-Methodist	Spartanburg, history; services held in 1815; church built in 1837; new church built in 1857 and remodeled in 1870 and 1896; new church built in 1915
8/24/1898	Journal	Churches-Methodist	Spartanburg, M. E. Church is being remodeled
10/5/1898	Journal	Churches-Methodist	Spartanburg, new bell at M. E. Church
2/9/1916	Herald	Churches-Methodist	Spartanburg, plans for new church
10/12/1881	Journal	Churches-Methodist	Union Chapel, new church at Union is completed and will be dedicated at 10 1/2 o'clock on October 23 by Rev. Munson of Wabash
4/13/1881	Journal	Churches-Methodist	Union Chapel, new church is to be erected on Martin Hoover's land near the site of old Union Meeting House in West River Township
4/3/1952	Journal-Herald	Churches-Methodist	Union Chapel, new classroom
10/19/1881	Journal	Churches-Methodist	Union Chapel, three miles west of Bloomingport, will be dedicated on October 23, 1881 by Rev. Munson
3/17/1909	Journal	Churches-Methodist	Union City M. E. Church to be dedicated next Sunday by Rev. W. D. Parr of Kokomo
8/26/1948	Journal-Herald	Churches-Methodist	Union City Methodist pipe organ
9/12/1907	Democrat	Churches-Methodist	Union City, cornerstone to be laid on new church
3/27/1907	Journal	Churches-Methodist	Union City, new church planned
5/26/1859	Journal	Churches-Methodist	Union City, new M. E. Church will be dedicated on June 12, 1859 by D. W. Clark
6/9/1859	Journal	Churches-Methodist	Union City, new M. E. Church will be dedicated on June 12, 1859 by D. W. Clark
9/13/1976	News-Gazette	Churches-Methodist	Union City, photo in 1890
5/1/1907	Herald	Churches-Methodist	Union City, plans for new church
10/19/1870	Journal	Churches-Methodist	Union City, spire of new church will be 150 feet
8/23/1876	Journal	Churches-Methodist	Unionport M. E. Church to be dedicated on September 17, 1876
6/28/1916	Herald	Churches-Methodist	Unionport, built in 1850, is being razed

Date	Source	Category	Description
6/29/1916	Democrat	Churches-Methodist	Unionport, church razed
8/23/1876	Journal	Churches-Methodist	Unionport, M. E. Church will be dedicated on September 17, 1876
9/19/1877	Journal	Churches-Methodist	Unionport, Methodists have a nice church
2/11/1874	Journal	Churches-Methodist	Vinegar Hill, M. E. Church is holding meetings
3/13/1889	Journal	Churches-Methodist	Winchester M. E. Church dedicated
10/1/1926	Daily News	Churches-Methodist	Winchester M. E. Church is being remodeled
11/11/1857	Journal	Churches-Methodist	Winchester M. E. Church to be dedicated on December 5 by Dr. Clark
12/27/1900	Democrat	Churches-Methodist	Winchester M. E. Church will be dedicated on December 30, 1900
7/7/1886	Journal	Churches-Methodist	Winchester M. E. Church will be dedicated on July 24, 1886
10/30/1926	Daily News	Churches-Methodist	Winchester M. E. Church will be reopened tomorrow
6/20/1888	Journal	Churches-Methodist	Winchester, 2nd M. E. Church (Colored) purchased A. M. E. Church in southwest part of town
6/20/1888	Herald	Churches-Methodist	Winchester, 2nd M. E. Church (Colored) will purchase old AME Church in south part of town from F. M. Way
9/12/1888	Journal	Churches-Methodist	Winchester, 2nd M. E. Church mentioned
3/5/1884	Journal	Churches-Methodist	Winchester, advertisement for bids on new church
6/10/1885	Journal	Churches-Methodist	Winchester, bids for new church will be received on June 18, 1885
1/5/1887	Journal	Churches-Methodist	Winchester, C. W. Diggs, new superintendent
2/26/1890	Herald	Churches-Methodist	Winchester, church has no tower, but one is planned
5/19/1886	Journal	Churches-Methodist	Winchester, colored church and M. E. Church using Snedeker's Block
10/25/1899	Journal	Churches-Methodist	Winchester, contract for new church to Will M. Carpeo for $13,733
2/27/1884	Journal	Churches-Methodist	Winchester, contract for new M. E. Church will be let on March 20, 1884
6/9/1875	Journal	Churches-Methodist	Winchester, contract for new parsonage
5/31/1900	Democrat	Churches-Methodist	Winchester, cornerstone laid
5/23/1900	Herald	Churches-Methodist	Winchester, cornerstone of new church will be laid on May 25, 1900
5/23/1900	Journal	Churches-Methodist	Winchester, cornerstone of new church will be laid on May 25, 1900
9/2/1885	Journal	Churches-Methodist	Winchester, cornerstone will be laid on September 2, 1885
3/13/1889	Journal	Churches-Methodist	Winchester, dedicated by Dr. Bayliss, editor of the Western Christian Advocate
3/13/1889	Herald	Churches-Methodist	Winchester, dedicated on March 10, 1889

9/1/1886	Herald	Churches-Methodist	Winchester, dedication by Rev. Payne; old church was razed in May 1885
9/1/1886	Journal	Churches-Methodist	Winchester, dedication of
7/21/1886	Journal	Churches-Methodist	Winchester, dedication postponed
8/11/1886	Herald	Churches-Methodist	Winchester, dedication will take place on August 29, not August 22
7/5/1899	Herald	Churches-Methodist	Winchester, fire destroys church
11/27/1895	Herald	Churches-Methodist	Winchester, frame church was built in 1835, 22 x 32
5/27/1885	Journal	Churches-Methodist	Winchester, General Stone's donation of $10,000 will allow the building of a new church
1/10/1883	Journal	Churches-Methodist	Winchester, H. W. Bowers has been Sunday School superintendent for past two years
12/30/1891	Journal	Churches-Methodist	Winchester, H. W. Bowers, superintendent
6/6/1888	Journal	Churches-Methodist	Winchester, Hampton Gettinger is awarded contract for addition to church
9/13/1899	Journal	Churches-Methodist	Winchester, Hampton Gettinger to design new church
1/5/1881	Journal	Churches-Methodist	Winchester, Henry Bowers is superintendent of Sabbath School
5/23/1888	Journal	Churches-Methodist	Winchester, history
12/5/1968	Journal-Herald	Churches-Methodist	Winchester, history of
7/19/1899	Journal	Churches-Methodist	Winchester, history of
5/30/1900	Herald	Churches-Methodist	Winchester, history of 1885 building
5/30/1900	Journal	Churches-Methodist	Winchester, history of Stone M. E. Church building
8/19/1966	News	Churches-Methodist	Winchester, history of, formed in 1832
3/30/1916	Democrat	Churches-Methodist	Winchester, history, church got first organ about 1866
4/20/1916	Democrat	Churches-Methodist	Winchester, history, first church was built in 1837; parsonage still stands; brick church was built in 1850; it was removed in April 1885; cornerstone of new church was laid on September 10, 1885; first used in August 1886
12/6/1911	Journal	Churches-Methodist	Winchester, J. E. Hinshaw is Superintendent of the Sunday School
7/31/1907	Journal	Churches-Methodist	Winchester, J. E. Hinshaw, Sunday School Superintendent
8/7/1907	Herald	Churches-Methodist	Winchester, J. E. Hinshaw, Sunday School Superintendent
7/1/1885	Journal	Churches-Methodist	Winchester, last services will be held in old church next Sabbath

5/23/1888	Journal	Churches-Methodist	Winchester, M. E. Church (Colored) meets at Snedeker's Hall
5/28/1884	Journal	Churches-Methodist	Winchester, M. E. Church (Colored) will attempt to build in Winchester
7/5/1899	Journal	Churches-Methodist	Winchester, M. E. Church burned
1/2/1901	Herald	Churches-Methodist	Winchester, M. E. Church dedication
12/9/1858	Journal	Churches-Methodist	Winchester, M. E. Church dedication is postponed until spring
11/19/1919	Herald	Churches-Methodist	Winchester, M. E. Church purchased parsonage on W. North Street
1/30/1889	Journal	Churches-Methodist	Winchester, M. E. Church will be dedicated in March
7/28/1886	Journal	Churches-Methodist	Winchester, M. E. Church will be dedicated on August 22, 1886
8/25/1886	Journal	Churches-Methodist	Winchester, M. E. Church will be dedicated on August 29, 1886 by Rev. C. P. Payne, D. D., President of Ohio Wesleyan University
8/11/1886	Journal	Churches-Methodist	Winchester, M. E. Church will be dedicated on August 29, 1886 by Rev. Dr. Payne
12/26/1900	Journal	Churches-Methodist	Winchester, M. E. Church will be dedicated on December 30, 1900
11/11/1858	Journal	Churches-Methodist	Winchester, M. E. Church will be dedicated on December 5, 1858 by Rev. Dr. Clark of Cincinnati [postponed until spring]
7/14/1886	Journal	Churches-Methodist	Winchester, M. E. Church will be dedicated on July 25, 1886
2/13/1889	Journal	Churches-Methodist	Winchester, M. E. Church will be dedicated on March 10, 1889 by Dr. J. H. Bayliss
5/9/1883	Journal	Churches-Methodist	Winchester, M. E. Church will build a new church
2/3/1897	Journal	Churches-Methodist	Winchester, M. E. Church will get pipe organ
11/15/1962	Journal-Herald	Churches-Methodist	Winchester, Methodist Church will be rededicated on November 25
1/31/1861	Journal	Churches-Methodist	Winchester, new bell; old one had broken
4/14/1886	Herald	Churches-Methodist	Winchester, new building planned; Hampton Gettinger, architect
12/19/1900	Herald	Churches-Methodist	Winchester, new pipe organ
4/12/1969	Journal-Herald	Churches-Methodist	Winchester, new pipe organ
5/12/1897	Journal	Churches-Methodist	Winchester, new pipe organ arrived
4/13/1916	Democrat	Churches-Methodist	Winchester, old church was razed in April 1885
5/12/1897	Herald	Churches-Methodist	Winchester, pipe organ delivered
6/2/1897	Journal	Churches-Methodist	Winchester, pipe organ recital
3/11/1961	Journal-Herald	Churches-Methodist	Winchester, plans for addition

Date	Source	Category	Description
1/23/1884	Journal	Churches-Methodist	Winchester, plans for new M. E. Church
6/2/1875	Journal	Churches-Methodist	Winchester, plans for new M. E. parsonage
7/5/1882	Journal	Churches-Methodist	Winchester, plans for semi-centennial
8/30/1882	Journal	Churches-Methodist	Winchester, R. Brandriff, pioneer letter
1/13/1968	Journal-Herald	Churches-Methodist	Winchester, remodeling and new pipe organ
1/20/1915	Journal	Churches-Methodist	Winchester, Rev. H. J. Norris to prepare a history of the M. E. Church in this county for a history of the North Indiana Conference
6/29/1888	Democrat	Churches-Methodist	Winchester, Second M. E. Church (Colored)
6/22/1888	Democrat	Churches-Methodist	Winchester, Second M. E. Church [Colored] to purchase AME Church in south part of town
10/4/1882	Journal	Churches-Methodist	Winchester, semi-centennial letters
1/22/1908	Journal	Churches-Methodist	Winchester, Sunday School Superintendent
7/28/1886	Herald	Churches-Methodist	Winchester, to be dedicated on August 22, 1886
10/7/1926	Democrat	Churches-Methodist	Winchester, to be rededicated on October 31, 1926 by Bishop Leete
6/20/1888	Journal	Churches-Methodist	Winchester, Trustees of Second M. E. Church are trying to purchase the AME Church of F. M. Way in the southwest part of town
6/24/1885	Journal	Churches-Methodist	Winchester, W. Gettinger got contract for new M. E. Church for $7868
6/20/1888	Journal	Churches-Methodist	Winchester, work commenced on completion of church
5/19/1886	Journal	Churches-Methodist	Winchester, work is progressing
7/8/1885	Journal	Churches-Methodist	Winchester, workmen began tearing down the old church on Monday
11/1/1860	Journal	Churches-Methodist	Windsor M. E. Church to be dedicated on November 25, 1860
12/12/1900	Journal	Churches-Methodist	Windsor, new church will be dedicated on December 16, 1900
6/26/1901	Herald	Churches-Methodist	Windsor, new M. E. Church
11/1/1860	Journal	Churches-Methodist	Windsor, new M. E. Church will be dedicated on November 25, 1860 by O. V. Lemon of Richmond
12/14/1961	Journal-Herald	Churches-Miscellaneous	Bible Deliverance Temple exists in or near Bloomingport
11/22/1923	Journal-Herald	Churches-Miscellaneous	Christian Science Church purchased dwelling at southeast corner of Franklin and East Streets in Winchester
5/27/1891	Journal	Churches-Miscellaneous	Christian Scientists at Losantville
12/4/1919	Democrat	Churches-Miscellaneous	Christian Scientists, Winchester, meets in Moose Lodge

Date	Source	Category	Description
9/6/1969	Journal-Herald	Churches-Miscellaneous	Church of God Chapel [near Unionport] history, built 1963
3/17/1909	Journal	Churches-Miscellaneous	Clear Creek Free Will Baptist established in 1881; building was later taken by the Christian Church [seems to be an error]
4/16/1873	Journal	Churches-Miscellaneous	County Sabbath Schools listed
3/11/1874	Journal	Churches-Miscellaneous	Days Creek Church, two miles west of Ridgeville
4/23/1873	Journal	Churches-Miscellaneous	Dunkirk Union Sabbath School, William Dimory, superintendent; Philip Retz, treasurer
7/27/1968	Journal-Herald	Churches-Miscellaneous	Faith Mission exists
12/10/1902	Journal	Churches-Miscellaneous	Farmland Holiness Association meets in Opera House
3/23/1892	Herald	Churches-Miscellaneous	Farmland, Free Methodist services held in Addington's Hall
1/15/1902	Journal	Churches-Miscellaneous	Honour Corner, effort to build church on Dunkirk Pike near Honour Corner
3/19/1940	Journal-Herald	Churches-Miscellaneous	Jehovah's Witnesses arrested in Winchester
7/27/1936	News-Democrat	Churches-Miscellaneous	Losantville, South Side Church, revival
8/13/1940	Journal-Herald	Churches-Miscellaneous	Lynn Apostolic Church dedicated on August 11
7/6/1950	Journal-Herald	Churches-Miscellaneous	Lynn Apostolic Church's name is changed to Lynn Tabernacle
12/31/1941	Journal-Herald	Churches-Miscellaneous	Lynn Apostolic Gospel Church celebrates third anniversary on January 1, 1942
11/28/1952	News	Churches-Miscellaneous	Lynn, Apostolic Church and Lynn Tabernacle both exist
8/17/1984	News-Gazette	Churches-Miscellaneous	Lynn, Trinity Faith and Deliverance Church, Green Street, non-denominational, exists
7/18/1952	News	Churches-Miscellaneous	Maxville Bethesada Temple exists
11/29/1947	Journal-Herald	Churches-Miscellaneous	Maxville Christian Church listed as "no services being held"
5/23/1981	News-Gazette	Churches-Miscellaneous	Maxville Community Church exists
11/9/1968	Journal-Herald	Churches-Miscellaneous	Maxville Community Church, Jerry Brumfield, pastor
6/1/1964	News	Churches-Miscellaneous	Maxville Evangelical Christian Church will be dedicated on June 7; Robert Shockney, pastor
1/27/1956	News	Churches-Miscellaneous	Maxville Full Gospel Temple exists
11/15/1960	Journal-Herald	Churches-Miscellaneous	Maxville U. E. A. Church opens
2/17/1967	News	Churches-Miscellaneous	Maxville, Barney Jester, pastor
6/19/1965	News	Churches-Miscellaneous	Maxville, National American Evangelical Christian Church Conference at Maxville; Robert A. Shockney is regional moderator

Date	Source	Category	Description
7/30/1980	News-Gazette	Churches-Miscellaneous	Mission of Faith Full Gospel exists, Audrey Rodriguez, pastor
5/14/1919	Herald	Churches-Miscellaneous	New Dayton has Union Sunday School
6/23/1927	Democrat	Churches-Miscellaneous	New Dayton, Anti-Slacker Class exists
4/30/1919	Herald	Churches-Miscellaneous	New Dayton, church and Sunday School started last Sunday by George Addington
11/5/1919	Herald	Churches-Miscellaneous	New Dayton, church has been remodeled; attendees listed
7/23/1919	Herald	Churches-Miscellaneous	New Dayton, church repair; Clarence Hunt will preach
9/24/1919	Herald	Churches-Miscellaneous	New Dayton, church to be repaired and re-roofed
6/25/1919	Herald	Churches-Miscellaneous	New Dayton, Elmer Thornburg to preach
2/5/1919	Herald	Churches-Miscellaneous	New Dayton, George E. Addington to start Sunday School and church at New Dayton [he became ill; it did not occur]
7/4/1929	Democrat	Churches-Miscellaneous	New Dayton, homecoming
5/7/1919	Herald	Churches-Miscellaneous	New Dayton, new officers of Sunday School listed
1/28/1920	Herald	Churches-Miscellaneous	New Dayton, new officers of Sunday School listed
12/30/1926	Democrat	Churches-Miscellaneous	New Dayton, Sunday School and Ladies Aid are active
12/31/1919	Herald	Churches-Miscellaneous	New Dayton, Sunday School continues
8/15/1981	News-Gazette	Churches-Miscellaneous	New Life Church, on U. S. 27, Larry Thomas, pastor
11/3/1948	News	Churches-Miscellaneous	New Pittsburg to be dedicated on November 7
8/17/1960	News	Churches-Miscellaneous	New Pittsburg, history of
6/10/1903	Journal	Churches-Miscellaneous	New Pittsburg, new M. E. and Christian Church will be dedicated on June 21, 1903
2/16/1876	Journal	Churches-Miscellaneous	Oaklin Church, Franklin Township, exists
2/13/1884	Journal	Churches-Miscellaneous	People's Church at Union Cemetery [Stoney Creek Township] will be dedicated this month by Father Bowen of Henry Co.
4/26/1906	Democrat	Churches-Miscellaneous	People's Church, Prof. Wattles converts gym (old German Church) into theatre
12/31/1902	Journal	Churches-Miscellaneous	Rural [Union Church], W. O. Bales apparently is pastor
5/4/1881	Journal	Churches-Miscellaneous	Rural, Sabbath School exists, Silas Hinshaw, superintendent
11/14/1952	News	Churches-Miscellaneous	Saratoga Gospel Temple, 20th anniversary
11/10/1959	Journal-Herald	Churches-Miscellaneous	Saratoga Gospel Temple, 27th anniversary
5/28/1884	Journal	Churches-Miscellaneous	Union Cemetery, church was dedicated on May 11, 1884

Date	Source	Category	Description
4/16/1884	Journal	Churches-Miscellaneous	Union Cemetery, church will be dedicated on second Sabbath in May by William Bowen
12/18/1907	Journal	Churches-Miscellaneous	Union Chapel Church (at Union Cemetery) was rededicated on December 15
8/2/1969	Journal-Herald	Churches-Miscellaneous	Union City American Evangelical Christian Church is "newly formed"
2/13/1970	News-Gazette	Churches-Miscellaneous	Union City American Evangelical Christian Church to be dedicated on February 22
1/9/1970	News-Gazette	Churches-Miscellaneous	Union City American Evangelical Christian Church was organized on July 13, 1969
4/10/1953	News	Churches-Miscellaneous	Union City Assembly of God will be dedicated on April 12; North Plum Street
11/9/1968	Journal-Herald	Churches-Miscellaneous	Union City churches listed, including Salvation Army at Carter and Union Streets
10/26/1979	News-Gazette	Churches-Miscellaneous	Union City Community Fellowship Church exists at 228 1/2 W. Pearl St.
6/17/1981	News-Gazette	Churches-Miscellaneous	Union City Evangelical Mennonite Church meets at UCCHS
9/18/1981	News-Gazette	Churches-Miscellaneous	Union City Evangelical Mennonite Church will be dedicated on October 4 at Jackson Pike and 28, established three years ago; this building was a modular
7/15/1891	Herald	Churches-Miscellaneous	Union City Free Methodist Church exists
7/30/1971	News-Gazette	Churches-Miscellaneous	Union City Open Bible Church is established at 135 Carter Street
9/17/1974	News-Gazette	Churches-Miscellaneous	Union City Open Bible Church was formed three years ago
12/29/1972	News-Gazette	Churches-Miscellaneous	Union City Pentecostal Assembly Church exists at 109 N. St.
7/6/1968	Journal-Herald	Churches-Miscellaneous	Union City Salvation Army exists
10/4/1981	News-Gazette	Churches-Miscellaneous	Union City welcomes two new churches: Evangelical Mennonite; Community Fellowship broke off from Calvary Assembly of God about two years ago; located on Pearl Street
4/11/1953	Journal-Herald	Churches-Miscellaneous	Union City, Calvary Assembly of God will be dedicated on April 12
9/24/1984	News-Gazette	Churches-Miscellaneous	Union City, church for sale at Carter and North Union, lots 562, 563, 564; church furnishing also sold
8/18/1972	News-Gazette	Churches-Miscellaneous	Union City, God's House of Prayer exists on W. Pearl Street
8/9/1906	Democrat	Churches-Miscellaneous	Union City, Pentecostal meetings held under the Western Ohio District of the Apostolic Holiness Union, led by A. J. Furstenberger, Quaker evangelist of Cardington, Ohio
8/28/1946	News	Churches-Miscellaneous	Winchester Apostolic Church exists on Western Ave.

Date	Source	Category	Description
12/2/1944	Journal-Herald	Churches-Miscellaneous	Winchester Apostolic Tabernacle dedicated at 600 Western Ave., church started one year ago
12/1/1978	News-Gazette	Churches-Miscellaneous	Winchester Cathedral is a Full Gospel Church
8/22/1978	News-Gazette	Churches-Miscellaneous	Winchester Cathedral, exists, one mile north of Courthouse on Main Street
10/14/1983	News-Gazette	Churches-Miscellaneous	Winchester Cathedral, Full Gospel, exists
4/3/1981	News-Gazette	Churches-Miscellaneous	Winchester Cathedral, history; began on May 28, 1977 in home, later purchased church on Western Avenue; plans for new building
8/27/1982	News-Gazette	Churches-Miscellaneous	Winchester Cathedral, located on Western Ave., addition; church established in 1978
6/17/1977	News-Gazette	Churches-Miscellaneous	Winchester Cathedral, new church; temporary location is one mile north on Main Street
12/3/1919	Journal	Churches-Miscellaneous	Winchester Christian Science Church purchases building at East South and Will Streets?
12/21/1911	Democrat	Churches-Miscellaneous	Winchester Christian Scientists meet in Central School
11/21/1959	Journal-Herald	Churches-Miscellaneous	Winchester Episcopal services to be held at American Legion at 7p.m. Sunday evening
12/24/1959	Journal-Herald	Churches-Miscellaneous	Winchester Episcopal, 304 S. East St. [American Legion] in church listing
12/9/1965	Journal-Herald	Churches-Miscellaneous	Winchester Gospel Tabernacle exists at Third and Meridian
4/14/1982	News-Gazette	Churches-Miscellaneous	Winchester Gospel Tabernacle exists at Third and Meridian
8/5/1947	Journal-Herald	Churches-Miscellaneous	Winchester Gospel Tabernacle nearly complete on North Main Street, Rev. Russell Castle, pastor
9/12/1947	News	Churches-Miscellaneous	Winchester Gospel Tabernacle on U. S. 27 will be dedicated on September 14
1/24/1936	News-Democrat	Churches-Miscellaneous	Winchester has a People's Church and a Science Church
5/29/1907	Herald	Churches-Miscellaneous	Winchester Mission Church in Beech Grove Addition was dedicated on May 26, 1907
11/16/1905	Democrat	Churches-Miscellaneous	Winchester People's Church is using the old German Church
11/22/1941	Journal-Herald	Churches-Miscellaneous	Winchester Pilgrim Holiness Church to be dedicated on November 23
5/27/1966	News	Churches-Miscellaneous	Winchester Pilgrim Holiness Church, history of
9/3/1977	News-Gazette	Churches-Miscellaneous	Winchester Union Mission exists
9/2/1966	News	Churches-Miscellaneous	Winchester Union Mission, history of
11/4/1954	Journal-Herald	Churches-Miscellaneous	Winchester United Pentecostal Church exists at 123 N. Jackson St.

Date	Source	Category	Description
11/30/1956	News	Churches-Miscellaneous	Winchester United Pentecostal Church will move to new building on Elm Street on December 2
5/14/1966	Journal-Herald	Churches-Miscellaneous	Winchester United Pentecostal Church, history of
3/17/1979	News-Gazette	Churches-Miscellaneous	Winchester United Pentecostal Church, remodeling
3/19/1960	Journal-Herald	Churches-Miscellaneous	Winchester, Assembly of God no longer listed in church directory
1/3/1957	Journal-Herald	Churches-Miscellaneous	Winchester, Bible Missionary Church exists on U. S. 27 in former Wesleyan Methodist Church
2/18/1909	Democrat	Churches-Miscellaneous	Winchester, Christian Science services are being held
11/18/1914	Herald	Churches-Miscellaneous	Winchester, Christian Science services are held in Moose Hall
10/30/1907	Herald	Churches-Miscellaneous	Winchester, Christian Science services being held
11/11/1914	Journal	Churches-Miscellaneous	Winchester, Christian Scientists have rented space in the Moose Lodge
12/3/1919	Journal	Churches-Miscellaneous	Winchester, Christian Scientists purchased lot on E. South and plan to build
9/15/1959	Journal-Herald	Churches-Miscellaneous	Winchester, Episcopalian meeting will be held on Thursday
12/16/1896	Journal	Churches-Miscellaneous	Winchester, First Spiritual Society meets in Snedeker's Hall
5/24/1963	News	Churches-Miscellaneous	Winchester, Four Square Gospel Church no longer appears in church listing
4/8/1960	News	Churches-Miscellaneous	Winchester, Four Square Gospel Church opened on Easter
12/2/1956	News	Churches-Miscellaneous	Winchester, Glad Tidings Assembly of God opens on December 12 at 123 N. Main Street
5/30/1888	Journal	Churches-Miscellaneous	Winchester, Hiatt, Dr. Jehu is erecting a church in his park northeast of town that will be free to all denominations
12/6/1905	Journal	Churches-Miscellaneous	Winchester, People's Church exists in W. Franklin Street under Rev. Wattles, member of Marion Meeting of Friends
12/20/1905	Journal	Churches-Miscellaneous	Winchester, People's Church, plan for permanent organization
12/21/1905	Democrat	Churches-Miscellaneous	Winchester, People's Church, proposition for permanent organization
2/27/1907	Herald	Churches-Miscellaneous	Winchester, People's Church, Rev. Wattles criticized religion
10/1/1908	Democrat	Churches-Miscellaneous	Winchester, People's Church, Rev. Wattles, formerly of this church, is a Socialist in Elwood
11/6/1959	News	Churches-Miscellaneous	Winchester, plans to establish an Episcopal Church
11/1/1905	Herald	Churches-Miscellaneous	Winchester, Rev. Wattles preaches at Old German Church

Date	Source	Category	Description
6/25/1925	Democrat	Churches-Miscellaneous	Winchester, Salvation Army Corps is withdrawn
6/12/1901	Journal	Churches-Miscellaneous	Winchester, Seventh-Day Adventist meeting are being held in the Evangelical Church
5/23/1907	Democrat	Churches-Miscellaneous	Winchester, Union Mission to be dedicated next Sunday
10/3/1958	News	Churches-Miscellaneous	Winchester, Union Mission will be rededicated on October 5; built in 1907
5/10/1958	Journal-Herald	Churches-Miscellaneous	Winchester, United Pentecostal Church is called "Faith Tabernacle"
8/4/1964	Journal-Herald	Churches-Miscellaneous	Winchester, United Pentecostal Church, 5th anniversary
4/12/1922	Democrat	Churches-Miscellaneous	Winchester, Unity Spiritual Church meets in Canada Block on west side of Square
11/24/1921	Democrat	Churches-Miscellaneous	Winchester, Unity Spiritualist Church meets in Redmen's Hall
1/13/1870	Journal	Churches-Miscellaneous	Winchester, Universalist Church exists
9/14/1963	Journal-Herald	Churches-Miscellaneous	Winchester, Wesleyan Holiness Church exists
5/28/1884	Journal	Churches-Miscellaneous	Windsor, Union Church dedication [on May 11?]
6/16/1875	Journal	Churches-Miscellaneous	Wood's Station, citizens will meet next Monday to plan the erection of a Free Union Meetinghouse
5/28/1953	Journal-Herald	Churches-Miscellaneous	Zion Faith Tabernacle no longer listed
7/18/1952	News	Churches-Miscellaneous	Zion Faith Tabernacle, Frank Kenyon, pastor, exists in rural county, existed in 1951
7/22/1939	Journal-Herald	Churches-Nazarene	Farmland Church of the Nazarene to be dedicated on July 23
5/11/1961	Journal-Herald	Churches-Nazarene	Farmland, addition
4/11/1942	Journal-Herald	Churches-Nazarene	Lynn Church of the Nazarene will be dedicated on April 12
1/17/1958	News	Churches-Nazarene	Lynn, church purchased new ground
5/4/1967	Journal-Herald	Churches-Nazarene	Lynn, dedicated on May 7
10/10/1958	News	Churches-Nazarene	Lynn, history of
9/6/1966	Journal-Herald	Churches-Nazarene	Lynn, new building under construction
5/3/1967	News	Churches-Nazarene	Lynn, new church cost $200,000
8/24/1942	Journal-Herald	Churches-Nazarene	Map of Nazarene Churches in Indiana
1/19/1950	Journal-Herald	Churches-Nazarene	Modoc Church of the Nazarene to be rededicated on January 22
9/25/1918	Journal	Churches-Nazarene	Modoc, church being built
6/18/1966	Journal-Herald	Churches-Nazarene	Modoc, fellowship building will be dedicated on June 19
5/20/1920	Democrat	Churches-Nazarene	Parker, Rev. Earl Cox filled appointment

Date	Source	Category	Description
10/22/1919	Herald	Churches-Nazarene	Pentecostal Church of the Nazarene name is changed to Church of the Nazarene
4/11/1958	News	Churches-Nazarene	Ridgeville, addition to be dedicated on April 13
8/8/1929	Journal-Herald	Churches-Nazarene	Winchester Church of the Nazarene nearly completed
4/19/1917	Democrat	Churches-Nazarene	Winchester First Pentecostal Church of the Nazarene was organized on November 9, 1916 with fifteen charter members
4/25/1917	Herald	Churches-Nazarene	Winchester First Pentecostal Church of the Nazarene was organized on November 9, 1916; currently looking for a location to meet
9/26/1929	Journal-Herald	Churches-Nazarene	Winchester Nazarene Church was dedicated last Sunday
8/20/1971	News-Gazette	Churches-Nazarene	Winchester, addition will be dedicated on August 29
4/4/1957	Journal-Herald	Churches-Nazarene	Winchester, annex will be dedicated on April 7
2/28/1929	Democrat	Churches-Nazarene	Winchester, bids on new church
7/12/1917	Democrat	Churches-Nazarene	Winchester, Church of the Nazarene was dedicated on July 8, 1917
6/13/1917	Journal	Churches-Nazarene	Winchester, church purchases old Main Street Christian Church
9/12/1929	Democrat	Churches-Nazarene	Winchester, church will be dedicated on September 22, 1929 by C. E. Hardy; Haldor Lillenas, famous hymnist, will be present
7/11/1917	Herald	Churches-Nazarene	Winchester, dedication by U. E. Harding
6/12/1918	Journal	Churches-Nazarene	Winchester, dedication was last Sunday
4/25/1917	Journal	Churches-Nazarene	Winchester, First Pentecostal Church of the Nazarene organized
7/18/1917	Journal	Churches-Nazarene	Winchester, H. Earl Cox, pastor
6/10/1966	News	Churches-Nazarene	Winchester, history of
12/12/1917	Herald	Churches-Nazarene	Winchester, J. H. Williams writes of the church
8/26/1970	News-Gazette	Churches-Nazarene	Winchester, new façade started
2/2/1928	Democrat	Churches-Nazarene	Winchester, plans to build new church
1/20/1927	Journal-Herald	Churches-Nazarene	Winchester, steeple removed from church
7/4/1917	Journal	Churches-Nazarene	Winchester, will be dedicated next Sunday by U. E. Harding
4/4/1929	Democrat	Churches-Nazarene	Winchester, work begins on new church; meetings are being held in the Moose Hall
10/11/1876	Journal	Churches-Presbyterian	Luce, Andrew was pastor of Winchester Presbyterian Church (1849-1857)

Date	Publication	Category	Description
1/17/1877	Journal	Churches-Presbyterian	Pleasant Ridge, Frances Jenkins's obituary says that the church "went down" in 1874
7/6/1968	Journal-Herald	Churches-Presbyterian	Union City, addition
7/13/1904	Herald	Churches-Presbyterian	Union City, foundation of new church is complete
11/16/1968	Journal-Herald	Churches-Presbyterian	Union City, rededication planned on November 17; siding and addition
7/30/1903	Democrat	Churches-Presbyterian	Union City, will build brick church
6/3/1961	Journal-Herald	Churches-Presbyterian	Winchester Presbyterian Church was enlarged in 1927
11/8/1928	Democrat	Churches-Presbyterian	Winchester, addition was dedicated on November 4, 1928
12/7/1881	Journal	Churches-Presbyterian	Winchester, Andrew Luce, former pastor of church here, came to organize new Presbyterian Church in Winchester
5/20/1903	Journal	Churches-Presbyterian	Winchester, bids for church
9/28/1887	Journal	Churches-Presbyterian	Winchester, builders turned church over to building committee
3/23/1982	News-Gazette	Churches-Presbyterian	Winchester, centennial
8/15/1883	Journal	Churches-Presbyterian	Winchester, church appointed a building committee
5/11/1904	Herald	Churches-Presbyterian	Winchester, church to be dedicated on May 29, 1904 by W. P. Kane, President of Wabash College
12/28/1887	Herald	Churches-Presbyterian	Winchester, church will be dedicated on January 1, 1888
12/28/1887	Journal	Churches-Presbyterian	Winchester, church will be dedicated on January 1, 1888 by Rev. Charles Little, D. D., of Wabash, Indiana
5/21/1903	Democrat	Churches-Presbyterian	Winchester, contract for new church let
1/12/1887	Journal	Churches-Presbyterian	Winchester, contract for new church to be let
7/29/1903	Herald	Churches-Presbyterian	Winchester, cornerstone laid
7/23/1903	Democrat	Churches-Presbyterian	Winchester, cornerstone laid on July 23, 1903
7/22/1903	Journal	Churches-Presbyterian	Winchester, cornerstone to be laid on July 23, 1903
7/22/1903	Herald	Churches-Presbyterian	Winchester, cornerstone will be laid on July 23, 1903
1/4/1888	Herald	Churches-Presbyterian	Winchester, dedicated last Sunday [filmed with 1887, but appears to be 1888]
1/4/1888	Journal	Churches-Presbyterian	Winchester, dedication of church; cost $3092 + $1050 + $800
6/1/1904	Herald	Churches-Presbyterian	Winchester, dedication; description of new building
3/23/1887	Journal	Churches-Presbyterian	Winchester, foundation is being laid
6/12/1982	News-Gazette	Churches-Presbyterian	Winchester, history and photo

Date	Source	Category	Description
6/24/1966	News	Churches-Presbyterian	Winchester, history of
3/1/1975	News-Gazette	Churches-Presbyterian	Winchester, new carillon
9/14/1887	Journal	Churches-Presbyterian	Winchester, new church will be completed this week
1/19/1887	Journal	Churches-Presbyterian	Winchester, notice to contractors
6/1/1904	Journal	Churches-Presbyterian	Winchester, photo
4/22/1914	Herald	Churches-Presbyterian	Winchester, photo of James P. Goodrich's class
12/26/1967	Journal-Herald	Churches-Presbyterian	Winchester, photo of original building
5/25/1904	Herald	Churches-Presbyterian	Winchester, pipe organ will be dedicated on May 26, 1904
9/1/1886	Herald	Churches-Presbyterian	Winchester, plans for new building
9/1/1886	Journal	Churches-Presbyterian	Winchester, plans for new church, frame, 48 x 70
9/1/1886	Journal	Churches-Presbyterian	Winchester, plans to build church
3/1/1882	Journal	Churches-Presbyterian	Winchester, Presbyterian Sunday School and Church are being organized
11/26/1884	Journal	Churches-Presbyterian	Winchester, Presbyterians have rented the second floor of the north side of the IOOF Building
10/11/1876	Journal	Churches-Presbyterian	Winchester, Rev. Andrew Luce was pastor in Winchester from 1849 to 1857
5/5/1915	Herald	Churches-Presbyterian	Winchester, Rev. Perry Hopper, pastor, photo
8/18/1886	Journal	Churches-Presbyterian	Winchester, subscriptions for new church
5/11/1904	Journal	Churches-Presbyterian	Winchester, to be dedicated on May 29, 1904
12/22/1927	Democrat	Churches-Presbyterian	Winchester, to build addition
4/19/1928	Democrat	Churches-Presbyterian	Winchester, work begins on addition
4/27/1892	Journal	Churches-U. B.	Bethel Chapel, Radical Brethren have about finished their new church
5/4/1892	Journal	Churches-U. B.	Bethel, dedication of the Radical Church will take place on May 29, 1892
1/20/1892	Herald	Churches-U. B.	Bethel, Radical U. B. Church at Bethel dissolved and plan new church on William Johnson's farm, west of "here," Liberals gained the day
4/27/1892	Herald	Churches-U. B.	Bethel, Radical U. B. new church completed
7/10/1889	Journal	Churches-U. B.	Bloomingport, more radical U. B. s than liberals at Bloomingport or New Hope
3/8/1889	Democrat	Churches-U. B.	Buena Vista U. B. Church existed in 1866 according to obituary of Mary E. Green

3/9/1887	Journal	Churches-U. B.	Buena Vista, obituary of Roena Ruble says church existed in 1868
7/20/1910	Journal	Churches-U. B.	Clark's (Stone Station) Schoolhouse; Susan Kolp obituary says she joined this church about 1868
7/24/1889	Journal	Churches-U. B.	Division in U. B. Church discussed in Martindale Items
12/21/1892	Journal	Churches-U. B.	Engle Schoolhouse was home to a U. B. Church 36 years ago (Lewis Cox obituary)
3/23/1887	Journal	Churches-U. B.	Farmland, plans to erect church
11/15/1893	Journal	Churches-U. B.	Losantville U. B. Church exists
6/15/1887	Herald	Churches-U. B.	Losantville U. B. Church purchased old Baptist Church and moved nearer "new part of town"
9/21/1888	Herald	Churches-U. B.	Losantville, purchased old Baptist Church and moved it near I B & W Railroad; dedicated on September 11, 1888
9/30/1891	Journal	Churches-U. B.	Losantville, Radical U. B. Church exists
5/27/1891	Journal	Churches-U. B.	Losantville, U. B. Church exists
1/18/1954	News	Churches-U. B.	Lynn U. B. Church photo
9/28/1898	Journal	Churches-U. B.	Lynn, liberal U. B. is nearly completed
5/25/1898	Herald	Churches-U. B.	Lynn, Liberal U. B.s to build a church in Lynn; Wesleyan Methodists holding services in Lynn
10/12/1898	Herald	Churches-U. B.	Lynn, U. B. church to be dedicated next Sabbath
9/28/1898	Herald	Churches-U. B.	Lynn, U. B. church to be dedicated on October 16, 1898
2/24/1941	Daily News	Churches-U. B.	Modoc U. B. Church burned on February 23
12/5/1900	Herald	Churches-U. B.	Modoc U. B. Church erecting new building at a cost of $2000
1/2/1901	Journal	Churches-U. B.	Modoc, new U. B. Church to be dedicated
1/2/1901	Herald	Churches-U. B.	Modoc, new U. B. Church will be dedicated on January 18, 1901 by C. J. Roberts
6/30/1897	Journal	Churches-U. B.	Modoc, U. B. Church is being remodeled
8/16/1893	Herald	Churches-U. B.	Mount Pleasant (Pinhook) will be dedicated on August 20, 1893 by J. T. Roberts of Indianapolis
8/7/1918	Journal	Churches-U. B.	Mount Pleasant U. B. Church, Greensfork Township, will be dedicated on August 25, 1918
3/2/1887	Journal	Churches-U. B.	Mount Pleasant, election of trustees
5/3/1900	Democrat	Churches-U. B.	New Liberty, Milton Wright preached there in 1865

Date	Source	Category	Description
5/18/1892	Herald	Churches-U. B.	Pleasant Dale, Economy Circuit U. B. Church (Radical), will be dedicated on May 29 by William Dillon, D. D.; located two miles south and 1.5 miles east of Lynn
5/18/1892	Journal	Churches-U. B.	Pleasantdale, U. B. Church will be dedicated on May 29, 1892 by William Dillon; it is two miles south and 1/2 mile east of Lynn
3/26/1903	Democrat	Churches-U. B.	Prospect U. B. Church "is not dead"
7/23/1903	Democrat	Churches-U. B.	Prospect, one mile east of New Pittsburg will be "reopened" on August 2, 1903
6/15/1892	Journal	Churches-U. B.	Radical United Brethren Churches exist at Pleasant Dale, Economy, Carlos City, and Bloomingport; McNew, Rust, and Moody are officials of the circuit
11/1/1893	Journal	Churches-U. B.	Saratoga Church to be dedicated on November 5
11/1/1893	Journal	Churches-U. B.	Saratoga Church will be dedicated on November 5, 1893 by Bishop Hatt of Ames, Iowa
11/22/1928	Democrat	Churches-U. B.	Saratoga reopened on November 18, 1928
12/9/1908	Journal	Churches-U. B.	Saratoga U. B. Church rededication Sunday by Rev. Dr. Fonts
1/15/1902	Journal	Churches-U. B.	Saratoga, church was rededicated on January 5, 1902; built in 1873; enlarged in 1893; redecorated in 1902
3/3/1954	News	Churches-U. B.	Saratoga, history and photos
4/5/1916	Journal	Churches-U. B.	Saratoga, new brick parsonage
4/6/1916	Democrat	Churches-U. B.	Saratoga, new parsonage
4/5/1916	Herald	Churches-U. B.	Saratoga, new parsonage, eight-room, two-story
5/21/1925	Democrat	Churches-U. B.	Selma [Delaware County], site of Klan funeral
12/14/1898	Journal	Churches-U. B.	Sparrow Creek U. B. Church remodeled; will be rededicated on December 18, 1898 by Bishop Haleck Floyd, D. D. of Dublin, Indiana
12/14/1898	Herald	Churches-U. B.	Sparrow Creek, will be rededicated on December 18, 1898 by Bishop Floyd; church was remodeled
6/5/1889	Journal	Churches-U. B.	United Brethren are split over secret orders
10/24/1894	Herald	Churches-U. B.	White River Chapel, being repaired
11/28/1906	Herald	Churches-U. B.	White River Chapel, work is being done
1/7/1926	Democrat	Churches-U. B.	Wilmore, A. C. writes history of White River Conference
9/23/1891	Herald	Churches-U. B.	Winchester U. B. Church meets in Presbyterian Church

Date	Source	Category	Description
1/15/1902	Herald	Churches-U. B.	Winchester, U. B. church to be organized in old Evangelical Church by the pastor of Saratoga U. B. Church
10/13/1875	Journal	Churches-U. B.	Zion U. B. Church, new building
4/27/1887	Journal	Churches-U. B.	Zion, Christian Life, leading member, died
7/7/1875	Journal	Churches-U. B.	Bethel Chapel, southeast of Lynn, arsonist burned church
12/16/1874	Journal	Churches-U. B.	Bloomingport, U. B. Church was dedicated last Sabbath
9/13/1876	Journal	Churches-U. B.	Prospect, U. B. Church, one mile east of New Pittsburg, will be dedicated on September 24, 1876 by Milton Wright
3/21/1877	Journal	Churches-U. B.	Zion, new church is not completed near Rome
10/13/1875	Journal	Churches-U. B.	Zion, U. B. Church erected one mile east of Harrisburg and one mile south of Steubenville
12/26/1982	News-Gazette	Churches-Wesleyan	Lynn, addition
3/26/1873	Journal	Churches-Wesleyan	Sparrow Creek, Susan Ward's obituary says she was a member of this church until death
3/29/1876	Journal	Churches-Wesleyan	White Chapel exists
10/5/1951	News	Churches-Wesleyan	Winchester Wesleyan Methodist Church at 1604 N. Main [was formerly Apostolic Church]
9/22/1886	Journal	Churches-Wesleyan	Carlos, exists
2/14/1912	Journal	Churches-Wesleyan	Shears Class, Elizabeth Mills's obituary says she was the last surviving member of the Wesleyan Class here, north of Huntsville
9/8/1909	Journal	Churches-Wesleyan	Shears Schoolhouse, Wesleyan Methodist Church existed there at one point in history; Hoagland obituary
6/7/1882	Journal	Churches-Wesleyan	White Chapel exists
8/25/1886	Journal	Churches-Wesleyan	White Chapel, mentioned
2/3/1886	Journal	Churches-Wesleyan	White Chapel, revival meeting
8/1/1862	Journal	Civil War	Burres at Farmland mentioned
10/9/1863	Journal	Civil War	Chickamauga, wounded listed
9/26/1862	Journal	Civil War	Conscientious objectors, 125 reported in Randolph County by enrolling officer
10/10/1862	Journal	Civil War	Conscientious objectors, list of
3/27/1863	Journal	Civil War	County School Examiner will withdraw teaching certificates of disloyal teachers in Greensfork Township

Date	Source	Category	Description
3/6/1863	Journal	Civil War	Deserters from Randolph County listed
4/25/1861	Journal	Civil War	Donors for war effort listed
2/20/1863	Journal	Civil War	Farmland, patriotic meeting at
8/22/1862	Journal	Civil War	Flag presented to George Carter's Company
5/16/1861	Journal	Civil War	Kansas Relief donors listed
2/27/1863	Journal	Civil War	Knights of the Golden Circle mentioned in Union City letter
4/25/1861	Journal	Civil War	Meeting to solicit volunteers for army; Judge James Brown, chairman; H. H. Neff, secretary
4/10/1863	Journal	Civil War	Olive Branch, Union Meeting held in schoolhouse
4/25/1861	Journal	Civil War	Randolph County Dragoons organized
4/17/1863	Journal	Civil War	Stoney Creek Schoolhouse, No. 10, Union Meeting held
4/25/1861	Journal	Civil War	Volunteers for army, list
6/19/1930	Democrat	Clubs and Organizations	4-H is organized in Green Township
6/26/1930	Democrat	Clubs and Organizations	4-H is organized in Washington Township
6/12/1930	Democrat	Clubs and Organizations	4-H was organized in Ward Township; it already existed elsewhere in the county
3/4/1908	Journal	Clubs and Organizations	4-H, Boys Corn Clubs to be organized
4/1/1908	Journal	Clubs and Organizations	4-H, Boys Corn Clubs, list of members
4/8/1908	Journal	Clubs and Organizations	4-H, Boys Corn Clubs, list of members
4/15/1908	Journal	Clubs and Organizations	4-H, Boys Corn Clubs, list of members
8/8/1960	News	Clubs and Organizations	4-H, history of in Randolph County
8/4/1977	News-Gazette	Clubs and Organizations	4-H, history of Randolph County 4-H Fair
4/14/1964	Journal-Herald	Clubs and Organizations	4-H, Monroe Central Modern Miss Club organized
4/2/1936	News-Democrat	Clubs and Organizations	4-H, new clubs organized
1/14/1944	News	Clubs and Organizations	Anti-Saloon League meeting at Winchester Friends Church
1/30/1889	Journal	Clubs and Organizations	Arba Protective Association exists
10/5/1887	Journal	Clubs and Organizations	Arba Protective Association exists
11/15/1911	Herald	Clubs and Organizations	Boy Scouts to be organized in Winchester
6/19/1957	News	Clubs and Organizations	CAR, Winchester CAR exists
2/10/1959	Journal-Herald	Clubs and Organizations	CAR, Winchester CAR exists
9/2/1958	Journal-Herald	Clubs and Organizations	Central Labor Council of Randolph County has 2200 members

Date	Source	Category	Description
1/2/1889	Journal	Clubs and Organizations	Cerro Gordo Protective Association exists
4/24/1895	Herald	Clubs and Organizations	Christian Endeavor societies exist at Bloomingport, Lynn, Cherry Grove
4/10/1901	Herald	Clubs and Organizations	Christian Endeavor, county convention
5/3/1876	Journal	Clubs and Organizations	Christian Temperance Society, Cherry Grove organized
10/19/1954	Journal-Herald	Clubs and Organizations	CIO exists in Randolph County
10/25/1975	News-Gazette	Clubs and Organizations	Civil War Roundtable
11/21/1974	News-Gazette	Clubs and Organizations	Civil War Roundtable, organized on November 17
4/11/1867	Journal	Clubs and Organizations	Cold Water Templars organized in Winchester [for youth?]
2/25/1965	Journal-Herald	Clubs and Organizations	County Cooks' Club, Pauline Edwards is president (1964-65)
8/30/1947	Journal-Herald	Clubs and Organizations	County Fair, history of old county fair
6/27/1941	Journal-Herald	Clubs and Organizations	DAR, Amy Moorman [Quaker] was regent of DAR in 1920
10/12/1910	Herald	Clubs and Organizations	DAR, Winchester Chapter organization
5/17/1911	Herald	Clubs and Organizations	DAR, Winchester Chapter received charter
1/26/1916	Herald	Clubs and Organizations	Eastern Indiana Horse Breeders organized; Emerson Addington, president
7/17/1878	Journal	Clubs and Organizations	Emersonian Musical Society of Winchester, historical sketch of
11/2/1922	Democrat	Clubs and Organizations	Farm Bureau county officers: M. A. Holloway, president; P. L. Ludwick, vice-president; A. R. Williams, secretary; Leroy Cox, treasurer
4/28/1933	Journal-Herald	Clubs and Organizations	Farm Bureau meeting at Huffman's Corner
9/17/1919	Journal	Clubs and Organizations	Farm Bureau, all townships now have organized Federation of Farmers
9/12/1973	News-Gazette	Clubs and Organizations	Farm Bureau, Eugene Lamb is county president
4/8/1926	Democrat	Clubs and Organizations	Farm Bureau, Farm Bureau repaired roof on Huffman Schoolhouse (Bear Creek)
8/20/1919	Herald	Clubs and Organizations	Farm Bureau, farmers organize
10/9/1919	Democrat	Clubs and Organizations	Farm Bureau, farmers organize
8/21/1919	Democrat	Clubs and Organizations	Farm Bureau, Federation of Farmers organizing
8/28/1919	Democrat	Clubs and Organizations	Farm Bureau, Federation of Farmers township meetings described; Miles Furnas is the temporary county chairman

Date	Source	Category	Description
4/8/1926	Journal-Herald	Clubs and Organizations	Farm Bureau, Franklin Township Farmers' Federation repaired the roof on Huffman's Corner Schoolhouse
2/2/1928	Democrat	Clubs and Organizations	Farm Bureau, Franklin Township meets at Huffman Schoolhouse
3/31/1927	Democrat	Clubs and Organizations	Farm Bureau, Franklin Township meets at Huffman's Corner; also East White River Farm Bureau exists
2/11/1926	Journal-Herald	Clubs and Organizations	Farm Bureau, Franklin Township will meet at Huffman's Corner Schoolhouse
2/1/1923	Democrat	Clubs and Organizations	Farm Bureau, Franklin Township, organized on Friday, August 22, 1919 by A. R. Williams; Charles Smithson was first president; H. H. Allen, secretary
1/30/1930	Journal-Herald	Clubs and Organizations	Farm Bureau, Franklin Twp. Meets at Huffman's Corner Schoolhouse
1/1/1931	Journal-Herald	Clubs and Organizations	Farm Bureau, Franklin Twp. Meets at Huffman's Corner Schoolhouse
3/9/1934	Journal-Herald	Clubs and Organizations	Farm Bureau, George E. Addington is County President
8/13/1964	Journal-Herald	Clubs and Organizations	Farm Bureau, George E. Addington organized the Randolph County Farm Bureau in 1919 [not really]
9/25/1934	Journal-Herald	Clubs and Organizations	Farm Bureau, George E. Addington resigns as head
2/16/1961	Journal-Herald	Clubs and Organizations	Farm Bureau, Greensfork Township and Monroe Central exist [and others]
2/1/1923	Democrat	Clubs and Organizations	Farm Bureau, history of Randolph County organization; organized on August 5, 1919 at the Randolph Hotel; Miles J. Furnas was the first temporary chairman; township chairmen were appointed; Franklin Township was the first to organize on August 22, 1919 by A. R. Williams; Charles Smithson was the first president and H. H. Allen was the first secretary; all townships were organized within a few weeks; it was then the Indiana Federation of Farmers Associations
7/16/1925	Democrat	Clubs and Organizations	Farm Bureau, Huntsville organization exists
2/21/1970	News-Gazette	Clubs and Organizations	Farm Bureau, local organizations: Greensfork, Monroe, Ward-Jackson, White River, Union, and Ward
10/18/1941	Journal-Herald	Clubs and Organizations	Farm Bureau, Louis Bookout resigns as county president
3/24/1927	Democrat	Clubs and Organizations	Farm Bureau, Lynn Farm Bureau organized on March 18, 1927; Spartanburg Farm Bureau organized on March 17, 1927

Date	Source	Category	Description
11/21/1957	Journal-Herald	Clubs and Organizations	Farm Bureau, Nettle Creek and West River merged as Union
11/22/1923	Democrat	Clubs and Organizations	Farm Bureau, new officers: C. C. Fisher, president
8/18/1927	Democrat	Clubs and Organizations	Farm Bureau, Randolph County Farm Bureau Co-Op is incorporated
10/22/1919	Journal	Clubs and Organizations	Farm Bureau, Randolph County Farmers are organized
10/22/1919	Herald	Clubs and Organizations	Farm Bureau, Randolph County Farmers Organization
10/1/1919	Journal	Clubs and Organizations	Farm Bureau, Randolph County Federation of Farmers was organized last week; Miles J. Furnas, president
11/3/1921	Democrat	Clubs and Organizations	Farm Bureau, Randolph County officers: Leroy Cox, chairman; T. E. Driver, vice-chairman; A. R. Williams, secretary; D. W. Wilmore, treasurer
1/20/1921	Democrat	Clubs and Organizations	Farm Bureau, Saratoga Unit of the Farmer's Federation was organized; John Addington was a director
1/29/1960	News	Clubs and Organizations	Farm Bureau, Stoney Creek, Green, and Monroe Townships merged into Monroe Central Farm Bureau
8/20/1919	Journal	Clubs and Organizations	Farm Bureau, temporary organization of Federation of Farmers was on last Friday; first meeting will be in Franklin Township Friday evening
9/4/1919	Democrat	Clubs and Organizations	Farm Bureau, township organization described
9/3/1919	Journal	Clubs and Organizations	Farm Bureau, township organization of Federation of Farmers described
1/25/1962	Journal-Herald	Clubs and Organizations	Farm Bureau, Ward and Jackson had separate Farm Bureau organizations
6/20/1958	News	Clubs and Organizations	Farm Bureau, Ward Township had only one organization
11/17/1963	Journal-Herald	Clubs and Organizations	Farm Bureau, Ward, White River Farm Bureaus exist [and others]
9/16/1975	News-Gazette	Clubs and Organizations	Farm Bureau, Washington-Greensfork exists
9/17/1975	News-Gazette	Clubs and Organizations	Farm Bureau, Washington-Greensfork exists
12/3/1968	Journal-Herald	Clubs and Organizations	Farm Bureau, Wayne-Jackson 50th anniversary
11/17/1968	Journal-Herald	Clubs and Organizations	Farm Bureau, Wayne-Jackson exists
2/28/1969	Journal-Herald	Clubs and Organizations	Farm Bureau, Wayne-Jackson exists
8/17/1971	News-Gazette	Clubs and Organizations	Farm Bureau, Wayne-Jackson exists
2/16/1972	News-Gazette	Clubs and Organizations	Farm Bureau, Wayne-Jackson exists
12/5/1968	Journal-Herald	Clubs and Organizations	Farm Bureau, White River exists
10/1/1971	News-Gazette	Clubs and Organizations	Farm Bureau, White River exists

Date	Source	Category	Description
3/9/1972	News-Gazette	Clubs and Organizations	Farm Bureau, White River exists
3/4/1920	Democrat	Clubs and Organizations	Farm Bureau, White River Farmers Federation split into two parts, east and west
8/27/1919	Journal	Clubs and Organizations	Farm Bureau, White River Township Federation of Farmers will be organized on August 29, 1919
4/10/1958	Journal-Herald	Clubs and Organizations	Farm Bureau, White River Township had only one township organization
3/22/1972	News-Gazette	Clubs and Organizations	Farmers' Achievement Banquet history; established in 1922
2/6/1953	Journal-Herald	Clubs and Organizations	Farmers' Achievement Banquet, 32nd anniversary
3/11/1914	Journal	Clubs and Organizations	Farmers' Club, Green Township, organized
3/19/1914	Democrat	Clubs and Organizations	Farmers Club, Jackson Township, organized
5/14/1914	Democrat	Clubs and Organizations	Farmers Club, Jefferson, exists
6/3/1914	Journal	Clubs and Organizations	Farmers' Club, Jefferson, organized previously
5/6/1914	Journal	Clubs and Organizations	Farmers' Club, McKinley, organized on April 9; Lincoln had been organized earlier
4/4/1906	Journal	Clubs and Organizations	Farmers Union, Deerfield Local Union, No. 1 exists
7/8/1954	News	Clubs and Organizations	Farmland Fire Department history
3/22/1982	News-Gazette	Clubs and Organizations	Full Gospel Businessmen established in Union City
1/11/1961	News	Clubs and Organizations	Gideons Auxiliary organized
3/7/1962	News	Clubs and Organizations	Girl Scouts, established in Winchester in October 1926
11/27/1895	Journal	Clubs and Organizations	Good Citizens League organized after a meeting at Winchester Friends Church
7/29/1891	Journal	Clubs and Organizations	Gospel Temperance Club (Murphy) recently organized in Winchester
4/28/1897	Journal	Clubs and Organizations	Green Township Sunday School Union organized
6/29/1887	Journal	Clubs and Organizations	Hawthorne Regulators organized
3/6/1918	Herald	Clubs and Organizations	Hawthorne Regulators reorganized for fourth time
8/24/1887	Journal	Clubs and Organizations	Hawthorne Regulators, members listed
5/23/1944	Journal-Herald	Clubs and Organizations	Historical society is needed in county
5/7/1956	News	Clubs and Organizations	Home Ec Clubs
5/5/1949	Journal-Herald	Clubs and Organizations	Home Ec Clubs, history
12/17/1949	Journal-Herald	Clubs and Organizations	Home Ec, 49ers Home Ec Club organized; 32nd club in county
12/29/1951	Journal-Herald	Clubs and Organizations	Home Ec, Apron Strings Home Ec Club

Date	Source	Category	Description
6/15/1983	News-Gazette	Clubs and Organizations	Home Ec, Farmland Club exists
9/10/1976	News-Gazette	Clubs and Organizations	Home Ec, Gingham Gals Club organized
5/7/1946	Journal-Herald	Clubs and Organizations	Home Ec, History of Home Economics clubs in Randolph County
5/8/1956	Journal-Herald	Clubs and Organizations	Home Ec, History of Home Economics clubs in Randolph County
11/1/1916	Herald	Clubs and Organizations	Home Ec, Huffman School House Home Ec club was organized in April 1915
4/9/1970	News-Gazette	Clubs and Organizations	Home Ec, Learn and Do Club and 70s Farmettes Club organized
5/20/1971	News-Gazette	Clubs and Organizations	Home Ec, Lickskillet Wildflowers Club, first mention of
4/26/1941	Journal-Herald	Clubs and Organizations	Home Ec, Mary Lynn Home Economics Club organized
2/23/1939	Journal-Herald	Clubs and Organizations	Home Ec, Nu Wa Home Economics Club organized
3/7/1964	Journal-Herald	Clubs and Organizations	Home Ec, Nu-Wa Club, 25th anniversary
5/17/1957	News	Clubs and Organizations	Home Ec, Ridgeville Home Ec Club organized; 38th in Randolph County
4/22/1969	Journal-Herald	Clubs and Organizations	Home Ec, Spacemates Club exists
5/6/1970	News-Gazette	Clubs and Organizations	Home Ec, Town and Country 70s Club formed
12/19/1929	Democrat	Clubs and Organizations	Home Economics, Modoc Club organized
10/11/1916	Journal	Clubs and Organizations	Independent Order of Coon Hunters organized
1/30/1961	News	Clubs and Organizations	Indiana Anti-Saloon League still exists, though very weak
1/17/1949	News	Clubs and Organizations	Jaycees organized in Winchester in December 1946
1/20/1983	News-Gazette	Clubs and Organizations	Jaycees, history, established in 1946 in Winchester
12/3/1957	Journal-Herald	Clubs and Organizations	Jaycees, Union City Jaycees established on December 2
2/29/1964	Journal-Herald	Clubs and Organizations	John Birch Society, Farmland Chapter, Harry Mills, Chairman; 70-80 present
7/15/1982	News-Gazette	Clubs and Organizations	Kappa Kappa Kappa, Psi Chapter, Winchester, 75th anniversary
8/4/1921	Democrat	Clubs and Organizations	Kiwanis, Union City Kiwanis Club organized on July 29, 1921
1/18/1956	News	Clubs and Organizations	Kiwanis, Winchester Kiwanis established in 1921
9/20/1950	News	Clubs and Organizations	Kiwanis, Winchester Kiwanis organized on February 3, 1921
1/20/1921	Democrat	Clubs and Organizations	Kiwanis, Winchester Kiwanis were organized on January 13, 1921
4/20/1922	Democrat	Clubs and Organizations	KKK Card Party [Tri Kappa?]
2/24/1886	Journal	Clubs and Organizations	Knights of Labor may be organized in Winchester

Date	Source	Category	Description
12/15/1886	Journal	Clubs and Organizations	Knights of Labor moved to GAR Hall
3/10/1886	Journal	Clubs and Organizations	Knights of Labor organized here last Friday
5/26/1953	Journal-Herald	Clubs and Organizations	Labor, list of labor organizations in Randolph County
9/25/1969	Journal-Herald	Clubs and Organizations	Lions Club, Farmland, history; established in May 1934 by Marion Club
5/13/1955	News	Clubs and Organizations	Lions Club, Lynn, 10th anniversary
7/3/1980	News-Gazette	Clubs and Organizations	Lions Club, Lynn, 35th anniversary
4/2/1980	News-Gazette	Clubs and Organizations	Lions Club, Lynn, new building
12/19/1952	News	Clubs and Organizations	Lions Club, Modoc Lions Club becomes Union Township Lions Club
5/23/1945	News	Clubs and Organizations	Lions Club, Parker chartered on May 22
10/28/1965	Journal-Herald	Clubs and Organizations	Lions Club, Parker, 20th anniversary
6/2/1970	News-Gazette	Clubs and Organizations	Lions Club, Parker, 25th anniversary
3/31/1975	News-Gazette	Clubs and Organizations	Lions Club, Parker, 30th anniversary, established 1945 by Muncie Club
6/26/1980	News-Gazette	Clubs and Organizations	Lions Club, Parker, 35th anniversary
7/27/1961	Journal-Herald	Clubs and Organizations	Lions Club, Parker, new clubhouse
6/20/1945	News	Clubs and Organizations	Lions Club, Ridgeville dedication of new hall
10/25/1937	Journal-Herald	Clubs and Organizations	Lions Club, Ridgeville Lions Club to be organized on October 26
9/26/1977	News-Gazette	Clubs and Organizations	Lions Club, Ridgeville, 40th anniversary
1/16/1976	News-Gazette	Clubs and Organizations	Lions Club, Saratoga, 25th anniversary, organized January 2, 1951 by Ridgeville Club
2/20/1964	Journal-Herald	Clubs and Organizations	Lions Club, Saratoga, new building
11/21/1947	News	Clubs and Organizations	Lions Club, Union City organized on November 20
12/1/1972	News-Gazette	Clubs and Organizations	Lions Club, Union City, 25th anniversary; organized on November 29, 1947
11/18/1977	News-Gazette	Clubs and Organizations	Lions Club, Union City, 30th anniversary
10/19/1981	News-Gazette	Clubs and Organizations	Lions Club, Union City, moved to Masonic Temple
11/30/1977	News-Gazette	Clubs and Organizations	Lions Club, Union Township, 30th anniversary
6/27/1938	Journal-Herald	Clubs and Organizations	Lions Club, Winchester begins second year
4/21/1962	Journal-Herald	Clubs and Organizations	Lions Club, Winchester established on April 7, 1937; Modoc on December 8, 1947; Union City on December 17, 1947

Date	Publication	Category	Description
11/16/1977	News-Gazette	Clubs and Organizations	Lions Club, Winchester, 40th anniversary
11/19/1947	News	Clubs and Organizations	Lions Clubs; Modoc will be chartered on December 8; Union City will be chartered on November 20
3/27/1981	News-Gazette	Clubs and Organizations	Little Hoosiers, chapters are organized at Morton, Willard, and White River
2/23/1954	Journal-Herald	Clubs and Organizations	Local 112, American Flint Glass Workers Union (OMCO), organized in 1915
8/31/1984	News-Gazette	Clubs and Organizations	Local 112, American Flint Glass Workers Union, history
2/27/1878	Journal	Clubs and Organizations	Murphy Club is properly called Christian Temperance Union
6/27/1877	Journal	Clubs and Organizations	Murphy Club organized at Harrisville
8/1/1877	Journal	Clubs and Organizations	Murphy Club reorganized in Winchester
1/16/1878	Journal	Clubs and Organizations	Murphy Club, Windsor, exists
7/8/1891	Journal	Clubs and Organizations	Murphy Gospel Union exists in Winchester
6/24/1961	Journal-Herald	Clubs and Organizations	National Federation of Agriculture, attempts to organize in Randolph County
3/7/1929	Democrat	Clubs and Organizations	National Hay Association Office is moved from Winchester to Indianapolis
1/5/1916	Journal	Clubs and Organizations	National Horse Thief Detective Association, Local Lodge No. 208, meets in MWA Hall
6/28/1916	Journal	Clubs and Organizations	National Horse Thief Detective Association, White River Lodge, No. 208, exists
12/14/1963	Journal-Herald	Clubs and Organizations	NFO, Randolph County National Farmers' Organization membership drive
1/29/1966	Journal-Herald	Clubs and Organizations	NFO, Randolph County organization exists
2/11/1969	Journal-Herald	Clubs and Organizations	NFO, Randolph County organization exists
3/25/1969	Journal-Herald	Clubs and Organizations	NFO, Randolph County organization exists
11/18/1969	Journal-Herald	Clubs and Organizations	NFO, Randolph County organization exists
2/18/1970	News-Gazette	Clubs and Organizations	NFO, Randolph County organization exists
1/27/1971	News-Gazette	Clubs and Organizations	NFO, Randolph County organization exists
2/1/1972	News-Gazette	Clubs and Organizations	NFO, Randolph County organization exists
1/23/1973	News-Gazette	Clubs and Organizations	NFO, Randolph County organization exists
4/26/1974	News-Gazette	Clubs and Organizations	NFO, Randolph County organization exists
3/15/1975	News-Gazette	Clubs and Organizations	NFO, Randolph County organization exists

Date	Source	Category	Description
8/12/1975	News-Gazette	Clubs and Organizations	NFO, Randolph County organization exists
5/18/1976	News-Gazette	Clubs and Organizations	NOW, Union City Chapter exists
9/14/1984	News-Gazette	Clubs and Organizations	Old Hunters Shoot, 85th annual
10/29/1879	Journal	Clubs and Organizations	Old Settlers, reorganization of
10/8/1879	Journal	Clubs and Organizations	Old Settlers, reorganization of
8/23/1899	Journal	Clubs and Organizations	Old Settlers, Ridgeville Old Settlers Reminiscences
8/20/1890	Journal	Clubs and Organizations	Old Settlers, Ridgeville, Thomas Addington is first president
4/7/1975	News-Gazette	Clubs and Organizations	Optimist Club to be formed in Winchester
10/1/1980	News-Gazette	Clubs and Organizations	Optimist Club was formed in Union City on September 27, 1980
4/21/1933	Journal-Herald	Clubs and Organizations	Phi Delta Kappa 21st anniversary
4/30/1947	News	Clubs and Organizations	Phi Delta Kappa Beta Eta Chapter, 25th anniversary
7/22/1948	Journal-Herald	Clubs and Organizations	Phi Delta Kappa is building new clubhouse
4/16/1949	Journal-Herald	Clubs and Organizations	Phi Delta Kappa of Winchester is largest in nation with 110 members
3/9/1984	News-Gazette	Clubs and Organizations	Planned Parenthood exists in Winchester
2/20/1907	Herald	Clubs and Organizations	Pleasant Hill Sunday School Association organized last week
4/14/1880	Journal	Clubs and Organizations	Porter's League exists at Huntsville
3/24/1880	Journal	Clubs and Organizations	Porter's Temperance Reform League exists at Neff
3/10/1880	Journal	Clubs and Organizations	Porter's Temperance Reform League meets in IOOF Hall in Losantville
1/14/1880	Journal	Clubs and Organizations	Porter's Temperance Reform League organized at Huntsville on January 3, 1880
8/2/1871	Journal	Clubs and Organizations	Randolph County Agricultural Association organized yesterday
3/12/1913	Journal	Clubs and Organizations	Randolph County Agricultural Association was organized last Saturday
3/12/1913	Journal	Clubs and Organizations	Randolph County Agricultural Association was organized last Saturday
10/25/1916	Journal	Clubs and Organizations	Randolph County Anti-Tuberculosis Society organized last Thursday; Lee L. Driver, president; Philip Kabel, secretary; J. E. Hinshaw, treasurer
2/12/1931	Journal-Herald	Clubs and Organizations	Randolph County Bar Association organized Thursday
6/4/1873	Journal	Clubs and Organizations	Randolph County Bar, members and dates of admission listed
4/22/1920	Democrat	Clubs and Organizations	Randolph County Brotherhood of Threshers organized

Date	Source	Category	Description
10/24/1917	Journal	Clubs and Organizations	Randolph County Cooperative Fair, officers listed
3/22/1969	Journal-Herald	Clubs and Organizations	Randolph County Council of Christian Education exists
11/20/1924	Democrat	Clubs and Organizations	Randolph County Council on Religious Education in session
5/15/1936	News-Democrat	Clubs and Organizations	Randolph County Dairy Herd Improvement Association was organized last week; Orval O. Hinshaw was one of the ten charter members
12/20/1900	Democrat	Clubs and Organizations	Randolph County Historical Association exists
8/28/1902	Democrat	Clubs and Organizations	Randolph County Historical Association meeting
12/12/1900	Journal	Clubs and Organizations	Randolph County Historical Association organized; H. W. Bowers, president
5/13/1968	News	Clubs and Organizations	Randolph County Historical Society buys house for a museum
8/26/1903	Journal	Clubs and Organizations	Randolph County Historical Society elected new officers
8/27/1903	Democrat	Clubs and Organizations	Randolph County Historical Society elected officers: Philip Kabel, president; C. W. Isenbarger, secretary and curator; Charles Daly, treasurer
10/25/1923	Democrat	Clubs and Organizations	Randolph County Historical Society elected officers: Philip Kabel, president; Judge Bales, vice-president; William Wright, secretary-treasurer
3/20/1973	News-Gazette	Clubs and Organizations	Randolph County Historical Society fireplace mantle
2/26/1953	Journal-Herald	Clubs and Organizations	Randolph County Historical Society is organized
7/12/1975	News-Gazette	Clubs and Organizations	Randolph County Historical Society Museum
7/18/1975	News-Gazette	Clubs and Organizations	Randolph County Historical Society Museum
7/24/1975	News-Gazette	Clubs and Organizations	Randolph County Historical Society Museum
7/3/1975	News-Gazette	Clubs and Organizations	Randolph County Historical Society Museum gets lattice work from I. P. Gray Home
10/16/1973	News-Gazette	Clubs and Organizations	Randolph County Historical Society Museum receives "Spirit of 76" painting by Nick Carter
9/30/1969	Journal-Herald	Clubs and Organizations	Randolph County Historical Society Museum was dedicated
9/22/1969	Journal-Herald	Clubs and Organizations	Randolph County Historical Society Museum will be dedicated on September 28
3/19/1983	News-Gazette	Clubs and Organizations	Randolph County Historical Society Museum, 1890 bridge plaque from 400 E and Mississinewa River donated
7/2/1981	News-Gazette	Clubs and Organizations	Randolph County Historical Society Museum, articles donated

Date	Source	Category	Description
10/1/1980	News-Gazette	Clubs and Organizations	Randolph County Historical Society Museum, donations to
6/7/1982	News-Gazette	Clubs and Organizations	Randolph County Historical Society Museum, donations, including temperance ledger
6/17/1975	News-Gazette	Clubs and Organizations	Randolph County Historical Society Museum, furnishing
2/28/1976	News-Gazette	Clubs and Organizations	Randolph County Historical Society Museum, Gordon GAR Drum and desk of Judge Monks donated
4/16/1976	News-Gazette	Clubs and Organizations	Randolph County Historical Society Museum, sandblasting
10/25/1980	News-Gazette	Clubs and Organizations	Randolph County Historical Society Museum, Way paintings were purchased by Randolph County Historical Society from Wayne County eleven years ago
6/17/1978	News-Gazette	Clubs and Organizations	Randolph County Historical Society Museum; old fence donated from Kizer-Marsh House
12/5/1900	Herald	Clubs and Organizations	Randolph County Historical Society organized
9/5/1900	Journal	Clubs and Organizations	Randolph County Historical Society organized; members listed
11/10/1921	Democrat	Clubs and Organizations	Randolph County Historical Society organized; Philip Kabel, president
5/10/1968	News	Clubs and Organizations	Randolph County Historical Society plans a museum
6/25/1975	News-Gazette	Clubs and Organizations	Randolph County Historical Society retains old officers; Joe Hamilton is County Historian
2/10/1953	Journal-Herald	Clubs and Organizations	Randolph County Historical Society to be organized
7/12/1923	Democrat	Clubs and Organizations	Randolph County Historical Society to give a historical pageant
6/17/1982	News-Gazette	Clubs and Organizations	Randolph County Historical Society, annex considered at museum
6/20/1906	Journal	Clubs and Organizations	Randolph County Historical Society, D. W. Lawrence bemoans end of
8/28/1901	Journal	Clubs and Organizations	Randolph County Historical Society, first regular meeting
10/9/1972	News-Gazette	Clubs and Organizations	Randolph County Historical Society, GR & I sign "Winchester" given to museum
4/23/1984	News-Gazette	Clubs and Organizations	Randolph County Historical Society, John Miller, author of Indiana Newspaper Bibliography, speaks
8/16/1984	News-Gazette	Clubs and Organizations	Randolph County Historical Society, new officers elected
6/28/1979	News-Gazette	Clubs and Organizations	Randolph County Historical Society, officers elected
8/12/1981	News-Gazette	Clubs and Organizations	Randolph County Historical Society, officers elected
7/6/1982	News-Gazette	Clubs and Organizations	Randolph County Historical Society, officers elected
7/3/1976	News-Gazette	Clubs and Organizations	Randolph County Historical Society, officers elected for two years
7/1/1977	News-Gazette	Clubs and Organizations	Randolph County Historical Society, officers elected for two years

Date	Source	Category	Description
12/1/1976	News-Gazette	Clubs and Organizations	Randolph County Historical Society, Robert Speiser, president
10/17/1979	News-Gazette	Clubs and Organizations	Randolph County Historical Society; Genealogical Society elects officers
9/15/1979	News-Gazette	Clubs and Organizations	Randolph County Historical Society; Genealogical Society organized
7/9/1919	Journal	Clubs and Organizations	Randolph County Holiness Association erected building
12/3/1919	Journal	Clubs and Organizations	Randolph County Holiness Association meeting held at Jericho
6/26/1918	Journal	Clubs and Organizations	Randolph County Holiness Association meeting held at Morgan Creek Friends [Wayne County]
8/29/1917	Journal	Clubs and Organizations	Randolph County Holiness Association organized; Asa Addington, president; Levi Cox, vice-president; H. E. Cox, secretary; Ed Heaston, treasurer; Executive Committee is Jesse Jackson, Ralph Lesley, R. E. Knotes, J. Thomas, Wm. Houk, Pearl Addington, and Lydia Meeks
2/11/1920	Herald	Clubs and Organizations	Randolph County Holiness Association, bids on tabernacle construction
7/17/1981	News-Gazette	Clubs and Organizations	Randolph County Holiness Association, Cecil Hinshaw, president
8/30/1916	Journal	Clubs and Organizations	Randolph County Holiness Association, first mention; members included Asa Addington, Elvan Thornburg, Edward Heaston, et al
7/26/1966	News	Clubs and Organizations	Randolph County Holiness Association, new tabernacle
10/12/1937	Journal-Herald	Clubs and Organizations	Randolph County Ministerial Association formed on October 11
5/27/1961	Journal-Herald	Clubs and Organizations	Randolph County Soil and Water Conservation District was organized on May 22
3/1/1871	Journal	Clubs and Organizations	Randolph County Soldiers Association organized
7/20/1926	Daily News	Clubs and Organizations	Randolph County Taxpayers Association organized by C. C. Fisher on July 19, 1926
12/31/1857	Journal	Clubs and Organizations	Randolph County Teachers Association met at Arba; next meeting will be at Jericho; W. Hill, president; Emily Horne, secretary
5/27/1858	Journal	Clubs and Organizations	Randolph County Teachers Association minutes
12/5/1900	Journal	Clubs and Organizations	Randolph County Teachers Association organized
1/28/1858	Journal	Clubs and Organizations	Randolph County Teachers Association will meet at Friends' schoolhouse at Poplar Run on 13th of 2nd Mo.

Date	Source	Category	Description
6/12/1970	News-Gazette	Clubs and Organizations	Randolph County United Fund established from Winchester-White River United Fund
4/11/1917	Journal	Clubs and Organizations	Randolph National Farm Loan Association organized
10/8/1964	News	Clubs and Organizations	Randolph Southern Ministerial Association was formerly the Lynn Ministerial Association
8/15/1917	Herald	Clubs and Organizations	Red Cross, chapters in Randolph County listed
7/4/1917	Herald	Clubs and Organizations	Red Cross, chapters organized at Huntsville and Saratoga
10/24/1917	Herald	Clubs and Organizations	Red Cross, eleven local chapters in Randolph County
5/15/1918	Journal	Clubs and Organizations	Red Cross, Huntsville Chapter meets in Masonic Building
6/27/1917	Journal	Clubs and Organizations	Red Cross, Huntsville Chapter to be organized
9/17/1919	Herald	Clubs and Organizations	Red Cross, Huntsville Red Cross meets in Masonic Lodge
7/4/1917	Journal	Clubs and Organizations	Red Cross, Modoc Chapter was already organized
5/2/1918	Democrat	Clubs and Organizations	Red Cross, Quaker Hill Red Cross exists
11/16/1964	News	Clubs and Organizations	Red Cross, Randolph County Chapter merges with Muncie Chapter
6/7/1917	Democrat	Clubs and Organizations	Red Cross, Randolph County Chapter organized
5/30/1917	Herald	Clubs and Organizations	Red Cross, Randolph County Chapter organized; Phillip Kabel, treasurer, et al
11/28/1917	Herald	Clubs and Organizations	Red Cross, Ward Township Red Cross organized at Jefferson on Friday evening
12/16/1959	News	Clubs and Organizations	Rotary Club, 40th anniversary in Winchester
5/14/1946	Journal-Herald	Clubs and Organizations	Rotary Club, Union City Rotary Club established in 1921
4/14/1971	News-Gazette	Clubs and Organizations	Rotary Club, Union City, organized April 27, 1921
9/8/1976	News-Gazette	Clubs and Organizations	Rotary Club, Union City, organized April 27, 1921, No. 904
12/10/1919	Journal	Clubs and Organizations	Rotary Club, Winchester, charter received
12/11/1919	Democrat	Clubs and Organizations	Rotary Club, Winchester, chartered; Lee L. Driver and J. E. Hinshaw are among the charter members
8/21/1919	Democrat	Clubs and Organizations	Rotary Club, Winchester, interest in organization
8/20/1919	Journal	Clubs and Organizations	Rotary Club, Winchester, is to be organized
12/10/1919	Herald	Clubs and Organizations	Rotary Club, Winchester, organized on Friday
9/11/1981	News-Gazette	Clubs and Organizations	Rural Couples, Friendly Chapter, 20th anniversary
9/7/1979	News-Gazette	Clubs and Organizations	Rural Couples, Progressive Chapter and Friendly Chapter exist

Date	Source	Category	Description
9/20/1958	Journal-Herald	Clubs and Organizations	Rural-Urban organization is practically extinct; had existed at Stone Station, Stoney Creek, Jericho, and near Arba
4/12/1871	Journal	Clubs and Organizations	Sabbath School Convention, Randolph County, held
8/6/1902	Journal	Clubs and Organizations	Stoney Creek Township Sunday School Convention, 9th annual
7/17/1907	Herald	Clubs and Organizations	Sunday School Association, Franklin Township Convention
5/20/1908	Herald	Clubs and Organizations	Sunday School Association, Franklin Township Convention held at Bear Creek
3/16/1976	News-Gazette	Clubs and Organizations	Sunday School Association, Franklin Township Sunday School Convention will be held at Ridgeville Church of the Nazarene on March 21, 1976
2/20/1907	Herald	Clubs and Organizations	Sunday School Association, Franklin Township Sunday School Convention, Elbert Russell, speaker
1/24/1912	Herald	Clubs and Organizations	Sunday School Association, history of Randolph County SS Association
5/14/1919	Herald	Clubs and Organizations	Sunday School Association, Monroe Township, 21st annual convention
3/22/1905	Herald	Clubs and Organizations	Sunday School Association, Nettle Creek-West River SS Association was organized on March 4, 1905
11/13/1930	Democrat	Clubs and Organizations	Sunday School Association, Randolph County Sunday School Association, new officers: Charles Heston, president
2/2/1916	Journal	Clubs and Organizations	Sunday School Association, Randolph County Sunday School Association, new officers; Lee L. Driver held no office
6/20/1888	Journal	Clubs and Organizations	Sunday School Association, Washington Township Sunday School Union and Ward Township Sunday School Union organized
6/5/1907	Journal	Clubs and Organizations	Sunday School Association, Washington Township, 20th annual convention
5/19/1909	Journal	Clubs and Organizations	Sunday School Association, White River Township Convention
3/3/1970	News-Gazette	Clubs and Organizations	Sunday School Convention held at Bear Creek Friends Church and Calvary United Methodist Church [Franklin Township]
11/30/1898	Herald	Clubs and Organizations	Teachers Association, Randolph County, organized in Winchester Friends Church
5/19/1859	Journal	Clubs and Organizations	Temperance Association, White Chapel (West River Township) exists
1/29/1873	Journal	Clubs and Organizations	Temperance Union organized in Winchester on January 14, 1873

Date	Source	Category	Description
3/22/1860	Journal	Clubs and Organizations	Temperance, Winchester Temperance Protection Society organized
2/18/1946	News	Clubs and Organizations	Union City, U. S. Disabled War Veterans to be organized on February 19
5/22/1982	News-Gazette	Clubs and Organizations	Union Little Hoosiers make plates [now at County Museum]
5/1/1965	Journal-Herald	Clubs and Organizations	United Church Women recently organized
11/11/1978	News-Gazette	Clubs and Organizations	United Fund, Randolph County, folded in 1964; reorganized in late 1960s, folded again in 1978
4/19/1923	Democrat	Clubs and Organizations	United Veterans of the Republic, Emmett Davidson Unit, organized; meets in JOUAM Hall
7/6/1922	Democrat	Clubs and Organizations	Vigilance Committee, Randolph County, recently formed
11/21/1942	Journal-Herald	Clubs and Organizations	War Mothers at Winchester, Losantville, Carlos, Huntsville, and Lynn
10/31/1942	Journal-Herald	Clubs and Organizations	War Mothers II, Lynn organizes
3/4/1943	Journal-Herald	Clubs and Organizations	War Mothers II, Winchester Unit No. 31 exists
1/9/1918	Journal	Clubs and Organizations	War Mothers to be organized in each township
5/12/1956	Journal-Herald	Clubs and Organizations	War Mothers, exist in Winchester and Union City
1/4/1952	News	Clubs and Organizations	War Mothers, Farmland Harmony Chapter American War Mothers
11/17/1956	Journal-Herald	Clubs and Organizations	War Mothers, Losantville Unit 187 exists
2/16/1957	Journal-Herald	Clubs and Organizations	War Mothers, Losantville unit exists
12/13/1958	Journal-Herald	Clubs and Organizations	War Mothers, Losantville unit exists
5/9/1959	Journal-Herald	Clubs and Organizations	War Mothers, Losantville unit exists
2/22/1952	News	Clubs and Organizations	War Mothers, Lynn Chapter to disband
4/5/1943	Journal-Herald	Clubs and Organizations	War Mothers, Lynn Unit No. 39
4/16/1943	Journal-Herald	Clubs and Organizations	War Mothers, Modoc No. 36
1/23/1951	Journal-Herald	Clubs and Organizations	War Mothers, No. 175 Union City and No. 31 Winchester exist
11/7/1942	Journal-Herald	Clubs and Organizations	War Mothers, organize at Carlos, Modoc, Huntsville
5/23/1918	Democrat	Clubs and Organizations	War Mothers, Randolph County Chapter exists
7/30/1952	News	Clubs and Organizations	War Mothers, Union City War Mothers organized in October 1950 by Ella Reitenour
3/15/1958	Journal-Herald	Clubs and Organizations	War Mothers, Winchester Unit exists
1/24/1959	Journal-Herald	Clubs and Organizations	War Mothers, Winchester Unit exists

Date	Source	Category	Description
3/26/1960	Journal-Herald	Clubs and Organizations	War Mothers, Winchester Unit exists
1/19/1961	Journal-Herald	Clubs and Organizations	War Mothers, Winchester Unit exists
1/26/1962	News	Clubs and Organizations	War Mothers, Winchester Unit No. 31 exists
1/21/1955	News	Clubs and Organizations	War Mothers, Winchester War Mothers exists
5/10/1860	Journal	Clubs and Organizations	Washingtonian Temperance Society, first mention
12/3/1902	Herald	Clubs and Organizations	Wayne Township Temperance Alliance, Walter Hinshaw, president
12/29/1927	Journal-Herald	Clubs and Organizations	WCTU at Bloomingport is Mary Bly Union
3/14/1929	Journal-Herald	Clubs and Organizations	WCTU exists at Carlos
10/6/1927	Journal-Herald	Clubs and Organizations	WCTU exists at Huntsville, Carlos, Losantville
12/29/1927	Journal-Herald	Clubs and Organizations	WCTU exists at Modoc
7/18/1929	Journal-Herald	Clubs and Organizations	WCTU exists at Modoc
10/8/1931	Journal-Herald	Clubs and Organizations	WCTU exists at Parker
9/5/1929	Journal-Herald	Clubs and Organizations	WCTU of county has 555 members and 13 unions
5/1/1912	Herald	Clubs and Organizations	WCTU organized last week in Union City
9/25/1912	Journal	Clubs and Organizations	WCTU, chapters and members in Randolph County listed
10/11/1928	Journal-Herald	Clubs and Organizations	WCTU, Elizabeth Stanley Loyal Temperance Legion, Martindale Division exists
3/27/1964	News	Clubs and Organizations	WCTU, Franklin Township Loyal Temperance Legion exists
3/4/1965	Journal-Herald	Clubs and Organizations	WCTU, Franklin Township Youth Temperance Council exists
4/9/1958	News	Clubs and Organizations	WCTU, Franklin Township Youth Temperance Council was organized on March 31
6/7/1961	News	Clubs and Organizations	WCTU, Franklin Township YTC exists
8/30/1950	News	Clubs and Organizations	WCTU, Grace Bookout reelected county president
8/17/1951	News	Clubs and Organizations	WCTU, Grace Bookout reelected county president
6/14/1938	Journal-Herald	Clubs and Organizations	WCTU, Greensfork WCTU to be organized on June 15
11/29/1916	Journal	Clubs and Organizations	WCTU, Huntsville WCTU organized
4/30/1969	Journal-Herald	Clubs and Organizations	WCTU, Parker Youth Temperance Council exists
3/28/1888	Journal	Clubs and Organizations	WCTU, Randolph County convention
1/6/1875	Journal	Clubs and Organizations	WCTU, Randolph County, organized [many Quakers involved]
8/25/1956	Journal-Herald	Clubs and Organizations	WCTU, Selva Davis replaces Thelma Riddlebarger as county president

Date	Source	Category	Description
8/17/1957	Journal-Herald	Clubs and Organizations	WCTU, Selvia Davis is elected county president
8/27/1947	News	Clubs and Organizations	WCTU, Tycia Lamb is in second year as county president
8/25/1961	News	Clubs and Organizations	WCTU, Vera Stanford reelected county president
7/1/1914	Journal	Clubs and Organizations	WCTU, Winchester has a newly organized union
6/22/1887	Journal	Clubs and Organizations	WCTU, Winchester, Amanda Way organized WCTU at M. E. Church
6/17/1914	Herald	Clubs and Organizations	WCTU, Winchester, reorganized on June 15, 1914
8/31/1953	News	Clubs and Organizations	WCTU, Youth Temperance Council of Union Township was organized on August 27
7/11/1888	Journal	Clubs and Organizations	West River Township Sunday School Union will be organized next Wednesday
8/26/1903	Herald	Clubs and Organizations	Winchester [Temperance] Alliance No. 183 will meet on August 29, 1903 to organize at First Christian Church; J. H. Williams, secretary
6/27/1917	Journal	Clubs and Organizations	Winchester Band history, organized at Kizer's Chapel about 1871
4/4/1917	Journal	Clubs and Organizations	Winchester Band, photo
4/22/1914	Journal	Clubs and Organizations	Winchester City Federation of Clubs organized last Thursday; clubs listed
3/7/1917	Journal	Clubs and Organizations	Winchester Cornet Band, photo from 1872
10/17/1929	Democrat	Clubs and Organizations	Winchester Golf Club disbands after nine years
1/18/1984	News-Gazette	Clubs and Organizations	Winchester Planned Parenthood exists
12/2/1903	Journal	Clubs and Organizations	Winchester Prohibition Alliance, No. 88 exists
12/6/1939	Journal-Herald	Clubs and Organizations	Winchester Townsend Club No. 1 exists
11/6/1965	Journal-Herald	Clubs and Organizations	Winchester United Fund exists
12/10/1938	Journal-Herald	Clubs and Organizations	Winchester Youth Center to open
3/2/1956	News	Clubs and Organizations	Winchester, Children of the American Revolution organized on February 28, 1956
11/16/1984	News-Gazette	Clubs and Organizations	Winchester, the Haven, a youth house, opens; many of the board members were from Bear Creek Friends Church
10/10/1964	News	Clubs and Organizations	Winchester-White River United Fund is defunct; Union City Fund is active
4/5/1928	Democrat	Clubs and Organizations	Women's clubs, list of; 24 in all
9/17/1976	News-Gazette	Clubs and Organizations	YMCA, photo of Union City YMCA about 1915
8/27/1979	News-Gazette	Clubs and Organizations	YMCA, Winchester Area, organized

Date	Source	Category	Description
6/4/1974	News-Gazette	Clubs and Organizations	Young Farmers, Earthbound Chapter exists [southern Randolph County]
5/1/1975	News-Gazette	Clubs and Organizations	Young Farmers, Earthbound Chapter exists [southern Randolph County]
10/24/1980	News-Gazette	Clubs and Organizations	Young Farmers, Earthbound Chapter exists [southern Randolph County]
3/26/1981	News-Gazette	Clubs and Organizations	Young Farmers, Earthbound Chapter exists [southern Randolph County]
3/14/1983	News-Gazette	Clubs and Organizations	Young Farmers, Earthbound Chapter exists [southern Randolph County]
4/24/1984	News-Gazette	Clubs and Organizations	Young Farmers, Earthbound Chapter exists [southern Randolph County]
8/7/1984	News-Gazette	Clubs and Organizations	Young Farmers, Earthbound Chapter exists [southern Randolph County]
8/30/1969	Journal-Herald	Clubs and Organizations	Young Farmers, Friendly Chapter [area northeast of Winchester]
4/15/1972	News-Gazette	Clubs and Organizations	Young Farmers, Friendly Chapter exists [near Ridgeville]
2/23/1980	News-Gazette	Clubs and Organizations	Young Farmers, Happy Harvesters Chapter, exists [Ridgeville area]
7/2/1974	News-Gazette	Clubs and Organizations	Young Farmers, Happy Sharecroppers Chapter exists [Modoc area]
3/31/1980	News-Gazette	Clubs and Organizations	Young Farmers, Happy Sharecroppers Chapter exists [Modoc area]
4/14/1972	News-Gazette	Clubs and Organizations	Young Farmers, Lynn Chapter and Lynn Hi Point Chapter exist
2/28/1968	News	Clubs and Organizations	Young Farmers, Lynn Chapter exists
6/2/1970	News-Gazette	Clubs and Organizations	Young Farmers, Lynn Chapter exists
10/3/1980	News-Gazette	Clubs and Organizations	Young Farmers, Lynn Chapter exists
2/4/1981	News-Gazette	Clubs and Organizations	Young Farmers, Lynn Chapter is 16 years old, third oldest in state
6/23/1972	News-Gazette	Clubs and Organizations	Young Farmers, Monroe Central Landhandlers Chapter exists
2/24/1972	News-Gazette	Clubs and Organizations	Young Farmers, Monroe Central Landhandlers Chapter organized
3/5/1975	News-Gazette	Clubs and Organizations	Young Farmers, Randolph Central Plowjockeys Chapter and Randolph Central Happy Harvesters Chapter exist
2/25/1969	Journal-Herald	Clubs and Organizations	Young Farmers, Randolph County Chapter [Lynn area] exists
8/6/1980	News-Gazette	Clubs and Organizations	Young Farmers, Rolling Hills Chapter exists [Lickskillet-Stone Station area]
6/30/1977	News-Gazette	Clubs and Organizations	Young Farmers, Rolling Hills Chapter organized, north of Winchester

Date	Source	Category	Description
6/22/1972	News-Gazette	Clubs and Organizations	Young Farmers, Union Chapter exists
2/29/1980	News-Gazette	Clubs and Organizations	Young Farmers, Union Chapter exists
5/6/1978	News-Gazette	Clubs and Organizations	Young Farmers, Union Chapter, 10th anniversary
4/24/1980	News-Gazette	Clubs and Organizations	Young Farmers, Union City Friendly Chapter exists
1/27/1971	News-Gazette	Clubs and Organizations	Young Farmers, Union organization and Lynn organization exist
4/13/1968	Journal-Herald	Clubs and Organizations	Young Farmers, Union Township Chapter organized
10/20/1984	News-Gazette	Clubs and Organizations	Y's Owls, 3rd anniversary
11/16/1922	Democrat	Klan	"Kluxers" handed out sample ballots that the election; Farmland was specifically mentioned
10/19/1922	Democrat	Klan	Brown, Eber M., editor of the Lynn Herald, is threatened by James L. Tolbert, Imperial Organizer of the Randolph County KKK
10/4/1922	Journal-Herald	Klan	Brown, Lester will give lecture on Klan at Union City on October 6
4/26/1923	Democrat	Klan	Fiery Cross, Klan newspaper, condemned John L. Smith, who confronted boys selling the Fiery Cross in Winchester
5/3/1923	Democrat	Klan	Fiery Cross, Klan newspaper, condemned the Winchester School Board for blocking a Bible reading plan
6/28/1923	Democrat	Klan	Huddleston, H. H., Kleagle of Randolph County Klan, called on the Winchester Democrat
10/18/1923	Democrat	Klan	Huddleston, Howard is seen in New Castle
10/4/1923	Democrat	Klan	Huddleston, Howard of New Castle, son of Charles T. Huddleston, Klan organizer, is on missing list
10/11/1923	Democrat	Klan	Huddleston, Howard, "no trace" of him
11/15/1923	Democrat	Klan	Huddleston, Howard, lost Klan organizer, is found in San Francisco
6/28/1923	Democrat	Klan	King, L. J. was Klan speaker on May 5 at Farmland High School
6/28/1923	Democrat	Klan	King, L. J., Klan speaker at Farmland on May 5, 1923 is exposed as not really being a former priest
9/18/1976	News-Gazette	Klan	Klan featured
11/15/1923	Democrat	Klan	Klan law is that of the jungle; no known Klan violence in Randolph County
10/9/1924	Journal-Herald	Klan	Klan meeting to be held in Courthouse yard on October 11
2/1/1923	Journal-Herald	Klan	Klan meeting was orderly at Union City Grand Opera House on Thursday, January 25

Date	Source	Topic	Description
9/6/1922	Journal-Herald	Klan	Ku Klux Klan at Union City M. E. Church (Union City and Winchester Provisional Klans exist)
9/27/1923	Journal-Herald	Klan	Ku Klux Klan Meeting at Funk's Lake on September 29
8/16/1923	Journal-Herald	Klan	Ku Klux Klan meetings Tuesday at Courthouse, Monday at Losantville, and Wednesday at Union City
9/6/1922	Journal-Herald	Klan	Ku Klux Klan met last Thursday evening in eastern Randolph County; 150 new members; "No true American should offer any opposition to the order"
5/10/1923	Journal-Herald	Klan	Ku Klux Klan spoke at Courthouse last Wednesday
9/18/1976	News-Gazette	Klan	Ku Klux Klan, history
5/8/1924	Democrat	Klan	Local Klan questionnaire about education and immigration reprinted
10/4/1922	Journal-Herald	Klan	Public meeting of Ku Klux Klan was held on September 28 in Fudge Field, one mile west of Winchester with 6000 present
10/25/1923	Democrat	Klan	Purdy, Alexander, editorial says that "Klan's way is not Christ's way"; Purdy says that some Quakers have joined the Klan
7/5/1923	Democrat	Klan	Thompson, W. H. received a note from the Klan for hiring a Negro painter at his home five miles southeast of Winchester
10/19/1922	Democrat	Klan	Trusler Post of the GAR condemns the Klan on October 14, 1922
10/18/1922	Journal-Herald	Klan	Trusler Post, GAR condemns Klan
9/14/1922	Democrat	Klan	Winchester Democrat anti-Klan editorial, "Prove All Things Hold Fast the Good" based on Romans 12
9/14/1922	Democrat	Klan	Winchester Democrat editorial against Klan
6/21/1923	Democrat	Klan	Winchester Democrat editorial on Randolph County Klan membership
11/9/1922	Democrat	Klan	Winchester Democrat editorial, "Does Randolph County Need the Ku Klux Klan?"
5/8/1924	Democrat	Klan	Winchester Democrat editorial, "Old Randolph Goes Klanward"; many Democrats are said to have voted in the Republican primary
10/12/1922	Democrat	Klan	Winchester Democrat prints "We have heard the Kall of the Klan," saying the Klan came into Randolph County under talk of a "Lincoln League" and a Masonic talk on Americanism
9/28/1922	Democrat	Klan	Winchester Democrat prints an editorial against the Ku Klux Klan
10/5/1922	Democrat	Klan	Winchester Democrat prints an editorial against the Ku Klux Klan

Date	Source	Topic	Description
9/14/1922	Democrat	Klan	Winchester Democrat prints its first editorial against the Ku Klux Klan
2/11/1926	Journal-Herald	Libraries	Farmland Library moved from National Bank to Norris Burris Room on South Main Street
1/20/1927	Journal-Herald	Libraries	Farmland, Marceille Stephenson resigned as director; Margaureite Taylor appointed
8/30/1968	Journal-Herald	Libraries	History of Libraries in Randolph County
7/14/1927	Journal-Herald	Libraries	Losantville Public Library opened
6/11/1943	Journal-Herald	Libraries	Lynn Library dedicated
6/24/1920	Democrat	Libraries	Lynn Public Library opened
11/3/1915	Herald	Libraries	Lynn, meeting to get library held in Friends Church
12/26/1972	News-Gazette	Libraries	Parker Library opens [not a public library]
5/20/1972	News-Gazette	Libraries	Ridgeville Public Library was established on January 1, 1912
2/6/1913	Democrat	Libraries	Ridgeville to get library
12/30/1903	Herald	Libraries	Union City, city accepts $10,000 for Carnegie Library
4/11/1867	Journal	Libraries	White River Township Library exists
11/20/1912	Herald	Libraries	Winchester Public Library Association was organized on November 23, 1906; in 1911 rented a house on Franklin Street
3/19/1913	Herald	Libraries	Winchester Public Library moved to W. E. Miller Building
3/16/1916	Democrat	Libraries	Winchester Public Library opened
7/19/1911	Journal	Libraries	Winchester Public Library opened at 117 E. Franklin Street
11/21/1912	Democrat	Libraries	Winchester Public Library, history
2/25/1915	Democrat	Libraries	Winchester to get Carnegie Library
3/28/1906	Herald	Libraries	Winchester, attempt to secure Carnegie Library
10/14/1914	Herald	Libraries	Winchester, attempt to secure Carnegie Library
7/7/1915	Journal	Libraries	Winchester, bids awarded for public library
8/21/1912	Journal	Libraries	Winchester, board of directors appointed
2/23/1916	Journal	Libraries	Winchester, Carnegie Library opened Monday for the first time
2/25/1915	Herald	Libraries	Winchester, Carnegie Library secured; Central School to be razed; fifth grade moved to old Christian Church on South Main Street
7/7/1915	Herald	Libraries	Winchester, contract is let
7/15/1915	Democrat	Libraries	Winchester, contract let for Carnegie Library
3/15/1916	Herald	Libraries	Winchester, formal opening on Friday
11/20/1912	Journal	Libraries	Winchester, history of

Date	Source	Category	Description
2/23/1916	Herald	Libraries	Winchester, new library opened Monday
2/16/1916	Herald	Libraries	Winchester, new library to open on February 21, 1916
11/12/1953	Journal-Herald	Lodges	Winchester has K of P, Spanish-American War Veterans, D of R, VFW, VFW Auxiliary, and D of A
11/27/1895	Herald	Lodges	Winchester women's organizations: OES, February 26, 1886; Ladies of Golden Eagle No. 4, January 6, 1894; Women's Relief Corps, January 27, 1887; Degree of Pocahontas No. 6, October 22, 1888; Daughters of Rebekah, May 22, 1856-no charter, reorganized on April 8, 1873
4/12/1972	News-Gazette	Lodges	Winchester World War I Veterans and Auxiliary exist
3/15/1968	News	Lodges	Winchester World War I Veterans No. 197 exists
3/16/1970	News-Gazette	Lodges	Winchester World War I Veterans No. 197 exists
1/20/1959	Journal-Herald	Lodges	Winchester, World War I Veterans and Auxiliary exist
2/12/1962	News	Lodges	Winchester, World War I Veterans and Auxiliary exist
5/22/1965	Journal-Herald	Lodges	Winchester, World War I Veterans and Auxiliary exist
4/16/1964	Journal-Herald	Lodges	Winchester, World War I Veterans exist
3/29/1928	Journal-Herald	Lodges-American Legion	American Legion has posts at Winchester, Ridgeville, Union City, and Lynn
1/13/1921	Democrat	Lodges-American Legion	Farmland American Legion exists
9/4/1945	Journal-Herald	Lodges-American Legion	Farmland Auxiliary exists
10/19/1965	Journal-Herald	Lodges-American Legion	Farmland, building to be dedicated on October 23
8/23/1943	News	Lodges-American Legion	Farmland, C. W. Owens, commander
3/3/1920	Herald	Lodges-American Legion	Farmland, Chauncy Botkin Post organized
3/4/1920	Democrat	Lodges-American Legion	Farmland, Chauncy Botkin Post organized on February 26, 1920
10/29/1963	Journal-Herald	Lodges-American Legion	Farmland, West Randolph Post American Legion, new building
6/13/1969	Journal-Herald	Lodges-American Legion	History of American Legion in Randolph County; Winchester Post was anti-Klan, fell to 34 members during the period; Lynn organized March 26, 1930, No. 274; Union City, No. 158, was organized November 1, 1919; Winchester Auxiliary was organized May 16, 1928; Union City Auxiliary was organized April 4, 1929
10/20/1947	News	Lodges-American Legion	Lynn, Harry Howell Auxiliary No. 374 exists
2/11/1938	Journal-Herald	Lodges-American Legion	Lynn, Harry Howell Auxiliary Unit 274 celebrated first anniversary

Date	Source	Category	Description
7/5/1922	Journal-Herald	Lodges-American Legion	Lynn, Harry Howell Post exists
3/27/1953	News	Lodges-American Legion	Lynn, Harry Howell Post No. 274, 31st anniversary
7/20/1954	Journal-Herald	Lodges-American Legion	Lynn, Harry Howell Post, organized November 29, 1922; Auxiliary organized in 1937
2/4/1939	Journal-Herald	Lodges-American Legion	Lynn, Harry Howell Unit 274, third anniversary
10/7/1937	Journal-Herald	Lodges-American Legion	Lynn, Harry Howell Unit No. 274, A. L. Auxiliary, exists
5/24/1928	Journal-Herald	Lodges-American Legion	Randolph Union No. 39 American Legion Auxiliary organized in Winchester
8/17/1972	News-Gazette	Lodges-American Legion	Ridgeville American Legion Auxiliary, No. 507, is organized
7/17/1972	News-Gazette	Lodges-American Legion	Ridgeville American Legion is building new building
1/14/1920	Herald	Lodges-American Legion	Ridgeville, American Legion organized in IOOF Hall
1/14/1971	News-Gazette	Lodges-American Legion	Ridgeville, American Legion Post No. 507 was chartered on January 11, 1971
10/30/1919	Democrat	Lodges-American Legion	Ridgeville, J. Earl Carpenter Post organized
11/5/1919	Journal	Lodges-American Legion	Ridgeville, J. Earl Carpenter Post organized
8/5/1920	Democrat	Lodges-American Legion	Saratoga American Legion organized
11/5/1919	Herald	Lodges-American Legion	Union City, American Legion organizes; Orville N. Stover Post
11/5/1919	Journal	Lodges-American Legion	Union City, charter for American Legion applied for; will be Orville Stover Post
3/14/1947	News	Lodges-American Legion	Union City, Orville Stover Post, No 158, 28th anniversary
11/23/1922	Democrat	Lodges-American Legion	Winchester American Legion Auxiliary organized
5/24/1923	Journal-Herald	Lodges-American Legion	Winchester American Legion Auxiliary organized on May 19
5/10/1928	Democrat	Lodges-American Legion	Winchester American Legion Auxiliary to be organized
4/7/1971	News-Gazette	Lodges-American Legion	Winchester American Legion gets 2500 signatures against the conviction of Calley [Vietnam]
8/21/1919	Democrat	Lodges-American Legion	Winchester American Legion organization
8/20/1919	Journal	Lodges-American Legion	Winchester American Legion organized in GAR Hall
5/17/1949	Journal-Herald	Lodges-American Legion	Winchester, American Legion Post No. 39 has built addition
8/13/1919	Herald	Lodges-American Legion	Winchester, American Legion to be organized on August 15, 1919 in GAR Hall, southeast corner of Square
10/29/1919	Herald	Lodges-American Legion	Winchester, list of charter members
3/12/1949	Journal-Herald	Lodges-American Legion	Winchester, list of commanders of Randolph Post No. 39
3/22/1923	Journal-Herald	Lodges-Ben Hur	Winchester has Ben-Hur lodge

Date	Source	Category	Description
3/25/1896	Journal	Lodges-Ben Hur	Winchester, Ben Hur organized in KGE Hall, Winchester Court, No. 71-32
4/8/1896	Journal	Lodges-Ben Hur	Winchester, Ben Hur will meet in POSA Hall, over Fudge's Store
3/27/1948	Journal-Herald	Lodges-Eagles	Union City, Hub City Aerie No. 2790, Fraternal Order of Eagles, organized on March 14
2/17/1943	Journal-Herald	Lodges-Elks	Elks Lodge exists at Union City
9/7/1967	Journal-Herald	Lodges-Elks	Union City Elks No. 1534 40th anniversary; organized May 16, 1927; building dedicated in 1938
2/5/1890	Journal	Lodges-F & A M	Deerfield, old Masonic Building burned last Friday
6/27/1867	Journal	Lodges-F & A M	Farmland F & A M to meet over Thornburg's room
10/12/1898	Journal	Lodges-F & A M	Farmland Masonic Lodge will be dedicated on Thursday
10/19/1964	News	Lodges-F & A M	Farmland, history of
10/26/1898	Journal	Lodges-F & A M	Farmland, Masonic Lodge dedication
10/19/1898	Journal	Lodges-F & A M	Farmland, Masonic Lodge to be dedicated tomorrow
12/8/1875	Journal	Lodges-F & A M	Farmland, Masons' new hall
8/15/1917	Journal	Lodges-F & A M	Farmland, new Masonic Hall will be dedicated on September 6, 1917
6/29/1887	Journal	Lodges-F & A M	Farmland, plans to organize Eastern Star
5/29/1895	Herald	Lodges-F & A M	Huntsville OES organized on May 25, 1895
7/1/1896	Journal	Lodges-F & A M	Huntsville, lodge recently moved into a new room [apparently a remodeling]
8/17/1898	Journal	Lodges-F & A M	Huntsville, Masons bought property of Ed Cox
5/29/1895	Journal	Lodges-F & A M	Huntsville, OES organized on May 25, 1895
6/20/1947	News	Lodges-F & A M	Job's Daughters No. 45 exists
3/27/1962	Journal-Herald	Lodges-F & A M	Job's Daughters, Winchester No. 45 and Union City No. 118 exist
4/26/1916	Journal	Lodges-F & A M	Knights Templar service in Winchester Friends Church
10/20/1909	Journal	Lodges-F & A M	Losantville F & A M lodge instituted
10/27/1909	Journal	Lodges-F & A M	Losantville Lodge instituted
4/15/1960	News	Lodges-F & A M	Losantville, new lodge hall
5/17/1905	Journal	Lodges-F & A M	Lynn Masonic Block under construction
4/17/1946	News	Lodges-F & A M	Lynn OES second anniversary
4/21/1944	News	Lodges-F & A M	Lynn Order of Eastern Star instituted
7/26/1871	Journal	Lodges-F & A M	New Pittsburg, Masons have a lodge
11/18/1982	News-Gazette	Lodges-F & A M	OES, history of past matrons
12/26/1877	Journal	Lodges-F & A M	Olive Branch, officers of Olive Lodge, No. 426

12/18/1878	Journal	Lodges-F & A M	Olive Lodge, members include Eli Hiatt, A. M. Addington, and George W. Addington
12/31/1879	Journal	Lodges-F & A M	Olive, officers listed
12/20/1906	Journal	Lodges-F & A M	Parker City Eastern Star instituted
6/5/1965	Journal-Herald	Lodges-F & A M	Parker DeMolay instituted on June 5
2/7/1967	Journal-Herald	Lodges-F & A M	Parker DeMolay received charter
11/29/1923	Journal-Herald	Lodges-F & A M	Parker F & A M moves to IOOF Building
10/21/1963	News	Lodges-F & A M	Parker, Job's Daughters, Bethel No. 124 exists
12/26/1963	Journal-Herald	Lodges-F & A M	Parker, Job's Daughters, Bethel No. 124 exists
2/12/1879	Journal	Lodges-F & A M	Ridgeville Masons plan new hall
6/3/1941	Journal-Herald	Lodges-F & A M	Summers Lodge consolidated into Winchester Lodge
9/12/1970	News-Gazette	Lodges-F & A M	Union City Bethel No. 118, Job's Daughters, 9th anniversary; established on August 12, 1961
9/11/1950	News	Lodges-F & A M	Union City DeMolay organized
1/7/1965	Journal-Herald	Lodges-F & A M	Union City Job's Daughters exists
10/28/1926	Democrat	Lodges-F & A M	Union City Masonic Lodge buys Post Office building
1/28/1966	News	Lodges-F & A M	Union City Masonic Temple was dedicated on January 22
4/27/1887	Journal	Lodges-F & A M	Union City, Eastern Star to be organized
7/11/1969	Journal-Herald	Lodges-F & A M	Union City, Turpen Lodge will rededicate new building on July 12
10/24/1959	Journal-Herald	Lodges-F & A M	Winchester Commandery No. 53, Knights Templar plans to merge with Muncie No. 18
5/15/1907	Herald	Lodges-F & A M	Winchester Commandery No. 53, Knights Templar, chartered
10/31/1959	Journal-Herald	Lodges-F & A M	Winchester Commandery No. 53, KT will not merge with Muncie No. 18
11/22/1905	Journal	Lodges-F & A M	Winchester Council, No. 20, R & S M instituted last Saturday
3/8/1961	News	Lodges-F & A M	Winchester DeMolay was organized in 1957
9/13/1957	News	Lodges-F & A M	Winchester DeMolay will be established on September 19
3/19/1963	Journal-Herald	Lodges-F & A M	Winchester DeMolay, history
5/22/1919	Democrat	Lodges-F & A M	Winchester F & A M Hall built in 1884
12/9/1946	News	Lodges-F & A M	Winchester Job's Daughters recently established
12/3/1946	Journal-Herald	Lodges-F & A M	Winchester Job's Daughters to be established on December 4
6/4/1984	News-Gazette	Lodges-F & A M	Winchester, 140th anniversary; Lynn Lodge consolidated in 1982
5/23/1906	Journal	Lodges-F & A M	Winchester, 50th anniversary of RAM
3/10/1886	Journal	Lodges-F & A M	Winchester, Eastern Star instituted on February 20, 1886

Date	Source	Category	Description
11/14/1906	Journal	Lodges-F & A M	Winchester, Hiatt, Enos published book on Winchester Lodge
6/11/1919	Journal	Lodges-F & A M	Winchester, history of
5/27/1944	Journal-Herald	Lodges-F & A M	Winchester, history of Masonic Lodges near Winchester with list of Masters
6/16/1984	News-Gazette	Lodges-F & A M	Winchester, Huntsville, Lynn, list of masters of lodges
4/18/1883	Journal	Lodges-F & A M	Winchester, last meeting of F & A. M. in old lodge room next Saturday
2/14/1877	Journal	Lodges-F & A M	Winchester, lodge is looking for a new home
4/25/1883	Journal	Lodges-F & A M	Winchester, Masons will moved to Temperance Hall
4/8/1908	Journal	Lodges-F & A M	Winchester, Randolph Chapter, Royal Arch Masons, jewel case is made from lumber of the old courthouse
7/26/1905	Journal	Lodges-F & A M	Winchester, Royal Arch Masons instituted last Thursday
6/13/1890	Democrat	Lodges-Farmers Alliance	Farmers Alliance Lodge No. 114 organized at Haysville on May 26, 1890
6/18/1890	Journal	Lodges-Farmers Alliance	Farmers Alliance, Harrisville Lodge No. 114 was organized on May 26, 1890
6/18/1890	Herald	Lodges-Farmers Alliance	Harrisville Lodge No. 114, Farmers Alliance, organized May 26, 1890
6/11/1890	Herald	Lodges-Farmers Alliance	Numerous branches of the Farmers' Alliance have been organized in Randolph County
2/8/1893	Journal	Lodges-Farmers' Alliance	Farmers' Alliance exists in Randolph County
9/3/1890	Journal	Lodges-Farmers' Alliance	Farmers' Alliance meeting at Morris Schoolhouse, Monroe Township
9/17/1890	Journal	Lodges-Farmers' Alliance	Huntsville, Farmers' Alliance attempts to organize in Huntsville with no success
9/10/1890	Journal	Lodges-Farmers' Alliance	Lickskillet, Farmers' Alliance exists
2/4/1891	Herald	Lodges-FMBA	Abbott's Schoolhouse, FMBA, Will Hinshaw spoke
9/10/1890	Journal	Lodges-FMBA	Barrax Corner, FMBA organized here Saturday night
9/14/1898	Herald	Lodges-FMBA	Cedar FMBA Fair, history; started at Goodview FMBA in 1892
9/16/1891	Herald	Lodges-FMBA	Cedar FMBA, William E. Hinshaw, speaker
4/8/1896	Herald	Lodges-FMBA	County FMBA exists
4/29/1891	Journal	Lodges-FMBA	County FMBA had 30 lodges and 900 members
6/11/1890	Herald	Lodges-FMBA	County FMBA met at Rural on June 3; N. T. Butts, president; W. E. Hinshaw, vice-president; W. T. Shockney, secretary; E. W. Hill, treasurer
5/29/1895	Herald	Lodges-FMBA	County FMBA picnic on Kemp Farm

Date	Source	Topic	Description
4/22/1891	Herald	Lodges-FMBA	County FMBA, W. E. Hinshaw elected president
6/13/1890	Democrat	Lodges-FMBA	County organization of FMBA occurred at Rural on June 3
12/2/1891	Journal	Lodges-FMBA	Elm Grove Schoolhouse, FMBA No. 4801 meets at, west of town
8/15/1894	Journal	Lodges-FMBA	FMBA Fair will be held at Cedar
10/26/1890	Journal	Lodges-FMBA	FMBA has 26 lodges in county
1/28/1891	Herald	Lodges-FMBA	Green Schoolhouse, FMBA, Will Hinshaw spoke
6/18/1890	Journal	Lodges-FMBA	Greensfork Township, School No. 6, first mention of FMBA
6/18/1890	Journal	Lodges-FMBA	Greensfork Township, Spartanburg, prospect of organizing FMBA
4/15/1891	Journal	Lodges-FMBA	Hinshaw, W. E. elected President of County FMBA
2/24/1892	Journal	Lodges-FMBA	Huntsville, FMBA Hall in mentioned
9/9/1891	Journal	Lodges-FMBA	Losantville FMBA exists
2/18/1891	Journal	Lodges-FMBA	Losantville, FMBA organized
4/3/1891	Democrat	Lodges-FMBA	Martindale Schoolhouse, FMBA to be organized
6/24/1891	Herald	Lodges-FMBA	Modoc FMBA
9/12/1890	Democrat	Lodges-FMBA	Osborn [Ozbun] Schoolhouse has FMBA
10/2/1895	Herald	Lodges-FMBA	Peacock, T. C. is county president
2/1/1893	Herald	Lodges-FMBA	Peacock, T. C. is county president of FMBA; B. F. Wilmore is county president of Farmers Alliance
6/8/1892	Journal	Lodges-FMBA	Poplar Run Lodge, No. 4667, FMBA exists
6/18/1890	Journal	Lodges-FMBA	Randolph County Farmers Mutual Benefit Association organized on June 3; N. T. Butts is president, W. E. Hinshaw is vice-president
4/8/1896	Journal	Lodges-FMBA	Randolph County FMBA will meet
5/18/1892	Journal	Lodges-FMBA	Randolph County, Lee L. Driver is president of county assembly
10/22/1890	Journal	Lodges-FMBA	Randolph County, N. T. Butts, county president; W. T. Shockney, secretary; W. E. Hinshaw and F. F. Canada, delegates; have 26 lodges and 650 members in county
4/8/1891	Journal	Lodges-FMBA	Randolph County, N. T. Butts, president of county assembly
4/15/1896	Journal	Lodges-FMBA	Randolph County, Solly Wright elected county president
1/3/1894	Journal	Lodges-FMBA	Randolph County, T. C. Peacock, president of county assembly
1/8/1896	Journal	Lodges-FMBA	Randolph County, T. C. Peacock, president of county assembly
4/3/1895	Journal	Lodges-FMBA	Randolph County, T. C. Peacock, president of county assembly
4/15/1891	Journal	Lodges-FMBA	Randolph County, W. E. Hinshaw elected president of county assembly

Date	Source	Category	Description
2/24/1892	Journal	Lodges-FMBA	Salem Lodge, No. 4785, FMBA exists; members are Winship, Sites, Evans, and Friddle
6/5/1895	Herald	Lodges-FMBA	Stoney Creek FMBAs to meet on grounds near Cedar
6/5/1895	Journal	Lodges-FMBA	Stoney Creek Township, third annual FMBA Fair
2/11/1891	Herald	Lodges-FMBA	White Hall Schoolhouse, FMBA
5/6/1891	Journal	Lodges-FMBA	White Hall Schoolhouse, FMBA No. 4188 meets there
9/12/1888	Journal	Lodges-GAR	Carlos City, Ira H. Davisson Camp, No. 151, SV mustered in last Wednesday evening
11/18/1891	Journal	Lodges-GAR	Carlos City, Jake Jackson Post, No. 536, GAR exists
9/5/1888	Journal	Lodges-GAR	Carlos City, Sons of Veterans Camp with sixteen members will be mustered in this evening
7/4/1888	Journal	Lodges-GAR	Carlos, Captain Jake Jackson Post organized with eighteen members
8/1/1888	Herald	Lodges-GAR	Carlos, GAR organized
12/25/1889	Journal	Lodges-GAR	Carlos, Ira Davison Camp, S of V, exists
1/1/1890	Journal	Lodges-GAR	Carlos, Ira Davisson Camp, Sons of Veterans, No. 151, exists
7/4/1888	Journal	Lodges-GAR	Carlos, Jake Jackson Post, GAR, organized
11/7/1906	Journal	Lodges-GAR	Farmland Camp, No. 9, Sons of Veterans organized Wednesday
3/3/1886	Journal	Lodges-GAR	Farmland GAR in IOOF Building
12/28/1887	Journal	Lodges-GAR	Farmland GAR moves from IOOF Building to IOGT Hall, over Hiatt's Tin Shop
12/17/1890	Journal	Lodges-GAR	Farmland GAR moves to Watson's Hall
11/28/1883	Journal	Lodges-GAR	Farmland, GAR and SV organized at Farmland
2/27/1889	Journal	Lodges-GAR	Farmland, GAR and SV quarters fitted up in D. Thornburg's Block
11/7/1883	Journal	Lodges-GAR	Farmland, GAR to be organized
3/3/1886	Journal	Lodges-GAR	Farmland, GAR will move to IOOF addition
11/21/1883	Journal	Lodges-GAR	Farmland, Moses Heron Post, No 261, GAR, organized last Saturday
5/9/1888	Journal	Lodges-GAR	Farmland, Newton McNees Camp, Sons of Veterans, mustered in last Friday evening
4/4/1888	Herald	Lodges-GAR	Farmland, S of V to be organized
4/4/1888	Journal	Lodges-GAR	Farmland, Sons of Veterans will be organized
5/2/1888	Journal	Lodges-GAR	Farmland, Sons of Veterans will be organized next Friday
2/19/1890	Journal	Lodges-GAR	Farmland, WRC organized on February 18, 1890
9/18/1889	Journal	Lodges-GAR	GAR bought 50 headstones for soldiers in Randolph County

Date	Source	Category	Description
4/20/1976	News-Gazette	Lodges-GAR	Gordon GAR Band, photo
6/17/1950	Journal-Herald	Lodges-GAR	Gordon's GAR Band from Huntsville
7/19/1961	News	Lodges-GAR	Hammers, Larry is member of Indianapolis Sons of Union Veterans
10/5/1916	Democrat	Lodges-GAR	Huntsville GAR disbands
9/27/1916	Journal	Lodges-GAR	Huntsville GAR Hall will be sold
10/17/1923	Journal-Herald	Lodges-GAR	Huntsville GAR reorganized in 1883
4/16/1890	Herald	Lodges-GAR	Huntsville, attempts to organize WRC
10/9/1901	Journal	Lodges-GAR	Huntsville, Frank Jones WRC celebrates twentieth anniversary
11/1/1893	Journal	Lodges-GAR	Huntsville, Frank Jones WRC is listed as No. 116
1/10/1906	Journal	Lodges-GAR	Huntsville, Frank Jones WRC, No. 116, exists
5/15/1890	Journal	Lodges-GAR	Huntsville, Frank Jones WRC, No. 249, organized on May 10, 1890
4/7/1897	Journal	Lodges-GAR	Huntsville, GAR and WRC have moved into the basement of the Masonic Hall
4/14/1897	Herald	Lodges-GAR	Huntsville, GAR and WRC moved to the first floor of the Masonic Block
5/5/1897	Journal	Lodges-GAR	Huntsville, GAR bought old school property
10/17/1883	Journal	Lodges-GAR	Huntsville, GAR instituted Monday evening
12/11/1889	Journal	Lodges-GAR	Huntsville, John R. Adamson Camp, No. 6, S of V exists
2/13/1907	Journal	Lodges-GAR	Huntsville, M. E. Conyers Camp, No. 10, SV, organized
6/29/1887	Herald	Lodges-GAR	Huntsville, S of V, No. 6, exists
2/6/1907	Journal	Lodges-GAR	Huntsville, Sons of Veterans organized
2/13/1907	Herald	Lodges-GAR	Huntsville, SUV organized last Thursday
4/16/1890	Journal	Lodges-GAR	Huntsville, WRC to be organized
6/19/1941	Journal-Herald	Lodges-GAR	King, Louis of Winchester is State Commander of Sons of Union Veterans
2/27/1884	Journal	Lodges-GAR	Losantville, J. E. Markle will institute a Grand Army post at Losantville next Tuesday evening
3/28/1888	Journal	Lodges-GAR	Lynn Sons of Veterans exists
6/1/1892	Journal	Lodges-GAR	Lynn Sons of Veterans has first anniversary
4/14/1897	Journal	Lodges-GAR	Lynn Sons of Veterans reorganized on Friday
3/21/1906	Herald	Lodges-GAR	Lynn Sons of Veterans to be instituted next week
5/24/1923	Journal-Herald	Lodges-GAR	Lynn WRC exists
1/30/1895	Herald	Lodges-GAR	Lynn WRC, Joe Cook Corps, No. 121, exists
6/10/1891	Journal	Lodges-GAR	Lynn, Captain R. W. Hamilton Camp, No. 292, SV, mustered in on Friday evening

Date	Source	Category	Description
2/6/1884	Journal	Lodges-GAR	Lynn, GAR Post to be instituted next Monday
4/12/1939	Journal-Herald	Lodges-GAR	Lynn, Joe Cook Post GAR disbanded in 1931 at death of Talt Nichols
2/13/1884	Journal	Lodges-GAR	Lynn, Joe Cook Post, No. 291, GAR organized last Monday
12/3/1890	Journal	Lodges-GAR	Lynn, Joe Cook WRC, No. 121, exists
4/4/1906	Journal	Lodges-GAR	Lynn, R. W. Hamilton Camp, No. 134, Sons of Veterans, established on March 28
3/9/1892	Journal	Lodges-GAR	Lynn, R. W. Hamilton Camp, No. 292, S of V, exists
6/10/1891	Herald	Lodges-GAR	Lynn, R. W. Hamilton Camp, No. 292, S of V, organized Friday
4/4/1906	Journal	Lodges-GAR	Lynn, R. W. Hamilton Camp, SV, No. 134, instituted Wednesday
4/4/1906	Herald	Lodges-GAR	Lynn, R. W. Hamilton Camp., No. 134, SUV, instituted last Wednesday
4/14/1897	Journal	Lodges-GAR	Lynn, S of V will be reorganized Friday
3/7/1906	Journal	Lodges-GAR	Lynn, Sons of Veterans Camp to be organized
3/28/1888	Journal	Lodges-GAR	Lynn, Sons of Veterans organized
2/28/1906	Herald	Lodges-GAR	Lynn, Sons of Veterans to organize soon
9/29/1886	Journal	Lodges-GAR	Lynn, SV will be organized
1/17/1906	Journal	Lodges-GAR	Lynn, WRC, No. 121 exists
5/11/1904	Journal	Lodges-GAR	Modoc, H. H. Neff Corps, No. 246, WRC at Modoc
1/27/1904	Journal	Lodges-GAR	Modoc, H. H. Neff, W. R. C. exists
3/5/1884	Journal	Lodges-GAR	Parker, GAR will be organized on March 7, 1884
3/19/1884	Journal	Lodges-GAR	Parker, Thomas K. Karnes Post, No. 313, GAR, organized on March 7, 1884
1/19/1887	Herald	Lodges-GAR	Ridgeville WRC, No. 33, exists
6/15/1887	Journal	Lodges-GAR	Ridgeville, David W. Ward Camp, S of V, organized last evening with 39 members
6/15/1887	Journal	Lodges-GAR	Ridgeville, David W. Ward Camp, Sons of Veterans, established at Ridgeville last night
5/28/1884	Journal	Lodges-GAR	Ridgeville, GAR organized
5/10/1911	Herald	Lodges-GAR	Ridgeville, GAR uses second floor of Ridgeville State Bank
5/5/1886	Herald	Lodges-GAR	Ridgeville, Ladies Auxiliary to GAR organized
6/22/1887	Herald	Lodges-GAR	Ridgeville, S of V instituted Tuesday of last week
2/21/1906	Journal	Lodges-GAR	Ridgeville, Sons of Veterans organized last night
2/28/1906	Herald	Lodges-GAR	Ridgeville, Sons of Veterans recently organized
6/1/1898	Herald	Lodges-GAR	Saratoga has GAR post

7/28/1886	Journal	Lodges-GAR	Shiloh Camp, Sons of Veterans, organized in Winchester on Wednesday night
8/21/1889	Herald	Lodges-GAR	Sons of Veterans have camps at Winchester, Union City, Spartanburg, Carlos, Farmland, Windsor, Ridgeville, and Huntsville
1/30/1901	Journal	Lodges-GAR	Spartanburg GAR transferred to Winchester
8/12/1891	Journal	Lodges-GAR	Spartanburg, Doc Morgan Camp No. 49, SUV, exists
3/3/1886	Journal	Lodges-GAR	Spartanburg, GAR post established last night
9/29/1886	Journal	Lodges-GAR	Spartanburg, SV to be established tomorrow
10/19/1881	Journal	Lodges-GAR	Union City GAR organized
11/28/1912	Democrat	Lodges-GAR	Union City S of V disbanded
11/25/1911	Democrat	Lodges-GAR	Union City Sons of Veterans Camp was organized on November 20, 1911
11/27/1912	Herald	Lodges-GAR	Union City Sons of Veterans disbands and merges with Winchester Camp
9/21/1870	Journal	Lodges-GAR	Union City, GAR Post exists
11/22/1911	Herald	Lodges-GAR	Union City, new S of V Camp to be organized next Monday
6/29/1887	Herald	Lodges-GAR	Union City, S of V instituted last Wednesday; a previous camp had "went down"
6/22/1887	Journal	Lodges-GAR	Union City, S of V will be instituted this evening
7/18/1906	Journal	Lodges-GAR	Union City, Sons of Veterans organizing
6/29/1887	Journal	Lodges-GAR	Union City, W. D. Stone Camp, Sons of Veterans, organized at Union City on Wednesday
4/7/1972	News-Gazette	Lodges-GAR	Winchester D of U exists
6/21/1972	News-Gazette	Lodges-GAR	Winchester D of U exists
2/23/1973	News-Gazette	Lodges-GAR	Winchester D of U exists
6/19/1973	News-Gazette	Lodges-GAR	Winchester Daughters of Union disbanded on June 11, 1973; organized in January 1934
4/7/1915	Journal	Lodges-GAR	Winchester GAR and SV moved to Holmes Block, southeast corner of the Square
10/12/1911	Democrat	Lodges-GAR	Winchester GAR moves from Central School to third floor of Ashton's Harness Shop after several years
10/11/1911	Journal	Lodges-GAR	Winchester GAR moves to 2nd and 3rd floors of the Central School Building
12/7/1921	Journal-Herald	Lodges-GAR	Winchester GAR moves to new quarters in Courthouse
1/27/1904	Journal	Lodges-GAR	Winchester GAR plans to purchase old Presbyterian Church
10/4/1866	Journal	Lodges-GAR	Winchester GAR Post organized

Date	Source	Category	Description
11/1/1911	Journal	Lodges-GAR	Winchester GAR, SV, and WRC move to Central School
5/24/1939	Journal-Herald	Lodges-GAR	Winchester has American Legion, AL Auxiliary, Spanish War Vets, SUV, Daughters of Union, WRC, and GAR
10/26/1922	Journal-Herald	Lodges-GAR	Winchester Ladies Auxiliary to the Sons of Veterans exists
12/4/1922	Journal-Herald	Lodges-GAR	Winchester Ladies Auxiliary to the Sons of Veterans is No. 16
5/11/1887	Herald	Lodges-GAR	Winchester S of V purchased cannon
11/20/1930	Journal-Herald	Lodges-GAR	Winchester SUV and Auxiliary exist
5/28/1946	Journal-Herald	Lodges-GAR	Winchester SUV and Spanish American War Veterans exist
5/29/1943	Journal-Herald	Lodges-GAR	Winchester SUV exists
5/18/1944	Journal-Herald	Lodges-GAR	Winchester SUV exists
5/30/1945	News	Lodges-GAR	Winchester SUV exists
5/3/1946	News	Lodges-GAR	Winchester SUV exists
3/18/1947	Journal-Herald	Lodges-GAR	Winchester SUV exists
5/28/1948	News	Lodges-GAR	Winchester SUV exists
5/27/1949	News	Lodges-GAR	Winchester SUV exists
2/9/1956	Journal-Herald	Lodges-GAR	Winchester SUV exists
9/8/1953	Journal-Herald	Lodges-GAR	Winchester SUV, No. 44, exists; Louis King is secretary-treasurer
12/9/1941	Journal-Herald	Lodges-GAR	Winchester SUV, Old 44, exists
4/14/1915	Herald	Lodges-GAR	Winchester WRC has new room over Hiatt's Hardware
8/9/1923	Democrat	Lodges-GAR	Winchester, "Old GAR Room" mentioned as being over Garfield Hiatt's Hardware Store
6/30/1886	Journal	Lodges-GAR	Winchester, Camp of Sons of Veterans to be organized this evening
3/17/1962	Journal-Herald	Lodges-GAR	Winchester, Daughters of the Union, Caroline Palmer Chapter of Winchester is largest local chapter in the United States
1/30/1934	Journal-Herald	Lodges-GAR	Winchester, Daughters of Union organized last week
1/16/1934	Journal-Herald	Lodges-GAR	Winchester, Daughters of Union to be organized
10/11/1911	Herald	Lodges-GAR	Winchester, GAR is moving to Central School from the third floor of Ashton's Harness Shop on the south side of the Square
5/3/1882	Journal	Lodges-GAR	Winchester, GAR is Nelson Trusler Post
1/15/1890	Journal	Lodges-GAR	Winchester, GAR meets in Mrs. Reed's hall
4/19/1911	Journal	Lodges-GAR	Winchester, GAR meets in three story brick building on the south side of the Square
4/19/1882	Journal	Lodges-GAR	Winchester, GAR Post organized

Date	Source	Category	Description
4/26/1882	Journal	Lodges-GAR	Winchester, GAR will meet in third story of old Herald Office, over Reinheimer's Grocery
5/16/1917	Journal	Lodges-GAR	Winchester, GAR, SV, and WRC meet at the southeast corner of the Square
9/5/1929	Democrat	Lodges-GAR	Winchester, history of Trusler Post; down to eight members
11/24/1921	Democrat	Lodges-GAR	Winchester, Ladies Auxiliary to the SUV organized on November 19, 1921; Camp is No. 16
11/21/1929	Journal-Herald	Lodges-GAR	Winchester, Nelson Trusler Post has eight members
1/24/1917	Herald	Lodges-GAR	Winchester, Nelson Trusler Post, surviving members listed
4/26/1905	Herald	Lodges-GAR	Winchester, S of V Camp revived
12/13/1911	Herald	Lodges-GAR	Winchester, S of V is now meeting at Central School
3/11/1915	Democrat	Lodges-GAR	Winchester, S of V moved from Central School to Richardson Block
8/4/1886	Herald	Lodges-GAR	Winchester, Sherman, not Shiloh, Camp, S of V
7/28/1886	Journal	Lodges-GAR	Winchester, Shiloh Camp, SV organized Wednesday with 21 members
4/19/1882	Journal	Lodges-GAR	Winchester, Sol Meredith Post, GAR, organized
3/5/1925	Journal-Herald	Lodges-GAR	Winchester, Sons of Veterans, WRC, and American Legion of Winchester lease Magee and Ward Hall, north side of square
12/14/1922	Democrat	Lodges-GAR	Winchester, SUV Auxiliary is one year old
1/30/1907	Journal	Lodges-GAR	Winchester, Trusler WRC observes 20th anniversary
5/22/1889	Journal	Lodges-GAR	Winchester, WRC presented banner to GAR
10/7/1896	Journal	Lodges-GAR	Winchester, WRC, No. 46, exists
3/12/1924	Democrat	Lodges-GAR	Winchester, WRC, Sons of Veterans, and American Legion move to Magee and Ward's Hall on north side of the Square
8/10/1887	Journal	Lodges-GAR	Windsor, General Tom Browne Camp, Sons of Veterans, No. 35, organized on March 23, 1887
3/2/1887	Journal	Lodges-GAR	Windsor, plans to organize Sons of Veterans
3/23/1887	Journal	Lodges-GAR	Windsor, Sons of Veterans established with 25 charter members
3/23/1887	Journal	Lodges-GAR	Windsor, Sons of Veterans to be organized
3/30/1887	Journal	Lodges-GAR	Windsor, Sons of Veterans, General Tom Browne Camp, was organized on March 23, 1887
10/30/1924	Democrat	Lodges-GAR	WRC exists at Lynn, Winchester, and Union City

10/30/1907	Journal	Lodges-GAR	WRC exists at Union City, No. 13, Ridgeville, No. 33, Winchester, No. 46, Trenton, No. 116, Lynn, No. 121, and Farmland, No. 137
10/31/1907	Democrat	Lodges-GAR	WRC exists at Union City, No. 13; Ridgeville, No. 33; Winchester, No. 46; Trenton, No. 116; Lynn, No. 121; and Farmland, No. 137
1/28/1874	Journal	Lodges-Grange	Bales Schoolhouse, Grangers will organize
6/11/1873	Journal	Lodges-Grange	Bartonia, Grange exists west of here at Liberty Hall
10/2/1934	Journal-Herald	Lodges-Grange	Bessie Snyder Grange exists
1/7/1874	Journal	Lodges-Grange	County Council of Patrons of Husbandry, constitution for
2/24/1938	Journal-Herald	Lodges-Grange	Deerfield Community Grange organized
9/13/1938	Journal-Herald	Lodges-Grange	Deerfield Juvenile Grange organized
4/22/1874	Journal	Lodges-Grange	Eight Mile Grange, exists at William Green's Schoolhouse
7/2/1873	Journal	Lodges-Grange	Fairview, Grange organized
4/26/1876	Journal	Lodges-Grange	Grange Hall to be built one mile south of Steubenville
7/2/1873	Journal	Lodges-Grange	Grange has organizations in Randolph County: 3 in White River, 1 in Washington, 1 in Green, 1 in Stoney Creek, and 1 in Wayne; 200 members in Randolph County
2/3/1916	Democrat	Lodges-Grange	Grange organized; Bert Fisher and Herman Keys, et al were original officers
10/10/1883	Journal	Lodges-Grange	Granges exist at Pleasant Grove, Pleasant Mound, Olive, New Dayton, Jackson, Green Township, Parker, and Sugar Creek
10/5/1921	Journal-Herald	Lodges-Grange	Greensfork Township Grange was organized at Arba on October 1
4/30/1884	Journal	Lodges-Grange	Harrisville, Grangers erected a building on Diehl's farm near Harrisville
11/17/1875	Journal	Lodges-Grange	Huntsville, Grangers are erecting a two-story hall
1/11/1935	Journal-Herald	Lodges-Grange	Jackson Grange exists
12/6/1916	Journal	Lodges-Grange	Local Grange mentioned
1/2/1875	Herald	Lodges-Grange	Losantville Grange No. 734, exists
5/1/1878	Journal	Lodges-Grange	New Dayton Grange, No. 292, exists
10/15/1873	Journal	Lodges-Grange	New Dayton, Grange No. 292, exists
1/23/1934	Journal-Herald	Lodges-Grange	New Grange to be established at Winchester
5/20/1891	Journal	Lodges-Grange	Parker Grange Hall is now a drug store
2/28/1877	Journal	Lodges-Grange	Parker had a Grange Hall
2/9/1916	Herald	Lodges-Grange	Randolph County Grange organized; C. C. Fisher, secretary; Herman Keys, treasurer; et al

2/2/1916	Journal	Lodges-Grange	Randolph County Grange organized; D. W. Climer, W. M.; C. C. Fisher, secretary; Herman Keys, treasurer
1/26/1916	Herald	Lodges-Grange	Randolph County Grange to be organized
10/1/1873	Journal	Lodges-Grange	Randolph County has fourteen Granges with 600-700 members
4/29/1874	Journal	Lodges-Grange	Randolph County, list of Granges
5/6/1874	Journal	Lodges-Grange	Randolph County, list of Granges
5/21/1957	Journal-Herald	Lodges-Grange	Ridgeville Grange No. 2422 was organized on May 18
3/11/1938	Journal-Herald	Lodges-Grange	Saratoga Grange organized on March 9
6/11/1890	Journal	Lodges-Grange	Spartanburg, Grangers revived two miles north
3/5/1879	Journal	Lodges-Grange	Steubenville, Grange is active
4/26/1876	Journal	Lodges-Grange	Steubenville, Grangers will build hall one mile south of
2/19/1873	Journal	Lodges-Grange	Stoney Creek Township, Grange will be organized
8/15/1877	Journal	Lodges-Grange	Sugar Creek Grange, No. 271; Pomona Grange, No 2; Randolph Pomona Grange all exist
8/4/1875	Journal	Lodges-Grange	Trenton Grange No. 363 existed
8/4/1875	Journal	Lodges-Grange	Trenton Grange No. 363 organized stock association
1/13/1921	Democrat	Lodges-Grange	Winchester Grange exists
6/21/1916	Herald	Lodges-Grange	Winchester Grange meets in MWA Hall
4/3/1918	Journal	Lodges-Grange	Winchester, Grange is moving from IORM Hall to MWA Hall
6/9/1875	Journal	Lodges-Grange	Winchester, Pomona Grange will be organized on June 24, 1875
11/19/1873	Journal	Lodges-Grange	Winchester, proceedings of organization of Grange near Winchester
6/30/1875	Journal	Lodges-Grange	Winchester, Randolph Pomona Grange instituted last Tuesday
3/2/1865	Journal	Lodges-IOGT	Deerfield, IOGT organized
9/7/1887	Journal	Lodges-IOGT	Farmland and Lynn, lodges instituted by Amanda Way
11/1/1866	Journal	Lodges-IOGT	Farmland IOGT exists
2/8/1888	Journal	Lodges-IOGT	Farmland IOGT exists
3/28/1888	Journal	Lodges-IOGT	Farmland Juvenile Templars exist
7/25/1888	Herald	Lodges-IOGT	Farmland, IOGT and Juvenile Temple exist
4/14/1875	Journal	Lodges-IOGT	Farmland, IOGT organized on January 31, 1875; now has 100 members
9/6/1871	Journal	Lodges-IOGT	Farmland, White River Lodge, NO. 703, IOGT exists
5/12/1875	Journal	Lodges-IOGT	Harrisville IOGT organized last Saturday, No. 197
12/10/1873	Journal	Lodges-IOGT	Huntsville IOGT exists

Date	Source	Category	Description
8/20/1873	Journal	Lodges-IOGT	Huntsville IOGT exists
11/27/1872	Journal	Lodges-IOGT	Huntsville IOGT organized
12/28/1870	Journal	Lodges-IOGT	Huntsville, Amanda Way reorganized IOGT on December 19, 1870
11/27/1872	Journal	Lodges-IOGT	Huntsville, IOGT organized
3/19/1873	Journal	Lodges-IOGT	Huntsville, IOGT organized on October 14, 1872 now has 80 members
9/7/1887	Journal	Lodges-IOGT	Lynn, Amanda Way and Mrs. Brookback organized an IOGT last week
4/11/1867	Journal	Lodges-IOGT	Morristown, Amanda Way organized IOGT lodge on March 30, 1867
6/22/1887	Journal	Lodges-IOGT	Ridgeville IOGT exists
8/17/1887	Journal	Lodges-IOGT	Ridgeville IOGT exists
11/24/1886	Herald	Lodges-IOGT	Ridgeville IOGT Lodge exists
5/29/1867	Journal	Lodges-IOGT	Union City IOGT exists
9/7/1887	Journal	Lodges-IOGT	Way, Amanda and Mrs. Brookbank established lodges at Union City, Farmland, and Lynn
9/6/1871	Journal	Lodges-IOGT	White River Lodge, No. 703, IOGT is at Farmland
10/11/1871	Journal	Lodges-IOGT	Winchester IOGT is No. 374
4/28/1875	Journal	Lodges-IOGT	Winchester IOGT lodge is the oldest in the state
5/9/1861	Journal	Lodges-IOGT	Winchester IOGT, No. 3, exists
5/10/1859	Journal	Lodges-IOGT	Winchester Lodge, No. 3, IOGT exists
6/22/1887	Journal	Lodges-IOGT	Winchester, Amanda Way Lodge No. 121, reorganized
6/22/1887	Journal	Lodges-IOGT	Winchester, Amanda Way reorganized IOGT with 31 charter members
2/28/1861	Journal	Lodges-IOGT	Winchester, Degree Lodge organized last Thursday evening
8/17/1887	Herald	Lodges-IOGT	Winchester, exists
1/7/1858	Journal	Lodges-IOGT	Winchester, IOGT meets at the corner of Washington and Main
10/11/1882	Journal	Lodges-IOGT	Winchester, Lodge of Good Templars organized Monday evening by A. M. Way, State Deputy
4/12/1860	Journal	Lodges-IOGT	Winchester, Temperance Hall is located at Main and Washington and home to IOGT and Randolph Division, No. 26, Sons of Temperance
6/16/1875	Journal	Lodges-IOGT	Windsor IOGT exists
4/7/1875	Journal	Lodges-IOGT	Windsor, IOGT organized Friday evening with 63 members
5/15/1878	Journal	Lodges-IOOF	Bloomingport, IOOF Hall is being built
4/10/1878	Journal	Lodges-IOOF	Bloomingport, plan to organize lodge [never happened]
4/25/1894	Journal	Lodges-IOOF	Carlos City D of R, No. 335, exists

Date	Source	Category	Description
7/6/1904	Herald	Lodges-IOOF	Carlos City, contract to be let for new IOOF Building
1/15/1908	Herald	Lodges-IOOF	Carlos City, D of R organized last Thursday evening
10/1/1890	Journal	Lodges-IOOF	Carlos City, D of R organized last Wednesday
11/25/1905	Journal	Lodges-IOOF	Carlos, lot 25 sold by IOOF to IORM
11/13/1963	News	Lodges-IOOF	Deerfield IOOF Lodge building razed
3/9/1892	Journal	Lodges-IOOF	Deerfield IOOF Lodge, No. 293, new hall built
11/30/1892	Journal	Lodges-IOOF	Deerfield IOOF Lodge, No. 297, new hall was dedicated on November 26
6/22/1892	Journal	Lodges-IOOF	Deerfield Lodge, No. 238, IOOF is building a two-story hall, 36 x 50; lodge was instituted on November 11, 1867
3/9/1892	Journal	Lodges-IOOF	Deerfield, bids for two-story IOOF Hall
6/15/1892	Journal	Lodges-IOOF	Deerfield, cornerstone of IOOF lodge will be laid on June 16, 1892
2/29/1888	Journal	Lodges-IOOF	Deerfield, Daughters of Rebekah established
11/30/1892	Herald	Lodges-IOOF	Deerfield, new hall (36 x 50) was dedicated on November 26, 1892
11/18/1903	Herald	Lodges-IOOF	Fairview, IOOF Lodge is building new hall
5/1/1924	Democrat	Lodges-IOOF	Farmland D of R gave up charter and united with Winchester
4/7/1921	Democrat	Lodges-IOOF	Farmland Encampment No. 386 was instituted on March 26, 1921
1/14/1880	Journal	Lodges-IOOF	Farmland IOOF Encampment discontinued
3/8/1900	Democrat	Lodges-IOOF	Farmland IOOF Encampment organized
10/12/1898	Herald	Lodges-IOOF	Farmland IOOF Hall dedicated last week
6/16/1859	Journal	Lodges-IOOF	Farmland IOOF Lodge organized Wednesday night
5/18/1867	Journal	Lodges-IOOF	Farmland IOOF lot sold to Curtis Thornburg
6/27/1867	Journal	Lodges-IOOF	Farmland IOOF to build new building (60 x 22)
5/14/1884	Journal	Lodges-IOOF	Farmland IOOF will build an addition
7/14/1886	Herald	Lodges-IOOF	Farmland, D of R to be instituted
1/19/1887	Journal	Lodges-IOOF	Farmland, Daughters of Rebekah organized on January 15, 1887 with twelve charter members
1/12/1860	Journal	Lodges-IOOF	Farmland, first officers of Farmland IOOF Lodge elected, including Chalkley Baldwin, treasurer
7/7/1981	News-Gazette	Lodges-IOOF	Farmland, gave safe to town; Gene Arnold and Wayne Holwayer were members
10/12/1898	Journal	Lodges-IOOF	Farmland, IOOF Hall dedicated
9/21/1898	Journal	Lodges-IOOF	Farmland, IOOF Hall will be dedicated on October 6, 1898

Date	Source	Category	Description
6/24/1885	Journal	Lodges-IOOF	Farmland, IOOF will build addition
7/12/1871	Journal	Lodges-IOOF	Farmland, Mt. Carmel Encampment, No. 110, instituted on June 20, 1871
12/21/1898	Herald	Lodges-IOOF	Farmland, Mt. Carmel Encampment, No. 110, reorganized
8/20/1981	News-Gazette	Lodges-IOOF	Farmland, safe moved to City Building
11/18/1896	Journal	Lodges-IOOF	Huntsville, IOOF Hall is nearly finished
8/19/1896	Journal	Lodges-IOOF	Huntsville, IOOF Hall will be repaired and remodeled
6/21/1889	Democrat	Lodges-IOOF	Huntsville, new Rebekah Lodge
9/2/1896	Journal	Lodges-IOOF	Huntsville, Orla Way will remodel the hall
5/15/1889	Journal	Lodges-IOOF	Huntsville, Rebekah Lodge will be instituted on Friday
8/19/1896	Journal	Lodges-IOOF	Huntsville, Trenton, bids for a new lodge room
5/15/1940	Journal-Herald	Lodges-IOOF	Huntsville, Will Edwards is remodeling old IOOF Building into grocery and garage
9/9/1896	Journal	Lodges-IOOF	Huntsville, workmen are laying foundation of new IOOF Hall
3/6/1907	Herald	Lodges-IOOF	Jordan, D of R organized
1/8/1890	Herald	Lodges-IOOF	Losantville, new hall
4/25/1900	Herald	Lodges-IOOF	Lynn, hall will be dedicated on May 8, 1900
8/8/1870	Journal	Lodges-IOOF	Lynn, IOOF Hall will be dedicated on August 13, 1870
12/27/1899	Herald	Lodges-IOOF	Lynn, lodge purchased town hall
5/2/1900	Journal	Lodges-IOOF	Lynn, new IOOF Building will be dedicated on May 8, 1900
10/21/1896	Journal	Lodges-IOOF	Modoc D of R to be organized by Huntsville D of R
10/14/1896	Journal	Lodges-IOOF	Modoc IOOF organized
10/14/1896	Herald	Lodges-IOOF	Modoc Lodge No. 725 organized last Friday night
10/18/1900	Democrat	Lodges-IOOF	Modoc Lodge No. 725, IOOF, exists
10/21/1896	Journal	Lodges-IOOF	Modoc, D of R will be instituted on Thursday
10/14/1896	Journal	Lodges-IOOF	Modoc, IOOF Lodge instituted last Friday
1/30/1906	Journal	Lodges-IOOF	New Pittsburg, IOOF organized by C. W. Paris last Thursday
3/28/1907	Democrat	Lodges-IOOF	Parker Encampment organized on March 22, 1907
12/19/1906	Journal	Lodges-IOOF	Parker IOOF will be dedicated on January 8, 1907
12/8/1875	Journal	Lodges-IOOF	Parker, IOOF Hall is 25 x 51
6/20/1906	Journal	Lodges-IOOF	Parker, IOOF to build a new building
6/20/1906	Herald	Lodges-IOOF	Parker, new IOOF building planned
5/16/1877	Journal	Lodges-IOOF	Parker, new IOOF Hall
9/8/1875	Journal	Lodges-IOOF	Parker, new lodge hall

Date	Source	Topic	Description
6/20/1877	Journal	Lodges-IOOF	Parker, new lodge hall will be dedicated on July 4, 1877
5/13/1969	Journal-Herald	Lodges-IOOF	Past Noble Grands organization, 60th anniversary
3/18/1903	Journal	Lodges-IOOF	Pittsburg D of R, No. 612, exists
6/22/1904	Herald	Lodges-IOOF	Randolph County, 1/5 of voters in Randolph County are Odd Fellows; 16 lodges in Randolph County
6/22/1904	Journal	Lodges-IOOF	Randolph County, 1/5 voters in county is an Odd Fellow
8/10/1887	Journal	Lodges-IOOF	Ridgeville D or R, No. 287, exists
5/22/1913	Democrat	Lodges-IOOF	Ridgeville IOOF Hall under construction
7/16/1913	Journal	Lodges-IOOF	Ridgeville IOOF let contract for a new building
4/6/1910	Herald	Lodges-IOOF	Ridgeville IOOF plans to build a new three-story block in the fall
3/5/1913	Journal	Lodges-IOOF	Ridgeville IOOF to build new building
2/11/1914	Journal	Lodges-IOOF	Ridgeville, dedication of new IOOF Hall will take place on February 23, 1914
8/10/1887	Journal	Lodges-IOOF	Ridgeville, Lodge No. 287, D. of R. instituted last Monday
7/17/1913	Democrat	Lodges-IOOF	Ridgeville, new IOOF Hall
5/25/1904	Herald	Lodges-IOOF	Saratoga, cornerstone to be laid on May 31, 1904
5/25/1904	Journal	Lodges-IOOF	Saratoga, cornerstone will be laid on May 31, 1904
11/16/1904	Journal	Lodges-IOOF	Saratoga, hall to be dedicated on Thanksgiving
3/23/1955	News	Lodges-IOOF	Saratoga, IOOF Building constructed in 1897; MWA Building constructed in 1900; IORM Building constructed c1900
3/2/1955	News	Lodges-IOOF	Saratoga, photo
1/1/1890	Journal	Lodges-IOOF	Spartanburg, Greensfork Encampment, IOOF exists
9/27/1899	Herald	Lodges-IOOF	Spartanburg, IOOF building will be dedicated on Thanksgiving
3/1/1899	Journal	Lodges-IOOF	Spartanburg, IOOF contemplates new hall
12/6/1899	Journal	Lodges-IOOF	Spartanburg, IOOF Hall dedicated
11/22/1899	Journal	Lodges-IOOF	Spartanburg, IOOF Hall will be dedicated on November 30, 1899
4/12/1899	Journal	Lodges-IOOF	Spartanburg, IOOF will build on southwest corner of Square
12/6/1899	Herald	Lodges-IOOF	Spartanburg, new hall dedicated last Thursday
3/8/1899	Journal	Lodges-IOOF	Spartanburg, new IOOF Hall will be built on the ground of the old Jerry Horn residence
9/27/1899	Journal	Lodges-IOOF	Spartanburg, new IOOF Hall will be dedicated on Thanksgiving
3/29/1899	Herald	Lodges-IOOF	Spartanburg, plans for new IOOF hall
4/25/1894	Journal	Lodges-IOOF	Trenton D of R, No. 308, exists

Date	Source	Category	Description
1/15/1908	Journal	Lodges-IOOF	Trenton IOOF Lodge, charter members listed: John Ross, John W. Hunt, Isaiah Oren, Dr. John W. Botkin, Milton Macy, Dr. R. L. Eikenbuerry, William Davidson, Isaac B. Harris, and T. W. Mills
1/15/1959	Journal-Herald	Lodges-IOOF	Winchester D of R and VFW exist
4/16/1973	News-Gazette	Lodges-IOOF	Winchester D of R celebrates 100th anniversary
11/15/1956	Journal-Herald	Lodges-IOOF	Winchester D of R exists
6/8/1957	Journal-Herald	Lodges-IOOF	Winchester D of R exists
11/6/1957	News	Lodges-IOOF	Winchester D of R exists
2/23/1960	Journal-Herald	Lodges-IOOF	Winchester D of R exists
1/21/1961	Journal-Herald	Lodges-IOOF	Winchester D of R exists
5/26/1962	Journal-Herald	Lodges-IOOF	Winchester D of R exists
2/5/1964	Journal-Herald	Lodges-IOOF	Winchester D of R exists
3/25/1965	Journal-Herald	Lodges-IOOF	Winchester D of R exists
1/24/1966	News	Lodges-IOOF	Winchester D of R exists
6/3/1968	News	Lodges-IOOF	Winchester D of R exists; charter is missing
1/17/1963	Journal-Herald	Lodges-IOOF	Winchester D of R, No. 101, Exists
3/15/1916	Journal	Lodges-IOOF	Winchester IOOF Building will be formally opened on March 31, 1916
5/21/1946	Journal-Herald	Lodges-IOOF	Winchester IOOF charter surrendered in January 1945; lawsuit
8/25/1915	Herald	Lodges-IOOF	Winchester IOOF Hall being remodeled
2/17/1916	Democrat	Lodges-IOOF	Winchester IOOF Hall enlarged; third floor added to the south
7/14/1915	Journal	Lodges-IOOF	Winchester IOOF to add third story to lodge building
12/31/1902	Journal	Lodges-IOOF	Winchester IOOF, history
5/23/1883	Journal	Lodges-IOOF	Winchester, bids on new hall on June 7, 1883
1/23/1889	Herald	Lodges-IOOF	Winchester, building built in 1883 at a cost of $20,000
5/19/1915	Journal	Lodges-IOOF	Winchester, contract advertised for enlarging IOOF Building
7/14/1915	Journal	Lodges-IOOF	Winchester, contract awarded for enlarging IOOF Building
8/8/1883	Journal	Lodges-IOOF	Winchester, cornerstone laying described
8/1/1883	Journal	Lodges-IOOF	Winchester, cornerstone laying program
6/20/1883	Journal	Lodges-IOOF	Winchester, ground broken for IOOF Block
12/31/1902	Journal	Lodges-IOOF	Winchester, history of
4/11/1883	Journal	Lodges-IOOF	Winchester, IOOF and K of P have moved to Richardson's third story
2/16/1916	Journal	Lodges-IOOF	Winchester, IOOF Building is completed
7/18/1883	Journal	Lodges-IOOF	Winchester, IOOF cornerstone will be laid on August 2, 1883

Date	Source	Category	Description
3/14/1883	Journal	Lodges-IOOF	Winchester, IOOF have rented third floor of Richardson's Building until their room is ready
3/7/1883	Journal	Lodges-IOOF	Winchester, IOOF Lodge proposes to build a new building
3/31/1915	Herald	Lodges-IOOF	Winchester, IOOF to build a third floor over the south part of the building and add apartments to the second floor
4/1/1915	Democrat	Lodges-IOOF	Winchester, IOOF will add third story to south
2/14/1877	Journal	Lodges-IOOF	Winchester, lodge is looking for a new home
7/9/1973	News-Gazette	Lodges-IOOF	Winchester, Past Noble Grands, 64th anniversary
3/24/1915	Journal	Lodges-IOOF	Winchester, plans to enlarge IOOF Block
12/23/1896	Journal	Lodges-IOOF	Windsor, D of R organized
3/28/1906	Herald	Lodges-IORM	Carlos City, D of P organized last Thursday night
6/25/1902	Journal	Lodges-IORM	Carlos City, IORM Lodge to be organized
7/16/1902	Journal	Lodges-IORM	Carlos City, Ulini Tribe was organized
7/9/1902	Journal	Lodges-IORM	Carlos City, Ulini Tribe, No. 332, will be organized on Saturday
3/28/1906	Journal	Lodges-IORM	Carlos, Degree of Pocahontas organized on March 22
12/18/1907	Journal	Lodges-IORM	Carlos, Pocataligo Council No. 246, D of P exists
7/17/1902	Democrat	Lodges-IORM	Carlos, Ulini Tribe, No. 332, IORM instituted
1/22/1890	Journal	Lodges-IORM	Farmland, D of P will be instituted at Farmland this evening
11/9/1898	Journal	Lodges-IORM	Farmland, IORM dedicated their hall last Tuesday
11/9/1898	Herald	Lodges-IORM	Farmland, IORM hall dedication
10/19/1898	Journal	Lodges-IORM	Farmland, IORM Hall will be dedicated on November 1, 1898
1/16/1889	Journal	Lodges-IORM	Farmland, IORM moved to hall over bank
3/28/1888	Herald	Lodges-IORM	Farmland, IORM organized in Watson's Hall
3/28/1888	Journal	Lodges-IORM	Farmland, IORM organized on March 20, 1888
2/19/1890	Journal	Lodges-IORM	Farmland, IORM will move over Bly and Thornburg's
10/7/1896	Journal	Lodges-IORM	Farmland, Oerika Council, No. 15, Degree of Pocahontas exists
1/29/1890	Journal	Lodges-IORM	Farmland, Ogarita Tribe, No. 15, D of P organized
1/29/1890	Herald	Lodges-IORM	Farmland, Orgarita D of P, No. 15, organized last Wednesday evening
3/7/1888	Journal	Lodges-IORM	Farmland, Red Men will organize
7/9/1902	Journal	Lodges-IORM	Harrisville, plans to organize IORM lodge [not clear if it happened]

Date	Source	Category	Description
6/25/1902	Journal	Lodges-IORM	Losantville, Monadnochs Tribe, IORM organized
9/25/1907	Herald	Lodges-IORM	Lynn IORM organized on September 24, 1907
8/19/1896	Journal	Lodges-IORM	Parker, D of P to be organized today
7/24/1895	Journal	Lodges-IORM	Parker, Improved Order of Red Men lodge organized
10/9/1895	Journal	Lodges-IORM	Parker, IORM will organize tomorrow
10/16/1895	Herald	Lodges-IORM	Parker, Katonka Lodge, No. 211, IORM, instituted at Parker last week
10/16/1895	Journal	Lodges-IORM	Parker, Katouka Tribe, IORM, organized last Thursday
10/7/1896	Journal	Lodges-IORM	Parker, Leota Council, No. 85, D of P, instituted last Wednesday
9/2/1903	Journal	Lodges-IORM	Ridgeville Haymakers instituted last week; also D of P at Saratoga
6/20/1885	Democrat	Lodges-IORM	Ridgeville IORM organized
3/12/1890	Journal	Lodges-IORM	Ridgeville, D of P to be organized tonight [it did not occur until later]
12/19/1900	Journal	Lodges-IORM	Ridgeville, Minnesela Council, No. 16, D of P exists
10/6/1911	Democrat	Lodges-IORM	Ridgeville, Waneta Haymakers, No. 73 1/2, exists
8/26/1903	Journal	Lodges-IORM	Saratoga D of P to be organized today
4/2/1902	Herald	Lodges-IORM	Saratoga, Kolola Tribe, No. 323, IORM instituted Wednesday night
3/27/1902	Democrat	Lodges-IORM	Saratoga, Kolola Tribe, No. 323, organized
12/30/1903	Journal	Lodges-IORM	Union City D of P to be organized
1/10/1906	Herald	Lodges-IORM	Union City, D of P is two years old last week
12/30/1903	Herald	Lodges-IORM	Union City, D of P to be organized tomorrow
9/26/1888	Herald	Lodges-IORM	Winchester D of P, No. 6, organized
11/3/1897	Journal	Lodges-IORM	Winchester Haymakers Hayloft, No. 72 1/2, exists
3/26/1902	Journal	Lodges-IORM	Winchester IORM Hall was dedicated on March 20, 1902
2/12/1902	Journal	Lodges-IORM	Winchester IORM Hall will be dedicated on March 20, 1902
3/12/1902	Journal	Lodges-IORM	Winchester IORM Hall will be dedicated on March 20, 1902
3/19/1902	Journal	Lodges-IORM	Winchester IORM Hall will be dedicated on March 20, 1902
1/15/1902	Journal	Lodges-IORM	Winchester IORM to be dedicated in February [actually on March 20]
8/7/1901	Herald	Lodges-IORM	Winchester, cornerstone of new hall laid Saturday evening
10/3/1888	Journal	Lodges-IORM	Winchester, D of P, No. 6, instituted in Winchester
3/26/1902	Herald	Lodges-IORM	Winchester, history; IORM chartered on January 20, 1884; Haymakers chartered on May 16, 1894
7/31/1901	Journal	Lodges-IORM	Winchester, IORM cornerstone to be laid on August 3, 1901

Date	Source	Category	Description
1/15/1902	Herald	Lodges-IORM	Winchester, IORM Hall to be dedicated
2/5/1902	Herald	Lodges-IORM	Winchester, IORM Hall will be dedicated on March 2, 1902
12/11/1889	Journal	Lodges-IORM	Winchester, IORM Room is in third story of Miller Building on south side of Square
12/26/1883	Journal	Lodges-IORM	Winchester, IORM will be established
3/16/1881	Journal	Lodges-IORM	Winchester, IORM will be organized tonight
11/20/1889	Journal	Lodges-IORM	Winchester, IORM will occupy a new hall
12/4/1889	Herald	Lodges-IORM	Winchester, lodge will be dedicated next Monday night
1/30/1884	Journal	Lodges-IORM	Winchester, Mohawk Tribe, No. 72, IORM, organized last Monday evening
12/19/1900	Journal	Lodges-IORM	Winchester, Nokomis Council, No. 6, D of P exists
3/26/1902	Herald	Lodges-IORM	Winchester, picture of new hall
9/26/1888	Journal	Lodges-IORM	Winchester, Pocahontas Degree instituted in Winchester Saturday evening
5/2/1900	Herald	Lodges-IORM	Winchester, Red Men will build new building
12/23/1903	Journal	Lodges-IORM	Windsor, IORM Hall burned
10/23/1923	Democrat	Lodges-IORM	Windsor, IORM hall burned
12/16/1896	Journal	Lodges-IORM	Windsor, IORM has new room
9/30/1896	Herald	Lodges-IORM	Windsor, Minnesota Tribe, No. 228, IORM, instituted on September 29, 1896
9/30/1896	Journal	Lodges-IORM	Windsor, Minnesota Tribe, No. 228, organized last Friday
2/6/1902	Democrat	Lodges-IORM	Windsor, new hall to be dedicated on March 20, 1902
3/27/1902	Democrat	Lodges-IORM	Windsor, new hall was dedicated
9/12/1936	Daily News	Lodges-JOUAM	JOUAM has lodges at Dunkirk, Portland, Pennville, Bellfontaine, Boundary, Saratoga, Union City, Muncie, Parker, Redkey, and Winchester
9/30/1926	Daily News	Lodges-JOUAM	JOUAM has lodges at Union City, Portland, Boundary, Muncie, Dunkirk, Richmond, Lynn, and Winchester
10/24/1935	News-Democrat	Lodges-JOUAM	JOUAM has lodges at Winchester, Union City, Saratoga, and Ridgeville
10/2/1901	Herald	Lodges-JOUAM	Losantville, Order of United American Mechanics hall being built
10/14/1926	Journal-Herald	Lodges-JOUAM	Lynn JOUAM exists
10/25/1952	Journal-Herald	Lodges-JOUAM	Ridgeville JOUAM exists
4/5/1951	Journal-Herald	Lodges-JOUAM	Ridgeville, No. 13, and Saratoga, No. 100, exist
3/15/1938	Journal-Herald	Lodges-JOUAM	Saratoga Lodge exists

Date	Source	Category	Description
5/25/1946	Journal-Herald	Lodges-JOUAM	Union City D of A, No. 21, exists
2/25/1938	Journal-Herald	Lodges-JOUAM	Union City Lodge exists
7/17/1907	Herald	Lodges-JOUAM	Union City, Order of United American Mechanics organized last Saturday evening
10/12/1939	Journal-Herald	Lodges-JOUAM	Winchester and Union City both had Daughters of America
5/23/1940	Journal-Herald	Lodges-JOUAM	Winchester and Union City both had Daughters of America
4/5/1928	Democrat	Lodges-JOUAM	Winchester and Union City had only JOUAM councils in Randolph County
2/7/1912	Herald	Lodges-JOUAM	Winchester Council JOUAM, No. 32, organized
1/31/1912	Journal	Lodges-JOUAM	Winchester Council, No. 32, JOUAM organized last Saturday in Hirsch Block
7/2/1938	Journal-Herald	Lodges-JOUAM	Winchester D of A exists
6/23/1927	Journal-Herald	Lodges-JOUAM	Winchester Daughters of America exists
5/23/1952	News	Lodges-JOUAM	Winchester JOUAM and D of A exist
12/15/1927	Journal-Herald	Lodges-JOUAM	Winchester JOUAM and Daughters of America meet in Pierce Hall
5/10/1963	News	Lodges-JOUAM	Winchester JOUAM exists
6/13/1912	Democrat	Lodges-JOUAM	Winchester JOUAM organized in February 1912
5/1/1951	Journal-Herald	Lodges-JOUAM	Winchester JOUAM purchases K of P Building; K of P still exists; photo of building
3/7/1929	Journal-Herald	Lodges-JOUAM	Winchester JOUAM tenth anniversary
8/29/1947	News	Lodges-JOUAM	Winchester JOUAM was organized in 1919
3/4/1940	Journal-Herald	Lodges-JOUAM	Winchester JOUAM, No. 51, 21st anniversary; Winchester Council, No. 27, D of A
8/27/1947	News	Lodges-JOUAM	Winchester JOUAM, photo in regalia
10/20/1933	Journal-Herald	Lodges-JOUAM	Winchester Lodge, No. 51, and Saratoga Lodge, No. 100, exist
3/12/1919	Journal	Lodges-JOUAM	Winchester Lodge, No. 51, JOUAM organized last Saturday evening; meeting was held in MWA Hall
3/5/1919	Journal	Lodges-JOUAM	Winchester Lodge, No. 57, JOUAM organized last Saturday
5/16/1900	Herald	Lodges-JOUAM	Winchester, attempt to organize JOUAM
4/5/1928	Democrat	Lodges-JOUAM	Winchester, Daughters of America have new quarters over Winchester Publishing Company with JOUAM; left Pierce Building
8/3/1922	Democrat	Lodges-JOUAM	Winchester, JOUAM Hall is on W. Franklin Street
7/3/1907	Herald	Lodges-JOUAM	Winchester, Order of United American Mechanics organized last Wednesday, June 26, 1907, in Red Men's Hall

Date	Source	Category	Description
7/3/1907	Journal	Lodges-JOUAM	Winchester, OUAM Lodge organized on Wednesday, June 26, 1907
1/24/1912	Journal	Lodges-JOUAM	Winchester, plans to organize lodge
6/7/1940	Journal-Herald	Lodges-JOUAM	Winchester, Pride of Winchester Council No. 27, D of A
5/3/1905	Herald	Lodges-K of C	Union City Knights of Columbus organized Sunday
12/25/1901	Journal	Lodges-K of P	DOKK described
3/24/1909	Herald	Lodges-K of P	Farmland K of P Building dedicated on March 18, 1909
3/17/1909	Journal	Lodges-K of P	Farmland K of P Building to be dedicated tomorrow
3/25/1909	Democrat	Lodges-K of P	Farmland K of P Building was dedicated last Thursday
3/24/1909	Journal	Lodges-K of P	Farmland K of P dedication
3/15/1923	Journal-Herald	Lodges-K of P	Farmland K of P lodge consolidated with Winchester lodge by surrender of charter
9/11/1907	Journal	Lodges-K of P	Farmland K of P to build new building
2/22/1923	Democrat	Lodges-K of P	Farmland Lodge consolidates with Winchester Lodge
3/17/1909	Journal	Lodges-K of P	Farmland, dedication of K of P Hall is tomorrow
12/9/1908	Herald	Lodges-K of P	Farmland, K of P Building nearing completion
6/22/1898	Journal	Lodges-K of P	Farmland, K of P organized
6/15/1898	Herald	Lodges-K of P	Farmland, K of P to organize on June 20, 1898
3/24/1897	Journal	Lodges-K of P	Farmland, K of P will be organized
6/15/1898	Journal	Lodges-K of P	Farmland, K of P will be organized
2/26/1890	Journal	Lodges-K of P	Farmland, K of P will soon be organized
9/2/1908	Journal	Lodges-K of P	Farmland, W. F. Pursley will erect the K of P Building
1/29/1886	Democrat	Lodges-K of P	Invincible Division, No. 15, U. R. K. of P. exists
8/2/1926	Daily News	Lodges-K of P	K of P Lodges exist at Lynn, Spartanburg, Winchester, and Union City
12/20/1925	Democrat	Lodges-K of P	Knights of Pythias lodges exist at Union City, Winchester, Lynn, Modoc, Parker, and Spartanburg
5/1/1907	Journal	Lodges-K of P	Lynn K of P building to be dedicated on May 23, 1907
5/16/1907	Democrat	Lodges-K of P	Lynn K of P Building will be dedicated on May 23, 1907
3/13/1901	Journal	Lodges-K of P	Lynn K of P plans new building
5/14/1884	Journal	Lodges-K of P	Lynn K of P will be instituted on May 23, 1884
12/15/1960	Journal-Herald	Lodges-K of P	Lynn Knights of Pythias Lodge is reactivated
5/22/1907	Herald	Lodges-K of P	Lynn, hall to be dedicated on May 23, 1907
10/20/1886	Journal	Lodges-K of P	Lynn, K of P Hall built in last year

Date	Source	Category	Description
5/28/1884	Journal	Lodges-K of P	Lynn, K of P organized
5/7/1884	Journal	Lodges-K of P	Lynn, K of P will be instituted
11/7/1906	Herald	Lodges-K of P	Lynn, new building nearing completion
5/29/1907	Journal	Lodges-K of P	Lynn, new K of P Hall; photo and article
11/27/1919	Democrat	Lodges-K of P	Lynn, organized in 1884
5/24/1954	News	Lodges-K of P	Lynn, photo of K of P in uniform and history
1/25/1893	Journal	Lodges-K of P	Lynn, Pythian Sisters exists
2/7/1906	Journal	Lodges-K of P	Lynn, Rathbones exist
6/22/1904	Journal	Lodges-K of P	Modoc Division, No. 24, Uniformed Rank, Knights of Pythias, established on June 20
4/22/1903	Journal	Lodges-K of P	Modoc K of P building will be dedicated on April 29, 1903
5/6/1903	Journal	Lodges-K of P	Modoc K of P dedication
4/23/1903	Democrat	Lodges-K of P	Modoc K of P Hall will be dedicated next Wednesday
8/22/1894	Journal	Lodges-K of P	Modoc K of P has fifth anniversary
9/6/1889	Democrat	Lodges-K of P	Modoc K of P instituted last Friday
9/4/1889	Journal	Lodges-K of P	Modoc K of P instituted last Friday with 22 members
10/22/1902	Herald	Lodges-K of P	Modoc K of P is building new hall
4/23/1902	Journal	Lodges-K of P	Modoc K of P will erect brick building
2/17/1892	Journal	Lodges-K of P	Modoc K of P, No. 229, exists
3/18/1896	Journal	Lodges-K of P	Modoc K of P, No. 229, exists
9/4/1889	Herald	Lodges-K of P	Modoc lodge organized
2/28/1900	Journal	Lodges-K of P	Modoc Rathbone Sisters exist
11/15/1899	Herald	Lodges-K of P	Modoc Rathbone Sisters exist
12/7/1892	Herald	Lodges-K of P	Modoc Temple No. 72, Pythian Sisters, organized on November 30, 1892
8/21/1907	Journal	Lodges-K of P	Modoc Temple, No. 72, Rathbone Sisters, exists
8/22/1894	Herald	Lodges-K of P	Modoc, 5th anniversary
4/23/1902	Herald	Lodges-K of P	Modoc, bids on K of P Hall
5/6/1903	Herald	Lodges-K of P	Modoc, dedication, photo
5/7/1903	Democrat	Lodges-K of P	Modoc, K of P Building is 49 x 80 and brick
4/22/1903	Herald	Lodges-K of P	Modoc, K of P No. 229, will be dedicated on April 29, 1903
7/17/1889	Herald	Lodges-K of P	Modoc, lodge to be organized
12/7/1892	Journal	Lodges-K of P	Modoc, Pythian Sisterhood organized last Tuesday
3/1/1917	Democrat	Lodges-K of P	Modoc, Union B. Hunt Lodge No. 229, K of P exists
6/24/1903	Herald	Lodges-K of P	Parker City, K of P Lodge organized on June 17, 1903
1/18/1896	Journal	Lodges-K of P	Parker City, K of P to be organized

Date	Source	Category	Description
6/10/1903	Herald	Lodges-K of P	Parker K of P Lodge to be organized
6/24/1903	Journal	Lodges-K of P	Parker, new lodge instituted at Parker last Wednesday
5/9/1912	Democrat	Lodges-K of P	Pythian Sisters have lodges at Union City, Modoc, Lynn, Parker, Winchester, and Ridgeville
5/8/1912	Journal	Lodges-K of P	Pythian Sisters Lodges exist at Union City, Winchester, Ridgeville
11/12/1919	Herald	Lodges-K of P	Randolph County has eight lodges
2/16/1910	Herald	Lodges-K of P	Ridgeville K of P will be instituted on February 24, 1910
3/2/1910	Journal	Lodges-K of P	Ridgeville Lodge established
1/11/1923	Democrat	Lodges-K of P	Ridgeville, Bob White Lodge, No. 637, K of P, consolidated with Winchester Lodge
3/2/1910	Herald	Lodges-K of P	Ridgeville, new K of P Lodge
7/24/1895	Journal	Lodges-K of P	Ridgeville, plan to organize K of P
12/3/1919	Journal	Lodges-K of P	Spartanburg K of P Lodge to move to IOOF Hall
6/22/1910	Journal	Lodges-K of P	Spartanburg K of P Lodge, No. 552, to be organized on Wednesday, June 29, 1910
7/6/1910	Journal	Lodges-K of P	Spartanburg Lodge, No. 552, organized in IOOF Room
7/6/1910	Herald	Lodges-K of P	Spartanburg, K of P organized on Wednesday
4/9/1919	Journal	Lodges-K of P	Union City K of P Lodge surrendered charter Thursday night
4/10/1919	Democrat	Lodges-K of P	Union City, K of P, No. 84 disbands; once owned Union Grand Theatre
10/17/1883	Journal	Lodges-K of P	Union City, Uniformed Rank, K of P will be instituted tonight
12/19/1894	Herald	Lodges-K of P	Winchester K of P Building dedication story
12/12/1894	Herald	Lodges-K of P	Winchester K of P Building to be dedicated tonight
12/17/1894	Journal	Lodges-K of P	Winchester K of P Hall dedicated Wednesday; Farmers and Merchants Bank located there
2/13/1901	Journal	Lodges-K of P	Winchester K of P has ninth anniversary
4/14/1880	Journal	Lodges-K of P	Winchester Lodge, No. 91, K of P, organized
5/7/1890	Herald	Lodges-K of P	Winchester Pythian Sisterhood, first anniversary
5/8/1889	Herald	Lodges-K of P	Winchester Pythian Sisters organized last Friday
3/29/1889	Democrat	Lodges-K of P	Winchester Pythian Sisters to be instituted [occurred in May 1889]
4/11/1906	Herald	Lodges-K of P	Winchester Temple No. 332, Rathbone Sisters, organized recently
3/13/1895	Journal	Lodges-K of P	Winchester Temple, No. 112, Rathbone Sisters, organized last Friday
11/27/1907	Journal	Lodges-K of P	Winchester Temple, No. 332, Pythian Sisters exists

Date	Source	Category	Description
4/5/1906	Democrat	Lodges-K of P	Winchester Temple, No. 332, Rathbone Sisters, organized on March 29, 1906
4/11/1906	Journal	Lodges-K of P	Winchester Temple, No. 332, Rathbone Sisters, organized recently
2/6/1895	Journal	Lodges-K of P	Winchester, a lodge of Rathbone Sisters will be organized in the near future
5/13/1903	Journal	Lodges-K of P	Winchester, DeBoulion Division, No. 22, Uniformed Rank, Knights of Pythias, reorganized
10/2/1885	Democrat	Lodges-K of P	Winchester, DeBuillion Uniformed Rank, K of P is organized on October 1
5/28/1902	Journal	Lodges-K of P	Winchester, Democratic Order of Knights of Khorassan, K of P Social Order, exists
4/11/1883	Journal	Lodges-K of P	Winchester, IOOF and K of P have moved to Richardson's third story
12/17/1894	Journal	Lodges-K of P	Winchester, K of P Block dedicated
12/8/1897	Journal	Lodges-K of P	Winchester, K of P Block, U. B. Hunt, P. T. Colgrove, Arla Brown
5/20/1885	Journal	Lodges-K of P	Winchester, K of P fitting up new hall
8/8/1894	Journal	Lodges-K of P	Winchester, K of P Hall will be dedicated on October 5, 1894
4/26/1893	Journal	Lodges-K of P	Winchester, K of P may put third story on new block in Winchester
3/31/1880	Journal	Lodges-K of P	Winchester, Knights of Pythias organized in IOOF Hall
4/14/1880	Journal	Lodges-K of P	Winchester, Knights of Pythias, No. 91, instituted last night
12/5/1894	Journal	Lodges-K of P	Winchester, new K of P Hall will be dedicated next Wednesday
11/13/1907	Herald	Lodges-K of P	Winchester, photo of building and history of lodge
5/2/1917	Herald	Lodges-K of P	Winchester, plans to reorganize the Uniform Rank, No. 91
2/7/1894	Herald	Lodges-K of P	Winchester, Pythian Block nearing completion
2/7/1906	Journal	Lodges-K of P	Winchester, Rathbone Sisters, plans to organize
5/8/1889	Journal	Lodges-K of P	Winchester, Temple of Pythian Sisterhood, No. 16, established here last Friday with a membership of 71
9/30/1885	Journal	Lodges-K of P	Winchester, Uniformed Rank, Knights of Pythias will be instituted soon
6/9/1897	Journal	Lodges-K of P	Winchester, Uniformed Rank, Knights of Pythias will be reorganized
12/4/1889	Herald	Lodges-K of P	Winchester, work on building
4/28/1909	Herald	Lodges-K of P	Windsor, K of P instituted April 27, 1909
4/21/1909	Journal	Lodges-K of P	Windsor, K of P organized yesterday
4/7/1909	Journal	Lodges-K of P	Windsor, K of P to be organized

3/24/1909	Journal	Lodges-K of P	Windsor, plans to organize lodge
2/19/1896	Herald	Lodges-KGE	Albany [Delaware County], KGE lodge instituted
1/31/1894	Journal	Lodges-KGE	Bartonia, KGE instituted last Monday
3/22/1905	Herald	Lodges-KGE	Farmland KGE organized last Wednesday; officially organized on March 24, 1905
6/29/1905	Democrat	Lodges-KGE	Farmland LGE was instituted last Saturday evening, June 24, 1905
3/29/1905	Journal	Lodges-KGE	Farmland, KGE was instituted on Friday, March 24, 1905
3/22/1905	Journal	Lodges-KGE	Farmland, KGE will be instituted on Friday, March 24, 1905
4/6/1905	Democrat	Lodges-KGE	Farmland, newly organized KGE lodge
8/6/1902	Journal	Lodges-KGE	Harrisville KGE will be dedicated on August 16, 1902
4/19/1944	News	Lodges-KGE	Harrisville Lodge history
8/7/1902	Democrat	Lodges-KGE	Harrisville, hall to be dedicated on August 16, 1902
8/13/1902	Herald	Lodges-KGE	Harrisville, hall to be dedicated on August 16, 1902
4/18/1894	Journal	Lodges-KGE	Harrisville, KGE, No. 9, organized last Saturday night in Fruit's House
2/27/1895	Journal	Lodges-KGE	Harrisville, Ladies of the Golden Eagle organized
5/14/1902	Herald	Lodges-KGE	Harrisville, lodge hall nearly complete
8/6/1902	Herald	Lodges-KGE	Harrisville, lodge hall to be dedicated a week from Saturday
6/19/1902	Democrat	Lodges-KGE	Harrisville, new hall
8/21/1902	Democrat	Lodges-KGE	Harrisville, new hall was dedicated
1/8/1902	Journal	Lodges-KGE	Harrisville, new KGE Building
4/2/1902	Journal	Lodges-KGE	Harrisville, new KGE building is planned
4/2/1902	Herald	Lodges-KGE	Harrisville, plans for new hall
1/1/1896	Journal	Lodges-KGE	Harrisville, Prosperity Temple No. 6, LGE exists
6/15/1905	Democrat	Lodges-KGE	Harrisville, Wise Guys Retreat organized; Winchester Retreat was No. 2
11/2/1898	Herald	Lodges-KGE	KGE exists at Union City, Winchester, Harrisville, Bartonia, Parker City, Windsor, and Modoc
4/10/1895	Herald	Lodges-KGE	Ladies of the Golden Eagle exist at Winchester, Union City, Bartonia, and Harrisville
9/8/1936	Daily News	Lodges-KGE	Ladies of the Golden Eagle have chapters at Union City, Harrisville, Anderson, and Troy in Indiana
6/26/1901	Journal	Lodges-KGE	LGE in Richmond is known as the "Quaker City Temple"
11/2/1898	Journal	Lodges-KGE	Lodges exist at Union City, Winchester, Harrisville, Bartonia, Parker City, Modoc, and Windsor

1/9/1901	Journal	Lodges-KGE	Modoc Eagle Hall mentioned
3/3/1897	Herald	Lodges-KGE	Modoc KGE was instituted last Friday evening
8/26/1896	Journal	Lodges-KGE	Modoc, KGE will be organized on Tuesday
3/3/1897	Journal	Lodges-KGE	Modoc, KGE, Castle, No. 14, instituted at Modoc on February 26
5/8/1895	Herald	Lodges-KGE	Parker City KGE exists
5/25/1898	Herald	Lodges-KGE	Parker KGE moved to new quarters
6/14/1905	Journal	Lodges-KGE	Parker KGE started last Friday, June 9
5/12/1897	Journal	Lodges-KGE	Parker KGE, No. 10, has third anniversary
5/2/1894	Herald	Lodges-KGE	Parker lodge organized Thursday night
4/18/1894	Herald	Lodges-KGE	Parker lodge to be organized
5/2/1894	Journal	Lodges-KGE	Parker, KGE instituted last Wednesday
5/12/1897	Journal	Lodges-KGE	Parker, LGE organized
1/18/1899	Herald	Lodges-KGE	Prosperity Temple, No. 6, LGE exists
11/23/1904	Journal	Lodges-KGE	Ridgeville KGE instituted last Thursday
2/1/1905	Journal	Lodges-KGE	Ridgeville KGE, No. 24, exists
5/10/1905	Journal	Lodges-KGE	Ridgeville LGE organized last Thursday evening
4/27/1905	Democrat	Lodges-KGE	Ridgeville, LGE will be instituted on May 4, 1905
1/15/1902	Herald	Lodges-KGE	Ridgeville, new KGE hall is being built
8/6/1902	Journal	Lodges-KGE	Rural, effort to organize KGE lodge
8/20/1902	Herald	Lodges-KGE	Rural, first KGE hall in the state [probably a mistaken reference to Harrisville]
8/27/1902	Herald	Lodges-KGE	Rural, KGE meeting
8/13/1902	Herald	Lodges-KGE	Rural, KGE to meet at Rural
3/2/1892	Journal	Lodges-KGE	Winchester, Canada Castle organized last Friday by Union City Castle
3/1/1893	Herald	Lodges-KGE	Winchester, Canada Castle organized on February 26, 1892
6/29/1892	Journal	Lodges-KGE	Winchester, Canada Castle, No. 9, KGE exists
3/6/1895	Herald	Lodges-KGE	Winchester, KGE 3rd anniversary; LGE is one year old; lodge in Richardson Building; five KGE lodges in Randolph County and four ladies temples
1/4/1912	Democrat	Lodges-KGE	Winchester, KGE exists
3/6/1901	Herald	Lodges-KGE	Winchester, KGE has lately purchased the second floor of the Richardson Building
12/23/1903	Journal	Lodges-KGE	Winchester, KGE Lodge moves to Canada Block

Date	Source	Category	Description
1/2/1895	Herald	Lodges-KGE	Winchester, KGE moved into former K of P Room
3/1/1893	Journal	Lodges-KGE	Winchester, KGE organized on February 26, 1892 in old Temperance Hall, now Canada's Hall
2/24/1892	Journal	Lodges-KGE	Winchester, KGE will be instituted next Friday in Canada's Block
3/1/1917	Democrat	Lodges-KGE	Winchester, KGE, 21st anniversary
2/23/1922	Democrat	Lodges-KGE	Winchester, KGE, 30th anniversary
3/6/1901	Journal	Lodges-KGE	Winchester, KGE, No. 7, has eighth anniversary; LGE is No. 4
1/24/1924	Journal-Herald	Lodges-KGE	Winchester, LGE of Winchester exists
3/3/1897	Journal	Lodges-KGE	Winchester, LGE, No. 4, exists
4/5/1905	Journal	Lodges-KGE	Winchester, Retreat No. 2 of the Wise Guys, KGE, was organized on March 28
6/26/1901	Journal	Lodges-KGE	Windsor, KGE exists
9/29/1897	Herald	Lodges-KGE	Windsor, KGE is building a two-story business block and hall
2/28/1900	Herald	Lodges-KGE	Windsor, KGE Lodge, third anniversary
3/3/1897	Herald	Lodges-KGE	Windsor, KGE was organized on February 25, 1897 by the Parker Castle
3/3/1897	Journal	Lodges-KGE	Windsor, KGE, Castle, No. 13, instituted at Windsor on February 25
5/15/1901	Journal	Lodges-KGE	Windsor, LGE exists
4/3/1889	Herald	Lodges-Miscellaneous	Ancient Order of the Orient reorganized in Stone's Block on the west side of the Square
10/14/1903	Journal	Lodges-Miscellaneous	Aristotle Lodge, No. 2, Order of the Pestalozzi of America, organized last Friday
6/5/1889	Journal	Lodges-Miscellaneous	Bloomingport has two secret orders
2/18/1891	Journal	Lodges-Miscellaneous	Council No. 1212, Grand Order of the Orient was organized last Wednesday at Losantville
1/29/1919	Journal	Lodges-Miscellaneous	Degree of Honor was instituted January 5
8/15/1912	Democrat	Lodges-Miscellaneous	Farmland, Woodmen of the World Lodge organized; Bruce Somerville, CC; S. M. Barker, AS; Cliff Lewellen, B; Harry Delk, E; Carl Painter, C; Add Mills, W; Harry Sunday, S
1/14/1880	Journal	Lodges-Miscellaneous	Huntsville, Porter's Temperance Lodge organized at Huntsville
11/29/1916	Journal	Lodges-Miscellaneous	Independent Order of Coon Hunters organized
7/15/1946	News	Lodges-Miscellaneous	Knights of Columbus exists in Union City
4/6/1978	News-Gazette	Lodges-Miscellaneous	Knights of Columbus, St. Mary's Council No. 983, Union City, exists
1/10/1883	Journal	Lodges-Miscellaneous	Knights of Honor exist in Winchester

Date	Source	Category	Description
1/15/1896	Journal	Lodges-Miscellaneous	Knights of Honor exist in Winchester
7/7/1886	Journal	Lodges-Miscellaneous	Knights of Honor exist in Winchester
6/30/1880	Journal	Lodges-Miscellaneous	Knights of Honor have rented third floor of Moorman's Building
10/13/1886	Journal	Lodges-Miscellaneous	Knights of Honor removed from GAR Hall to Moorman Building on northeast corner of Square
7/9/1879	Journal	Lodges-Miscellaneous	Knights of Honor will occupy old Temperance Hall in Winchester
6/25/1879	Journal	Lodges-Miscellaneous	Knights of Honor, Magnolia Lodge will be established
5/17/1882	Journal	Lodges-Miscellaneous	Knights of Honor, new hall in old Herald Office
3/30/1887	Journal	Lodges-Miscellaneous	Knights of Honor, No. 1672, described; eight years old
6/22/1887	Journal	Lodges-Miscellaneous	Knights of Morality existed at Huntsville
3/30/1887	Journal	Lodges-Miscellaneous	Knights of Morality, exist at Huntsville
4/6/1887	Journal	Lodges-Miscellaneous	Knights of Morality, for boys, has recently been established at Huntsville
2/2/1887	Journal	Lodges-Miscellaneous	Knights of Rest is new lodge at Farmland
7/29/1970	News-Gazette	Lodges-Miscellaneous	Knights of the Golden Circle described near Emmettsville in 1860s
5/5/1909	Herald	Lodges-Miscellaneous	Knights of the Golden Circle, history of in Randolph County
5/7/1946	Journal-Herald	Lodges-Miscellaneous	Lodges of Winchester: Moose, D of A, D of R; IOOF no longer exists
3/10/1880	Journal	Lodges-Miscellaneous	Losantville, Porter League organized
3/23/1887	Herald	Lodges-Miscellaneous	Magnolia Lodge, No. 1672, Knights of Honor is eight years old
1/15/1896	Journal	Lodges-Miscellaneous	Magnolia Lodge, No. 1672, Knights of Honor, exists
6/27/1888	Journal	Lodges-Miscellaneous	Magnolia Lodge, No. 1672, Knights of Honor, exists
4/7/1932	Journal-Herald	Lodges-Miscellaneous	McKinley Camp No. 66, USWV exists
2/15/1922	Journal-Herald	Lodges-Miscellaneous	McKinley Post, No. 66, U. S. Spanish-American War Veterans, organized on February 8
6/10/1903	Journal	Lodges-Miscellaneous	Order of Pestaloggi [sic] formed by Jay County Teachers
10/14/1903	Journal	Lodges-Miscellaneous	Order of Pestalozzi organized in Winchester
4/14/1982	News-Gazette	Lodges-Miscellaneous	Phi Delta Kappa, 70th anniversary
5/26/1897	Journal	Lodges-Miscellaneous	Protective Home of America lodge described
5/19/1897	Journal	Lodges-Miscellaneous	Protective Home of America lodge will be established in Winchester tomorrow
9/16/1947	Journal-Herald	Lodges-Miscellaneous	Randolph Ship, 103, NCUSA exists

Date	Source	Category	Description
7/30/1903	Democrat	Lodges-Miscellaneous	Ridgeville, Knights of Rest exist
1/9/1895	Journal	Lodges-Miscellaneous	Soldiers Union organized in January 1867
2/2/1945	News	Lodges-Miscellaneous	Spanish-American War Veterans exist
1/17/1947	News	Lodges-Miscellaneous	Spanish-American War Veterans exist
11/24/1951	Journal-Herald	Lodges-Miscellaneous	Spanish-American War Veterans exist
7/13/1926	Daily News	Lodges-Miscellaneous	Supreme Lodge Order of Protective Americans of the U. S. incorporated; all are Winchester people: nativist, public school, etc.; 75 members in subordinate chapter in Winchester; secret order
6/14/1973	News-Gazette	Lodges-Miscellaneous	Union City, Randolph County Fraternal Order of Police Lodge No. 150, membership list
11/16/1898	Journal	Lodges-Miscellaneous	Union Veterans Union Camp, No. 1 reorganized in Winchester
1/8/1890	Journal	Lodges-Miscellaneous	Union Veterans Union organized last Saturday night in Winchester
1/15/1890	Journal	Lodges-Miscellaneous	Union Veterans Union, Winchester Command, No. 1 organized
10/18/1947	Journal-Herald	Lodges-Miscellaneous	Winchester Disabled American Veterans organized recently
1/28/1920	Journal	Lodges-Miscellaneous	Winchester Lodge, No. 34, Degree of Honor exists
12/29/1921	Democrat	Lodges-Miscellaneous	Winchester Lodge, No. 34, Degree of Honor exists, it was a lodge for women
12/17/1955	Journal-Herald	Lodges-Miscellaneous	Winchester Spanish-American War Veterans exists
2/25/1960	Journal-Herald	Lodges-Miscellaneous	Winchester World War I Veterans No. 197 exists
1/18/1961	News	Lodges-Miscellaneous	Winchester World War I Veterans No. 197 exists
2/16/1956	Journal-Herald	Lodges-Miscellaneous	Winchester, Barracks No. 197, Veterans of WWI USA, first anniversary meeting
1/29/1919	Journal	Lodges-Miscellaneous	Winchester, Degree of Honor, for ladies, was organized on January 5, 1919
5/8/1924	Democrat	Lodges-Miscellaneous	Winchester, Protected Home Circle Lodge organized
11/15/1860	Journal	Lodges-Miscellaneous	Winchester, Social Temple exists in Temperance Hall
1/3/1936	Journal-Herald	Lodges-Miscellaneous	Winchester, Spanish-American War Veterans exists
12/22/1859	Journal	Lodges-Miscellaneous	Winchester, Temple of Honor organized last Saturday
2/12/1890	Journal	Lodges-Miscellaneous	Winchester, Union Veterans Union, No. 1, organized
4/5/1923	Democrat	Lodges-Miscellaneous	Winchester, Unit of United Veterans of the Republican is organized
3/14/1955	News	Lodges-Miscellaneous	Winchester, Veterans of World War I of the USA exists

Date	Source	Category	Description
1/24/1955	News	Lodges-Miscellaneous	Winchester, Veterans of World War I organized on January 23
5/24/1860	Journal	Lodges-Miscellaneous	Winchester, Washingtonian Temperance Society met in M. E. Church
8/14/1912	Herald	Lodges-Miscellaneous	Woodmen of the World, Farmland, organization
6/2/1915	Journal	Lodges-Moose	Union City had Moose Lodge
6/25/1913	Journal	Lodges-Moose	Union City, Loyal Order of Moose Lodge instituted Sunday
11/5/1913	Journal	Lodges-Moose	Winchester, Loyal Order of Moose, Randolph Lodge, No. 827 exists
4/28/1915	Herald	Lodges-Moose	Winchester, Moose Home grand opening was last Friday evening
8/9/1928	Democrat	Lodges-Moose	Winchester, Moose Home on North Street has been vacant for some time
12/5/1929	Journal-Herald	Lodges-Moose	Winchester, Moose Lodge building is for sale
9/2/1914	Herald	Lodges-Moose	Winchester, Moose Lodge Building nearly complete
3/20/1913	Democrat	Lodges-Moose	Winchester, Moose Lodge instituted
12/18/1924	Journal-Herald	Lodges-Moose	Winchester, Moose Lodge is bankrupt
9/16/1969	Journal-Herald	Lodges-Moose	Winchester, Moose Lodge meets at 120 N. Main St.
9/30/1914	Herald	Lodges-Moose	Winchester, Moose Lodge moves into new quarters
3/27/1969	Journal-Herald	Lodges-Moose	Winchester, Moose Lodge No. 1977 was organized on March 16
3/19/1913	Herald	Lodges-Moose	Winchester, Moose Lodge No. 827, organized in IORM Hall
9/24/1925	Democrat	Lodges-Moose	Winchester, Moose Lodge organized
3/19/1913	Journal	Lodges-Moose	Winchester, Moose Lodge organized Sunday
4/23/1913	Journal	Lodges-Moose	Winchester, Moose Lodge recently organized
7/11/1984	News-Gazette	Lodges-Moose	Winchester, Moose Lodge refused to serve blacks at AFL-CIO dinner in Winchester
10/23/1945	Journal-Herald	Lodges-Moose	Winchester, Moose Lodge to be instituted
1/16/1969	Journal-Herald	Lodges-Moose	Winchester, Moose Lodge to be organized
1/29/1969	Journal-Herald	Lodges-Moose	Winchester, Moose Lodge to be organized
10/29/1913	Journal	Lodges-Moose	Winchester, Moose Lodge to build hall
11/6/1913	Democrat	Lodges-Moose	Winchester, Randolph Lodge, No. 827, is building on North Street
3/9/1946	Journal-Herald	Lodges-Moose	Winchester, Women of the Moose established in Winchester
1/16/1946	News	Lodges-Moose	Winchester, Women of the Moose to be organized on January 18
1/23/1902	Democrat	Lodges-MWA	Farmland, MWA instituted
3/17/1909	Herald	Lodges-MWA	Huntsville, MWA organized Friday, March 12, 1909

Date	Source	Topic	Description
6/23/1909	Journal	Lodges-MWA	Lynn Camp, No. 13184, MWA instituted last Tuesday
6/21/1935	Journal-Herald	Lodges-MWA	Lynn, MWA does not exist
6/24/1909	Democrat	Lodges-MWA	Lynn, MWA instituted in Hinshaw's Hall
6/23/1909	Herald	Lodges-MWA	Lynn, MWA instituted this week
6/23/1909	Journal	Lodges-MWA	Lynn, MWA Lodge, No. 13184, organized in E. J. Hinshaw's Hall last Tuesday night
4/12/1911	Herald	Lodges-MWA	MWA exists at Saratoga, Ridgeville, Farmland, Huntsville, Lynn, Union City, and two in Winchester
2/6/1901	Journal	Lodges-MWA	MWA lodges exist at Union City, Ridgeville, Saratoga, and Winchester
3/30/1904	Herald	Lodges-MWA	Parker, MWA organized on March 25, 1904
12/4/1901	Herald	Lodges-MWA	Saratoga, MWA and RNA built new two-story frame hall (32 x 65) dedication Thursday; MWA organized in August 1896
10/23/1901	Journal	Lodges-MWA	Saratoga, MWA hall being built
12/4/1901	Journal	Lodges-MWA	Saratoga, MWA hall dedicated last Thursday
3/20/1969	Journal-Herald	Lodges-MWA	Saratoga, MWA has 267 members
7/1/1903	Journal	Lodges-MWA	Saratoga, Royal Neighbors Lodge exists
3/5/1903	Democrat	Lodges-MWA	Saratoga, Royal Neighbors of America exists
2/12/1902	Journal	Lodges-MWA	Saratoga, Victoria Camp, No. 2381, RNA, exists
10/31/1975	News-Gazette	Lodges-MWA	Saratoga. MWA Lodge exists
12/16/1908	Journal	Lodges-MWA	Winchester Camp, No. 4680, Royal Neighbors of America exists
9/6/1899	Herald	Lodges-MWA	Winchester Camp, No. 6950, organized on August 30, 1899 by Saratoga Camp, No. 4125
9/6/1899	Journal	Lodges-MWA	Winchester, MWA Camp, No. 6950, organized last Wednesday
3/4/1914	Journal	Lodges-MWA	Winchester, MWA camps are consolidated; S. C. Mendenhall was a member
7/19/1906	Democrat	Lodges-MWA	Winchester, MWA No. 7440 leased Hirsch Building
7/5/1911	Herald	Lodges-MWA	Winchester, MWA remodeled third floor of Hirsch Block
8/30/1899	Herald	Lodges-MWA	Winchester, MWA to be organized on Wednesday evening, August 30, 1899
8/30/1899	Journal	Lodges-MWA	Winchester, MWA will be organized today at K of P Hall
2/12/1914	Democrat	Lodges-MWA	Winchester, No. 6950 merged into No. 7440; meets in Hirsch Block
7/18/1906	Journal	Lodges-MWA	Winchester, Randolph County MWA, No. 7440, organized in Hirsch Building on July 12
1/24/1924	Journal-Herald	Lodges-MWA	Winchester, Royal Neighbors Lodge 4680 exists

Date	Source	Category	Description
1/23/1907	Journal	Lodges-MWA	Winchester, Royal Neighbors Lodge organized
9/26/1912	Democrat	Lodges-Owls	Winchester Owls organize
9/11/1912	Journal	Lodges-Owls	Winchester, Nest of Owls organized in MWA Hall
8/21/1912	Herald	Lodges-Owls	Winchester, Order of Owls being formed
8/12/1914	Journal	Lodges-Owls	Winchester, Owls leased third floor of MWA Hall
9/11/1912	Herald	Lodges-Owls	Winchester, Owls organize in MWA Hall
9/25/1912	Herald	Lodges-Owls	Winchester, Owls organized last Sunday in IORM Hall with 257 members
9/25/1912	Journal	Lodges-Owls	Winchester, Owls organized; officers listed
10/10/1912	Democrat	Lodges-Phi Delta Kappa	Winchester Phi Delta Kappa established
7/17/1895	Journal	Lodges-POSA	Farmland, POSA organized at Farmland, C. W. Paris, p.p.
6/26/1895	Journal	Lodges-POSA	Farmland, POSA will be organized at Farmland next week
7/17/1895	Journal	Lodges-POSA	Lynn, POSA organized at Lynn, Miles J. Furnas, p. p.
6/26/1895	Journal	Lodges-POSA	Lynn, POSA will be organized at Lynn on Friday
9/4/1895	Journal	Lodges-POSA	Parker, POSA organized last Friday
2/12/1896	Herald	Lodges-POSA	Patriotic Order Sons of America has lodges at Lynn, Farmland, Parker, and Ridgeville
8/7/1895	Herald	Lodges-POSA	Patriotic Order Sons of America meeting in Eagle Hall, Richardson Building, Winchester
8/14/1895	Herald	Lodges-POSA	Patriotic Order Sons of America will meet in Red Men's Hall over D. Fudge's Furniture Store, Winchester
5/29/1895	Herald	Lodges-POSA	Winchester, Patriotic Order Sons of America to be organized in K of P Hall on Saturday
6/5/1895	Journal	Lodges-POSA	Winchester, Patriotic Order, Sons of America (POSA) organized
5/29/1895	Journal	Lodges-POSA	Winchester, Patriotic Order, Sons of America will be organized
6/19/1895	Journal	Lodges-POSA	Winchester, POSA described
6/5/1895	Journal	Lodges-POSA	Winchester, POSA organized Saturday
8/21/1895	Journal	Lodges-POSA	Winchester, POSA will meet on third floor of Masonic Block
2/1/1882	Journal	Lodges-Sons of Temperance	Farmland has Sons of Temperance lodge
4/27/1881	Journal	Lodges-Sons of Temperance	Farmland, Sons of Temperance Lodge exists
2/15/1882	Journal	Lodges-Sons of Temperance	Farmland, Sons of Temperance meet in Hewitt Building
2/7/1882	Journal	Lodges-Sons of Temperance	Huntsville, Sons of Temperance
6/13/1867	Journal	Lodges-Sons of Temperance	Huntsville, Sons of Temperance and IOGT exist

Date	Source	Category	Description
4/12/1871	Journal	Lodges-Sons of Temperance	Huntsville, Sons of Temperance Hall is on East State Street
2/7/1882	Journal	Lodges-Sons of Temperance	Huntsville, Sons of Temperance will be organized
7/13/1857	Journal	Lodges-Sons of Temperance	Huntsville, Summit Division, No. 354, Sons of Temperance is nearly seven years old
7/13/1858	Journal	Lodges-Sons of Temperance	Huntsville, Summit Division, No. 354, Sons of Temperance, exists; J. Z. Paschall, Richard Jobes, John Jenkins are among the members
8/9/1871	Journal	Lodges-Sons of Temperance	Randolph Division, Sons of Temperance, in 26th year
1/11/1882	Journal	Lodges-Sons of Temperance	Winchester, Division of Sons of Temperance will be organized this evening
4/25/1867	Journal	Lodges-Sons of Temperance	Winchester, Randolph Division, No. 26, exists
8/7/1945	Journal-Herald	Lodges-VFW	Union City, VFW organized on August 4 in CIO Hall
5/27/1936	News-Democrat	Lodges-VFW	Union City, Zeller Fifer Post No. 2457, VFW, chartered April 10, 1932; exists
6/9/1945	Journal-Herald	Lodges-VFW	Winchester, VFW advertisement to organize
11/15/1962	Journal-Herald	Lodges-VFW	Winchester, VFW exists; moved from South Side of Square to GAR Room in Courthouse
3/31/1932	Journal-Herald	Lodges-VFW	Winchester, VFW to be organized on April 5
8/3/1945	News	Lodges-VFW	Winchester, VFW, No. 1633, will be instituted on August 5
5/13/1909	Democrat	Miscellaneous	"Nigger Holler" referenced
10/27/1897	Herald	Miscellaneous	"Reminiscences of Adams, Jay, and Randolph Counties" is being sold by Women's Relief Corps
1/25/1882	Journal	Miscellaneous	African-Americans, Charles H. Smothers, of Randolph County, is first colored man elected justice of the peace in Indiana
3/22/1871	Journal	Miscellaneous	African-Americans, first colored men serve on jury in Randolph County
3/26/1977	News-Gazette	Miscellaneous	African-Americans, history of in Randolph County
1/25/1882	Journal	Miscellaneous	African-Americans, John Roberts, of Nettle Creek, is first colored man elected township assessor in Indiana
5/5/1880	Journal	Miscellaneous	African-Americans, Randolph County is first county in state to issue a certificate of election to a colored man
5/7/1873	Journal	Miscellaneous	African-Americans, Solomon R. Ward is now constable of Nettle Creek; township already has colored justice of the peace
10/7/1950	Journal-Herald	Miscellaneous	Arba, history

Date	Source	Category	Description
4/23/1952	News	Miscellaneous	Armistice Day photo, November 11, 1918
11/6/1901	Herald	Miscellaneous	Automobile, built by E. R. Hiatt and W. J. Davisson
7/13/1910	Journal	Miscellaneous	Bald eagle, Oron O. Carter shot a bald eagle south of Parker
6/11/1873	Journal	Miscellaneous	Bartonia described
1/24/1894	Journal	Miscellaneous	Basketball first mentioned
10/20/1886	Journal	Miscellaneous	Bear Creek is being straightened
3/27/1889	Journal	Miscellaneous	Beaver Dam Lake in Nettle Creek Township formerly covered 1300 acres; only 1/4 left; mastodon tusks found
7/25/1894	Journal	Miscellaneous	Birchville described; Birch Shellheimer
3/13/1878	Journal	Miscellaneous	Birchville is 3/4 mile northeast of Winchester
1/17/1917	Journal	Miscellaneous	Birth of Nation is showing at Union City
1/16/1918	Journal	Miscellaneous	Blizzard occurred in Randolph County
1/29/1978	News-Gazette	Miscellaneous	Blizzard of 1978 (no paper from January 26-January 28)
2/25/1978	News-Gazette	Miscellaneous	Blizzard of 1978 special section
1/23/1918	Herald	Miscellaneous	Blizzard, terrible blizzard "worst ever"
4/6/1887	Journal	Miscellaneous	Brightsville is the same as Lickskillet
4/21/1886	Journal	Miscellaneous	Brightville is located on the Huntsville-Mount Pleasant Road, near schoolhouse No. 5, near the headwaters of Bear Creek [It was Mull or Lickskillet]
8/19/1891	Journal	Miscellaneous	Brooks Lake being built near Winchester
6/27/1900	Herald	Miscellaneous	Buena Vista and Unionport, history of
7/4/1900	Herald	Miscellaneous	Buena Vista and Unionport, history of, continued
7/11/1900	Herald	Miscellaneous	Buena Vista and Unionport, history of, continued
1/2/1907	Herald	Miscellaneous	Cabin Creek Bog, ghost?
8/22/1960	News	Miscellaneous	Cabin Creek Bog, history of
10/9/1976	News-Gazette	Miscellaneous	Carlos, Bloomingport history
5/3/1882	Journal	Miscellaneous	Carlos, embryo of town on West River-Washington Township line and railroad; don't know if it will be called Coggshellville or Hoovertown
5/10/1882	Journal	Miscellaneous	Carlos, town was originally called "Browne"
9/16/1891	Journal	Miscellaneous	Census figures for 1890
9/16/1891	Herald	Miscellaneous	Census figures for 1890 for county
4/12/1911	Journal	Miscellaneous	Census figures for 1910 for Randolph County
12/8/1960	Journal-Herald	Miscellaneous	Census figures for 1960

Date	Source	Category	Description
8/22/1961	Journal-Herald	Miscellaneous	Census figures for 1960 by town and township
2/6/1971	News-Gazette	Miscellaneous	Census figures for 1970
6/19/1930	Democrat	Miscellaneous	Census figures, Randolph County lost population by 1433 between 1920 and 1930
1/3/1912	Herald	Miscellaneous	Census figures, Randolph County official census statistics for 1910
1/3/1948	Journal-Herald	Miscellaneous	Centennial Farm families listed
2/18/1874	Journal	Miscellaneous	Chapultepec, headquarters of Patrons of Husbandry in east part of White River Township
9/3/1902	Journal	Miscellaneous	Cherry Grove Camp Meeting held for first time
8/28/1982	News-Gazette	Miscellaneous	Circle X, history
5/28/1931	Democrat	Miscellaneous	Civil War veterans at Main Street Christian Church
9/4/1895	Journal	Miscellaneous	Civil War, D. E. Hoffman is carving the monument of the 84th Indiana for Chickamauga Battlefield
1/3/1872	Journal	Miscellaneous	Clark's Station, name changed to Stone Station
8/11/1886	Journal	Miscellaneous	College Corner is 1/2 mile west of White River Township, No. 1 School
7/30/1890	Journal	Miscellaneous	Corners, the, is located one-quarter mile from Elkhorn Valley
6/1/1881	Journal	Miscellaneous	Cotton Wood is two miles south of Possom [sic] Valley
6/1/1881	Journal	Miscellaneous	Cotton Wood Schoolhouse is near Farmland
5/13/1937	Daily News	Miscellaneous	Crow contest at Farmland, photo
6/21/1882	Journal	Miscellaneous	Cyclone hit southern part of Randolph County
6/24/1896	Journal	Miscellaneous	Cyclone struck Ridgeville
3/27/1918	Journal	Miscellaneous	Daylight Saving Time enacted
6/21/1973	News-Gazette	Miscellaneous	Draft Office moved to Richmond
1/11/1911	Journal	Miscellaneous	Drain tile, 1858 drain tile at Bloomingport described
11/3/1965	News	Miscellaneous	Drainage, history of in Randolph County
11/6/1895	Journal	Miscellaneous	Earthquake felt in Winchester
3/8/1882	Journal	Miscellaneous	Explosion at Stone Station
1/30/1913	Democrat	Miscellaneous	Fair Grounds, Old Fairgrounds sold to Fudge
5/6/1885	Journal	Miscellaneous	Fairgrounds, changes at discussed
10/9/1863	Journal	Miscellaneous	Fairgrounds, new
1/29/1913	Herald	Miscellaneous	Fairgrounds, old Fairgrounds sold
5/17/1916	Journal	Miscellaneous	Fairview, history of
1/31/1906	Journal	Miscellaneous	Farmers' Institute officers listed
7/22/1858	Journal	Miscellaneous	Farmland described
12/13/1911	Journal	Miscellaneous	Farmland got electricity on Saturday night

Date	Source	Category	Description
12/13/1911	Herald	Miscellaneous	Farmland now has electricity
1/18/1911	Journal	Miscellaneous	Farmland will probably be electrified
7/6/1922	Democrat	Miscellaneous	Farmland, new fire truck
8/5/1903	Herald	Miscellaneous	Farmland, now a dry town
9/24/1908	Democrat	Miscellaneous	Farmland, plans for electric street lights
11/16/1922	Democrat	Miscellaneous	Farmland, work on the water tower on the old school grounds
6/21/1977	News-Gazette	Miscellaneous	Fire Department insert
2/12/1957	Journal-Herald	Miscellaneous	Fire Numbers are issued in White River Township
9/3/1913	Herald	Miscellaneous	Fire Prevention Day held
10/11/1911	Journal	Miscellaneous	Fire Prevention Day mentioned
7/31/1918	Journal	Miscellaneous	Fire truck, Winchester's new fire truck pictured
1/15/1937	Daily News	Miscellaneous	Flood in Randolph County; bridge near Huffman's Corner was washed out
4/2/1913	Journal	Miscellaneous	Flood of 1913
3/26/1913	Herald	Miscellaneous	Flood, big 1913 flood described
6/26/1918	Journal	Miscellaneous	Frost, severe frost occurred last night; like that of June 1856
9/19/1929	Journal-Herald	Miscellaneous	Fudge Mound is being excavated
8/29/1929	Democrat	Miscellaneous	Fudge Mound is being opened/excavated
12/19/1929	Democrat	Miscellaneous	Fudge Mound relics are being send to the State Historical Bureau
9/19/1929	Democrat	Miscellaneous	Fudge Mound, excavation under the direction of Frank M. Setzler of the University of Chicago; everything is being photographed
3/31/1871	Journal	Miscellaneous	Germans of Winchester celebrated German victory in Europe
6/14/1952	Journal-Herald	Miscellaneous	ghoti=fish; gh as in tough; o as in women; ti as in nation
7/3/1982	News-Gazette	Miscellaneous	Golf, history of in Randolph County
9/15/1932	Journal-Herald	Miscellaneous	Goodrich Park Cabin placed; built by W. W. Moffitt in 1874
6/17/1903	Herald	Miscellaneous	Grasshopperville, name of community near Huntsville
11/27/1968	Journal-Herald	Miscellaneous	Greensfork Township, history of
2/2/1887	Journal	Miscellaneous	Ground Hog's Day, today is
10/12/1887	Herald	Miscellaneous	Harrisville, history of
10/19/1887	Herald	Miscellaneous	Harrisville, history of
10/5/1887	Herald	Miscellaneous	Harrisville, history of
11/9/1887	Herald	Miscellaneous	Harrisville, history of
9/21/1888	Herald	Miscellaneous	Harrisville, history of
9/28/1887	Herald	Miscellaneous	Harrisville, history of
8/24/1887	Journal	Miscellaneous	Hawthorne Regulators reorganized on June 24, 1887

Date	Source	Category	Description
5/26/1880	Journal	Miscellaneous	Hiawatha or Mull has five dwellings, a blacksmith shop, a shoe shop, a saw mill, and a schoolhouse with J. H. Williams as the teacher
10/28/1943	Journal-Herald	Miscellaneous	Highest point in Indiana is in Randolph County
2/26/1896	Herald	Miscellaneous	Highest point in Indiana is in Randolph County, near Bloomingport
6/21/1916	Herald	Miscellaneous	Highest point, Randolph County, highest point in state is located in Randolph County southeast of Arba
12/20/1871	Journal	Miscellaneous	Hinshaw Station, name changed to Snow Hill Station
7/2/1946	Journal-Herald	Miscellaneous	Historical society is needed in county
3/8/1876	Journal	Miscellaneous	History of Randolph County given
10/4/1934	Democrat	Miscellaneous	History of Winchester and Randolph County
1/21/1984	News-Gazette	Miscellaneous	History photos
10/27/1897	Journal	Miscellaneous	History, "Reminiscences of Adams, Jay, and Randolph" described
8/2/1882	Journal	Miscellaneous	History, additional artists, Summer and Berry, are here to sketch for the history book
4/12/1893	Journal	Miscellaneous	History, B. F. Bowen is working on forthcoming county history
2/14/1883	Journal	Miscellaneous	History, county history is being delivered by Captain Kingman
1/24/1883	Journal	Miscellaneous	History, county history is expected in next few days
2/7/1883	Journal	Miscellaneous	History, county history is not here yet
9/20/1882	Journal	Miscellaneous	History, county history men have removed headquarters to Union City
11/15/1899	Journal	Miscellaneous	History, Indianapolis Journal says that Randolph County was named for North Carolina county
5/31/1882	Journal	Miscellaneous	History, Journal supports the new county history book
6/28/1882	Journal	Miscellaneous	History, Mr. F. M. Gilbert, sketching artist for county history, is here; those who want residences to appear should contact Kingman
8/23/1882	Journal	Miscellaneous	History, new county history is thought to be the largest ever published for any county in the state
6/7/1882	Journal	Miscellaneous	History, old courthouse should appear in new county history book
2/1/1893	Journal	Miscellaneous	History, Portrait and Biographical Record of Delaware and Randolph Counties planned
1/12/1887	Journal	Miscellaneous	History, Randolph County in 1840 described
12/13/1882	Journal	Miscellaneous	History, the county history is expected about the holidays

6/14/1882	Journal	Miscellaneous	History, township maps to be examined for correctness for county history book
10/19/1881	Journal	Miscellaneous	History, Tucker requests histories of lodges and other organizations
10/12/1881	Journal	Miscellaneous	History, Tucker's history is near completion
12/1/1880	Journal	Miscellaneous	History, Tucker's history transferred to Kingman Brothers
6/22/1881	Journal	Miscellaneous	History, Tucker's history will soon be ready for distribution
7/19/1882	Journal	Miscellaneous	History, work of illustrating county history is on-going
6/27/1883	Journal	Miscellaneous	Hunt's Cross Roads is located south of Losantville
10/2/1954	Journal-Herald	Miscellaneous	Huntsville Poem
2/20/1895	Journal	Miscellaneous	Huntsville wants telephone line to Modoc
6/4/1968	Journal-Herald	Miscellaneous	Huntsville, history
6/6/1900	Herald	Miscellaneous	Huntsville, history of
6/4/1913	Herald	Miscellaneous	Huntsville, Memorial Day originated in Huntsville
4/18/1900	Herald	Miscellaneous	Huntsville, Memorial Day, history of
2/6/1901	Journal	Miscellaneous	Huntsville, pioneer days described
9/16/1955	News	Miscellaneous	Huntsville, poem
5/22/1962	Journal-Herald	Miscellaneous	Indiana Governor's Mansion from 1919 to 1945 is being razed
4/28/1859	Journal	Miscellaneous	Indiana, Bourbon County will be formed with Russellville as county seat from parts of Parke, Putnam, and Montgomery Counties
10/23/1878	Journal	Miscellaneous	Indians; Skeletons found in Painter's Gravel Bank, Franklin Township
10/16/1918	Herald	Miscellaneous	Influenza closes schools and churches
1/27/1979	News-Gazette	Miscellaneous	Jackson Township history
3/22/1938	Journal-Herald	Miscellaneous	Jay County REMC put up first light pole
5/20/1914	Herald	Miscellaneous	Jones, Bob to hold services in Winchester
12/13/1911	Herald	Miscellaneous	Kabel, Philip plans to write new history of Randolph County with others
12/27/1911	Herald	Miscellaneous	Kabel, Philip will not write new history of Randolph County due to lack of interest
1/3/1883	Journal	Miscellaneous	Lake George, northwest of Farmland between Oak Grove and Rose Hill; George Keever lives there
11/22/1876	Journal	Miscellaneous	Lickskillet is also known as Hiawatha
5/15/1918	Journal	Miscellaneous	Lickskillet, Marion Hubbard is "mayor"; County Treasurer Melville Mull and Assessor James A. White are from that place
3/24/1949	Journal-Herald	Miscellaneous	Lickskillet, story of the name

Date	Source	Category	Description
8/18/1948	News	Miscellaneous	Lion (?) near Lynn
2/3/1859	Journal	Miscellaneous	Losantville described; has Regular Baptist Church and Christian Church; new district schoolhouse erected with township funds
10/16/1901	Journal	Miscellaneous	Losantville featured
9/15/1960	Journal-Herald	Miscellaneous	Losantville, name of town is officially changed from Bronson
2/7/1912	Herald	Miscellaneous	Losantville, origins
10/2/1942	Journal-Herald	Miscellaneous	Lynn Civil War Cannon to scrap drive
11/13/1901	Herald	Miscellaneous	Lynn featured
2/28/1912	Herald	Miscellaneous	Lynn to get electricity
4/23/1902	Herald	Miscellaneous	Lynn, citizens fought a pool hall at Lynn, among them were Miles Furnas, Henry Pickett, and Isaac Furnas
8/11/1886	Herald	Miscellaneous	Lynn's oldest settlers
11/16/1898	Journal	Miscellaneous	Maps, new township map of county is being printed by the surveyor's office for the first time in nearly twenty years
6/8/1977	News-Gazette	Miscellaneous	Mardi Gras, history of, started in 1947
6/29/1881	Journal	Miscellaneous	Masesville is one mile west of Emmettsville
11/6/1895	Journal	Miscellaneous	Mastodon at Earlham College, most of it from Randolph County; also the Earlham College beaver came from Randolph County
10/10/1888	Journal	Miscellaneous	Mastodon skeleton found on farm of William Bookout
10/20/1897	Journal	Miscellaneous	Mastodon tusks found on Fudge Farm, west of Winchester
9/11/1889	Journal	Miscellaneous	Mastodon, remains of another one found; this one on Larkin Howe Farm
3/27/1912	Herald	Miscellaneous	Maxville Dam washed away
3/28/1912	Democrat	Miscellaneous	Maxville Dam washed away
9/20/1871	Journal	Miscellaneous	Maxville is named for Robinson McIntire
3/7/1917	Journal	Miscellaneous	Mexican Conflict, Company F, 2nd Indiana returned from the Mexican Border
4/26/1882	Journal	Miscellaneous	Mexico is west of Farmland
9/9/1903	Herald	Miscellaneous	Modoc featured
12/5/1946	Journal-Herald	Miscellaneous	Modoc War Memorial to be dedicated on December 8, 1946
11/19/1903	Democrat	Miscellaneous	Modoc was named after "Modoc Bitters"; has K of P, IOOF, GAR, WRC, Pocahontas, Rebeccas, Eagles, Rathbone Sisters
6/18/1968	Journal-Herald	Miscellaneous	Modoc's name came from "Modoc Bitters," not cigars

Date	Source	Category	Description
4/3/1984	News-Gazette	Miscellaneous	Monroe Central tornado of 1974 remembered
5/17/1980	News-Gazette	Miscellaneous	Mound Builders of Randolph County
9/3/1902	Herald	Miscellaneous	Name, Randolph County, Geographer of U. S. Geological Survey says that Randolph County is named for Thomas Randolph
9/3/1902	Journal	Miscellaneous	Name, Randolph County, Henry Garrett of the U. S. Geological Survey says it was named for Thomas Randolph
10/22/1913	Herald	Miscellaneous	National Guard, history of Company F, IVI
6/19/1895	Journal	Miscellaneous	Native Americans, Lynn Mound is a burial ground
10/24/1894	Journal	Miscellaneous	Native Americans, skeletons unearthed west of Lynn
4/23/1913	Journal	Miscellaneous	Neff, all buildings at Neff (house and barn) destroyed by fire last Friday
5/21/1873	Journal	Miscellaneous	New Dayton, described
4/26/1947	Journal-Herald	Miscellaneous	New Dayton, identification of historic photograph
7/27/1960	News	Miscellaneous	Nixon, Richard, photo with Herbert Hoover
4/7/1875	Journal	Miscellaneous	Olive Branch has church of various denominations, schoolhouse with William Dail as teacher, and Masonic Lodge
5/13/1948	Journal-Herald	Miscellaneous	Orphan's Home is "run by Quaker Church"
11/27/1962	Journal-Herald	Miscellaneous	Orphan's Home, Moorman heirs claim property
3/10/1961	News	Miscellaneous	Orphan's Home, Moorman, is only privately-owned orphanage in the state; in trouble
5/23/1906	Herald	Miscellaneous	Parker featured
11/10/1971	News-Gazette	Miscellaneous	Parker history
3/14/1894	Herald	Miscellaneous	Parker is now a city with Winchester and Union City (?)
2/5/1913	Journal	Miscellaneous	Parker now has electricity; every town has it except Saratoga, which has contracted for it, and three towns in the southwest part of the county
4/21/1972	News-Gazette	Miscellaneous	Parker Reservoir and Maxville
4/29/1972	News-Gazette	Miscellaneous	Parker Reservoir and Windsor
4/8/1972	News-Gazette	Miscellaneous	Parker Reservoir map
2/20/1975	News-Gazette	Miscellaneous	Parker Reservoir not authorized to be built
1/12/1972	News-Gazette	Miscellaneous	Parker Reservoir planned
1/21/1975	News-Gazette	Miscellaneous	Parker, name of town is changed to Parker City by town board
11/13/1976	News-Gazette	Miscellaneous	Parker, photos and history
7/6/1957	Journal-Herald	Miscellaneous	Photos, historic

Date	Paper	Category	Description
9/20/1968	Journal-Herald	Miscellaneous	Photos, old
2/6/1901	Herald	Miscellaneous	Pioneers described
6/25/1931	Democrat	Miscellaneous	Plat book, free with subscription to the Winchester Democrat
3/9/1892	Journal	Miscellaneous	Poleville is one and a half miles east of Martindale
3/29/1893	Herald	Miscellaneous	Portrait and Biographical Record of Delaware and Randolph Counties planned
11/8/1893	Herald	Miscellaneous	Portrait and Biographical Record of Delaware and Randolph Counties will be ready in February
5/4/1881	Journal	Miscellaneous	Possum Valley is 2.5 miles southeast of Fairview
1/31/1912	Herald	Miscellaneous	Queer names in Winchester directory
3/19/1959	Journal-Herald	Miscellaneous	Randolph County 1877 Directory mentioned
6/29/1950	Journal-Herald	Miscellaneous	Randolph County census figures: 1940-26,766; 1950-27,157
12/6/1911	Journal	Miscellaneous	Randolph County Directory by Masslick is now in the hands of the printer
3/12/1908	Democrat	Miscellaneous	Randolph County Directory is being completed
1/18/1912	Democrat	Miscellaneous	Randolph County Directory published by Commercial Directory Company of Marion, cost $4
1/17/1912	Journal	Miscellaneous	Randolph County Directory, H. B. Masslich, president of Commercial Directory Company of Marion, released directory for 1912-13
1/2/1963	News	Miscellaneous	Randolph County has 68 license plate prefix
8/28/1901	Journal	Miscellaneous	Randolph County Historical Society is organized on August 24 with C. W. Paris, President, D. W. Lawrence, Secretary, George E. Addington, Vice-President, and Phillip Kabel, Treasurer
6/20/1906	Journal	Miscellaneous	Randolph County Historical Society, letter from D. W. Lawrence bemoans demise of
10/4/1934	Democrat	Miscellaneous	Randolph County history
5/7/1913	Journal	Miscellaneous	Randolph County History by Smith and Driver first mentioned
3/8/1876	Journal	Miscellaneous	Randolph County history in newspaper
9/16/1914	Journal	Miscellaneous	Randolph County History, arrival of Smith and Driver's history book
8/16/1913	Journal	Miscellaneous	Randolph County history, being written
9/23/1914	Journal	Miscellaneous	Randolph County History, Killdeer Paradise Items criticizes Smith and Driver's history; discusses mills
12/6/1911	Journal	Miscellaneous	Randolph County history, Philip Kabel plans to write a new history

Date	Source	Category	Description
4/19/1911	Journal	Miscellaneous	Randolph County is focus of April IUT Magazine
8/7/1918	Herald	Miscellaneous	Randolph County is one hundred years old this week
10/31/1968	Journal-Herald	Miscellaneous	Randolph County poem
8/17/1968	Journal-Herald	Miscellaneous	Randolph County Sesquicentennial Edition
3/20/1968	News	Miscellaneous	Randolph County Sesquicentennial emblems
8/19/1968	Journal-Herald	Miscellaneous	Randolph County Sesquicentennial history
3/10/1939	Journal-Herald	Miscellaneous	Randolph County was first in state to use drain tile (1856) and to have a silo (near Lynn)
2/1/1938	Journal-Herald	Miscellaneous	Randolph County Young People's Contest, 14th anniversary
2/23/1910	Herald	Miscellaneous	Randolph County, new atlas of
3/18/1908	Herald	Miscellaneous	Randolph County, new directory
5/13/1908	Herald	Miscellaneous	Randolph County, new directory is completed
10/22/1919	Journal	Miscellaneous	Randolph County, poem about
9/5/1894	Herald	Miscellaneous	Reunion of Co. A, 84th IVI at Mills Lake
9/10/1938	Journal-Herald	Miscellaneous	Revolutionary Soldiers
11/16/1906	Herald	Miscellaneous	Ridgeville dam dynamited
11/15/1906	Democrat	Miscellaneous	Ridgeville Dam is blown
8/28/1913	Democrat	Miscellaneous	Ridgeville Dam replaced
10/2/1901	Journal	Miscellaneous	Ridgeville featured
5/31/1911	Herald	Miscellaneous	Ridgeville Fire Department organized
7/1/1903	Herald	Miscellaneous	Ridgeville Soldiers Monument dedicated on Thursday, June 25, 1903
7/2/1903	Democrat	Miscellaneous	Ridgeville Soldiers Monument dedicated recently
6/24/1903	Journal	Miscellaneous	Ridgeville soldier's monument will be unveiled on June 25, 1903
1/2/1913	Democrat	Miscellaneous	Ridgeville to get electricity; Winchester furnishes electricity to Union City, Lynn, Farmland, and Saratoga
6/21/1916	Journal	Miscellaneous	Ridgeville, history of
8/21/1895	Herald	Miscellaneous	Ridgeville, story of Lake Pequannah and new dam
4/28/1875	Journal	Miscellaneous	Rome, a village four miles north of Farmland
1/10/1917	Journal	Miscellaneous	Round Top is located six miles northwest of Winchester; once had round top log cabins
12/20/1911	Journal	Miscellaneous	Sampletown described in old assessor's book; the center of the town was the brick house occupied by Charles Johnson
7/25/1975	News-Gazette	Miscellaneous	Saratoga, centennial section

Date	Source	Category	Description
2/23/1955	News	Miscellaneous	Saratoga, history of
1/27/1886	Journal	Miscellaneous	Shacklingsburg is 1.5 miles south of Maxville
2/24/1904	Herald	Miscellaneous	Shady Side is community near Hopewell M. P. Church
5/7/1913	Herald	Miscellaneous	Smith and Driver's county history book planned
5/8/1913	Democrat	Miscellaneous	Smith and Driver's county history book planned
8/7/1913	Democrat	Miscellaneous	Smith and Driver's county history is a "centennial history" of Randolph County
8/6/1913	Journal	Miscellaneous	Smith and Driver's History of Randolph County, plans for
7/29/1955	News	Miscellaneous	Snow Hill photograph
4/9/1919	Journal	Miscellaneous	Socum was the name of settlement at the Mississinewa Bridge on Mt. Holly Road by Clough Farm
10/29/1879	Journal	Miscellaneous	Soldiers' Monument Association, advertisement
6/26/1878	Journal	Miscellaneous	Sooner Town is one mile north and one mile east of Buena Vista
4/27/1898	Journal	Miscellaneous	Spanish-American War declared
4/27/1898	Herald	Miscellaneous	Spanish-American War, enlistees
8/18/1965	News	Miscellaneous	Spanish-American War, last veteran in Randolph County dies
11/26/1903	Democrat	Miscellaneous	Spartanburg is center of 1900 U. S. population according; Indianapolis News says "the country is settled largely by Quakers"
6/13/1900	Herald	Miscellaneous	Spartanburg, history of
9/25/1901	Journal	Miscellaneous	Spartanburg, history of
6/13/1900	Herald	Miscellaneous	Spartanburg, history of continued
10/18/1871	Journal	Miscellaneous	State nicknames listed
4/10/1918	Journal	Miscellaneous	State Normal School, new school at Muncie
3/26/1890	Journal	Miscellaneous	Stone Station, explosion at
3/26/1890	Herald	Miscellaneous	Stone Station, explosion near
10/13/1907	Journal	Miscellaneous	Stoney Creek Township, Lee L. Driver says official records spell it "Stoney Creek"
10/18/1969	Journal-Herald	Miscellaneous	Stringtown, Short Street in Winchester from city limits to 100 E
1/26/1916	Herald	Miscellaneous	Tax receipt, old, William Reece was county treasurer in 1844
2/16/1916	Herald	Miscellaneous	Tax receipts, old, 1836, T. W. Coats, treasurer of Randolph County; 1839, William Kizer, treasurer of Randolph County
4/13/1898	Herald	Miscellaneous	Taxpayers, large taxpayers mentioned
7/2/1884	Journal	Miscellaneous	Taxpayers, list of "heavy taxpayers"
7/9/1884	Journal	Miscellaneous	Taxpayers, list of "heavy taxpayers"

Date	Publication	Category	Description
3/28/1883	Journal	Miscellaneous	Telephones are being installed in Randolph County; some were installed last year
6/10/1874	Journal	Miscellaneous	Temperance Convention
4/1/1874	Journal	Miscellaneous	Temperance, Ladies Temperance League of Winchester is active
4/1/1874	Journal	Miscellaneous	Temperance, Losantville, ladies closed saloon
3/25/1874	Journal	Miscellaneous	Temperance, Winchester, ladies crusade described
7/8/1936	News-Democrat	Miscellaneous	Temperature reached 108 degrees in Randolph County
4/30/1879	Journal	Miscellaneous	Timothy Crossing is located near Rural
6/4/1879	Journal	Miscellaneous	Timothy Crossing is three miles south of Winchester on the Pike
2/15/1936	News-Democrat	Miscellaneous	Toilets, many outside toilets were being rebuilt by the WPA
6/23/1897	Journal	Miscellaneous	Tornado hit Randolph County, Profs. Baker and Driver were caught in it on a train
3/12/1956	News	Miscellaneous	Towns, how they acquired their names, including Lickskillet
10/14/1903	Journal	Miscellaneous	Underground Railroad, described in letter from Daniel Lawrence
12/9/1908	Herald	Miscellaneous	Underground Railroad, house west of Winchester razed; may have been UGRR station
8/12/1914	Journal	Miscellaneous	Underground Railroad, Reverdy Puckett's father, Levi, hid slaves in a cave
2/11/1903	Journal	Miscellaneous	Underground Railroad, serial story started
9/6/1974	News-Gazette	Miscellaneous	Union City Quasquicentennial Edition
7/2/1977	News-Gazette	Miscellaneous	Ward Township Fire Department history
3/14/1957	Journal-Herald	Miscellaneous	Ward Township Volunteer Fire Department; history of; organized on January 1, 1956
3/8/1905	Herald	Miscellaneous	Washington Township, history of
6/8/1881	Journal	Miscellaneous	White Oak is two miles north and one mile east of Farmland
12/16/1952	Journal-Herald	Miscellaneous	White River Fire Department, first run
8/27/1903	Democrat	Miscellaneous	Winchester as Blodgett of the Indianapolis News saw it
11/20/1912	Herald	Miscellaneous	Winchester census; foreign born countries listed
8/14/1901	Journal	Miscellaneous	Winchester City Directory is inaccurate
5/30/1906	Journal	Miscellaneous	Winchester City Directory published by Captain Nelson Pegg
5/31/1906	Democrat	Miscellaneous	Winchester City Directory published by Captain Nelson Pegg
6/6/1906	Journal	Miscellaneous	Winchester city directory published by Nelson Pegg, L. H. Harris, and Oscar Jones

Date	Source	Category	Description
5/28/1983	News-Gazette	Miscellaneous	Winchester Fire Department, history of
6/4/1983	News-Gazette	Miscellaneous	Winchester Fire Department, history of
5/2/1911	Herald	Miscellaneous	Winchester firemen, photo composite
4/17/1944	News	Miscellaneous	Winchester history (photo)
7/17/1907	Herald	Miscellaneous	Winchester in 2007; predictions
4/7/1909	Herald	Miscellaneous	Winchester is getting house numbers
2/3/1972	News-Gazette	Miscellaneous	Winchester is something else [advertising insert]
3/24/1915	Herald	Miscellaneous	Winchester names in telephone directory
11/15/1975	News-Gazette	Miscellaneous	Winchester parks, history of
11/17/1975	News-Gazette	Miscellaneous	Winchester parks, history of
11/18/1975	News-Gazette	Miscellaneous	Winchester parks, history of
11/19/1975	News-Gazette	Miscellaneous	Winchester parks, history of
1/18/1949	Journal-Herald	Miscellaneous	Winchester Rural Routes decreased from eleven to eight in 1918 then to four in 1933
7/28/1939	Journal-Herald	Miscellaneous	Winchester South Side Park opens
2/17/1915	Herald	Miscellaneous	Winchester Tile Dir., names in
2/2/1887	Herald	Miscellaneous	Winchester twenty years ago and now
3/13/1889	Journal	Miscellaneous	Winchester will get electric street lights
3/8/1871	Journal	Miscellaneous	Winchester, "Goose Pasture" is that part of town lying east of Main Street [?]
8/20/1955	Journal-Herald	Miscellaneous	Winchester, "Island" and "Quaker Hill" sections
11/23/1904	Herald	Miscellaneous	Winchester, "Smoky Row" is southwest part of Winchester
3/5/1931	Democrat	Miscellaneous	Winchester, Central States Directory is planned
8/11/1915	Herald	Miscellaneous	Winchester, Goodrich Park donated to city
3/11/1978	News-Gazette	Miscellaneous	Winchester, history of elec. in Winchester
5/30/1906	Herald	Miscellaneous	Winchester, new city directory issued
3/24/1955	Journal-Herald	Miscellaneous	Winchester, new water tower
8/5/1954	Journal-Herald	Miscellaneous	Winchester, northeast section was called "Island," southeast section was called "Quaker Hill"
11/4/1903	Herald	Miscellaneous	Winchester, old timer's letter about Winchester in 1834
7/25/1883	Journal	Miscellaneous	Winchester, Quaker Hill area is Cheney and Watson's Addition, east of Salt Creek
2/28/1918	Democrat	Miscellaneous	Winchester, reminiscences of early days
10/7/1908	Herald	Miscellaneous	Winchester, what Winchester has: lodges, churches, etc.

Date	Publication	Category	Description
6/3/1972	News-Gazette	Miscellaneous	Winchester, Where else but Winchester [advertising]
9/17/1873	Journal	Miscellaneous	Windsor described
6/19/1907	Herald	Miscellaneous	Windsor, history
10/28/1920	Democrat	Miscellaneous	Women, first women served on juries in Randolph County; Olynthus Cox, jury commissioner
11/3/1875	Journal	Miscellaneous	Women's suffrage convention will be held in Winchester on November 23 and 24
10/7/1983	News-Gazette	Miscellaneous	Youth Explosion '83
3/8/1984	News-Gazette	Miscellaneous	Youth Explosion, mentions Kim Mills, pastor of Bear Creek Friends Church
2/8/1954	Journal-Herald	Newspapers	Attempt to establish a Republican newspaper on February 9
5/26/1911	Democrat	Newspapers	Democrat, published in Diggs Block by C. K. Rockwell
8/26/1981	News-Gazette	Newspapers	Famous Front Pages
9/22/1880	Journal	Newspapers	Farmland Campaigner is new newspaper
7/13/1904	Herald	Newspapers	Farmland Enterprise sold to Batchelor and W. T. Davis
5/9/1888	Journal	Newspapers	Farmland Enterprise, Clint West purchased the Farmland Times and renamed it the Farmland Enterprise
4/22/1908	Journal	Newspapers	Farmland Enterprise, Editor Harris goes to Pierceton; Joe F. Ferry will take over
4/24/1907	Journal	Newspapers	Farmland Enterprise, Henry F. Harris purchases paper from Penery, who will continue with the Losantville Journal
6/10/1908	Journal	Newspapers	Farmland Enterprise, I. C. Penery repurchased
7/13/1904	Journal	Newspapers	Farmland Enterprise, J. O. Batchelor and W. T. Davis purchased
3/20/1918	Herald	Newspapers	Farmland Enterprise, Roy R. Webster purchased
3/13/1918	Journal	Newspapers	Farmland Enterprise, Roy Webster replaces I. C. Penery as editor
5/8/1878	Journal	Newspapers	Farmland News established this week
3/12/1879	Journal	Newspapers	Farmland Press died on March 6, 1879
5/15/1878	Journal	Newspapers	Farmland Press established by C. M. White
5/15/1878	Journal	Newspapers	Farmland Press established by C. M. White; seventh newspaper in Randolph County
10/23/1878	Journal	Newspapers	Farmland Press is printed on press of old Winchester Gazette
4/18/1906	Herald	Newspapers	Farmland Reporter established by Fred C. West, son of W. C. West
4/18/1906	Journal	Newspapers	Farmland Reporter established by Fred West
3/10/1909	Herald	Newspapers	Farmland Reporter, W. C. West died

Date	Type	Category	Description
3/14/1888	Journal	Newspapers	Farmland Times folded
8/19/1885	Journal	Newspapers	Farmland Times will be edited by Manor and Barnell of Muncie
11/19/1947	News	Newspapers	Farmland, Randolph County Enterprise sold
4/2/1925	Democrat	Newspapers	Farmland, Randolph County Enterprise sold by Penery to Bolich and Webster
1/6/1909	Journal	Newspapers	Farmland, Randolph County Enterprise transferred to the Enterprise Printing Company under I. C. Penery
8/8/1906	Journal	Newspapers	Four County Enterprise established by I. C. Penery at Losantville
4/6/1934	Journal-Herald	Newspapers	Gazette Publishing Company buys Hub City Gazette and makes it a daily, Democrat paper
6/1/1962	News	Newspapers	Gazette Publishing Company, Jerry Davis resigns as editor of all papers
6/10/1938	Journal-Herald	Newspapers	Journal-Herald Company, John W. Macy sold interest
1/3/1939	Journal-Herald	Newspapers	Journal-Herald Company, Nate Mendenhall is president
12/11/1962	Journal-Herald	Newspapers	Journal-Herald Corporation, John E. Bales, president
2/1/1947	Journal-Herald	Newspapers	Journal-Herald Corporation, Meeks Cockerill is president
2/24/1951	Journal-Herald	Newspapers	Journal-Herald Corporation, Meeks Cockerill is president
3/28/1953	Journal-Herald	Newspapers	Journal-Herald Corporation, Meeks Cockerill is president
3/24/1954	News	Newspapers	Journal-Herald Corporation, Meeks Cockerill reelected president
6/15/1938	Journal-Herald	Newspapers	Journal-Herald Corporation, Nate Mendenhall is new president
10/2/1934	Journal-Herald	Newspapers	Journal-Herald editor I. M. Bridgman died October 1
7/14/1933	Journal-Herald	Newspapers	Journal-Herald is already being printed twice a week
9/8/1941	Journal-Herald	Newspapers	Journal-Herald returns being a morning newspaper
2/26/1937	Journal-Herald	Newspapers	Journal-Herald sold to Journal-Herald Corporation, Robert M. Kist, editor
3/23/1946	Journal-Herald	Newspapers	Journal-Herald, "Observations" re-established by Bob Kist, "Randolph County still Republican"
12/23/1937	Journal-Herald	Newspapers	Journal-Herald, J. W. Macy is president of corporation; it was a daily
8/4/1954	News	Newspapers	Kist, A. A., co-publisher of Union City Times-Gazette and Winchester News, died August 3
11/17/1915	Herald	Newspapers	Losantville Independent exists
12/10/1913	Journal	Newspapers	Losantville Independent, an independent paper, is edited by F. G. Finch and published by I. C. Penery

Date	Paper	Category	Description
10/9/1901	Journal	Newspapers	Losantville Journal has been established by Rush Deardorff
4/6/1904	Journal	Newspapers	Losantville Journal sold by Eph Ruth to Losantville Journal Company
6/27/1906	Journal	Newspapers	Losantville Journal sold to I. C. Penery by Dr. Oderkirk [Penery made it the Four County Enterprise]
10/9/1901	Herald	Newspapers	Losantville Journal, edited and published by R. E. Deardoff
9/28/1904	Journal	Newspapers	Losantville Journal, G. H. Oderkirk, publisher
7/11/1906	Herald	Newspapers	Losantville Journal, I. C. Penery purchases
4/6/1904	Herald	Newspapers	Losantville Journal, sold by Eph Ruth after one year to the Losantville Journal Company
9/13/1899	Journal	Newspapers	Losantville News, O. T. Kendall replaces Mr. Templin as editor
3/19/1908	Democrat	Newspapers	Losantville, Four County Enterprise has been sold; plant will be moved to Lewisville
3/18/1908	Journal	Newspapers	Losantville, Four County Enterprise moved to Lewisville
8/8/1906	Journal	Newspapers	Losantville, Four County Enterprise, volume I issued by I. C. Penery
4/5/1899	Journal	Newspapers	Losantville, Tri County News established by F. Clyde Templin
5/24/1899	Herald	Newspapers	Losantville, Tri County News exists
6/7/1899	Journal	Newspapers	Losantville, Tri County News, Clyde Templin, editor
9/12/1912	Democrat	Newspapers	Lynn Herald and Farmland Enterprise lean toward Bull Moose Progressivism
2/26/1952	Journal-Herald	Newspapers	Lynn Herald changed to Randolph County Herald by Joe Hamilton
11/16/1898	Journal	Newspapers	Lynn Herald established
5/3/1905	Journal	Newspapers	Lynn Herald moved to new building
8/9/1916	Herald	Newspapers	Lynn Herald moves into new cement block building
9/8/1943	News	Newspapers	Lynn Herald sold by Virgil Creek after eleven years to Joe Hamilton
6/7/1899	Journal	Newspapers	Lynn Herald souvenir edition issued last week
2/25/1920	Herald	Newspapers	Lynn Herald, Eber Brown purchased from Frank Wright
7/27/1898	Herald	Newspapers	Lynn Herald, owned by O. R. and R. C. Hamilton, discontinued after volume 6, No. 41 to move to a larger town
5/14/1902	Herald	Newspapers	Lynn Herald, owned by S. L. Light and Frank Wright
3/4/1903	Journal	Newspapers	Lynn Herald, S. H. Light sold the paper to Frank Wright after nearly five years
4/30/1902	Herald	Newspapers	Lynn Herald, S. L. Light sold 1/2 interest to Frank Wright
6/7/1899	Herald	Newspapers	Lynn Herald, souvenir edition published

Date	Type	Category	Description
10/3/1883	Journal	Newspapers	Lynn Observer established last week
4/8/1885	Journal	Newspapers	Lynn Observer is a thing of the past; Jim moved to Union City, Ohio to establish a Democratic newspaper; he was a Republican here
1/11/1893	Journal	Newspapers	Lynn Observer is three months old
7/27/1898	Journal	Newspapers	Lynn Tribune failed; Hamiltons moved press to Carlisle, Ohio
8/28/1895	Journal	Newspapers	Lynn Tribune sold to J. M. Hamilton
10/26/1892	Journal	Newspapers	Lynn Tribune was established last Friday; C. E. Ward, editor
8/29/1883	Journal	Newspapers	Lynn will get the former Red Rey [sic] Observer
11/9/1898	Journal	Newspapers	Lynn, Mr. Light is new printer
8/14/1889	Journal	Newspapers	Lynn, new newspaper
3/6/1953	News	Newspapers	Lynn, Randolph County Herald sold to Kist and Buckmaster
2/28/1912	Herald	Newspapers	Modoc Herald, Drollinger will move to Bryant; plant will not be rebuilt [was it Tribune or Herald?]
1/31/1912	Herald	Newspapers	Modoc Tribune, plant burns; Harry L. Drollinger, publisher
5/15/1976	News-Gazette	Newspapers	New-Gazette Saturday Extra issued for first time
9/8/1973	News-Gazette	Newspapers	New-Gazette will move from 119 E. North St. to 224 W. Franklin; moved in 1963 from 117 N. Meridian; Union City Office moved in 1973 from 236 to 232 W. Pearl St.
3/9/1974	News-Gazette	Newspapers	New-Gazette, A. M. Gibbons resigned as editor
11/13/1976	News-Gazette	Newspapers	News and Journal-Herald press moved from old Journal-Herald Building to East North Street in 1963, then to 224 W. Franklin in December 1975
9/13/1979	News-Gazette	Newspapers	News-Gazette and Journal-Herald continued to appear on advertising into the 1980s, but not on banner after 1976
6/29/1976	News-Gazette	Newspapers	News-Gazette Bicentennial Edition
3/7/1973	News-Gazette	Newspapers	News-Gazette has multiple editors; Janet Fuller is city editor
1/3/1974	News-Gazette	Newspapers	News-Gazette moved to 224 W. Franklin St.
5/31/1968	News	Newspapers	News-Gazette will be established on July 1; the Union City office will remain at 236 W. Pearl
2/26/1972	News-Gazette	Newspapers	News-Gazette, Christen P. Heide is new managing editor
9/29/1972	News-Gazette	Newspapers	News-Gazette, Christen P. Heide resigns as editor
11/13/1976	News-Gazette	Newspapers	News-Gazette, history of, Jerry Collins, editor
8/30/1977	News-Gazette	Newspapers	News-Gazette, Janet Fuller named editor

Date	Source	Category	Description
4/16/1974	News-Gazette	Newspapers	News-Gazette, Jerry Collins is appointed news editor
8/17/1977	News-Gazette	Newspapers	News-Gazette, Richard Wise, editor and publisher
1/5/1984	News-Gazette	Newspapers	News-Gazette, Richard Wise, editor and publisher
1/10/1917	Journal	Newspapers	Old newspapers in Randolph County discussed
10/24/1894	Herald	Newspapers	Parker City News, edited by J. B. McKinney; Parker City Times, edited by Mr. Canady; Press, edited by Mr. Harris; Winchester Democrat reestablished by Mr. Fawcet of LaGrange
9/29/1897	Journal	Newspapers	Parker City Times, Bert Canady, editor
2/2/1898	Journal	Newspapers	Parker City Times, E. N. Canaday, editor
10/24/1894	Journal	Newspapers	Parker City Times, under Canaday Publishing Company, established this week; A. D. McKinney, publisher; E. N. Canady established paper
7/12/1893	Journal	Newspapers	Parker News established by C. L. Reed as editor
4/11/1894	Journal	Newspapers	Parker News folded; equipment moved to Redkey
5/2/1894	Journal	Newspapers	Parker News revived
7/26/1893	Herald	Newspapers	Parker News, published in former Stone church
4/19/1899	Journal	Newspapers	Parker Review established by Hall and Ashcraft
3/21/1921	Democrat	Newspapers	Parker Review is reestablished after lapsing for over a year by McNutt; the old editor, Mr. Ashcraft, had died
2/16/1922	Democrat	Newspapers	Parker Review is sold by E. F. McNutt to Frank J. Barron
11/22/1923	Journal-Herald	Newspapers	Parker Review suspended
10/22/1925	Journal-Herald	Newspapers	Parker Review suspended, Poe Trinkle, publisher
9/3/1902	Journal	Newspapers	Parker Review, Ashcraft is editor
4/19/1899	Herald	Newspapers	Parker Review, first issue, published by Hall and Ashcraft
2/27/1901	Journal	Newspapers	Parker Review, O. M. Hall sold his share to E. L. Ashcraft, who will continue
2/2/1898	Herald	Newspapers	Parker Times, building burned
5/8/1936	Journal-Herald	Newspapers	Portland case results in new Democrat newspaper in Randolph County
2/22/1899	Journal	Newspapers	Randolph County Christian established; J. R. Cortner, editor
2/1/1899	Herald	Newspapers	Randolph County Christian; first issue coming in a few weeks
11/30/1898	Herald	Newspapers	Randolph County Christian; semi-monthly newspaper started by New Light Christians

Date	Paper	Category	Description
2/25/1961	Journal-Herald	Newspapers	Randolph County Historical Review established
5/22/1907	Herald	Newspapers	Randolph County Republican editors listed
4/22/1885	Journal	Newspapers	Ridgeville Banner has been consolidated into the Winchester Democrat
4/22/1885	Journal	Newspapers	Ridgeville Banner will be removed to Winchester and consolidated with the defunct Democrat to establish a new Democrat paper about May 1
11/10/1886	Journal	Newspapers	Ridgeville Enterprise discontinued; moved to Portland
5/14/1879	Journal	Newspapers	Ridgeville Enterprise established
8/18/1886	Journal	Newspapers	Ridgeville Enterprise exists
11/17/1886	Herald	Newspapers	Ridgeville Enterprise suspends
2/27/1889	Herald	Newspapers	Ridgeville has two newspapers, published by C. C. Lyons and Day Brothers
11/16/1881	Journal	Newspapers	Ridgeville Leader established
10/31/1883	Journal	Newspapers	Ridgeville Leader is two years old
11/21/1883	Journal	Newspapers	Ridgeville Leader will be Democratic paper
1/23/1884	Journal	Newspapers	Ridgeville Leader will remove to Winchester
2/26/1924	Democrat	Newspapers	Ridgeville News changed to "Randolph County News"
6/6/1877	Journal	Newspapers	Ridgeville News established by W. H. Richardson
12/27/1900	Democrat	Newspapers	Ridgeville News has been purchased by J. C. Stanley from Britt and Nelson
6/8/1892	Herald	Newspapers	Ridgeville News has Mugwump editor
11/13/1901	Journal	Newspapers	Ridgeville News moved to new home
2/1/1900	Democrat	Newspapers	Ridgeville News sold
5/8/1895	Journal	Newspapers	Ridgeville News was sold by Oscar A. White to W. W. Weaver
4/5/1899	Journal	Newspapers	Ridgeville News, Devor is editor
10/2/1895	Journal	Newspapers	Ridgeville News, F. L. Kendell replaces W. W. Weaver as publisher
5/20/1920	Democrat	Newspapers	Ridgeville News, Fred Baker reestablishes the paper
12/26/1900	Journal	Newspapers	Ridgeville News, J. G. Stanley replaces Jacob Britt as editor
6/12/1912	Journal	Newspapers	Ridgeville News, James G. Stanley has leased the paper to Charles M. Trader and the Union City Eagle to Don Ward
4/14/1909	Herald	Newspapers	Ridgeville News, Omar Peelle replaces James Stanley as editor; Stanley moved to Union City
8/25/1909	Herald	Newspapers	Ridgeville News, Omar Peelle resigns as manager

Date	Source	Category	Description
10/2/18895	Journal	Newspapers	Ridgeville News, sold by M. M. Weaver to F. L. Kendell
10/2/1919	Democrat	Newspapers	Ridgeville News, Stanley sold out to William P. Cuppy
5/24/1906	Democrat	Newspapers	Ridgeville News, Stanley, editor
2/17/1897	Journal	Newspapers	Ridgeville News, T. A. Devor replaces F. L. Kendall
2/17/1897	Herald	Newspapers	Ridgeville News, T. A. Devor took over from F. L. Taylor
4/1/1920	Democrat	Newspapers	Ridgeville News, under Stanley, may be discontinued
5/8/1895	Journal	Newspapers	Ridgeville News, W. W. Weaver replaces Oscar A. White as editor
9/22/1880	Journal	Newspapers	Ridgeville Rambler is new newspaper
6/18/1902	Journal	Newspapers	Ridgeville Record established by Earl Coble
9/30/1903	Journal	Newspapers	Ridgeville Record sold
9/24/1903	Democrat	Newspapers	Ridgeville Record, Earl Coble sold the paper to "Decatur people"
7/9/1903	Democrat	Newspapers	Ridgeville Record, Earl Coble, editor
7/29/1903	Herald	Newspapers	Ridgeville Record, Earl Coble, editor
6/18/1902	Herald	Newspapers	Ridgeville Record, established recently by Earl Coble
10/22/1879	Journal	Newspapers	Ridgeville Register ceased publication
8/7/1878	Journal	Newspapers	Ridgeville Register exists
12/4/1878	Journal	Newspapers	Ridgeville Register has moved to Crown Point
3/20/1878	Journal	Newspapers	Ridgeville Register is new newspaper
3/6/1940	Journal-Herald	Newspapers	Ridgeville Reporter, established in 1880 with A. L. Kitselman as editor
9/24/1913	Journal	Newspapers	Ridgeville Star suspends after 2.5 years
3/26/1913	Journal	Newspapers	Ridgeville Star, Milton Bolerjack sold the paper several weeks ago
3/22/1911	Journal	Newspapers	Ridgeville Star, Milton S. Bolerjack; independent in politics
12/19/1912	Democrat	Newspapers	Ridgeville Star, sold by Bolerjack to Mr. Drollinger
9/11/1889	Journal	Newspapers	Ridgeville Times suspended publication
3/6/1889	Journal	Newspapers	Ridgeville Times, C. C. Lyons establishes, a Democratic paper
3/6/1889	Herald	Newspapers	Ridgeville Times, C. C. Lyons, publisher, first issue last week, Democrat paper; Ridgeville News, published by Day Brothers, is independent
10/26/1881	Journal	Newspapers	Ridgeville Times, Franklin replaces Lemaux as editor
8/31/1881	Journal	Newspapers	Ridgeville Times, William Lemaux replaces Dr. Harrison as editor
2/20/1889	Journal	Newspapers	Ridgeville, C. C. Lyons will start Democrat/Independent paper

Date	Type	Category	Description
3/15/1957	News	Newspapers	Ridgeville, Gazette Publishing Company purchased newspaper
3/1/1911	Journal	Newspapers	Ridgeville, Milton Bolerjack will start the Evening Star newspaper
3/3/1886	Journal	Newspapers	Ridgeville, new newspaper established
4/14/1875	Journal	Newspapers	Ridgeville, plans for a newspaper
9/17/1925	Journal-Herald	Newspapers	Saratoga Independent discontinued, C. E. Ward, publisher, moves to Union City
11/18/1903	Herald	Newspapers	Saratoga Independent established by Ora G. Pogue
12/10/1913	Journal	Newspapers	Saratoga Independent has been reestablished as a Democrat paper by Ida Barnum and will be printed by the Ridgeville News
5/24/1917	Democrat	Newspapers	Saratoga Independent has been revived under Charles Ward
4/18/1917	Journal	Newspapers	Saratoga Independent has suspended publication
1/31/1912	Herald	Newspapers	Saratoga Independent is sold to F. O. Sowers of Union City
5/14/1908	Democrat	Newspapers	Saratoga Independent sold to Riley Barnum and son, Gath, by L. E. Worster; Worster had owned it for four years
12/3/1913	Journal	Newspapers	Saratoga Independent will be reestablished after the holidays
2/12/1914	Democrat	Newspapers	Saratoga Independent, Cyrus Bousman took over ownership on April 28, 1913 from C. O. Drollinger; Suspended until December 1913; Stanley was editor (?)
6/12/1912	Journal	Newspapers	Saratoga Independent, Frank Sowers, editor
2/17/1904	Herald	Newspapers	Saratoga Independent, Levi Lambert to become editor
10/24/1906	Journal	Newspapers	Saratoga Independent, Lew Wooster, publisher
11/19/1903	Democrat	Newspapers	Saratoga, newspaper has been established by Ora V. Pogue
10/28/1903	Journal	Newspapers	Saratoga, Ora Pogue will start a newspaper
1/19/1865	Journal	Newspapers	Union [City] Eagle exists
7/24/1902	Democrat	Newspapers	Union City [Daily] Eagle suspends publication after eleven years; W. S. Ensign is publisher
7/23/1902	Journal	Newspapers	Union City Daily Eagle suspended last Saturday after eleven years
6/6/1888	Journal	Newspapers	Union City Daily Express has suspended publication
3/25/1896	Journal	Newspapers	Union City Daily Times established Monday
10/10/1877	Journal	Newspapers	Union City Eagle is building a new building
9/5/1906	Journal	Newspapers	Union City Eagle passed to new management

Date	Source	Category	Description
1/10/1906	Herald	Newspapers	Union City Eagle purchased by James Stanley
1/3/1906	Journal	Newspapers	Union City Eagle sold by M. P. Davis to James Stanley
10/6/1915	Journal	Newspapers	Union City Eagle, Eagle Publishing Company formed
10/15/1919	Herald	Newspapers	Union City Eagle, H. R. Millette, of Ansonia, purchased paper from Clyde N. Chattin
10/2/1919	Democrat	Newspapers	Union City Eagle, Hilton R. Millette replaces P. C. Chattin as manager
7/25/1906	Herald	Newspapers	Union City Eagle, J. R. Dennison took over since Stanley is now postmaster
8/7/1872	Journal	Newspapers	Union City Eagle, John Commons starts as editor
4/16/1879	Journal	Newspapers	Union City Eagle, Masslich, editor
2/14/1883	Journal	Newspapers	Union City Eagle, Masslick [sic] sold Eagle to S. R. Bell, who formed a partnership with Mr. Ensign of the News; the papers are combined
2/17/1915	Journal	Newspapers	Union City Eagle, Mearl Ward replaces Don Ward as editor
8/17/1887	Journal	Newspapers	Union City Eagle, S. R. Bell sold interest to his partner, W. S. Ensign
5/24/1906	Democrat	Newspapers	Union City Eagle, Stanley, editor
5/12/1886	Journal	Newspapers	Union City Express changed from a quarto to a folio
6/10/1885	Journal	Newspapers	Union City Express exists
10/19/1870	Journal	Newspapers	Union City Gazette established by N. R. Brice, formerly of the Winchester Gazette
2/21/1877	Journal	Newspapers	Union City has new Democratic newspaper
7/3/1901	Journal	Newspapers	Union City Independent established by Hull Printing Company (David Hull)
3/13/1872	Journal	Newspapers	Union City Independent established; Union City Gazette sold to Maslich of Union City Eagle; Gazette editor [A. Jaqua] established Independent
7/14/1897	Herald	Newspapers	Union City News discontinued after one year
7/12/1882	Journal	Newspapers	Union City News, Theodore Shockney, editor
4/3/1939	Journal-Herald	Newspapers	Union City newspapers to consolidate
3/14/1877	Journal	Newspapers	Union City Plain Dealer established by Bro. Mitchener
7/24/1878	Journal	Newspapers	Union City Plain Dealer exists
11/21/1861	Journal	Newspapers	Union City Times established by J. and I. Simmons
3/31/1915	Journal	Newspapers	Union City Times is moving to the Shank Block
3/9/1933	Journal-Herald	Newspapers	Union City Times switched from daily to semi-weekly

Date	Type	Category	Description
11/25/1874	Journal	Newspapers	Union City Times will move from old M. E. Church to Hartzell's new building
7/9/1925	Journal-Herald	Newspapers	Union City Times, Editor Patchell died
8/11/1921	Democrat	Newspapers	Union City Times, George Patchell retires as editor
4/2/1873	Journal	Newspapers	Union City Times, John Commons, editor
12/12/1877	Journal	Newspapers	Union City Times, Patchel and Sipe have purchased it from Fields, who kept it only one week
9/30/1943	Journal-Herald	Newspapers	Union City Times-Gazette, Don Ward replaces Gib Swaim and editor
8/23/1952	Journal-Herald	Newspapers	Union City Times-Gazette, Jerry Davis resigns as editor
4/25/1963	Journal-Herald	Newspapers	Union City Times-Gazette, John H. Larimer, editor from 1959-1963, died on April 24; had also edited the Journal-Herald for six months
11/9/1953	News	Newspapers	Union City Times-Gazette, Joseph R. Lay is new editor
6/12/1954	Journal-Herald	Newspapers	Union City Times-Gazette, Richard Wise is now editor
2/11/1957	News	Newspapers	Union City Times-Gazette, Richard Wise resumes editorial duties; had been in Air Force since 1955
6/23/1886	Journal	Newspapers	Winchester Advertiser, second issue appeared last week
12/19/1900	Herald	Newspapers	Winchester Daily Courier has existed for two years; started by Harry B. Shockley, then under Will Watson; purchased by Herald Company and became Daily Herald; Winchester Advertiser exists
12/13/1900	Democrat	Newspapers	Winchester Daily Courier, established two years ago by Harry B. Shockley, sold to Herald Company and became Daily Herald
5/20/1914	Herald	Newspapers	Winchester Daily Herald exists
12/24/1902	Herald	Newspapers	Winchester Daily Herald folds today
12/9/1908	Herald	Newspapers	Winchester Daily Herald recently started
12/12/1900	Journal	Newspapers	Winchester Daily Herald succeeds Daily Courier on Saturday
12/24/1902	Journal	Newspapers	Winchester Daily Herald suspends today
12/12/1894	Journal	Newspapers	Winchester Daily Journal will appear Monday
9/4/1941	Journal-Herald	Newspapers	Winchester Daily News established by Arthur K. Remmel on May 15, 1941, folded in 1915; was an independent newspaper
6/17/1926	Democrat	Newspapers	Winchester Daily News is established from the Democrat's Office
1/13/1927	Journal-Herald	Newspapers	Winchester Daily News suspended

Date	Type	Category	Description
11/10/1915	Journal	Newspapers	Winchester Daily News, established by D. W. Callahan
6/14/1926	Daily News	Newspapers	Winchester Daily News, first issue; published by Winchester Publishing Company; non-partisan
11/29/1860	Journal	Newspapers	Winchester Democrat "has squatted"
5/6/1885	Journal	Newspapers	Winchester Democrat appeared Friday; J. J. Gorrell, editor; Dr. C. C. Hiatt, associate
1/3/1861	Journal	Newspapers	Winchester Democrat ceased publication
10/14/1894	Journal	Newspapers	Winchester Democrat ceased publication
10/3/1894	Herald	Newspapers	Winchester Democrat ceases
7/29/1925	Democrat	Newspapers	Winchester Democrat editorial, "Farewell! And Stand Fast For Democracy!" states that the Randolph County Klan was not violent; though highly misguided
3/22/1860	Journal	Newspapers	Winchester Democrat established by I. C. Dille in Strohm's Building on the first of next week
9/27/1871	Journal	Newspapers	Winchester Democrat established by the Democrat Company, J. H. Keys and James Williamson
2/13/1884	Journal	Newspapers	Winchester Democrat established last week
10/5/1894	Journal	Newspapers	Winchester Democrat folded
12/3/1884	Journal	Newspapers	Winchester Democrat has not been published for two weeks
9/11/1913	Democrat	Newspapers	Winchester Democrat is housed in Engle Building, corner of Franklin and Main Streets
6/21/1917	Democrat	Newspapers	Winchester Democrat is moving from Engle Building to Kelley Block after four years
6/13/1935	Democrat	Newspapers	Winchester Democrat is purchased by Gazette Publishing Company; moved to office of Daily News in Davis Block
6/11/1919	Herald	Newspapers	Winchester Democrat is sold back to D. W. Callahan after only a few days
7/5/1911	Herald	Newspapers	Winchester Democrat is sold to D. W. Callahan
12/24/1884	Journal	Newspapers	Winchester Democrat may be revived with C. C. Peelle as editor
6/20/1917	Herald	Newspapers	Winchester Democrat moved to Kelley Block, second floor
1/7/1915	Democrat	Newspapers	Winchester Democrat office is in the Engle Building
6/10/1920	Democrat	Newspapers	Winchester Democrat office moved to Franklin Street in the National Poland China Home Building; was previously in the Kelley Block

Date	Source	Category	Description
6/4/1919	Herald	Newspapers	Winchester Democrat sold by D. W. Callahan to C. I. Miller; Callahan had owned it since July 1, 1911
12/17/1873	Journal	Newspapers	Winchester Democrat sold to parties of Hartford City
12/13/1871	Journal	Newspapers	Winchester Democrat transferred from Mr. Keys to J. E. Williamson
12/31/1884	Journal	Newspapers	Winchester Democrat was formerly edited by John R. Polk
6/18/1925	Democrat	Newspapers	Winchester Democrat was started by Joseph J. Gorrell in 1885; he ran it for six years
2/11/1885	Journal	Newspapers	Winchester Democrat will be resurrected soon
2/6/1884	Journal	Newspapers	Winchester Democrat will make its appearance this week
4/19/1885	Journal	Newspapers	Winchester Democrat will start Friday, edited by C. C. Hiatt and Mr. Garrell of Ridgeville Banner
1/2/1902	Democrat	Newspapers	Winchester Democrat, A. C. Hindsley, publisher; located in Diggs Block, opposite the post office
7/14/1897	Journal	Newspapers	Winchester Democrat, A. J. Daniels takes over
2/3/1897	Journal	Newspapers	Winchester Democrat, A. L. Hindsley replaces J. L. Smith as editor
11/23/1898	Journal	Newspapers	Winchester Democrat, Alva C. Hindsley takes over
6/20/1917	Journal	Newspapers	Winchester Democrat, D. W. Callahan has moved paper to the Kelley Block; all three newspapers in Winchester are in one block
3/25/1920	Democrat	Newspapers	Winchester Democrat, D. W. Callahan sold his interest to A. M. Browne; paper is under the management of J. L. Turner and owned by the Winchester Publishing Company
6/5/1919	Democrat	Newspapers	Winchester Democrat, D. W. Callahan sold the paper to C. I. Miller; office is located in the Kelley Block at Washington and Meridian
6/4/1919	Journal	Newspapers	Winchester Democrat, D. W. Callihan [sic] sold paper to C. I Miller
7/7/1886	Journal	Newspapers	Winchester Democrat, Dr. C. C. Hiatt sold his interest
2/11/1885	Journal	Newspapers	Winchester Democrat, equipment has been purchased by a syndicate to reestablish a paper
1/7/1885	Journal	Newspapers	Winchester Democrat, equipment of will be sold
8/10/1892	Journal	Newspapers	Winchester Democrat, Erastus Lollas, chairman of the county central committee, has taken over as editor
4/5/1911	Herald	Newspapers	Winchester Democrat, Hindsley sold paper to C. K. Rockhill
6/14/1899	Journal	Newspapers	Winchester Democrat, J. L. Smith is again editor

Date	Paper	Category	Description
9/25/1895	Journal	Newspapers	Winchester Democrat, J. L. Smith of Dana takes over from Mr. Williams on first of month
6/14/1899	Herald	Newspapers	Winchester Democrat, J. L. Smith purchased 1/2 interest
11/6/1901	Journal	Newspapers	Winchester Democrat, J. L. Smith retires as editor
6/11/1925	Democrat	Newspapers	Winchester Democrat, J. L. Turner, publisher; J. L. Smith, editor
8/13/1919	Herald	Newspapers	Winchester Democrat, J. L. Turner joins D. W. Callahan
1/5/1933	Democrat	Newspapers	Winchester Democrat, J. L. Turner, editor
8/19/1925	Democrat	Newspapers	Winchester Democrat, J. L. Turner, publisher; W. R. Kiracofe, editor
7/29/1925	Democrat	Newspapers	Winchester Democrat, John L. Smith retires for the fourth time
3/3/1921	Democrat	Newspapers	Winchester Democrat, John L. Turner is manager; office is on Franklin Street
2/24/1927	Democrat	Newspapers	Winchester Democrat, John L. Turner, publisher; no editor listed
10/3/1894	Herald	Newspapers	Winchester Democrat, L. G. Ellingham moved to paper to Decatur
12/13/1860	Journal	Newspapers	Winchester Democrat, Mr. Lon Dynes has purchased the Winchester Democrat office and will merge with the Journal
1/12/1860	Journal	Newspapers	Winchester Democrat, plans to establish a Democratic newspaper at this place
11/10/1915	Herald	Newspapers	Winchester Evening News is launched by Winchester Democrat
5/20/1914	Journal	Newspapers	Winchester Evening News, Arthur K. Remmell began publication last Thursday
8/19/1914	Journal	Newspapers	Winchester Evening News, daily newspaper published here since May, suspended Saturday
5/13/1914	Journal	Newspapers	Winchester Evening News, Remmel, Arthur K. to establish a daily newspaper in the Pretlow Block
4/19/1876	Journal	Newspapers	Winchester Gazette, Jonesboro Herald is printed on old press of
5/13/1914	Herald	Newspapers	Winchester Herald Building is located at 117 N. Meridian Street
1/6/1875	Journal	Newspapers	Winchester Herald has been established recently by J. G. Brice
12/25/1901	Herald	Newspapers	Winchester Herald history; Established by Brice in Canada Block; then E. L. Watson ran it, then Lee Ault and R. A. Leavell, then Thos. Harrison, then Watson alone, then Addington and Commons and W. O. Pierce, etc. Canada Block has since been replaced by K. of P. Building

Date	Type	Category	Description
2/11/1885	Journal	Newspapers	Winchester Herald moved to the basement of the Masonic Block
2/4/1891	Herald	Newspapers	Winchester Herald will move to building north of Dennis Kelley's building
8/27/1902	Herald	Newspapers	Winchester Herald, C. C. Peele retires from Herald; S. S. Watson, manager
3/17/1915	Herald	Newspapers	Winchester Herald, C. C. Peelle has been co-owner for eight years
9/5/1877	Journal	Newspapers	Winchester Herald, Charley Harrison leaves; Watson is now sole owner
12/31/1884	Journal	Newspapers	Winchester Herald, Emerson Addington has purchased it
9/21/1910	Herald	Newspapers	Winchester Herald, Frank P. Litschert, city editor
2/11/1903	Herald	Newspapers	Winchester Herald, new building
2/25/1903	Herald	Newspapers	Winchester Herald, new building on North Meridian Street
4/28/1958	News	Newspapers	Winchester Herald, old photo of office
9/10/1902	Herald	Newspapers	Winchester Herald, plans to raze old Herald Office and replace it with a new one
6/8/1887	Herald	Newspapers	Winchester Herald, S. S. Watson replaces W. O. Pierce as editor
5/11/1892	Herald	Newspapers	Winchester Herald, U. B. Hunt purchased interest in
1/3/1894	Herald	Newspapers	Winchester Herald, U. B. Hunt resigns as editor
3/1/1893	Herald	Newspapers	Winchester Herald, U. B. Hunt, editor
1/4/1893	Herald	Newspapers	Winchester Journal moved to new building
2/5/1919	Herald	Newspapers	Winchester Journal of 1866 described
9/15/1886	Journal	Newspapers	Winchester Journal of August 23, 1860 described
3/18/1920	Democrat	Newspapers	Winchester Journal to sold to Winchester Herald
6/23/1870	Journal	Newspapers	Winchester Journal, A. C. Beeson and E. J. Marsh, proprietors
11/21/1894	Herald	Newspapers	Winchester Journal, A. C. Beeson becomes president of Randolph County Bank; sons took over newspaper
1/13/1865	Journal	Newspapers	Winchester Journal, Andrew J. Neff, editor and proprietor
4/28/1859	Journal	Newspapers	Winchester Journal, B. F. Diggs, editor, refers to "our Quaker upbringing"
4/19/1911	Journal	Newspapers	Winchester Journal, bound volumes from 1858-62 are received
5/5/1859	Journal	Newspapers	Winchester Journal, C. D. Smith sells paper to John W. Jarnagin; B. F. Diggs continues as editor
12/6/1871	Journal	Newspapers	Winchester Journal, E. J. Marsh leaves

Date	Type	Category	Description
8/15/1862	Journal	Newspapers	Winchester Journal, G. H. Bonebrake left partnership with Dynes after five months
4/6/1887	Journal	Newspapers	Winchester Journal, General Browne gave the office bound volumes for 1858 to 1861
7/3/1872	Journal	Newspapers	Winchester Journal, J. M. Hodson purchases an interest
6/29/1881	Journal	Newspapers	Winchester Journal, J. M. Hodson sells interest to A. C. Beeson
1/23/1863	Journal	Newspapers	Winchester Journal, L. G. Dynes sold paper to Dr. J. E. Beverly
12/19/1862	Journal	Newspapers	Winchester Journal, L. G. Dynes sold paper to J. E. Beverly
1/1/1864	Journal	Newspapers	Winchester Journal, name of paper changed to Randolph County Journal
6/9/1870	Journal	Newspapers	Winchester Journal, office in the National Bank Building, third story; E. B. Walkup retires as editor, and Lytle
10/28/1896	Journal	Newspapers	Winchester Journal, T. M. Paschall describes original press
12/5/1894	Journal	Newspapers	Winchester Journal, Will and Charles Beeson took over the paper from their father
1/1/1890	Journal	Newspapers	Winchester Journal, Will E. and Charles H. Beeson join father in newspaper
3/17/1920	Journal	Newspapers	Winchester Journal-Herald formed; Journal Building had been used for 25 years
3/2/1937	Journal-Herald	Newspapers	Winchester Journal-Herald is sold to the Winchester Journal-Herald Corporation; members are John W. Moore, Jr., H. Emerson Butts, M. L. Snyder, Robert Kist, manager; the paper will be printed/published by the Gazette Publishing Company in the Journal-Herald Office at 117 N. Meridian Street; John Oliver was the manager since Harry Rowe resigned in December
8/16/1922	Journal-Herald	Newspapers	Winchester Journal-Herald sold to I. M. Bridgman of Brookville
7/2/1968	Journal-Herald	Newspapers	Winchester Journal-Herald will continue as a rural, afternoon paper; New-Gazette will be a morning, city paper
9/26/1963	Journal-Herald	Newspapers	Winchester Journal-Herald, Anna Marie Gibbons, editor
2/4/1965	Journal-Herald	Newspapers	Winchester Journal-Herald, Anna Marie Gibbons, editor
6/21/1960	Journal-Herald	Newspapers	Winchester Journal-Herald, Bob Kist, editor since 1937, died on June 20
10/9/1965	Journal-Herald	Newspapers	Winchester Journal-Herald, circulation is 3494

Date	Title	Category	Description
12/22/1960	Journal-Herald	Newspapers	Winchester Journal-Herald, Jerry Davis is editor
10/11/1965	News	Newspapers	Winchester News, Richard Wise, publisher; A. M. Gibbons, editor
8/26/1936	Daily News	Newspapers	Winchester News-Democrat became the Winchester Daily News
5/27/1936	News-Democrat	Newspapers	Winchester News-Democrat moved to 210 S. Main Street from the Davis Building
1/18/1936	News-Democrat	Newspapers	Winchester News-Democrat, Russell E. Wise, president of Gazette Publishing Company; George Mills, manager; Paul R. Honn, editor
10/8/1963	Journal-Herald	Newspapers	Winchester newspaper printing plant moved from 117 N. Meridian Street to 119 E. North St.
7/1/1943	Journal-Herald	Newspapers	Winchester newspapers go to tri-weeklies (Journal-Herald on Tuesday, Thursday, Saturday; News on Monday, Wednesday, Friday)
11/29/1969	Journal-Herald	Newspapers	Winchester newspapers to combine into News-Gazette and Journal-Herald; Janet Harris was editor of Journal-Herald; will be editor of Union City edition of News-Gazette and Journal-Herald; A. M. Gibbons will be editor of News-Gazette
10/27/1886	Journal	Newspapers	Winchester Organizer ceased
7/28/1886	Journal	Newspapers	Winchester Organizer, C. C. Hiatt's new paper, appeared last Friday
7/21/1886	Journal	Newspapers	Winchester Organizer, new paper to be established by Dr. C. C. Hiatt
11/28/1894	Journal	Newspapers	Winchester Press ceases after three weeks
9/30/1903	Journal	Newspapers	Winchester Press established
10/24/1894	Journal	Newspapers	Winchester Press established this week by John Harris and Company; neutral in politics
11/28/1894	Journal	Newspapers	Winchester Press failed after three weeks
9/30/1903	Journal	Newspapers	Winchester Press is started by Joseph Day, Frank McNees, and Rush Deardorff
12/5/1894	Journal	Newspapers	Winchester Republican established by W. P. Needham last week
1/12/1898	Herald	Newspapers	Winchester Republican, owned by W. P. Needham, sold and moved away, leaving nine papers in Randolph County
1/12/1898	Journal	Newspapers	Winchester Republican, William P. Needham, publisher, suspends the publication
3/9/1904	Herald	Newspapers	Winchester Saturday Press suspends

Date	Publication	Category	Description
7/28/1870	Journal	Newspapers	Winchester, Democratic paper will start in Winchester about August 18, 1870
7/21/1870	Journal	Newspapers	Winchester, Democratic paper will start in Winchester next week
11/11/1874	Journal	Newspapers	Winchester, Journal has removed to new building
12/24/1966	Journal-Herald	Newspapers	Winchester, old newspaper building in 100 block of N. Meridian, built in 1903, is razed; Gazette Publishing Company purchased Journal-Herald Company's stock in 1962
2/23/1881	Journal	Newspapers	Winchester, Phantasmagorian established last week by W. P. Needham
10/21/1963	News	Newspapers	Winchester, photos of old newspaper office
4/14/1875	Journal	Newspapers	Winchester, plans for a German language newspaper
7/1/1858	Journal	Newspapers	Winchester, Randolph County Journal, J. E. Beverly resigns as editor
12/31/1857	Journal	Newspapers	Winchester, Randolph County Journal, J. E. Beverly starts as editor
12/31/1857	Journal	Newspapers	Winchester, Randolph County Journal, published by Beverly and Smith
8/5/1874	Journal	Newspapers	Winchester, Randolph County News, an independent newspaper, exists
1/24/1867	Journal	Newspapers	Winchester, Randolph Journal
9/20/1866	Journal	Newspapers	Winchester, Randolph Journal
7/8/1858	Journal	Newspapers	Winchester, Randolph Journal, B. F. Diggs is new editor
4/20/1916	Democrat	People	Abshire, James, photograph
3/7/1917	Journal	People	Addington, A. Everette [sic] had some sight in one eye after surgery
10/23/1918	Journal	People	Addington, Archie Allen, Randolph County native, is a school principal in Bloomington at age 22
7/6/1904	Herald	People	Addington, Benjamin 80th birthday
6/29/1904	Journal	People	Addington, Benjamin birthday celebration
11/7/1906	Journal	People	Addington, Benjamin died Monday
11/14/1906	Journal	People	Addington, Benjamin obituary
6/29/1904	Journal	People	Addington, Benjamin, 80th birthday
2/28/1912	Herald	People	Addington, E. H., Grand Master of Grand Lodge of Louisiana, F. & A. M., is Randolph County native
12/15/1886	Journal	People	Addington, Emerson moved to New Orleans
9/10/1919	Journal	People	Addington, Everett plans to attend Indiana University
1/25/1923	Democrat	People	Addington, Evert A., featured
10/1/1919	Journal	People	Addington, Evert enrolled at Indiana University

Date	Source	Category	Description
4/8/1885	Journal	People	Addington, George died
11/11/1908	Journal	People	Addington, George E. will reside with his father-in-law
11/23/1922	Democrat	People	Addington, George suffered a nervous breakdown and is in Oxford Sanitarium
4/24/1878	Journal	People	Addington, J. S. now a resident of Hancock County
9/3/1902	Herald	People	Addington, John L. v. John Wilson (1849) case in Randolph County about witchcraft
3/6/1878	Journal	People	Addington, John L., former county commissioner, died in Ackley, Iowa
11/13/1878	Journal	People	Addington, Lindsey elected sheriff in Worth County, Missouri as a Greenback Republican
6/4/1913	Journal	People	Addington, Luther E. is first minister in Randolph County to own an automobile
4/21/1915	Journal	People	Addington, Luther E. removed as mail carrier
6/22/1916	Democrat	People	Addington, Luther gave temperance talks at Cedar and Poplar Run Friends Churches
9/7/1904	Herald	People	Addington, Oliver B. is horse thief
12/21/1968	Journal-Herald	People	Addington, Rev. and Mrs. Luther, 70th anniversary
12/19/1969	News-Gazette	People	Addington, Rev. and Mrs. Luther, 71st anniversary
9/11/1918	Journal	People	Addington, Rev. Luther E. moved from Pennville to Portland
3/19/1966	Journal-Herald	People	Addington, Rev. Luther E., photo
11/8/1957	News	People	Addington, Rev. Luther returns to Randolph County
1/31/1912	Herald	People	Addington, Rev. Thomas obituary
1/31/1912	Journal	People	Addington, Rev. Thomas obituary
12/15/1909	Journal	People	Addington, Rev. Thomas, 80th birthday
1/24/1979	News-Gazette	People	Addington, Richard, Union City police chief, photo
7/6/1881	Journal	People	Addington, Thomas is building new residence
4/28/1897	Journal	People	Addington, Thomas will publish "Jim Baker"
2/26/1902	Journal	People	Addington, Thomas wrote "A Manual of Parliamentary Laws"
5/11/1898	Journal	People	Addington, Thomas, book "Jim Baker" is available for 50 cents
7/7/1897	Journal	People	Addington, Thomas; "Jim Baker" is published in newspaper
10/27/1897	Journal	People	Addington, Thomas; "Jim Baker" last installment in newspaper
4/21/1909	Journal	People	Addington, Zack, old school teacher, buried at Jericho
7/10/1936	News-Democrat	People	Adelsparger, C. C., founder of Union City Body Company, died

Date	Publication	Category	Description
11/26/1902	Journal	People	Aiken, Robert, photo and obituary; member of Cherry Grove Friends Church
4/24/1907	Herald	People	Aker, Andrew (1823-1907) died; member of Winchester Friends Church
4/25/1907	Democrat	People	Aker, Andrew died; member of Winchester Friends Church
12/20/1955	Journal-Herald	People	Albertson, Ollie is Lynn Quaker
11/9/1892	Journal	People	Alexander, Clement F., obituary
11/13/1878	Journal	People	Anthony, Susan B. will be in Union City on the 26th
8/3/1963	Journal-Herald	People	Bailey, Dallas is new commander of American Legion
8/15/1953	Journal-Herald	People	Bailey, Gail planned to give his 8500 books to Wilmington College
3/18/1978	News-Gazette	People	Bailey, Gail, collection
9/16/1943	Journal-Herald	People	Baird, Lee, Superintendent of Delaware County Schools for twenty years, died, native of Randolph County
5/7/1931	Democrat	People	Baker, Oscar, biography
1/31/1917	Journal	People	Baldwin, Chalkley died
10/11/1916	Herald	People	Baldwin, Chalkley, 100 years old, registered to vote; staunch Republican
1/31/1917	Herald	People	Baldwin, Chalkley, died
7/19/1916	Journal	People	Baldwin, Chalkley, photo
9/6/1905	Herald	People	Baldwin, John E., balloonist, killed
9/13/1905	Herald	People	Baldwin, John E., did he commit suicide?
10/23/1889	Journal	People	Bales, Alonzo is teacher at Ponfrey School
10/12/1898	Journal	People	Bales, Alonzo, photo
9/1/1921	Democrat	People	Bales, Joel F., Civil War veteran, is buried at White River Friends Cemetery
3/13/1918	Herald	People	Bales, Rev. William Oliver, son of Evan and Louise (Hester) Bales; 1856 Fremont pole raising described
9/18/1964	News	People	Barnes, Leroy is chairman of Randolph County ASC
6/24/1908	Journal	People	Barr, Sarah wrote letter defending women's rights
5/30/1906	Journal	People	Batchelor, J. O. announced for county superintendent in 1907
11/14/1906	Journal	People	Batchelor, J. O. is living at Fort Wayne but is maintaining his residence at Farmland so that he can run for county superintendent
12/13/1893	Journal	People	Beard, Elkanah and Irena are going to Archer, Florida
12/11/1895	Journal	People	Beard, Elkanah and Irena left for Lake Kerr, Florida

Date	Source	Category	Description
5/1/1872	Journal	People	Beard, Elkanah and Irena returned to Lynn last week from India
2/15/1905	Herald	People	Beard, Elkanah died
6/1/1881	Journal	People	Beard, Elkanah has moved to his house, south of Quaker Church in Winchester
2/15/1905	Journal	People	Beard, Elkanah obituary and photo
6/21/1882	Journal	People	Beard, Elkanah, letter from Europe
3/15/1871	Journal	People	Beard, Elkanah, letter from India
4/12/1871	Journal	People	Beard, Elkanah, letter from India
6/6/1949	News	People	Beck, Paul is new county superintendent of schools
5/2/1957	Journal-Herald	People	Beck, Paul is reappointed county superintendent
5/2/1961	Journal-Herald	People	Beck, Paul is reappointed county superintendent
6/5/1961	News	People	Beck, Paul is son of Wiley and Mary Beck
5/4/1953	News	People	Beck, Paul reelected county superintendent
6/18/1963	Journal-Herald	People	Beck, Paul resigns as county superintendent; was member of State Board of Education after 1958
1/6/1974	News-Gazette	People	Beck, Paul, former county superintendent, dies
9/18/1942	Journal-Herald	People	Beeson, A. C. and family photos
6/24/1903	Herald	People	Beeson, A. C. died
6/24/1903	Journal	People	Beeson, A. C. died
4/13/1934	Journal-Herald	People	Beeson, Charles photo
9/18/1942	Journal-Herald	People	Beeson, William and Charles, photos
9/7/1916	Democrat	People	Benson, J. B., of Winchester, will head Vermilion Grove [Friends] Academy in Illinois
6/11/1958	News	People	Bentz, Walter, trustee of Green Township, commits suicide
9/22/1875	Journal	People	Bergman, Harvey and Alice Smith married by Rev. Henry Merrill
5/9/1888	Journal	People	Beverly, Dr. John E. died in Winchester
8/24/1910	Journal	People	Binford, Rev. Joseph O., Quaker minister, died
11/16/1898	Herald	People	Biographies of new county officials
6/21/1967	News	People	Bly, Mary biography
3/15/1946	News	People	Bolinger, Cecil is member of Winchester Friends Church
1/24/1958	News	People	Bolinger, Leonard is member of Winchester Friends Church
8/10/1919	Journal	People	Boltz, John H. died
9/10/1919	Herald	People	Boltz, John H. died
7/16/1913	Journal	People	Boltz, John H., of Winchester, is a member of the State Board of Accounts

Date	Source	Category	Description
4/13/1945	News	People	Boltz, Mrs. John died
10/27/1897	Journal	People	Bond, John H., obituary
12/23/1908	Herald	People	Bosworth, L. U. to erect house west of town
2/1/1964	Journal-Herald	People	Botkin Farm history, near Huntsville
11/8/1899	Herald	People	Botkin, Dr. John biography
4/21/1965	News	People	Botkin, William E. house burns
10/18/1899	Herald	People	Bowen, Ephraim biography
12/12/1917	Journal	People	Bowers, Elma died November 30, 1917; married September 30, 1905
5/18/1887	Journal	People	Bowers, H. W. accepted superintendency of Portland Schools
5/15/1889	Journal	People	Bowers, H. W. appointed superintendent at Portland for third year
11/19/1913	Journal	People	Bowers, H. W. changed houses on Meridian Street in Winchester
11/1/1916	Journal	People	Bowers, H. W. died
11/1/1916	Herald	People	Bowers, H. W. died Sunday, aged 66
1/2/1901	Journal	People	Bowers, H. W. is associated with Winchester M. E. Church
7/24/1901	Journal	People	Bowers, H. W. is named principal of Portland High School
6/26/1901	Journal	People	Bowers, H. W. is principal at Portland [Jay County]
10/18/1882	Journal	People	Bowers, H. W. is secretary of Randolph County Republican Central Committee
8/26/1908	Journal	People	Bowers, H. W. is the son of Mrs. Hannah Hull
5/28/1902	Journal	People	Bowers, H. W. left Portland for Winchester to take charge of bookstore
10/7/1885	Journal	People	Bowers, H. W. married Ella Bowen on September 30, 1885
6/17/1891	Journal	People	Bowers, H. W. named principal of Winchester High School
11/8/1916	Herald	People	Bowers, H. W. obituary
11/8/1916	Journal	People	Bowers, H. W. obituary
5/20/1891	Journal	People	Bowers, H. W. resigned as superintendent at Portland and will return to Winchester
9/13/1882	Journal	People	Bowers, H. W. teaching at Winchester High School
6/3/1885	Journal	People	Bowers, H. W. unanimously reelected county superintendent
4/10/1878	Journal	People	Bowers, H. W. will continue teaching in Winchester
7/20/1887	Journal	People	Bowers, H. W. will live at Arch and Wayne Streets in Portland
7/21/1880	Journal	People	Bowers, Henry earned M. A. from Asbury University

Date	Source	Category	Description
3/1/1882	Journal	People	Bowers, Henry is secretary of White River Township Republican Committee
10/7/1885	Journal	People	Bowers, Henry married Ella Bowen on September 30, 1885
7/3/1878	Journal	People	Bowers, Henry resigned as superintendent of Winchester M. E. Sunday School
5/18/1887	Journal	People	Bowers, Henry W. appointed Superintendent of Portland Schools
9/23/1896	Journal	People	Bowers, Henry W. goes to Union City as superintendent
5/23/1894	Herald	People	Bowers, Henry W. is graduate of Winchester Schools and DePauw, '77
3/10/1915	Herald	People	Bowers, Henry W. purchases property at the corner of Meridian and Will
7/3/1895	Journal	People	Bowers, Henry W. starts as principal of Union City
11/1/1916	Journal	People	Bowers, Henry Willard died Sunday, October 30
11/8/1916	Journal	People	Bowers, Henry Willard obituary
12/5/1917	Journal	People	Bowers, Mrs. Elma died
12/5/1917	Journal	People	Bowers, Mrs. H. W. (Ella) died last Friday
12/5/1917	Herald	People	Bowers, Mrs. H. W. died at Reid Hospital on Thursday night, aged 54, daughter of B. F. Bowen
1/31/1917	Journal	People	Bowers, Mrs. Henry is sister of George Bowen
5/31/1916	Herald	People	Branson, James R., Farmland native, is now city editor of Indianapolis News
5/19/1897	Journal	People	Branson, Joseph B. died
7/27/1965	Journal-Herald	People	Branson, Paul is new county agent
5/5/1977	News-Gazette	People	Brantingham, Dorothy, wife of Friends Superintendent, is native of Salem, Ohio
1/30/1889	Journal	People	Brice, J. G., obituary
1/23/1889	Herald	People	Brice, John Grant, obituary
5/22/1918	Journal	People	Brice, Margaret Elizabeth, wife of James G., died in Tonganoxie, Kansas
10/17/1877	Journal	People	Brice, Rev. J. G. is moving to Kansas City after 35 years in Randolph County
11/12/1903	Democrat	People	Bright, Mary A, wife of Sheriff George Bright, died; funeral at Winchester Friends Church
10/21/1959	News	People	Briner, Lee, former sheriff, member of Winchester Friends Church
2/10/1945	Journal-Herald	People	Brooks, Rev. Rachel photo
1/31/1953	Journal-Herald	People	Brooks, Rev. Rachel photo
6/27/1981	News-Gazette	People	Brooks, Rev. Rachel, biography and photos

Date	Source	Category	Description
8/14/1889	Journal	People	Brown, Judge James died in Mankato, Minnesota
11/28/1888	Journal	People	Brown, Judge James reminiscences of the early days in Winchester
10/10/1888	Journal	People	Brown, Judge James, political recollections
6/6/1888	Journal	People	Brown, Judge James, reminiscences
8/8/1888	Journal	People	Brown, Judge James, reminiscences
9/12/1888	Journal	People	Brown, Judge James, reminiscences of Judge Anthony and Winchester
11/21/1888	Journal	People	Brown, Judge James, reminiscences of the early days in Winchester
6/13/1888	Journal	People	Brown, Judge James, reminiscences, including Presbyterian Church
7/21/1886	Journal	People	Brown, Judge James, who moved to Mankato in 1865, is visiting here
5/25/1865	Journal	People	Brown, Judge left for Mankato
5/5/1949	Journal-Herald	People	Brown, Mrs. Gilvie of Farmland is president of state Home Ec Clubs
5/19/1920	Journal-Herald	People	Brown, Rev. W. C., autobiography
3/30/1898	Journal	People	Brown, W. C. is PC of GAR, No. 60
7/15/1903	Journal	People	Brown, W. C., Quaker minister, biography
1/27/1915	Herald	People	Browne, Gen. Thomas, personal things sold by daughter
7/22/1891	Journal	People	Browne, General Thomas died
8/2/1893	Journal	People	Browne, O. K. murdered
1/17/1972	News-Gazette	People	Bryan, Merle, Monroe Central administrator, biography
11/4/1908	Journal	People	Bryan, William Jennings was in Winchester last Saturday
4/26/1876	Journal	People	Burres, Ann M., obituary
2/14/1949	Journal-Herald	People	Burres, Captain William
3/22/1899	Journal	People	Burres, Captain William died at Farmland
7/13/1881	Journal	People	Burres, Captain, wound of 1863 discussed
9/2/1891	Journal	People	Burres, Mrs. Samuel died in Farmland
11/17/1880	Journal	People	Burres, S. C. is sick
9/8/1880	Journal	People	Burres, Samuel C. and daughters have moved to Windsor
7/12/1893	Journal	People	Burres, Samuel died at Farmland
11/8/1876	Journal	People	Burres, Sarah, obituary
3/29/1899	Journal	People	Burres, William, obituary
12/22/1897	Journal	People	Burton, David S., obituary
5/7/1902	Herald	People	Butler, E. H., former school superintendent, hangs self

10/26/1916	Journal	People	Butts, Louisa Macy, originally a Quaker
6/12/1878	Journal	People	Butts, N. T. is finishing a brick residence near Mt. Zion
8/27/1902	Herald	People	Butts, Nathan T. died
8/23/1876	Journal	People	Butts, Rev. Nathan T. is preparing to build a new residence
8/2/1952	Journal-Herald	People	Butts, Viola appointed county historian in June
2/23/1970	News-Gazette	People	Butts, Viola died, was Randolph County Historian
12/3/1968	Journal-Herald	People	Butts, Viola is Randolph County Historian
1/23/1878	Journal	People	Byrd, Green H. will move from Farmland to Fairview
11/15/1899	Herald	People	Cadwallader, Nathan biography
4/25/1917	Herald	People	Cadwallader, Nathan had a birthright in the Friends Church
6/4/1913	Herald	People	Caldwell, F. S., of Winchester, appointed to State Court of Appeals
2/18/1885	Journal	People	Campbell, William M., former sheriff, obituary
10/5/1898	Journal	People	Canada, Silas A., photo
9/21/1892	Journal	People	Canada, W. W. , picture
9/15/1970	News-Gazette	People	Canada, W. W. biography and photos
7/26/1980	News-Gazette	People	Canada, W. W. biography and photos
5/19/1921	Democrat	People	Canada, W. W. died; funeral at Winchester Friends Church
6/2/1921	Democrat	People	Canada, W. W. was a "birthright and faithful Quaker"; Republican County Chairman, 1890-97; U. S. Consul to Vera Cruz, 1897-1917
11/17/1915	Journal	People	Canada, W. W., of Winchester, has been U. S. Consul at Vera Cruz since 1897
4/22/1914	Journal	People	Canada, W. W., of Winchester, is the U. S. Consul at Vera Cruz; conflict with Mexico
1/27/1915	Journal	People	Capper, Arthur, photo, Governor of Kansas, Quaker
1/5/1910	Herald	People	Capron, Rev. and Mrs. Levi golden anniversary
3/2/1910	Herald	People	Capron, Rev. and Mrs. Levi, photo
7/12/1916	Herald	People	Carter, Martitia, of Indianapolis, visited Farmland
6/28/1954	News	People	Carter, Nick
9/27/1973	News-Gazette	People	Carter, Nick, paintings
4/30/1959	Journal-Herald	People	Cassady, Rev. Mark photo
3/21/1935	Democrat	People	Chamness, Rev. Leander died
6/12/1918	Journal	People	Chamness, Rev. Mahlon died; buried at Nettle Creek
2/28/1906	Journal	People	Cheesman, D. S. photo
4/8/1903	Journal	People	Cheney, Judge died Sunday

Date	Source	Category	Description
4/8/1903	Herald	People	Cheney, Judge died; photo
4/15/1903	Journal	People	Cheney, Judge obituary
9/5/1888	Journal	People	Chenoweth family are all Republicans
6/8/1933	Democrat	People	Chenoweth, Glen is reelected county superintendent
6/5/1945	Journal-Herald	People	Chenoweth, Glen is reelected county superintendent
6/6/1929	Journal-Herald	People	Chenoweth, Glen O. elected County Superintendent
9/15/1921	Democrat	People	Chenoweth, Glen O. marries Martha Hawkins on September 8, 1921
1/27/1965	News	People	Chenoweth, Glen O., former county superintendent, died on January 27; born August 8, 1894
6/6/1929	Democrat	People	Chenoweth, Glen was elected county superintendent on Monday
6/2/1949	Journal-Herald	People	Chenoweth, Glen will finish term as county superintendent on August 16
3/13/1953	News	People	Childress, Morris, Church of God and personal history
9/3/1964	News	People	Clark, John Paul, is birthright Quaker and member of Friends Church, attends Presbyterian Church
6/14/1882	Journal	People	Clark, Nannie Goodrich died at Economy
10/26/1898	Journal	People	Clark, Thomas H., photo
5/9/1894	Journal	People	Clark, William D. and Stephen Warrick had horse race on way to Winchester
4/30/1931	Democrat	People	Clevenger, Troy, Winchester Police Chief, killed
9/25/1878	Journal	People	Coats, John, died
7/14/1875	Journal	People	Coats, Mrs. John died
9/4/1895	Journal	People	Coats, Reunion, history of John and Sally Coats
4/17/1918	Journal	People	Coats, Seth D. died
4/17/1918	Herald	People	Coats, Seth D. obituary
10/3/1906	Journal	People	Coffin Family history; Charity Coats Coffin smoked a pipe
9/10/1890	Journal	People	Coffin, Charity Coats, picture and obituary
2/10/1886	Journal	People	Coffin, Charles F., case of [Richmond Quaker]
11/26/1913	Journal	People	Coffin, George, chief of police in Indianapolis, is the son of Thomas Coffin, a native of Randolph County
11/11/1914	Journal	People	Coffin, George, new sheriff of Marion County, is grandson of Stephen and Charity Coats Coffin, son of William Coffin of Randolph County
10/24/1900	Journal	People	Coffin, Lewis is building new residence west of Martindale
4/6/1955	News	People	Coggeshall doctors

Date	Source	Category	Description
9/27/1882	Journal	People	Coggeshall, Caleb, father of county commissioner, buried at Cherry Grove
8/27/1890	Journal	People	Coggeshall, William R., former commissioner, died
1/23/1907	Journal	People	Colgrove, General is buried at Lake Kerr, Florida and will be moved to Arlington National Cemetery at some point
1/16/1907	Journal	People	Colgrove, General, resolution of respect due to death of
1/16/1907	Herald	People	Colgrove, Judge Silas dead
4/16/1913	Journal	People	Collins, Ernest B., Farmland native, is Speaker of the House in Alaska Territory
4/15/1915	Democrat	People	Collins, Ernest B., Farmland native, is Speaker of the House in Alaska Territory
7/2/1913	Democrat	People	Commons, John R., economist at University of Wisconsin, is Winchester native
5/25/1892	Journal	People	Commons, John R., Winchester native, is appointed professor of political economy at Indiana University
6/12/1895	Journal	People	Commons, John R., Winchester native, resigns from Indiana University to go to Syracuse
5/4/1881	Journal	People	Conway, Charles; Jim Lasley is his grandson
12/10/1983	News-Gazette	People	Cook, Chase featured; "being history-minded in Randolph County sometimes is a little like being a stock broker on Wall Street"
4/13/1881	Journal	People	Cooper, John resigned from Richmond Schools to go to Evansville
7/28/1886	Journal	People	Cooper, Prof. John, formerly of here, appointed superintendent of schools in Leavenworth, Kansas
3/24/1942	Journal-Herald	People	Cope, Stanton, Randolph County boy at Swarthmore College, is All-American in soccer
5/13/1920	Democrat	People	Cornell, Rev. Frank is naturalized as a citizen
6/4/1919	Herald	People	Cornell, Rev. Frank, photo
4/29/1920	Democrat	People	Cornell, Rev. Frank, photo
2/24/1916	Democrat	People	Cornell, Ward, son of Frank, pastor of Winchester Friends Church, is in the Canadian Army
9/29/1886	Journal	People	Cottom, James S., obituary
9/20/1905	Journal	People	Cox boy [Murray] now living with Ira Johnsons
12/23/1874	Journal	People	Cox, Cyrus A. married Linnie A. Pierce on November 17 by Elkanah Beard
3/6/1878	Journal	People	Cox, Cyrus now has medical degree

Date	Publication	Section	Description
10/2/1924	Democrat	People	Cox, Everett and Myrtle attended White River Friends Church
3/23/1865	Journal	People	Cox, Foster eloped and left wife
8/2/1905	Journal	People	Cox, Henry B. photo and obituary
6/22/1946	Journal-Herald	People	Cox, Kenneth "Jack" raised in White River Friends Church
4/12/1928	Journal-Herald	People	Cox, Mary Nichols is "old school teacher"
9/14/1936	Daily News	People	Cox, Mary Nichols is a former teacher at Clark School, southeast of Winchester
8/13/1925	Democrat	People	Cox, Mr. and Mrs. Addison, golden anniversary
7/30/1902	Journal	People	Cox, Olynthus pictured in last Thursday's Muncie Star
7/18/1906	Herald	People	Cox, Rev. Levi and Homer, tent meeting was forcibly closed down in Winchester
9/17/1919	Journal	People	Cox, Rev. Levi filled regular appointment at Upland
12/16/1908	Journal	People	Cox, Silas has moved to Winchester
2/6/1901	Journal	People	Cox, W. M. obituary; Quaker minister
4/30/1873	Journal	People	Cox, William B. obituary
7/13/1898	Journal	People	Cromer, George W., photo
9/20/1893	Journal	People	Cubberley, E. P. was speaker at Teachers' Institute
6/23/1979	News-Gazette	People	Daly Family featured
6/8/1970	News-Gazette	People	Daly, Dr. Walter J., son of Walter, a Randolph County native, is head of Medical Department of IUPUI
10/6/1927	Democrat	People	Daly, U. G. spoke at Mount Pleasant Friends Church
10/6/1927	Democrat	People	Daly, U. G., a "sprinter" tried to run away from him
11/22/1916	Herald	People	Daly, W. A. W. died
11/22/1916	Journal	People	Daly, W. A. W. died
11/19/1884	Journal	People	Daly, W. A. W. sworn in as deputy sheriff
6/4/1925	Democrat	People	Daly, W. H., Randolph County native, is new warden of prison at Michigan City
10/25/1916	Herald	People	Daly, Wm., farm, seven miles south of Winchester, for sale
10/12/1904	Journal	People	Daugherty, Harry will speak in Winchester on October 18, 1904
3/12/1902	Journal	People	Davenport, Rev. D. S., Christian minister, photo
6/23/1875	Journal	People	Davis, J. S., new residence in Farmland
2/3/1897	Journal	People	Davis, Kora is a Democrat
4/4/1944	Journal-Herald	People	Davisson, Jack "like all good Quakers you can rely on the honesty and sincerity of his convictions"
5/23/1968	Journal-Herald	People	Davisson, Jack died

Date	Source	Category	Description
9/10/1919	Herald	People	Davisson, W. J. died
4/17/1902	Democrat	People	Davisson, W. J. is building automobile with his cousin, Enos Hiatt
4/2/1884	Journal	People	Day, J. T., secretary of Franklin Township Republican Convention [he was later the Democrat mayor of Dunkirk]
7/28/1897	Journal	People	Denney, J. W. and E. A. McKee purchased the Seymour Democrat
10/17/1888	Journal	People	Denney, J. W. and Flora Deal will be married soon
4/4/1883	Journal	People	Denney, J. W. goes to Danville next week
2/18/1903	Herald	People	Denney, J. W. has been living in Dolores, Colorado for two years
5/8/1901	Journal	People	Denney, J. W. has moved from Alabama to Colorado
12/20/1900	Democrat	People	Denney, J. W. is a member of the Ruskin Socialist Colony near Way Cross, Georgia; "Ruskin Colony"
3/31/1886	Herald	People	Denney, J. W. is a teacher at Parker
11/1/1900	Democrat	People	Denney, J. W. is living in Ruskin, Georgia
6/5/1889	Herald	People	Denney, J. W. is reelected county superintendent
5/15/1895	Herald	People	Denney, J. W. is son-in-law of Peter Deal
4/8/1885	Journal	People	Denney, J. W. is taking a college course at Richmond
4/4/1883	Journal	People	Denney, J. W. is teaching at Maxville
6/10/1941	Journal-Herald	People	Denney, J. W. now living in Denver, Colorado
6/15/1892	Herald	People	Denney, J. W. purchased Hirsch Drug Store
6/7/1893	Herald	People	Denney, J. W. reelected county superintendent
7/6/1892	Journal	People	Denney, J. W. sold interest in drug store to his partner
9/1/1897	Herald	People	Denney, J. W., house on farm, located one mile south and one mile east of Olive Branch burned
9/1/1897	Journal	People	Denney, J. W., largest house in the county on the John Huffman Farm near Lickskillet, now owned by John W. Denney, burned
6/8/1887	Journal	People	Denney, J. W., new county superintendent, was principal at Windsor (1886-87)
6/30/1886	Herald	People	Denney, J. W., teaching at Windsor
4/23/1884	Journal	People	Denney, John W. "Willard," formerly of Nettle Creek, now teaching in White River, will attend school at Portland
8/4/1897	Herald	People	Denney, John W. became partner in Seymour Democrat

6/8/1887	Herald	People	Denney, John W. elected county superintendent on 19th ballot; was not a candidate until the 14th
10/28/1896	Journal	People	Denney, John W. is for free silver
1/18/1911	Journal	People	Denney, John W. lives at Anderson, Missouri; is in ill health and has quit teaching
6/24/1891	Journal	People	Denney, John Wesley, mentioned
5/17/1882	Journal	People	Denney, Willard is attending Pen Art Hall School at Delaware, Ohio
5/18/1916	Democrat	People	Dennis, David W., of Earlham, taught his first school two miles from Farmland in 1865 [probably Cedar]
1/15/1890	Journal	People	Denny [sic], J. W., elected Republican delegate; so was Charles Paris
12/19/1906	Journal	People	Denny [sic], John elected county superintendent in Colorado as a Free Silver Republican
12/14/1898	Journal	People	Denny [sic], John W. is teaching in Tennessee City, Tennessee
9/7/1881	Journal	People	Denny, Willard is organizing prohibition temperance clubs in Nettle Creek Township
8/24/1904	Journal	People	Dick, Philip K. photo
1/15/1957	Journal-Herald	People	Dickerson, Charles is principal at Williamsburg [Wayne County]
6/19/1963	News	People	Dickerson, Charles will become county superintendent on July 1; biographical information
3/13/1872	Journal	People	Diggs, Armsbee obituary
5/29/1912	Herald	People	Diggs, Calvin W. obituary and photo
4/3/1912	Journal	People	Diggs, Jesse obituary
10/6/1897	Journal	People	Diggs, Marshall Way
4/25/1888	Journal	People	Diggs, Thomas and Eunice, golden anniversary
12/26/1939	Journal-Herald	People	Diggs, William S., Winchester mayor from April 1, 1893 to September 10, 1898, died
6/15/1904	Herald	People	Dines, Leonidas G. "Lon," former editor of the Journal, died last Monday morning
6/7/1968	News	People	Dishler, Leota photo
4/20/1881	Journal	People	Dodd, Salathiel, born March 21, 1802 in Marshall Co., Vir.; died April 6, 1881; married May 1, 1828; member Olive Branch Church
5/22/1863	Journal	People	Doty sold to Abraham Roe (at New Dayton)
3/30/1940	Journal-Herald	People	Douglas, Rev. Charles died; member of F & A M and Scottish Rite
9/18/1918	Journal	People	Driver family went to Muncie to see a play or film
9/23/1903	Journal	People	Driver is catcher and 1/2 pitcher of Winchester High School team

Date	Source	Category	Description
10/22/1902	Journal	People	Driver is quarterback of Winchester High School football team
5/26/1886	Herald	People	Driver, "Dady" [Joab] will run the dutchman's engine this fall [traction engine at lumber yard?]
2/17/1897	Journal	People	Driver, Clarence and others built an igloo in his back yard
6/19/1907	Journal	People	Driver, Clarence has accepted a position in Dayton, Ohio
7/9/1902	Journal	People	Driver, Clarence hurt by toy cannon
4/19/1905	Journal	People	Driver, Clarence is catcher on WHS baseball team
11/24/1915	Journal	People	Driver, Elverson moved back from Florida
1/6/1915	Journal	People	Driver, Hal, brother of Lee and Randolph County native, is superintendent of schools at Aurora
6/18/1913	Journal	People	Driver, Herschel graduates from Mechanical Engineering Department at Purdue
9/1/1886	Journal	People	Driver, Jacob arrived in Randolph County on June 22, 1821
12/27/1893	Journal	People	Driver, Jacob died
3/3/1886	Journal	People	Driver, Jacob is ill
1/3/1894	Journal	People	Driver, Jacob, obituary
10/3/1877	Journal	People	Driver, Joab built house east of Farmland School
7/26/1876	Journal	People	Driver, Joab elected marshal of Farmland Hayes and Wheeler Republican Club; Charles W. Paris, secretary
10/3/1877	Journal	People	Driver, Joab has bought an acre of land east of Farmland schoolhouse and will build a residence
8/18/1875	Journal	People	Driver, Joab is building a house in Farmland
11/28/1883	Journal	People	Driver, Joab is charter member of Farmland GAR
7/26/1882	Journal	People	Driver, Joab is engineer at Stanley and Harbour's Mill
12/26/1877	Journal	People	Driver, Joab moved into his new house; has eye injury
2/21/1877	Journal	People	Driver, Joab sold his milk cow and lost money
9/11/1878	Journal	People	Driver, Joab sold his saw mill
10/3/1862	Journal	People	Driver, Joab wounded at Antietam
4/13/1887	Journal	People	Driver, Joab, "Dada Driver has had a very sick child"
3/18/1885	Journal	People	Driver, Joab, "Daddy Driver smiles and says it is another boy"
4/25/1888	Journal	People	Driver, Joab, obituary
11/14/1877	Journal	People	Driver, Joab's house is nearly finished
4/2/1879	Journal	People	Driver, Joab's little boy has been quite ill

Date	Source	Category	Description
1/25/1911	Journal	People	Driver, L. L. and Charles Hinshaw were the pronouncers at the spelling contest
4/13/1910	Journal	People	Driver, L. L. and Oscar Baker attend Northern Indiana State Teachers Association at Fort Wayne
7/19/1911	Journal	People	Driver, L. L. and others played lawn tennis
7/26/1911	Journal	People	Driver, L. L. and others played lawn tennis in Muncie
10/21/1908	Journal	People	Driver, L. L. and Trustee J. H. Sheppard visited West River Township schools
4/29/1891	Journal	People	Driver, L. L. appointed member of Finance Committee of County FMBA
12/7/1910	Journal	People	Driver, L. L. at dedication of Jackson School; for the first time in his life he got all the fried chicken he wanted to eat
12/16/1908	Journal	People	Driver, L. L. attended dinner for outgoing trustees, including J. H. Sheppard
7/7/1909	Journal	People	Driver, L. L. attended state meeting of county superintendents at Indianapolis last week
5/3/1911	Journal	People	Driver, L. L. has an exhibit of drawing from Lynn School
8/16/1911	Journal	People	Driver, L. L. has been invited to participate in the state tennis tournament
8/23/1911	Journal	People	Driver, L. L. has hay fever and will have to decline the invitation to speak at the Henry County Teachers' Institute
10/5/1910	Journal	People	Driver, L. L. inspected new schools in Green, Ward, and Jackson Townships on Thursday
7/5/1911	Journal	People	Driver, L. L. is at County Superintendents' meeting in Indianapolis
6/8/1910	Journal	People	Driver, L. L. is going to Purdue to son's graduation
1/18/1911	Journal	People	Driver, L. L. is in charge of the county spelling contest
12/9/1903	Journal	People	Driver, L. L. is member of the Winchester MWA and Summers Lodge F & A M
6/7/1911	Journal	People	Driver, L. L. is unanimously reelected county superintendent
5/18/1910	Journal	People	Driver, L. L. presented diplomas at White River Township commencement "in his scholarly manner"
7/6/1910	Journal	People	Driver, L. L. spent part of the week in Indianapolis
5/11/1910	Journal	People	Driver, L. L. was in Indianapolis yesterday

Date	Source	Category	Description
2/15/1911	Journal	People	Driver, L. L. was with Trustee Lee for bids on Modoc School
1/20/1909	Journal	People	Driver, L. L. will hold examinations
2/11/1885	Journal	People	Driver, L. L., Monroe Township teacher, was in town
10/18/1899	Journal	People	Driver, Lee and Amos Maple installed lockers in the basement of Winchester High School
8/19/1896	Journal	People	Driver, Lee and family returned from Bear Lake
8/24/1898	Journal	People	Driver, Lee and family returned from Turkey Lake
12/29/1897	Journal	People	Driver, Lee and Oscar Baker are at ISTA
12/28/1898	Journal	People	Driver, Lee and Oscar Baker at ISTA
8/25/1897	Journal	People	Driver, Lee and Oscar Baker returned from Nashville Exposition
3/9/1898	Journal	People	Driver, Lee and Oscar Baker went to science teachers meeting in Richmond
5/4/1898	Journal	People	Driver, Lee and Oscar Baker will open a Normal and Summer School in Central Building for six weeks
12/30/1896	Journal	People	Driver, Lee and others at ISTA
1/1/1896	Journal	People	Driver, Lee and others attended ISTA in Indianapolis last week
2/25/1885	Journal	People	Driver, Lee and others closed their schools in Monroe Township
8/22/1894	Journal	People	Driver, Lee and son in Winchester on bicycle
8/5/1896	Journal	People	Driver, Lee and Tom Ashton and families left for Turkey Lake
10/25/1911	Journal	People	Driver, Lee at Nettle Creek Township Institute on Saturday
1/22/1896	Journal	People	Driver, Lee at Parker IOOF
2/19/1896	Journal	People	Driver, Lee attended the funeral of Mrs. Jacob Meeks at Mount Pleasant
6/5/1907	Herald	People	Driver, Lee chosen county superintendent of schools
11/21/1917	Herald	People	Driver, Lee in demand as national speaker
3/28/1894	Journal	People	Driver, Lee injured building his house
3/14/1917	Herald	People	Driver, Lee is appointed Assistant State Superintendent of Public Instruction [He did not accept]
6/18/1919	Herald	People	Driver, Lee is appointed State High School Inspector; can the county match their salary offer?
8/25/1915	Herald	People	Driver, Lee is appointed to State Central Committee [of ISTA?]
6/6/1907	Democrat	People	Driver, Lee is elected new county superintendent of schools
4/3/1912	Herald	People	Driver, Lee is giving Randolph County history lecture

Date	Source	Category	Description
8/28/1895	Journal	People	Driver, Lee is in Winchester looking for a house
1/31/1912	Herald	People	Driver, Lee is new vice-president of Randolph County SS Association
5/28/1919	Herald	People	Driver, Lee is one of opening speakers at National Education Association convention in Milwaukee
7/2/1913	Herald	People	Driver, Lee is President of County Superintendents Association of Indiana
6/10/1914	Herald	People	Driver, Lee is President of County Superintendents Association of Indiana
3/13/1918	Herald	People	Driver, Lee is president of State Supervisors and Inspectors of Rural Schools
6/6/1917	Herald	People	Driver, Lee is reelected county superintendent; vote was 7-5 with two Democrats voting for him
7/3/1918	Journal	People	Driver, Lee L. addressed an educational meeting at Cleveland on Monday
2/17/1915	Journal	People	Driver, Lee L. addressed Randolph County Sunday School Association; reelected vice-president
3/12/1919	Journal	People	Driver, Lee L. and A. C. Wilmore led movement to put soldiers' monument in Woodlawn Cemetery
9/19/1917	Journal	People	Driver, Lee L. and A. L. Hodgson left Monday for Huntington to attend a convention
5/29/1912	Journal	People	Driver, Lee L. and C. M. Kelley are in Indianapolis attending the Masonic Grand Lodge
4/21/1886	Journal	People	Driver, Lee L. and Carrie Wood marriage license
9/2/1914	Journal	People	Driver, Lee L. and Charles Mahan will got to Decatur tomorrow; Driver will deliver an illustrated lecture on the township school
6/29/1898	Journal	People	Driver, Lee L. and family left for Vawter Park, where he will attend nine weeks term of Bloomington University
9/4/1901	Journal	People	Driver, Lee L. and family visited Oscar M. Wood
8/27/1902	Journal	People	Driver, Lee L. and family visited Oscar Wood at Parker
4/16/1919	Journal	People	Driver, Lee L. and Oscar Baker at district oratorical contest at Portland
3/3/1915	Journal	People	Driver, Lee L. and Oscar Baker left Wednesday to attend the National Association of School Superintendents Meeting in Cincinnati

Date	Source	Category	Description
5/24/1905	Journal	People	Driver, Lee L. and S. A. Canada are attending Grand Lodge of Masons in Indianapolis
1/7/1920	Journal	People	Driver, Lee L. and state inspector at Lincoln on December 29
3/26/1902	Journal	People	Driver, Lee L. and tennis players have built tennis courts at the high school
6/26/1918	Journal	People	Driver, Lee L. and wife and mother visited Herschel at Toledo
7/28/1915	Journal	People	Driver, Lee L. and wife are in Martinsville; she is taking baths and resting
7/23/1919	Journal	People	Driver, Lee L. and wife are in the East, where he will deliver a number of educational addresses
3/21/1900	Journal	People	Driver, Lee L. and wife entertained a crowd of young people at their home Friday evening
1/15/1908	Journal	People	Driver, Lee L. announces license exams
10/15/1913	Journal	People	Driver, Lee L. assisted with the funeral of Warren Burkett, a teacher
9/8/1915	Journal	People	Driver, Lee L. at County Teachers' Institute at Rockford, Illinois
9/9/1914	Journal	People	Driver, Lee L. at Decatur
10/25/1911	Journal	People	Driver, Lee L. at Indianapolis
1/2/1907	Journal	People	Driver, Lee L. at ISTA in Indianapolis
10/21/1914	Journal	People	Driver, Lee L. at Lincoln Farmers' Club on November 5
2/19/1919	Journal	People	Driver, Lee L. at State Teachers' Meeting in Pennsylvania last week
5/24/1905	Journal	People	Driver, Lee L. at state university
11/26/1913	Journal	People	Driver, Lee L. attended a meeting of Henry County teachers last Friday
9/18/1918	Journal	People	Driver, Lee L. attended District Meeting of Board of Instruction for Registrants at Ft. Wayne
6/30/1915	Journal	People	Driver, Lee L. attended funerals of Aunt Catherine Driver and Uncle Joseph McNees
1/2/1901	Journal	People	Driver, Lee L. attended State Teachers Meeting at Indianapolis
5/2/1900	Journal	People	Driver, Lee L. attended the District Republican Convention to selected delegates to the National Convention on May 10, 1900
1/1/1908	Journal	People	Driver, Lee L. attended the ISTA last week
12/12/1906	Journal	People	Driver, Lee L. attended Township Institute at Huntsville
12/11/1912	Journal	People	Driver, Lee L. attended West River Township Sunday School Convention
6/26/1912	Journal	People	Driver, Lee L. attends Franklin Township Sunday School Convention

Date	Source	Category	Description
7/23/1913	Journal	People	Driver, Lee L. became vice-president of the Randolph County Sunday School Association; Orebaugh moved up to president
6/16/1897	Journal	People	Driver, Lee L. becomes Winchester High School math teacher
10/12/1904	Journal	People	Driver, Lee L. built halltree for lab coats in high school chemistry lab
7/12/1893	Journal	People	Driver, Lee L. called on Journal Office
3/25/1908	Journal	People	Driver, Lee L. commended by teachers of Losantville School
1/27/1904	Journal	People	Driver, Lee L. daughter born to
7/16/1919	Journal	People	Driver, Lee L. declined appointment as State High School Inspector
8/7/1918	Journal	People	Driver, Lee L. delivered a patriotic address at Bartonia Sunday afternoon
5/15/1912	Journal	People	Driver, Lee L. delivered a talk on "The Organized Class, a Working Force" at the Greensfork Township Sunday School Convention at Brown Chapel
6/13/1917	Journal	People	Driver, Lee L. delivered commencement address at Drewersburg, Franklin County, last Thursday; will go to Daviess County on Friday
3/10/1915	Journal	People	Driver, Lee L. delivered his illustrated lecture on consolidated schools near Fort Wayne Saturday evening
10/22/1960	Journal-Herald	People	Driver, Lee L. dies in Florida
1/6/1904	Journal	People	Driver, Lee L. elected 8th District Vice-President of ISTA
12/9/1903	Journal	People	Driver, Lee L. elected Advisor of MWA Camp
1/31/1912	Journal	People	Driver, Lee L. elected president of the 8th, 9th, and 11th District County Superintendents Association at Kokomo last Thursday
12/16/1903	Journal	People	Driver, Lee L. elected S. W. of Summers Lodge
11/1/1916	Journal	People	Driver, Lee L. elected to the Executive Committee of the ISTA last week
12/20/1905	Journal	People	Driver, Lee L. elected W. M. of Summers Lodge
10/30/1912	Journal	People	Driver, Lee L. entertained the Superintendents of the 8th, 9th, and 10th [sic] Districts here
5/29/1918	Journal	People	Driver, Lee L. gave an address near Aurora last Thursday evening
12/11/1912	Journal	People	Driver, Lee L. gave an illustrated lecture at Jackson last Friday
6/18/1913	Journal	People	Driver, Lee L. gave commencement address at New Goshen on Saturday

Date	Source	Category	Description
8/26/1914	Journal	People	Driver, Lee L. gave illustrated lecture to Adams County Teachers' Institute
6/4/1913	Journal	People	Driver, Lee L. gave teachers examination to 70 teachers
4/9/1913	Journal	People	Driver, Lee L. gave the commencement address at Deedsville, Miami County
3/20/1901	Journal	People	Driver, Lee L. had charge of singing at WHS Monday morning
5/30/1900	Journal	People	Driver, Lee L. handed out diplomas at Winchester High School commencement and gave a speech
6/18/1919	Journal	People	Driver, Lee L. has been hired as High School Inspector for the state [he turned it down]
12/31/1913	Journal	People	Driver, Lee L. has been named chairman of the legislative committee of the Indiana State Teachers Association
7/24/1918	Journal	People	Driver, Lee L. has been sick
11/18/1914	Journal	People	Driver, Lee L. has given all pennies to his daughter Agnes since 1909
11/21/1917	Journal	People	Driver, Lee L. has returned from North Dakota and Arkansas
8/8/1917	Journal	People	Driver, Lee L. has returned from the Dakotas
5/1/1918	Journal	People	Driver, Lee L. held examination for 89 teaching applicants
10/18/1911	Journal	People	Driver, Lee L. helped put the new seats in the school at Huntsville
7/3/1895	Journal	People	Driver, Lee L. hired as eighth grade teacher in Winchester; will resign from Parker City Schools
5/19/1915	Journal	People	Driver, Lee L. hit himself with an ax; it bounced off a clothesline while he was cutting a cherry tree; he was not hurt
7/27/1904	Journal	People	Driver, Lee L. in I. U. Catalogue
11/5/1913	Journal	People	Driver, Lee L. in quarantine
2/20/1889	Journal	People	Driver, Lee L. is "prosperous young farmer of Monroe Township"
10/8/1919	Journal	People	Driver, Lee L. is a member of the board of directors of the Winchester Rotary Club
4/24/1918	Journal	People	Driver, Lee L. is a member of the committee in charge of state educational week
9/10/1913	Journal	People	Driver, Lee L. is a member of the Education Committee and the Executive Committee of the County Fall Festival Association
12/29/1915	Journal	People	Driver, Lee L. is a member of the membership committee of the Monroe Township Farmers' Institute

6/12/1918	Journal	People	Driver, Lee L. is acting chairman of Thrift Stamp Campaign; war saving stamp drive
3/14/1917	Journal	People	Driver, Lee L. is again offered the job of State High School Inspector
12/18/1901	Journal	People	Driver, Lee L. is against cigarettes
4/22/1914	Journal	People	Driver, Lee L. is at commencement each night this week
12/18/1918	Journal	People	Driver, Lee L. is at teachers' association meeting in Pennsylvania
12/27/1916	Journal	People	Driver, Lee L. is at the State Teachers Association of New Jersey in Atlantic City Friday of this week
7/3/1918	Journal	People	Driver, Lee L. is attending the NEA at Pittsburgh
6/26/1918	Journal	People	Driver, Lee L. is chair of War Saving and Stamp Canvass
9/15/1915	Journal	People	Driver, Lee L. is chairman of education committee of Randolph County Fall Festival and Home Coming
11/8/1916	Journal	People	Driver, Lee L. is chairman of the Executive Committee of the ISTA
3/12/1913	Journal	People	Driver, Lee L. is delivering an illustrated talk on consolidated schools in Miami County this week
2/20/1889	Journal	People	Driver, Lee L. is described as "a young farmer"
1/20/1904	Journal	People	Driver, Lee L. is elected treasurer of Winchester City Republican Committee
12/18/1912	Journal	People	Driver, Lee L. is elected W. M. of Summers Lodge
8/1/1900	Journal	People	Driver, Lee L. is enrolled at Indiana University
5/2/1888	Journal	People	Driver, Lee L. is erecting a very fine residence north of Parker
11/7/1917	Journal	People	Driver, Lee L. is going to North Dakota and Arkansas
6/21/1916	Journal	People	Driver, Lee L. is headed to New York City next month
6/21/1905	Journal	People	Driver, Lee L. is home from state university for a weeks' vacation
10/3/1917	Journal	People	Driver, Lee L. is in Indianapolis to prepare for ISTA, October 31 through November 3, 1917
11/5/1919	Journal	People	Driver, Lee L. is in the east, delivering talks at Columbia University and in Pennsylvania and New Jersey
12/17/1902	Journal	People	Driver, Lee L. is J. W. of Summers Lodge, No. 637
7/17/1901	Journal	People	Driver, Lee L. is listed in IU Catalogue
10/27/1915	Journal	People	Driver, Lee L. is member of Executive Committee of Indiana State Teachers Association

Date	Source	Category	Description
9/11/1918	Journal	People	Driver, Lee L. is named chairman of the Board of Instructions for Registrants [for Randolph County]
1/4/1911	Journal	People	Driver, Lee L. is now a grandpa "proudly"
3/7/1917	Journal	People	Driver, Lee L. is offered the job of State High School Inspector
7/23/1919	Journal	People	Driver, Lee L. is on advisory committee of County Fair and Stock Show
1/30/1918	Journal	People	Driver, Lee L. is on program of Randolph County Sunday School Convention
3/12/1919	Journal	People	Driver, Lee L. is on program tonight at Blackford County Sunday School Association
1/15/1913	Journal	People	Driver, Lee L. is on the program of the 31st annual convention of the Randolph County Sunday School Association, January 23-24, 1913; his subject is "Making Teaching Easier and More Interesting"
7/5/1916	Journal	People	Driver, Lee L. is on way to New York City
9/1/1915	Journal	People	Driver, Lee L. is one of 15 members of the State Historical Commission speaking tour
9/27/1911	Journal	People	Driver, Lee L. is one of the organizers of the Association of County Superintendents of the 8th, 9th, and 11th Congressional Districts at Marion last Wednesday
10/22/1919	Journal	People	Driver, Lee L. is one of vice-chairmen of Randolph County organization for Roosevelt Memorial
12/6/1911	Journal	People	Driver, Lee L. is preparing a historical review of the county for the schools
10/25/1916	Journal	People	Driver, Lee L. is president of new County Anti-Tuberculosis Society
6/10/1914	Journal	People	Driver, Lee L. is president of the County Superintendents Association of Indiana; will give opening address at convention
2/19/1908	Journal	People	Driver, Lee L. is president of White River Township Sunday School Institute [new president elected in March]
6/6/1917	Journal	People	Driver, Lee L. is reelected county superintendent
1/29/1913	Journal	People	Driver, Lee L. is reelected vice-president of the Randolph County Sunday School Association
3/18/1914	Journal	People	Driver, Lee L. is speaker at White River Township Teachers' Institute on March 21, 1914
10/8/1913	Journal	People	Driver, Lee L. is speaker on tour of Randolph County Sunday School Association, October 13-19, 1913

Date	Source	Category	Description
7/7/1915	Journal	People	Driver, Lee L. is speaking in Adams County
4/3/1918	Journal	People	Driver, Lee L. is spending the week in Arkansas
8/21/1918	Journal	People	Driver, Lee L. is spending the week in Athens, Ohio
1/9/1907	Journal	People	Driver, Lee L. is teacher of and trustee of Ben-Hur
12/10/1919	Journal	People	Driver, Lee L. is vice-president of new Rotary Club
1/15/1913	Journal	People	Driver, Lee L. is vice-president of the Randolph County Sunday School Association
2/7/1900	Journal	People	Driver, Lee L. is White River Township Delegate to District Republican Convention
1/13/1904	Journal	People	Driver, Lee L. is Winchester 5 Republican precinct committeeman
2/27/1901	Journal	People	Driver, Lee L. lectured on Longfellow at WHS
1/14/1920	Journal	People	Driver, Lee L. left for a two weeks visit to Pennsylvania
2/20/1918	Journal	People	Driver, Lee L. left for Washington, D. C. and Atlantic City
1/15/1913	Journal	People	Driver, Lee L. left Monday for Indianapolis to attend the State Board of Education meeting
9/25/1918	Journal	People	Driver, Lee L. left Saturday for Bloomington and universities and schools in Wisconsin and Iowa, where he will deliver addresses for the remainder of the week.
10/9/1918	Journal	People	Driver, Lee L. left the first of the week to fill a number of educational engagements in Wisconsin
12/8/1915	Journal	People	Driver, Lee L. left yesterday for Lebanon, Pennsylvania, to deliver a talk on the consolidated school system
8/5/1903	Journal	People	Driver, Lee L. listed in catalogue of I. U.
4/21/1915	Journal	People	Driver, Lee L. made student appointment to training at Culver for two weeks
2/13/1961	News	People	Driver, Lee L. memorial of Randolph County Historical Society for
9/23/1914	Journal	People	Driver, Lee L. met with 13 of 14 county principals on Saturday
11/19/1919	Journal	People	Driver, Lee L. moved to Paul Gray's house on W. Washington; the property he vacated on the east side of town is being occupied by its owner, Mart McDonald
8/24/1892	Journal	People	Driver, Lee L. not listed at county teachers' institute
12/2/1903	Journal	People	Driver, Lee L. on Executive Committee of County Teachers' Association

12/4/1907	Journal	People	Driver, Lee L. on Executive Committee of County Teachers' Association
5/7/1902	Journal	People	Driver, Lee L. presented diplomas at Farmland High School; Hal Driver graduated
5/16/1906	Journal	People	Driver, Lee L. presented diplomas at Winchester High School commencement
3/6/1918	Journal	People	Driver, Lee L. presided over a County Council of Defense meeting at Main Street Church on Sunday
8/29/1900	Journal	People	Driver, Lee L. promoted to principalship of Winchester High School
6/12/1919	Democrat	People	Driver, Lee L. receives M. A. degree from Earlham College
6/9/1911	Democrat	People	Driver, Lee L. reelected county superintendent
2/4/1914	Journal	People	Driver, Lee L. reelected vice-president of the Randolph County Sunday School Association
2/7/1900	Journal	People	Driver, Lee L. refused to excuse anyone from the assembly room during the fire Wednesday afternoon. Wonder why?
11/12/1913	Journal	People	Driver, Lee L. released after three weeks in quarantine yesterday; daughter has diphtheria
2/13/1918	Journal	People	Driver, Lee L. reported the sale of thrift stamps in schools
7/3/1895	Journal	People	Driver, Lee L. resigned from Parker Schools to teach eighth grade at Winchester
12/24/1919	Journal	People	Driver, Lee L. resigns as county superintendent effective January 10
1/28/1920	Journal	People	Driver, Lee L. retired on Saturday [January 24, 1920]; nine one-room schools remain
4/10/1918	Journal	People	Driver, Lee L. returned from Arkansas, where he delivered his illustrated lecture on consolidated schools
8/12/1903	Journal	People	Driver, Lee L. returned from Bloomington, where he was attending school
12/22/1915	Journal	People	Driver, Lee L. returned from Pennsylvania
7/19/1916	Journal	People	Driver, Lee L. returned from the east
3/6/1918	Journal	People	Driver, Lee L. returned from the east, where he had been on invitation to deliver a number of addresses to national educational bodies
10/2/1918	Journal	People	Driver, Lee L. returned Wednesday from a professional visit at Stevens Point, Wisconsin

Date	Source	Category	Description
2/25/1903	Journal	People	Driver, Lee L. spent music time talking on the work of the General Assembly
1/28/1920	Journal	People	Driver, Lee L. spoke about Randolph County Schools to Rotary Club
5/4/1904	Journal	People	Driver, Lee L. spoke and presented diplomas at Farmland High School commencement
2/25/1914	Journal	People	Driver, Lee L. spoke at Harrison Township, Blackford County
2/17/1915	Journal	People	Driver, Lee L. spoke at Huntsville Parent-Teacher Meeting
10/11/1916	Journal	People	Driver, Lee L. spoke at Indiana Day at Winchester Friends Church
10/9/1901	Journal	People	Driver, Lee L. spoke on cigarette smoking at Winchester High School
10/27/1915	Journal	People	Driver, Lee L. spoke on Randolph County at the Union City Community Welfare Entertainment
8/11/1915	Journal	People	Driver, Lee L. spoke to Old Settlers Reunion at Economy yesterday
4/2/1919	Journal	People	Driver, Lee L. spoke to Pennsylvania legislative committee
2/18/1900	Journal	People	Driver, Lee L. students had surprise birthday party for
11/11/1914	Journal	People	Driver, Lee L. suggests that all schools should observe Riley Day
3/7/1906	Journal	People	Driver, Lee L. suggests the study of parliamentary law
8/19/1908	Journal	People	Driver, Lee L. supplied electric fans to the County Institute
6/26/1912	Journal	People	Driver, Lee L. to attend the State County Superintendents Meeting at Lafayette
4/23/1913	Journal	People	Driver, Lee L. to give a lecture on Randolph County at Ridgeville
10/26/1904	Journal	People	Driver, Lee L. to play bass violin in W. H. S. orchestra
11/19/1913	Journal	People	Driver, Lee L. to speak before the Union City Parent-Teacher Meeting on Wednesday
7/26/1916	Journal	People	Driver, Lee L. told of James Whitcomb Riley's family in Randolph County at M. E. Sunday School
7/1/1914	Journal	People	Driver, Lee L. took teachers examination at Muncie; 65 took it in Randolph County
4/4/1906	Journal	People	Driver, Lee L. took up subscription for Athletic Association
1/29/1919	Journal	People	Driver, Lee L. tried to save Grant Gilmore, whose car was stalled on the Interurban track
1/13/1892	Journal	People	Driver, Lee L. visited Journal Office
2/18/1903	Journal	People	Driver, Lee L. was at Farmland on Thursday attending Masonic Lodge
1/17/1917	Journal	People	Driver, Lee L. was at Union City for Indiana University alumni meeting

7/2/1913	Journal	People	Driver, Lee L. was elected president of the County School Superintendents Association of Indiana at Bloomington last week
3/3/1920	Journal	People	Driver, Lee L. was here visiting consolidated schools
3/5/1919	Journal	People	Driver, Lee L. was in Chicago last week for National Educational Meeting
5/21/1913	Journal	People	Driver, Lee L. was in Pike County last week and in Hamilton County yesterday
2/11/1885	Journal	People	Driver, Lee L. was in Winchester; he is teaching in Monroe Township
2/14/1917	Journal	People	Driver, Lee L. was not elected to any office in the Randolph County Sunday School Association
6/13/1917	Journal	People	Driver, Lee L. was one of the principal speakers at the state meeting of county superintendents
5/2/1917	Herald	People	Driver, Lee L. was principal speaker at flag raising at Masonic Building
2/18/1914	Journal	People	Driver, Lee L. was speaker at the Green Township Teachers' Institute
5/22/1918	Journal	People	Driver, Lee L. went to Camp Taylor to see Max Diggs, John Ferris, Ray Crist
10/10/1917	Journal	People	Driver, Lee L. went to Camp Taylor to try to see soldiers from Randolph County
11/27/1918	Journal	People	Driver, Lee L. went to Greenfield to see the unveiling of the Riley Statue
7/25/1917	Journal	People	Driver, Lee L. went to North Dakota to help in county institute work
10/17/1917	Journal	People	Driver, Lee L. went to the State Board of Accounts to get waiver for the new boiler at Farmland
3/29/1916	Journal	People	Driver, Lee L. will address the Huntsville PTA on April 7, 1916
5/29/1912	Journal	People	Driver, Lee L. will address the Washington Township Sunday School Convention Thursday of next week
6/17/1914	Journal	People	Driver, Lee L. will address the West River Township Sunday School Convention on June 21, 1914
5/31/1899	Journal	People	Driver, Lee L. will be a speaker at the White River Township Sunday School convention next Sunday
5/23/1917	Journal	People	Driver, Lee L. will be at Cambridge City on Friday to deliver a commencement address on "Centralized Vocational Schools"
2/18/1914	Journal	People	Driver, Lee L. will be at the Huntsville Parent-Teachers' Association Meeting on February 20, 1914
5/21/1919	Journal	People	Driver, Lee L. will deliver Memorial address at New Dayton

1/17/1912	Journal	People	Driver, Lee L. will give a historical lecture in the court room on January 18, 1912
12/15/1915	Journal	People	Driver, Lee L. will give a lecture at Schoolhouse No. 5 in Franklin Township
3/6/1918	Journal	People	Driver, Lee L. will give an illustrated lecture on the Revolutionary Period at the Presbyterian Church on March 14; sponsored by Daughters of the American Revolution for the war relief fund
5/5/1915	Journal	People	Driver, Lee L. will give commencement address at Eaton, Indiana
10/2/1918	Journal	People	Driver, Lee L. will go to a social meeting at the new school in Wayne Township
5/1/1912	Journal	People	Driver, Lee L. will hand out diplomas at Stoney Creek, West River
4/21/1915	Journal	People	Driver, Lee L. will have charge of Indiana's educational exhibit at San Francisco
9/11/1918	Journal	People	Driver, Lee L. will preside over seeing off 29 soldiers
10/4/1916	Journal	People	Driver, Lee L. will represent the ISTA at the annual meeting of Charities and Corrections at Indianapolis on October 16-17, 1916
2/3/1915	Journal	People	Driver, Lee L. will speak on "The Teacher" at the Randolph County Sunday School Association Convention on February 11 and 12, 1915
1/16/1918	Journal	People	Driver, Lee L. will speak on war savings stamps at Green Township Farmers Institute
8/14/1918	Journal	People	Driver, Lee L. writes article for the centennial of Randolph County
2/26/1908	Journal	People	Driver, Lee L., exam for 8th grade graduates
12/31/1919	Journal	People	Driver, Lee L., family will stay in Winchester until June
3/6/1912	Journal	People	Driver, Lee L., historical lecture at Harrisville lasted two hours
3/13/1912	Journal	People	Driver, Lee L., historical lecture at Huntsville on March 16 and at Green on March 22; was at Modoc last Friday
1/24/1912	Journal	People	Driver, Lee L., historical lecture described
2/14/1912	Journal	People	Driver, Lee L., historical lecture given at Losantville
1/31/1912	Journal	People	Driver, Lee L., historical lecture given at Spartanburg
2/21/1912	Journal	People	Driver, Lee L., historical lecture will be given at Harrisville, Saratoga, and Farmland

3/6/1912	Journal	People	Driver, Lee L., historical lecture will be given at McKinley on March 15, 1912
3/25/1896	Journal	People	Driver, Lee L., is charter member of Winchester Court, Ben Hur and original captain
10/15/1913	Journal	People	Driver, Lee L., lecture at Purdue
7/16/1913	Journal	People	Driver, Lee L., meeting of Randolph County Sunday School Association Council to be held in his office
4/16/1913	Journal	People	Driver, Lee L., member of the Sons of Veterans [?]
5/28/1919	Journal	People	Driver, Lee L., Milwaukee papers praise him; he is going to NEA June 28-July 5, 1919
10/13/1897	Journal	People	Driver, Lee L., mother visited
6/4/1919	Journal	People	Driver, Lee L., petition to raise salary
12/31/1919	Journal	People	Driver, Lee L., Rotary Club honors
6/24/1914	Journal	People	Driver, Lee L., speech at County Superintendents Association meeting described
8/9/1899	Journal	People	Driver, Lee L., Sunday School class of will meet August 10
11/26/1902	Journal	People	Driver, Lee L., surprise on "Leotus Lincoln Driver"
3/21/1917	Journal	People	Driver, Lee L., West River Township teachers support retention of Driver as superintendent
3/23/1904	Journal	People	Driver, Lee L., White River Township Republican Chairman, called township convention
6/11/1919	Journal	People	Driver, Lee L.; Earlham College will confer BA [sic] on
9/25/1918	Journal	People	Driver, Lee L.; Supt. Lewellen of New Castle was in Winchester for 4th Liberty Loan and said that Lee L. Driver was of national repute in educational circles
8/8/1900	Journal	People	Driver, Lee L.'s Sunday School class went on an excursion
4/12/1916	Journal	People	Driver, Lee L.'s talks "are always pleasing" [Huntsville]
11/15/1899	Journal	People	Driver, Lee lectured on ants at high school
6/21/1899	Journal	People	Driver, Lee left for a summer course at Winona Lake
8/30/1893	Journal	People	Driver, Lee lost house to fire
2/27/1907	Journal	People	Driver, Lee moved from Dick Kemp's house to James Moorman property on East North Street
11/19/1919	Herald	People	Driver, Lee moved from E. Washington Street
9/4/1895	Journal	People	Driver, Lee moved into Dennis Kelley's property on South Meridian Street
2/27/1895	Journal	People	Driver, Lee of Farmland was in Winchester last Saturday

Date	Source	Category	Description
10/2/1954	Journal-Herald	People	Driver, Lee receives Pennsylvania Ambassador Award; was originally a carpenter
9/7/1904	Journal	People	Driver, Lee recovered stolen watch
6/7/1911	Herald	People	Driver, Lee reelected County Superintendent of Schools without opposition
12/24/1919	Herald	People	Driver, Lee resigns as county superintendent
7/28/1897	Journal	People	Driver, Lee returned from Bloomington to go to Turkey Lake
7/21/1897	Journal	People	Driver, Lee returned from Indiana University for his mother-in-law's funeral
8/14/1895	Journal	People	Driver, Lee returned from Terre Haute; will move to Winchester when he can find a house
10/18/1958	Journal-Herald	People	Driver, Lee sent books to Monroe Central and said, "to me Randolph County is the center of the universe"
4/19/1899	Journal	People	Driver, Lee spoke at the 19th anniversary of the Winchester Lodge, K of P
6/7/1917	Democrat	People	Driver, Lee succeeds self as county superintendent
10/15/1919	Herald	People	Driver, Lee to lecture at National Convention of Rural Schools in Sioux Falls, SD
2/9/1898	Journal	People	Driver, Lee visited Farmland
5/14/1960	Journal-Herald	People	Driver, Lee was called "Ottie" in youth
9/18/1895	Journal	People	Driver, Lee went to the funeral of J. W. Jones, a teacher, at Parker
4/2/1884	Journal	People	Driver, Lee will go to Danville next Monday to pursue studies
7/26/1952	Journal-Herald	People	Driver, Lee writes of old jail and need for county museum
8/14/1954	Journal-Herald	People	Driver, Lee, bicycle story
7/1/1903	Journal	People	Driver, Lee, Hal, and Clarence attending summer term at Indiana University
8/30/1893	Herald	People	Driver, Lee, house, two miles north of Parker, burned
1/27/1897	Journal	People	Driver, Lee, infant child of died
4/5/1899	Journal	People	Driver, Lee, Oscar Baker, and Amos Maple attended a State Teachers' Association meeting at Fort Wayne
2/9/1898	Journal	People	Driver, Lee, pictures taken of his room in school
6/16/1897	Journal	People	Driver, Lee, promoted; left for Indiana University for the summer term
5/17/1917	Democrat	People	Driver, Lee, reappointment as county superintendent is opposed by Winchester Democrat newspaper
3/19/1977	News-Gazette	People	Driver, Lee, remembered by North Carolina visitor from 1919

Date	Source	Category	Description
3/23/1904	Herald	People	Driver, Lee, White River Township Republican Chairman
9/1/1897	Journal	People	Driver, Levi visited Lee Driver; Levi is teaching in Knox County
12/23/1896	Journal	People	Driver, Mary E., of Farmland, visited Lee Driver in Winchester
1/21/1874	Journal	People	Driver, Mollie E., letter from Farmland
1/12/1898	Journal	People	Driver, Mr. is preparing a catalogue of the Smithsonian Reports so that they are easier to use
6/30/1915	Journal	People	Driver, Mrs. Lee L. entertained the Priscilla Club
6/18/1902	Journal	People	Driver, Mrs. Lee L. is improving from illness
7/10/1901	Journal	People	Driver, Mrs. Lee L. left for Bloomington
8/11/1915	Journal	People	Driver, Mrs. Lee L. returned from Martinsville
11/14/1906	Journal	People	Driver, Mrs. Lee L. returned from Purdue
11/20/1901	Journal	People	Driver, Mrs. loaned organ to Winchester High School
9/8/1880	Journal	People	Driver, Mrs. Mary E. baptized by Samuel McNees
1/2/1918	Journal	People	Driver, Mrs. Mary will spend the winter in Florida
12/16/1885	Journal	People	Driver, Otta is camping in the woods
5/14/1884	Journal	People	Driver, Otto is home from school at Danville
12/9/1896	Journal	People	Driver, Prof. & Mrs. are the parents of a baby girl
4/5/1899	Journal	People	Driver, Prof. Lee was elected treasurer of the State High School Association last week at Fort Wayne
8/28/1895	Journal	People	Driver, Prof. Lee was in our city last Saturday, looking for a house to move into
9/20/1899	Journal	People	Driver, Prof.'s class held an entertainment to benefit the new M. E. Church
8/25/1897	Journal	People	Driver, Professor Lee moved to property on E. South St. formerly occupied by Charles Hiatt
1/1/1896	Journal	People	Driver, Professor Lee's family visited near Parker last week
3/4/1896	Journal	People	Driver, Professor visited Farmland
12/24/1895	Journal	People	Driver, Professor wants "more pupils" for Christmas
2/26/1896	Journal	People	Driver, Professor, surprise 29th birthday party; has taught school since he was 16
4/19/1893	Journal	People	Eaton, A. K., first auditor of Randolph County, letter from
7/25/1944	Journal-Herald	People	Edger, E. E. and Jane photos
8/6/1925	Democrat	People	Edger, E. S. died

Date	Publication	Section	Description
3/18/1915	Democrat	People	Edger, E. S. photograph
8/4/1880	Journal	People	Edwards, Eli, obituary; Quaker
8/15/1906	Journal	People	Edwards, Rev. Frank was recently recorded as a Friends minister and preaches every Sunday at Charlottesville
7/29/1914	Journal	People	Edwards, Rev. Frank, Quaker minister, is a son of J. L. Edwards of Martindale
5/13/1926	Democrat	People	Eilar, Jesse is elected County Superintendent of Henry County
2/7/1906	Herald	People	Ellis, Rev. Elwood confesses to adultery
9/21/1904	Herald	People	Ellis, Rev. Elwood O. dropped from membership by Friends Church in Richmond
7/20/1904	Herald	People	Ellis, Rev. Elwood O., Quaker minister of Richmond, has been found
7/13/1904	Herald	People	Ellis, Rev. Elwood O., Quaker minister of Richmond, is missing
6/9/1880	Journal	People	Elzroth, John died at home of grandson, Cal Hiatt at Amboy; he was 94
9/28/1898	Journal	People	Engle, Calvin, photo
8/27/1890	Journal	People	Engle, Isaac, picture and obituary
4/11/1917	Journal	People	Engle, Judge is candidate for state constitutional convention
11/2/1870	Journal	People	Ferris, James S., biography
10/12/1870	Journal	People	Ferris, Rev. James S. obituary
4/12/1952	Journal-Herald	People	Fetters, Mr. and Mrs. C. C. golden anniversary
3/13/1930	Democrat	People	Fidler, Eugene is a son of Ed and Cecil (Harbour) Fidler; [Cecil was a daughter of Dempsey Harbour]
11/16/1957	Journal-Herald	People	Fields, John, county councilman, died; father of Wallace and Weldon
4/19/1968	Journal-Herald	People	Fisher, Rev. and Mrs. Orville, golden anniversary
3/26/1968	Journal-Herald	People	Flatter, Rev. and Mrs. Adam, golden anniversary
12/4/1901	Journal	People	Flood, J. L. obituary
1/29/1890	Journal	People	Flood, John criticized
8/31/1881	Journal	People	Flood, John is fixing up a little stylish for a Quaker
5/23/1888	Journal	People	Flood, Uncle John joined IORM
5/4/1898	Journal	People	Flood, Uncle John would go to Cuba, if needed [Spanish-American War]
9/10/1925	Democrat	People	Focht, Ferman C. died
2/20/1901	Journal	People	Foreman, Sylvanus, old soldier, buried at Bear Creek
3/7/1883	Journal	People	Forkner, Amer, last Democratic sheriff elected in Randolph County, died in Richmond last week

Date	Publication	Category	Description
1/6/1915	Herald	People	Fox, S. D. died; had been Winchester City Clerk since 1898; was town trustee from 1879-81
11/19/1984	News-Gazette	People	Fraze Family awarded Hoosier Homestead Farm Award; S. P. Burton Family earlier
11/15/1905	Journal	People	Frazier, Rev. Elihu, Friends minister, formerly of this county, lives at Summitville
5/15/1878	Journal	People	Frist, Cora is teaching at Small Schoolhouse, near Lynn
3/30/1898	Journal	People	Fulgham, Amy, obituary
3/23/1898	Journal	People	Fulgham, Amy, Quaker minister, died in Clinton County, Ohio
2/21/1948	Journal-Herald	People	Furnas, Miles J. is a 50-year Mason
6/20/1890	Democrat	People	Furnas, Miles J. is member of FMBA
3/17/1909	Herald	People	Furnas, Miles J. may run for Congress
10/8/1954	News	People	Furnas, Miles J. obituary
7/29/1896	Journal	People	Furnas, Robert W., ex-Governor of Nebraska, is cousin of Furnas Brothers of Lynn
6/27/1907	Democrat	People	Furstenberger, Rev. A. J., photo [Quaker minister]
11/13/1973	News-Gazette	People	Gaddis, Gail featured
1/28/1903	Herald	People	Garrett, Fremont died
5/2/1900	Herald	People	Garrett, Fremont, reminiscences
10/11/1871	Journal	People	Garrett, Nathan, former sheriff and auditor, died
11/7/1907	Democrat	People	Ginger, Sam, biography and photo
1/5/1943	Journal-Herald	People	Gist, Ollie photo
6/2/1936	News-Democrat	People	Goodrich and Watson pictured in a political cartoon
6/9/1936	News-Democrat	People	Goodrich and Watson pictured in a political cartoon
1/2/1918	Herald	People	Goodrich, Elizabeth P. died
1/2/1918	Journal	People	Goodrich, Elizabeth P. died
3/7/1917	Journal	People	Goodrich, Governor signed limited women's suffrage law
9/15/1915	Herald	People	Goodrich, James P. announces candidacy for governor
7/14/1897	Herald	People	Goodrich, James P. elected County Republican Chairman to replace W. W. Canada
12/14/1887	Journal	People	Goodrich, James P., residence burned
4/6/1898	Journal	People	Goodrich, John and Elizabeth, frame residence burned on Residence Street
3/21/1888	Journal	People	Goodrich-Frist wedding
2/20/1895	Journal	People	Gray, Gov. Isaac died in Mexico
10/16/1975	News-Gazette	People	Gray, Isaac P. photos

Date	Publication	Category	Description
2/20/1895	Herald	People	Gray, Isaac P., dead
9/3/1983	News-Gazette	People	Gray, Jesse, story in Saturday Extra
11/27/1907	Herald	People	Gray, Pierre died
2/11/1926	Journal-Herald	People	Greist, O. H.
11/8/1947	Journal-Herald	People	Greist, O. H. died November 6 at Plainfield, buried in Indianapolis
11/7/1947	News	People	Greist, O. H. died November 6; biographical information
1/7/1920	Journal	People	Greist, O. H. elected county superintendent
1/18/1923	Journal-Herald	People	Greist, O. H. is member of Main Street Christian Church
6/9/1921	Democrat	People	Greist, O. H. is reelected County Superintendent
6/4/1925	Democrat	People	Greist, O. H. is reelected County Superintendent
10/6/1859	Journal	People	Griffis, James, former legislator, died
7/30/1931	Journal-Herald	People	Gutheil, William is son of Arthur and Cora (Diggs), grandson of Marshall and Elizabeth (Addington) Diggs
6/22/1898	Herald	People	Hadley, Judge John V. of Hinshaw Murder Case is candidate for State Supreme Court
5/15/1912	Journal	People	Haisley, Franklin obituary
4/10/1889	Journal	People	Hall, Sarah Hunt, wife of Rev. Colbrath Hall and daughter of Rev. William Hunt, obituary
9/15/1983	News-Gazette	People	Hamilton, Dorothy, noted author in Delaware County, is member of Friends Memorial Church, Muncie
7/3/1976	News-Gazette	People	Hamilton, Joe died; mother was Emma (Keggeris) Hamilton
8/21/1972	News-Gazette	People	Hamilton, Joe is a historian of Randolph County
7/9/1966	Journal-Herald	People	Hancock, Brig. Gen. Robinson is Randolph County native
10/2/1912	Journal	People	Harding, Warren G. gave a speech at the Courthouse
10/12/1904	Journal	People	Harding, Warren G. was at Opera House on Wednesday
10/21/1914	Journal	People	Hardwick, Rev. John moved to Van Wert, Ohio
6/9/1909	Herald	People	Harris, Eliza, the real Eliza Harris of "Uncle Tom's Cabin"
1/12/1881	Journal	People	Harris, Emily J. died
2/17/1909	Journal	People	Harris, Jonathan, old solider and lifelong Quaker, died; buried at Poplar Run
4/5/1938	Journal-Herald	People	Harris, Milford L. was member at Poplar Run and on County Council
10/15/1890	Herald	People	Harrison, Benjamin passed through Winchester

7/24/1889	Journal	People	Harrison, Elizabeth (Flood), obituary; daughter of Rev. Jonathan Flood and widow of Jesse Harrison; mother of J. B. Harrison
5/18/1953	News	People	Harrison, Herb is new postmaster of Winchester
8/6/1884	Journal	People	Harrison, J. B. visited; living in New England
6/26/1907	Journal	People	Harrison, J. B., former county superintendent [examiner] died
10/21/1858	Journal	People	Harrison, J. B., Rev., married Phebe J. Claever [sic] of Shelby County, Indiana on October 17, 1858
4/22/1858	Journal	People	Harrison, J. B., secretary of Temperance Meeting
10/12/1870	Journal	People	Harrison, Jesse died in Green Township; father of Rev. J. B. Harrison of New York City; had lived in Randolph County for 23 years
10/23/1889	Journal	People	Harrison, Jesse, will probated; dated August 2, 1868; he died in 1870
10/15/1890	Journal	People	Harrison, President passed through on Monday
10/8/1890	Journal	People	Harrison, President will pass through on Monday
4/14/1875	Journal	People	Harvey, Nathan, a Quaker of New Castle, taught Senator Morton at Salisbury
9/18/1878	Journal	People	Henizer, Fred died
1/30/1895	Journal	People	Herron, Mrs. Senith died
11/3/1915	Herald	People	Hiatt, Adam R. died
11/3/1915	Journal	People	Hiatt, Adam R. died
3/28/1946	Journal-Herald	People	Hiatt, Bertha, widow of Rev. C. E. died March 26 at Knightstown
10/21/1891	Herald	People	Hiatt, Dr. Jehu, obituary
10/21/1891	Journal	People	Hiatt, Dr., obituary
9/22/1880	Journal	People	Hiatt, Eli, Sr. ruptured himself; little hope of recovery
11/17/1880	Journal	People	Hiatt, Eli, Sr., obituary
4/8/1914	Journal	People	Hiatt, Enos R. admitted to the bar
4/17/1941	Journal-Herald	People	Hiatt, G. Walter died in Louisiana
9/24/1935	Journal-Herald	People	Hiatt, G. Walter has lived in Bastrop, Louisiana, for more then 20 years
5/28/1919	Herald	People	Hiatt, Mrs. Charles died; burial at Westfield
8/2/1860	Journal	People	Hiatt, Pleasant is secretary of Harrisville Republican Club
5/12/1875	Journal	People	Hiatt, Pleasant visited Winchester
4/21/1859	Journal	People	Hiatt, Pleasant will commence a school at Salem
2/1/1871	Journal	People	Hiatt, Pleasant, Kansas letter
3/17/1897	Journal	People	Hiatt, Rev. C. E. will erect a new residence

Date	Source	Category	Description
8/18/1921	Democrat	People	Hiatt, Rev. Charles E. is named superintendent of Indiana Yearly Meeting of Friends
3/15/1944	News	People	Hiatt, Rev. Charles E. obituary
4/1/1952	Journal-Herald	People	Hiatt, Rev. Wilda died
8/14/1901	Journal	People	Hill, Benoni obituary
12/2/1858	Journal	People	Hill, Daniel is in the General Assembly; others say to compliment someone, "He is as reliable as the Quaker from Randolph [meaning Hill]"
10/4/1882	Journal	People	Hill, Daniel, formerly of Randolph County, is Prohibitionist candidate for Congress from Wilmington, Ohio
8/29/1883	Journal	People	Hill, George and Asenath, golden anniversary
11/29/1899	Journal	People	Hill, Rev. Daniel died at Richmond
4/15/1896	Journal	People	Hill, Rev. Daniel married Mrs. Baily [sic]
8/15/1917	Journal	People	Hinckle, Rev. Milo is preparing to go to Jamaica as a missionary
9/9/1972	News-Gazette	People	Hinshaw family, "When you say Hinshaw . . ."
6/11/1919	Journal	People	Hinshaw, Alva is preparing to go to South America
10/22/1919	Journal	People	Hinshaw, Alva O. is headed for Bolivia
8/12/1914	Journal	People	Hinshaw, Alva to go to Plainfield to Bible School
3/27/1872	Journal	People	Hinshaw, B. C. murder case
4/3/1872	Journal	People	Hinshaw, B. C. murder case; hung jury
11/12/1873	Journal	People	Hinshaw, Barney C. will sell his residence, 1.5 miles northeast of town
8/20/1873	Journal	People	Hinshaw, Barney found not guilty on grounds of self-defense
9/27/1871	Journal	People	Hinshaw, Barney, trial set for next week
4/9/1975	News-Gazette	People	Hinshaw, Clyde M., photo
10/9/1901	Journal	People	Hinshaw, J. B. died
5/2/1883	Journal	People	Hinshaw, J. Calvin is building a new house in Washington Township
5/30/1917	Journal	People	Hinshaw, J. E. is appointed Liberty Loan Chairman for Randolph County
9/12/1917	Journal	People	Hinshaw, J. E. is appointed Second Liberty Loan Chairman for Randolph County
9/12/1917	Herald	People	Hinshaw, J. E. is Randolph County Chairman of the Second Liberty Loan
11/2/1898	Journal	People	Hinshaw, Jacob E., photo
9/8/1897	Journal	People	Hinshaw, Job, obituary
8/23/1977	News-Gazette	People	Hinshaw, Kenneth died

Date	Source	Category	Description
1/11/1944	Journal-Herald	People	Hinshaw, L. D. died
1/10/1944	News	People	Hinshaw, L. D. was member of Lynn Methodist Church
12/7/1898	Journal	People	Hinshaw, Lindley family arrived in Randolph County
11/1/1961	News	People	Hinshaw, Mitchell, active Republican, dies; member of Friends Church
1/16/1895	Journal	People	Hinshaw, Mr. and Mrs. Will shot by burglars in Belleville, Indiana
6/16/1921	Democrat	People	Hinshaw, Rev. Meredith obituary; funeral by Rev. Luther E. Addington
7/3/1901	Herald	People	Hinshaw, Rev. S. S. obituary
7/3/1901	Journal	People	Hinshaw, Rev. S. S. obituary
9/11/1895	Journal	People	Hinshaw, Rev. Will E., trial at Danville
11/20/1976	News-Gazette	People	Hinshaw, Rev. William, "Saint or Devil"?
11/14/1877	Journal	People	Hinshaw, S. S. is grocer at Lynn
9/26/1900	Herald	People	Hinshaw, S. S. refuses Democrat nomination for commissioner
4/8/1974	News-Gazette	People	Hinshaw, Shorty is auto racer
2/12/1873	Journal	People	Hinshaw, Solomon obituary
4/24/1895	Journal	People	Hinshaw, Thirza, coroner of Hendricks County ruled that she was killed by unknown persons
2/27/1895	Journal	People	Hinshaw, Thursa [sic], autopsy in Winchester
1/16/1895	Herald	People	Hinshaw, W. E. and wife shot at Belleville
2/6/1895	Journal	People	Hinshaw, W. E. arrested for the murder of his wife
7/28/1897	Journal	People	Hinshaw, W. E. case cited from Indianapolis People
2/22/1900	Democrat	People	Hinshaw, W. E. case of
11/27/1902	Democrat	People	Hinshaw, W. E. case revived again
2/24/1886	Journal	People	Hinshaw, W. E. closed his school at Snow Hill
10/9/1895	Journal	People	Hinshaw, W. E. found guilty at Danville
12/27/1900	Democrat	People	Hinshaw, W. E. get a furlough
11/14/1906	Journal	People	Hinshaw, W. E. goes back to prison
11/15/1906	Democrat	People	Hinshaw, W. E. goes back to prison
11/16/1906	Herald	People	Hinshaw, W. E. goes back to prison
9/21/1892	Journal	People	Hinshaw, W. E. goes to Hendricks County to teach
5/29/1895	Journal	People	Hinshaw, W. E. indicted in Hendricks County
5/13/1915	Democrat	People	Hinshaw, W. E. is allowed to attend funeral of U. B. Hunt
6/25/1903	Democrat	People	Hinshaw, W. E. is an artist; see the Indianapolis News for Saturday, June 20, 1903

Date	Source	Category	Description
1/30/1895	Journal	People	Hinshaw, W. E. is here after death of wife
1/24/1917	Journal	People	Hinshaw, W. E. is here with relatives
2/13/1895	Journal	People	Hinshaw, W. E. is in Winchester
7/27/1898	Journal	People	Hinshaw, W. E. is now prison photographer and assists in chapel
1/25/1917	Democrat	People	Hinshaw, W. E. is temporarily paroled by Goodrich
1/18/1905	Journal	People	Hinshaw, W. E. paroled
1/11/1905	Herald	People	Hinshaw, W. E. paroled by Governor Durbin
1/10/1918	Democrat	People	Hinshaw, W. E. paroled in January 1917 and went to Arizona; married Anna Freeman in Arizona; Parole Board recommends a pardon
4/26/1905	Herald	People	Hinshaw, W. E. preached at Rural
3/12/1903	Democrat	People	Hinshaw, W. E. to be paroled
3/30/1905	Democrat	People	Hinshaw, W. E. was trading horses in Belleville
1/9/1918	Journal	People	Hinshaw, W. E. will likely be pardoned
4/15/1896	Journal	People	Hinshaw, W. E., appeal filed
1/12/1905	Democrat	People	Hinshaw, W. E., biography and parole
3/6/1895	Journal	People	Hinshaw, W. E., case
12/23/1896	Journal	People	Hinshaw, W. E., case of goes to the Indiana Supreme Court on January 8, 1897
9/15/1897	Journal	People	Hinshaw, W. E., Hendricks County Grand Jury reopens case
9/18/1895	Journal	People	Hinshaw, W. E., it is expected that he will be acquitted
1/25/1899	Journal	People	Hinshaw, W. E., prison chaplain thinks him innocent
11/13/1895	Journal	People	Hinshaw, W. E., taken to prison; made principal of prison school
11/3/1945	Journal-Herald	People	Hinshaw, W. M. golden wedding anniversary
6/18/1954	News	People	Hinshaw, W. W. golden anniversary
10/3/1958	News	People	Hinshaw, Warren photo
4/7/1897	Journal	People	Hinshaw, Will denied new trial
4/27/1905	Democrat	People	Hinshaw, Will preached at Rural
10/19/1905	Democrat	People	Hinshaw, Will preached at Rural
8/20/1890	Journal	People	Hinshaw, William C., case of
7/2/1890	Journal	People	Hinshaw, William C., murder of
9/23/1909	Democrat	People	Hinshaw, William E., letter from
7/31/1895	Journal	People	Hinshaw, Ziimri and Meredith visited Will at Danville
7/28/1897	Herald	People	Hinshaw; Noah Baney confesses to Thirza Hinshaw murder
8/11/1897	Journal	People	Hinshaw-Baney Case
12/1/1973	News-Gazette	People	Hitchcock, Brig. Gen. Robinson, Randolph County native, died

Date	Source	Category	Description
6/25/1884	Journal	People	Hobbs, Barnabus C. [Quaker], nominated for Superintendent of Public Instruction by Republicans
6/22/1892	Journal	People	Hobbs, Barnabus Coffin, former President of Earlham College, died at Bloomingdale, Indiana
8/21/1878	Journal	People	Hockett, Nathan, obituary
10/25/1905	Journal	People	Hodgin, Rev. Jonathan, Quaker minister, died
2/24/1916	Democrat	People	Hoffman, D. E. reminiscences
3/7/1935	Democrat	People	Hollingsworth, Rev. Isaac H. died; father of Fred of Arba
10/9/1863	Journal	People	Hollowell, Luke, house burned
4/18/1935	Democrat	People	Hoover, Former President Herbert visited James P. Goodrich in Winchester
11/20/1878	Journal	People	Horn, Jacob died at the residence of I. L. Addington; he was a lifelong Quaker
7/8/1896	Herald	People	Hough, Thomas, founder of Spartanburg Union Church and Cemetery, was born a Quaker on January 18, 1807 in Steubenville, Ohio; got Spartanburg Schoolhouse built in 1856
8/11/1897	Journal	People	House, Mrs. John (formerly Mrs. John Oyler), mother-in-law of Will Hinshaw, filed for divorce
10/13/1897	Journal	People	Huddleston, Dr., is remodeling house at East and South Streets
4/4/1964	Journal-Herald	People	Huddleston, Eric, Winchester High School Class of 1906, is famous architect
6/15/1898	Journal	People	Huffman, Henry D. organized first Sunday School in Randolph County about 1830 near Maxville
3/1/1876	Journal	People	Huffman, Henry D., obituary
3/10/1983	News-Gazette	People	Huffman, Rev. and Mrs. Roy, golden anniversary
3/4/1914	Journal	People	Huffman, Rev. Herbert, Quaker minister, visited family here
8/21/1945	Journal-Herald	People	Huffman, Wilbur received Bronze Star
9/20/1916	Herald	People	Hughes, Charles Evans, Republican candidate for President, will be in Winchester on September 21, 1916
2/23/1915	Journal	People	Hull, Hannah obituary; mother of Henry W. Bowers
1/23/1889	Journal	People	Hunnicutt, A. C., obituary
2/13/1901	Herald	People	Hunt Family of Huntsville
3/9/1892	Journal	People	Hunt, Charles S. is M. E. minister
5/10/1916	Journal	People	Hunt, Clarence is taking courses at Westfield
11/8/1893	Journal	People	Hunt, Comfort Jenkins, obituary
1/20/1892	Journal	People	Hunt, Dr. Pleasant, Quaker doctor of Farmland, died; buried at Cedar

Date	Source	Category	Description
6/16/1984	News-Gazette	People	Hunt, Marsha biography
4/23/1964	Journal-Herald	People	Hunt, Marsha, of the Defenders television show, is a native of Huntsville
12/12/1935	News-Democrat	People	Hunt, Marsha, Randolph County native, stars in the film, "The Virginia Judge"
10/29/1879	Journal	People	Hunt, Miles settled in West River with his father in 1826
3/15/1905	Journal	People	Hunt, Mrs. Rhoda is teaching at Washington Township, No. 14
1/27/1892	Journal	People	Hunt, Pleasant, obituary
2/27/1918	Journal	People	Hunt, Rev. Clarence moved from Westfield to the McCracken Farm, northwest of this city
6/16/1875	Journal	People	Hunt, Rev. Milton died (October 5, 1833-May 12, 1875); married Lydia Oxford on June 6, 1857 in Iroquois County, Ill.
4/7/1875	Journal	People	Hunt, Rev. William, obituary; donated land for Huntsville Cemetery nearly 50 years ago
7/2/1903	Democrat	People	Hunt, U. B. announced candidacy for governor
5/5/1915	Journal	People	Hunt, Union B. died
5/6/1915	Democrat	People	Hunt, Union B. died
8/10/1898	Herald	People	Hunt, Union B. of Randolph County is Republican nominee for Indiana Secretary of State
5/13/1915	Democrat	People	Hunt, Union B., former Vice-President Charles Fairbanks was one of his pallbearers
5/12/1915	Herald	People	Hunt, Union B., James E. Watson delivered address at funeral; said James P. Goodrich was Hunt's best friend
5/5/1915	Herald	People	Hunt, Union B., obituary and photo; had daughter, Mrs. Kenneth Davis of Indianapolis
7/13/1898	Journal	People	Hunt, Union B., photo
5/6/1903	Herald	People	Hunt, Union B., photo and house
6/4/1902	Journal	People	Hunt, William S. photo
9/25/1968	Journal-Herald	People	Hunt, William S. was once trustee of West River Township for 12 years [long ago]
10/5/1904	Journal	People	Hutchens, Edward, Quaker minister in Ohio Yearly Meeting, is a native of Washington Township, Randolph County
1/14/1984	News-Gazette	People	Hutchens, George is member of Lynn Friends Church
7/30/1902	Journal	People	Hutchens, Postmaster pictured in last Thursday's Muncie Star

Date	Source	Category	Description
7/26/1899	Journal	People	Indiana University Catalogue lists Leottis Lincoln Driver, Arlam Roy Williams, and James Otterbein Batchelor
9/30/1958	Journal-Herald	People	James, Rev. Morris photo
10/15/1879	Journal	People	Jarnigan, Mrs. J. W. goes to Iowa to speak on women's rights
5/11/1910	Journal	People	Jay, Allen, Quaker minister of Richmond, died
10/10/1894	Journal	People	Jenkins, John died; member of Pleasant Ridge Presbyterian Church until it disbanded about 1862; son of Jacob and Hannah Jenkins of Apple Pie Ridge; born February 7, 1810
12/15/1933	Journal-Herald	People	Jessup, Dr. Walter A., age 56, is native of Randolph County, President of the University of Iowa (1916-1933) and head of Carnegie Foundation
1/13/1892	Journal	People	Jessup, Rev. and Mrs. Jehu, Quaker minister of Wayne County, golden anniversary
4/22/1896	Journal	People	Jessup, Rev. Jehu, Quaker minister of Wayne County, died
5/3/1899	Journal	People	Jessup, Rev. Levi died at Lynn
5/10/1899	Journal	People	Jessup, Rev. Levi, obituary
8/23/1916	Herald	People	Jessup, Walter T., formerly of Winchester and grandson of Carey Goodrich, is the new president of Iowa State University
8/24/1916	Democrat	People	Jessup, Walter T., President of Iowa State University, is a son of Albert and Anna (Goodrich) Jessup of Modoc
4/3/1907	Journal	People	Jessup, Walter, Randolph County native and son of Albert Jessup, is superintendent of schools at Madison
1/11/1978	News-Gazette	People	Johnson, Dick is "lifelong Quaker"
9/16/1926	Journal-Herald	People	Johnson, Elijah marker erected in Jericho Cemetery
9/4/1878	Journal	People	Johnson, Elijah says man can be white on outside and black on inside
8/1/1888	Herald	People	Johnson, Elijah, "colored" criticized Republican Party
11/21/1888	Journal	People	Johnson, Elijah, colored minister of the Friends Church, died
6/5/1895	Journal	People	Johnson, Hannah, widow of Elijah, died in Winchester
9/28/1904	Journal	People	Johnson, I. V. D. R., Christian minister, obituary and photo
11/23/1910	Journal	People	Johnson, Ira and Ola and Murray Cox left to attend school at Cleveland, Ohio
10/18/1911	Journal	People	Johnson, Ira and wife and Murray Cox returned to Cleveland, Ohio

Date	Source	Category	Description
10/11/1893	Journal	People	Johnson, Ira C. is appointed trustee of White's Institute
5/3/1900	Democrat	People	Johnson, Rev. I. V. D. R. joined New Liberty U. B. Church in 1865 under Milton Wright
5/31/1900	Democrat	People	Johnson, Rev. I. V. D. R., part two
7/20/1892	Journal	People	Johnson, Rev. Ruth died
11/15/1928	Journal-Herald	People	Johnson, Rev. Wallace obituary
9/13/1928	Democrat	People	Johnson, Rev. Wallace, Quaker minister, died in California
10/12/1910	Journal	People	Johnson, Rev. Zelma will be ordained as a minister at New Liberty on October 30, 1910
7/27/1892	Journal	People	Johnson, Ruth, obituary
2/19/1896	Journal	People	Johnson, Silas, obituary
5/1/1948	Journal-Herald	People	Johnson, Tony is member of Lynn Friends Church
9/23/1914	Democrat	People	Jones, Bob to hold services in Winchester
12/11/1982	News-Gazette	People	Jones, David; Davey Martin-Jones, motion picture critic, is Winchester native
8/22/1894	Journal	People	Jones, Jane Puckett Hinshaw, Quaker minister, obituary
8/15/1894	Journal	People	Jones, Jane, Friends' minister, died
11/20/1978	News-Gazette	People	Jones, Jim, Guyana massacre, was Randolph County native
11/23/1887	Journal	People	Jones, Mr. and Mrs. Endsley, 50th anniversary
6/12/1956	Journal-Herald	People	Jones, Robert G. leaves Union for Greenfield High School
12/28/1911	Democrat	People	Kabel, Philip abandons plans to write new history of Randolph County
9/8/1915	Herald	People	Kabel, Philip appointed to represent Randolph County on Central Committee [for Indiana Centennial]
6/24/1966	News	People	Kabel, Philip died
10/4/1911	Herald	People	Kabel, Philip gets more Indian relics
12/18/1913	Democrat	People	Kabel, Philip got armadillo and moccasins to add to his collection
12/6/1911	Democrat	People	Kabel, Philip plans to write new history of Randolph County
8/1/1956	News	People	Kabel, Philip resigns as County Welfare Director
2/7/1950	Journal-Herald	People	Kabel, Phillip featured in Indianapolis Star
8/16/1923	Journal-Herald	People	Kabel, Phillip is president of Farmers and Merchants Bank
12/6/1911	Journal	People	Kabel, Phillip plans to write a new county history for Lewis Publishers, Chicago
7/8/1903	Journal	People	Kelley, Dennis retires
4/12/1911	Herald	People	Kelley, Dennis, died
7/15/1926	Daily News	People	Kelley, Dr. C. M. died; Mason, IORM, JOUAM

Date	Source	Category	Description
10/7/1908	Journal	People	Kelley, Dr. C. M. is a Democrat
10/26/1910	Herald	People	Kelley, Dr. C. M. is a Democrat
1/12/1887	Journal	People	Kelley, Dr. Clifton moved here from Palestine, Ohio
3/5/1981	News-Gazette	People	Keys, Hazel is founder of Local 203, GBBA
2/28/1906	Journal	People	Keys, Joseph and Betsy
3/7/1906	Herald	People	King, Albert, Sheriff, photo in Muncie Star last Friday
6/21/1960	Journal-Herald	People	Kist, Bob died
3/10/1909	Herald	People	Kitselman, Mahala, mother of Kitselman Brothers, died; daughter of Robert and Hannah Starbuck of Whitewater; born October 19, 1833; died February 26, 1909
3/16/1922	Democrat	People	Kittrell, Rev. John died; had a son, Anon
11/27/1901	Journal	People	Kizer, Henry P. photo
12/4/1901	Herald	People	Kizer, T. W. obituary
10/25/1899	Herald	People	Kizer, Thomas W. biography
12/4/1901	Journal	People	Kizer, Thomas W. photo
5/7/1953	Journal-Herald	People	Koch, Buenace, Randolph County native, is new superintendent of Jay County schools
2/14/1936	Journal-Herald	People	Lacy, John W., native of Randolph County, was chief justice of Wyoming Territorial Court, died
2/13/1936	News-Democrat	People	Lacy, John W., Winchester native, former judge of the Wyoming Territorial Court, died in Cheyenne
11/6/1963	News	People	Lapar, Dr. first elected to city council
10/16/1980	News-Gazette	People	Lapar, Dr. William was a Democrat before coming to Randolph County
7/29/1874	Journal	People	Lasley, Dan will continue as superintendent of Lynn Schools
7/29/1874	Journal	People	Lasley, Daniel at Lynn (1874-1875)
3/11/1874	Journal	People	Lasley, Daniel teaching at Lynn
9/13/1899	Herald	People	Lasley, Peter biography
4/7/1909	Journal	People	Lawrence, Daniel goes from Friends Academy at North Branch, Kansas, to Friendsville, Tennessee
2/25/1953	News	People	Leavell, State Senator Charles died
10/9/1918	Herald	People	Leggett, George, mayor of Winchester, killed in automobile accident
10/9/1918	Journal	People	Leggett, George, mayor of Winchester, killed in automobile accident
10/10/1918	Democrat	People	Leggett, Mayor George of Winchester killed
2/15/1882	Journal	People	Lesley, Dan is admitted to the bar to practice law

Date	Publication	Section	Description
6/3/1908	Herald	People	Lesley, Daniel died in Oregon last week; born May 17, 1849; member of the IOOF
7/27/1881	Journal	People	Lesley, Daniel is building new house
6/3/1908	Journal	People	Lesley, Daniel, former county superintendent, died
2/19/1919	Herald	People	Levering, Rev. George, Quaker minister, died in Greensboro, North Carolina
2/9/1937	Daily News	People	Lincoln, Abraham; Narra Lewis, 80, Blue Springs, Missouri, remembers seeing Lincoln in Farmland when she was six or seven years old; his train stopped to take on wood and he spoke to the crowd assembled at the station; her parents, Mr. and Mrs. John H. Lewis, moved to Missouri in 1883
11/9/1892	Herald	People	Lincoln, Robert Todd passed through Winchester
11/9/1892	Journal	People	Lincoln, Robert Todd passed through Winchester
2/16/1951	News	People	Litschert, Frank P., Randolph County native and editor of National Republic, died
9/24/1879	Journal	People	Lloyd, William R., obituary; was Farmland teacher
11/9/1965	Journal-Herald	People	Long, Rev. Frank J. is living at Wapakoneta, Ohio
6/25/1975	News-Gazette	People	Long, Shelley, actress, at Parker Fair
11/16/1887	Journal	People	Luce, Rev. Andrew died in Wabash County
7/27/1898	Journal	People	Luellen, Oliver F. died
3/24/1915	Herald	People	Lykins, Eliza Wright obituary
1/27/1951	Journal-Herald	People	Lykins, Rev. Claude photo
12/4/1901	Herald	People	Macy, David obituary
11/11/1908	Herald	People	Macy, J. W. and James S. Engle, biographies and photos
2/10/1915	Herald	People	Macy, J. W., portrait hung in the Courtroom
8/28/1912	Herald	People	Macy, John W. died
8/28/1912	Journal	People	Macy, John W. died
11/26/1977	News-Gazette	People	Macy, John W., Jr. featured in Saturday Extra
12/5/1973	News-Gazette	People	Macy, John W., Jr., "Winchester As I Remember It"
2/28/1877	Journal	People	Macy, W. P. is building residence on his farm [north of Farmland]
10/29/1913	Herald	People	Macy, W. W. obituary
7/14/1897	Herald	People	Maple, Amos C., principal of Winchester High School, married a Knightstown Quaker, Lula Hadley
5/5/1880	Journal	People	Mark, Mary Jane (Mrs. Moses), obituary
5/13/1891	Journal	People	Mark, Rev. Moses died in Illinois

Date	Publication	Category	Description
1/10/1961	Journal-Herald	People	Marlatt, Earl; story of hymn, "Are Ye Able?"
12/29/1897	Journal	People	Marsh, A. O., photo
4/13/1898	Journal	People	Marsh, Albert O., photo
1/1/1919	Herald	People	Marsh, B. F. died
10/30/1912	Herald	People	Marsh, Judge A. O. died
2/26/1890	Journal	People	Martin, Elisha, brickmaker, described
8/12/1874	Journal	People	Martindale, Elijah died in New Castle
9/26/1964	News	People	Mayo, General Paul to retire
7/20/1964	News	People	Mayo, General Paul, a Winchester native, is Chief of Finance for U. S. Army
3/11/1974	News-Gazette	People	Mayo, General Paul, Winchester native, died
7/1/1891	Journal	People	McClelland, Judge Beattie, formerly of Winchester, died last Friday at Columbus, Indiana
11/12/1919	Journal	People	McDougle, Theo opened tin shop in Winchester
9/20/1871	Journal	People	McIntyre, Robinson, founder of Maxville, died
9/26/1894	Journal	People	McKinley, Governor William, of Ohio, passed through
7/5/1900	Democrat	People	McNees, Andrew, biography
7/19/1900	Democrat	People	McNees, Andrew, biography
7/19/1952	Journal-Herald	People	McNees, Harvey E. died
6/21/1900	Democrat	People	McNees, James H., biography
8/11/1880	Journal	People	Mendenhall, Hiram and Martha, biography
6/15/1910	Herald	People	Mendenhall, Hiram, Philip Kabel has a tintype of him
7/13/1910	Journal	People	Mendenhall, Hiram, Phillip Kabel has a tintype of him
10/27/1875	Journal	People	Meredith, General Sol, funeral preached by C. F. Coffin [Wayne County]
8/20/1977	News-Gazette	People	Miles, Walter O., actor, is Union City, Indiana, native
8/31/1942	Journal-Herald	People	Miller, John Allen, formerly County Treasurer, died, son of Oliver and Mollie (Botkin) Miller and father of Orpha Osborn
3/26/1914	Democrat	People	Miller, John, former county commissioner, was son of William and Sarah, immigrants from Ireland; he was also the grandfather of J. Blair Mills
8/18/1897	Herald	People	Miller, Oliver, Civil War veteran
1/19/1876	Journal	People	Miller, Peter S., obituary
11/8/1916	Herald	People	Miller, W. E. dead; built block in 1883; enlarged in 1898

Date	Source	Category	Description
6/25/1913	Journal	People	Miller, W. T. is building a new house just south of Martindale Church
4/16/1890	Journal	People	Milligan, Dr. C. E. has located in Winchester
12/30/1920	Democrat	People	Milligan, Winifred H. is president of County European Relief Committee
4/20/1944	Journal-Herald	People	Millis, Frank T., later Treasurer of State, was a Quaker from southern Indiana
4/13/1898	Journal	People	Mills, Joel, obituary
1/24/1912	Journal	People	Mills, M. L., of new Mills Building, is a Quaker
10/4/1893	Journal	People	Milner, Isaiah C. died
6/24/1891	Herald	People	Moffit, Zimri, biography
1/8/1913	Herald	People	Monks, Chief Justice Leander J. retired on January 5, 1913; had served 18 years
1/27/1904	Herald	People	Monks, Coats, and Bell all featured in new "Legislative and State Manual"
8/17/1910	Herald	People	Monks, G. W. dead
10/18/1916	Herald	People	Monks, Judge writes history of Indiana Bar
4/23/1919	Herald	People	Monks, Leander died
4/23/1919	Journal	People	Monks, Leander J. died
5/6/1926	Journal-Herald	People	Monks, Merrett lost in GOP Primary for township trustee
4/2/1946	Journal-Herald	People	Moore, Clyde W. of Farmland appointed to Alcoholic Beverage Commission
5/20/1959	News	People	Moorman, Anne is prom queen
5/14/1890	Journal	People	Moorman, Frank elected president of Winchester Town Board
3/31/1915	Journal	People	Moorman, Frank, first owner of a tractor in Randolph County to be mentioned
10/17/1888	Herald	People	Moorman, James gave $1000 to Women's Suffrage Society of Indiana
2/20/1907	Herald	People	Moorman, James is new superintendent of White's Institute
9/26/1888	Journal	People	Moorman, James, died at Union City
10/17/1888	Journal	People	Moorman, James, obituary
10/10/1888	Journal	People	Moorman, James, will of
1/4/1899	Journal	People	Moorman, John A. died
1/11/1899	Journal	People	Moorman, John A., photo and obituary
11/20/1918	Journal	People	Moorman, Luther L. obituary and photo
7/18/1900	Herald	People	Moorman, Stephen biography
9/28/1904	Journal	People	Moorman, T. F. photo in August issue of School Board Journal
1/5/1876	Journal	People	Moorman, Tarlton, obituary

6/21/1899	Herald	People	Moorman, Thomas biography
12/27/1905	Journal	People	Moorman, Thomas obituary and photo
6/12/1901	Journal	People	Moorman, Thomas photo
3/15/1905	Journal	People	Moorman, Thomas photo
9/5/1917	Journal	People	Morris, Marion, of Washington Township, has written a book
10/22/1902	Journal	People	Morris, Rev. B. F., former pastor of Farmland Friends Church, died
9/20/1968	Journal-Herald	People	Mote, Judge, Randolph County native, died; member of State Court of Appeals (1962-66) and State Supreme Court (1966-68)
11/22/1899	Herald	People	Murray, William E. biography
1/12/1921	Journal-Herald	People	Murray, William E. died on December 28, 1920
5/23/1958	News	People	Myers, Russell, pastor of First Friends Church in Canton, Ohio, is Arba native
3/9/1887	Journal	People	Needham, W. P. wrote a book
6/22/1887	Journal	People	Needham, W. P.'s book is "Phantasmagorian Theology"
10/8/1902	Herald	People	Neff, H. H. died; was independent Whig candidate for auditor in 1841; there were two other candidates; Eaton, Democrat, won
6/12/1901	Journal	People	Neff, H. H. photo
3/15/1899	Herald	People	Neff, H. H., reminiscences
10/8/1902	Journal	People	Neff, Henry H. photo and obituary
4/27/1904	Herald	People	Neff, Jay H., formerly of Winchester, is mayor of Kansas City
9/1/1915	Journal	People	Neff, Jay, Winchester native, died; had been mayor of Kansas City, elected in 1904
1/13/1892	Journal	People	Neff, John, obituary
10/13/1984	News-Gazette	People	Nelson, Jackie, noted scholar on Indiana Quakers, is a Modoc native; taught five years at Randolph Southern; graduated from Ball State in 1969, married to Van Nelson
1/1/1908	Journal	People	Newman, Al, former sheriff, died; funeral at Bloomingport Friends Church; buried at Cherry Grove
11/21/1877	Journal	People	Nicholson, Timothy, Richmond Quaker, is appointed to board of State Normal School
2/14/1906	Journal	People	Oren, Ruby "of Cedar"
6/3/1874	Journal	People	Osborn, John, of Economy, obituary
1/28/1914	Herald	People	Osborn, Worth died
1/28/1914	Journal	People	Osborn, Worth died
7/10/1912	Journal	People	Osborn, Worth has new barn
2/20/1878	Journal	People	Overman, Joseph, Quaker of Wayne County, obituary

Date	Source	Category	Description
10/12/1898	Journal	People	Overman, Thomas J., photo
3/19/1913	Herald	People	Overman, Thomas, former sheriff, died
2/11/1874	Journal	People	Oyler, John has joined Mt. Zion
9/16/1914	Journal	People	Oyler, John obituary
5/27/1914	Journal	People	Oyler, John T., author of "Thoughts for Thinkers," is a native of Randolph County; now lives at Kansas City
2/28/1894	Herald	People	Oyler, John, of Rural, builds bicycles
12/31/1913	Journal	People	Oyler, Ota is a Democrat
1/15/1908	Journal	People	Ozbun, Isaac, photograph and obituary
5/30/1894	Journal	People	Ozburn, John, Quaker minister formerly of Farmland, died in Kansas
9/14/1983	News-Gazette	People	Painter, Dr. Lowell is retiring
1/9/1901	Journal	People	Paris, Arch and John are sons of C. W.
6/30/1875	Journal	People	Paris, C. W. is principal of Union City High School
11/17/1880	Journal	People	Paris, C. W. is teacher at Lewis Schoolhouse
1/20/1892	Journal	People	Paris, C. W. is teacher at Oak Grove
12/31/1890	Journal	People	Paris, C. W. is worshipful master of Farmland Masonic Lodge
3/2/1892	Journal	People	Paris, C. W. resides one mile east of Farmland and one mile north of Maxville
5/6/1908	Journal	People	Paris, C. W. sold farm and moved to town
8/5/1908	Journal	People	Paris, C. W. to move west
8/27/1879	Journal	People	Paris, C. W. will move to Adonijah Painter's farm near Farmland on September 1, 1879
4/18/1888	Journal	People	Paris, Charles closed term of school at Parker
2/19/1924	Democrat	People	Paris, Charles died; had ten children
6/7/1899	Herald	People	Paris, Charles elected to four-year term as county superintendent
6/21/1911	Journal	People	Paris, Charles is living in Farmland
12/26/1883	Journal	People	Paris, Charles is tyler of Farmland Masonic Lodge
4/22/1908	Herald	People	Paris, Charles purchased Weiler's property on Main Street and will move there
6/4/1903	Democrat	People	Paris, Charles reelected county superintendent on second ballot
7/31/1912	Herald	People	Paris, Charles W. is delegate to State Progressive Convention
8/22/1877	Journal	People	Paris, Charles W. is new deputy clerk
8/5/1908	Journal	People	Paris, Charles W. is planning to move to Colorado
11/19/1873	Journal	People	Paris, Charles W. member Farmland F & A M and M. E. Church

Date	Source	Category	Description
8/1/1877	Journal	People	Paris, Charles W. moved from Farmland to Winchester
9/24/1913	Journal	People	Paris, Charles W. moved to Richmond, California
9/24/1913	Journal	People	Paris, Charles W. moved to Richmond, California
4/15/1874	Journal	People	Paris, Charles W. starts as superintendent of Farmland M. E. Sunday School
6/9/1897	Herald	People	Paris, Charles was successful candidate for county superintendent last Monday; elected on 12th ballot
10/23/1901	Journal	People	Paschall, Mary A. died
10/12/1898	Journal	People	Paschall, Mary A., biography
12/11/1901	Journal	People	Paschall, Mary A., story in Indianapolis Journal
10/23/1901	Herald	People	Paschall, Mary, obituary
3/13/1901	Journal	People	Peacock, Benjamin died; son of Judge William; Judge came to Randolph County, near Carlos, in 1818 from Mount Holly, New Jersey, and died in 1838
9/14/1910	Herald	People	Peacock, Harry was principal at Modoc three years and Losantville for one year in the 1890s
9/17/1982	News-Gazette	People	Peacock, Myrna is new county health nurse
7/17/1895	Journal	People	Peele, John Cox obituary, son of William and Sally Cox Peele, Quakers
7/9/1902	Herald	People	Peele, Judge died
4/10/1930	Democrat	People	Penery, Ira C. died; former editor of the Farmland Enterprise
9/7/1887	Journal	People	Perry, Willis died
1/10/1906	Journal	People	Pickett, Benjamin, book written on the family of
12/23/1908	Journal	People	Pickett, J. W. and Fanny, golden wedding anniversary; photo
8/25/1897	Journal	People	Pickett, John B., obituary
3/11/1896	Journal	People	Pickett, Mr. and Mrs. John W. moved back to Winchester from the country
10/29/1965	News	People	Pickett, Rev. Mildred Allen, died aged 71; member of OES at Winchester
12/24/1890	Journal	People	Pier, Rev. Frankie died in Spring Valley, Ohio
3/28/1888	Journal	People	Pier, Rev. Frankie, Friends minister, sketch of
12/30/1908	Journal	People	Pierson, Levi F., Civil War veteran, died
5/8/1930	Democrat	People	Pretlow, Dr. J. J. died in Seattle
9/15/1897	Journal	People	Puckett, Hannah (Mrs. Joel), Quaker minister, died in Muncie; buried at Maxville
10/6/1897	Journal	People	Puckett, Hannah, obituary

Date	Source	Category	Description
4/13/1971	News-Gazette	People	Puckett, Troy, died; played major league baseball for one year as the pitcher of the Phillies in September 1911
9/20/1911	Herald	People	Puckett, Troy, of Winchester, is playing for the Philadelphia Phillies
1/27/1969	Journal-Herald	People	Pursley, Robert, biography, Randolph County native
12/16/1972	News-Gazette	People	Quaker Names: Unthank, Macy
11/9/1898	Journal	People	Ralston, John W. died at Carthage
6/12/1971	News-Gazette	People	Ralston, Penny, noted African-American native of Modoc, says she experienced no racism in her life before going to Ball State
7/12/1966	Journal-Herald	People	Reece, Rev. Harry biography
9/22/1943	News	People	Reed, Merritt C., Delaware County Superintendent, is 1922 graduate of Parker High School
9/23/1943	Journal-Herald	People	Reed, Merritt C., Parker City native, elected Superintendent of Delaware County Schools
2/1/1893	Journal	People	Reed, Nathan died
2/1/1893	Herald	People	Reed, Nathan, obituary
5/24/1899	Herald	People	Reed, Phebe, widow of Nathan, died; member of Winchester Friends Church
4/18/1975	News-Gazette	People	Reed, Sheriff Dan shot
3/30/1887	Journal	People	Reeder, Martin and wife joined Friends Church
8/18/1897	Herald	People	Reeder, Martin obituary; worked on Underground Railroad with Daniel Worth, Dr. Hiram P. Bennett, and Paul W. Way
7/19/1882	Journal	People	Reeder, Martin, reminiscences of early Winchester
7/30/1890	Journal	People	Reeder, Mary Martin died
6/22/1898	Journal	People	Rees, Hulda, obituary
6/6/1945	News	People	Reitenour, Monisa photo
3/5/1873	Journal	People	Renbarger, Abraham obituary
3/12/1975	News-Gazette	People	Retter, Carson, biography
9/16/1874	Journal	People	Reynard, Sarah obituary
11/1/1911	Journal	People	Richardson, John died
5/5/1875	Journal	People	Richardson, John will modernize his residence
9/18/1878	Journal	People	Rickner, Smith and Cornelius Addington are going to move to Adams County this fall
12/23/1874	Journal	People	Riley, George is brother-in-law of J. E. Neff
10/7/1936	Daily News	People	Riley, James Whitcomb, memorial for planned in Randolph County

Date	Publication	Section	Description
7/30/1962	News	People	Riley, James Whitcomb, monument for family erected at Fountain Park Cemetery
3/4/1914	Journal	People	Riley, James Whitcomb, Philip Kabel is completing a genealogy for him; his parents were from Randolph County
3/6/1979	News-Gazette	People	Riley, James Whitcomb; Randolph County connections
10/1/1890	Journal	People	Rine, Dr. E. W. recently moved here from Ohio
10/21/1896	Journal	People	Rine, Mrs. Dr. is a sister of Mrs. F. S. Caldwell
1/26/1910	Herald	People	Roe, Abe died
4/19/1899	Journal	People	Roe, Abe, 80th birthday
4/12/1899	Herald	People	Roe, Abraham, birthday
6/5/1907	Herald	People	Roosevelt, Theodore's train passed through
9/23/1939	Journal-Herald	People	Ross, Oran E
10/18/1916	Herald	People	Ryan, Pony, obituary; member of Winchester Friends Church
8/2/1911	Herald	People	Ryan, Pony, origin of his nickname
10/19/1916	Democrat	People	Ryan, Pony, Quaker
9/23/1970	News-Gazette	People	Saltzberg, Art, is Stuart Zaltsberg, a Winchester native, WOWO radio personality
3/4/1984	News-Gazette	People	Satkamp, Willie, retires from UCCHS
4/20/1904	Herald	People	Sayers, Mrs. W. J. photo in last Sunday's Muncie Star
8/1/1906	Herald	People	Sayers, Rev. W. J., son died
12/22/1947	News	People	Sayers, Rev. William J. obituary
4/29/1965	Journal-Herald	People	Scaglia, Duke, county agent for three years, to resign
4/5/1916	Journal	People	Schultz, Clyde is partner is Central Auto Company of Union City
9/6/1951	Journal-Herald	People	Scientists from Randolph County listed
6/7/1905	Herald	People	Shaw, Fred has Indian museum at his home
10/12/1888	Democrat	People	Shaw, Gideon died
10/17/1888	Herald	People	Shaw, Gideon obituary; born March 22, 1821 in Warren County, Ohio
10/24/1888	Journal	People	Shaw, Gideon, obituary
11/1/1876	Journal	People	Shaw, Gideon, Sr., is the only Democratic Quaker in Randolph County [He was no longer a member.]
6/12/1878	Journal	People	Shaw, R. C. is preparing to build a new residence
12/16/1896	Journal	People	Shaw, R. C., "Across the Plains in '49" described
9/9/1914	Herald	People	Sheeley, Abraham died; photo
2/17/1904	Herald	People	Sheeley, Caroline Palmer obituary

Date	Publication	Category	Description
9/6/1945	Journal-Herald	People	Sheppard, W. J., former POW
8/30/1945	Journal-Herald	People	Sheppard, W. J., POW is liberated
10/1/1959	Journal-Herald	People	Shockney, Rev. Robert A. photo
5/3/1928	Journal-Herald	People	Shockney, Theodore died
5/3/1928	Democrat	People	Shockney, Theodore died in Florida
12/8/1875	Journal	People	Shockney, Theodore, teacher of Wayne Township, arrested on charges of seduction
3/25/1914	Herald	People	Shreeve, Miss Louie, daughter of Jacob, of Union City, is first woman admitted to Randolph County Bar
3/29/1951	Journal-Herald	People	Sickels, George, mailbox appears in Ripley's Believe It or Not
3/23/1892	Journal	People	Simmons, Benjamin, county recorder, obituary
1/30/1901	Herald	People	Smith, Durant family
4/5/1893	Journal	People	Smith, Durant, family history
8/11/1870	Journal	People	Smith, George A. sold out to Daniel B. Miller and will go to Jasper County, Missouri
2/13/1930	Journal-Herald	People	Smith, J. L. died
1/16/1976	News-Gazette	People	Smith, J. R. died; principal of Spartanburg (1957-59), Driver Junior High (1959-68), UCCHS (1972-74)
12/30/1874	Journal	People	Smith, Jeremiah died in Winchester
1/6/1875	Journal	People	Smith, Jeremiah obituary
6/29/1865	Journal	People	Smith, Jeremiah, reminiscences of Randolph County
2/13/1930	Democrat	People	Smith, John L., former editor of the Winchester Democrat, died
9/16/1920	Democrat	People	Smith, Mrs. Louisa, Winchester history
4/15/1858	Journal	People	Smith, O. H. reminiscences of Winchester
8/22/1888	Journal	People	Smithson, George W. was a Whig and is a Republican
7/22/1891	Journal	People	Smithson, George W., obituary
8/16/1916	Herald	People	Smithson, Ira barn burns
7/27/1933	Democrat	People	Smithson, Ira, storm blew down barn on his farm
11/4/1885	Journal	People	Smithson, Shack has been in Nebraska
8/20/1890	Journal	People	Soldiers, list of old soldiers
8/14/1889	Journal	People	Soldiers, list of old soldiers in White River Township
8/25/1897	Journal	People	Stakebake, A. J. died
8/25/1897	Herald	People	Stakebake, A. J. obituary
3/23/1892	Journal	People	Stakebake, A. J. picture
5/2/1888	Journal	People	Stakebake, Andrew Jackson mentioned
2/1/1888	Journal	People	Stanley, Charles H., formerly of Farmland, died

Date	Source	Category	Description
6/16/1971	News-Gazette	People	Stanley, Dr. Wendell, Nobel winner and Ridgeville native, died
9/5/1982	News-Gazette	People	Stewart, Gene and Gary
3/18/1858	Journal	People	Stone, Asahel's house burned
7/5/1860	Journal	People	Stone, Asahel's new brick house struck by lightning
9/28/1887	Journal	People	Stone, General and Mrs., 50th anniversary
2/25/1891	Journal	People	Stone, General died
5/19/1875	Journal	People	Stone, General is improving his grounds
3/4/1891	Journal	People	Stone, General, obituary
9/21/1892	Journal	People	Stone, Lydia, obituary
5/27/1957	News	People	Strickler, Casey, County Auditor, dead
12/16/1885	Journal	People	Study, L. W. died
12/16/1885	Journal	People	Study, L. W., obituary
4/12/1911	Herald	People	Summers, Charles O. photo
4/5/1911	Journal	People	Summers, Charles O., photo
5/17/1922	Journal-Herald	People	Sunday, Billy to be in Winchester on Saturday
5/23/1955	News	People	Swaim, W. F., former trustee of Washington Township, member at Lynn Friends Church
5/3/1899	Herald	People	Swain, Ira biography
3/17/1947	News	People	Swander, Rev. Charles died
6/9/1942	Journal-Herald	People	Sweet, Rev. Charles obituary
10/21/1908	Journal	People	Taft, William Howard will be in Winchester on October 24, 1908
10/28/1908	Journal	People	Taft, William Howard, photo of him in Winchester
8/3/1881	Journal	People	Taxpayers, list of "heavy taxpayers"
2/19/1890	Journal	People	Teal, Asa, biography
2/12/1890	Journal	People	Teal, Asa, obituary
3/5/1981	News-Gazette	People	Thomas, Gaynelle (Mrs. Rev. Percy), obituary
4/24/1980	News-Gazette	People	Thomas, Rev. and Mrs. Alva, golden anniversary
3/6/1979	News-Gazette	People	Thompson, Walter, former publisher of Randolph County News, died
7/8/1908	Journal	People	Thornburg family photo
2/17/1964	News	People	Thornburg Farm, history
3/23/1967	Journal-Herald	People	Thornburg, Alonzo is 100 years old
10/14/1967	Journal-Herald	People	Thornburg, C. L. is 50-year Mason
8/10/1926	Daily News	People	Thornburg, E. H., DVM, of Lynn, photo
11/10/1973	News-Gazette	People	Thornburg, Ivan featured
12/9/1978	News-Gazette	People	Thornburg, L. Ivan biography

7/21/1927	Democrat	People	Thornburg, Marvin, south of Winchester on Lynn Pike, owns the first combine in Randolph County, a John Deere
3/8/1916	Herald	People	Thornburg, Opal is a sophomore at McKinley [later Archivist of Earlham College]
4/14/1983	News-Gazette	People	Thornburg, Rev. and Mrs. Marcell, golden anniversary
7/29/1953	News	People	Thornburg, Rev. Elvan dead
12/13/1941	Journal-Herald	People	Thornburg, Rev. Elvan photo
5/14/1913	Journal	People	Thornburg, Rev. Lee Harris, Friends minister, died
8/25/1954	News	People	Thornburg, Rev. N. H. biography
9/5/1888	Journal	People	Thornburg, Rhoda, family are all Republicans
1/16/1919	Democrat	People	Thornburg, W. H., former sheriff, died; buried at Cherry Grove
1/15/1919	Herald	People	Thornburg, W. H., former sheriff, died; member of Friends Church; funeral at Cherry Grove
1/15/1919	Journal	People	Thornburg, W. H., former sheriff, obituary
1/21/1920	Journal	People	Thornburg, W. H., photo
4/4/1877	Journal	People	Thornburg, William H. is JP in Washington Township
3/29/1980	News-Gazette	People	Toney, Ansel biography
7/31/1924	Democrat	People	Townsend, John, Revolutionary Veteran, father-in-law of Joseph Addington, is buried at Fountain City; remains were moved from Goshen in Wayne County
8/12/1908	Journal	People	Townsend, John, story of
5/8/1975	News-Gazette	People	Tucker, Bernice Caldwell, Winchester native, writes book about childhood entitled, "Yesterday"
4/15/1885	Journal	People	Tucker, Ebenezer died at Union City last Saturday
10/29/1879	Journal	People	Tucker, Ebenezer is preparing to write a history of Randolph County
9/4/1878	Journal	People	Tucker, Ebenezer is running for county superintendent
12/1/1880	Journal	People	Tucker, Ebenezer's history transferred to Kingman Brothers
6/16/1880	Journal	People	Tucker, Ebenzer read history at Old Settlers Meeting
4/6/1946	Journal-Herald	People	Unger, Frank chairman of Democrat Central Committee for twelve years; came to Randolph County from Clinton County in 1918
4/2/1947	News	People	Van Deventer, Florence Rinard, Farmland native, is entertainment star

Date	Publication	Category	Description
12/14/1971	News-Gazette	People	Van Deventer, Fred, husband of Florence Reynard of Farmland, television star, died
1/30/1895	Journal	People	Vanderburg, George W., obituary
4/5/1916	Journal	People	Veal, George, photo, former county treasurer
8/27/1956	News	People	Veit, Herman F. replaces William Grimes on County Council
5/2/1906	Journal	People	Vinnedge, Mrs. John W. died
9/20/1923	Democrat	People	Vorhis, Hetty died; funeral by Rev. Frank Cornell; she was not a church member
7/31/1889	Journal	People	Voters, old voters in Randolph County listed
8/7/1889	Journal	People	Voters, old voters in Randolph County listed
1/25/1957	News	People	Wagner, Rev. William, Friends pastor, biography
10/10/1958	News	People	Wagner, Rev. William, Friends pastor, biography
12/16/1963	News	People	Wagner, Rev. William, Friends pastor, biography
8/14/1964	News	People	Wagner, Rev. William, Friends pastor, biography; married to former Dorothy Smith of Marion
6/11/1925	Democrat	People	Wall, F. J., Ridgeville native, is elected Superintendent of Cass County Schools
7/19/1967	News	People	Walter, Rev. John R. died; buried in Garlands Brook Cemetery, Columbus
8/12/1944	Journal-Herald	People	Ward, Don died
7/6/1936	News-Democrat	People	Ward, Dr. M. S., native of Union City, is the new president of Ferris Institute
7/13/1892	Journal	People	Ward, Thomas, obituary
7/13/1892	Herald	People	Ward, Thomas, obituary; unsuccessful Whig candidate for sheriff in 1841
11/2/1898	Journal	People	Warner, George W., photo
8/10/1936	News-Democrat	People	Watson political cartoon
9/21/1936	Daily News	People	Watson political cartoon
3/3/1909	Journal	People	Watson, Enos died
3/3/1909	Herald	People	Watson, Enos L. died
11/15/1980	News-Gazette	People	Watson, James E. biography
2/15/1893	Journal	People	Watson, James E. has retired from the practice of law and will join the ministry of the M. E. Church [never happened]
1/3/1937	Daily News	People	Watson, James writes "As I Knew Them"
4/19/1928	Democrat	People	Watson, James, kicked off his Presidential campaign

9/28/1881	Journal	People	Watson, Jim resigned as teacher to go to Greencastle; Jim Goodrich will replace him at White River School No. 16
7/19/1911	Journal	People	Watson, Rev. Clyde, Quaker minister, was a Winchester native
7/30/1948	News	People	Watson, Sen. James history
10/18/1905	Journal	People	Wattles, Rev. W. D., now of Winchester, is a member of Marion Monthly Meeting of Friends
7/4/1917	Herald	People	Watts, Ann (Diggs), wife of Isaiah, born on August 1, 1842, daughter of Littlebury and Hannah (Mendenhall) Diggs, birthright Quaker?
7/19/1971	News-Gazette	People	Watts, Chester, Randolph County native, of the U. S. Naval Observatory, died
8/14/1907	Herald	People	Way, Amanda 79th birthday
5/28/1884	Journal	People	Way, Amanda and Lou Way are in Washington, DC
4/27/1881	Journal	People	Way, Amanda and Oscar Porter went to Kansas last week
6/20/1888	Journal	People	Way, Amanda and politics
6/22/1887	Journal	People	Way, Amanda at Winchester M. E. Church
12/23/1858	Journal	People	Way, Amanda called for a meeting on women's property rights at the courthouse
7/26/1911	Herald	People	Way, Amanda celebrates 83rd birthday
3/5/1914	Democrat	People	Way, Amanda death notice
3/11/1914	Herald	People	Way, Amanda died
3/4/1914	Journal	People	Way, Amanda died in California
4/18/1900	Journal	People	Way, Amanda has been nominated by the Prohibitionists in Idaho for Congress
3/14/1861	Journal	People	Way, Amanda has commenced a 3-months school in the south schoolhouse in Winchester
2/2/1876	Journal	People	Way, Amanda here
2/7/1882	Journal	People	Way, Amanda in Farmland for temperance work
2/15/1882	Journal	People	Way, Amanda is at Parker
7/16/1879	Journal	People	Way, Amanda is visiting here and soliciting aid for the colored people of Kansas
1/19/1887	Journal	People	Way, Amanda letter from in regard to death of Jesse Way
2/21/1872	Journal	People	Way, Amanda licensed to preach in the M. E. Church
3/18/1914	Journal	People	Way, Amanda obituary
11/22/1882	Journal	People	Way, Amanda organized "Temperance Army" for the children of Winchester

1/24/1861	Journal	People	Way, Amanda organized an IOGT in Muncie on Wednesday of last week
11/29/1876	Journal	People	Way, Amanda preached at Friends Church last Sabbath
3/27/1872	Journal	People	Way, Amanda preached at M. E. Church
6/15/1887	Journal	People	Way, Amanda preached at Winchester Friends Church
1/21/1858	Journal	People	Way, Amanda present at Temperance Meeting
11/14/1861	Journal	People	Way, Amanda receives letter from John Stewart Way in the army
3/29/1882	Journal	People	Way, Amanda recently lectured at Bloomingport
10/19/1887	Journal	People	Way, Amanda returned to Kansas
4/13/1881	Journal	People	Way, Amanda returned to Winchester to nurse her nephew, Oscar Porter
5/29/1867	Journal	People	Way, Amanda visited last week; is Grand Worthy Chief Templar of Indiana; returned to Indianapolis on Friday last
12/22/1875	Journal	People	Way, Amanda was here last week
7/26/1871	Journal	People	Way, Amanda will be at IOGT in Winchester
6/6/1888	Journal	People	Way, Amanda will lecture on local option at City Hall on Thursday evening
9/17/1884	Journal	People	Way, Amanda will preach at Mt. Zion next Sabbath
12/7/1870	Journal	People	Way, Amanda will speak at Huntsville on December 19, 1870
7/8/1858	Journal	People	Way, Amanda will take charge of the Progressive Department of the Crystal Fountain newspaper
6/14/1980	News-Gazette	People	Way, Amanda, biography
8/26/1858	Journal	People	Way, Amanda, Crystal Fountain newspaper failed
12/29/1886	Journal	People	Way, Amanda, letter from
3/25/1914	Journal	People	Way, Amanda, siblings listed; she did her first temperance work at age 16
11/18/1891	Journal	People	Way, F. M. moved to Oakland, California
1/5/1887	Journal	People	Way, Henry P., body of removed from old to new cemetery
5/6/1858	Journal	People	Way, James P. moved to new residence
1/23/1889	Journal	People	Way, James P., obituary
8/3/1892	Journal	People	Way, Judith Wilson died
8/10/1892	Journal	People	Way, Judith Wilson, obituary
8/1/1892	Herald	People	Way, Judith, obituary
5/31/1911	Herald	People	Way, Marion died

Date	Source	Category	Description
7/14/1875	Journal	People	Way, Miss Amanda addressed temperance meeting last Sabbath; will be at Ridgeville on Friday
2/17/1897	Journal	People	Way, Miss Amanda has been pensioned for her services in the Civil War
6/16/1875	Journal	People	Way, Miss Amanda, of Kansas, is visiting here
5/22/1901	Herald	People	Way, Moorman opposed the death penalty and used plan language
8/24/1881	Journal	People	Way, Moorman, resolutions on death of
12/16/1896	Journal	People	Way, Mrs. William, daughter of John Wright, died in Illinois
2/1/18983	Journal	People	Way, William, reminiscences
2/5/1983	News-Gazette	People	Whitehead, Lloyd, biography
2/12/1983	News-Gazette	People	Whitehead, Lloyd, biography
5/26/1984	News-Gazette	People	Whitehead, Lloyd, writes "Autumn Leaves"
9/14/1933	Democrat	People	Williams, A. R. is on National Committee of National Education Association
4/17/1936	News-Democrat	People	Williams, A. R. obituary and photo; taught 4 years in Franklin Township (1891-95); then went to Hiawatha, Kansas; was superintendent there (1902-04); superintendent in Perry, Oklahoma (1904-06); superintendent in Broken Bow, Oklahoma (1906-08); farmed (1908-23); teacher at Jackson (1923-26); member of the Presbyterian Church and Rotary Club; earned an AB from Indiana University and an MA from Columbia University
5/7/1931	Democrat	People	Williams, A. R., biography; was at Perry, Oklahoma, and other places; had a master's degree from Columbia University
10/12/1898	Journal	People	Williams, A. R., of Randolph County, elected president of the senior class of Indiana University
6/20/1894	Journal	People	Williams, Arlie left for Danville
5/27/1914	Herald	People	Williams, Jan, Winchester native, is "world's great clarinetist"
11/19/1879	Journal	People	Williams, Joel H., teaching record: six terms at Green, No. 7; before at Hill, Shiloh, Walnut Corner, Hubbard, and Bales
5/10/1905	Herald	People	Williams, L. L. is "prosperous citizen"
3/2/1887	Journal	People	Williams, L. L. plans to build new dwelling
8/17/1887	Journal	People	Williams, L. L., fine mansion will soon be completed
3/16/1887	Journal	People	Williams, L. L., J. C. Bundy will erect a new residence for him this summer

Date	Source	Category	Description
5/7/1890	Journal	People	Williams, Luther granted a pension of $20/month
2/26/1890	Journal	People	Williams, Luther is "one of Franklin Township's staunch Republicans"
9/20/1911	Journal	People	Williams, Luther L. bought a new EMF auto
2/7/1917	Herald	People	Williams, Luther L. died
12/16/1908	Herald	People	Willis, Rebecca biography, recently deceased
9/12/1900	Journal	People	Willis, Rebecca Reynard used plain language and dress
12/23/1908	Herald	People	Willis, Rebecca, artifacts of her house described
8/8/1888	Journal	People	Wilmore, Willis, obituary
7/10/1965	Journal-Herald	People	Wilson, Jim of Farmland killed in military plane crash
7/3/1918	Herald	People	Winemiller, Julia, author, is member of Winchester Friends Church
1/24/1981	News-Gazette	People	Wise, Robert biography
4/23/1966	Journal-Herald	People	Wise, Robert E., Winchester native, wins Academy Award; biography
9/17/1935	Journal-Herald	People	Wise, Russell "known more familiarly as Randolph County's beer baron"
3/7/1961	Journal-Herald	People	Wise, Russell died on March 6
9/8/1927	Journal-Herald	People	Wisehart, Roy of Union City named State Superintendent of Public Instruction
8/15/1981	News-Gazette	People	Wisener, Monisa appointed county historian
12/10/1977	News-Gazette	People	Wisener, Monisa featured in Saturday Extra
4/5/1916	Herald	People	Wood, C. H., former superintendent of Winchester Schools, dead
6/27/1894	Journal	People	Wood, Charles H. is member of Mt. Pleasant M. E. Church
2/11/1914	Journal	People	Wood, Henry F. reelected County Republican Chairman
9/18/1895	Journal	People	Wood, Margaret is visiting Lee Driver and family
7/21/1897	Journal	People	Wood, Margaret, obituary
7/14/1897	Journal	People	Wood, Mrs. Margaret, mother of Mrs. Lee L. Driver, died
6/17/1885	Journal	People	Wood, W. H., obituary; died on May 23, 1885
11/3/1859	Journal	People	Worth, Daniel and North Carolina Quakers
6/21/1917	Democrat	People	Worth, Rev. Aaron, famous Wesleyan minister and Prohibitionist, was born in Randolph County
4/19/1943	Journal-Herald	People	Wright, Frank died
11/13/1918	Journal	People	Wright, Frank is first three-term legislator from Randolph County
7/19/1962	News	People	Wright, Fred and Doris photo

Date	Source	Category	Description
1/6/1915	Journal	People	Wright, Grant completes six years on township board; now on county council
10/19/1898	Journal	People	Wright, Hicks K., photo
6/22/1881	Journal	People	Wright, Marjory, obituary
10/21/1903	Journal	People	Wright, Mary Ann (Heaston) obituary
6/30/1886	Journal	People	Wright, Mrs. Jennie (Branson), wife of trustee Harvey, buried at Cedar
3/8/1980	News-Gazette	People	Wright, Richard E. biography
6/23/1915	Journal	People	Wright, William obituary; Quaker minister
5/19/1936	News-Democrat	People	Yost, Jesse, recollections and photo
5/12/1979	News-Gazette	People	Yost, John W. photo
4/14/1886	Journal	Politics	"Old Adage: Vote early and vote often"
6/16/1880	Journal	Politics	1825 election returns
1/18/1893	Journal	Politics	1844 Whig Ticket described [it was actually 1846]
8/11/1880	Journal	Politics	1844 Whig ticket described; clarified in issue of August 18, 1880
7/15/1885	Journal	Politics	1848 election reminiscences
3/21/1906	Journal	Politics	1856 newspaper and Republican county ticket described
12/16/1908	Journal	Politics	Almonrode, T. A. appointed County Assessor
4/15/1975	News-Gazette	Politics	American Party formed in Randolph County; Michael Stigleman, Lynn, Chairman; Julia Beeson, Farmland, Vice-Chairman
3/20/1963	News	Politics	Americans for Conservative Action, Randolph County Chapter organized
3/28/1963	Journal-Herald	Politics	Americans for Conservative Action, Randolph County Chapter organized on April 9
5/11/1963	Journal-Herald	Politics	Americans for Conservative Action, Randolph County Chapter, George Daly is president
6/3/1891	Journal	Politics	Assessor, J. F. Middleton appointed county assessor
3/16/1892	Journal	Politics	Assessor, office described
5/27/1891	Journal	Politics	Auditor, county commissioners will select
10/17/1969	Journal-Herald	Politics	Ball State students support Nixon's Vietnam policy
5/13/1926	Democrat	Politics	Beeson, Charles is elected County Republican Chairman
10/5/1940	Journal-Herald	Politics	Beeson, I. F. is Prohibition nominee for State Auditor
4/15/1946	News	Politics	Beetley, F. C., Trustee of Greensfork Township, died
9/8/1880	Journal	Politics	Bloomingport, 40 of 41 voters in Bloomingport are Republicans
1/17/1906	Journal	Politics	Boltz, John elected County Republican Chairman

Date	Source	Category	Description
1/17/1906	Herald	Politics	Boltz, John H. is elected County Republican Chairman
1/6/1972	News-Gazette	Politics	Botkin, Joseph, county councilman, died
7/12/1916	Herald	Politics	Bragg, J. W. resigns as justice of the peace; W. E. Kendell resigns as justice of the peace at Losantville
5/27/1891	Journal	Politics	Bronson (Losantville) town council mentioned
4/14/1897	Herald	Politics	Bronson (Losantville), election will be held first Monday in May
1/6/1892	Journal	Politics	Bronson, town was already incorporated
12/20/1926	Daily News	Politics	Brown will resign as prosecuting attorney; attempt to bribe
12/23/1926	Journal-Herald	Politics	Brown, Eber resigned as prosecutor
10/7/1858	Journal	Politics	Brown, Judge, dialogue between Brown and a Quaker
7/14/1932	Democrat	Politics	Brown, Omer, county auditor, is indicted
7/8/1952	Journal-Herald	Politics	Brown, Russell W. named to county council
5/9/1977	News-Gazette	Politics	Brown, Russell, County Auditor, dies
10/20/1915	Journal	Politics	Browne, James replaces H. F. Wood as County Republican Chairman
10/3/1900	Herald	Politics	Bryan, W. J. will visit Winchester "next Friday"
11/5/1908	Democrat	Politics	Bryan, William Jennings was in Winchester on October 31, 1908
5/6/1950	Journal-Herald	Politics	Buckingham, Ray elected County Democrat Chairman; Gutheil is reelected as Republican chair
5/12/1952	News	Politics	Buckingham, Ray is reelected County Democrat Chairman; Gutheil is reelected as Republican chair
12/18/1895	Herald	Politics	Butts, Nathan T., county chairman, People's Party
5/16/1894	Herald	Politics	Butts, Nathan T., county chairman, People's Party
6/2/1915	Journal	Politics	Callahan, D. W. elected County Democrat Chairman to replace E. S. Edger
3/16/1916	Democrat	Politics	Callahan, D. W. replaces Chattain as County Democrat Chairman
6/2/1915	Herald	Politics	Callahan, D. W. replaces E. S. Edger as Democrat County Chairman
6/3/1915	Democrat	Politics	Callahan, D. W. replaces E. S. Edger as Democrat County Chairman; Edger served for three years
1/17/1894	Herald	Politics	Canada named County Republican Chairman to replace A. O. Marsh, who served four years
12/7/1979	News-Gazette	Politics	Carpenter, Noel, resigns as County Assessor effective December 31
3/27/1895	Herald	Politics	Carter, C. R. is new County Prohibition Chairman; C. Hinshaw, secretary; A. Stanley, treasurer

Date	Source	Category	Description
3/15/1916	Herald	Politics	Chairman: J. M. Browne, Republican; D. W. Callahan, Democrat; Stephen Clevenger, Progressive; Other Progressive officers are Will Glunt, vice-chairman; Merl Ward, secretary; and S. C. Mendenhall, treasurer
11/20/1919	Democrat	Politics	Chattin, Clyde replaces E. S. Edger as County Democrat Chairman
6/15/1910	Herald	Politics	Chenoweth, Chris replaces Bowen, deceased, as county commissioner
10/4/1894	Journal	Politics	Circuit Court Judge, L. J. Monks resigned; G. D. Williamson appointed
3/22/1905	Herald	Politics	Cities, mayors to take office in September 1906 and serve until January 1910; only one councilman will serve per district
8/24/1916	Democrat	Politics	Citizens Ticket is combination of Democrats, Progressives, and Prohibitionists
8/30/1916	Herald	Politics	Citizens Ticket is combination of Democrats, Progressives, and Prohibitionists
9/20/1916	Journal	Politics	Citizens Ticket nominated [Democrats, Progressives, Prohibitionists]
11/8/1905	Journal	Politics	City and town election results; Democrats won in Lynn
3/15/1905	Herald	Politics	City and town elections switched to November for four years
5/8/1902	Democrat	Politics	City election results
5/11/1904	Journal	Politics	City election results
11/5/1913	Herald	Politics	City election results
11/5/1913	Journal	Politics	City election results
11/6/1913	Democrat	Politics	City election results
3/7/1941	Daily News	Politics	City elections postponed until 1943; law was changed in 1933
4/3/1901	Herald	Politics	City officers elected in 1903 will serve only two years
5/5/1909	Herald	Politics	City Treasurer's office abolished
4/20/1892	Journal	Politics	Civil Engineer, J. E. Hinshaw replaced C. C. Yunker as civil engineer of county
8/22/1952	News	Politics	Clark, John P. appointed to county council
1/8/1902	Journal	Politics	Coats, George W. appointed justice of the peace
2/13/1860	Journal	Politics	Coffin, Stephen, trustee of White River Township, died
11/12/1925	Democrat	Politics	Coggshell replaces Walter Bowers as commissioner
12/3/1919	Journal	Politics	Comer is trustee of White River Township

Date	Source	Category	Description
9/27/1916	Journal	Politics	Commissioner districts were established in 1858: Jackson, Wayne, and Greensfork=Eastern District; what is now County Road 500 W is the western line
4/11/1917	Journal	Politics	Committee on Food Supplies, members listed
4/21/1880	Journal	Politics	Constables, list of in county
8/16/1860	Journal	Politics	Constitutional Union Meeting, Bell and Everett Meeting held in Winchester; referred to as "Know Nothing Meeting"
8/22/1860	Journal	Politics	Constitutional Union Meeting, Jeremiah Smith attended; only three Bell men were present
4/27/1951	News	Politics	Coroner, Gullet resigns as
7/18/1917	Herald	Politics	County Agent, A. L. Hodgson is new county agent
3/10/1920	Journal	Politics	County Agent, A. L. Hodgson resigned
3/10/1920	Herald	Politics	County Agent, A. L. Hodgson resigns after three years
7/11/1917	Journal	Politics	County Agent, A. L. Hodgson selected
12/10/1913	Journal	Politics	County Agent, Charles Mahan is appointed first one
10/4/1916	Journal	Politics	County Agent, County Board of Education abolished the office
10/4/1916	Herald	Politics	County Agent, office abandoned; Mahan had served three years
4/16/1913	Journal	Politics	County Agent, request for appointment of
5/17/1939	Journal-Herald	Politics	County Agents, history of
2/17/1875	Journal	Politics	County Assessor, office abolished
9/13/1905	Journal	Politics	County budget listed
5/3/1899	Journal	Politics	County Council, commissioners establish districts for
8/9/1899	Journal	Politics	County Council, W. C. Diggs elected president
5/24/1899	Journal	Politics	County Councilmen appointed
10/10/1861	Journal	Politics	County election results
10/17/1862	Journal	Politics	County election results
10/18/1866	Journal	Politics	County election results
10/20/1859	Journal	Politics	County election results
10/16/1878	Journal	Politics	County election results by precinct
8/12/1903	Journal	Politics	County expenses estimate for 1904 (salaries)
8/28/1901	Journal	Politics	County officials' salaries listed
1/7/1936	News-Democrat	Politics	County officials, photos of
2/1/1911	Journal	Politics	County option will be repealed

3/23/1892	Journal	Politics	County Recorder, William G. Moulton replaces Benjamin W. Simmons, deceased
12/16/1908	Journal	Politics	County Temperance Organization
8/27/1962	News	Politics	Cox, Jack is appointed sheriff
3/20/1969	Journal-Herald	Politics	Darling, Clarence, County Recorder, died
3/22/1969	Journal-Herald	Politics	Darling, Winifred appointed County Recorder
10/29/1873	Journal	Politics	Daugherty, James trustee of Monroe Township
5/13/1940	Journal-Herald	Politics	Davisson and Unger both re-elected as county chairmen
5/11/1942	Journal-Herald	Politics	Davisson and Unger both re-elected as county chairmen
5/8/1944	News	Politics	Davisson and Unger both re-elected as county chairmen
5/6/1948	Journal-Herald	Politics	Davisson, Jack is criticized
5/11/1948	Journal-Herald	Politics	Davisson, Jack is criticized
5/9/1938	Journal-Herald	Politics	Davisson, Jack is elected County Republican chairman
5/16/1956	News	Politics	Davisson, Jack is reelected as treasurer of Republican District Committee
9/28/1949	News	Politics	Davisson, Jack resigns as County Republican Chairman
10/1/1949	Journal-Herald	Politics	Davisson, Jack resigns as County Republican Chairman
8/31/1910	Herald	Politics	Democrat convention
4/10/1918	Herald	Politics	Democrat county ticket listed
11/6/1912	Herald	Politics	Democrat landslide
8/18/1880	Journal	Politics	Democrat nominees listed
6/10/1914	Herald	Politics	Democrat ticket listed
6/24/1874	Journal	Politics	Democratic Convention held
12/12/1861	Journal	Politics	Democratic Mass Meeting in Winchester; seventeen present
12/19/1861	Journal	Politics	Democratic Mass Meeting, proceedings of
5/14/1962	News	Politics	Democratic Party, Chester Dunn is in fourth term as chairman
6/2/1915	Journal	Politics	Democratic Party, D. W. Callahan, elected chairman
7/13/1892	Journal	Politics	Democratic sheriff was elected in 1841
5/15/1878	Journal	Politics	Democrats and Independents will hold a joint convention on May 25, 1878
11/20/1889	Herald	Politics	Democrats and Prohibitionists join forces in Randolph County
4/9/1890	Journal	Politics	Democrats elected township assessors in Greensfork and Nettle Creek
12/11/1976	News-Gazette	Politics	Democrats in Randolph County, interviews

Date	Source	Category	Description
9/30/1920	Democrat	Politics	Democrats run as "Independent Ticket" in Randolph County
9/26/1862	Journal	Politics	Democrats, A. F. Teal, chairman of Democratic Central Committee of Randolph County
12/20/1876	Journal	Politics	Democrats, Asa Teal is county chairman
1/9/1878	Journal	Politics	Democrats, Asa Teal, county chairman
2/27/1878	Journal	Politics	Democrats, Asa Teal, county chairman
6/30/1880	Journal	Politics	Democrats, Asa Teal, county chairman
8/28/1878	Journal	Politics	Democrats, Asa Teal, county chairman
8/4/1880	Journal	Politics	Democrats, Asa Teal, county chairman
6/14/1882	Journal	Politics	Democrats, Asa Teal, county chairman, convention will be held on June 24, 1882
11/4/1896	Journal	Politics	Democrats, C. C. Lyons was Democratic chairman in late 1888, replacing Mr. Brown of Ward Township
6/3/1874	Journal	Politics	Democrats, Chairman, G. W. H. Riley is chairman of County Democrat Central Committee
4/8/1896	Journal	Politics	Democrats, Charley Smith chosen county chairman
3/30/1892	Journal	Politics	Democrats, convention and nominees
5/19/1886	Journal	Politics	Democrats, convention to be held on May 29, 1886
7/5/1882	Journal	Politics	Democrats, county convention held last Saturday
2/13/1878	Journal	Politics	Democrats, county convention minutes
6/21/1882	Journal	Politics	Democrats, county convention postponed until July 1, 1882
3/17/1886	Journal	Politics	Democrats, county convention will be held next Saturday
3/10/1880	Journal	Politics	Democrats, county convention; Asa Teal, county chairman
5/7/1884	Journal	Politics	Democrats, county nominees listed; Henry Hinshaw, commissioner of Eastern District
3/21/1888	Journal	Politics	Democrats, county ticket listed
2/16/1898	Journal	Politics	Democrats, Dr. C. M. Kelley elected county chairman; Ed K. Semans elected secretary; no ticket but favor free silver
6/2/1886	Journal	Politics	Democrats, E. E. McGriff, county chairman; also convention proceedings
10/27/1886	Journal	Politics	Democrats, Emerson McGriff, county chairman
11/10/1886	Journal	Politics	Democrats, Emerson McGriff, county chairman, will move to Decatur

Date	Source	Category	Description
8/10/1892	Journal	Politics	Democrats, Erastus Lollar is county chairman
4/11/1894	Journal	Politics	Democrats, F. S. Caldwell elected county chairman
5/6/1891	Journal	Politics	Democrats, G. D. Williamson, county chairman
5/1/1872	Journal	Politics	Democrats, G. W. H. Riley, Chairman of County Democrat-Liberal Republican Central Committee
8/21/1872	Journal	Politics	Democrats, G. W. H. Riley, Chairman of County Democrat-Liberal Republican Central Committee
3/15/1876	Journal	Politics	Democrats, George W. H. Riley, County Chairman
9/20/1866	Journal	Politics	Democrats, Heaston, N. P. is Chairman of Democratic Central Committee
7/1/1914	Journal	Politics	Democrats, J. L. Smith will write the history of the Democratic Party of this county for a history
4/5/1876	Journal	Politics	Democrats, minutes of county convention; Captain Asa Teal elected chairman of County Central Committee
4/16/1890	Journal	Politics	Democrats, Mort Miller elected county chairman; ticket listed
11/20/1863	Journal	Politics	Democrats, Peace Democrat Meeting five miles southeast of Winchester
10/31/1888	Journal	Politics	Democrats, W. S. Brown, county chairman
3/22/1871	Journal	Politics	Democrats, William H. Dimery [sic] warned his colored brethren that the Democratic party was but a snake in the grass
5/6/1891	Journal	Politics	Democrats, Williamson, G. D. is chairman of County Democrat Central Committee
9/27/1944	News	Politics	Dewey, Thomas, Presidential candidate's train passed through Winchester on September 27
10/15/1940	Journal-Herald	Politics	Draft Board: William E. Harrison, Mitchell A. Hinshaw, and Charles W. Bowman
5/30/1917	Journal	Politics	Draft Registrars and Conscription Committee, listed
3/23/1933	Democrat	Politics	Dry Forces hold township meetings
10/20/1932	Democrat	Politics	Dry Forces organize; George E. Addington, chairman
2/3/1909	Journal	Politics	Dry Majority is 2451 for county option prohibition; wets lost all precincts in county
12/7/1943	Journal-Herald	Politics	Dry organization formed at Winchester Christian Church
6/8/1933	Democrat	Politics	Dry, Randolph County goes 2-1 Dry
3/15/1911	Herald	Politics	Drys, Farmland and Parker to remain dry; Union City will vote on March 30, 1911

Date	Source	Category	Description
2/15/1911	Herald	Politics	Drys, organize in meeting at Winchester Friends Church; J. E. Hinshaw on the program
4/5/1911	Herald	Politics	Drys, Union City voted to go wet
12/6/1917	Democrat	Politics	Dunn appointed county prosecutor; Chenoweth is in the army
6/12/1962	Journal-Herald	Politics	Dunn, Chet is County Democrat Chairman
12/5/1917	Journal	Politics	Dunn, Ernest E. appointed prosecutor; Prosecutor Chenoweth went into the army
2/15/1912	Democrat	Politics	Edger, E. S. is new County Democrat Chairman
1/28/1914	Herald	Politics	Edger, E. S. is reelected County Democrat Chairman
1/28/1914	Journal	Politics	Edger, E. S. is reelected County Democrat Chairman
1/29/1914	Democrat	Politics	Edger, E. S. is reelected County Democrat Chairman
1/25/1893	Journal	Politics	Edger, Edward was a Democrat
6/9/1880	Journal	Politics	Edwards, William; Cal Edwards has commission of; he was first judge in Randolph County
10/21/1858	Journal	Politics	Election results by precinct
11/10/1886	Journal	Politics	Election results by precinct
11/4/1908	Journal	Politics	Election results; trustees, etc.
4/5/1882	Journal	Politics	Elections results for nominating elections in Monroe and Nettle Creek Townships; and county
12/30/1915	Democrat	Politics	Engle appointed to county council to replace J. D. Miller, resigned
1/13/1904	Journal	Politics	Engle, James S. elected County Republican Chairman
1/13/1904	Herald	Politics	Engle, James S. elected new County Republican Chairman on second ballot
1/13/1904	Journal	Politics	Engle, James S. is new County Republican Chairman
11/7/1906	Journal	Politics	Fairbanks, Vice-President Charles was in Winchester
12/10/1946	Journal-Herald	Politics	Farabee, H. C. will be Greensfork Trustee until the end of the year
12/22/1875	Journal	Politics	Farmland corporation limits will be extended to take in school building
1/22/1925	Journal-Herald	Politics	Farmland Council, Howard Hill succeeds Luther Thornburg, who resigned
5/16/1877	Journal	Politics	Farmland election
5/8/1901	Herald	Politics	Farmland election results
10/20/1915	Journal	Politics	Farmland election results
4/28/1880	Journal	Politics	Farmland election results
5/10/1899	Herald	Politics	Farmland election results
5/13/1885	Journal	Politics	Farmland election results
5/16/1877	Journal	Politics	Farmland election results

Date	Source	Category	Description
5/17/1876	Journal	Politics	Farmland election results
5/18/1885	Journal	Politics	Farmland election results
5/25/1881	Journal	Politics	Farmland election results
5/3/1882	Journal	Politics	Farmland election results
5/4/1892	Journal	Politics	Farmland election results
5/6/1896	Journal	Politics	Farmland election results
5/7/1879	Journal	Politics	Farmland election results
5/8/1878	Journal	Politics	Farmland election results
5/11/1887	Herald	Politics	Farmland election results: Elisha Graham (2), J. S. Davis (3); Isaac Gillam, marshal; John Thornburg, treasurer; H. D. Good, clerk; one of these was a Democrat, the first ever elected in Farmland
11/10/1915	Herald	Politics	Farmland election results: Ford, marshal; Harrison, clerk; Garver Bly, treasurer; Frank Mills (1), M. M. Boots (3)
5/8/1901	Journal	Politics	Farmland election results; all Republicans win
5/12/1897	Journal	Politics	Farmland election results; all Republicans win
11/8/1905	Herald	Politics	Farmland election returns: Harrison, clerk; Bales, treasurer; Oswald (1), W. E. Williams (2), Harve Taylor (3)
6/27/1867	Journal	Politics	Farmland is now incorporated
12/15/1875	Journal	Politics	Farmland is now incorporated; plans to organize a school board
11/12/1919	Journal	Politics	Farmland officers listed
1/11/1922	Journal-Herald	Politics	Farmland officers listed
12/15/1875	Journal	Politics	Farmland reincorporated
1/29/1890	Herald	Politics	Farmland, "more Republicans to the square in Farmland than any town in Indiana"
12/15/1897	Journal	Politics	Farmland, article in Portland Sun says that Democrats were barred from voting in Farmland during Civil War
5/26/1984	News-Gazette	Politics	Farmland, Barney Jester replaces Raymond Howell on town board
7/8/1975	News-Gazette	Politics	Farmland, Betty Ludwig replaces Frances Main as clerk-treasurer
7/2/1879	Journal	Politics	Farmland, David Wasson replaces Linn Thornburg as JP
12/4/1984	News-Gazette	Politics	Farmland, Gary Moore and Mark Ingle are on town board
10/13/1948	News	Politics	Farmland, Ira Smithson (2) and Leslie Cox (3) joined Farmland Town Board
4/25/1877	Journal	Politics	Farmland, J. W. Macy resigns as marshal; E. R. Robbins replaces him

Date	Source	Category	Description
6/9/1909	Herald	Politics	Farmland, James G. Nixon (D) replaces Williams on Farmland Board [he was not actually a Democrat]
6/10/1909	Democrat	Politics	Farmland, James Nixon, Democrat, replaced William E. Williams, Republican, on town board [later reported indicated that he was not a Democrat]
4/25/1877	Journal	Politics	Farmland, John W. Macy resigned as marshal; E. R. Robbins appointed
12/31/1879	Journal	Politics	Farmland, Lindley Thornburg and E. T. Spence replaced J. H. B. McNees and N. E. Gray on town board
2/1/1923	Democrat	Politics	Farmland, Lonnie Woodard replaces S. H. Davisson as marshal after two years
10/5/1910	Journal	Politics	Farmland, M. M. Boots replaces George Davis as marshal
6/28/1876	Journal	Politics	Farmland, New Jersey Democratic delegates were greeted by cheers for Hayes at Farmland
6/16/1909	Journal	Politics	Farmland, Nixon, new town board member, is not a Democrat as previously reported
2/7/1867	Journal	Politics	Farmland, petition to incorporate
10/10/1966	News	Politics	Farmland, Richard Shockney replaces Keith Mills on town board
11/4/1965	Journal-Herald	Politics	Farmland, Russell Hammer replaces Gerald Williams on town board
12/29/1936	Daily News	Politics	Farmland, Stewart Hobley resigns as justice of the peace
4/4/1912	Democrat	Politics	Farmland, Theodore Roosevelt won Farmland Republican primary
11/5/1913	Journal	Politics	Farmland, two Progressives and three Republicans elected; Union City went Democrat
2/5/1879	Journal	Politics	Farmland, W. J. Davisson resigns from town board
9/8/1971	News-Gazette	Politics	Fields, Lowell, appointed to County Council
9/7/1971	News-Gazette	Politics	Fields, Weldon, county councilman, died
10/17/1890	Democrat	Politics	FMBA and Farmers Alliance meeting today to form a political ticket
1/14/1914	Journal	Politics	Fox, S. D. and William Y. Puckett, city officials, photos
4/7/1880	Journal	Politics	Franklin Township election results for township offices
10/4/1928	Democrat	Politics	Franklin Township, A. B. Wall, trustee, killed
2/3/1937	Daily News	Politics	Franklin Township, David Mosier appointed justice of the peace to replace T. A. Almonrode
1/18/1882	Journal	Politics	Franklin Township, George Addington appointed trustee in place of I. N. Stratton, removed by court

Date	Source	Category	Description
9/10/1873	Journal	Politics	Franklin Township, James Addington is constable
4/4/1883	Journal	Politics	Franklin Township, Levi James replaces G. Sims as JP
1/4/1882	Journal	Politics	Franklin Township, S. S. Franklin replaces D. W. Porter as JP
9/16/1896	Journal	Politics	Free Silver ticket listed
4/6/1898	Journal	Politics	Free Silver, Democrat, Populist, Prohibitionist joint ticket named
3/23/1898	Journal	Politics	Free Silver, Democrats, People's and Prohibitionists met to nominate a joint Free Silver Ticket
3/10/1859	Journal	Politics	Garrett, Elisha starts as county auditor
5/24/1947	Journal-Herald	Politics	Gist, Oliver, Mayor of Union City since 1933, died; he had replaced Williamson
10/6/1915	Herald	Politics	Goodrich Rally, 10,000 people attend
1/17/1900	Journal	Politics	Goodrich, James P. elected County Republican Chairman
8/7/1901	Herald	Politics	Goodrich, James P. elected State Republican Chairman
1/29/1902	Journal	Politics	Goodrich, James P. elected State Republican Chairman
1/17/1900	Journal	Politics	Goodrich, James P. elected to State Republican Committee
11/7/1900	Herald	Politics	Goodrich, James P. is County and District Republican Chairman
1/17/1900	Herald	Politics	Goodrich, James P. reelected County Republican Chairman
1/19/1898	Herald	Politics	Goodrich, James P. reelected County Republican Chairman
1/20/1904	Journal	Politics	Goodrich, James P. reelected State Republican Chairman
2/9/1910	Herald	Politics	Goodrich, James P. retires as State Republican Chairman
1/22/1868	Journal	Politics	Goodrich, John B. was previous chairman of County Central Committee
9/20/1866	Journal	Politics	Goodrich, John B., chairman Union (Republican) Party
2/16/186	Journal	Politics	Goodrich, John B., chairman Union Party
3/5/1886	Democrat	Politics	Gray, Pierre resigns as Democrat County Chairman; E. E. McGriff starts
6/16/1958	News	Politics	Green Township, Clyde F. Thornburg named trustee to succeed Walter Bentz, deceased
1/12/1876	Journal	Politics	Green Township, S. S. Clark replaces Vice H. Hubbard, resigned, as JP
6/16/1886	Journal	Politics	Green Township, Steubenville Precinct moved to Brinkley
2/19/1890	Journal	Politics	Green Township, W. H. Harrison is Republican nominee for trustee and F. M. Green is nominee for assessor

Date	Source	Category	Description
8/16/1876	Journal	Politics	Greenback, "Independent" ticket listed
10/20/1880	Journal	Politics	Greenbackers got 75 votes in Randolph County
10/2/1878	Journal	Politics	Greenbackers, B. F. Wilmore is chairman of National Greenback County Central Committee
5/8/1878	Journal	Politics	Greenbackers, B. F. Wilmore is county chairman of the Independent Central Committee
9/1/1880	Journal	Politics	Greenbackers, B. F. Wilmore, chairman, National Greenback Party of Randolph County
7/26/1876	Journal	Politics	Greenbackers, Independent convention on August 12, 1876 to select Greenback Ticket; B. F. Wilmore, chairman, County Central Committee
5/22/1878	Journal	Politics	Greenbackers, Independent mass convention and ticket
11/10/1886	Journal	Politics	Greenbackers, only 19 Greenback votes in Randolph County
1/8/1914	Democrat	Politics	Greensfork Township, George O. Wise replaces Bunch, resigned, as trustee
1/7/1914	Herald	Politics	Greensfork Township, George Wise appointed to replace John Bunch, resigned, as trustee
1/7/1914	Journal	Politics	Greensfork Township, John Bunch resigns as trustee; George Wise appointed to replace him
7/17/1901	Journal	Politics	Greensfork Township, John I. Thomas resigned as justice of the peace to become postmaster at Crete
6/6/1894	Journal	Politics	Greensfork Township, John W. Taylor, trustee, died; John H. Taylor appointed
6/6/1894	Herald	Politics	Greensfork Township, Johnny Taylor, trustee, died
7/25/1972	News-Gazette	Politics	Greensfork Township, Paul C. Macy, trustee, died
9/15/1875	Journal	Politics	Greensfork Township, Thomas Hough replaces John Harlan as JP
7/29/1914	Journal	Politics	Greensfork Township, Trustee Bunch resigns
10/22/1931	Democrat	Politics	Greensfork Township, William R. Mann, trustee, died
1/14/1914	Journal	Politics	Greenville article on Randolph County Republicans
1/17/1872	Journal	Politics	Gullett, Alex resigns as Wayne Trustee; James Woodbury appointed
10/12/1949	News	Politics	Gutheil, William is named County Republican Chairman
9/13/1984	News-Gazette	Politics	Hahn, Greg, Winchester native, is Democrat candidate for State Attorney General

Date	Source	Category	Description
8/25/1861	Journal	Politics	Halliday, E. F. replaces John W. Jarnagin as county treasurer
10/12/1904	Journal	Politics	Harding, Warren G. campaigns in Winchester for Republicans
8/1/1888	Journal	Politics	Harrison Voters of 1840 listed
7/25/1888	Herald	Politics	Harrison Voters of 1840: Thomas Moorman, James Moorman, Thomas Ward, George Cox, Stephen Harris, Job Harris, Isom Harris, etc.
12/16/1969	News-Gazette	Politics	Harrison, Herb, County Treasurer, resigns; Opal McGuire is appointed
5/8/1969	Journal-Herald	Politics	Hendrickson, Chester, County Clerk, dies
8/23/1876	Journal	Politics	Hiatt, Ephraim is nominated by Republicans for County Surveyor
2/2/1910	Herald	Politics	Hiatt, Walter G. is elected County Republican Chairman
2/23/1933	Journal-Herald	Politics	Hill replaces Grant Wright and Warren Fudge replaces Wise on County Council
2/23/1933	Democrat	Politics	Hill, D. W. replaces Grant Wright, deceased, and Warren Fudge replaces Marcus Wise on County Council
8/26/1908	Journal	Politics	Hindsley is County Democrat Chairman
3/23/1904	Journal	Politics	Hindsley, A. C. elected County Democrat Chairman
3/28/1906	Journal	Politics	Hindsley, A. C. elected County Democrat Chairman
3/29/1906	Democrat	Politics	Hindsley, A. C. elected County Democrat Chairman
3/26/1908	Democrat	Politics	Hindsley, A. C. elected County Democrat Chairman
12/13/1911	Democrat	Politics	Hindsley, A. C. is County Democrat Chairman
12/27/1911	Herald	Politics	Hindsley, A. C. is County Democrat Chairman
3/25/1908	Journal	Politics	Hindsley, Alva elected County Democrat Chairman
3/28/1906	Herald	Politics	Hindsley, Alva is County Democrat Chairman
5/10/1893	Herald	Politics	Hinshaw, J. E. is county engineer
9/23/1941	Journal-Herald	Politics	Hinshaw, Mitchell resigns from draft board
1/27/1927	Journal-Herald	Politics	Hinshaw, O. W. appointed coroner
9/27/1900	Democrat	Politics	Hinshaw, S. S. refuses Democrat nomination for commissioner
4/20/1900	Democrat	Politics	Hinshaw, Simpson nominated for commissioner by Democrats [he declined the nomination]
6/30/1952	News	Politics	Hodson, William, county councilman, died
9/27/1916	Journal	Politics	Hughes, Charles E., Republican candidate for President, spoke at Franklin Street and GR & I

Date	Source	Category	Description
7/17/1889	Journal	Politics	Huntsville Corporation exists
5/18/1881	Journal	Politics	Huntsville election results
5/19/1880	Journal	Politics	Huntsville election results
1/23/1891	Democrat	Politics	Huntsville gave up its corporation; had 23 voters
11/10/1915	Herald	Politics	Huntsville has first justice of the peace in many years, Avery Jones
2/18/1858	Journal	Politics	Huntsville Republican meeting
12/24/1890	Journal	Politics	Huntsville, citizens voted to vacate incorporation
5/26/1886	Journal	Politics	Huntsville, Clyde Lynch, Republican, elected marshal
5/26/1875	Journal	Politics	Huntsville, our town is now incorporated
1/15/1902	Journal	Politics	Hutchens, Thomas W. is elected Chairman of the County Republican Central Committee
1/9/1918	Herald	Politics	Hutchins, Thomas reappointed county attorney
1/15/1902	Herald	Politics	Hutchins, Thomas, is new County Republican Chairman
9/16/1874	Journal	Politics	Independent Central Committee, B. F. Bundy, chairman
2/16/1876	Journal	Politics	Independent Greenback meeting held
9/2/1874	Journal	Politics	Independent ticket listed
12/2/1874	Journal	Politics	Independents [Greenbackers], T. W. Reece was one of organizers of the new party at Indianapolis last week
11/7/1975	News-Gazette	Politics	Ingle, Elna accused of fraud as County Clerk
5/9/1969	Journal-Herald	Politics	Ingle, Elna appointed County Clerk
5/29/1976	News-Gazette	Politics	Ingle, Elna resigns as County Clerk
12/26/1907	Democrat	Politics	Jack, Harry, county treasurer-elect, died
3/21/1888	Herald	Politics	Jackson, William King was only Republican trustee ever in Jackson Township
5/10/1978	News-Gazette	Politics	Jefferis, Alan is elected 10th District Republican Chairman
6/14/1980	News-Gazette	Politics	Jefferis, Alan of Randolph County is delegate to Republican National Convention
5/8/1978	News-Gazette	Politics	Jefferis, Alan reelected County Republican Chairman; Bud Landess reelected County Democrat Chairman
5/13/1974	News-Gazette	Politics	Jefferis, Allen is elected Republican County Chairman; Shirley Wright is elected Republican County Vice-Chairman; Bud Landess is reelected County Democrat Chairman
5/10/1976	News-Gazette	Politics	Jefferis, Allen is reelected Republican County Chairman; Bud Landess is reelected County Democrat Chairman

Date	Source	Category	Description
1/14/1972	News-Gazette	Politics	Jefferis, Duane is appointed to County Council
5/31/1957	News	Politics	Johnson, Tony is named County Auditor to replace Casey Strickler, deceased
7/9/1890	Journal	Politics	JP trouble
11/16/1898	Journal	Politics	JPs elected listed
4/10/1863	Journal	Politics	Justices of the peace, election of
11/11/1874	Journal	Politics	Justices of the peace, list of those elected
4/17/1878	Journal	Politics	Justices of the Peace, list of those elected
4/30/1890	Journal	Politics	Justices of the Peace, list of those elected: 28 Republicans, eight Democrats; also new assessors listed
1/24/1861	Journal	Politics	Kansas Relief meeting held
11/29/1916	Herald	Politics	Keagy, W., Union City councilman, died
3/1/1966	Journal-Herald	Politics	Keever, Albert was elected surveyor in 1964 but did not qualify, so Arthur Purdy continued to serve [until end of 1966]
2/25/1926	Democrat	Politics	Keever, Pearl G. appointed township assessor to replace Josiah Lamm, who died
1/11/1888	Journal	Politics	King, William, trustee of Jackson Township is a Republican
11/7/1894	Journal	Politics	King, William, trustee of Jackson Township is a Republican
4/4/1861	Journal	Politics	Kizer, T. W. elected White River Township Trustee
9/29/1859	Journal	Politics	Kizer, Thomas W. is Republican candidate for coroner
7/4/1890	Democrat	Politics	Knights of Labor, FMBA, and Farmers Alliance will hold a joint meeting on July 12
9/5/1890	Democrat	Politics	Knights of Labor, FMBA, Farmers Alliance and Grange will hold a joint meeting
3/12/1973	News-Gazette	Politics	Landess, Alonzo "Bud" is elected County Democrat Chairman
5/12/1970	News-Gazette	Politics	Lapar, Dr. William is reelected County Republican Chairman; Don Staley is reelected County Democrat Chairman
9/3/1969	Journal-Herald	Politics	Lapar, Dr. William named County Republican Chairman
5/8/1972	News-Gazette	Politics	Lapar, Dr. William reelected County Republican Chairman; Don Staley reelected County Democrat Chairman
6/6/1877	Journal	Politics	Liberty Party Convention remembered
2/1/1899	Herald	Politics	Liberty Party, reminiscences of party in Indiana

Date	Source	Category	Description
3/20/1878	Journal	Politics	Liberty Precinct discontinued; Bloomingport and Wood's Station Precincts established
2/13/1951	Journal-Herald	Politics	Lincoln Club, Dr. Norwood Brigance, not George Craig, at Lincoln Club dinner
2/10/1945	Journal-Herald	Politics	Lincoln Club, Randolph County has oldest Lincoln Club in the U. S.
2/10/1948	Journal-Herald	Politics	Lincoln Club, Randolph County Lincoln Club "is the father of them all"
2/9/1952	Journal-Herald	Politics	Lincoln Club, Randolph County's is first Lincoln Club in USA
2/12/1948	Journal-Herald	Politics	Lincoln Club, Randolph County's Lincoln Club was the first in the U. S.
2/14/1861	Journal	Politics	Lincoln, Abraham did NOT come through Randolph County on way to Washington
4/16/1884	Journal	Politics	List of trustees and JPs elected
2/4/1909	Democrat	Politics	Local Option Election, drys carried every precinct in county; Large margins included S. Lynn (141-29), Bloomingport (99-13), Arba (84-18), and Hubbard (107-3)
3/26/1902	Journal	Politics	Lollar, Enos is elected Chairman of County Democrat Party
1/9/1934	Journal-Herald	Politics	Longnecker replaces Dunn on County Council
8/21/1872	Journal	Politics	Losantville correspondent says 9/10 of Baptists in the area are Democrats
5/5/1897	Journal	Politics	Losantville election results; no contests
12/3/1982	News-Gazette	Politics	Losantville, has not had a town election in 50 years
12/29/1949	Journal-Herald	Politics	Losantville, James S. Seagraves, town clerk off and on since 1903, died
6/20/1980	News-Gazette	Politics	Losantville, Joe Hinshaw has been marshal since March 1979
11/6/1981	News-Gazette	Politics	Losantville, Joseph P. Hinshaw is appointed to town board to replace Terry Green; Betty F. Barnett and Marvin McNees continue; Martha Culy resigns as clerk-treasurer effective January 1; Leah Abrams appointed
10/12/1982	News-Gazette	Politics	Losantville, Michael Turner starts as marshal
8/8/1980	News-Gazette	Politics	Losantville, Robert Cross, Jr. resigns from town board; other members are Richard James and Tony Green; Martha Culy is clerk-treasurer
10/2/1981	News-Gazette	Politics	Losantville, Terry Green resigns from town board

Date	Source	Category	Description
8/10/1982	News-Gazette	Politics	Losantville, town board consists of Marvin McNees, Betty Barnett, Joseph P. Hinshaw; Leah Abrams is clerk-treasurer
9/16/1971	News-Gazette	Politics	Losantville, Verlin Jones replaces Charles V. Macy on town board
1/6/1970	News-Gazette	Politics	Losantville, Wayne Metsker starts on town board to replace Cliff Farmer, who died in December
7/2/1980	News-Gazette	Politics	Losantvillle, Joe Hinshaw resigns as marshal
9/30/1911	Democrat	Politics	Lynn dry, 7-1
5/4/1887	Journal	Politics	Lynn election results
5/5/1886	Journal	Politics	Lynn election results
11/6/1913	Democrat	Politics	Lynn election results: Moody, marshal; Hodgin, clerk; Swain, east district; Chenoweth, south district; all are Republicans
11/9/1905	Democrat	Politics	Lynn election results: Republican clerk and treasurer; Democrats won council seats: Charles Longfellow, 1; Charles Davis, 2; B. F. Barnes; 3
1/22/1890	Journal	Politics	Lynn incorporated prior to this time
4/20/1898	Journal	Politics	Lynn Republican ticket listed
5/25/1910	Journal	Politics	Lynn, A. C. Quigg, Republican, replaces John Roland on Lynn Town Board
11/4/1939	Journal-Herald	Politics	Lynn, Adam Flatter retiring as Clerk-Treasurer
2/9/1973	News-Gazette	Politics	Lynn, Bill Ratts appointed to town board
5/4/1978	News-Gazette	Politics	Lynn, Charles Shaw appointed to town board
4/25/1900	Herald	Politics	Lynn, election results (all Republicans): Ezra Nye, 3; S. H. Light, treasurer; G. V. Hodgen, clerk; Thomas Norton, marshal;
12/27/1975	News-Gazette	Politics	Lynn, history of town board
2/14/1978	News-Gazette	Politics	Lynn, Howard Miller resigns from town board
6/27/1883	Journal	Politics	Lynn, incorporating election will be held on July 7, 1883
7/11/1883	Journal	Politics	Lynn, incorporation, vote was unanimous
8/23/1983	News-Gazette	Politics	Lynn, Irene Addington resigns as clerk-treasurer after 19 years; Larry Girton resigns from town board
1/4/1973	News-Gazette	Politics	Lynn, James Ponder resigns from town board
9/7/1983	News-Gazette	Politics	Lynn, Kay Straley appointed clerk-treasurer; Joe Ralston White appointed to town board
7/9/1981	News-Gazette	Politics	Lynn, Larry Case replaces William Elliott on town board

Date	Source	Category	Description
2/9/1984	News-Gazette	Politics	Lynn, Linda McFarland replaces Walter Thomas, deceased, on town board
12/6/1958	Journal-Herald	Politics	Lynn, Owen Dunlap resigns from town board
4/26/1899	Herald	Politics	Lynn, Republican nominees listed
4/22/1896	Journal	Politics	Lynn, Republican ticket listed
3/9/1978	News-Gazette	Politics	Lynn, Stanley Sims replaces Howard Miller on town board; Robert Sheppard replaces Bob McFarland on town board
4/28/1978	News-Gazette	Politics	Lynn, Stanley Sims resigns from town board
5/7/1981	News-Gazette	Politics	Lynn, William Elliott resigns from town board
4/22/1976	News-Gazette	Politics	Lynn, William McFarland, marshal for 28 years is retiring; William H. Trinder has been marshal of Losantville for 25 years; Ed Huddleston has been marshal at Farmland for 18 years
10/7/1896	Journal	Politics	Lyons, C. C., former chairman of the County Democratic Central Committee, is now a Republican
1/4/1980	News-Gazette	Politics	Macy, Helen appointed County Assessor
8/22/1877	Journal	Politics	Macy, J. W. takes clerk's office today; D. C. Braden takes recorder's office
5/15/1924	Democrat	Politics	Macy, John W. is elected Republican County Chairman (he is anti-Klan); Charles A. Wall is elected Democrat County Chairman
5/11/1922	Democrat	Politics	Macy, John W. is elected Republican County Chairman; J. L. Turner is elected Democrat County Chairman to replace Chattin
1/15/1902	Herald	Politics	Macy, John W. is new judge
5/11/1922	Democrat	Politics	Macy, John W. to succeed Harvey E. McNees as County Republican Chairman; McNees served eight years
12/2/1966	News	Politics	Macy, John W., Jr. is retiring as Judge
1/7/1914	Herald	Politics	Mahan, Charles is new County Agricultural Agent
2/18/1965	Journal-Herald	Politics	Marlin, Kenneth [no longer 10th District Republican Chairman]
6/10/1955	News	Politics	Marlin, Kenneth is new chairman of Republican Central Committee
6/22/1961	Journal-Herald	Politics	Marlin, Kenneth of Farmland is elected 10th District Republican Chairman through May 1962
5/16/1962	News	Politics	Marlin, Kenneth of Farmland is reelected Chairman of Tenth District Republican Central Committee

Date	Source	Category	Description
5/14/1956	News	Politics	Marlin, Kenneth reelected as Republican Chairman; Chester Dunn is new Democrat Chairman
5/12/1958	News	Politics	Marlin, Kenneth reelected as Republican Chairman; Chester Dunn is reelected as Democrat Chairman
5/9/1960	News	Politics	Marlin, Kenneth reelected as Republican Chairman; Chester Dunn is reelected as Democrat Chairman
1/20/1892	Herald	Politics	Marsh, A. O. reelected County Republican Chairman
11/14/1906	Journal	Politics	Martin, "Abe" comments on Winchester politics
6/2/1886	Herald	Politics	McGriff, E. E., Chairman County Democrat Central Committee
2/14/1941	Daily News	Politics	McGuire, Albert J. served 11 years and 5 months as White River trustee; wife was a daughter of Henry Addington
1/3/1970	News-Gazette	Politics	McGuire, Opal appointed County Treasurer to begin on January 2
9/22/1859	Journal	Politics	McKew, Arthur is Republican commissioner candidate
1/9/1918	Herald	Politics	McNees out; Leggett in as Winchester mayor
5/15/1918	Herald	Politics	McNees, H. E. reelected County Republican Chairman
9/5/1917	Herald	Politics	McNees, H. E. replaces J. M. Browne as County Republican Chairman
9/5/1917	Journal	Politics	McNees, Harvey is appointed County Republican Chairman to replace James M. Brown, resigned
5/16/1918	Democrat	Politics	McNees, Harvey reelected County Republican Chairman; D. W. Callahan reelected County Democrat Chairman
5/15/1918	Herald	Politics	McNees, Harvey re-elected Republican chairman
9/6/1917	Democrat	Politics	McNees, Harvey replaces J. M. Browne as County Republican Chairman
5/12/1920	Journal-Herald	Politics	McNees, Harvey, reelected County Republican Chairman
5/11/1964	News	Politics	Mendenhall, Bill is elected Republican County Chairman; Jim Wall is elected Democrat County Chairman
4/10/1962	Journal-Herald	Politics	Mendenhall, Bill is new County Republican Chairman
5/14/1962	News	Politics	Mendenhall, Bill is reelected County Republican Chairman; Chester Dunn is reelected County Democratic Chairman
5/9/1966	News	Politics	Mendenhall, Bill is reelected Republican County Chairman; Jim Wall is reelected Democrat County Chairman

Date	Source	Category	Description
5/13/1968	News	Politics	Mendenhall, Bill is reelected Republican County Chairman; Jim Wall is reelected Democrat County Chairman
8/22/1969	Journal-Herald	Politics	Mendenhall, Bill, County Republican Chairman, died; was member of Winchester Friends Church
12/8/1936	Daily News	Politics	Mendenhall, Brazilla C. replaces Edgar Hill on County Council
2/27/1936	News-Democrat	Politics	Mendenhall, Nate, county prosecutor, will not seek reelection; was appointed in 1932 and elected in 1932 and 1934
8/26/1981	News-Gazette	Politics	Modoc Board: Tom Fields, Thomas Larrison, Dane Fields
11/15/1911	Herald	Politics	Modoc election results: Charley Skinner, clerk; Emmet Harris, treasurer; Charley Downing, marshal;
5/8/1901	Herald	Politics	Modoc election results: Robert M. Busear, marshal; M. V. Hanscom, clerk; Thomas F. Whelan, treasurer; Sylvester Willis, Enoch Behringer, Peter Stepanek, trustees
11/12/1913	Herald	Politics	Modoc election results: W. C. Shoemaker, James Edwards, Charles Graham, trustees; Will Mendenhall, clerk; V. B. Harris, treasurer; Charles M. Manning, marshal
11/4/1981	News-Gazette	Politics	Modoc Police Department is abolished
6/30/1909	Herald	Politics	Modoc Republican nominees listed: Charles Skinner, clerk; D. E. Barker, treasurer; Charles Downing, marshal; William Howell (south), M. V. Maulsby (middle), Will Shoemaker (north)
1/6/1982	News-Gazette	Politics	Modoc, Dane Smith resigns from town board
11/24/1982	News-Gazette	Politics	Modoc, Donna Johnston appointed clerk-treasurer, effective January 1, 1983; resigns from town board
4/7/1982	News-Gazette	Politics	Modoc, Donna Johnston appointed to town board
1/5/1983	News-Gazette	Politics	Modoc, Donna Johnston starts as clerk-treasurer; Fields and Larrison are town board members
3/29/1899	Herald	Politics	Modoc, election is in favor of incorporation; 41-15
5/24/1899	Herald	Politics	Modoc, election results: A. A. Conarroe, C. E. Skinner, trustees; George Graham, clerk; H. A. Gaddis, treasurer; William James, marshal
3/30/1898	Journal	Politics	Modoc, election to incorporate was not held
2/4/1981	News-Gazette	Politics	Modoc, has no marshal
3/19/1913	Herald	Politics	Modoc, John Bradie replaces Charles Lowning [sic] as marshal

Date	Source	Category	Description
10/7/1981	News-Gazette	Politics	Modoc, Nancy Larrison is clerk-treasurer
10/6/1982	News-Gazette	Politics	Modoc, Nancy Larrison resigns as clerk-treasurer effective December 31
3/15/1899	Journal	Politics	Modoc, petition for incorporation granted by commissioners
1/8/1981	News-Gazette	Politics	Modoc, Rick Hunt resigns from town board
3/4/1981	News-Gazette	Politics	Modoc, Tom Fields replaces Rick Hunt on town board; other members are Dane Smith and Tom Larrison; Nancy Larrison is clerk-treasurer
11/9/1983	News-Gazette	Politics	Modoc, will not hold election; none held for several years
12/29/1859	Journal	Politics	Monks, George W. is County Republican Chairman
3/13/1872	Journal	Politics	Monks, L. J. elected Republican chairman
4/22/1908	Journal	Politics	Monks, L. J. of Winchester is Chief Justice of Indiana
9/13/1911	Herald	Politics	Monroe Township, A. B. Somerville resigns from township board; B. F. Sumwalt is appointed
9/15/1911	Democrat	Politics	Monroe Township, A. B. Somerville resigns from township board; Benjamin F. Sumwalt replaces him
1/18/1882	Journal	Politics	Monroe Township, Adam Slonaker will be trustee another term
3/28/1894	Journal	Politics	Monroe Township, Barclay Smith is JP
5/4/1967	Journal-Herald	Politics	Monroe Township, Joseph A. Butler, township trustee, died
1/4/1968	Journal-Herald	Politics	Monroe Township, Ray Thompson is appointed trustee to replace Rema Butler, who resigned effective December 31, 1967
5/10/1967	News	Politics	Monroe Township, Rema Butler is appointed trustee
12/9/1957	News	Politics	Monroe, Green, Stoney Creek, movement to consolidate civil townships
3/22/1871	Journal	Politics	Morristown, petition to incorporate town
6/9/1915	Journal	Politics	Mullen Precinct is established in Ward Township; will vote at No. 9 Schoolhouse
11/25/1957	News	Politics	Murray, John D. appointed to county council to replace John Fields, deceased
7/11/1888	Herald	Politics	Music for "Tippecanoe and Morton, Too"
4/15/1874	Journal	Politics	Nettle Creek Township, C. B. Murray resigns as JP
3/19/1890	Journal	Politics	Nettle Creek Township, Democratic ticket listed
4/21/1875	Journal	Politics	Nettle Creek Township, Hicks K. Wright, trustee, died; Lemuel Wiggins appointed

Date	Source	Category	Description
9/19/1888	Journal	Politics	Nettle Creek Township, John P. Edwards appointed constable
4/26/1882	Journal	Politics	Nettle Creek Township, Joseph Bookout elected assessor
2/26/1890	Journal	Politics	Nettle Creek Township, Republican nominees listed
3/28/1883	Journal	Politics	Nettle Creek Township, Solomon Ward, colored, appointed JP
10/16/1976	News-Gazette	Politics	News-Gazette endorses Dick Lugar
10/15/1976	News-Gazette	Politics	News-Gazette endorses Phil Sharp
3/20/1901	Journal	Politics	Newspaper lists old county Republican ticket
10/6/1952	News	Politics	Nixon, Richard will be at Richmond or Paoli, both Quaker strongholds
1/11/1969	Journal-Herald	Politics	Nixon, Richard, story on his religion
10/15/1913	Herald	Politics	Nixon, Sater appointed county coroner to replace D. C. Roney, resigned
11/7/1973	News-Gazette	Politics	Nixon's very own church
1/31/1942	Journal-Herald	Politics	No "skip" election
5/15/1918	Journal	Politics	Nominees listed; county and township
10/11/1871	Journal	Politics	Obituary says Nathan Garrett was sheriff (1835-1839), Jeremiah Smith was sheriff (1835), T. G. Noble was sheriff (1839+), Nathan Garrett was auditor (1844-1859), and Elisha Garrett was auditor (1859+).
11/21/1894	Journal	Politics	Officers, when the new officers take their positions
4/10/1863	Journal	Politics	Olive Branch Schoolhouse, Union meeting held
5/8/1948	Journal-Herald	Politics	Oliver, Robert C. is reelected Democrat County Chairman
4/4/1950	Journal-Herald	Politics	Painter, Lowell was coroner from 1932 to 1950
3/21/1894	Journal	Politics	Parker is incorporated as Parker City
2/7/1894	Journal	Politics	Parker voted for incorporation, 85 to 5
11/10/1909	Herald	Politics	Parker, Democrats were elected marshal and clerk
12/17/1974	News-Gazette	Politics	Parker, Edwin Graham replaces Paul Smith on town board
1/3/1970	News-Gazette	Politics	Parker, James Jones appointed to town board
11/19/1964	News	Politics	Parker, Jim Wright is elected clerk-treasurer
8/2/1979	News-Gazette	Politics	Parker, Neil Reed replaces Richard Hammer on town board
11/2/1959	News	Politics	Parker, Paul Beck elected to town board
12/2/1969	News-Gazette	Politics	Parker, Ralph Griffith resigns from town board
4/24/1901	Herald	Politics	Parker, Republican nominees listed
11/10/1915	Journal	Politics	Parker, Republicans won all offices

Date	Source	Category	Description
6/22/1976	News-Gazette	Politics	Parker, Rick Hammer replaces Keever on town board; Don Hiatt to resign from town board effective June 30
4/19/1899	Herald	Politics	Parker, town election nominees listed
12/1/1954	News	Politics	Parker, Wayman Jacobs replaces George Murphey, deceased, as clerk-treasurer
5/18/1976	News-Gazette	Politics	Parker, Wayman Keever resigns from town board
1/3/1973	News-Gazette	Politics	Patty, Vernon appointed County Surveyor
6/14/1976	News-Gazette	Politics	Peach, Suzanne is appointed County Clerk
2/24/1940	Journal-Herald	Politics	Peacock, Harry is Prohibition nominee for Lieutenant Governor
6/16/1897	Journal	Politics	Pension Board at Union City will be transferred to Winchester
5/29/1878	Journal	Politics	People's Convention [Democrats and Greenbackers]
6/17/1874	Journal	Politics	People's Convention held
5/31/1882	Journal	Politics	People's Convention is called for June 10, 1882
5/22/1878	Journal	Politics	People's Convention will be held on May 25, 1878 [joint Democrat and Greenbacker]
3/25/1874	Journal	Politics	People's Convention, call for
5/27/1896	Herald	Politics	People's Party convention
8/11/1897	Herald	Politics	People's Party of Randolph County, Marion Harter, Chairman; B. F. Wilmore, secretary
8/22/1894	Herald	Politics	People's Party, Nathan T. Butts, chairman
1/20/1892	Journal	Politics	People's Party, W. E. Hinshaw is chairman
6/9/1897	Herald	Politics	People's Party, White River Township meeting
6/28/1882	Journal	Politics	People's Ticket listed
3/15/1916	Journal	Politics	Political reorganization: James M. Browne, Republican chairman; D. W. Callihan [sic], Democrat chairman; Stephen Clevenger, Progressive chairman; S. C. Mendenhall, Progressive treasurer
5/13/1896	Journal	Politics	Populist meeting planned
1/20/1897	Herald	Politics	Populists of Randolph County will meet on January 30 to determine future
7/2/1890	Journal	Politics	Populists, call for mass reform convention on July 12, 1890 with Farmers' Alliance, FMBA, and Knights of Labor
2/16/1898	Journal	Politics	Populists, Marion Harter reelected county chairman; party will have a ticket (free silver)

Date	Source	Category	Description
1/22/1896	Journal	Politics	Populists, Marion Harter, county chairman of People's Party
5/18/1898	Journal	Politics	Populists, Marion Harter, county chairman of People's Party
7/1/1896	Journal	Politics	Populists, Marion Harter, county chairman of People's Party
9/23/1896	Journal	Politics	Populists, Marion Harter, county chairman of People's Party
2/19/1898	Journal	Politics	Populists, Marion Harter, county chairman of People's Party; will have convention on February 10, 1898
10/30/1895	Journal	Politics	Populists, Nathan T. Butts, county chairman
3/7/1894	Journal	Politics	Populists, People's Convention will be held on March 15, 1894
3/16/1892	Journal	Politics	Populists, People's Party convention and nominees
1/24/1894	Journal	Politics	Populists, People's Party will meet on January 27, 1894
5/16/1894	Journal	Politics	Populists, People's Party, N. T. Butts, county chairman
10/29/1890	Journal	Politics	Populists, People's ticket is called "a farce"
8/25/1897	Journal	Politics	Populists, Populist Party picnic; oppose union with Democrats
1/20/1897	Journal	Politics	Populists, Randolph County Populists will meet
7/16/1890	Journal	Politics	Populists, Reform convention held
2/17/1892	Journal	Politics	Populists, W. E. Hinshaw is county chairman of People's Party
5/31/1893	Journal	Politics	Populists, W. E. Hinshaw will speak at People's Party picnic
6/11/1973	News-Gazette	Politics	Precincts changed
6/13/1888	Journal	Politics	Precincts changed in Jackson and West River
9/15/1886	Journal	Politics	Precincts changed in West River, Green, Ward, and Franklin Townships
2/7/1882	Journal	Politics	Precincts described
1/23/1974	News-Gazette	Politics	Precincts reduced from 41 to 24
4/10/1872	Journal	Politics	Primary election results
4/15/1874	Journal	Politics	Primary election results
4/3/1872	Journal	Politics	Primary election results
4/8/1874	Journal	Politics	Primary election results
2/10/1916	Democrat	Politics	Progressive organization filed county ticket
7/24/1912	Herald	Politics	Progressives of Randolph County to organize on July 29
7/24/1912	Journal	Politics	Progressives, call for county to organize
3/11/1914	Journal	Politics	Progressives, candidates for county and township offices listed
1/27/1916	Democrat	Politics	Progressives, Carl Thompson ends term as County Chairman

Date	Source	Category	Description
1/19/1916	Journal	Politics	Progressives, Carl Thompson resigns as County Chairman
1/14/1914	Journal	Politics	Progressives, committeemen for White River Township listed
1/29/1914	Democrat	Politics	Progressives, committeemen listed
10/9/1912	Herald	Politics	Progressives, county ticket listed
8/28/1912	Herald	Politics	Progressives, delegates listed
8/12/1914	Herald	Politics	Progressives, E. S. Jaqua, former Progressive, attended a meeting on July 30 with Will Hayes to rejoin the Republican Party
3/11/1914	Herald	Politics	Progressives, G. Walter Hiatt is County Chairman
4/2/1914	Democrat	Politics	Progressives, G. Walter Hiatt is County Chairman
1/7/1914	Journal	Politics	Progressives, L. Ray Lenich is County Chairman; Wm. H. Bales is secretary
1/8/1914	Democrat	Politics	Progressives, L. Ray Lenich is County Chairman; Wm. H. Bales is secretary
1/21/1914	Journal	Politics	Progressives, L. Ray Lenich is elected district chairman
1/28/1914	Herald	Politics	Progressives, L. Ray Lenich is reelected County Chairman; committeemen listed
2/4/1914	Journal	Politics	Progressives, L. Ray Lenich resigned as county chairman; G. Walter Hiatt elected to replace him
1/21/1914	Journal	Politics	Progressives, list of committeemen
11/10/1915	Journal	Politics	Progressives, meeting held; Merl S. Ward chaired the meeting since G. W. Hiatt is no longer eligible
1/26/1916	Journal	Politics	Progressives, no successor named to Carl Thompson as County Chairman
7/31/1912	Journal	Politics	Progressives, organization of party
9/11/1912	Herald	Politics	Progressives, Rally in Courthouse
3/16/1916	Democrat	Politics	Progressives, Stephen Clevenger starts as County Chairman
2/11/1914	Journal	Politics	Progressives, William Smith, JP writes in support of the Progressive Party
10/12/1912	Journal	Politics	Progressives, Winchester Journal condemned Progressive ticket
5/21/1948	News	Politics	Prohibition Article (Quakers)
1/27/1892	Journal	Politics	Prohibition convention
4/14/1945	Journal-Herald	Politics	Prohibition County Convention
3/10/1915	Journal	Politics	Prohibition Party Central Committee re-elected: James Frazier, chairman; Harry Oxley, secretary; J. E. Thompson, treasurer
3/1/1911	Journal	Politics	Prohibition Party meeting held, township chairmen listed

Date	Source	Category	Description
9/9/1944	Journal-Herald	Politics	Prohibition Party names county candidates
9/22/1932	Journal-Herald	Politics	Prohibition Party to reorganize on September 24
2/1/1905	Journal	Politics	Prohibition Party, E. L. Conklin replaces J. H. Cummins as county chairman; J. H. Williams continues as secretary-treasurer
2/15/1900	Democrat	Politics	Prohibition Party, John R. Lamb, county chairman
2/15/1911	Journal	Politics	Prohibition Party, Worth Osborn, chair
1/27/1909	Journal	Politics	Prohibition Party, Worth Osborn, chair; John Hinshaw, secretary
1/13/1909	Journal	Politics	Prohibition Party, Worth Osborn, county chairman
10/31/1906	Herald	Politics	Prohibition ticket listed
3/7/1912	Democrat	Politics	Prohibition ticket listed
4/14/1943	Journal-Herald	Politics	Prohibitionists have reorganized due to the failure of local option
3/18/1915	Democrat	Politics	Prohibitionists reelect old officers: James Frazier, chairman; Oxley, secretary; J. E. Thompson, treasurer
3/10/1915	Journal	Politics	Prohibitionists reelect old officers; James Frazier, chairman
3/18/1915	Democrat	Politics	Prohibitionists reelected all county officers: James Frazier, county chairman; Harry Oxley, secretary; J. E. Thompson, treasurer
4/12/1943	Journal-Herald	Politics	Prohibitionists will meet Tuesday night to reorganize
11/5/1890	Journal	Politics	Prohibitionists, beat Democrats in Hubbard Precinct and will get a judge and clerk there; probably the only ones in Indiana
2/19/1896	Journal	Politics	Prohibitionists, C. R. Carter elected county chairman
4/21/1886	Journal	Politics	Prohibitionists, candidates listed
4/28/1886	Journal	Politics	Prohibitionists, convention
12/9/1885	Journal	Politics	Prohibitionists, convention
3/23/1892	Journal	Politics	Prohibitionists, convention and nominees
9/24/1884	Journal	Politics	Prohibitionists, convention called by John Richardson, J. W. Denney, and W. F. Hunt
3/1/1911	Journal	Politics	Prohibitionists, County Central Committee reorganized; Worth Osborn, Chairman; Byron Fennimore, secretary/treasurer
10/1/1884	Journal	Politics	Prohibitionists, county committee appointed; six townships represented
3/17/1886	Journal	Politics	Prohibitionists, county convention will be held on April 15, 1886

Date	Source	Category	Description
4/4/1917	Journal	Politics	Prohibitionists, county party is reorganized; Michael Lahey, chairman; Alma Ozborn [sic], secretary
10/13/1932	Democrat	Politics	Prohibitionists, county party reorganized
3/9/1904	Herald	Politics	Prohibitionists, county ticket listed
10/22/1913	Journal	Politics	Prohibitionists, donors listed
2/1/1905	Herald	Politics	Prohibitionists, E. L. Conklin elected County Chairman in place of J. H. Cummins; J. H. Williams reelected Secretary-Treasurer
2/1/1905	Journal	Politics	Prohibitionists, E. L. Conklin replaces J. H. Cummins as County Chairman
6/25/1947	News	Politics	Prohibitionists, four Randolph Countians at National Convention: Mattie Brumfield, Alice Peacock, Harry Oxley, and Grace Bookout
5/15/1948	Journal-Herald	Politics	Prohibitionists, G. W. Wilhelm is County Chairman
2/25/1914	Journal	Politics	Prohibitionists, Harry Peacock elected County Chairman
10/23/1912	Herald	Politics	Prohibitionists, Harry Peacock is County Chairman
2/26/1914	Democrat	Politics	Prohibitionists, Harry Peacock is new County Chairman; Job Potter, Calvin Johnson, et al were there
6/14/1916	Journal	Politics	Prohibitionists, Harry Peacock of Randolph County is candidate for State Auditor
6/27/1906	Journal	Politics	Prohibitionists, Harry Peacock, county chairman; A. J. Hinshaw, secretary; Joel H. Williams, treasurer; El Conklin, Worth Osborn, Frank Beeson, central committee
2/15/1906	Democrat	Politics	Prohibitionists, Harry Peacock, County Chairman; John Hinshaw, secretary
11/1/1952	Journal-Herald	Politics	Prohibitionists, Horace Smith of Wayne County is nominee for Treasurer of State
11/3/1958	News	Politics	Prohibitionists, Horace Smith of Wayne County is nominee for Treasurer of State
8/5/1896	Journal	Politics	Prohibitionists, it is not known if local Prohibitionists will split
2/16/1916	Herald	Politics	Prohibitionists, James Frazier, County Chairman
3/10/1915	Journal	Politics	Prohibitionists, James Frazier, county chairman; Harry Oxley, secretary; J. E. Thompson, treasurer
1/8/1903	Democrat	Politics	Prohibitionists, John Cortner is past county-chairman; J. H. Cummins is new chairman; J. H. Williams is secretary; Davidson Cheesman in treasurer

Date	Source	Category	Description
2/21/1900	Journal	Politics	Prohibitionists, John R. Lamb elected County Chairman
2/15/1900	Democrat	Politics	Prohibitionists, John R. Lamb is County Chairman
3/13/1895	Journal	Politics	Prohibitionists, John Richardson, county chairman
3/24/1886	Journal	Politics	Prohibitionists, John Richardson, county chairman
1/25/1888	Journal	Politics	Prohibitionists, John Richardson, county chairman; J. B. Bristol, secretary
3/14/1894	Journal	Politics	Prohibitionists, John Richardson, county chairman; William M. Ross, secretary; C. O. Harris, treasurer
3/14/1907	Democrat	Politics	Prohibitionists, L. M. Hinshaw is County Chairman
8/15/1900	Herald	Politics	Prohibitionists, meetings at Poplar Run, Jericho, Cherry Grove, Martindale; John R. Lamb, county chairman
3/29/1917	Democrat	Politics	Prohibitionists, Michael Lahey replaces N. W. Gray, resigned, as County Chairman
4/4/1917	Journal	Politics	Prohibitionists, Michael Lahey, county chairman; Alma Osborn, secretary
2/1/1888	Journal	Politics	Prohibitionists, minutes of convention
3/15/1917	Democrat	Politics	Prohibitionists, N. W. Gray is County Chairman
3/16/1916	Democrat	Politics	Prohibitionists, N. W. Gray replaces James Frazier as County Chairman
9/5/1962	News	Politics	Prohibitionists, off state ballot for first time since 1880s; no local party
2/21/1912	Herald	Politics	Prohibitionists, Osborn, Worth is County Chairman
7/22/1896	Journal	Politics	Prohibitionists, plans to organize the National Party [Prohibitionist splinter group] in Randolph County
6/14/1916	Herald	Politics	Prohibitionists, Randolph Countians: Harry Peacock is nominee for Auditor of State; Lum Carter is alternate delegate to National Convention; Albert Stanley, formerly of Winchester, is nominee for Lieutenant Governor
3/15/1916	Journal	Politics	Prohibitionists, Rev. N. W. Gray is elected County Chairman; candidates listed
3/6/1912	Journal	Politics	Prohibitionists, ticket listed
5/28/1890	Journal	Politics	Prohibitionists, ticket listed; James Brown, chairman of convention
2/23/1898	Journal	Politics	Prohibitionists, W. M. Ross calls for Prohibition organization in Randolph County
2/17/1904	Herald	Politics	Prohibitionists, Winchester city ticket listed

Date	Source	Category	Description
3/27/1907	Journal	Politics	Prohibitionists, Worth Osborn elected County Chairman
1/27/1909	Journal	Politics	Prohibitionists, Worth Osborn is elected County Chairman; John Hinshaw, Secretary
3/18/1908	Herald	Politics	Prohibitionists, Worth Osborn, County Chairman
2/15/1911	Herald	Politics	Prohibitionists, Worth Osborn, County Chairman
3/1/1911	Herald	Politics	Prohibitionists, Worth Osborn, county chairman, Byrom Fennimore, secretary and treasurer
3/28/1907	Democrat	Politics	Prohibitionists, Worth Osborn, County Chairman; A. J. Hinshaw, secretary; Harry V. Hitz, treasurer
7/11/1883	Journal	Politics	Prosecuting Attorney, Thomas A. Spence, died
6/3/1920	Democrat	Politics	Purdy, Arthur appointed county surveyor to replace Walter Batchelor, who resigned
5/6/1938	Journal-Herald	Politics	Purdy, Arthur has been Republican chair for four years; will not seek re-election
5/15/1934	Journal-Herald	Politics	Purdy, Arthur is new Republican county chair; Frank Unger is Democrat chair
12/23/1966	News	Politics	Purdy, Arthur is retiring as County Surveyor
12/22/1964	News	Politics	Purdy, Arthur retires as county surveyor
10/16/1912	Journal	Politics	Randolph County 1862 election results reprinted
10/19/1870	Journal	Politics	Randolph County election results
10/21/1874	Journal	Politics	Randolph County election results
10/18/1876	Journal	Politics	Randolph County election results by precinct
11/11/1896	Journal	Politics	Randolph County election results by precinct
11/16/1892	Journal	Politics	Randolph County election results by precinct
11/16/1898	Journal	Politics	Randolph County election results by precinct
11/7/1894	Journal	Politics	Randolph County election results by precinct
11/22/1882	Journal	Politics	Randolph County elections results by precinct
2/3/1909	Herald	Politics	Randolph County goes dry; Hubbard 3 wets to 107 drys, etc.
11/16/1910	Journal	Politics	Randolph County is only county in state to never elect a Democrat to county office since Civil War
2/25/1858	Journal	Politics	Randolph County Republican Convention proceedings
2/1/1911	Herald	Politics	Randolph County, County Option prohibition expires
5/23/1877	Journal	Politics	Recorders, history of in Randolph County

Date	Source	Category	Description
4/7/1859	Journal	Politics	Reed, Nathan elected White River Township Trustee
3/1/1893	Journal	Politics	Reed, Nathan was a Whig and a Universalist; was sheriff from August 28, 1844 to September 6, 1846 by appointment and from September 6, 1846 to August 28, 1848 by election; was first township trustee under new constitution
4/19/1860	Journal	Politics	Republican candidates, biographies
1/5/1860	Journal	Politics	Republican county convention, proceedings
2/25/1874	Journal	Politics	Republican county convention, proceedings
2/9/1876	Journal	Politics	Republican county convention, proceedings; W. E. Murray, chairman, central committee
9/15/1886	Journal	Politics	Republican county ticket from 1860 listed
3/19/1890	Journal	Politics	Republican nominating election results
3/23/1892	Journal	Politics	Republican nominating election results
3/26/1890	Journal	Politics	Republican nominating election results in table form
3/7/1888	Herald	Politics	Republican Party used nominating convention instead of an election
2/2/1910	Journal	Politics	Republican Party, G. Walter Hiatt is new chairman of GOP Central Committee
3/15/1916	Journal	Politics	Republican Party, James M. "Mal" Browne, chair; Democratic Party, D. W. Callahan, chair; Progressive Party, Stephen Mendenhall, chair
2/26/1896	Journal	Politics	Republican primary election results
3/14/1894	Journal	Politics	Republican primary election results
2/12/1890	Journal	Politics	Republican township tickets for Stoney Creek, White River, and Greensfork listed
3/31/1886	Journal	Politics	Republican township tickets listed
1/30/1965	Journal-Herald	Politics	Republican Women, Miriam Hinshaw, president
2/22/1882	Journal	Politics	Republican, county convention
2/22/1882	Journal	Politics	Republican, John W. Macy reelected county chairman
1/20/1892	Journal	Politics	Republicans, A. O. Marsh reelected as county chairman
1/22/1890	Journal	Politics	Republicans, A. O. Marsh replaces J. W. Macy as county chairman
1/6/1892	Journal	Politics	Republicans, A. O. Marsh, county chairman
12/27/1893	Journal	Politics	Republicans, A. O. Marsh, county chairman
1/23/1878	Journal	Politics	Republicans, Asahel Stone, county chairman
2/3/1886	Journal	Politics	Republicans, B. F. Boltz elected county chairman

Date	Source	Category	Description
10/27/1886	Journal	Politics	Republicans, B. F. Boltz, county chairman
1/19/1898	Journal	Politics	Republicans, committeeman listed
2/10/1892	Journal	Politics	Republicans, convention minutes
3/7/1888	Journal	Politics	Republicans, convention selected Republican nominees (not in a primary election)
1/25/1888	Journal	Politics	Republicans, county convention minutes
1/31/1894	Journal	Politics	Republicans, county convention minutes
2/12/1896	Journal	Politics	Republicans, county convention minutes
2/13/1878	Journal	Politics	Republicans, county convention minutes
2/20/1884	Journal	Politics	Republicans, county convention minutes
2/3/1886	Journal	Politics	Republicans, county convention minutes
2/5/1890	Journal	Politics	Republicans, county convention minutes
2/2/1898	Journal	Politics	Republicans, County Republican team
2/19/1864	Journal	Politics	Republicans, County Union Convention proceedings
7/3/1878	Journal	Politics	Republicans, delegates to Congressional Convention included Ira Johnson, W. H. Thornburg, W. H. Mendenhall, Cornelius Metsker, Frank Boroughs, Joseph DeVoss, L. H. Karns, George W. Addington, L. L. Williams, and others
2/26/1914	Democrat	Politics	Republicans, Frank Wright, W. D. Parker, C. P. Friedline were listed
2/9/1876	Journal	Politics	Republicans, General Stone, president of County Central Committee
9/26/1862	Journal	Politics	Republicans, George A. Smith, chairman of Republican Central Committee of Randolph County
9/20/1866	Journal	Politics	Republicans, Goodrich, John B. is Chairman of Union Central Committee
4/1/1864	Journal	Politics	Republicans, J. B. Goodrich, chairman of County Central Committee
7/14/1897	Journal	Politics	Republicans, J. P. Goodrich elected county chairman
2/13/1878	Journal	Politics	Republicans, J. W. Macy is elected county chairman
1/28/1880	Journal	Politics	Republicans, J. W. Macy, county chairman
10/31/1888	Journal	Politics	Republicans, J. W. Macy, county chairman
1/25/1888	Journal	Politics	Republicans, John W. Macy elected county chairman
2/1/1882	Journal	Politics	Republicans, John W. Macy is county chairman

Date	Source	Category	Description
2/20/1884	Journal	Politics	Republicans, John W. Macy is elected county chairman
1/3/1872	Journal	Politics	Republicans, L. J. Monks, Chairman, County Republican Central Committee
2/11/1874	Journal	Politics	Republicans, L. J. Monks, Chairman, County Republican Central Committee
7/28/1870	Journal	Politics	Republicans, L. J. Monks, Chairman, County Republican Central Committee
10/4/1882	Journal	Politics	Republicans, L. W. Study replaces J. W. Macy as county chairman
1/16/1884	Journal	Politics	Republicans, L. W. Study, county chairman; H. W. Bowers, secretary
3/10/1886	Journal	Politics	Republicans, nominating election results
4/9/1884	Journal	Politics	Republicans, nominating election results
2/23/1898	Journal	Politics	Republicans, primary election results
1/24/1872	Journal	Politics	Republicans, proceedings of county convention
4/10/1980	News-Gazette	Politics	Republicans, takeover attempt in Randolph County by Moral Majority
2/25/1874	Journal	Politics	Republicans, W. E. Murray elected chairman of the County Republican Central Committee
1/22/1896	Journal	Politics	Republicans, W. W. Canada reelected county chairman
7/7/1897	Journal	Politics	Republicans, W. W. Canada resigns as county chairman
1/17/1894	Journal	Politics	Republicans, W. W. Canada, county chairman
3/20/1895	Herald	Politics	Richardson, John is Prohibition chair
10/21/1909	Democrat	Politics	Ridgeville Democrat and Republican tickets listed
5/15/1901	Journal	Politics	Ridgeville election results
5/16/1888	Journal	Politics	Ridgeville election results
5/19/1880	Journal	Politics	Ridgeville election results
5/27/1885	Journal	Politics	Ridgeville election results
5/4/1892	Journal	Politics	Ridgeville election results
5/6/1896	Journal	Politics	Ridgeville election results
5/7/1903	Democrat	Politics	Ridgeville election results: Guy Wilmore, Republican, clerk; M. T. Sumption, Republican, treasurer; Joseph Iliff, Republican, marshal; John Wright, Democrat, 1; Charles Barrett, Democrat, 2; Will McCurdy, Democrat, 3
4/13/1898	Journal	Politics	Ridgeville Republican ticket listed
10/18/1911	Herald	Politics	Ridgeville, A. Morrical, clerk; Robert Conner, M. S. Thompson, J. D. Barger, trustees
4/12/1899	Herald	Politics	Ridgeville, Addington is marshal

Date	Source	Category	Description
9/8/1909	Journal	Politics	Ridgeville, Alex Wood resigns; Will Ford, Republican, elected marshal
5/26/1976	News-Gazette	Politics	Ridgeville, Chris Lay resigns from town board
6/18/1981	News-Gazette	Politics	Ridgeville, Clayton Addington (Democrat) is appointed to town board
6/16/1978	News-Gazette	Politics	Ridgeville, David Hoover resigns from town board
6/5/1981	News-Gazette	Politics	Ridgeville, David Northcutt (Democrat) resigns from town board
8/15/1979	News-Gazette	Politics	Ridgeville, Debbie Heniscey (Republican) appointed clerk-treasurer
5/3/1899	Herald	Politics	Ridgeville, election results: All Republicans elected, M. R. Hiatt, council; Thomas L. Addington, marshal; Joseph LaFollette, clerk; M. T. Sumption, treasurer
8/4/1978	News-Gazette	Politics	Ridgeville, Foust, Merrill appointed to town board
3/29/1958	Journal-Herald	Politics	Ridgeville, Gegenheimer replaces Taylor as clerk-treasurer
1/6/1984	News-Gazette	Politics	Ridgeville, new town board consists of Jeannie Holt, Linda Lee Harshman, James L. Ray; Arlinda Hardwick is clerk-treasurer
5/4/1979	News-Gazette	Politics	Ridgeville, Pam May, clerk-treasurer, resigns
11/12/1919	Journal	Politics	Ridgeville, Republicans elected; Farmland officers listed
10/8/1982	News-Gazette	Politics	Ridgeville, staggered term for south board member passed
12/7/1904	Journal	Politics	Road supervisor elections described
3/28/1917	Herald	Politics	Road Supervisor, legislature abolished the office
12/20/1905	Journal	Politics	Road supervisor, list of those elected
3/14/1917	Journal	Politics	Road Supervisor, office abolished
11/30/1916	Democrat	Politics	Road Supervisor, office created by 1915 law; supervisors will be elected on December 16
12/20/1911	Journal	Politics	Road supervisors, list of those elected
12/12/1972	News-Gazette	Politics	Robbins, Merl resigns as County Surveyor
12/15/1972	News-Gazette	Politics	Robbins, Merl, County Surveyor, accused of taking bribes
8/13/1962	News	Politics	Roberson, Gib resigns as sheriff
8/14/1962	News	Politics	Roberson, Gib resigns as sheriff
4/3/1912	Herald	Politics	Roosevelt forces carried Eighth District Republican Convention
10/10/1900	Journal	Politics	Roosevelt, Theodore is coming to Winchester on October 11, 1900
10/17/1900	Journal	Politics	Roosevelt, Theodore was here; 20,000 persons attended

Date	Source	Category	Description
10/3/1900	Herald	Politics	Roosevelt, Theodore will visit Winchester on October 11, 1900
10/17/1900	Herald	Politics	Roosevelt, Theodore, story of his visit
11/11/1908	Journal	Politics	Ross, Elmer, County Assessor, died
11/12/1908	Democrat	Politics	Ross, Elmer, County Assessor, died
11/11/1908	Herald	Politics	Ross, Elmer, County Assessor, died; father of Oran Ross
7/2/1942	Journal-Herald	Politics	Ross, F. O. of Modoc is Prohibition nominee for Treasurer of State
11/7/1929	Journal-Herald	Politics	Ross, Oran elected mayor of Winchester; Charles I. Williamson, Republican, is elected mayor of Union City
2/4/1914	Journal	Politics	Russell, Elbert, Quaker of Richmond, will run for Congress as a Progressive
12/27/1882	Journal	Politics	Russell, Surveyor, mentioned
10/18/1967	News	Politics	Saratoga Election
11/10/1915	Herald	Politics	Saratoga election results, all elected on the Citizens ticket: Marshal Glesha Barr, Councilman H. J. Hinkle, Treasurer Ralph Johnson; all are actually Democrats
6/20/1907	Democrat	Politics	Saratoga elects first officers (all on Citizens Ticket): E. D. Shadday, west; John W. Owens, south; Wm. Hill, north; Tilden H. Warren, clerk-treasurer
6/19/1907	Journal	Politics	Saratoga incorporated as a town
5/23/1907	Democrat	Politics	Saratoga incorporates as a town
4/17/1907	Journal	Politics	Saratoga plans to incorporate
4/24/1907	Herald	Politics	Saratoga to vote on incorporation
5/6/1903	Journal	Politics	Saratoga to vote on incorporation on May 19, 1903
5/21/1903	Democrat	Politics	Saratoga voted down incorporation
3/2/1982	News-Gazette	Politics	Saratoga, Bob Smiley reappointed marshal
1/8/1982	News-Gazette	Politics	Saratoga, Bob Smiley resigns after 12 years as marshal
12/29/1975	News-Gazette	Politics	Saratoga, Merritt Manning resigns after 20 years on town board
4/23/1903	Democrat	Politics	Saratoga, plans to incorporate
5/15/1907	Journal	Politics	Saratoga's incorporation election is next week
5/22/1907	Journal	Politics	Saratoga's incorporation election passed by 2 votes
5/9/1906	Journal	Politics	Sayers, Rev. and John T. Cornelius are Prohibitionists
5/12/1982	News-Gazette	Politics	Scheidt, Virgil is Chairman of 2nd District Republican Party
12/18/1863	Journal	Politics	Scott, T. L. is county auditor
11/7/1861	Journal	Politics	Scott, Thomas L. starts as county auditor

Date	Source	Category	Description
10/16/1902	Democrat	Politics	Semans, E. M. is County Democrat Chairman
2/14/1900	Journal	Politics	Semans, Ed elected County Democrat Chairman
3/26/1902	Herald	Politics	Semans, Ed is reelected County Democrat Chairman
2/15/1900	Democrat	Politics	Semans, Ed M. is elected County Democrat Chairman; John R. Lamb is elected County Prohibition Chairman
2/14/1900	Herald	Politics	Semans, Ed, seems to be County Democrat Chairman
2/15/1900	Democrat	Politics	Semans, Ed. M. is elected Chairman of the Democrat Central Committee
3/27/1902	Democrat	Politics	Semans, Ed. M. will continue as Democrat County Chairman
11/1/1876	Journal	Politics	Shaw, Gideon Sr. is the only Democratic Quaker in Randolph County [He was not actually a Quaker]
5/19/1977	News-Gazette	Politics	Shepherd, Bernard appointed County Auditor
5/10/1982	News-Gazette	Politics	Shepherd, Bernard reelected County Republican Chairman; Bud Landess reelected County Democrat Chairman
5/14/1984	News-Gazette	Politics	Shepherd, Bernard reelected County Republican Chairman; Bud Landess reelected County Democrat Chairman
1/7/1874	Journal	Politics	Sheriff Ford died; W. W. Macy appointed
3/16/1898	Journal	Politics	Sheriff, James W. Simmons appointed to replace David B. Strahan, resigned
8/12/1896	Journal	Politics	Silver Ticket, Democrats, Populists, and Prohibitionists in Randolph County will nominate a silver ticket
6/27/1940	Journal-Herald	Politics	Simmons, J. W., County Auditor died; Catherine Simmons to succeed him
11/29/1899	Journal	Politics	Slonaker, Adam, county commissioner, died
2/16/1860	Journal	Politics	Smith, George A. is chairman of Randolph County Republican Central Committee
3/1/1860	Journal	Politics	Smith, George A. is chairman of Randolph County Republican Central Committee
6/11/1860	Journal	Politics	Smith, Jeremiah is chairman of Randolph County Democratic Central Committee
10/29/1916	Journal	Politics	Socialist Party, all but two candidates from Union City
9/30/1914	Journal	Politics	Socialist Party, most Socialists are in Union City
9/30/1914	Journal	Politics	Socialist ticket listed
10/25/1916	Journal	Politics	Socialist ticket listed

Date	Source	Category	Description
11/2/1916	Democrat	Politics	Socialists had county ticket; A. W. Wagner is County Chairman; all but two candidates were from Union City
11/15/1916	Herald	Politics	Socialists had county ticket; largest vote was in Union City
3/29/1906	Democrat	Politics	Socialists hold meeting in People's Church in Winchester
7/17/1912	Journal	Politics	Socialists organize in Randolph County, William Hetzler, chairman
10/23/1918	Journal	Politics	Socialists run no ticket in Randolph County, neither do Prohibitionists
10/3/1906	Herald	Politics	Socialists, convention
9/27/1905	Herald	Politics	Socialists, convention will be held in Winchester on October 4, 1905
10/4/1906	Democrat	Politics	Socialists, county ticket
8/24/1910	Journal	Politics	Socialists, county ticket
9/26/1906	Herald	Politics	Socialists, J. M. Best is County Chairman; convention will be held at People's Church
9/26/1906	Journal	Politics	Socialists, J. M. Best, County Chairman of Central Committee, will nominate a county ticket at convention at the People's Church
9/2/1908	Herald	Politics	Socialists, M. L. Fisher is County Chairman
11/16/1904	Journal	Politics	Socialists, no county ticket
10/18/1905	Journal	Politics	Socialists, nominees for city offices
10/5/1904	Journal	Politics	Socialists, plan to organize party in Randolph County
10/19/1905	Democrat	Politics	Socialists, run a city ticket in Winchester
8/17/1910	Journal	Politics	Socialists, S. J. H. Trine is County Chairman of Socialist Central Committee
8/17/1910	Herald	Politics	Socialists, S. J. H. Trine, County Chairman
10/3/1906	Journal	Politics	Socialists, ticket listed
8/24/1910	Herald	Politics	Socialists, ticket listed
7/17/1912	Journal	Politics	Socialists, William Heltzler, county chairman; Frank Poffenbarger, secretary; Calvin Swisher, treasurer
2/16/1973	News-Gazette	Politics	Staley, Don, Democrat Chairman since 1969, died
1/26/1970	News-Gazette	Politics	Staley, Donald appointed Democrat County Chairman
12/8/1966	Journal-Herald	Politics	Stohler, Zane is appointed judge of Randolph Circuit Court
1/13/1870	Journal	Politics	Stone, Asahel is Chairman of the Republican Central Committee
4/17/1863	Journal	Politics	Stoney Creek No. 10, Union meeting held
1/22/1890	Journal	Politics	Stoney Creek Township, A. H. Oren resigns as JP
12/17/1879	Journal	Politics	Stoney Creek Township, John A. Bond resigns as constable

Date	Source	Category	Description
4/15/1874	Journal	Politics	Stoney Creek Township, T. W. Thornburg resigns as JP
10/21/1874	Journal	Politics	Stoney Creek, claims that new trustee is Democrat [he was not]
8/16/1976	News-Gazette	Politics	Stoney Creek, George Cline, trustee, died
2/14/1977	News-Gazette	Politics	Stoney Creek, Perry Thomas named trustee
10/4/1882	Journal	Politics	Study, L. W. replaces John W. Macy as County Republican Chairman
1/23/1884	Journal	Politics	Surveyor, A. M. Russell will not seek reelection
5/14/1884	Journal	Politics	Surveyor, A. M. Russell, fled county
3/27/1912	Herald	Politics	Taft forces won Randolph County primary election
10/28/1908	Herald	Politics	Taft Rally
2/21/1912	Herald	Politics	Taft, President is endorsed by Winchester Herald
7/5/1911	Herald	Politics	Taft, President stopped in Winchester
7/7/1911	Democrat	Politics	Taft, President, train through Winchester
10/21/1908	Herald	Politics	Taft, William Howard will visit Winchester next Saturday
7/12/1975	News-Gazette	Politics	Tanner, Raymond is appointed first judge of County Court
12/16/1908	Journal	Politics	Temperance forces are led by Thomas W. Hutchens, president
3/13/1978	News-Gazette	Politics	Thornburg, Howard, member of Stoney Creek Advisory Board and pastor of Union Chapel Christian Church
11/12/1913	Journal	Politics	Town election results
11/3/1915	Journal	Politics	Town election results
11/6/1935	News-Democrat	Politics	Town election results
5/7/1873	Journal	Politics	Town election results; marshals are now appointed by town boards
5/8/1901	Journal	Politics	Town elections results
6/21/1980	News-Gazette	Politics	Town Marshals
6/21/1899	Journal	Politics	Township advisory boards appointed
9/6/1899	Journal	Politics	Township Advisory Boards; Circuit Court appointed John Miller and A. R. Abshire in place of William T. Miller and Rufus King in Washington Township and Milfred Addington in place of George E. Addington in Franklin Township
1/4/1871	Journal	Politics	Township assessors listed
4/5/1899	Journal	Politics	Township assessors listed
3/10/1875	Journal	Politics	Township Assessors, list of those appointed
4/10/1878	Journal	Politics	Township assessors, list of those elected

Date	Source	Category	Description
2/13/1878	Journal	Politics	Township election law of 1877 described
11/16/1904	Journal	Politics	Township election results
2/22/1888	Journal	Politics	Township election results
4/5/1860	Journal	Politics	Township election results
11/11/1908	Journal	Politics	Township election returns
2/21/1894	Journal	Politics	Township elections moved from April to November and terms for four years
3/2/1904	Journal	Politics	Township nominees listed
4/5/1876	Journal	Politics	Township nominees listed
8/7/1889	Journal	Politics	Township officers will be elected for a limit of one four-year term beginning in 1890; office will be assumed in August
10/19/1870	Journal	Politics	Township officers, list of those elected
10/25/1876	Journal	Politics	Township officers, list of those elected
4/26/1882	Journal	Politics	Township officers, list of those elected
10/25/1905	Journal	Politics	Township tax rates listed
11/20/1872	Journal	Politics	Township trustees and assessors, newly elected listed
1/7/1915	Democrat	Politics	Township Trustees elected in 1908 served through 1914, except John C. Bunch of Greensfork, who resigned and was replaced by George O. Wise
9/18/1863	Journal	Politics	Township Trustees listed: P. Hiatt, Robert Murphy, Joseph Brown, William C. Hendricks, Anthony W. Jarnagin, David T. Hiatt, H. C. Thornburg, Olney Whipple, T. W. Kizer, R. B. Cougill, Rufus K. Mills
4/4/1877	Journal	Politics	Township trustees will be elected in April 1878 for two years; eligible for only one term
11/14/1894	Journal	Politics	Township trustees, assessors, and JPs elected listed
11/11/1914	Journal	Politics	Township trustees, Don Ward of the Union City Eagle says that one of the Democrat trustees is actually a Progressive [it was Gantz of Green Township]
4/4/1888	Journal	Politics	Township trustees, eight Republicans and four Democrats; gain of one Democrat
3/7/1894	Journal	Politics	Township trustees, list of Republican nominees for
4/14/1886	Journal	Politics	Township trustees, list of those elected
4/3/1878	Journal	Politics	Township trustees, list of those elected
4/9/1890	Journal	Politics	Township trustees, list of those elected: ten Republicans and two Democrats

Date	Source	Category	Description
10/21/1874	Journal	Politics	Township Trustees, list of those elected; W. W. Smith of Ward Township is a Republican
11/4/1914	Journal	Politics	Township trustees, majority of new trustees are Democrats
4/4/1917	Journal	Politics	Township trustees, new law allows them to succeed themselves
4/19/1882	Journal	Politics	Township trustees, Republicans elected 11 of 12
3/28/1917	Journal	Politics	Township trustees, salaries listed
3/10/1897	Journal	Politics	Township trustees, terms extended to 1900
4/10/1878	Journal	Politics	Township trustees: nine Republicans and three Democrats
1/26/1916	Journal	Politics	Treasurer, old tax receipts show that T. W. Coats was county treasurer in 1838; William Kizer was county treasurer in 1839
7/8/1891	Journal	Politics	Treasurers, old county treasurers listed on tax receipts
7/29/1891	Journal	Politics	Treasurers, old tax receipts from Daniel Petty
1/4/1905	Herald	Politics	Trustees, old and new township trustees listed
11/6/1950	News	Politics	Trustees, photo of
1/9/1953	News	Politics	Trustees, photo of
12/17/1954	News	Politics	Trustees, photo of
4/23/1946	Journal-Herald	Politics	Unger to resign as Democrat chair; Robert C. Oliver will succeed him
10/23/1936	Journal-Herald	Politics	Unger, Frank is Democrat County Chairman
5/11/1936	News-Democrat	Politics	Unger, Frank is reelected County Democrat Chairman; Arthur B. Purdy is reelected County Republican Chairman
5/9/1938	Journal-Herald	Politics	Unger, Frank is reelected to third term as County Democrat Chairman
10/7/1909	Democrat	Politics	Union City Democrat ticket listed
5/11/1898	Journal	Politics	Union City election results
2/22/1888	Herald	Politics	Union City election results: Frank H. Bowen, mayor; Noah B. Lewis, treasurer; J. L. Heck, clerk; W. M. Reeves, marshal
11/4/1909	Democrat	Politics	Union City election results: William Harris, Democrat, mayor; Ross Sutton, Democrat, clerk; Elmer Kerr, Democrat, treasurer; Adolphus Adams, H. D. Rosenbush, Milo Oliver, Charles Reitenour, William Keagy, all Democrats, councilmen
7/18/1929	Journal-Herald	Politics	Union City Mayor Lee M. Welbourne died
3/2/1904	Herald	Politics	Union City Republican nominees listed
4/5/1911	Journal	Politics	Union City voted wet by 5 votes
11/7/1917	Journal	Politics	Union City went Republican

Date	Source	Category	Description
5/12/1886	Journal	Politics	Union City, C. H. Cadwallader, Republican, elected mayor
9/20/1969	Journal-Herald	Politics	Union City, Carol Macy resigns as clerk-treasurer; was elected in 1963 and 1967
1/13/1981	News-Gazette	Politics	Union City, council consists of Fenton, Abel, Leahey, Barga, Thum
1/10/1906	Herald	Politics	Union City, Democrats control City Council
2/9/1982	News-Gazette	Politics	Union City, Doug Fenton (Republican) resigns from city council
3/3/1886	Journal	Politics	Union City, election results; C. H. Cadwallader elected mayor
11/10/1909	Herald	Politics	Union City, election returns (all Democrats): William Harris, mayor; Ross C. Sutton, clerk; Elmer Kerr, treasurer; Adolphus Adams, H. G. Rosenbush, Milo Oliver, Charles Reitchous, William Keagy, councilmen
12/3/1941	Journal-Herald	Politics	Union City, Frank Bowen started as mayor in 1888
5/15/1878	Journal	Politics	Union City, James B. Ross elected mayor
3/9/1982	News-Gazette	Politics	Union City, Joanne Cotter (Republican) appointed to city council
7/18/1929	Democrat	Politics	Union City, Mayor Lee Welbourne died
7/25/1933	Journal-Herald	Politics	Union City, Oliver Gist is new mayor
10/6/1980	News-Gazette	Politics	Union City, Terry Mendenhall (Democrat) resigns from town board
2/15/1882	Journal	Politics	Union City, Theodore Shockney is mayor
12/23/1896	Journal	Politics	Union City, Thomas Jones, mayor, died
10/2/1969	Journal-Herald	Politics	Union City, Wanda Wook started as clerk-treasurer
8/9/1860	Journal	Politics	Union Convention (Bell and Everett) on August 11 at Courthouse
12/22/1972	News-Gazette	Politics	Union Township, Ed Enghaus appointed trustee
12/11/1972	News-Gazette	Politics	Union Township, Robert Foutz resigns as trustee
4/8/1964	News	Politics	Union, Jim Bragg replaces Raymond Fouts on advisory board
8/19/1969	Journal-Herald	Politics	Veit, Herman died, had resigned from County Council earlier in the year
11/12/1884	Journal	Politics	Vote of Randolph County
7/11/1906	Journal	Politics	Voting machines purchased for cities in Randolph County
2/16/1933	Democrat	Politics	Wall, Charles A. is Democrat County Chairman
12/11/1930	Democrat	Politics	Wall, Charles A. is reelected County Democrat Chairman

Date	Source	Category	Description
12/11/1930	Journal-Herald	Politics	Wall, Charles is chairman of Democrat Central Committee
5/19/1932	Democrat	Politics	Wall, Charles is elected 10th District Democrat Chairman
5/13/1926	Democrat	Politics	Wall, Charles is reelected County Democrat Chairman
5/12/1932	Democrat	Politics	Wall, Charles is reelected County Democrat Chairman
5/12/1932	Journal-Herald	Politics	Wall, Charles reelected Democrat chairman
1/14/1970	News-Gazette	Politics	Wall, James resigns as Democrat County Chairman; had served since 1964
11/6/1918	Journal	Politics	Ward Township elects first Republican trustee since Hawthorne in the 1870s
4/19/1882	Journal	Politics	Ward Township, Benjamin Hawthorne is first straight-out Republican trustee in Ward Township [later found to be untrue]
7/20/1910	Journal	Politics	Ward Township, Benjamin Hawthorne, a trustee in the 1800s was a Republican
4/9/1931	Democrat	Politics	Ward Township, David Reitenour, township assessor, died
4/26/1882	Journal	Politics	Ward Township, Henry W. Fields and William W. Smith were previous Republicans who were trustees of Ward Township
10/17/1961	Journal-Herald	Politics	Ward Township, Lowell Mock appointed trustee to replace Charles Mock, deceased
2/18/1914	Journal	Politics	Ward Township, Thomas Johnson, Democrat, is trustee
12/24/1873	Journal	Politics	Ward Township, trustee is a Liberal Republican
4/6/1865	Journal	Politics	Washington Township election results
9/13/1882	Journal	Politics	Washington Township, Bascom and Johnson have resigned as JPs
7/2/1969	Journal-Herald	Politics	Washington Township, Charles Engle appointed trustee through January 31, 1970
1/14/1944	News	Politics	Washington Township, Cyrus Johnson replaces L. D. Hinshaw as trustee; Johnson is Mason and K of P
4/12/1871	Journal	Politics	Washington Township, IVDR Johnson elected Justice of the Peace
2/14/1877	Journal	Politics	Washington Township, Jesse Cook resigned as JP
3/22/1871	Journal	Politics	Washington Township, John Johnson, Justice of the Peace, died
8/24/1904	Journal	Politics	Washington Township, S. L Nichols resigns as trustee; Grant Johnson is appointed to serve until January 1
6/27/1969	Journal-Herald	Politics	Washington Township, Vance Eisenhour, township trustee, died

Date	Source	Category	Description
3/3/1909	Journal	Politics	Watson, Enos L. was elected surveyor in 1852 and 1856; elected prosecuting attorney for common pleas in 1856 and 1858
8/14/1952	Journal-Herald	Politics	Watters, Chauncey resigns from county council
11/5/1890	Journal	Politics	Wayne County, some Republicans were defeated [but not in Randolph]
11/21/1962	News	Politics	Wayne Township, Addington named trustee
1/17/1872	Journal	Politics	Wayne Township, Alex Gullett resigns as trustee; James Woodbury appointed to replace him
6/24/1874	Journal	Politics	Wayne Township, Amos W. Peacock appointed constable
11/29/1899	Journal	Politics	Wayne Township, John W. Williams replaces Orla Green as JP
8/26/1968	Journal-Herald	Politics	Wayne Township, Leland Addington, trustee, died
2/21/1924	Democrat	Politics	Wayne Township, Louis Stump, Democrat, resigns as township assessor; Victor Wildermuth, Democrat, appointed
8/29/1968	Journal-Herald	Politics	Wayne Township, Mrs. Leland Addington appointed trustee
11/12/1962	News	Politics	Wayne Township, Ralph Byrum, trustee, died
7/20/1984	News-Gazette	Politics	Welch, Don appointed to County Council
4/16/1890	Journal	Politics	West River Township election results
12/19/1861	Journal	Politics	West River Township, R. K. Mills is trustee
6/16/1886	Journal	Politics	West River Township, South Precinct moved to Carlos City
3/14/1877	Journal	Politics	West River Township, W. P. Harris appointed JP
9/17/1879	Journal	Politics	West River Township, W. S. Robertson replaces William R. Parsons as JP
6/2/1886	Journal	Politics	West River Township, William P. Harris filed bond as JP
3/12/1902	Herald	Politics	Whigs, old Whig ticket [probably for 1848] found: Ralph M. Pomeroy for representative; William Kizer for sheriff; William A. Peele for prosecuting attorney; Nathaniel Kemp for commissioner; Joseph Merryfield for coroner; Jesse Way for assessor
5/24/1899	Journal	Politics	White River Township Advisory Board appointed
4/19/1882	Journal	Politics	White River Township election results
4/4/1867	Journal	Politics	White River Township election results
4/6/1865	Journal	Politics	White River Township election results

Date	Source	Category	Description
4/7/1859	Journal	Politics	White River Township election results
4/7/1886	Journal	Politics	White River Township election results
4/9/1890	Journal	Politics	White River Township election results
4/4/1861	Journal	Politics	White River Township election results; T. W. Kizer elected trustee
3/22/1882	Journal	Politics	White River Township nominating election results
11/1/1882	Journal	Politics	White River Township Precincts described
8/4/1927	Journal-Herald	Politics	White River Township, A. J. McGuire appointed trustee; John Culy died
11/16/1910	Herald	Politics	White River Township, board, justices of the peace, and constables listed
12/27/1916	Herald	Politics	White River Township, David Cox resigns from advisory board; James Austin Barnes appointed
3/12/1890	Journal	Politics	White River Township, Democratic ticket listed
3/25/1903	Journal	Politics	White River Township, Enos Tisor replaces Nate Curtis as assessor
1/4/1917	Democrat	Politics	White River Township, James A. Barnes replaces David Cox on advisory board
12/27/1916	Herald	Politics	White River Township, James Austin Barnes replaces Dave Cox on advisory board
5/10/1871	Journal	Politics	White River Township, Nathan Reed to replace Jacob Elzroth as JP
5/17/1871	Journal	Politics	White River Township, Nathan Reed to replace Jacob Elzroth as JP
12/17/1948	News	Politics	White River Township, Robert W. Jones replaces Warren Wall, deceased, as township assessor
4/26/1974	News-Gazette	Politics	White River Township, Rosemary Holdeman appointed justice of the peace to replace James Macy; will serve until 1975
12/13/1860	Journal	Politics	White River Township, Stephen Coffin, township trustee, died
10/25/1899	Herald	Politics	White River Township, Thomas W. Kizer was elected trustee in the spring of 1860
4/18/1888	Journal	Politics	White River Township, William D. Chapman will succeed W. W. Canada as JP
1/31/1912	Journal	Politics	White River Township, William S. Freeman appointed township assessor to replace Marcus Reynard, resigned
7/10/1984	News-Gazette	Politics	Wigger, Marv resigns from County Council
4/19/1946	News	Politics	Wilhelm, George W. is County Prohibition Party Chairman
9/6/1905	Journal	Politics	William Wasson replaces Charles Hook on county council

Date	Source	Category	Description
7/7/1933	Journal-Herald	Politics	Williamson, Charles L. resigns as Union City mayor; George Heuber appointed
8/27/1940	Journal-Herald	Politics	Willkie Rally photo, D. M. Simmons, C. H. Leavell, Orla Keener
1/3/1935	Democrat	Politics	Wilson Day, 10th anniversary; first one in United States?
9/19/1912	Democrat	Politics	Wilson, Woodrow was at Union City
4/8/1896	Journal	Politics	Winchester city Republican primary election results
5/8/1878	Journal	Politics	Winchester corporation election results
4/29/1874	Journal	Politics	Winchester corporation Republican ticket listed
5/10/1860	Journal	Politics	Winchester election results
5/3/1871	Journal	Politics	Winchester election results
5/3/1882	Journal	Politics	Winchester election results
5/4/1881	Journal	Politics	Winchester election results
5/4/1887	Journal	Politics	Winchester election results
5/4/1898	Journal	Politics	Winchester election results
5/5/1880	Journal	Politics	Winchester election results
5/5/1886	Journal	Politics	Winchester election results
5/6/1885	Journal	Politics	Winchester election results
5/6/1891	Journal	Politics	Winchester election results
5/7/1879	Journal	Politics	Winchester election results
5/7/1884	Journal	Politics	Winchester election results
5/8/1872	Journal	Politics	Winchester election results
5/8/1889	Journal	Politics	Winchester election results
5/9/1877	Journal	Politics	Winchester election results
5/9/1888	Journal	Politics	Winchester election results
11/6/1913	Democrat	Politics	Winchester election results (4 tickets in field: Republican, Democrat, Progressive, and Socialist): C. G. Hiatt, Republican, and E. H. Bailey, Republican, at-Large; B. N. Botkin, Republican, first; Henry Abel, Progressive, second; Russell Coats, Republican, third; S. D. Fox, Republican, clerk;
5/14/1902	Herald	Politics	Winchester election results (all Republicans): Hutchens, mayor; Fox, clerk; Coats, treasurer; Daly, marshal; W. Y. Puckett and H. E. McNees (1), J. M. Seagraves and H. B. Puckett (2), and B. S. Hunt and S. Clevenger (3), councilmen
11/4/1909	Democrat	Politics	Winchester election results: Democrats were elected to the city council for the first time ever; two Democrats were elected to the town board in 1886; they were Frank Preston and J. C. Hirsch

Date	Source	Category	Description
3/14/1894	Herald	Politics	Winchester election results: Diggs, mayor; I. N. Stout, marshal; W. P. Needham, clerk; S. D. Coats, treasurer; Puckett and William Chapman (1), Slagle and Bailey (2), and Clevenger and William Lenkensdorfer (3)
5/11/1904	Herald	Politics	Winchester election results: Focht, mayor; Nathan Curtis, marshal; Samuel Fox, clerk; S. D. Coats, treasurer; B. S. Hunt and O. H. Barnhill (1), R. B. Puckett and Z. T. Romizer (2), and Wm. Y. Puckett and J. E. Hinshaw (3), councilmen; all are Republicans
5/7/1890	Herald	Politics	Winchester election results: Frank M. Preston (Democrat), 2nd; Thomas W. Kizer (Republican), 3rd; William P. Needham, clerk; Ira D. Hawthorne, marshal; W. H. Hippenheimer, treasurer
3/23/1898	Herald	Politics	Winchester election results: Hutchens, mayor; S. D. Fox, clerk; U. S. Daly, marshal; Perry Leavell, 1; Lewis A. Payne, 2; Stephen Clevenger, 3
5/4/1887	Herald	Politics	Winchester election results: John W. Jackson, trustee; James M. Fletcher, marshal; William P. Needham, clerk; P. E. Goodrich, treasurer
4/13/1892	Herald	Politics	Winchester election results: Norton (2), Tripp (3), Coffin, marshal; Needham, clerk; Thomas, treasurer
4/15/1891	Herald	Politics	Winchester election results: William Y. Puckett, 1st; Francis M. Dodd, marshal; William P. Needham, clerk; Elmore A. Thomas, treasurer
5/7/1890	Journal	Politics	Winchester election results; Democrat elected in one ward
5/4/1892	Journal	Politics	Winchester election results; Republicans elected entire ticket
12/4/1907	Herald	Politics	Winchester is first dry city in the state
1/27/1904	Herald	Politics	Winchester Nominating Election
3/23/1898	Journal	Politics	Winchester nominating election results
4/19/1893	Herald	Politics	Winchester nominating election results: Diggs, mayor; W. P. Needham, clerk; S. D. Coats, treasurer; John Coffin, marshal; U. B. Hunt (1), Marshal F. Bailey (2), Omar R. Tripp, William Y. Puckett (1), Levi Slagle (2), Stephen Clevenger (3)
4/8/1896	Herald	Politics	Winchester nominating election results: William Y. Puckett (1), S. T. Remmel (2), Hiram D. Moorman (3)

1/1/1914	Democrat	Politics	Winchester outgoing city council: Link Reinheimer, Republican; J. M. Browne, Republican; W. U. Davis, Democrat; Wm. Y. Puckett, Republican; Ot Burke, Democrat had replaced Albert Norton
3/7/1917	Herald	Politics	Winchester Primary election results: Mayor Leggett; Clerk N. R. Chenoweth; Council at-Large R. J. Litschert; 1 B. N. Botkin; 2 Charles Protsman; 3 Russell J. Coats
9/13/1905	Herald	Politics	Winchester Primary: Parry, mayor; Chenoweth, treasurer; Fox, clerk; W. Y. Puckett (1), Robert Puckett (2), Clevenger and B. S. Hunt (tie in 3), Taylor Romizer and William Horn (at-large)
10/20/1909	Journal	Politics	Winchester Prohibition Ticket listed: John E. Thompson for mayor, Oliver Coats for treasurer, Joel Williams for clerk, Jonathan Johnson for first district, Bernard P. Harris for second district, Ezra Troxell for third district
5/14/1890	Journal	Politics	Winchester Town Board, history of
4/16/1913	Herald	Politics	Winchester, Albert Norton, city councilman, died
4/23/1913	Journal	Politics	Winchester, Albert Norton, city councilman, recently died
5/12/1886	Journal	Politics	Winchester, all offices are Republican for the first time in several years
10/11/1905	Herald	Politics	Winchester, B. S. Hunt won primary for city council
5/11/1892	Journal	Politics	Winchester, Billy Needham elected to fourteenth consecutive term as clerk of Winchester
3/18/1926	Democrat	Politics	Winchester, Carl McCamish replaces Charles Harrison, resigned, on city council
12/4/1962	Journal-Herald	Politics	Winchester, Charles McRose appointed to City Council to replace Mike Make
4/17/1918	Herald	Politics	Winchester, Charles Protsman, city councilman in district 2, resigned
5/12/1984	News-Gazette	Politics	Winchester, Charles Wolf (Republican), member of city council, died
3/29/1893	Journal	Politics	Winchester, city election will soon be called
5/16/1861	Journal	Politics	Winchester, corporation election results
5/3/1876	Journal	Politics	Winchester, corporation election results
5/5/1875	Journal	Politics	Winchester, corporation election results
7/3/1901	Herald	Politics	Winchester, Daly, U. G. resigns as marshal after three years

Date	Source	Category	Description
3/16/1955	News	Politics	Winchester, Davis, Irene (Democrat), Winchester Clerk-Treasurer is member of Winchester Friends Church
11/3/1909	Herald	Politics	Winchester, election results; first Democrats elected since incorporation as a city; Union City's mayor-elect is a Democrat
5/8/1889	Herald	Politics	Winchester, election returns
11/3/1909	Journal	Politics	Winchester, first Democrats elected to city council
1/9/1918	Herald	Politics	Winchester, George E. Leggett replaces Harvey McNees as mayor
10/9/1918	Journal	Politics	Winchester, George E. Leggett, mayor, killed in auto accident Monday afternoon
11/7/1917	Journal	Politics	Winchester, George Leggett elected mayor
3/7/1917	Journal	Politics	Winchester, George W. Leggett is Republican nominee for mayor
5/26/1984	News-Gazette	Politics	Winchester, Helen Segraves (Republican) appointed to city council
6/17/1937	Journal-Herald	Politics	Winchester, Henry Abel, Republican on City Council, died
10/8/1982	News-Gazette	Politics	Winchester, James Blansett, city councilman, died
1/22/1902	Journal	Politics	Winchester, James Segraves elected to city council
11/4/1982	News-Gazette	Politics	Winchester, Junior Byrum is appointed to city council
9/16/1908	Herald	Politics	Winchester, Lincoln Reinheimer replaces William Horn on city council
5/9/1894	Journal	Politics	Winchester, lots cast for terms of city councilmen
10/23/1918	Herald	Politics	Winchester, Merl Chenoweth appointed mayor to replace George Leggett, deceased
1/12/1915	Democrat	Politics	Winchester, Nate Chenoweth appointed city clerk; replaced S. D. Fox, deceased, who had served since 1898
11/1/1905	Journal	Politics	Winchester, only nominees for mayor are Republican and Socialist
12/28/1921	Journal-Herald	Politics	Winchester, Oran Ross replaces Merl Chenoweth as mayor
7/23/1938	Journal-Herald	Politics	Winchester, Oscar G. Puckett, Republican, appointed Clerk-Treasurer of Winchester; Orla L. Davis, Democrat, resigned
9/5/1906	Herald	Politics	Winchester, Parry succeeds Focht as mayor
3/8/1893	Journal	Politics	Winchester, petition to incorporate as a city
10/20/1909	Herald	Politics	Winchester, Prohibitionist city ticket listed
4/19/1893	Journal	Politics	Winchester, Republican nominating election

Date	Publication	Category	Description
3/21/1900	Herald	Politics	Winchester, Republican nominees: W. Y. Puckett, 1; C. E. Magee, 2; J. H. Kinkead, 3
5/6/1858	Journal	Politics	Winchester, Republicans elected to town council
1/6/1915	Journal	Politics	Winchester, Samuel D. Fox, city clerk, died; N. R. Chenoweth replaces him
9/8/1954	News	Politics	Winchester, Shepherd, Bernard appointed to city council
9/4/1954	Journal-Herald	Politics	Winchester, Smith, Quentin resigned from city council
10/18/1905	Herald	Politics	Winchester, Socialists nominate a ticket
5/6/1874	Journal	Politics	Winchester, Temperance candidates beat anti-temperance candidates
8/4/1937	Journal-Herald	Politics	Winchester, Theodore Orebaugh appointed to City Council
5/5/1859	Journal	Politics	Winchester, town election results
5/2/1894	Journal	Politics	Winchester, W. S. Diggs reelected mayor
9/2/1908	Herald	Politics	Winchester, William Horn resigns from city council
9/2/1908	Journal	Politics	Winchester, William Horn resigns from the city council
9/10/1931	Journal-Herald	Politics	Wise and Watters replace Hiatt and Jaqua on County Council
5/10/1954	News	Politics	Wise, Russell E. begins as chairman of County Democrat Committee
6/11/1919	Herald	Politics	Women's Franchise League is to be organized in Winchester on June 13, 1919
6/18/1919	Herald	Politics	Women's Franchise League organized
10/19/1870	Journal	Politics	Women's suffrage, Amanda M. Way, Mary F. Thomas, and Mrs. M. T. Clark will lecture on women's suffrage and temperance
2/1/1912	Democrat	Politics	Wood, H. F. is new County Republican Chairman
1/31/1912	Herald	Politics	Wood, Henry F. is new County Republican Chairman
12/9/1981	News-Gazette	Politics	Wright, Shirley, Indiana Supreme Court rules she won Clerk's race in 1980
7/7/1936	News-Democrat	Politics	Young Democrats, Randolph County, organized on July 6, 1936
3/24/1936	News-Democrat	Politics	Young Republicans have been active in last three campaigns
8/24/1936	News-Democrat	Politics	Young Republicans, plans to organize in Randolph County
10/21/1965	Journal-Herald	Politics	Young Republicans, Randolph County organization re-established
12/27/1905	Journal	Post Offices	Bloomingport Post Office discontinued; only Arba, Deerfield, and Spartanburg are post offices not on a railroad in Randolph County

Date	Source	Category	Description
12/27/1905	Journal	Post Offices	Bloomingport Post Office was discontinued on December 23
12/6/1905	Journal	Post Offices	Bloomingport Post Office will be discontinued
8/10/1887	Journal	Post Offices	Bloomingport, I. N. Beeson resigned as postmaster over two years ago, but there is no Democrat to replace him
11/23/1881	Journal	Post Offices	Bloomingport, Isaac N. Beeson appointed postmaster
11/12/1879	Journal	Post Offices	Bloomingport, John Batchelor is postmaster
7/14/1897	Herald	Post Offices	Bragg P. O. reestablished; Randolph County has 36 post offices
12/24/1895	Journal	Post Offices	Bragg Post Office discontinued; mail to Brinkley
7/7/1897	Journal	Post Offices	Bragg Post Office reestablished
4/1/1896	Journal	Post Offices	Bragg, there will be a post office at Bragg
4/11/1888	Journal	Post Offices	Bragg's, petition for post office at, four miles north and one mile east of Farmland
5/23/1888	Journal	Post Offices	Bragg's, post office established at Bragg's Store with A. Bragg as postmaster
8/17/1881	Journal	Post Offices	Brinkley Post Office established at Shedville with James McProud as postmaster
8/14/1918	Journal	Post Offices	Carlos and Crete rural carriers abandoned
9/25/1901	Journal	Post Offices	Carlos City, J. W. Cox appointed postmaster
11/13/1901	Herald	Post Offices	Carlos City, J. W. Cox became postmaster three weeks ago
1/1/1902	Journal	Post Offices	Carlos City, John W. Cox is postmaster
9/10/1902	Journal	Post Offices	Carlos City, John W. Cox resigned as postmaster
1/3/1883	Journal	Post Offices	Carlos City, new post office established at Rosebud called Carlos City with John C. Batchelor as postmaster
4/20/1976	News-Gazette	Post Offices	Carlos may lose post office
3/31/1886	Journal	Post Offices	Castle Post Office moved 3/4 mile north of old Castle to residence of George Mangas
6/2/1886	Journal	Post Offices	Castle Post Office reestablished
4/9/1902	Journal	Post Offices	Cerro Gordo Post Office abandoned
9/24/1902	Journal	Post Offices	Cerro Gordo, at closing of post office, one cent was owed to postmaster
3/27/1907	Herald	Post Offices	Clark, Rural, and Snow Hill Post Offices will be discontinued after March 31, 1907
10/11/1871	Journal	Post Offices	Clark's Station, application for a post office, five miles north of Winchester

Date	Source	Category	Description
1/3/1883	Journal	Post Offices	Crete Post Office established with Isaac Jordan as postmaster
7/17/1901	Journal	Post Offices	Crete, John I. Thomas becomes postmaster
6/2/1875	Journal	Post Offices	Emmetsville, Post Office established; Samuel Bretch, postmaster
2/27/1901	Journal	Post Offices	Emmettsville Post Office discontinued; mail will go to Redkey
9/18/1918	Herald	Post Offices	Farabee, Hattie is first woman mail carrier in Randolph County
11/27/1889	Journal	Post Offices	Farmland Post Office moved to west of IOOF Block
5/21/1936	News-Democrat	Post Offices	Farmland, Jesse Hoppes appointed postmaster
7/24/1919	Democrat	Post Offices	Farmland, Oren Hurst, Democrat, is postmaster
1/22/1868	Journal	Post Offices	Farmland, post office is moved to Terrell's Saddlery
12/21/1898	Journal	Post Offices	Goodview Post Office discontinued
3/24/1886	Journal	Post Offices	Goodview Post Office moved from Pinch; now 4.5 miles from Unionport and 2.75 miles from Fallen Timber
4/1/1920	Democrat	Post Offices	Harrisville Post Office closed
4/14/1920	Journal-Herald	Post Offices	Harrisville Post Office to close
5/5/1909	Journal	Post Offices	Harrisville, Luther Coats has been appointed post master
3/24/1909	Journal	Post Offices	Harrisville, Luther Coats took over as postmaster on March 15
3/25/1920	Democrat	Post Offices	Harrisville, Otis Coats resigns as postmaster; post office to close
6/15/1892	Herald	Post Offices	Horn Post Office established at Olive Branch with Charles T. Bolinger as post master
5/25/1892	Journal	Post Offices	Horn Post Office established at Olive Branch with John T. Bolinger and postmaster
7/1/1885	Journal	Post Offices	Huntsville, attempt to remove Mrs. Paschal [sic] as postmaster
5/21/1902	Journal	Post Offices	Huntsville, John Hardwick resigned as postmaster
7/8/1885	Journal	Post Offices	Huntsville, Mrs. Paschal [sic], postmaster
11/18/1885	Journal	Post Offices	Huntsville, Mrs. Paschall has not been replaced
4/5/1876	Journal	Post Offices	Johnson Post Office established in 1874; J. O. Lane is present postmaster
2/11/1874	Journal	Post Offices	Johnson's Station, post office established; J. M. Thomas, postmaster
11/26/1890	Journal	Post Offices	Lavaca Post Office at Maxville closed; mail sent to Farmland
8/6/1890	Journal	Post Offices	Lavaca Post Office established at Maxville with T. W. White as postmaster

11/27/1895	Journal	Post Offices	Lewellen's Corner, petition for a post office at Nigger Holler to be called Lewellen's Corner [not granted]
10/16/1897	Journal	Post Offices	Lickskillet has post office
10/6/1897	Journal	Post Offices	Lickskillet, effort to secure a post office
5/1/1961	News	Post Offices	Losantville, gets new post office building
9/24/1962	News	Post Offices	Lynn Post Office building dedication
5/21/1936	News-Democrat	Post Offices	Lynn, Clarence Washler appointed postmaster
6/30/1961	News	Post Offices	Lynn, new post office building
7/3/1878	Journal	Post Offices	Melancthon, new post office
8/14/1878	Journal	Post Offices	Melancton Post Office established in Nettle Creek Township; government made mistake in the name; it was supposed to be "Melancthon"; Charles H. Burroughs, postmaster
2/11/1880	Journal	Post Offices	Melancton Post Office moved to Pinch with Goodlope Wright as postmaster
11/26/1879	Journal	Post Offices	Melancton, effort to move post office to Pinch
8/29/1984	News-Gazette	Post Offices	Modoc, Marjorie Card, postmaster since 1972, retiring
11/14/1883	Journal	Post Offices	Modoc, petition to abolish Swain's Hill Post Office and establish a new one at West River Summit. The IB & W folks have built a depot there and christened it "Modoc"
1/2/1884	Journal	Post Offices	Modoc, the post office at Swain's Hill has been changed to West River Summit and the name changed to Modoc
10/13/1897	Journal	Post Offices	Mull Post Office established at Lickskillet
2/4/1891	Journal	Post Offices	Neff Post Office discontinued; mail sent to Losantville
3/13/1878	Journal	Post Offices	Neff Post Office discontinued; mail sent to Windsor
3/27/1878	Journal	Post Offices	Neff Post Office will be reestablished when the building is complete
3/20/1907	Journal	Post Offices	New Pittsburg Post Office discontinued; will be served by Ridgeville Rural Route
3/5/1902	Journal	Post Offices	Parker Post Office changed to Parker City due to confusion with Parker, Ohio
11/20/1907	Herald	Post Offices	Parker Post Office moved to IOOF Building
3/1/1962	Journal-Herald	Post Offices	Parker, history of
10/19/1898	Journal	Post Offices	Parker, rural free delivery first mentioned

Date	Publication	Category	Description
12/25/1912	Herald	Post Offices	Post Card craze is dying out
4/15/1903	Journal	Post Offices	Randolph County Rural Mail Service Map, county will be fully covered this year
12/30/1915	Democrat	Post Offices	Randolph County's rural routes to be motorized; fifth county in state to do so
7/12/1899	Journal	Post Offices	Randolph, Fremont Wright replaced John Smith
1/15/1919	Herald	Post Offices	Ridgeville, G. D. Williamson, postmaster, died
5/24/1962	Journal-Herald	Post Offices	Ridgeville, history of
5/21/1936	News-Democrat	Post Offices	Ridgeville, J. E. McFarland appointed postmaster
3/31/1909	Herald	Post Offices	Ridgeville, Russell Addington named postmaster
4/1/1909	Democrat	Post Offices	Ridgeville, Russell W. Addington is new postmaster
3/20/1889	Herald	Post Offices	Ridgeville, Sylvester Addington is new postmaster
4/10/1889	Journal	Post Offices	Ridgeville, Sylvester Addington is new postmaster
3/21/1907	Democrat	Post Offices	Rural and New Pittsburg post offices have been discontinued
3/20/1907	Journal	Post Offices	Rural Post Office and Clarke Post Office will be discontinued; will be served by Winchester Rural Routes
4/18/1900	Journal	Post Offices	Rural routes described
10/7/1903	Journal	Post Offices	Rural routes described
8/15/1918	Democrat	Post Offices	Rural routes described
4/19/1900	Democrat	Post Offices	Rural routes listed
7/15/1874	Journal	Post Offices	Rural, Rural Post Office established at Wood's Station; John C. Barnes, postmaster
7/21/1980	News-Gazette	Post Offices	Saratoga, new building
12/11/1895	Journal	Post Offices	Sherman Post Office discontinued
12/24/1895	Journal	Post Offices	Sherman Post Office discontinued; mail to Horn
7/6/1881	Journal	Post Offices	Sherman Post Office is established at New Dayton
8/3/1881	Journal	Post Offices	Sherman, L. W. Sherman, postmaster
4/3/1907	Journal	Post Offices	Snow Hill Post Office closed on March 30
4/3/1907	Journal	Post Offices	Snow Hill Post Office closed on March 30, 1907; mail to Winchester
4/7/1859	Journal	Post Offices	Snow Hill Post Office established
6/13/1883	Journal	Post Offices	Snow Hill, Jacob E. Hinshaw is postmaster
1/16/1907	Journal	Post Offices	Spartanburg Post Office closed yesterday
1/2/1907	Journal	Post Offices	Spartanburg, post office will be discontinued on January 15 and put on Crete Rural Route

Date	Source	Category	Description
5/14/1879	Journal	Post Offices	Swain's Hill Post Office established; Ira Swain, postmaster
11/14/1883	Journal	Post Offices	Swain's Hill, petition to abolish post office and establish a new one at West River Summit. The IB & W folks have built a depot there are christened it "Modoc"
1/2/1884	Journal	Post Offices	Swain's Hill, the post office has been changed to West River Summit and the name changed to Modoc
7/30/1902	Journal	Post Offices	Trenton Post Office to be discontinued tomorrow
2/13/1901	Herald	Post Offices	Trenton, Mary Ann Paschall, postmistress
12/11/1901	Journal	Post Offices	Trenton, Mary Ann Paschall, postmistress, is featured in Indianapolis Journal of December 6
2/17/1915	Journal	Post Offices	Union City, Don Ward named postmaster
10/27/1975	News-Gazette	Post Offices	Union City, history of
2/24/1936	News-Democrat	Post Offices	Union City, new post office building to be dedicated on Saturday
6/25/1936	News-Democrat	Post Offices	Union City, Orvah Hindsley is new postmaster
3/14/1906	Herald	Post Offices	Unionport and Bartonia Post Offices discontinued
6/19/1878	Journal	Post Offices	Unionport Post Office established; A. A. Mendenhall, postmaster
8/14/1878	Journal	Post Offices	Unionport, Post Office at Unionsport is "Unionport"
5/16/1917	Herald	Post Offices	Winchester Post Office is moved from Kizer Building to Kelley Block
4/12/1917	Democrat	Post Offices	Winchester Post Office is moved to Kelley Block
10/1/1884	Journal	Post Offices	Winchester Post Office removed to Journal Building
1/31/1917	Herald	Post Offices	Winchester Post Office to be moved
4/11/1917	Herald	Post Offices	Winchester Post Office to move to Kelley Block
6/10/1858	Journal	Post Offices	Winchester Post Office will be moved
1/22/1919	Herald	Post Offices	Winchester, B. E. Hinshaw is new postmaster
8/6/1902	Herald	Post Offices	Winchester, C. L. Hutchens succeeds E. W. Scott as postmaster
5/5/1915	Journal	Post Offices	Winchester, E. S. Edgar replaces S. S. Watson as postmaster
3/17/1915	Herald	Post Offices	Winchester, E. S. Edger is appointed postmaster
12/11/1918	Herald	Post Offices	Winchester, E. S. Edger resigns as postmaster
8/11/1932	Democrat	Post Offices	Winchester, excavation for post office
12/1/1962	Journal-Herald	Post Offices	Winchester, Mike Make replaces Herb Harrison, who retired, as postmaster
6/11/1931	Democrat	Post Offices	Winchester, plans for a new post office

Date	Source	Category	Description
2/17/1859	Journal	Post Offices	Winchester, post office moved to southeast corner of Square
11/13/1901	Journal	Post Offices	Windsor, Opal Post Office discontinued
12/19/1900	Journal	Post Offices	Windsor, Opal Post Office established
6/20/1963	Journal-Herald	Post Offices	Zip codes announced
8/1/1877	Journal	Schools	White River Township, Trustee Coats receives bids for brick and frame on schoolhouse question
11/17/1886	Journal	Schools	176 teachers in Randolph County
5/7/1919	Journal	Schools	Attendance officer, Charles Puckett reelected
5/5/1915	Journal	Schools	Attendance Officer, G. Walter Hiatt elected to replace James Fletcher
5/7/1913	Journal	Schools	Attendance officer, James M. Fletcher elected Attendance Officer; replaces office of Truant Officer; term is one year
5/25/1898	Journal	Schools	Baccalaureate services at Winchester Friends Church; Baker and Driver spoke
2/22/1972	News-Gazette	Schools	Basketball sectional sites, history of
3/4/1914	Journal	Schools	Basketball, first girls basketball game ever played at Winchester High School
6/18/1963	Journal-Herald	Schools	Beck, Paul resigns as county superintendent
10/26/1922	Democrat	Schools	Beech Grove School burned on October 19, 1922; students are being sent to Lynn
2/21/1912	Herald	Schools	Beech Grove, a five-room school will be built on the site of No. 2 in Washington Township
3/27/1912	Journal	Schools	Beech Grove, bids received on new schoolhouse at No. 2; patrons want the school to be one mile south
3/6/1912	Journal	Schools	Beech Grove, bids will be received on March 23, 1912 for schoolhouse at site of No. 2
6/12/1912	Journal	Schools	Beech Grove, built during Civil War to replace one that burned; will be moved to new schoolhouse lot to serve as a barn
3/27/1912	Herald	Schools	Beech Grove, contract is let for new school; Fred Huffman, construction, $11,580; Hoosier Warming and Ventilation, heating, $1948
4/3/1912	Herald	Schools	Beech Grove, hearing on April 17 on location of new school
4/24/1912	Journal	Schools	Beech Grove, Lee L. Driver granted petition to move the school location to Retter Corner; will be a four-room school
12/18/1912	Journal	Schools	Beech Grove, new consolidated school has been christened "Beech Grove"

4/25/1912	Democrat	Schools	Beech Grove, new location for school, one mile south, will consolidate Nos. 1, 2, 3, 5, 6 in Washington Twp.
4/24/1912	Herald	Schools	Beech Grove, new location is selected one mile south; will consolidate Numbers 1, 2, 3, 5, and 7
2/14/1912	Journal	Schools	Beech Grove, petition for new five room school on site of No. 2 in Washington Township
1/15/1913	Herald	Schools	Beech Grove, photo of school appeared in Muncie Star, cost $15,000
12/19/1912	Democrat	Schools	Beech Grove, school opened Monday of last week
12/4/1912	Journal	Schools	Beech Grove, school will begin next Monday at Washington Township North School
4/3/1912	Journal	Schools	Beech Grove, the trustee and a majority of the patrons petitioned for a change of location; hearing will occur before Lee L. Driver on April 17, 1912
12/11/1912	Journal	Schools	Beech Grove, Washington Township North School is now open
6/20/1917	Journal	Schools	Bloomingport, bids for school awarded
5/30/1917	Journal	Schools	Bloomingport, bids taken on June 15
8/27/1879	Journal	Schools	Bloomingport, foundation for new schoolhouse
11/6/1878	Journal	Schools	Bloomingport, Joel Williams will take charge
7/11/1917	Journal	Schools	Bloomingport, land purchased in northwest part of town for school
6/20/1917	Herald	Schools	Bloomingport, new four-room school planned; contract to Stanley Brothers of Ridgeville for $8670; plumbing contract to Hobbick for $1425; will consolidate Numbers 8, 9, 11, 12, 14, leaving only three districts schools in Randolph County
11/12/1879	Journal	Schools	Bloomingport, new schoolhouse
7/11/1917	Journal	Schools	Bloomingport, new site selected; contract awarded to Stanley Brothers and H. F. Hobbick
6/24/1915	Democrat	Schools	Bloomingport, No. 12, bids for remodeling
6/24/1915	Democrat	Schools	Bloomingport, notice of letting of contract for remodeling
3/29/1917	Democrat	Schools	Bloomingport, School No. 12 is condemned; plans for new four-room school
6/21/1917	Democrat	Schools	Bloomingport, Stanley Brothers of Ridgeville are awarded contract for new school; $8,670; it will consolidate Districts 8, 9, 11, 12, and 14; Hobbick got the plumbing bid for $1425

Date	Source	Category	Description
11/3/1880	Journal	Schools	Booher's Schoolhouse mentioned
12/27/1866	Journal	Schools	Brice, J. G. is county examiner
4/18/1981	News-Gazette	Schools	Building projects and where they stand
1/31/1981	News-Gazette	Schools	Building projects and where they stand: Deerfield, Monroe Central Elementary, remodeling at Union
4/16/1873	Journal	Schools	Burnworth's Schoolhouse mentioned
11/23/1887	Journal	Schools	Carlos City School has two teachers: Alice Nichols and Mattie Botkin
5/25/1892	Journal	Schools	Carlos City School is joint school between Washington and West River
11/13/1895	Journal	Schools	Carlos City, "school of two rooms just east of city"
7/25/1912	Democrat	Schools	Carlos City, bids for repair
3/3/1921	Democrat	Schools	Carlos City, contract let for school; Bickel Brothers, construction, $24,825; A. J. Moser, heating and ventilating, $5500; H. F. Hobbick, plumbing, $2820; S. J. Fisher, Jr., wiring, $655; total is $33,975
2/17/1886	Journal	Schools	Carlos City, new school
3/18/1920	Democrat	Schools	Carlos City, petition for new school building and high school
5/19/1921	Democrat	Schools	Carlos City, school bonds are sold
4/7/1921	Democrat	Schools	Carlos City, school building work held up
1/11/1922	Journal-Herald	Schools	Carlos City, school dedication on Friday, Rev. Martin and Supt. Greist, speakers
1/4/1922	Journal-Herald	Schools	Carlos City, school will begin Monday in new building
6/2/1920	Journal-Herald	Schools	Carlos, bids for school on June 24
6/30/1921	Democrat	Schools	Carlos, bonds sold for school
12/12/1953	Journal-Herald	Schools	Carlos, Canada's Corner School, 1886, two-room school
3/3/1921	Democrat	Schools	Carlos, contract let for new school
8/27/1955	Journal-Herald	Schools	Carlos, history of school
6/10/1920	Democrat	Schools	Carlos, notice to contractors of plans to build school
3/10/1920	Herald	Schools	Carlos, patrons want a high school
5/27/1920	Democrat	Schools	Carlos, plans completed for new schoolhouse; old building to be used for elementary grades
7/1/1920	Democrat	Schools	Carlos, school will not be built now; bids are too high
9/18/1878	Journal	Schools	Catey's Schoolhouse mentioned
10/4/1911	Herald	Schools	Certificates are issued by the state for Jefferson, Jackson, McKinley, Lincoln, Modoc, and Green Schools
6/6/1933	Journal-Herald	Schools	Chenoweth, Glen O. reelected county superintendent

Date	Source	Topic	Description
9/21/1870	Journal	Schools	Chenoweth's, Jarnigan's, Peelle's Brick schools mentioned
4/29/1874	Journal	Schools	City/town schools described
5/6/1874	Journal	Schools	City/town schools described
9/4/1901	Journal	Schools	Clarence Johnson Schoolhouse is mentioned
5/15/1901	Journal	Schools	Common school graduates listed
4/19/1905	Journal	Schools	Common school graduates listed
5/6/1903	Journal	Schools	Common school graduates listed (197 total)
2/14/1956	Journal-Herald	Schools	Conferences; Farmland still in East-Central Conference
9/16/1908	Herald	Schools	Consolidation advocated
1/29/1959	Journal-Herald	Schools	Consolidation bill passed by General Assembly
11/16/1954	Journal-Herald	Schools	Consolidation election totals from the past: November 1946, Winchester 1222-605, White River 307-445; May 1950, Winchester 1190-624, White River 314-521; November 1950, White River 410-442, Wayne 369-177
9/13/1935	Journal-Herald	Schools	Consolidation of White River Schools proposed with new building west of Winchester
6/26/1912	Herald	Schools	Consolidation raises high school entering from 21% to 90-92%
9/10/1913	Journal	Schools	Consolidation, "The schools of this county are considered models by many educational people of other counties and states"
7/14/1915	Journal	Schools	Consolidation, "The Story of Rural School Consolidation in Indiana" at San Francisco
8/30/1911	Journal	Schools	Consolidation, A. E. Winship is an instructor at the Randolph County Teachers' Institute
10/21/1914	Herald	Schools	Consolidation, A. O. Neal, State Inspector, and IU and State Normal School officials visit
3/3/1915	Herald	Schools	Consolidation, Asst. Commissioner of Education of New Jersey and man from Wisconsin visit schools in Randolph County
10/27/1915	Journal	Schools	Consolidation, Calvin N. Kendal [sic], Commissioner of Education of New Jersey, is here
2/2/1916	Democrat	Schools	Consolidation, Canadian visitors
1/28/1920	Journal	Schools	Consolidation, Chinese delegation visited Randolph County Schools
4/22/1926	Democrat	Schools	Consolidation, county annual is distributed
12/24/1925	Democrat	Schools	Consolidation, county annual to be published
2/3/1927	Democrat	Schools	Consolidation, county annual, the Hoosier Pioneer, contract is let

Date	Source	Topic	Description
4/28/1927	Democrat	Schools	Consolidation, county annual, the Hoosier Pioneer, is completed
4/21/1915	Journal	Schools	Consolidation, county graduates listed
4/24/1918	Journal	Schools	Consolidation, county graduates listed
12/26/1917	Journal	Schools	Consolidation, county schools newsletter is selected and edited by the county superintendent
1/9/1964	Journal-Herald	Schools	Consolidation, county superintendent post eliminated in Randolph County
10/30/1912	Herald	Schools	Consolidation, county superintendents praise Randolph County
8/12/1914	Journal	Schools	Consolidation, Dr. A. E. Winship at County Teachers' Institute
10/2/1912	Journal	Schools	Consolidation, Dr. Aley, former State Superintendent of Public Instruction, selects Lynn School as the ideal modern school in his history of Indiana [a photo appears in the book, but no identification or story]
10/27/1915	Herald	Schools	Consolidation, Dr. Kendell [sic], Commissioner of Education of New Jersey, compliments the schools of Randolph County
4/7/1915	Herald	Schools	Consolidation, Dr. Richard Lesee of Petersborough, Ontario visits Randolph County
5/29/1956	Journal-Herald	Schools	Consolidation, Driver, Lee tried consolidation with Winchester in 1909; says Wilson and Jefferson were unnecessary schools
7/7/1915	Journal	Schools	Consolidation, E. E. Jones of Northwestern will be at Teachers' Institute on August 23, 1915
3/14/1917	Journal	Schools	Consolidation, E. M. Hurlbert, Secretary of National Research Society is here visiting Lee L. Driver
8/11/1959	Journal-Herald	Schools	Consolidation, every district is represented on Randolph County School Committee
3/22/1911	Journal	Schools	Consolidation, Green High School is accredited; the state has recommissioned the high schools of Union City, Farmland, Ridgeville, and Monroe
4/22/1914	Journal	Schools	Consolidation, high school graduates in the county have the same course of study as those in the city
3/5/1955	Journal-Herald	Schools	Consolidation, How it's progressing; petition for consolidation in Ward Township gets 53%; some favor consolidation of Ridgeville, Ward, Jackson, and Pike Township of Jay County

Date	Source	Category	Description
3/10/1961	News	Schools	Consolidation, Indiana Supreme Court rules School Reorganization Act of 1959 is valid; Winchester was test case
11/5/1919	Herald	Schools	Consolidation, J. L. McBrien, head of Rural Schools Development Department, praises Randolph County Schools
11/8/1963	News	Schools	Consolidation, last one-room schools in Indiana to close in the spring
11/19/1919	Journal	Schools	Consolidation, law about passing school hacks quoted
4/24/1912	Journal	Schools	Consolidation, Lee L. Driver got a letter from O. M. Elliott, Superintendent of Twin Falls, Idaho, asking for information about consolidation; Elliott is a native of Harrisville
10/23/1912	Journal	Schools	Consolidation, Lee L. Driver is in Indianapolis; Lynn, Spartanburg, Parker are commissioned high schools; Losantville, Modoc, McKinley, Green, Jefferson, Saratoga are certified high schools; Huntsville, Jackson, and Lincoln are accredited high schools; a certified school has a school year of eight or more months; a commissioned high school has a school year of seven or more months; an accredited school is one not yet having a senior class
1/10/1917	Journal	Schools	Consolidation, Lee L. Driver says that virtually all Randolph County teachers were at the ISTA last fall
4/21/1915	Journal	Schools	Consolidation, Lee L. Driver will have charge of Indiana's educational exhibit at San Francisco
4/18/1917	Journal	Schools	Consolidation, list of county graduates
1/24/1912	Journal	Schools	Consolidation, manual training and domestic science will be added next year at McKinley
4/16/1913	Journal	Schools	Consolidation, Martindale Items mentions "red school hack"
5/24/1917	Democrat	Schools	Consolidation, Mexican visitors
6/20/1917	Journal	Schools	Consolidation, motorized auto hacks are being demonstrated in county
7/10/1907	Herald	Schools	Consolidation, New law, schools must have 12 pupils to remain open
7/10/1907	Journal	Schools	Consolidation, new laws deal with county superintendent, school book dealers, and small districts
2/28/1912	Journal	Schools	Consolidation, no school hacks ran near Martindale Thursday and Friday due to drifted roads

Date	Publication	Category	Description
11/23/1936	Daily News	Schools	Consolidation, one-room schools are fading away; 1,363 of 6000 remain open in Indiana
1/10/1912	Journal	Schools	Consolidation, petition for school at the intersection of Washington, West River, and White River Townships
3/6/1912	Journal	Schools	Consolidation, petition for school at the intersection of Washington, West River, and White River Townships is not possible due to debt limits in the townships
8/13/1913	Journal	Schools	Consolidation, plans for County Teachers Institute, which included A. E. Winship of the Journal of Education
11/12/1960	Journal-Herald	Schools	Consolidation, plans for school consolidation presented: four-unit plan and one-unit plan
4/23/1919	Journal	Schools	Consolidation, plans to give intelligence tests to pupils of graduating classes in a meeting led by Lee L. Driver with county superintendents and principals
5/30/1917	Journal	Schools	Consolidation, Quinteres, Mexican educational official, will probably not visit due to schools being closed for the summer
3/22/1916	Herald	Schools	Consolidation, Randolph County featured in the Indiana Daily Times
5/7/1913	Journal	Schools	Consolidation, Randolph County has lost 100 school children in the past year
2/4/1915	Democrat	Schools	Consolidation, Randolph County has the largest number of commissioned high schools of any county in the state
8/23/1916	Herald	Schools	Consolidation, Randolph County school boosted in Philadelphia North American
4/21/1915	Herald	Schools	Consolidation, Randolph County school exhibit at World's Fair at San Francisco
8/25/1915	Herald	Schools	Consolidation, Randolph County school exhibit at World's Fair at San Francisco
2/4/1915	Democrat	Schools	Consolidation, Randolph County School praised in U. S. Bureau of Education bulletin
5/11/1916	Democrat	Schools	Consolidation, Randolph County schools are "boosted" in the Christian Science Monitor of Monday, May 3, 1916; "Consolidated Schools Please Indiana People"
2/2/1916	Democrat	Schools	Consolidation, Randolph County schools are featured in the "Evening Examiner" and the "Farm and Dairy" of Peterborough, Ontario

Date	Source	Category	Description
2/3/1915	Herald	Schools	Consolidation, Randolph County Schools are praised by the U. S. Bureau of Education in a bulletin called, "Consolidated Schools"; focuses on Randolph County; Randolph County has the largest number of commissioned high schools in the state
5/10/1916	Journal	Schools	Consolidation, Randolph County will represent rural school in State Centennial Display; Indianapolis will represent urban schools
5/8/1912	Journal	Schools	Consolidation, Randolph County's school enrollment is down due to loss to city schools
3/14/1912	Democrat	Schools	Consolidation, request for centralized school at Washington Twp., No. 6
1/22/1919	Journal	Schools	Consolidation, school officials from Kentucky visited
1/25/1961	News	Schools	Consolidation, School Reorganization Committee favors four-unit plan by 5-4 vote
10/29/1913	Herald	Schools	Consolidation, schools visited by officials of Miami County
3/4/1914	Journal	Schools	Consolidation, snow closes some schools
3/5/1902	Journal	Schools	Consolidation, some trustees in county favor it
2/9/1916	Herald	Schools	Consolidation, Spartanburg featured in "Farm and Dairy" of Peterboro, Ontario
4/16/1913	Journal	Schools	Consolidation, State Board of Education issues commissions to schools
6/19/1907	Journal	Schools	Consolidation, state board plans for rural schools
10/21/1914	Journal	Schools	Consolidation, state high school inspector here
2/28/1917	Journal	Schools	Consolidation, state high school inspector here
9/25/1912	Journal	Schools	Consolidation, State Superintendent Charles Greathouse praised Randolph County Schools with a picture of Parker School that appeared in another newspaper
4/1/1914	Journal	Schools	Consolidation, Superintendent of Daviess County visited last Thursday
3/5/1919	Journal	Schools	Consolidation, superintendents from Pennsylvania and North Carolina visit
5/24/1916	Journal	Schools	Consolidation, thanks from National Conference of Charities and Corrections and Indianapolis for exhibit on schools
10/16/1918	Journal	Schools	Consolidation, there will be medical inspections of all school children

Date	Source	Category	Description
4/11/1906	Journal	Schools	Consolidation, township graduates listed
3/22/1916	Journal	Schools	Consolidation, township trustees delivered diploma examination returns to Lee L. Driver
4/11/1947	News	Schools	Consolidation, trustees reject one county unit plan
1/15/1919	Journal	Schools	Consolidation, Union City Times said that people fought the passing of the little red schoolhouse
1/10/1917	Herald	Schools	Consolidation, visit by the Superintendent of Elementary Schools of Kentucky
5/13/1914	Journal	Schools	Consolidation, visitor from Purdue University
4/2/1919	Journal	Schools	Consolidation, visitors came from Kentucky and Adams County, Indiana
6/20/1917	Journal	Schools	Consolidation, visitors from Arkansas
10/22/1913	Journal	Schools	Consolidation, visitors from Miami County toured schools
3/3/1915	Journal	Schools	Consolidation, visitors from New Jersey and Wisconsin tour schools
1/15/1913	Journal	Schools	Consolidation, visitors from Pulaski County come to see schools
5/9/1962	News	Schools	Consolidation, voters favor two of three proposed districts [Randolph Southern rejected]
5/1/1962	Journal-Herald	Schools	Consolidation, voting on school issues nothing new for Randolph County persons
8/20/1913	Journal	Schools	Consolidation, Wayne County, Indiana officials visited Randolph County schools
8/25/1951	Journal-Herald	Schools	Consolidation, Webster Township, Wayne County and Rush County had consolidation before 1888
12/29/1921	Democrat	Schools	Consolidation; Country Gentlemen magazine says Randolph County has a fine school system
7/20/1864	Journal	Schools	Cooper, John is County School Examiner
7/7/1870	Journal	Schools	Cooper, Professor John moved to town
9/3/1913	Journal	Schools	County Agent, Lee L. Driver was at Purdue yesterday and secured the appointment of a county agent for this county
4/16/1913	Journal	Schools	County Athletic Association Track Meet will be held at Fairgrounds on April 25, 1913
1/10/1949	News	Schools	County basketball tourney first held in 1948
8/7/1907	Journal	Schools	County Board of Education, regular meeting
6/14/1871	Journal	Schools	County Examiner, A. J. Stakebake appointed for three year term

4/19/1871	Journal	Schools	County Examiner, J. G. Brice, report of
3/20/1872	Journal	Schools	County Examiner's report
5/7/1919	Journal	Schools	County high school graduates listed
4/24/1863	Journal	Schools	County School Examiner's report
8/1/1877	Journal	Schools	County Superintendent should be provided with an office in the Courthouse
12/31/1919	Journal	Schools	County superintendent will be elected on January 2, 1920
8/8/1877	Journal	Schools	County Superintendent will have an office in the Courthouse
8/3/1887	Journal	Schools	County Superintendent, Bowers letter about again
6/29/1887	Journal	Schools	County Superintendent, Bowers says in letter he was underpaid as
2/6/1907	Journal	Schools	County superintendent, candidates for the office listed
5/29/1907	Journal	Schools	County superintendent, candidates for the office listed
6/9/1897	Journal	Schools	County Superintendent, Charles Paris elected on the 12th ballot
6/4/1873	Journal	Schools	County Superintendent, Charles W. Paris elected; Theodore Shockney was also a candidate
6/7/1899	Journal	Schools	County Superintendent, Charles W. Paris reelected without opposition
6/23/1875	Journal	Schools	County Superintendent, Dan Lesley is new county superintendent
6/6/1877	Journal	Schools	County Superintendent, Dan Lesley is reelected
6/4/1879	Journal	Schools	County Superintendent, Daniel Lesley elected to third term as
6/8/1881	Journal	Schools	County Superintendent, Daniel Lesley reelected last Monday
6/6/1907	Democrat	Schools	County Superintendent, Driver is elected county superintendent; Paris received no votes
6/11/1873	Journal	Schools	County Superintendent, Examiner Stakebake turned over books to Charles Paris
6/3/1885	Journal	Schools	County Superintendent, H. W. Bowers unanimously reelected
6/6/1883	Journal	Schools	County Superintendent, Henry W. Bowers is elected over Dan Lesley, who served eight years
6/3/1891	Journal	Schools	County Superintendent, J. W. Denney reelected on first ballot
5/27/1891	Journal	Schools	County Superintendent, J. W. Denney, Elias Boltz, and W. W. Canada are candidates
6/8/1887	Journal	Schools	County Superintendent, J. W. Denny [sic] elected superintendent on twentieth ballot
6/5/1889	Journal	Schools	County Superintendent, J. W. Denny [sic] reelected unanimously

9/4/1895	Journal	Schools	County Superintendent, J. W. Denny [sic] will hold office as county superintendent until 1897 due to Supreme Court overturning law changing the election
6/7/1893	Journal	Schools	County Superintendent, John W. Denney reelected for the fourth time; it was unanimous
7/29/1874	Journal	Schools	County Superintendent, law was passed by a Democrat Superintendent of Public Instruction; a Republican legislature, and a Democrat Governor
12/31/1919	Herald	Schools	County Superintendent, new one to be elected
2/11/1926	Democrat	Schools	County Superintendent, new one to be elected today
5/23/1907	Democrat	Schools	County Superintendent, new one to be elected; Driver, Paris, Mote, and Smith are candidates
8/22/1929	Journal-Herald	Schools	County superintendent, new Superintendent, Glen O. Chenoweth, takes office
1/8/1920	Democrat	Schools	County Superintendent, O. H. Greist is named to post; Montgomery County native; Central Normal School, Wabash College, Chicago University; Taught at Shoals, Carlisle; three years superintendent of Union City Schools; member of Church of Christ and Turpen Lodge
9/30/1885	Journal	Schools	County Superintendent, report of
5/1/1907	Journal	Schools	County superintendent, Troy Smith of Saratoga is candidate
6/2/1897	Journal	Schools	County Superintendent, trustees will elect
5/21/1873	Journal	Schools	County Superintendent, trustees will elect; candidates are S. T. McProud, Charles Paris, Daniel Lesley, B. F. Wilmore
12/11/1872	Journal	Schools	County Superintendent, Winchester Journal opposes bill establishing office
8/15/1877	Journal	Schools	County Superintendent's office is on first floor of Courthouse
5/7/1914	Democrat	Schools	County Track Meet, Losantville won
4/28/1927	Journal-Herald	Schools	County track meet, Lynn won
2/5/1925	Journal-Herald	Schools	County Unit Bill opposed by 2000 Randolph County voters
4/9/1981	News-Gazette	Schools	Deerfield, bids opened
4/16/1981	News-Gazette	Schools	Deerfield, contracts awarded
11/8/1982	News-Gazette	Schools	Deerfield, dedication
11/4/1982	News-Gazette	Schools	Deerfield, dedication is Sunday; Dr. Thomas Mullen, speaker; cost $2,532,299.17; 40,059 square feet

Date	Source	Category	Description
7/15/1981	News-Gazette	Schools	Deerfield, Gary Kizer will be principal when school opens in 1982-83
5/12/1981	News-Gazette	Schools	Deerfield, groundbreaking
5/6/1981	News-Gazette	Schools	Deerfield, groundbreaking is planned for May 11
3/11/1981	News-Gazette	Schools	Deerfield, plans to build are approved despite strong opposition
4/14/1982	News-Gazette	Schools	Deerfield, school may be ready by June
9/4/1981	News-Gazette	Schools	Deerfield, steel going up
6/4/1975	News-Gazette	Schools	Delaware Community [Delaware County] sale of furniture from old schools
3/25/1971	News-Gazette	Schools	Driver Junior High School "Blue Hawks"
4/22/1974	News-Gazette	Schools	Driver Junior High School, construction underway
7/8/1975	News-Gazette	Schools	Driver Junior High School, Robert Farlow is new principal
3/2/1910	Journal	Schools	Driver, L. L. and Oscar Baker attend County Superintendents Association in Indianapolis
6/5/1907	Journal	Schools	Driver, L. L. elected county superintendent
8/16/1948	News	Schools	Driver, Lee calls for high school consolidation
1/28/1920	Journal	Schools	Driver, Lee L. retired Saturday, nine one-room schools remain
8/23/1916	Herald	Schools	Driver, Lee L., annual report
9/26/1947	News	Schools	East Central Conference; Farmland and Union City are charter members
4/24/1947	Journal-Herald	Schools	East-Central Athletic Conference established on April 23; Farmland is member
12/30/1947	Journal-Herald	Schools	East-Central Athletic Conference, Farmland and Union City are members
11/16/1953	News	Schools	East-Central Conference has thirteen teams
11/28/1953	Journal-Herald	Schools	East-Central Conference membership: Liberty, Morton Memorial, Centerville, Farmland, Spiceland, Union City, Middletown, Morristown, Cambridge City, Knightstown, Hagerstown, Milroy, and Brookville
12/11/1951	Journal-Herald	Schools	East-Central Conference, Farmland and Lynn are members
2/5/1955	Journal-Herald	Schools	East-Central Conference, Farmland and Union City are members
2/7/1957	Journal-Herald	Schools	East-Central Conference, list of members
10/6/1951	Journal-Herald	Schools	East-Central Conference, Lynn applied for membership
10/27/1956	Journal-Herald	Schools	East-Central Conference, Union City is still member; Farmland is not
8/15/1984	News-Gazette	Schools	Employees of all county schools listed

Date	Source	Category	Description
11/9/1936	Daily News	Schools	Farmland and Parker, bands organized
12/14/1983	News-Gazette	Schools	Farmland and Parker, school buildings to be razed
12/22/1875	Journal	Schools	Farmland corporation has no school; want committee to take schoolhouse over
10/13/1937	Journal-Herald	Schools	Farmland county baseball champions
10/28/1955	News	Schools	Farmland dropped out of East-Central Conference
9/9/1874	Journal	Schools	Farmland Graded School, C. S. Atkinson, superintendent, Daugherty, trustee
1/13/1870	Journal	Schools	Farmland Graded School, Lee Ault, principal
2/23/1860	Journal	Schools	Farmland has two school districts
11/8/1905	Journal	Schools	Farmland High School receives commission
10/14/1935	News-Democrat	Schools	Farmland is county baseball champion
11/16/1950	Journal-Herald	Schools	Farmland is in East Central Conference
2/13/1937	Daily News	Schools	Farmland joined IHSAA in 1919
10/29/1954	News	Schools	Farmland participates in MEC basketball
6/14/1882	Journal	Schools	Farmland School Board listed
4/17/1889	Journal	Schools	Farmland School Board: Dennis Thornburg replaces Rev. I. V. D. R. Johnson
12/12/1877	Journal	Schools	Farmland School Board: J. S. Davis, L. A. Gable, W. W. Fowler
2/19/1919	Journal	Schools	Farmland School Corporation put under township control
10/6/1909	Journal	Schools	Farmland School opened; largest school in Randolph County
11/18/1909	Democrat	Schools	Farmland School to be dedicated on Wednesday
11/17/1909	Journal	Schools	Farmland Schoolhouse to be dedicated on Wednesday of next week
5/3/1952	Journal-Herald	Schools	Farmland senior composite photo
3/19/1884	Journal	Schools	Farmland teachers for 1884-85: J. R. Hancock, superintendent; Frank Smith, Mrs. Hancock, Vina Moorman, teachers
4/1/1885	Journal	Schools	Farmland teachers for 1885-86: C. W. Paris, Principal; H. D. Good, intermediate; Rosa Huffman, primary
9/4/1924	Journal-Herald	Schools	Farmland teachers listed, Howard Hill, principal
9/1/1915	Journal	Schools	Farmland teachers listed; John W. Reynolds, superintendent; Bert Herman, principal
3/13/1907	Journal	Schools	Farmland will erect a new school

Date	Source	Category	Description
6/15/1904	Journal	Schools	Farmland, A. J. Pursley, H. D. Good, N. Oswald are school board; J. O. Batchelor, superintendent
3/10/1909	Journal	Schools	Farmland, agitation over new schoolhouse
11/18/1903	Herald	Schools	Farmland, Austin G. Morris replaces J. O. Batchelor as principal of high school
11/11/1903	Journal	Schools	Farmland, Austin Morris replaces Batchelor as superintendent
9/4/1878	Journal	Schools	Farmland, Benton Webb, Superintendent, J. W. Ralston and L. Moorman, teachers
12/9/1908	Journal	Schools	Farmland, bid for new school is awarded to Adamson of Hartford City for $27,471
11/25/1908	Journal	Schools	Farmland, bids for new school will be received on December 7, 1908
4/29/1908	Herald	Schools	Farmland, board of education purchased lots for $2475 for new school
4/8/1885	Journal	Schools	Farmland, C. Paris elected principal
3/18/1874	Journal	Schools	Farmland, C. S. Atkinson is superintendent
7/14/1875	Journal	Schools	Farmland, C. S. Atkinson resigned as superintendent after two years; goes to Jonesboro
4/15/1885	Journal	Schools	Farmland, C. W. Paris elected superintendent
6/21/1876	Journal	Schools	Farmland, C. W. Paris, principal, J. W. Ralston, instructor, Melvina Moorman, primary
12/1/1909	Journal	Schools	Farmland, Dr. Hurty did not attend the school dedication
7/15/1914	Journal	Schools	Farmland, E. E. Zimmerman, Superintendent; Harriette McArthur, Principal
6/25/1913	Journal	Schools	Farmland, E. E. Zimmerman, Superintendent; J. R. Godlove, Principal
7/2/1913	Democrat	Schools	Farmland, E. E. Zimmerman, superintendent; J. R. Godlove, principal
7/23/1914	Democrat	Schools	Farmland, E. Zimmerman, superintendent; McArthur, principal
5/16/1906	Journal	Schools	Farmland, first commencement of commissioned high school
8/20/1969	Journal-Herald	Schools	Farmland, Gayle Replogle is principal
5/11/1898	Herald	Schools	Farmland, George C. Powers, superintendent and principal
8/10/1951	News	Schools	Farmland, Gerald F. Irwin is principal
4/12/1950	News	Schools	Farmland, Gerald French resigned as principal, served since 1943
7/7/1886	Journal	Schools	Farmland, H. D. Good appointed superintendent
2/22/1882	Journal	Schools	Farmland, Hancock is superintendent

Date	Source	Category	Description
7/5/1911	Journal	Schools	Farmland, Harry McKinsie replaces Caswell as superintendent of schools; Paul Kunscik is principal
11/26/1879	Journal	Schools	Farmland, Ira Branson, superintendent, May Meredith and Flo Deal, teachers
4/23/1879	Journal	Schools	Farmland, Ira M. Branson will be superintendent next year
7/13/1892	Journal	Schools	Farmland, J. D. White is superintendent; last year it was O. B. Zell
5/10/1905	Journal	Schools	Farmland, J. O. Batchelor continues
11/8/1905	Journal	Schools	Farmland, J. O. Batchelor is superintendent; high school is commissioned
6/15/1904	Journal	Schools	Farmland, J. O. Batchelor replaces A. G. Morris as superintendent
11/5/1903	Democrat	Schools	Farmland, J. O. Batchelor resigned from schools effective in November
4/11/1906	Journal	Schools	Farmland, J. O. Batchelor resigns after five years as superintendent
6/9/1950	News	Schools	Farmland, J. R. Clark was principal (1917-20) and Howard Hill was principal (1920-28)
8/11/1880	Journal	Schools	Farmland, J. V. Stuart, principal
2/23/1860	Journal	Schools	Farmland, J. W. Keener fired over a black female student
9/24/1902	Journal	Schools	Farmland, James Batchelor, superintendent
1/29/1902	Journal	Schools	Farmland, James O. Batchelor replaces Prof. Bobbitt as superintendent
8/12/1971	News-Gazette	Schools	Farmland, Jerry Moore starts as principal
4/20/1881	Journal	Schools	Farmland, John Hancock, superintendent, 1881-82
5/10/1882	Journal	Schools	Farmland, John Hancock, superintendent; Mary Meredith, Vina Moorman, Nellie Slonaker, teachers
9/6/1916	Journal	Schools	Farmland, John Reynolds, superintendent
6/8/1916	Democrat	Schools	Farmland, joint school contract made; eastern part of Monroe Township will go to Farmland School; school will be jointly governed by Russell Fodrea, president of town school board, and Ira Smithson, township trustee
10/17/1959	Journal-Herald	Schools	Farmland, MEC cross country champions
10/7/1961	Journal-Herald	Schools	Farmland, MEC cross country champions; third straight
3/3/1909	Herald	Schools	Farmland, meeting held in opposition to a new school building
6/18/1919	Journal	Schools	Farmland, Monroe Township took over property of Farmland High School

Date	Source	Category	Description
9/24/1890	Journal	Schools	Farmland, new school building will be ready by October
9/9/1908	Herald	Schools	Farmland, new school planned
4/30/1908	Democrat	Schools	Farmland, new school planned for highest point in town
12/11/1863	Journal	Schools	Farmland, new schoolhouse is being built in the east part of town; will not be ready until April; west district building is being repaired
11/24/1909	Herald	Schools	Farmland, new schoolhouse to be dedicated by Lee Ault, U. O. Cox, J. W. Macy, and J. N. Hurty on November 24, 1909
11/24/1909	Journal	Schools	Farmland, new schoolhouse to be dedicated this afternoon
11/1/1866	Journal	Schools	Farmland, Norveil is the teacher in the East District; James L. Davis is teacher in West District
7/1/1891	Journal	Schools	Farmland, O. B. Zell, superintendent/principal
5/27/1926	Journal-Herald	Schools	Farmland, old brick schoolhouse being torn down
5/2/1906	Journal	Schools	Farmland, Omar Caswell starts as superintendent
9/21/1910	Herald	Schools	Farmland, Omar Caswell, superintendent; Frank Forry, high school principal
12/8/1972	News-Gazette	Schools	Farmland, photo of 1907-08 basketball team
2/3/1909	Journal	Schools	Farmland, project is rebid
6/11/1890	Journal	Schools	Farmland, public school is being repaired with an addition to the south
6/19/1919	Democrat	Schools	Farmland, school corporation dissolved; township takes over building and debt of $16,000
4/20/1984	News-Gazette	Schools	Farmland, school razed
2/26/1890	Herald	Schools	Farmland, school to be remodeled and enlarged
12/1/1909	Herald	Schools	Farmland, school was dedicated
6/7/1916	Journal	Schools	Farmland, school will be jointly governed by town and Monroe Township
11/17/1909	Herald	Schools	Farmland, school will be opened on October 5, 1909
5/5/1953	Journal-Herald	Schools	Farmland, senior class photo
9/4/1954	Journal-Herald	Schools	Farmland, summer baseball league champions
3/26/1890	Journal	Schools	Farmland, third story of school to be removed
8/13/1965	News	Schools	Farmland, Thomas Gourley is new principal
6/18/1919	Herald	Schools	Farmland, town school is placed under township control
2/16/1860	Journal	Schools	Farmland, troubles over black student

Date	Source	Topic	Description
2/23/1860	Journal	Schools	Farmland, troubles over black student
9/11/1913	Democrat	Schools	Farmland, Uphaus is principal
11/24/1875	Journal	Schools	Farmland, W. Lloyd, superintendent
12/29/1875	Journal	Schools	Farmland, W. R. Lloyd, superintendent
10/10/1875	Journal	Schools	Farmland, William R. Floyd, superintendent
5/21/1890	Herald	Schools	Farmland, work on the new school will begin at once
2/10/1909	Herald	Schools	Farmland's new school building; has 23 rooms
6/30/1915	Herald	Schools	Fire escapes new at Lincoln and McKinley
9/9/1914	Herald	Schools	Fire escapes put on Winchester High School, Lynn High School; planned for County Infirmary
5/23/1978	News-Gazette	Schools	First County Track Meet: Winchester, boys; Union City, girls
11/23/1870	Journal	Schools	First public colored school taught in Cabin Creek settlement
3/8/1876	Journal	Schools	First schoolhouse built in 1822 on Paul Way farm, southwest of Winchester
7/17/1907	Journal	Schools	Franklin Township and Greensfork Township; both are nearly free from debt
6/12/1912	Journal	Schools	Franklin Township enjoined from building a consolidated school.
9/18/1918	Herald	Schools	Franklin Township has schools at No. 2, 3, 5, and 6
1/29/1958	News	Schools	Franklin Township rejects merger with Ward-Jackson, 311-382
9/13/1899	Journal	Schools	Franklin Township teachers listed
1/27/1958	News	Schools	Franklin Township to vote on consolidation with Ward-Jackson on Tuesday
8/29/1912	Democrat	Schools	Franklin Township troubles; Stoney Creek No. 7 is to be repaired
9/20/1911	Herald	Schools	Franklin Township, $18,000 consolidated school planned at Shack Smithson corner
5/8/1912	Journal	Schools	Franklin Township, Architect Huffman of Decatur is making plans for consolidated school on Smithson Farm
2/5/1879	Journal	Schools	Franklin Township, Bear Creek Schoolhouse, Charlie Hiatt, teacher
10/4/1860	Journal	Schools	Franklin Township, Bear Creek Schoolhouse, near A. P. Steele's [Franklin Twp. No. 5]
8/28/1912	Journal	Schools	Franklin Township, bids for large schoolhouse in Franklin Township; suit has been filed; will go to trial on September 2, 1912

Date	Source	Category	Description
6/7/1916	Journal	Schools	Franklin Township, bids on next Saturday for construction of new schoolhouse in southwest part of township [No. 3]; also sale of Riverside [No. 1]
8/6/1942	Journal-Herald	Schools	Franklin Township, Days Creek School reunion
9/24/1913	Journal	Schools	Franklin Township, dismissal of Hollowell v. Zimmerman, trustee case
4/10/1924	Democrat	Schools	Franklin Township, Huffman Schoolhouse was sold Saturday to John Dull for $267; he plans to make a house of it
8/11/1915	Herald	Schools	Franklin Township, Huffman, new schoolhouse is being built
8/25/1915	Herald	Schools	Franklin Township, Huffman, new schoolhouse is being constructed slowly due to weather
5/20/1915	Democrat	Schools	Franklin Township, Huffman, notice of letting for addition to schoolhouse
8/25/1886	Herald	Schools	Franklin Township, Huffman, schoolhouse nearly enclosed
11/3/1915	Herald	Schools	Franklin Township, Huffman, the schoolhouse is almost completed
9/15/1875	Journal	Schools	Franklin Township, Huffman, Wesley Williams, teacher
5/26/1915	Journal	Schools	Franklin Township, Huffman's Corner, bids for improving and enlarging school will be received on June 12, 1915
11/18/1920	Democrat	Schools	Franklin Township, Huffman's Corner, Clark Payne is new teacher
4/16/1873	Journal	Schools	Franklin Township, Huffman's Schoolhouse mentioned
8/28/1912	Journal	Schools	Franklin Township, injunction against consolidation in Ridgeville
6/13/1912	Democrat	Schools	Franklin Township, injunction issued by Judge Engle on June 10, bars building of consolidated school
9/20/1911	Journal	Schools	Franklin Township, Lee L. Driver was there because they will probably build a new high school in the coming year
11/21/1888	Herald	Schools	Franklin Township, list of teachers
8/22/1912	Democrat	Schools	Franklin Township, more school troubles, request to re-established Nos. 2, 3, 4, 5
3/27/1895	Herald	Schools	Franklin Township, Mosier, Arlie Williams, teacher
12/15/1875	Journal	Schools	Franklin Township, Mosier's School, M. Bosworth, teacher
8/28/1912	Herald	Schools	Franklin Township, new school to be built in center of township
8/15/1894	Journal	Schools	Franklin Township, No. 1, petition to restrain trustee from changing location
2/23/1898	Journal	Schools	Franklin Township, No. 1, Riverside School, Poorman, teacher

Date	Source	Category	Description
4/5/1899	Journal	Schools	Franklin Township, No. 1, Trustee Bolander [sic] will erect a new schoolhouse on the Joel Ward farm near Ridgeville this summer
10/2/1950	News	Schools	Franklin Township, No. 1-Baker, No. 2-Nicholson, No.3-Smithson
7/8/1914	Journal	Schools	Franklin Township, No. 2, Nicholson, bids will be received on July 23, 1914 for the construction of a schoolhouse
7/2/1914	Democrat	Schools	Franklin Township, No. 2, Nicholson, notice of letting for new frame building
4/23/1879	Journal	Schools	Franklin Township, No. 3 and No. 6, new schools will be built this summer
5/24/1916	Journal	Schools	Franklin Township, No. 3, bids for construction of schoolhouse on June 10, 1916
2/13/1889	Journal	Schools	Franklin Township, No. 6, Sater Smithson, teacher
6/20/1912	Democrat	Schools	Franklin Township, Nos. 1, 3, 4, and 6 all condemned by State Board of Health
1/19/1887	Journal	Schools	Franklin Township, Olive Branch School, John Pierce teacher
11/16/1887	Journal	Schools	Franklin Township, Olive Branch School, John Pierce teacher
10/1/1873	Journal	Schools	Franklin Township, Olive Branch School, R. T. Maltbie, teacher
9/15/1875	Journal	Schools	Franklin Township, Olive Branch, Alfred Addington, teacher
4/5/1893	Journal	Schools	Franklin Township, Olive Branch, Arlie Williams's school closed on March 24
4/25/1877	Journal	Schools	Franklin Township, Olive Branch, Charley Hiatt taught three months at
7/15/1914	Journal	Schools	Franklin Township, Olive Branch, frame of schoolhouse damaged in a windstorm
7/1/1914	Journal	Schools	Franklin Township, Olive Branch, Glen Meyers will repair the school at a cost of $2100; additions and alterations
9/28/1881	Journal	Schools	Franklin Township, Olive Branch, Henry Cortner is in third year as teacher
1/8/1879	Journal	Schools	Franklin Township, Olive Branch, Henry Cortner, teacher
11/24/1880	Journal	Schools	Franklin Township, Olive Branch, Henry Cortner, teacher
10/27/1880	Journal	Schools	Franklin Township, Olive Branch, Henry J. Cortner, teacher
11/27/1878	Journal	Schools	Franklin Township, Olive Branch, honor roll includes Effie Addington, Schuyler C. Williams, Frank Addington
3/21/1888	Journal	Schools	Franklin Township, Olive Branch, J. S. Pierce, teacher

Date	Source	Category	Description
11/16/1887	Herald	Schools	Franklin Township, Olive Branch, John Pierce, teacher
2/26/1896	Herald	Schools	Franklin Township, Olive Branch, Mr. Gantz, teacher
4/17/1878	Journal	Schools	Franklin Township, Olive Branch, Mr. Hiatt, teacher
9/13/1899	Herald	Schools	Franklin Township, Olive Branch, new school built by J. C. Bundy and Charles Bolinger
4/11/1924	Democrat	Schools	Franklin Township, Olive Branch, Robert Stephens purchased the schoolhouse on Saturday
11/26/1879	Journal	Schools	Franklin Township, Olive Branch, W. E. Murray, teacher
2/19/1890	Journal	Schools	Franklin Township, Olive Branch, W. H. Hall, teacher
3/31/1880	Journal	Schools	Franklin Township, Olive Branch, William E. Murray, teacher
7/3/1912	Herald	Schools	Franklin Township, patrons will vote on consolidation of township; four district schools condemned
9/23/1911	Democrat	Schools	Franklin Township, plans for $23,000 consolidated school at Shack Smithson Corner to avoid paying tuition to send students to Ridgeville H. S.
9/20/1911	Journal	Schools	Franklin Township, plans for consolidated school at Shack and Smithson Corner, near center of township
2/23/1898	Journal	Schools	Franklin Township, Riverside, teacher problems
8/28/1912	Herald	Schools	Franklin Township, school bid is held up
6/26/1912	Journal	Schools	Franklin Township, school election for joint school in Ridgeville
8/29/1860	Journal	Schools	Franklin Township, schoolhouse near Stanley's Mill on Bear Creek mentioned
8/13/1913	Journal	Schools	Franklin Township, State ex rel James M. Hollowell v. Albert Zimmerman, trustee of Franklin Township
9/13/1905	Journal	Schools	Franklin Township, Teachers listed
1/14/1958	Journal-Herald	Schools	Franklin Township, vote on consolidation with Ward-Jackson on January 28
7/24/1912	Herald	Schools	Franklin Township, voters favor joint school; Franklin 115-71; Ridgeville 208-29; would have separate corporations with a joint school
9/29/1875	Journal	Schools	Franklin Township, Walnut Corner, Mattie May, teacher
4/17/1878	Journal	Schools	Franklin Township, Walnut Corner, Mr. Whipple, teacher
10/12/1904	Herald	Schools	Franklin Township, Walnut Corner, new schoolhouse; old building was brick; new building badly needed

Date	Source	Category	Description
6/23/1886	Herald	Schools	Franklin Township,, Huffman, Alex Huffman purchased Huffman School House to move to farm to use as a barn
2/15/1957	News	Schools	Franklin, Ward, Jackson consolidation proposed
3/22/1957	News	Schools	Franklin, Ward, Jackson consolidation vote is April 9
7/25/1912	Democrat	Schools	Franklin-Ridgeville, election for new school carries: Ridgeville 208 yes-29 no; Franklin Township, 115 yes-71 no
6/27/1912	Democrat	Schools	Franklin-Ridgeville, special election called on building of joint school
4/2/1879	Journal	Schools	Frannklin Township, Bear Creek, E. H. Addington, teacher
9/17/1977	News-Gazette	Schools	Freedom Christian Academy
9/2/1978	News-Gazette	Schools	Freedom Christian Academy
1/24/1981	News-Gazette	Schools	Freedom Christian Academy
9/2/1978	News-Gazette	Schools	Freedom Christian Academy established on August 29; Bible Baptist Academy will soon start
3/2/1937	Daily News	Schools	Green joined IHSAA in 1918; did not play in tournament in 1923, 1928-30; 1934, or 1935
12/16/1963	News	Schools	Green School razed; Losantville, Modoc, Huntsville, and McKinley already razed
5/17/1963	News	Schools	Green School will be sold
1/9/1889	Journal	Schools	Green Township teachers listed
11/10/1954	News	Schools	Green Township will vote on consolidation with Delaware County during week of December 20
1/13/1892	Journal	Schools	Green Township, No. 4 burned on Thursday; it was built three years ago
5/11/1881	Journal	Schools	Green Township, Cottonwood Schoolhouse is two miles south of Possum Valley near Cabinville [probably Gantz Schoolhouse]
8/23/1911	Herald	Schools	Green Township, debt limit prevents rebuilding of two condemned schoolhouses
9/3/1913	Journal	Schools	Green Township, Emanuel Zimmerman took an informal referendum on length of school term
8/14/1878	Journal	Schools	Green Township, Fairview, schoolhouse badly needed
1/18/1864	Journal	Schools	Green Township, McCracken School mentioned
3/15/1949	Journal-Herald	Schools	Green Township, McCracken Schoolhouse was later replaced by McCamish Schoolhouse
12/27/1882	Journal	Schools	Green Township, new school built near Shedville with Ed Gunkle as teacher

Date	Source	Category	Description
10/26/1910	Herald	Schools	Green Township, new school opened on October 25, 1910
9/27/1893	Journal	Schools	Green Township, No. 1 is being rebuilt
3/29/1893	Journal	Schools	Green Township, No. 1, Schoolhouse damaged by storm
8/13/1913	Herald	Schools	Green Township, No. 2, suit over school
10/17/1888	Journal	Schools	Green Township, No. 4, D. B. Nibarger has just completed a new schoolhouse
5/11/1892	Journal	Schools	Green Township, No. 4, new schoolhouse
5/16/1888	Herald	Schools	Green Township, No. 4, plans for new frame schoolhouse
1/27/1892	Journal	Schools	Green Township, No. 4, resumed school in old brick house that was vacated when new building opened
7/8/1874	Journal	Schools	Green Township, No. 4, schoolhouse to be moved one-half mile west ; makes third schoolhouse in this district in the lifetime of the first settlers
1/26/1887	Journal	Schools	Green Township, No. 5, a brick building, damaged by fire last Thursday night
10/13/1909	Herald	Schools	Green Township, No. 6 closed and sent to No. 5; patrons want it reopened
10/7/1909	Democrat	Schools	Green Township, No. 6, some patrons want the school reopened
10/6/1909	Journal	Schools	Green Township, No. 6, suit to reopen
10/14/1909	Democrat	Schools	Green Township, No. 6, trustee refuses to reopen the school
10/13/1909	Herald	Schools	Green Township, No. 6, trustee says will not reopen
2/25/1880	Journal	Schools	Green Township, No. 7, J. H. Williams, teacher
8/9/1905	Herald	Schools	Green Township, No. 8, students are being hauled to No. 5 this fall and winter
12/18/1889	Journal	Schools	Green Township, Shedville Schoolhouse mentioned
6/4/1913	Journal	Schools	Green Township, suit against Zimmerman, trustee, over school issues
2/4/1955	News	Schools	Green Township-Delaware County merger never voted on
5/18/1910	Journal	Schools	Green, contract to J. W. Morris for $17,595 + $2945
10/10/1938	Journal-Herald	Schools	Green, county baseball champs
10/16/1939	Journal-Herald	Schools	Green, county baseball champs
10/9/1940	Journal-Herald	Schools	Green, county baseball champs
10/10/1942	Journal-Herald	Schools	Green, county baseball champs
12/14/1910	Journal	Schools	Green, dedicated yesterday by Dr. Hurty and F. S. Caldwell

Date	Source	Category	Description
12/14/1910	Herald	Schools	Green, dedication by Dr. Hurty on December 13, 1910
4/20/1910	Journal	Schools	Green, legal notice of bids for new school
8/16/1954	News	Schools	Green, petitions plan for consolidation of Green Township with Delaware County
4/27/1910	Herald	Schools	Green, plans for new school
9/29/1954	News	Schools	Green, plans to consolidate with DeSoto in Delaware County
3/22/1911	Herald	Schools	Green, school is now accredited
11/18/1935	News-Democrat	Schools	Green, will have a basketball team again after two seasons out; Big 18 is Big 18 again; Green plays at Albany
8/1/1917	Journal	Schools	Greensfork Township purchased a Studebaker auto hack
12/27/1866	Journal	Schools	Greensfork Township schools described
9/6/1899	Journal	Schools	Greensfork Township teachers listed
9/21/1898	Journal	Schools	Greensfork Township teachers listed, including Milton Benson of Snow Hill at No. 13
9/11/1895	Journal	Schools	Greensfork Township teachers listed: 1, 2, 3, 5, 6, 8, 9, 10, 11, 12, 13
5/4/1904	Journal	Schools	Greensfork Township, Arba, Lone Star Reporter is school newspaper
5/20/1920	Democrat	Schools	Greensfork Township, Arba, school to be remodeled after being damaged by a tornado
7/11/1917	Journal	Schools	Greensfork Township, bids for auto hacks
5/15/1954	Journal-Herald	Schools	Greensfork Township, Brown Schoolhouse photos
9/11/1954	Journal-Herald	Schools	Greensfork Township, Clark Schoolhouse, near Lynn, two rooms, used by Wesleyan Methodist Church for three years, razed in the early 1930s
6/14/1916	Journal	Schools	Greensfork Township, Clark, No. 3, Gray and Son of Farmland awarded contract for $2,929.50
11/13/1901	Journal	Schools	Greensfork Township, Clark, schoolhouse damaged by fire Thursday [probably last week]
5/17/1916	Journal	Schools	Greensfork Township, Clark's Schoolhouse, Greensfork No. 3, bids for new building
2/1/1905	Journal	Schools	Greensfork Township, Hart's Glory, brick from burnt schoolhouse to be sold on February 11, 1905
6/7/1905	Journal	Schools	Greensfork Township, Hart's Glory, frame school building begun on June 5
7/27/1881	Journal	Schools	Greensfork Township, list of teachers; No. 1, colored

Date	Source	Category	Description
6/14/1916	Herald	Schools	Greensfork Township, new school [No. 3] will be built by S. Gray and Son for $2,929
12/19/1912	Democrat	Schools	Greensfork Township, No. 11, discrimination suit of closure
5/31/1916	Journal	Schools	Greensfork Township, No. 3, bids for construction of new schoolhouse on Tuesday of next week
6/8/1916	Democrat	Schools	Greensfork Township, No. 3, bids for new frame schoolhouse in southwest corner of township; $2,929.50; students cannot go to Lynn since it is in a different township
1/18/1905	Journal	Schools	Greensfork Township, No. 8, 2.5 miles southeast of Spartanburg, burned last Thursday
1/19/1905	Democrat	Schools	Greensfork Township, No. 8, two-and-a-half miles southeast of Spartanburg, burned on January 12, 1905
2/27/1913	Democrat	Schools	Greensfork Township, Number 11 School closed in spring of 1912; Number 9 is open (?)
1/24/1907	Democrat	Schools	Greensfork Township, Pinhook School burned on January 22, 1907
1/30/1907	Journal	Schools	Greensfork Township, Pinhook School No. 1 burned last Tuesday night
7/25/1900	Journal	Schools	Greensfork Township, Pinhook will get new schoolhouse
3/30/1916	Democrat	Schools	Greensfork Township, Pinhook, history of school
4/15/1915	Democrat	Schools	Greensfork Township, Pocket School, to be sold at auction on April 24, 1915
5/15/1878	Journal	Schools	Greensfork Township, Small Schoolhouse, near Lynn, Cora Frist, teacher
10/29/1913	Journal	Schools	Greensfork Township, State ex rel Harvey Thornburg v. John Bunch, trustee, dismissed
11/19/1884	Journal	Schools	Greensfork Township, Union Literary Institute receives public funds
6/16/1915	Journal	Schools	Greensfork Township, Witter, bids to remodel will be received on July 3, 1915
6/10/1915	Democrat	Schools	Greensfork Township, Witter, notice of letting of contract for addition and repair
2/8/1905	Journal	Schools	Greensfork, Hart's Glory, brick sold
1/23/1907	Herald	Schools	Greensfork, Pinhook, schoolhouse burned on January 22, 1907
9/15/1897	Herald	Schools	Greensfork, teachers listed; no school in district four or eight
6/10/1915	Democrat	Schools	Greensfork, Witter, bids for addition

Date	Source	Category	Description
11/16/1925	Journal-Herald	Schools	Greist, O. H. appointed Executive Secretary of Teachers' Pension Board effective February 1, 1926
1/7/1920	Herald	Schools	Greist, O. H. to replace L. L. Driver as county superintendent
3/1/1982	News-Gazette	Schools	Gymnastics meet, county
1/2/1863	Journal	Schools	Hiatt, Pleasant is county school examiner
7/11/1862	Journal	Schools	Hiatt, Pleasant is county school examiner
1/13/1865	Journal	Schools	Hiatt, Pleasant, county school examiner
2/28/1956	Journal-Herald	Schools	Horseshoe, history of
9/30/1950	Journal-Herald	Schools	Horseshoe, new one presented; old one presented by Union City American Legion in March 1923
1/15/1947	News	Schools	Horseshoes; winner's, loser's, second team
3/2/1939	Journal-Herald	Schools	Huntsville "Red Birds"
2/29/1940	Journal-Herald	Schools	Huntsville "Red Birds"
2/15/1941	Daily News	Schools	Huntsville "Red Birds"
2/27/1941	Daily News	Schools	Huntsville "Red Birds"
2/26/1942	Journal-Herald	Schools	Huntsville "Red Birds"
2/24/1943	Journal-Herald	Schools	Huntsville "Red Birds"
2/23/1944	News	Schools	Huntsville "Red Birds"
2/19/1945	News	Schools	Huntsville "Red Birds"
3/8/1940	Journal-Herald	Schools	Huntsville "Red Men"
1/23/1947	Journal-Herald	Schools	Huntsville "Red Men"
11/3/1947	News	Schools	Huntsville "Red Men"
10/22/1948	News	Schools	Huntsville "Red Men"
11/4/1948	Journal-Herald	Schools	Huntsville "Red Men"
9/11/1895	Journal	Schools	Huntsville had no school tax [meaning corporation was disbanded]
4/29/1908	Journal	Schools	Huntsville High School and Modoc High School issued diplomas
12/10/1913	Journal	Schools	Huntsville High School has been certified
3/4/1908	Journal	Schools	Huntsville High School mentioned
11/6/1936	Daily News	Schools	Huntsville is victim of graduation; several players graduated, including Leary Hinshaw; red and black were the colors
2/26/1937	Daily News	Schools	Huntsville joined IHSAA in 1920
12/4/1912	Journal	Schools	Huntsville No. 5, College Corner No. 8, and No. 10 schools to be sold
12/11/1912	Journal	Schools	Huntsville School to be dedicated on December 20 by John I Huffman
9/19/1894	Journal	Schools	Huntsville Schools commence on Monday, September 24
10/3/1894	Journal	Schools	Huntsville Schools commenced on Tuesday, September 25

Date	Source	Category	Description
4/4/1894	Journal	Schools	Huntsville, "new school building"
10/8/1919	Journal	Schools	Huntsville, addition was formally dedicated by Lee L. Driver on Thursday [October 2, 1919]
12/19/1912	Democrat	Schools	Huntsville, addition will be dedicated on December 20
3/13/1918	Journal	Schools	Huntsville, addition will have gymnasium and kitchen
2/21/1912	Journal	Schools	Huntsville, bid for new school awarded to A. M. Waltz for $10,500; heating bid to A. H. Johnson for $2,410.
4/17/1918	Journal	Schools	Huntsville, bids for addition rejected; it will be bid again on May 2, 1918
4/17/1918	Herald	Schools	Huntsville, bonds for addition
3/6/1918	Journal	Schools	Huntsville, contract for addition to school to be let on March 29
5/8/1918	Journal	Schools	Huntsville, contract for addition to Zach Wood for $11,300; heating and plumbing to Tibbetts and Adkins for $3,050
2/21/1912	Herald	Schools	Huntsville, contract is awarded for new school; A. L. Waltz, construction, $10,500; American Warming and Ventilating, heating, for $2,320; many country schools will be abolished when it opens
5/16/1918	Democrat	Schools	Huntsville, contract let for addition to school
12/25/1912	Herald	Schools	Huntsville, dedicated
12/25/1912	Journal	Schools	Huntsville, dedication of school; Lee L. Driver presided
2/24/1897	Journal	Schools	Huntsville, Jerry Bly purchased old schoolhouse
8/15/1894	Journal	Schools	Huntsville, May Foster is plastering new schoolhouse
9/26/1894	Herald	Schools	Huntsville, new building
10/3/1894	Herald	Schools	Huntsville, new building consolidates three schools
8/1/1894	Journal	Schools	Huntsville, new school building is nearing completion
1/24/1912	Journal	Schools	Huntsville, plan to build a four-room school
12/11/1912	Journal	Schools	Huntsville, program for dedication to take place on December 20, 1912
2/26/1919	Journal	Schools	Huntsville, PTA dissolved to form Farmers' Institute; Lee L. Driver was present
4/25/1917	Journal	Schools	Huntsville, PTA reorganized; Lee L. Driver was present; Lee Gaddis is president of the organization
1/2/1895	Journal	Schools	Huntsville, report on upper grades; Alta Bromagen, principal
5/14/1931	Democrat	Schools	Huntsville, S. H. Possee, principal, died; wife was Elma Abshire, daughter of A. R. Abshire

Date	Source	Topic	Description
10/8/1919	Herald	Schools	Huntsville, school building dedication
8/9/1876	Journal	Schools	Huntsville, School tax district allowed
6/19/1912	Journal	Schools	Huntsville, storm damaged part of the new school
5/19/1897	Journal	Schools	Huntsville, Trenton High School commencement planned
2/20/1918	Journal	Schools	Huntsville, trustee, superintendent, and advisory board approved plans for addition
12/11/1912	Herald	Schools	Huntsville, will be dedicated on December 20, 1912 by John I. Hoffman and A. L. Bales
4/4/1894	Journal	Schools	Huntsville, work on new school will commence in the near future
6/6/1894	Journal	Schools	Huntsville, work on new schoolhouse begins this week
3/1/1917	Democrat	Schools	Indiana School for Negroes, 172 acre site in Randolph County was deeded in 1848
11/13/1918	Journal	Schools	Influenza, schools reopened after being closed
2/24/1937	Daily News	Schools	Jackson joined IHSAA in 1919
12/7/1910	Journal	Schools	Jackson School dedicated on December 2 by Charles Greathouse
8/13/1958	News	Schools	Jackson School houses elementary classes
11/16/1910	Journal	Schools	Jackson School will be dedicated on December 2, 1910
9/21/1910	Herald	Schools	Jackson Township has schools at Number 2, 3, 4, 6, 7, 8, 9, 10 and Jackson
9/6/1860	Journal	Schools	Jackson Township, Devor's Schoolhouse exists in Jackson Township
3/28/1917	Journal	Schools	Jackson Township, Mangas School not sold due to injunction; Jessup School not sold due to low bids
1/31/1917	Journal	Schools	Jackson Township, Mangas School will be sold on February 26, and Jessup School will be sold on February 28
2/19/1890	Herald	Schools	Jackson Township, New Lisbon, brick schoolhouse will be erected this spring
12/5/1883	Journal	Schools	Jackson Township, New Pittsburg, petition for new school
7/8/1915	Democrat	Schools	Jackson Township, No. 10, notice of letting for remodeling
9/12/1912	Democrat	Schools	Jackson Township, No. 3, Jessup; No. 7, Lisbon; No. 8, Mt. Holly; No. 9, Middleton; No. 10, Pittsburg
5/29/1872	Journal	Schools	Jackson Township, No. 5 is known as Warren's Schoolhouse
10/16/1902	Democrat	Schools	Jackson Township, Warren Schoolhouse exists
4/21/1921	Democrat	Schools	Jackson won county track meet

Date	Source	Topic	Description
6/3/1915	Democrat	Schools	Jackson, 26 X 30 addition will be built this summer
2/3/1915	Journal	Schools	Jackson, bids awarded for addition
5/4/1910	Journal	Schools	Jackson, contract let to Glass and Humphries for $13,518.53
5/4/1910	Herald	Schools	Jackson, contracts let for new school
10/19/1950	Journal-Herald	Schools	Jackson, county baseball champions
12/7/1910	Journal	Schools	Jackson, dedicated last Friday by Lee L. Driver, F. S. Caldwell, and State Superintendent Charles Greathouse
11/23/1910	Herald	Schools	Jackson, dedication will take place on December 2, 1910 with Charles Greathouse as the speaker
12/7/1910	Herald	Schools	Jackson, dedication; building cost $17,000
3/23/1910	Herald	Schools	Jackson, new school planned
1/12/1915	Democrat	Schools	Jackson, notice of letting for addition
12/7/1953	News	Schools	Jackson, Ralph W. Johnson, principal, died
12/10/1962	News	Schools	Jackson, school sold for $4,100 on December 8, 1962
5/13/1957	News	Schools	Jackson, should it consolidate with Union City?
4/24/1958	Journal-Herald	Schools	Jackson, students to be sent to Ward
12/16/1953	News	Schools	Jackson, Willie Satkamp appointed principal
10/24/1959	Journal-Herald	Schools	Jefferson and Jackson buildings will be sold on November 7
2/18/1937	Daily News	Schools	Jefferson joined IHSAA in 1919
12/3/1959	Journal-Herald	Schools	Jefferson School Building sold to Weldon Huber for $2000
2/21/1918	Democrat	Schools	Jefferson School to be enlarged; addition of four rooms and a gym planned
2/1/1911	Journal	Schools	Jefferson School was dedicated last Wednesday
1/18/1911	Journal	Schools	Jefferson School will be dedicated next Wednesday
2/13/1918	Journal	Schools	Jefferson, 291 voters of Ward Township petitioned for a much needed addition to Jefferson School
2/28/1912	Journal	Schools	Jefferson, A. H. Kenna replaces Grace Bray as principal
3/21/1917	Journal	Schools	Jefferson, addition planned, but bids for it were rejected as too high
2/13/1918	Journal	Schools	Jefferson, bids for an addition will be received on March 8, 1918
4/6/1910	Journal	Schools	Jefferson, bids for new school in Ward Township
3/30/1910	Herald	Schools	Jefferson, C. E. Losch architect of planned school in Ward Township

Date	Source	Category	Description
3/20/1918	Herald	Schools	Jefferson, contract let for addition
2/1/1911	Herald	Schools	Jefferson, dedicated on Wednesday by Assistant State Superintendent Bunnell; building cost $18,167.90
6/16/1915	Journal	Schools	Jefferson, Dora DeLong replaces J. C. Burgess as principal; Burgess is going to Modoc
12/8/1958	News	Schools	Jefferson, injunction filed to block sale of building
3/9/1910	Herald	Schools	Jefferson, plans for a new school building at Deerfield
3/23/1910	Herald	Schools	Jefferson, plans for a new school; also plans for Green School
12/15/1958	News	Schools	Jefferson, plans to sell building are dropped
4/18/1958	News	Schools	Jefferson, there will be no school in the building next year
2/4/1955	News	Schools	Jefferson-Saratoga consolidation talk
2/24/1955	Journal-Herald	Schools	Jefferson-Saratoga consolidation talk
3/3/1955	Journal-Herald	Schools	Jefferson-Saratoga consolidation talk
1/26/1983	News-Gazette	Schools	Key, girls' basketball key presented by Frank Miller Lumber Company
11/2/1870	Journal	Schools	Lasley, Daniel teaching at Winchester
5/19/1950	News	Schools	Lincoln and McKinley high schools are consolidated
9/7/1910	Journal	Schools	Lincoln given full accreditation on Saturday
7/30/1926	Daily News	Schools	Lincoln High School is discontinued
8/26/1926	Journal-Herald	Schools	Lincoln High School patrons oppose closure
8/19/1926	Journal-Herald	Schools	Lincoln High School to be closed
8/17/1926	Daily News	Schools	Lincoln High School, petitions signed to stop closure
2/16/1937	Journal-Herald	Schools	Lincoln is presented with Lincoln etching, "first rural consolidated school in the U. S."
11/27/1934	Journal-Herald	Schools	Lincoln referred to as "Eagles"
12/29/1926	Daily News	Schools	Lincoln School opens today
5/8/1957	News	Schools	Lincoln School sale set again for tomorrow
4/12/1957	News	Schools	Lincoln School sold
3/28/1929	Democrat	Schools	Lincoln School will be remodeled with gymnasium and classrooms
3/3/1937	Daily News	Schools	Lincoln was last county team to join the IHSAA, in 1923; did not play in a sectional until 1929; referred to as "Eagles"
3/3/1938	Journal-Herald	Schools	Lincoln was last in Randolph County to join IHSAA (1923)
11/4/1914	Journal	Schools	Lincoln won county track meet
10/16/1971	News-Gazette	Schools	Lincoln, "first rural consolidated school in U. S." is being razed

10/16/1912	Herald	Schools	Lincoln, addition is complete
3/28/1912	Democrat	Schools	Lincoln, addition, legal notice
4/17/1912	Journal	Schools	Lincoln, bid for addition awarded to Otis Williams for $9,771; heating to Hoosier Warming Co. for $3,025
5/27/1908	Journal	Schools	Lincoln, bids are to be taken; plans were drawn by Hampton Gettinger
3/20/1912	Journal	Schools	Lincoln, bids for addition will be received on April 12, 1912
4/10/1912	Journal	Schools	Lincoln, bids on addition on Friday
6/18/1908	Democrat	Schools	Lincoln, bids received
3/18/1957	News	Schools	Lincoln, building and land are for sale
1/3/1912	Herald	Schools	Lincoln, C. F. Wood resigns as principal; Morton Longnecker replaces him
10/21/1926	Journal-Herald	Schools	Lincoln, case to Jay County Court
4/17/1912	Herald	Schools	Lincoln, contract is let for addition; Odes Williams, construction, $9771; Hoosier Ventilation and Warming, $3830
12/2/1926	Journal-Herald	Schools	Lincoln, court ruled for trustee
11/27/1926	Daily News	Schools	Lincoln, decision is made in school case
2/10/1909	Journal	Schools	Lincoln, dedication planned
2/17/1909	Journal	Schools	Lincoln, dedication; Prof. Will Howe gave the dedication address in place of Supt. Aley
7/14/1909	Journal	Schools	Lincoln, efforts to "put in a high school near Maxville"
2/13/1937	Daily News	Schools	Lincoln, etching of Abraham Lincoln presented to Lincoln School yesterday
8/29/1969	Journal-Herald	Schools	Lincoln, first graduating class was in 1914
6/12/1912	Journal	Schools	Lincoln, first high school graduates
9/15/1909	Herald	Schools	Lincoln, first regular term of school opens in the building
5/13/1914	Journal	Schools	Lincoln, G. W. Hiatt has been ordered by the state to erect a fire escape at Lincoln
4/29/1929	Journal-Herald	Schools	Lincoln, gym and new classrooms planned
5/30/1929	Democrat	Schools	Lincoln, hearing about improvements
12/30/1926	Democrat	Schools	Lincoln, high school grades resume at Lincoln today
8/5/1926	Democrat	Schools	Lincoln, high school is discontinued at Lincoln
8/18/1909	Journal	Schools	Lincoln, high school will be added
9/20/1943	News	Schools	Lincoln, history and photographs
2/17/1909	Herald	Schools	Lincoln, is dedicated by Will Howe of Indiana University; cost $13,971.67
2/8/1911	Journal	Schools	Lincoln, L. P. Lasley, principal, died

Date	Source	Category	Description
1/25/1911	Herald	Schools	Lincoln, L. P. Lesley resigns as principal; C. H. Wood replaces him
4/11/1946	Journal-Herald	Schools	Lincoln, McKinley, and Winchester discuss consolidation
8/26/1967	Journal-Herald	Schools	Lincoln, migrants are housed in
1/3/1912	Journal	Schools	Lincoln, Morton Longnecker appointed principal to replace Charles H. Wood, resigned
1/4/1912	Democrat	Schools	Lincoln, Morton Longnecker replaces C. H. Woods as principal
9/7/1910	Herald	Schools	Lincoln, new high school now has a two-year commission
5/7/1908	Democrat	Schools	Lincoln, new school building planned
9/4/1926	Daily News	Schools	Lincoln, patrons filed lawsuit to keep high school open; among the petitioners were C. C. Fisher and C. L Heaston
8/25/1926	Daily News	Schools	Lincoln, patrons make statement about transfer of high school grades
8/26/1926	Democrat	Schools	Lincoln, patrons make statement about transfer of high school grades
2/14/1912	Journal	Schools	Lincoln, petition for a four-room addition
8/19/1926	Democrat	Schools	Lincoln, petitions signed to reopen high school
5/6/1908	Journal	Schools	Lincoln, plans for a new school to be build one mile east of Maxville
1/25/1957	News	Schools	Lincoln, school abandoned; McKinley is 1-6; White River is 7-12
2/18/1909	Democrat	Schools	Lincoln, school building is dedicated; only two district schools sent there this year
2/11/1909	Democrat	Schools	Lincoln, school building is finished
11/6/1926	Daily News	Schools	Lincoln, school case is continued
11/12/1926	Daily News	Schools	Lincoln, school case is under advisement
11/18/1926	Journal-Herald	Schools	Lincoln, school case undecided
9/16/1926	Journal-Herald	Schools	Lincoln, school cased continued
4/13/1972	News-Gazette	Schools	Lincoln, school has been razed
9/15/1909	Journal	Schools	Lincoln, school opened with 147 pupils, including 23 in high school
2/3/1909	Journal	Schools	Lincoln, school starts on Monday; Pupils from No. 6 and No. 7 will be transferred to the new building
2/3/1909	Herald	Schools	Lincoln, school to begin; officials visited Selma School to study it
9/9/1926	Journal-Herald	Schools	Lincoln, school trouble
5/2/1929	Democrat	Schools	Lincoln, some patrons oppose improvements and want a centralized school with McKinley west of Winchester; against unnecessary gymnasium
11/5/1926	Daily News	Schools	Lincoln, trial is nearing an end
11/4/1926	Daily News	Schools	Lincoln, trial is still in session

Date	Source	Category	Description
11/3/1926	Daily News	Schools	Lincoln, trial opens in Portland over Lincoln's high school grades
11/4/1926	Democrat	Schools	Lincoln, trial opens in Portland over Lincoln's high school grades
6/24/1908	Journal	Schools	Lincoln, Wilson Carson awarded bid for $10,253.54.
5/9/1912	Democrat	Schools	Lincoln, work begins on addition
3/3/1937	Daily News	Schools	Lincoln's team is referred to as "Wolves"
10/26/1935	News-Democrat	Schools	Lincoln's team referred to as "Eagles"
12/5/1936	Daily News	Schools	Lincoln's team referred to as "Eagles"
12/15/1936	Daily News	Schools	Lincoln's team referred to as "Eagles"
2/20/1937	Daily News	Schools	Lincoln's team referred to as "Eagles"
1/23/1937	Daily News	Schools	Lincoln's team referred to as "Eaglets"
1/30/1937	Daily News	Schools	Lincoln's team referred to as "Eaglets"
11/26/1936	Daily News	Schools	Lincoln's teams referred to as "Presidents" and "Eaglets"
4/11/1946	Journal-Herald	Schools	Losantville and Modoc discuss consolidation
2/15/1937	Daily News	Schools	Losantville joined IHSAA in 1920
6/22/1957	Journal-Herald	Schools	Losantville School will be sold on July 22; Modoc and Huntsville already sold
4/29/1914	Journal	Schools	Losantville won county track meet
8/9/1905	Journal	Schools	Losantville, Al Sanders is building the new school
2/25/1947	Journal-Herald	Schools	Losantville, baseball champions for two years
6/2/1920	Journal-Herald	Schools	Losantville, bids for addition on June 13
6/29/1898	Journal	Schools	Losantville, bids for new schoolhouse on July 2, 1898
3/4/1903	Journal	Schools	Losantville, contemplation of a new schoolhouse
10/7/1946	News	Schools	Losantville, county baseball champions
2/3/1859	Journal	Schools	Losantville, district school erected south of town by township funds, perhaps first in county so funded
7/4/1888	Journal	Schools	Losantville, graded school is being built
6/24/1891	Journal	Schools	Losantville, Harvey Cook purchased the lot west of town on which the old schoolhouse stood
11/21/1877	Journal	Schools	Losantville, Lemuel Wiggins is erecting a new brick schoolhouse
5/31/1945	Journal-Herald	Schools	Losantville, Modoc, Huntsville meeting to plan consolidation of schools
8/8/1888	Herald	Schools	Losantville, new schoolhouse

Date	Source	Topic	Description
8/29/1888	Herald	Schools	Losantville, new schoolhouse will soon be ready
10/19/1904	Herald	Schools	Losantville, no school; condemned six weeks ago
8/30/1905	Journal	Schools	Losantville, Nos. 8 and 9 transferred to No. 6; No. 10 is Modoc
5/13/1920	Democrat	Schools	Losantville, notice to contractors of plans for an addition
3/23/1968	Journal-Herald	Schools	Losantville, old gym, built c1918, became casket factory in 1961, burned
9/28/1887	Journal	Schools	Losantville, one of the schools at Losantville will be dispensed with this year
5/16/1888	Herald	Schools	Losantville, plans for two-room school
11/8/1905	Journal	Schools	Losantville, school opened on Monday, November 6, 1905; 200 students in 5 rooms
11/8/1905	Herald	Schools	Losantville, schoolhouse completed; cost $12,000
7/16/1968	Journal-Herald	Schools	Losantville, three-room school built in 1878; razed in 1903-05; new building was first used in fall of 1905 with only two outlying schools consolidated
7/12/1905	Journal	Schools	Losantville, work is progressing on new schoolhouse
6/13/1955	News	Schools	Lynn addition is nearing completion; 8 elementary classrooms; cost $225,000
8/27/1954	News	Schools	Lynn addition progressing
9/15/1875	Journal	Schools	Lynn Graded School under charge of Daniel Lesley
1/6/1886	Journal	Schools	Lynn has town school
10/23/1936	Journal-Herald	Schools	Lynn is county baseball champion
3/1/1937	Daily News	Schools	Lynn joined IHSAA in 1909, then dropped out and rejoined in 1921; referred to as "Bulldogs"
5/7/1884	Journal	Schools	Lynn listed separately in school enumeration
6/15/1892	Journal	Schools	Lynn School Board: Dr. Blair, Dr. Cox, and N. R. Chenoweth
5/29/1901	Journal	Schools	Lynn School Corporation dissolved; Washington Township will build a new building
10/3/1912	Democrat	Schools	Lynn School pictured in Aley and Aley's "The Story of Indiana"
5/24/1899	Journal	Schools	Lynn teachers listed
5/6/1896	Journal	Schools	Lynn teachers listed
5/10/1928	Journal-Herald	Schools	Lynn to build gymnasium
4/16/1954	News	Schools	Lynn, $200,000 addition planned
2/8/1888	Journal	Schools	Lynn, 3-story brick school erected
1/2/1889	Journal	Schools	Lynn, A. C. Hunnicutt resigned
6/8/1887	Journal	Schools	Lynn, A. C. Hunnicutt will continue as principal

Date	Source	Category	Description
6/16/1954	News	Schools	Lynn, addition begun
9/28/1885	Journal	Schools	Lynn, addition is nearly complete
5/10/1928	Democrat	Schools	Lynn, addition of gymnasium and auditorium planned for this summer
2/13/1954	Journal-Herald	Schools	Lynn, addition planned
9/23/1885	Journal	Schools	Lynn, addition to school
7/20/1954	Journal-Herald	Schools	Lynn, addition underway
7/6/1904	Journal	Schools	Lynn, Austin Morris starts as principal
4/1/1978	News-Gazette	Schools	Lynn, basketball, 1907-08
6/2/1909	Journal	Schools	Lynn, bids for a four-room addition to school
7/7/1909	Journal	Schools	Lynn, bids opened for addition
8/7/1901	Journal	Schools	Lynn, contract for school is awarded for $12,448
10/25/1952	Journal-Herald	Schools	Lynn, football team in 1903; Quaker fathers, including Amos Hodgin and Ira Johnson, were opposed
8/29/1955	News	Schools	Lynn, history of schools; c1886-2 rooms added
4/22/1908	Journal	Schools	Lynn, issued high school diplomas
1/9/1889	Herald	Schools	Lynn, J. E. Beeson replaces A. C. Hunnicutt, deceased, as superintendent
4/29/1976	News-Gazette	Schools	Lynn, James Longenbaugh, elementary principal for three years, fired
5/26/1973	News-Gazette	Schools	Lynn, John Bright resigns as principal
7/2/1969	Journal-Herald	Schools	Lynn, John Bright starts as principal
4/27/1957	Journal-Herald	Schools	Lynn, MEC track champions
5/3/1958	Journal-Herald	Schools	Lynn, MEC track champions
5/1/1961	News	Schools	Lynn, MEC track champions
5/27/1909	Democrat	Schools	Lynn, notice to bidders of plans for addition
8/27/1955	Journal-Herald	Schools	Lynn, opening of addition on August 28
5/27/1909	Democrat	Schools	Lynn, plans to remodel school building with four-room addition
8/20/1873	Journal	Schools	Lynn, Prof. Atkinson resigns to take charge of schools in Farmland
9/6/1955	Journal-Herald	Schools	Lynn, scenes at opening of Lynn School
9/10/1902	Herald	Schools	Lynn, school dedication on September 10, 1902 by J. J. Mills, Frank Posey, and Dr. Hurty, and others
9/10/1902	Journal	Schools	Lynn, Washington Township High School dedicated; Posey, Hurty, et al there
12/24/1902	Journal	Schools	Lynn, Washington Township High School is commissioned by the state

Date	Source	Category	Description
9/3/1902	Journal	Schools	Lynn, Washington Township Nos. 4 and 10 are abandoned; hacks will transport the students to Lynn
8/27/1902	Journal	Schools	Lynn, Washington Township Public School will be dedicated on September 4, 1902 with Mills, Posey, Hurty, Cottom, et al
8/23/1979	News-Gazette	Schools	Maranatha Baptist Christian Academy advertised
8/25/1979	News-Gazette	Schools	Maranatha Baptist Christian Academy, K-12, will start in fall
2/23/1955	News	Schools	Mascots, Gus Shafer drawing of
10/21/1950	Journal-Herald	Schools	McKinley "Presidents" still even after consolidation
5/28/1960	Journal-Herald	Schools	McKinley being razed
11/13/1950	News	Schools	McKinley first called "Little Giants"
7/15/1914	Journal	Schools	McKinley is getting electric lights
2/27/1937	Daily News	Schools	McKinley joined IHSAA in 1921
5/28/1960	Journal-Herald	Schools	McKinley School is razed
2/2/1921	Journal-Herald	Schools	McKinley School must have addition
7/7/1921	Democrat	Schools	McKinley School to be improved
3/10/1920	Herald	Schools	McKinley to be enlarged with four-room addition and gymnasium
4/22/1948	Journal-Herald	Schools	McKinley won county cross country championship
4/28/1948	News	Schools	McKinley won county cross country championship
3/22/1911	Journal	Schools	McKinley, advisory board orders new schoolhouse to be built in eastern White River Township
2/3/1921	Democrat	Schools	McKinley, bids for an addition
5/17/1911	Journal	Schools	McKinley, bids for new school next Saturday
5/24/1911	Herald	Schools	McKinley, bids for new six-room school; Glass and Humphries of Muncie got bid for $22,905.33; heating contract went to American Warming and Ventilating for $3300
5/3/1911	Journal	Schools	McKinley, bids for schoolhouse east of town
5/3/1957	News	Schools	McKinley, class of 1957 photo
7/21/1921	Democrat	Schools	McKinley, contracts let for addition; Anderson and Hunnicutt, contractors, $27,850; Hobbick, $7400
10/13/1941	Journal-Herald	Schools	McKinley, county baseball champions
4/5/1951	Journal-Herald	Schools	McKinley, county track champions
4/23/1955	Journal-Herald	Schools	McKinley, county track champions
2/9/1922	Democrat	Schools	McKinley, Lee L. Driver will dedicate the addition of a gymnasium and auditorium on February 24, 1922

Date	Source	Category	Description
5/26/1911	Democrat	Schools	McKinley, Muncie contractor to build six room school
1/29/1922	Democrat	Schools	McKinley, new addition is being equipped
3/10/1909	Journal	Schools	McKinley, petition made to abandon four district schools in eastern White River Township
7/2/1920	Journal-Herald	Schools	McKinley, plans for addition to
3/29/1911	Journal	Schools	McKinley, plans for new school are being drawn by Hauk of Bluffton
5/10/1916	Journal	Schools	McKinley, Ralph Butcher resigns as principal to go to Wayne
9/13/1911	Herald	Schools	McKinley, Ralph Butler is new principal
12/25/1912	Journal	Schools	McKinley, Ralph E. Butcher is superintendent
10/31/1950	Journal-Herald	Schools	McKinley, school consolidation meeting held on October 31
2/23/1922	Democrat	Schools	McKinley, school to be dedicated on Friday
3/2/1922	Democrat	Schools	McKinley, school was dedicated on February 24, 1922 by Lee L. Driver
12/8/1915	Journal	Schools	McKinley, Superintendent Miller of Fountain City visited
12/22/1955	Journal-Herald	Schools	McKinley, track champions
4/26/1911	Journal	Schools	McKinley, Trustee Walter Hiatt purchased ground for the new school; it will be called "McKinley"
7/19/1911	Journal	Schools	McKinley, Virges Wheeler will take charge of the high school
11/27/1936	Daily News	Schools	McKinley's team referred to as "Bulldogs"
11/30/1936	Daily News	Schools	McKinley's team referred to as "Presidents"
4/5/1957	News	Schools	MEC Champions 1956-57: Baseball-Spartanburg; Cross Country-Ridgeville; Basketball-Parker
10/16/1959	News	Schools	MEC Champions: Farmland, cross country; Parker and Union City-Wayne tied in baseball
10/5/1960	News	Schools	MEC Champions: Farmland, cross country; Parker, baseball
5/7/1963	Journal-Herald	Schools	MEC Champions: track, Union; cross country, Farmland; baseball, Spartanburg; basketball, Union
10/16/1958	Journal-Herald	Schools	MEC Champions: Union City-Wayne, baseball; Parker-cross country
9/10/1963	Journal-Herald	Schools	Mid-Central Conference [baseball] members: Ridgeville, Williamsburg, Fountain City, Spartanburg, Union, Lynn
5/28/1964	Journal-Herald	Schools	Mid-Central Conference: Randolph Southern, Fountain City-Whitewater, Webster-Williamsburg, and Ridgeville
5/4/1964	News	Schools	Mid-Central track meet; Union has joined MEC

9/6/1962	News	Schools	Mid-Eastern Conference consists of Lynn, Ridgeville, Parker, Union, Farmland, and Spartanburg
8/23/1953	News	Schools	Mid-Eastern Conference established, all but Winchester are members
9/26/1953	Journal-Herald	Schools	Mid-Eastern Conference, all county schools are members except Winchester
1/5/1954	Journal-Herald	Schools	Mid-Eastern Conference, Farmland not in MEC Basketball competition; conference has baseball, basketball, volleyball, track, and ping pong
8/2/1871	Journal	Schools	Mills Schoolhouse mentioned
12/29/1953	Journal-Herald	Schools	Mississinewa Valley Conference membership: Mississinewa, Royerton, Fairmount, Winchester, Portland
4/5/1956	Journal-Herald	Schools	Mississinewa Valley Conference, Eastern Howard joined
8/26/1961	Journal-Herald	Schools	Mississinewa Valley Conference, formed in 1952 with Winchester, Portland, Royerton, Mississinewa; Fairmount joined in 1953; Eastern was included from 1956-1961; Highland and Hagerstown joined in 1961
2/20/1968	Journal-Herald	Schools	Mississinewa Valley Conference: Mississinewa, Portland, Delta, Eastbrook, Winchester
10/18/1955	Journal-Herald	Schools	Mississinewa Valley Conference; Eastern of Greentown joined; members are Fairmount, Royerton, Mississinewa, Portland, Winchester, and Eastern
2/29/1940	Journal-Herald	Schools	Modoc "Tigers" ?
2/20/1895	Journal	Schools	Modoc has high school grades
11/12/1890	Journal	Schools	Modoc has high school instructor
2/20/1937	Daily News	Schools	Modoc joined IHSAA in 1916; referred to as "blue and gold netters"
11/1/1911	Journal	Schools	Modoc School dedicated by John F. Haines
12/14/1910	Journal	Schools	Modoc School, contract for to be let next week
9/4/1963	News	Schools	Modoc, "No School Today" [seems to indicate that Modoc School had been recently razed]
12/7/1910	Journal	Schools	Modoc, bids for new school
1/11/1911	Journal	Schools	Modoc, bids rejected
11/2/1911	Democrat	Schools	Modoc, dedication; John Haines, Superintendent of Hamilton County, speaker
8/9/1911	Herald	Schools	Modoc, frame schoolhouse, No. 9, to be sold on August 26, 1911

2/8/1911	Journal	Schools	Modoc, J. W. Norris is awarded contract for $13,942
1/18/1911	Journal	Schools	Modoc, new bids will be received on February 4, 1911
10/8/1890	Herald	Schools	Modoc, new school almost complete
10/6/1911	Democrat	Schools	Modoc, new school opened
6/4/1890	Herald	Schools	Modoc, new, three-room, joint township school will be erected at Modoc
10/5/1910	Journal	Schools	Modoc, plans for a joint school
9/4/1913	Democrat	Schools	Modoc, Principal Trueblood is from Salem, Indiana
10/25/1911	Journal	Schools	Modoc, program for dedication
7/20/1910	Herald	Schools	Modoc, school building is condemned
10/25/1911	Herald	Schools	Modoc, school will be dedicated on October 27, 1911 by C. A. Greathouse [Greathouse was absent]
7/27/1910	Journal	Schools	Modoc, schoolhouse condemned
11/1/1911	Herald	Schools	Modoc, schoolhouse was dedicated Friday afternoon by John Haines, superintendent of Hamilton County
8/20/1890	Journal	Schools	Modoc, three room schoolhouse being built
7/30/1914	Democrat	Schools	Monroe (Parker), George M. Elliott, superintendent; B. P. Beeson, principal
1/19/1910	Journal	Schools	Monroe (Parker), new school; bids for furniture
1/18/1984	News-Gazette	Schools	Monroe Central approves plans to give schools sites to towns as parks
4/4/1974	News-Gazette	Schools	Monroe Central destroyed by tornado
8/29/1983	News-Gazette	Schools	Monroe Central Elementary School opens today
11/12/1963	Journal-Herald	Schools	Monroe Central High School will be dedicated on November 17 with State Superintendent William E. Wilson as the main speaker
9/19/1963	Journal-Herald	Schools	Monroe Central is not in a baseball conference
9/14/1960	News	Schools	Monroe Central to sign lease for new building; opponents plan remonstrance
7/11/1979	News-Gazette	Schools	Monroe Central, architect selected for new elementary school
5/7/1974	News-Gazette	Schools	Monroe Central, architect selected for new high school
10/17/1958	News	Schools	Monroe Central, architectural plans; no gym is planned
12/14/1961	Journal-Herald	Schools	Monroe Central, bids are opened for new school

Date	Source	Category	Description
11/14/1961	Journal-Herald	Schools	Monroe Central, bids for new school will be opened on December 12
5/23/1961	Journal-Herald	Schools	Monroe Central, bids on new school expire
3/24/1982	News-Gazette	Schools	Monroe Central, board approved construction contracts for elementary school
1/4/1984	News-Gazette	Schools	Monroe Central, board hears from towns about demolition of schools
5/6/1983	News-Gazette	Schools	Monroe Central, boys and girls county track champions
9/27/1983	News-Gazette	Schools	Monroe Central, boy's county cross country champions
5/18/1976	News-Gazette	Schools	Monroe Central, construction contracts are signed; $4,869,771.19; groundbreaking will be on May 21 at 3 p.m.
4/21/1982	News-Gazette	Schools	Monroe Central, construction of new elementary school to begin today
11/19/1976	News-Gazette	Schools	Monroe Central, construction of new high school is progressing
1/16/1978	News-Gazette	Schools	Monroe Central, county wrestling champions
10/16/1978	News-Gazette	Schools	Monroe Central, dedication
7/28/1977	News-Gazette	Schools	Monroe Central, Don Elder, biography
12/2/1981	News-Gazette	Schools	Monroe Central, elementary building under fire
7/3/1982	News-Gazette	Schools	Monroe Central, elementary construction
1/20/1982	News-Gazette	Schools	Monroe Central, elementary project gets state approval
7/31/1982	News-Gazette	Schools	Monroe Central, Farmland and Parker buildings will be razed
1/6/1982	News-Gazette	Schools	Monroe Central, final decision has not been made on elementary building
2/7/1979	News-Gazette	Schools	Monroe Central, first steps toward new elementary school
11/18/1963	News	Schools	Monroe Central, hundreds attend dedication; cost $816,000; William E. Wilson, speaker
6/12/1973	News-Gazette	Schools	Monroe Central, John Robbins starts as high school principal
5/7/1966	Journal-Herald	Schools	Monroe Central, John Wright resigns as principal
11/24/1982	News-Gazette	Schools	Monroe Central, Larry Hall will be new principal of elementary school
8/6/1959	Journal-Herald	Schools	Monroe Central, Leo Arvin replaces Leonard O. Hewitt as superintendent
8/2/1957	News	Schools	Monroe Central, Leonard Hewitt starts as superintendent
1/25/1978	News-Gazette	Schools	Monroe Central, March 1 is tentative completion date for new high school
9/19/1963	Journal-Herald	Schools	Monroe Central, mascot will be "Golden Bears"

374

Date	Source	Category	Description
7/8/1966	News	Schools	Monroe Central, Merle Bryan named high school principal
3/13/1973	News-Gazette	Schools	Monroe Central, Merle Bryan named superintendent
10/19/1960	News	Schools	Monroe Central, more signatures against lease arrangements; 669 signatures from all over district
3/21/1978	News-Gazette	Schools	Monroe Central, moving date is set for mid-April
4/8/1978	News-Gazette	Schools	Monroe Central, new building featured in Saturday Extra
4/25/1962	News	Schools	Monroe Central, new building will be ready by fall of 1963
10/16/1981	News-Gazette	Schools	Monroe Central, new elementary school will cost about $7 million
3/18/1963	News	Schools	Monroe Central, new high school will be ready to open in fall; 60,000 square feet; $825,000
3/8/1978	News-Gazette	Schools	Monroe Central, occupancy of new building is at least six weeks away
3/18/1982	News-Gazette	Schools	Monroe Central, patrons discuss new elementary school
12/15/1972	News-Gazette	Schools	Monroe Central, Paul Beck to retire as superintendent
11/25/1974	News-Gazette	Schools	Monroe Central, pen and ink drawing of old building
6/12/1957	News	Schools	Monroe Central, Philip Guy resigns as superintendent
8/8/1956	News	Schools	Monroe Central, Phillip A. Guy, superintendent
8/23/1956	Journal-Herald	Schools	Monroe Central, Phillip A. Guy, superintendent
11/7/1959	Journal-Herald	Schools	Monroe Central, plans for new building by 1961
10/12/1978	News-Gazette	Schools	Monroe Central, rededication set for Sunday, October 15; Dr. Merl Strom, professor at Ball State, will be speaker
10/14/1960	News	Schools	Monroe Central, remonstrance against lease agreement for new building; all 40 signers had Farmland addresses
11/9/1981	News-Gazette	Schools	Monroe Central, remonstrance halts elementary building plans; signed by Board Member Clifford Coulter, all three township trustees, and fifty-four others
11/30/1981	News-Gazette	Schools	Monroe Central, residents give their viewpoints on elementary building
2/19/1968	News	Schools	Monroe Central, Robert Starbuck replaces Clyde Thornburg on school board
4/5/1963	Journal-Herald	Schools	Monroe Central, school attendance districts listed
3/7/1984	News-Gazette	Schools	Monroe Central, school board approves towns purchasing school sites
2/15/1963	News	Schools	Monroe Central, school nears completion

Date	Source	Category	Description
1/21/1957	News	Schools	Monroe Central, six proposed plans for reorganization
1/13/1976	News-Gazette	Schools	Monroe Central, sketch of new school; 104,118 square feet; $4,788,399; gym capacity of 2250
12/17/1981	News-Gazette	Schools	Monroe Central, state approves elementary school project
4/14/1978	News-Gazette	Schools	Monroe Central, the "big move" is underway
4/14/1962	Journal-Herald	Schools	Monroe Central, work is underway on school; delayed a year by legal action
4/14/1962	Journal-Herald	Schools	Monroe Central, work is underway on school; Repp and Mundt are general contractors
5/22/1976	News-Gazette	Schools	Monroe Central, work will begin on new high school; 32 classrooms; gym capacity of 2250
2/2/1865	Journal	Schools	Monroe Township teachers listed
3/19/1884	Journal	Schools	Monroe Township, Ben Hill, Joseph Day, teacher
11/14/1877	Journal	Schools	Monroe Township, Canada's Schoolhouse, 1.5 miles north of Farmland near William Miller's, Frank Smith, teacher
3/16/1881	Journal	Schools	Monroe Township, Confederate Cross Roads, Frank Smith, teacher (Rose Hill Items)
4/20/1881	Journal	Schools	Monroe Township, Hickory Grove, Pauline Green, teacher
2/25/1885	Journal	Schools	Monroe Township, John W. Bradrick (Hill), Lee Driver, J. R. Slonaker, N. O. Cox, Lida Brooks are township teachers
11/14/1877	Journal	Schools	Monroe Township, Lewis Schoolhouse, Abel Gillespie, teacher
11/17/1880	Journal	Schools	Monroe Township, Lewis Schoolhouse, C. W. Paris, teacher
6/14/1876	Journal	Schools	Monroe Township, Lewis Schoolhouse, Hattie Burres, teacher
8/6/1884	Journal	Schools	Monroe Township, Lewis, new schoolhouse at C. Lewis
1/2/1901	Journal	Schools	Monroe Township, No. 1, J. W. Jones, teacher, died; Bessie Paris replaced him
3/12/1879	Journal	Schools	Monroe Township, No. 1, S. D. Christopher, teacher
11/24/1880	Journal	Schools	Monroe Township, No. 3, J. W. Braderick, teacher
5/31/1882	Journal	Schools	Monroe Township, No. 6, bid for new school to Samuel Wright for $475
9/26/1912	Democrat	Schools	Monroe Township, No. 6, lawsuit
3/18/1874	Journal	Schools	Monroe Township, Oak Grove, Ben Fertick is teacher

Date	Source	Category	Description
7/17/1878	Journal	Schools	Monroe Township, Oak Grove, brick schoolhouse to be built in fall
1/20/1892	Journal	Schools	Monroe Township, Oak Grove, C. W. Paris, teacher
3/1/1882	Journal	Schools	Monroe Township, Oak Grove, Flora Meeks is teacher
10/27/1880	Journal	Schools	Monroe Township, Oak Grove, Flora Meeks, teacher
11/17/1880	Journal	Schools	Monroe Township, Oak Grove, Mr. Fletcher Meeks, teacher
8/28/1878	Journal	Schools	Monroe Township, Oak Grove, school nearly completed; built by Mr. French of Farmland
1/11/1888	Journal	Schools	Monroe Township, Rehobeth, Mollie Hill and D. F. Hill, teachers
5/17/1916	Journal	Schools	Monroe, autos were there; cost enough to pay for the school
7/9/1913	Journal	Schools	Monroe, faculty: V. I. Brown, superintendent; George Elliott, principal
2/2/1865	Journal	Schools	Monroe, Stoney Creek, White River, Wayne teachers and schools described
7/29/1914	Journal	Schools	Monroe, teachers listed: George M. Elliott, superintendent; B. P. Beeson, principal
2/25/1955	News	Schools	Monroe-Green-Stoney Creek consolidation committee formed; Noel Thornburg, chairman
4/6/1956	News	Schools	Monroe-Green-Stoney Creek consolidation petitions circulated
2/16/1955	News	Schools	Monroe-Green-Stoney Creek consolidation steps taken
3/21/1955	News	Schools	Monroe-Green-Stoney Creek consolidation to be called "Lee Driver Consolidated School Corporation"
5/9/1956	News	Schools	Monroe-Green-Stoney Creek merger approved by voters
3/30/1955	News	Schools	Monroe-Green-Stoney Creek merger resolution
5/23/1955	News	Schools	Monroe-Green-Stoney Creek trustees have petitions mandating consolidation election
5/3/1956	Journal-Herald	Schools	Monroe-Green-Stoney Creek, notice of consolidation plan
9/5/1888	Journal	Schools	Murray Schoolhouse, John Green's, west of
2/7/1906	Journal	Schools	Music, 44 organs and pianos in the schoolhouses of Randolph County
5/11/1910	Journal	Schools	Nettle Creek Township (Losanville), commencement of four year high school held
8/30/1899	Journal	Schools	Nettle Creek Township teachers listed
9/30/1896	Journal	Schools	Nettle Creek Township teachers listed: 1, 2, 3, 4, 5, 6 (Losantville), 8, 9, 10 (Modoc)

Date	Source	Category	Description
9/4/1895	Journal	Schools	Nettle Creek Township teachers listed; schools exist at 1, 2, 3, 4, 5, 6 (Losantville), 8, 9, 10 (Modoc)
11/5/1919	Journal	Schools	Nettle Creek Township, No. 1 will be sold next Saturday
7/17/1912	Journal	Schools	Nettle Creek Township, [No. 7] new building to be built
7/24/1912	Journal	Schools	Nettle Creek Township, [No. 7] was damaged by a storm a few weeks ago; will be replaced
5/2/1900	Herald	Schools	Nettle Creek Township, Barrax Corner, old schoolhouse is now a stable; was frame building
7/24/1912	Journal	Schools	Nettle Creek Township, bids for new schoolhouse
11/22/1882	Journal	Schools	Nettle Creek Township, Burrough's, new schoolhouse is completed
2/14/1872	Journal	Schools	Nettle Creek Township, Colored people's schoolhouse in Nettle Creek Township is No. 10
1/31/1872	Journal	Schools	Nettle Creek Township, Colored people's schoolhouse in Nettle Creek Township, township convention there
3/22/1871	Journal	Schools	Nettle Creek Township, colored school, first district colored school in Randolph County, closed on March 11, 1871 [for the year]
5/15/1895	Journal	Schools	Nettle Creek Township, Concord School No. 4 is near Modoc
10/30/1895	Journal	Schools	Nettle Creek Township, Concord School No. 4 is near Modoc, Omer Ross, teacher
3/17/1897	Journal	Schools	Nettle Creek Township, Diamond Hill School is Nettle Creek No. 7
10/24/1888	Journal	Schools	Nettle Creek Township, Isaac Wood Schoolhouse, No. 10, Nettle Creek Township
5/15/1878	Journal	Schools	Nettle Creek Township, Lemuel Wiggins appointed trustee of Nettle Creek on April 22, 1875; elected in October 1876; erected five brick schoolhouses; redistricted in 1877; dropped one district; beat in the nominating election in 1878
12/18/1894	Journal	Schools	Nettle Creek Township, Lindsey School, Nettle Creek Twp. No. 2, burned; 1.25 miles south of Neff
9/2/1908	Journal	Schools	Nettle Creek Township, No. 1 is nearly completed
10/30/1919	Democrat	Schools	Nettle Creek Township, No. 1, notice of sale
10/22/1919	Journal	Schools	Nettle Creek Township, No. 1, notice of sale of school property on November 8, 1919
5/10/1911	Journal	Schools	Nettle Creek Township, No. 2, Lindsey School, bids for new school on June 3, 1911

Date	Source	Category	Description
12/17/1894	Journal	Schools	Nettle Creek Township, No. 2, Lindsey School, burned
5/12/1911	Democrat	Schools	Nettle Creek Township, No. 2, Lindsey School, new frame one-room schoolhouse
1/2/1895	Journal	Schools	Nettle Creek Township, No. 2, school has been repaired; foundation and walls survived the fire
3/8/1882	Journal	Schools	Nettle Creek Township, No. 2, schoolhouse has been ornamented with a bell
12/21/1881	Journal	Schools	Nettle Creek Township, No. 2, Willard Denney is teacher
2/13/1878	Journal	Schools	Nettle Creek Township, No. 7 is Routh Schoolhouse
9/11/1912	Journal	Schools	Nettle Creek Township, No. 7 will be rebuilt or remodeled
1/21/1920	Journal	Schools	Nettle Creek Township, No. 7, notice of sale of school property on February 14, 1920
7/18/1912	Democrat	Schools	Nettle Creek Township, No. 7, Section 26, bids for new building
9/11/1912	Journal	Schools	Nettle Creek Township, No. 7; West River, No. 3; Stoney Creek, No. 7 due to get new or remodeled buildings
8/30/1905	Journal	Schools	Nettle Creek Township, No. 8 to No. 6 and No. 9 to No. 7
9/20/1866	Journal	Schools	Nettle Creek Township, No. 9 has new building
7/3/1912	Journal	Schools	Nettle Creek Township, old brick schoolhouse damaged by storm
9/6/1860	Journal	Schools	Nettle Creek Township, Routh's Schoolhouse exists in Nettle Creek Township
4/26/1860	Journal	Schools	Nettle Creek Township, Snodgrass Schoolhouse exists [Nettle Creek No. 9]
6/13/1883	Journal	Schools	Nettle Creek Township, teachers listed
7/13/1904	Herald	Schools	Nettle Creek Township, two schoolhouses in township condemned
12/3/1879	Journal	Schools	Nettle Creek Township, Willard Denny is teacher at new schoolhouse
4/18/1917	Journal	Schools	New Jersey pamphlet focused on Randolph County Schools
10/3/1953	Journal-Herald	Schools	No county baseball champions
9/25/1954	Journal-Herald	Schools	No county baseball champions
3/6/1912	Journal	Schools	North Washington, bids for on site of No. 2
3/27/1912	Journal	Schools	North Washington, contract awarded to Fred Huffman for $11,580; heating and ventilation to Hoosier Warming Co. for $1,948

Date	Source	Topic	Description
3/6/1912	Journal	Schools	North Washington, petition to build on Fred Retter Farm
12/29/1886	Journal	Schools	Oak Ridge School House mentioned; Miss Hattie Strahan, teacher
2/9/1887	Journal	Schools	Oak Ridge School, Jarrett, Hunt, Keener, Diggs, and Jones families
6/3/1903	Journal	Schools	Paris, C. W. reelected county superintendent
12/28/1898	Journal	Schools	Paris, Charles W. and Trustee Isenbarger visited high school in Williamsburg, Indiana
6/3/1903	Herald	Schools	Paris, Charles was reelected county superintendent on second ballot; Driver was also a candidate
3/3/1909	Journal	Schools	Parker abandoned school corporation effective May 10
3/3/1909	Herald	Schools	Parker City School Board abolished effective May 10, 1909
10/17/1906	Journal	Schools	Parker City, high school is now commissioned; lot has been purchased for a new building
4/16/1919	Journal	Schools	Parker City, old school building sold to William Murray for $225
4/20/1910	Herald	Schools	Parker City, State Superintendent Aley will speak at dedication on Wednesday, May 4, 1910
11/3/1936	Daily News	Schools	Parker Flyers
1/9/1937	Daily News	Schools	Parker Flyers
1/8/1938	News	Schools	Parker Flyers
2/24/1875	Journal	Schools	Parker is to have a brick schoolhouse this summer (Farmland Items)
2/23/1937	Daily News	Schools	Parker joined IHSAA in 1921; referred to as "Panthers"
4/23/1925	Journal-Herald	Schools	Parker opened new gym
3/6/1937	Daily News	Schools	Parker Panthers
3/4/1938	Journal-Herald	Schools	Parker Panthers
3/4/1909	Democrat	Schools	Parker School Town is abandoned effective May 10, 1909
6/8/1898	Journal	Schools	Parker teachers listed
8/25/1909	Herald	Schools	Parker to build new school
4/9/1925	Journal-Herald	Schools	Parker to opened new annex on April 14, 1925
10/17/1933	Journal-Herald	Schools	Parker won county baseball championship
7/7/1909	Journal	Schools	Parker, bids for new school
3/6/1984	News-Gazette	Schools	Parker, building will be completely razed by end of week
10/8/1902	Journal	Schools	Parker, C. L. Reed resigns as teacher
1/29/1890	Journal	Schools	Parker, C. L. Reed, principal
8/14/1907	Herald	Schools	Parker, Carl Mote starts as superintendent

Date	Publication	Category	Description
10/19/1933	Democrat	Schools	Parker, county baseball champions
10/6/1947	News	Schools	Parker, county baseball champions
10/15/1958	News	Schools	Parker, cross country champions
5/4/1910	Journal	Schools	Parker, dedication of new school is today
6/24/1908	Herald	Schools	Parker, Ernest B. Freshwater replaces Carl Mote as superintendent
4/9/1925	Democrat	Schools	Parker, formal opening of annex will be held on April 14, 1925 by H. N. Sherwood, Superintendent of Public Instruction
4/21/1875	Journal	Schools	Parker, ground broken for new schoolhouse
6/5/1907	Herald	Schools	Parker, J. G. Elsteun resigns as superintendent
7/10/1895	Herald	Schools	Parker, L. J. Shetterly develops plans for Parker School House
2/16/1910	Herald	Schools	Parker, new school building planned
1/2/1889	Herald	Schools	Parker, new schoolhouse for primary department finished and occupied last Monday
11/28/1888	Journal	Schools	Parker, new schoolhouse for primary grades completed
12/8/1875	Journal	Schools	Parker, new schoolhouse is 34 x 50, 2 stories with cupola
4/24/1924	Democrat	Schools	Parker, notice of letting contract for addition
6/17/1909	Democrat	Schools	Parker, notice to contractors
8/5/1909	Democrat	Schools	Parker, notice to contractors of rebidding
8/26/1909	Democrat	Schools	Parker, plans for new school
5/19/1909	Journal	Schools	Parker, plans for school
3/10/1984	News-Gazette	Schools	Parker, residents have fond memories of school
5/21/1913	Journal	Schools	Parker, Roy C. Keever resigned as superintendent after four years; V. I. Brown elected to replace him
2/16/1910	Journal	Schools	Parker, school began in the new building; new commission issued to the high school
7/14/1875	Journal	Schools	Parker, schoolhouse is waiting on brick
8/1/1956	News	Schools	Parker, summer league baseball champions
4/27/1910	Herald	Schools	Parker, Supt. Aley will speak at dedication
10/3/1877	Journal	Schools	Parker, work on schoolhouse
10/6/1909	Herald	Schools	Parker's new school building
1/10/1912	Journal	Schools	Petition for joint school near line of West River, White River, and Washington Townships
3/19/1977	News-Gazette	Schools	Photos from 1919
10/12/1892	Journal	Schools	Poleville School mentioned

Date	Source	Category	Description
7/13/1892	Journal	Schools	Principals for next year: J. D. White, Farmland; George F. Addleman, Lynn; C. P. Callett, Ridgeville
9/19/1917	Journal	Schools	Principals, four new principals went into office in Randolph County
9/24/1965	News	Schools	Ran-Del Summer Baseball League Conference: Ridgeville, Albany, DeSoto, Center, Monroe Central, Selma, Union
2/9/1965	Journal-Herald	Schools	Randolph Central, architect's plan for new Driver H. S.
10/1/1982	News-Gazette	Schools	Randolph Central, auction of contents of Ward and Ridgeville will be October 5
3/13/1984	News-Gazette	Schools	Randolph Central, board approves converting Driver Junior High into Driver Middle School; White River Elementary School will cease at the end of the school year
5/14/1964	Journal-Herald	Schools	Randolph Central, board renews efforts to buy Goodrich site
9/29/1982	News-Gazette	Schools	Randolph Central, board votes to demolish Ward and Ridgeville; will not sell either; Deerfield will be dedicated on November 7
2/22/1984	News-Gazette	Schools	Randolph Central, considers converting junior high into middle school, moving kindergarten to the Field House, making Baker 1-2 and Morton 3-5
4/10/1964	News	Schools	Randolph Central, court rules against school board condemnation of Goodrich land
1/8/1965	News	Schools	Randolph Central, Donald Hahn appointed to school board to replace Lloyd Schafer
3/14/1979	News-Gazette	Schools	Randolph Central, Dr. Ed Glenn to retire as superintendent
6/26/1968	News	Schools	Randolph Central, Dr. Glenn hired as superintendent
2/13/1964	Journal-Herald	Schools	Randolph Central, drawing of new high school
5/14/1964	Journal-Herald	Schools	Randolph Central, Driver High School has a golf team
8/8/1984	News-Gazette	Schools	Randolph Central, elementary district lines (on both sides of road will go to Deerfield)
5/16/1984	News-Gazette	Schools	Randolph Central, elementary districts redrawn: 300 N to U. S. 27, then south to 225 N to 200 E, then south to UC Pike; everyone north goes to Deerfield
5/10/1972	News-Gazette	Schools	Randolph Central, elementary principals: Gene Richardson, Baker; John Kidder, Morton; Cleo Bookout, Ridgeville, Ralph Fowler, White River; William Cole will replace Fowler next year

Date	Source	Category	Description
8/11/1965	News	Schools	Randolph Central, enlarge plans for new Randolph Central High School
7/3/1962	News	Schools	Randolph Central, first school board
11/19/1982	News-Gazette	Schools	Randolph Central, Gary Keesling starts as superintendent
6/9/1965	News	Schools	Randolph Central, groundbreaking for new high school will be held on June 10
6/4/1964	Journal-Herald	Schools	Randolph Central, hope to begin work on new high school by fall
7/17/1973	News-Gazette	Schools	Randolph Central, John Kidder is principal of Morton Elementary and Ward Elementary
4/27/1968	Journal-Herald	Schools	Randolph Central, Merritt Beck resigns as superintendent effective June 30
5/3/1974	News-Gazette	Schools	Randolph Central, Mrs. Ivan Brenner leaves administration building to school corporation
12/15/1964	News	Schools	Randolph Central, new bus barn at site of McKinley
6/8/1964	News	Schools	Randolph Central, new high school to cost $1.5 million
1/12/1966	News	Schools	Randolph Central, new high school will be "Winchester Community High School," on a 4-1 vote by the board
1/27/1982	News-Gazette	Schools	Randolph Central, Phil Wray goes from Morton to Driver and White River; Coe out at White River; Robert Farlow out at Driver; Richardson will be principal at Baker and Morton
1/16/1969	Journal-Herald	Schools	Randolph Central, plans to build new Willard; plans to raze Winchester High School; White River Elementary served all students in the township
3/25/1981	News-Gazette	Schools	Randolph Central, purchased 15 acres of land for $42,000
7/3/1979	News-Gazette	Schools	Randolph Central, Ron Meyers is new superintendent
7/14/1982	News-Gazette	Schools	Randolph Central, Ron Myers resigns as superintendent
10/2/1963	News	Schools	Randolph Central, school board makes offer for Goodrich Park site for high school
1/31/1964	News	Schools	Randolph Central, school board votes to condemn Goodrich site for new high school
3/19/1983	News-Gazette	Schools	Randolph Central, school memorabilia is placed in superintendent's office
3/13/1963	News	Schools	Randolph Central, sites for new high school discussed
9/10/1962	News	Schools	Randolph Central, superintendent's office moved from high school to basement of library

Date	Source	Category	Description
8/11/1982	News-Gazette	Schools	Randolph Central, Ward and Ridgeville Schools to be demolished
4/25/1964	Journal-Herald	Schools	Randolph Central, White River Elementary, new fight song
9/5/1967	Journal-Herald	Schools	Randolph Central, Winchester Community, first day for was September 1 [in old building]
5/26/1965	News	Schools	Randolph Central, work to start on new high school; Baystone Construction Company, $803,541; Hutzel Mechanical, $320,440; Hatfield Elect., $72,448
5/23/1974	News-Gazette	Schools	Randolph Central; Joel Taylor will replace Cleo Bookout as principal at Ridgeville; John Kidder resigns as principal of Ward, will continue at Morton; Gary Kiser will be new Ward principal
3/11/1965	Journal-Herald	Schools	Randolph Central; will new high school be "Driver" or not?
9/1/1920	Journal-Herald	Schools	Randolph County Athletic and Literary Association formed
12/4/1912	Journal	Schools	Randolph County Athletic Association organized
4/26/1916	Journal	Schools	Randolph County graduates listed
10/5/1870	Journal	Schools	Randolph County had 91 schoolhouses in 1856
9/21/1870	Journal	Schools	Randolph County has 128 schoolhouses, 8116 school children
2/4/1920	Herald	Schools	Randolph County has 7258 students in school
8/21/1913	Democrat	Schools	Randolph County has 8850 pupils; first year since 1845 that there has been no exclusively colored school
5/10/1899	Journal	Schools	Randolph County school enumeration
6/18/1919	Journal	Schools	Randolph County Seminary history; brick building was completed in 1841 at a cost of $2200; discontinued as a seminary in 1851
3/27/1863	Journal	Schools	Randolph County Seminary, John Cooper, principal; trustees listed
4/8/1858	Journal	Schools	Randolph County Teachers Association held at Jericho; schools are maintained at Winchester, Arba, Poplar Run, Union City, Salem, Jericho, and perhaps others
9/15/1915	Journal	Schools	Randolph County teachers listed
9/8/1897	Journal	Schools	Randolph County teachers listed
5/11/1898	Journal	Schools	Randolph County, school enumeration
8/26/1908	Journal	Schools	Randolph County, statistics
1/4/1962	Journal-Herald	Schools	Randolph Eastern, 2300 signatures on petitions for formation of

12/30/1981	News-Gazette	Schools	Randolph Eastern, A. M. Bennett resigns as superintendent effective June 30 after ten years
7/10/1981	News-Gazette	Schools	Randolph Eastern, addition and renovation of high school to cost $1.5 million
7/28/1966	Journal-Herald	Schools	Randolph Eastern, Dee Hand resigns as superintendent after eleven years
9/24/1969	Journal-Herald	Schools	Randolph Eastern, Delbert Hatton is superintendent; Kenneth Ayres is high school principal
7/14/1982	News-Gazette	Schools	Randolph Eastern, Eugene Huddleston starts as superintendent
4/1/1982	News-Gazette	Schools	Randolph Eastern, Eugene Huddleston to be new superintendent
7/27/1983	News-Gazette	Schools	Randolph Eastern, James Adcock appointed to school board
6/29/1983	News-Gazette	Schools	Randolph Eastern, James Carpenter resigns from school board
6/27/1984	News-Gazette	Schools	Randolph Eastern, Joe Mathias resigns from school board
12/12/1974	News-Gazette	Schools	Randolph Eastern, North Side, board signs contracts for addition to
10/31/1961	Journal-Herald	Schools	Randolph Eastern, petitions for establishment go into circulation this week
10/28/1981	News-Gazette	Schools	Randolph Eastern, remodeling of high school cost up
1/25/1962	Journal-Herald	Schools	Randolph Eastern, school corporation is created and certified by court
7/11/1984	News-Gazette	Schools	Randolph Eastern, Walter Hap appointed to school board
9/26/1962	News	Schools	Randolph Southern (Union-Washington-Greensfork), election called for November 6
11/7/1962	News	Schools	Randolph Southern (Union-Washington-Greensfork), voted down
4/25/1974	News-Gazette	Schools	Randolph Southern Jr.-Sr. High School, groundbreaking was held on April 24; building will be 92,000 square feet
2/3/1965	News	Schools	Randolph Southern Junior High School housed at Spartanburg
6/8/1976	News-Gazette	Schools	Randolph Southern will be dedicated on June 13 with Dr. Charles Fields, Executive Director of the Indiana Association of Public School Superintendents, as speaker; cost $3.8 million
1/8/1975	News-Gazette	Schools	Randolph Southern, building is progressing
1/26/1983	News-Gazette	Schools	Randolph Southern, Carolyn Haggard starts as superintendent

Date	Source	Category	Description
11/15/1972	News-Gazette	Schools	Randolph Southern, citizens form committee to combat building of new high school
11/29/1973	News-Gazette	Schools	Randolph Southern, contracts are signed for new building
6/14/1976	News-Gazette	Schools	Randolph Southern, dedication
11/24/1982	News-Gazette	Schools	Randolph Southern, Gary Keesling resigns as superintendent after nearly 4.5 years
8/17/1978	News-Gazette	Schools	Randolph Southern, Gerald Keesling starts as superintendent
8/9/1968	Journal-Herald	Schools	Randolph Southern, Harry Rinehart named principal
2/20/1964	Journal-Herald	Schools	Randolph Southern, high schools will be consolidated in 1964-65 school year
6/16/1973	News-Gazette	Schools	Randolph Southern, Howard Addison named principal of high school and Lynn Elementary
9/3/1965	News	Schools	Randolph Southern, John McBride is new superintendent
6/22/1983	News-Gazette	Schools	Randolph Southern, Larry Marker named high school principal
1/3/1964	News	Schools	Randolph Southern, Lloyd D. Frazer is new superintendent
8/28/1965	Journal-Herald	Schools	Randolph Southern, Lloyd Frazer resigns as superintendent
4/2/1964	Journal-Herald	Schools	Randolph Southern, mascot will be "Rebels"; colors will be kelly green and white
5/3/1978	News-Gazette	Schools	Randolph Southern, Maynard Myers elected to school board
3/10/1977	News-Gazette	Schools	Randolph Southern, Maynard Myers replaces Danny Cross on school board
9/4/1963	News	Schools	Randolph Southern, merger approved between Greensfork and Washington
10/26/1973	News-Gazette	Schools	Randolph Southern, Merrill Nicholson replaces Stanley Arthur on school board
8/28/1975	News-Gazette	Schools	Randolph Southern, new building
1/27/1976	News-Gazette	Schools	Randolph Southern, new building will be occupied on Tuesday, January 27
1/5/1976	News-Gazette	Schools	Randolph Southern, new gym will be opened on January 7 against Union; 2100 capacity
11/15/1973	News-Gazette	Schools	Randolph Southern, new high school should cost about $3,544,000
10/30/1963	News	Schools	Randolph Southern, plans for merger near completion
5/11/1973	News-Gazette	Schools	Randolph Southern, proposed new high school building; Fanning and Howey, architects

Date	Source	Category	Description
7/14/1976	News-Gazette	Schools	Randolph Southern, Robert Shumaker starts as high school principal; Eugene Hime is elementary principal
3/1/1983	News-Gazette	Schools	Randolph Southern, Shumaker resigns as high school principal
1/26/1983	News-Gazette	Schools	Randolph Southern, Shumaker suspended, Marker acting principal at high school
6/14/1978	News-Gazette	Schools	Randolph Southern, Vincent Haviza fired as superintendent
7/3/1967	News	Schools	Randolph Southern, Vincent Haviza is appointed superintendent to replace John McBride
5/21/1962	News	Schools	Randolph Southern, vote will be taken again in November [Union, Washington, and Greensfork Townships]
11/12/1980	News-Gazette	Schools	Randolph Southern, William P. Allen replaces Maynard Myers on school board
9/8/1909	Journal	Schools	Religious affiliation of Randolph County teachers listed: 72 Methodists, 20 Friends, 56 Christians, 5 Congregationalists, 16 Presbyterians, 1 Episcopalian, 2 United Brethren, 1 Universalist, 1 German Reformed, 2 Lutheran, 2 Catholic, 21 with no affiliation
12/30/1891	Journal	Schools	Ridgeville College changes to new management
1/27/1892	Journal	Schools	Ridgeville College transferred to Congregationalists
12/20/1866	Journal	Schools	Ridgeville College, Free Will Baptists will locate a college at Liber, Jay County
12/20/1866	Journal	Schools	Ridgeville College, Free Will Baptists will locate a college at Ridgeville
12/15/1979	News-Gazette	Schools	Ridgeville College, history
10/19/1887	Journal	Schools	Ridgeville College, meeting to consider moving it
2/14/1941	Daily News	Schools	Ridgeville gymnasium remodeled
1/20/1909	Journal	Schools	Ridgeville High School receives its first commission from the state
2/11/1937	Daily News	Schools	Ridgeville joined IHSAA in 1919; beat Muncie in 1920; went to finals at Bloomington and were defeated by Milroy (no regional in those days); 1921 won regional bust lost to Muncie in the finals at Bloomington
1/3/1924	Democrat	Schools	Ridgeville School building was dedicated by L. N. Hines
2/18/1920	Journal	Schools	Ridgeville School Corporation dissolved; Franklin Township will erect a modern school
8/25/1915	Journal	Schools	Ridgeville School officials listed

Date	Source	Topic	Description
4/29/1874	Journal	Schools	Ridgeville Schools have been incorporated one year
3/9/1949	News	Schools	Ridgeville went to state basketball finals in 1920, held at Cow Barn
4/4/1867	Journal	Schools	Ridgeville will get college; railroad has arrived
4/16/1890	Journal	Schools	Ridgeville will have $12,000 new schoolhouse
9/19/1900	Journal	Schools	Ridgeville, "school war," majority of town board wants to abolish high school
2/27/1952	News	Schools	Ridgeville, 1920 won Muncie Sectional, lost at Bloomington; 1921 won Scottsburg Regional
8/29/1912	Democrat	Schools	Ridgeville, bids on new joint school held up
2/10/1921	Democrat	Schools	Ridgeville, bids rejected for new school
4/22/1983	News-Gazette	Schools	Ridgeville, community group organizes to secure school land
5/25/1922	Democrat	Schools	Ridgeville, contract let for new school
6/26/1912	Journal	Schools	Ridgeville, election to be held on July 23 for a joint school with Franklin Twp.
3/16/1922	Democrat	Schools	Ridgeville, Franklin Township plans for new school immediately results in fighting
7/24/1912	Journal	Schools	Ridgeville, Franklin Twp. votes yes, 115 to 71; Ridgeville votes yes, 332 to 100 for joint school; vote was on July 23, 1912
8/10/1898	Herald	Schools	Ridgeville, H. W. Bortner, superintendent
8/23/1900	Democrat	Schools	Ridgeville, high school abandoned; high school students will go to Ridgeville College
5/19/1966	Journal-Herald	Schools	Ridgeville, last days of Ridgeville High School, Max Reynolds, principal
7/14/1964	Journal-Herald	Schools	Ridgeville, M. M. Reynolds is principal
5/30/1918	Democrat	Schools	Ridgeville, M. S. Grahg returns as superintendent
10/13/1956	Journal-Herald	Schools	Ridgeville, MEC cross country champions
11/1/1893	Herald	Schools	Ridgeville, new school nearly completed
1/6/1921	Democrat	Schools	Ridgeville, new school site is chosen, west side of GR & I Railroad and south of 2nd Street [this site was never used]
4/30/1890	Herald	Schools	Ridgeville, new schoolhouse almost completed
1/1/1890	Herald	Schools	Ridgeville, new schoolhouse foundation done
2/27/1889	Herald	Schools	Ridgeville, new schoolhouse planned

Date	Publication	Category	Description
5/5/1921	Democrat	Schools	Ridgeville, no new school for Franklin Township; bids are too high
4/20/1922	Democrat	Schools	Ridgeville, notice for letting of contract for construction of a school building in Franklin Township
8/3/1922	Democrat	Schools	Ridgeville, notice of sale of school bonds
2/11/1938	Journal-Herald	Schools	Ridgeville, old school burned on October 24, 1892
8/15/1917	Journal	Schools	Ridgeville, Ray Addington, principal and son of B. F. Addington, has resigned to join the army
4/27/1922	Democrat	Schools	Ridgeville, remonstrance against school
2/18/1920	Herald	Schools	Ridgeville, school board dissolved; new building to be erected, leaving only five one-room schools in county
10/14/1982	News-Gazette	Schools	Ridgeville, school is being demolished
11/4/1965	Journal-Herald	Schools	Ridgeville, seems to have not been a member of any athletic conference
5/24/1922	Journal-Herald	Schools	Ridgeville, State Comm. Granted permission to build school in Ridgeville; contract to Glen Myers for $62,301; plumbing to Tibbetts and Co. for $19,031; wiring to Lenkensdofer for $850; old building sold to Meyers for $6,250
2/19/1920	Democrat	Schools	Ridgeville, town board of education is dissolved; property and management go to Franklin Township
6/11/1983	News-Gazette	Schools	Ridgeville, Ward, school lands sold at auction
10/26/1892	Journal	Schools	Ridgeville's new school was totally destroyed by fire Sunday night
11/19/1873	Journal	Schools	Rose Schoolhouse Sunday School, J. R. Wright, superintendent
10/26/1935	News-Democrat	Schools	Saratoga "red and white"
1/13/1909	Herald	Schools	Saratoga gets a four-year high school certificate from the state; F. K. Williamson, superintendent, and Anna Bailey, principal
3/18/1908	Journal	Schools	Saratoga High School to add two rooms
2/17/1937	Daily News	Schools	Saratoga joined IHSAA in 1914
6/9/1915	Journal	Schools	Saratoga, advertisement for bids for addition on June 17, 1915
5/27/1915	Democrat	Schools	Saratoga, bids for addition
3/18/1896	Journal	Schools	Saratoga, brick schoolhouse burned last Thursday; it was only ten years old
6/23/1915	Journal	Schools	Saratoga, Glen Meyers of Ridgeville to build addition for $2497

Date	Source	Category	Description
2/10/1927	Democrat	Schools	Saratoga, new building was first used on January 31, 1927; 180 x 160; includes gymnasium and auditorium; dedication will occur on February 10, 1927
8/17/1898	Herald	Schools	Saratoga, new school building
2/10/1927	Journal-Herald	Schools	Saratoga, new school dedicated
6/17/1915	Democrat	Schools	Saratoga, notice of letting for addition
8/5/1908	Journal	Schools	Saratoga, school nearly complete
6/14/1876	Journal	Schools	Saratoga, two new schoolhouses to be built this summer: one in Saratoga and another north of Saratoga
3/18/1908	Herald	Schools	Saratoga, two-room addition planned; one year added to high school course to make it a four-year high school
4/7/1909	Herald	Schools	Saratoga, W. C. Williamson resigns as principal
3/3/1937	Daily News	Schools	Saratoga's team is referred to as "Red Birds"
3/5/1937	Daily News	Schools	Saratoga's team is referred to as "Red clad warriors"; Modoc is referred to as "black and gold"
3/26/1919	Journal	Schools	School boards, law passed to ensure bipartisan school boards
2/25/1953	News	Schools	School colors listed
3/19/1873	Journal	Schools	School Examiner, report
9/29/1880	Journal	Schools	Schools mentioned: Platt's in Greensfork; Braden No. 10 in West River; Swamp Valley in Nettle Creek?; Lindsey in Nettle Creek; Burrows in Nettle Creek; Routh's in Nettle Creek; Salem in West River; Concord in Nettle Creek?; and Coddington in Wayne
1/7/1976	News-Gazette	Schools	Sectional tournament will be moved to Jay County
8/6/1884	Journal	Schools	Seven new schoolhouses in Randolph County this year
6/25/1884	Journal	Schools	Several new schools will be erected this year
8/24/1881	Journal	Schools	Snow Hill Schoolhouse is near Mt. Zion
4/26/1922	Journal-Herald	Schools	Spartanburg addition bid on May 31
1/12/1948	News	Schools	Spartanburg defeats McKinley in first county basketball tourney
1/13/1909	Herald	Schools	Spartanburg gets a four-year high school certificate from the state; Charles C. Mann, superintendent, and Mary Cox, principal
2/16/1937	Daily News	Schools	Spartanburg has never won a tourney

Date	Source	Category	Description
10/7/1908	Journal	Schools	Spartanburg School to be dedicated on October 10 by Lawrence McTurnan
9/30/1908	Journal	Schools	Spartanburg School will be dedicated on October 10, 1908
4/24/1954	Journal-Herald	Schools	Spartanburg wins MEC all conference title; also track champions
3/8/1923	Journal-Herald	Schools	Spartanburg, addition dedicated on March 1, cost $65,000
3/4/1908	Journal	Schools	Spartanburg, bids for school
4/1/1908	Journal	Schools	Spartanburg, bids for school; it will be a township high school; cost $22,000
5/27/1908	Herald	Schools	Spartanburg, cornerstone laying Saturday
5/20/1908	Journal	Schools	Spartanburg, cornerstone of new school is to be laid on May 23
5/7/1908	Democrat	Schools	Spartanburg, cornerstone will be laid on May 23, 1908
5/13/1908	Journal	Schools	Spartanburg, cornerstone will be laid on May 23, 1908
10/4/1948	News	Schools	Spartanburg, county baseball champions
10/6/1956	Journal-Herald	Schools	Spartanburg, county baseball champions
4/30/1953	Journal-Herald	Schools	Spartanburg, county track champions
5/5/1951	Journal-Herald	Schools	Spartanburg, county track champions
5/7/1954	News	Schools	Spartanburg, county track champions for second year
4/29/1950	Journal-Herald	Schools	Spartanburg, county track champions; McKinley won in 1949, the first year
10/14/1908	Journal	Schools	Spartanburg, dedication of school
5/26/1973	News-Gazette	Schools	Spartanburg, Ed Weston retires as principal
12/20/1939	Journal-Herald	Schools	Spartanburg, new gym to be dedicated this evening
4/2/1908	Democrat	Schools	Spartanburg, new school building
8/5/1908	Journal	Schools	Spartanburg, new school is being completed
3/5/1908	Democrat	Schools	Spartanburg, notice of letting
1/19/1922	Democrat	Schools	Spartanburg, plans to build new gym to be completed by September 1, 1922
5/10/1922	Journal-Herald	Schools	Spartanburg, sale of bonds on May 31
10/14/1908	Herald	Schools	Spartanburg, school dedicated by Lawrence McTurnan, Assistant State Superintendent of Public Instruction
3/8/1923	Democrat	Schools	Spartanburg, school dedication [gymnasium]

Date	Publication	Category	Description
4/26/1976	News-Gazette	Schools	Spartanburg, school sold to Williams Manufacturing Co. for $21,000
10/1/1908	Democrat	Schools	Spartanburg, school will be dedicated on October 10, 1908
4/28/1976	News-Gazette	Schools	Spartanburg, school will be used as gate factory
8/12/1957	News	Schools	Spartanburg, summer league baseball champions
4/12/1911	Journal	Schools	State Board of Health condemned White River Nos. 10, 11, 12, West River No. 11, and Jackson No. 9
9/18/1878	Journal	Schools	Statistics of Randolph County Schools
4/24/1958	Journal-Herald	Schools	Stoney Creek and Green High Schools to be closed; land purchased for new Monroe Central for $21,000
2/15/1964	Journal-Herald	Schools	Stoney Creek being razed
10/11/1916	Herald	Schools	Stoney Creek gets six new school wagons
2/12/1937	Daily News	Schools	Stoney Creek joined the IHSAA in 1919
6/14/1917	Democrat	Schools	Stoney Creek School will be dedicated on June 23, 1917
12/28/1916	Democrat	Schools	Stoney Creek School will open on January 1, 1917
6/13/1917	Journal	Schools	Stoney Creek to be dedicated on June 23, with Governor Goodrich and State Superintendent Horace Ellis as speakers
9/15/1886	Herald	Schools	Stoney Creek Township has ten schoolhouses; also Herron Tollgate
12/4/1878	Journal	Schools	Stoney Creek Township teachers listed
9/13/1899	Journal	Schools	Stoney Creek Township teachers listed
9/29/1897	Journal	Schools	Stoney Creek Township teachers listed
7/14/1915	Journal	Schools	Stoney Creek Township, Branson Harbour v. Trustee and Advisory Board in Jay Circuit Court
9/13/1911	Herald	Schools	Stoney Creek Township, names of district schools listed
12/5/1877	Journal	Schools	Stoney Creek Township, Neff Schoolhouse No. 7 mentioned
1/8/1890	Journal	Schools	Stoney Creek Township, Neff, new schoolhouse planned to replace one recently burned
3/12/1890	Journal	Schools	Stoney Creek Township, No. 1 is known as White River School and Seman's School
8/19/1914	Journal	Schools	Stoney Creek Township, No. 5 closed due to lack of attendance
8/19/1914	Herald	Schools	Stoney Creek Township, No. 5 has been closed due to lack of attendance; there was no school at Numbers 2, 5, or 9+

Date	Source	Category	Description
8/27/1914	Democrat	Schools	Stoney Creek Township, No. 5, closed
5/8/1885	Journal	Schools	Stoney Creek Township, No. 5, Hubbard's
5/23/1917	Journal	Schools	Stoney Creek Township, No. 5, will be sold on June 8, 1917
9/13/1876	Journal	Schools	Stoney Creek Township, No. 7 is Bailey Schoolhouse
12/11/1912	Journal	Schools	Stoney Creek Township, No. 7 is now open
9/11/1912	Journal	Schools	Stoney Creek Township, No. 7 will be rebuilt or remodeled
9/6/1905	Journal	Schools	Stoney Creek Township, No. 7, Laura Fetters, teacher
1/1/1890	Herald	Schools	Stoney Creek Township, No. 7, Neff, new schoolhouse being built
2/15/1882	Journal	Schools	Stoney Creek Township, Poplar Run, L. M. Jackson is teacher of new term
7/2/1884	Journal	Schools	Stoney Creek Township, schoolhouse will be built near Union Cemetery in coming summer
9/11/1878	Journal	Schools	Stoney Creek Township, Seman's Schoolhouse, Stoney Creek Township, J. M. Branson, teacher
7/19/1882	Journal	Schools	Stoney Creek Township, several brick schoolhouses will be built
10/25/1912	Democrat	Schools	Stoney Creek Township, Smullen School is not ready
11/13/1889	Journal	Schools	Stoney Creek Township, Smullen Schoolhouse, one mile east of Neff, destroyed by fire last week
5/27/1914	Journal	Schools	Stoney Creek Township, suit to compel building of a high school
6/9/1915	Journal	Schools	Stoney Creek Township, suit, State ex rel Branson Harbour v. Trustee and Advisory Board
7/24/1889	Journal	Schools	Stoney Creek Township, Windsor, 8 room school in southeast part of town
9/23/1885	Journal	Schools	Stoney Creek Township, Windsor, addition
10/20/1886	Journal	Schools	Stoney Creek Township, Windsor, J. W. Denney is principal
9/22/1875	Journal	Schools	Stoney Creek Township, Windsor, new school completed
6/9/1875	Journal	Schools	Stoney Creek Township, Windsor, new schoolhouse planned
8/4/1875	Journal	Schools	Stoney Creek Township, Windsor, old school property sold; new ready by October
6/29/1955	News	Schools	Stoney Creek votes down consolidation with Monroe and Green
12/20/1916	Journal	Schools	Stoney Creek will open on January 1, 1917; Randolph is probably first county in state to have a high school in each township

Date	Source	Topic	Description
4/22/1914	Herald	Schools	Stoney Creek, "consolidated school is the chief topic of conversation"
9/15/1915	Journal	Schools	Stoney Creek, a high school has been opened in Stoney Creek No. 8 [or No. 3?] with 20 students
2/17/1916	Democrat	Schools	Stoney Creek, all bids are rejected
2/16/1916	Journal	Schools	Stoney Creek, all bids for construction rejected
3/8/1916	Journal	Schools	Stoney Creek, bids for school on April 1, 1916; advertisement
3/22/1916	Journal	Schools	Stoney Creek, bids for school on April 14, 1916 and advertisement
1/19/1916	Journal	Schools	Stoney Creek, bids for school on February 11, 1916
2/16/1916	Herald	Schools	Stoney Creek, bids rejected as too high
4/19/1916	Journal	Schools	Stoney Creek, contract awarded to Mann and Christen for $21,438 and heating and ventilating to H. F. Hobbick for $1575
2/9/1916	Herald	Schools	Stoney Creek, contract let
4/19/1916	Herald	Schools	Stoney Creek, contract let: Mann and Cristen of Decatur, construction for $21,438; W. H. Johnson and Son of Indianapolis, heating for $1865; H. F. Hobbick, plumbing for $1575
4/20/1916	Democrat	Schools	Stoney Creek, contract let; Mann and Cristen of Decatur, construction, $21,438 and others
2/9/1916	Journal	Schools	Stoney Creek, contract to be let on Friday
6/27/1917	Herald	Schools	Stoney Creek, dedicated by J. P. Goodrich
6/20/1917	Herald	Schools	Stoney Creek, dedication will take place on June 23, 1917 with Governor Goodrich and Horace Ellis as speakers
11/18/1915	Democrat	Schools	Stoney Creek, ground is purchased for a new school building
9/16/1915	Democrat	Schools	Stoney Creek, high school opens in No. 8 building
11/4/1935	News-Democrat	Schools	Stoney Creek, home basketball games are played in Hoppes Hall
9/1/1915	Journal	Schools	Stoney Creek, Judge Denney of Jay Circuit Court overruled motion for new trial in school case
7/21/1915	Herald	Schools	Stoney Creek, Judge Denney of Portland ordered construction of a new schoolhouse in Stoney Creek Township
10/3/1963	Journal-Herald	Schools	Stoney Creek, legal notice of sale planned for October 19
6/28/1917	Democrat	Schools	Stoney Creek, new school dedication Saturday
9/1/1915	Herald	Schools	Stoney Creek, new school will be constructed

Date	Source	Category	Description
7/21/1915	Journal	Schools	Stoney Creek, order to build school by Jay Circuit Court
1/27/1916	Democrat	Schools	Stoney Creek, plans completed
11/17/1915	Herald	Schools	Stoney Creek, purchased ground for school
6/17/1914	Herald	Schools	Stoney Creek, school trouble
6/20/1917	Journal	Schools	Stoney Creek, school will be dedicated next Saturday
1/10/1917	Journal	Schools	Stoney Creek, students will move into the consolidated building next Monday; it was not ready on January 1
5/27/1914	Herald	Schools	Stoney Creek, suit by state and Trustee Puckett to force advisory board to build new high school building
11/3/1915	Journal	Schools	Stoney Creek, township purchased five acres of Blaine Thornburg for school
8/17/1948	Journal-Herald	Schools	Stories of gyms and toilets
5/3/1954	News	Schools	Summer baseball league organized
6/7/1882	Journal	Schools	Teacher statistics from county superintendent
2/27/1863	Journal	Schools	Teachers' Association, Pleasant Hiatt, president
3/29/1916	Journal	Schools	Teachers' examination, 193 took it; largest number ever
8/21/1907	Journal	Schools	Teachers Institute, better attendance this year because of the way Driver credits attendance
10/30/1863	Journal	Schools	Teachers licensed, list
9/14/1898	Journal	Schools	Teachers listed for Nettle Creek and White River Townships
9/7/1898	Journal	Schools	Teachers listed for West River, Stoney Creek, Monroe, Jackson, Wayne, and Franklin Townships
9/14/1887	Journal	Schools	Teachers of several townships listed
9/22/1915	Herald	Schools	Teachers supplied for Stoney Creek 1, 4, 6, 7, 10, 3; West River 11, 2; Nettle Creek 1, 2, 5, 7; Ward 1, 3, 9, 11; Franklin 1, 3, 4, 5, 2; Greensfork 1, 2, 3, 8; Washington 9; Wayne 2; Monroe 1, 6, 7; Jackson 7, 9, 10; White River 1, 4, 5, 21
9/4/1901	Journal	Schools	Teachers, list of county teachers
8/30/1905	Journal	Schools	Teachers, list of county teachers
8/29/1906	Journal	Schools	Teachers, list of county teachers
4/3/1872	Journal	Schools	Teachers, list of in county
5/27/1874	Journal	Schools	Teachers, list of in county
6/9/1875	Journal	Schools	Teachers, list of in county
4/9/1873	Journal	Schools	Town school boards established by new law

Date	Source	Category	Description
3/12/1873	Journal	Schools	Town schools are to be under town control say commissioners
5/10/1899	Journal	Schools	Township graduates listed
5/5/1897	Journal	Schools	Township graduates listed
4/30/1913	Herald	Schools	Track Meet, first ever, held at Old Fair Grounds
4/29/1914	Herald	Schools	Track Meet, second annual, Losantville won
4/22/1896	Journal	Schools	Transfer rules described
10/16/1962	Journal-Herald	Schools	Tri-Eastern Conference consists of Union City, Cambridge City, Centerville, Liberty, Knightstown; baseball and tennis will be added in 1963-64; football and wrestling will be added in 1964-65
5/1/1918	Journal	Schools	Truant officer, Charles Puckett elected
5/5/1915	Herald	Schools	Truant officer, G. Walter Hiatt appointed
5/3/1916	Herald	Schools	Truant officer, G. Walter Hiatt reelected
5/8/1901	Journal	Schools	Truant officer, Henry Wood reelected
5/7/1902	Journal	Schools	Truant officer, J. M. Fletcher elected
5/6/1914	Herald	Schools	Truant Officer, J. M. Fletcher reappointed
5/6/1903	Journal	Schools	Truant officer, J. M. Fletcher reelected
9/4/1901	Journal	Schools	Truant officer, Jesse Yost replaces Henry Wood
5/7/1913	Herald	Schools	Truant officer, office created
1/10/1970	News-Gazette	Schools	Union City Catholic Schools to be closed at the end of the school year
10/24/1963	Journal-Herald	Schools	Union City Community High School is the name of the school
2/22/1964	Journal-Herald	Schools	Union City Community High School is the name of the school
8/15/1974	News-Gazette	Schools	Union City Community High School, Paul G. Weaver replaces J. R. Smith as principal
2/9/1937	Daily News	Schools	Union City has finest tourney record in county; joined IHSAA in 1905; played first tourney at Richmond in 1916; in 1917, 1918, and 1920 at Muncie; in 1921 at Winchester
2/19/1919	Journal	Schools	Union City High School burned
6/30/1875	Journal	Schools	Union City High School, Charles W. Paris selected as principal
8/19/1896	Journal	Schools	Union City High School, H. W. Bowers, principal
9/7/1963	Journal-Herald	Schools	Union City played first varsity football game ever
12/4/1969	News-Gazette	Schools	Union City South Side; building should be repaired [UC Edition]
12/5/1955	News	Schools	Union City still in East-Central Conference

Date	Source	Category	Description
4/16/1890	Journal	Schools	Union City will have $32,000 new schoolhouse
11/13/1961	News	Schools	Union City will revive football, dropped about 1906
9/28/1982	News-Gazette	Schools	Union City wins second straight boys cross country championship
11/30/1982	News-Gazette	Schools	Union City, addition to high school
10/11/1955	Journal-Herald	Schools	Union City, baseball champion, no game (?)
12/22/1955	Journal-Herald	Schools	Union City, baseball, cross country champions
6/18/1919	Herald	Schools	Union City, bids on school
2/24/1982	News-Gazette	Schools	Union City, board signs contracts to remodel UCCHS for $1.5 million
7/19/1956	Journal-Herald	Schools	Union City, city council approves new school building
3/18/1920	Democrat	Schools	Union City, contract let for new school; Hunnicutt and Anderson, construction, $170,660; Arnold and Company, plumbing, $16,613, and electrical, $2250
11/27/1956	Journal-Herald	Schools	Union City, contracts are signed for new school with 18 classrooms
8/5/1920	Democrat	Schools	Union City, cornerstone laid on July 30, 1920
12/13/1945	News	Schools	Union City, E. Phillips Blackburn resigns as superintendent; served 1940-45 and replaced Harlie Garver, who served 1927-1940
11/24/1954	News	Schools	Union City, East Side and West Side discuss merger
2/2/1953	News	Schools	Union City, East Side and West Side merger appears hopeless
2/1/1955	Journal-Herald	Schools	Union City, East Side and West Side working toward consolidation
8/12/1885	Journal	Schools	Union City, F. Truedley, superintendent
5/29/1964	News	Schools	Union City, first season for tennis
11/30/1964	News	Schools	Union City, first wrestling team; first in county
11/25/1981	News-Gazette	Schools	Union City, go ahead given for remodeling of UCCHS
12/3/1956	News	Schools	Union City, groundbreaking for new high school was November 30
7/3/1895	Journal	Schools	Union City, H. W. Bowers hired as principal
9/23/1896	Journal	Schools	Union City, H. W. Bowers named superintendent to replace Mrs. Susan G. Patterson, deceased
6/12/1901	Journal	Schools	Union City, H. W. Bowers reelected superintendent for seventh term
2/2/1957	Journal-Herald	Schools	Union City, high school to be constructed in four units
6/20/1906	Herald	Schools	Union City, Hines resigns; Blossom starts as superintendent of schools
5/30/1877	Journal	Schools	Union City, J. C. Eagle, superintendent

Date	Source	Category	Description
4/8/1908	Herald	Schools	Union City, J. O. Batchelor resigns as superintendent
6/26/1907	Journal	Schools	Union City, J. O. Batchelor starts as principal
7/5/1911	Journal	Schools	Union City, John P. King replaces J. W. Stott as superintendent of schools
12/13/1979	News-Gazette	Schools	Union City, Kenneth Ayers appointed principal of West Side to replace William Smith, who served seven years
10/13/1955	Journal-Herald	Schools	Union City, MEC cross country champions
10/12/1957	Journal-Herald	Schools	Union City, MEC cross country champions
7/9/1984	News-Gazette	Schools	Union City, North Side, walls being put up to end open concept
1/25/1984	News-Gazette	Schools	Union City, Northside Elementary School, plans to enclose classrooms
7/28/1909	Herald	Schools	Union City, O. H. Blossom resigns as superintendent
11/30/1982	News-Gazette	Schools	Union City, open house for addition will be December 2; cost $1.5 million
4/13/1979	News-Gazette	Schools	Union City, Paul Weaver resigns as high school principal
4/16/1890	Herald	Schools	Union City, plans for $22,000 schoolhouse
6/15/1956	News	Schools	Union City, plans for new high school building
8/6/1879	Journal	Schools	Union City, Professor Meade is new superintendent
2/25/1880	Journal	Schools	Union City, Professor Meade, superintendent, died last Sunday
5/11/1957	Journal-Herald	Schools	Union City, proposed layout of new school plant
6/19/1958	Journal-Herald	Schools	Union City, remodeling of old high school
2/4/1920	Journal	Schools	Union City, school bids taken on Monday, February 23
11/6/1954	News	Schools	Union City, school board asks city council to approve school site purchase on Plum Street
2/19/1919	Herald	Schools	Union City, school burns
11/24/1982	News-Gazette	Schools	Union City, Steve Hinshaw resigns as football coach after seven years
4/1/1965	Journal-Herald	Schools	Union City, tennis established in 1964
5/12/1966	Journal-Herald	Schools	Union City, tennis team exists
6/28/1979	News-Gazette	Schools	Union City, Thomas J. Goldsberry named high school principal
8/5/1978	News-Gazette	Schools	Union City, Vincent Haviza starts as elementary principal; Howe goes to Mississinewa Valley
12/27/1957	News	Schools	Union City, Wayne Elementary students will move into elementary wing of Union City High School, which opens on January 6, 1958

Date	Source	Category	Description
5/18/1957	Journal-Herald	Schools	Union City, Wayne school officials invite Jackson to consolidate
12/5/1979	News-Gazette	Schools	Union City, William Smith resigns as principal of West Side Middle School
8/21/1963	News	Schools	Union City-Wayne [sic] sports schedule [was already UCCHS]
10/3/1957	Journal-Herald	Schools	Union City-Wayne High School member of East-Central Conference
1/9/1958	Journal-Herald	Schools	Union City-Wayne is member of East-Central Conference
1/14/1958	Journal-Herald	Schools	Union City-Wayne is member of Mid-Eastern Conference
4/21/1956	Journal-Herald	Schools	Union City-Wayne merger called to vote on May 8
12/20/1960	Journal-Herald	Schools	Union City-Wayne seems not to be in East-Central Conference
3/24/1959	Journal-Herald	Schools	Union City-Wayne, aerial photo shows progress
10/15/1962	News	Schools	Union City-Wayne, B team football is being played
10/4/1957	News	Schools	Union City-Wayne, bids opened for third unit of high school, industrial arts wing
11/6/1958	Journal-Herald	Schools	Union City-Wayne, construction of gym to begin immediately; cost $299,192.50
10/28/1957	News	Schools	Union City-Wayne, MEC cross country champions
5/2/1959	Journal-Herald	Schools	Union City-Wayne, MEC track champions
10/28/1960	News	Schools	Union City-Wayne, not in East-Central Conference
6/13/1958	News	Schools	Union City-Wayne, petitions ask for construction of a gym; work to start about September 1, 1958
7/8/1959	News	Schools	Union City-Wayne, photo of gym construction
10/22/1960	Journal-Herald	Schools	Union City-Wayne, plans for 4 classroom addition before September 1961
4/23/1977	News-Gazette	Schools	Union Literary Institute featured in Saturday Extra
10/7/1937	Journal-Herald	Schools	Union Literary Institute to be sold on October 28
5/19/1859	Journal	Schools	Union Literary Institute, building to be constructed by Martin A. Reeder
3/26/1919	Journal	Schools	Union Literary Institute, lawsuit over property
3/11/1942	Journal-Herald	Schools	Union Literary Institute, lawsuit over trust funds, school closed on July 11, 1900
11/27/1924	Journal-Herald	Schools	Union Literary Institute, suits over land
8/24/1887	Journal	Schools	Union Literary Institute, trustees election

Date	Source	Category	Description
11/12/1957	Journal-Herald	Schools	Union Township High School gym was dedicated on November 9 with Robert G. Jones as primary speaker
5/15/1963	News	Schools	Union Township plans consolidation with Stoney Creek Township, Henry County
10/15/1958	News	Schools	Union Township voters turn down metropolitan school district, 347-451
2/11/1950	Journal-Herald	Schools	Union Township, complete record of consolidation
2/7/1950	Journal-Herald	Schools	Union Township, merger complete
5/17/1957	News	Schools	Union Township, plans to sell Huntsville, Losantville, and Modoc buildings on June 17
5/7/1964	Journal-Herald	Schools	Union won first MCC track meet
9/20/1955	Journal-Herald	Schools	Union, advertisement for bids for new school
8/17/1982	News-Gazette	Schools	Union, Alan Tasson starts as principal of high school
12/12/1961	Journal-Herald	Schools	Union, bids for addition for agriculture and industrial arts will be opened early next year
10/13/1955	Journal-Herald	Schools	Union, bids opened for new school
8/30/1973	News-Gazette	Schools	Union, Bill Townsend resigns as elementary principal
6/8/1971	News-Gazette	Schools	Union, Bill Townsend starts as elementary principal; Leslie Slinker resigns as superintendent
8/6/1964	Journal-Herald	Schools	Union, Blountsville School is open
4/8/1981	News-Gazette	Schools	Union, building project to build auxiliary gym and ag building
7/31/1968	Journal-Herald	Schools	Union, Carl Hylton resigns as principal of Randolph Southern to accept principalship at Union High School
11/17/1981	News-Gazette	Schools	Union, completion of gym is delayed
9/19/1968	Journal-Herald	Schools	Union, construction of elementary school begins
6/2/1966	Journal-Herald	Schools	Union, Dan Waterfill resigns as principal after two years service
2/8/1982	News-Gazette	Schools	Union, dedication
2/2/1982	News-Gazette	Schools	Union, dedication is reset for Sunday, February 7
1/28/1982	News-Gazette	Schools	Union, dedication is Sunday; cost $1,925,877
1/5/1982	News-Gazette	Schools	Union, dedication planned for January 31
9/12/1984	News-Gazette	Schools	Union, Dennis Fox is new superintendent
11/3/1981	News-Gazette	Schools	Union, elementary gym construction is on schedule
6/27/1952	News	Schools	Union, High School students may go to Modoc
9/27/1951	Journal-Herald	Schools	Union, land purchased for new school

Date	Source	Category	Description
1/15/1974	News-Gazette	Schools	Union, Leslie Pence resigns as superintendent
7/12/1971	News-Gazette	Schools	Union, Leslie Pence starts as superintendent
8/3/1963	Journal-Herald	Schools	Union, Leslie Slinker is new superintendent; Blountsville School is still open (grades 1-6)
4/8/1964	News	Schools	Union, Leslie Slinker, principal (1963-64) is named superintendent; Dan Waterfill is named principal
8/20/1964	Journal-Herald	Schools	Union, Leslie Slinker, superintendent; Gerald Shelton, principal
2/2/1974	News-Gazette	Schools	Union, Lyle Bonnell moved from high school principal to superintendent after two years
6/23/1966	Journal-Herald	Schools	Union, Max Reynolds is named principal
7/13/1968	Journal-Herald	Schools	Union, Max Reynolds resigns as principal
4/28/1956	Journal-Herald	Schools	Union, MEC track champions
3/24/1964	Journal-Herald	Schools	Union, member of Mid-Central and Mid-Eastern Conference; Lynn is member of MCC, also
12/1/1969	News-Gazette	Schools	Union, new building was dedicated by Senator Hartke
2/6/1953	News	Schools	Union, new metal building is called "Annex"
7/19/1952	Journal-Herald	Schools	Union, new metal building planned
6/27/1952	News	Schools	Union, new metal building planned at Modoc School; elementary students will go to Huntsville and Losantville
6/23/1964	Journal-Herald	Schools	Union, no longer in Mid-Central Conference
11/9/1978	News-Gazette	Schools	Union, Patsy R. Smith starts as elementary principal
6/3/1963	News	Schools	Union, petitions call for vote on merger with Stoney Creek Township, Henry County
4/19/1951	Journal-Herald	Schools	Union, planning for new building
5/17/1968	News	Schools	Union, plans for addition
5/2/1968	Journal-Herald	Schools	Union, plans to build $930,000 elementary addition to close Blountsville School
3/17/1981	News-Gazette	Schools	Union, plans to remodel high school
9/16/1977	News-Gazette	Schools	Union, Richard Hays is new principal of elementary school
10/9/1978	News-Gazette	Schools	Union, Richard Hays, elementary principal, dies
7/12/1978	News-Gazette	Schools	Union, Richard Hoffmeyer is new high school principal
9/1/1977	News-Gazette	Schools	Union, Robert Poffenbarger replaces Lyle Bonnell as superintendent
8/5/1980	News-Gazette	Schools	Union, Robert Poffenbarger resigns as superintendent

Date	Source	Category	Description
10/9/1952	Journal-Herald	Schools	Union, school colors are royal blue and grey; mascot is rockets
11/1/1957	News	Schools	Union, school will be dedicated on November 3 by Wilbur Young, State Superintendent of Public Instruction
11/8/1969	Journal-Herald	Schools	Union, Senator Hartke will dedicate new addition on November 30
10/3/1955	News	Schools	Union, sketch of new Union Township High School
6/27/1963	Journal-Herald	Schools	Union, Stoney Creek Township in Henry County will merge with Union to form a new school district
8/4/1984	News-Gazette	Schools	Union, Terry Munday resigns as superintendent to go to Blackford; started in 1980 to replace Poffenbarger
9/18/1980	News-Gazette	Schools	Union, Terry Mundy starts as superintendent
2/12/1974	News-Gazette	Schools	Union, Tim Heller named high school principal
8/2/1971	News-Gazette	Schools	Union, Wayne B. Pearl replaces Carl Hylton as high school principal
2/25/1958	Journal-Herald	Schools	Ward and Jackson Schools were separate until the spring of 1958
8/6/1955	Journal-Herald	Schools	Ward school reorganization is in court
2/5/1864	Journal	Schools	Ward Township schools and teachers; also Ridgeville, Green, and Monroe (partial)
9/6/1899	Journal	Schools	Ward Township teachers listed
12/19/1918	Democrat	Schools	Ward Township, Clear Creek, Enos L. Watson taught in log Clear Creek Schoolhouse in about 1848; it was a subscription school
12/18/1918	Journal	Schools	Ward Township, Clear Creek, history
7/12/1911	Journal	Schools	Ward Township, Deerfield, Frank Walker will fix up the old brick schoolhouse for a store
2/25/1914	Journal	Schools	Ward Township, Democratic primary contest for trustee was "based largely on the school problem"; winner (Evans) was a teacher at Jefferson
9/13/1893	Journal	Schools	Ward Township, No. 10, built at a cost of $500
3/18/1896	Herald	Schools	Ward Township, No. 3, burned last Thursday
2/7/1917	Journal	Schools	Ward Township, No. 6 to be sold on February 24, 1917
6/14/1916	Herald	Schools	Ward Township, Ralph Johnson, principal, will be superintendent
11/24/1875	Journal	Schools	Ward Township, Saratoga, plans for new schoolhouse
7/1/1896	Herald	Schools	Ward Township, St. Jink, schoolhouse rebuilt by Sol Brown and Newton Towell; it is ready for plaster

Date	Source	Category	Description
6/14/1876	Journal	Schools	Ward Township, two new brick schoolhouses will be build this summer, one at Saratoga and one north
9/13/1955	Journal-Herald	Schools	Ward, action to halt merger amended
7/11/1962	News	Schools	Ward, high school and junior high pupils will be sent to Driver; Ridgeville unchanged
11/29/1957	News	Schools	Ward, Jackson trustees vote to consolidate with Franklin as Tri School Corporation
6/13/1957	Journal-Herald	Schools	Ward, Jackson vote for merger
9/10/1955	Journal-Herald	Schools	Ward, mascot is "comets"; colors are red and white
4/2/1957	Journal-Herald	Schools	Ward, Pike Township, Jay County will transfer students from Ward to Jay County
8/12/1955	News	Schools	Ward, school decision is up to Judge Macy
6/8/1957	Journal-Herald	Schools	Ward-Jackson consolidation election will be June 12
2/18/1926	Democrat	Schools	Warren, Russell is new county superintendent of schools
9/13/1905	Journal	Schools	Washington and West River Township teachers listed
2/19/1890	Journal	Schools	Washington Township has fourteen districts
4/19/1871	Journal	Schools	Washington Township has sixteen schools
12/12/1888	Journal	Schools	Washington Township teachers listed
2/19/1890	Journal	Schools	Washington Township teachers listed
8/30/1899	Journal	Schools	Washington Township teachers listed
2/29/1888	Journal	Schools	Washington Township, Beech Grove School is also known as Lesley's School
12/28/1956	News	Schools	Washington Township, Beech Grove, photo
12/10/1954	News	Schools	Washington Township, Beech Grove, photo of frame schoolhouse
7/21/1915	Journal	Schools	Washington Township, Bloomingport, all bids for school rejected
6/30/1915	Journal	Schools	Washington Township, Bloomingport, bids for remodeling on July 15, 1915
4/4/1917	Journal	Schools	Washington Township, Bloomingport, schoolhouse condemned; probably means a new schoolhouse will be built
11/16/1892	Journal	Schools	Washington Township, Cherry Grove, Daniel Lawrence is teaching school at Cherry Grove for the advanced pupils of Osborn School

Date	Source	Category	Description
1/4/1882	Journal	Schools	Washington Township, Cherry Grove, Judge Monks did not sustain the action of Joel Mills, but found that the district had been abolished
12/28/1881	Journal	Schools	Washington Township, Cherry Grove, Judge Monks sustained the decision of Joel Mills, trustee of Washington Township, in suspending the school at Cherry Grove
5/21/1873	Journal	Schools	Washington Township, Hinshaw Schoolhouse is near Snow Hill
2/20/1878	Journal	Schools	Washington Township, Hinshaw Schoolhouse, A. R. Abshire closed a very successful school
5/24/1871	Journal	Schools	Washington Township, Hinshaw's School, flourishing Sabbath School organized, south of this city
11/28/1888	Journal	Schools	Washington Township, Hunt's Schoolhouse, No. 3, Washington Township
4/18/1888	Journal	Schools	Washington Township, J. F. Hunt Schoolhouse is near Martindale
9/6/1911	Journal	Schools	Washington Township, No. 1, bids will be received on September 23, 1911 for a new building
12/15/1880	Journal	Schools	Washington Township, No. 1, Fudge School house burned on Wednesday due to a defective flue
9/26/1912	Democrat	Schools	Washington Township, No. 1, suit to save school, which was recently repaired at a cost of $1050
10/11/1911	Journal	Schools	Washington Township, No. 1, work has begun on new building
4/2/1890	Journal	Schools	Washington Township, No. 10 is known as Johnson School
2/19/1890	Journal	Schools	Washington Township, No. 11, W. E. Hinshaw, teacher
6/19/1863	Journal	Schools	Washington Township, No. 2, burned last week; frame house that cost $550
8/17/1865	Journal	Schools	Washington Township, No. 2, construction delayed due to illness of Mr. Morris
11/22/1893	Journal	Schools	Washington Township, No. 3, Otis Hinshaw, teacher
6/7/1905	Journal	Schools	Washington Township, No. 4 and No. 10 will be sold on June 17, 1905
6/21/1905	Herald	Schools	Washington Township, No. 4 sold to Samuel Clements for $285 and No. 10 sold to Elkanah Johnson for $111
6/21/1905	Journal	Schools	Washington Township, No. 4 sold to Samuel Clements; No. 10 sold to Elkanah Johnson
6/14/1905	Herald	Schools	Washington Township, No. 4, Vinegar Hill, and No. 10, Johnson's, will be sold on June 17, 1905
3/28/1888	Journal	Schools	Washington Township, No. 5 is Brumfield's Schoolhouse

Date	Source	Category	Description
3/20/1878	Journal	Schools	Washington Township, No. 8 is Jacob Bales Schoolhouse
4/20/1892	Journal	Schools	Washington Township, Ozbun, No. 11, W. E. Hinshaw closed his third term of school here
1/31/1912	Journal	Schools	Washington Township, petition for a school to replace Nos. 1, 2, 3, 5, and 6
7/10/1889	Journal	Schools	Washington Township, Ponfrey Schoolhouse near Bloomingport
10/23/1889	Journal	Schools	Washington Township, Ponfrey, Alonzo Bales is teacher
11/12/1913	Journal	Schools	Washington Township, Rockhill School sold
11/20/1913	Democrat	Schools	Washington Township, Rockhill School sold
12/31/1902	Journal	Schools	Washington Township, Rockhill School, Washington Twp. No. 3
11/14/1913	Herald	Schools	Washington Township, Rockhill, school sold to T. F. Moorman; originally purchased from J. F. Hunt in 1862 for $15
6/22/1881	Journal	Schools	Washington Township, Rural, foundation for new brick schoolhouse is being laid
6/29/1881	Journal	Schools	Washington Township, Rural, new brick schoolhouse is being erected to replace the one burned last winter
8/14/1912	Journal	Schools	Washington Township, Rural, new school will not be ready for school this fall [No. 1]
3/28/1912	Democrat	Schools	Washington Township, school contract awarded to Fred Huffman for $11,580
2/24/1886	Herald	Schools	Washington Township, Snow Hill, W. E. Hinshaw, teacher
6/17/1908	Journal	Schools	Washington Township, Swamp Valley abandoned
6/30/1952	News	Schools	Washington Township, Swamp Valley photo, closed in 1917
3/28/1906	Journal	Schools	Washington Township, Swamp Valley School, No. 9, exists
9/4/1970	News-Gazette	Schools	Washington Township, Swamp Valley still stands
2/19/1913	Journal	Schools	Washington Township, Swamp Valley, No. 9, school is being used
12/18/1907	Journal	Schools	Washington Township, W. T. Miller School mentioned [also known as Jackson School]
7/22/1963	News	Schools	Washington-Greensfork, Trustees resolve to merge schools; to be called "Lynn-Burg"
4/17/1954	Journal-Herald	Schools	Wayne Advisory Board asked to defend merger plans with Union City
7/29/1955	News	Schools	Wayne election is certified by canvassing board; consolidation failed
3/24/1955	Journal-Herald	Schools	Wayne is being polled on school merger: Union City or White River?

Date	Source	Category	Description
2/25/1937	Daily News	Schools	Wayne joined IHSAA in 1919; referred to as "Tigers"
5/5/1954	News	Schools	Wayne rejects consolidation with Union City, 152 to 404
1/9/1913	Democrat	Schools	Wayne School dedicated
1/8/1913	Journal	Schools	Wayne School dedicated last Friday
12/11/1912	Journal	Schools	Wayne School is not complete; district schools are being used
5/29/1958	Journal-Herald	Schools	Wayne School to be sold on June 14, 1958
5/26/1927	Journal-Herald	Schools	Wayne School to get addition
7/20/1955	News	Schools	Wayne School vote will go to Circuit Court; Wayne 102 yes-183 no; Wilson 262 yes-182 no; overall 364 yes-365 no
8/1/1906	Journal	Schools	Wayne Township is clear of indebtedness [White River Township described earlier]
9/7/1938	Journal-Herald	Schools	Wayne Township school reunions vote to consolidate
9/6/1899	Journal	Schools	Wayne Township teachers listed
9/4/1918	Journal	Schools	Wayne Township, "new school building"; probably Wilson
8/26/1857	Journal	Schools	Wayne Township, Balaka Schoolhouse at Salem
10/10/1894	Herald	Schools	Wayne Township, Chenoweth Schoolhouse, Z. T. Addington, teacher
7/24/1872	Journal	Schools	Wayne Township, Chenoweth's Schoolhouse east of Bartonia
4/29/1874	Journal	Schools	Wayne Township, Coats Schoolhouse located in Wayne Township, two miles east of White River No. 1
5/9/1952	News	Schools	Wayne Township, Coddington School north of Lisbon (Harvey Moist)
12/4/1889	Journal	Schools	Wayne Township, Compromise Schoolhouse finished
10/28/1914	Journal	Schools	Wayne Township, effort to build a new school in northern part
12/10/1919	Herald	Schools	Wayne Township, Harrisville School to be sold on December 26, 1919; leaves no district schools in Wayne Township
11/23/1887	Herald	Schools	Wayne Township, Harrisville, history of schools; new brick schoolhouse in spring of 1887, completed on September 1, 1887; cost $2,668; designed by Hampton Gettinger; had 52 foot tower
11/16/1887	Herald	Schools	Wayne Township, Harrisville, history of schools; No. 3 built 1839; about 1860 new frame 20 x 40; brick in 1875
3/22/1911	Journal	Schools	Wayne Township, Harrisville, Jericho, and one school near Union City oppose centralization

Date	Source	Topic	Description
5/20/1920	Democrat	Schools	Wayne Township, Harrisville, Stuart Pierce purchased the schoolhouse from John Watson, who had purchased it in December 1919; will be dismantled to build a house
1/24/1912	Journal	Schools	Wayne Township, Hayesville School No. 4 burned Monday of last week; pupils transferred to No. 3
2/21/1912	Herald	Schools	Wayne Township, Hayesville, patrons want a new school to replace the burned building
6/12/1912	Journal	Schools	Wayne Township, Hayesville, patrons want a new school; do not wish to attend consolidated school
4/26/1882	Journal	Schools	Wayne Township, Jericho, a new schoolhouse will be built this summer [was it?]
9/8/1927	Democrat	Schools	Wayne Township, Jericho, history; first school was taught by Miriam Hill in log house thirty rods west of old cemetery; new house was built opposite Roscoe Harris's land; it had two windows and one door; new schoolhouse was built east of present meetinghouse; Body Friends built schoolhouse on Frank Thornburg's land and called it West Jericho; the 1819 building was taken over by Anti-Slavery Friends; new schoolhouse was later built south of cemetery with public money; Conservative Friends built a schoolhouse near center of Levi Thornburg's farm; it was later moved to hill on north side of road west of Ora Robinsons
8/7/1889	Journal	Schools	Wayne Township, Jericho, plans to build a new schoolhouse one mile east of
7/7/1886	Herald	Schools	Wayne Township, No 8, historical sketch of schools taught forty years ago [No. 8]
9/1/1915	Journal	Schools	Wayne Township, No. 1 burned; thought to be arson
1/2/1895	Journal	Schools	Wayne Township, No. 1 dropped due to transfers
7/22/1909	Democrat	Schools	Wayne Township, No. 1 will be transferred to No. 10, which will be enlarged
1/2/1919	Democrat	Schools	Wayne Township, No. 10 "good brick" sold to W. H. Sipe for $436; No. 4 sold to Preston Woodbury for $409; No. 2 sold to Stephen Clevenger for $300; leaves only Harrisville as the only district school in township

Date	Source	Category	Description
1/8/1919	Journal	Schools	Wayne Township, No. 10 sold to W. H. Sipe for $436; No. 4 Hayesville sold to P. N. Woodbury for $409; No. 2 Coddington sold to Stephen Clevenger for $300; Harrisville is only one unsold; only Wayne and Wilson are used
9/9/1896	Journal	Schools	Wayne Township, No. 10, new schoolhouse being built
9/13/1917	Democrat	Schools	Wayne Township, No. 10, reunion; Theodore Shockney was first teacher 42 years ago
5/5/1886	Herald	Schools	Wayne Township, No. 2, new school planned; also at the district south of Harrisville
5/9/1890	Democrat	Schools	Wayne Township, No. 4 is known as Woodbury School
7/17/1912	Journal	Schools	Wayne Township, No. 4 rebuilt by Zack Woods for $1638.41. Ready by September 16; old one burned last winter.
6/20/1912	Democrat	Schools	Wayne Township, No. 4, bids let
2/8/1912	Democrat	Schools	Wayne Township, No. 4, new building; old building was destroyed by fire on January 15, 1912
1/17/1912	Herald	Schools	Wayne Township, No. 4, schoolhouse burned on Monday, January 15, 1912; students sent to Harrisville for the rest of the year
1/9/1918	Journal	Schools	Wayne Township, No. 8 and Bartonia to be sold on January 30
11/20/1866	Journal	Schools	Wayne Township, No. 8 moved north near railroad
11/22/1866	Journal	Schools	Wayne Township, No. 8, schoolhouse moved north to old railroad tracks
5/1/1918	Journal	Schools	Wayne Township, No. 8; J. K. Mote is tearing down one of the old landmarks of this vicinity, the No. 8 schoolhouse, which he purchased in January
3/6/1863	Journal	Schools	Wayne Township, Pleasant Hill Schoolhouse near Bartonia mentioned
9/9/1914	Journal	Schools	Wayne Township, school is delayed due to lack of wagons; only three schools left in the township
1/24/1867	Journal	Schools	Wayne Township, teachers
3/29/1911	Journal	Schools	Wayne Township, vigorous opposition to centralized school
5/8/1957	News	Schools	Wayne votes yes on Union City merger
12/24/1913	Herald	Schools	Wayne, "Elm Hill School" mentioned near Bartonia
5/1/1912	Journal	Schools	Wayne, bid awarded to G. W. Carson for $18,491; heating to American Heating and Ventilation for $3,142

Date	Source	Category	Description
8/23/1916	Journal	Schools	Wayne, bids for schoolhouse in Wayne Township
4/10/1912	Journal	Schools	Wayne, bids will be received on April 25, 1912
5/2/1912	Democrat	Schools	Wayne, contract let for new building
4/10/1912	Herald	Schools	Wayne, contract will be let for new building on April 25, 1912
10/8/1951	News	Schools	Wayne, county baseball champions
10/21/1952	Journal-Herald	Schools	Wayne, county baseball champions
10/6/1952	News	Schools	Wayne, county baseball champions for second consecutive year
8/17/1956	News	Schools	Wayne, election for consolidation with White River as Randolph Central is September 18
7/26/1955	Journal-Herald	Schools	Wayne, Judge Macy rules on school consolidation
1/1/1913	Journal	Schools	Wayne, new school has an enrollment of 110 with 19 in the high school
4/11/1912	Democrat	Schools	Wayne, new township school is planned
8/3/1955	News	Schools	Wayne, recount sought in school election
8/14/1956	Journal-Herald	Schools	Wayne, remonstrance is filed; will vote on consolidation
11/30/1972	News-Gazette	Schools	Wayne, school is being razed
12/18/1912	Journal	Schools	Wayne, school started Monday at Wayne for the first time
10/17/1936	Daily News	Schools	Wayne, Tigers are handicapped since they have no gym; Big 18 Conference is mentioned
2/20/1957	News	Schools	Wayne, trustee will act first on petition for consolidation with Union City
9/19/1956	News	Schools	Wayne, turns down merger with White River by 42 votes; Wayne 180 yes-108 no; Wilson 153 yes-267 no
2/7/1957	Journal-Herald	Schools	Wayne, upper six grades will be closed at end of school year
4/9/1947	Journal-Herald	Schools	Wayne-Jackson consolidation proposed
1/23/1950	News	Schools	Wayne-Jackson-Union City consolidation discussed
3/26/1954	News	Schools	Wayne-Union City consolidation "hinged" in Wayne Primary
3/8/1950	News	Schools	Wayne-Union City consolidation discussed
1/19/1953	News	Schools	Wayne-Union City consolidation discussed
2/11/1953	News	Schools	Wayne-Union City consolidation discussed
1/29/1954	News	Schools	Wayne-Union City consolidation discussed
2/20/1954	Journal-Herald	Schools	Wayne-Union City consolidation discussed
2/25/1954	Journal-Herald	Schools	Wayne-Union City consolidation discussed

Date	Source	Category	Description
7/9/1955	Journal-Herald	Schools	Wayne-Union City consolidation resolution
5/9/1956	News	Schools	Wayne-Union City merger defeated by two votes; Wayne 378 yes-380 no; Union City 991 yes-112 no
7/22/1955	News	Schools	Wayne-Union City merger petition is filed in Circuit Court
3/21/1957	Journal-Herald	Schools	Wayne-Union City merger, petition calls for vote on
3/19/1957	Journal-Herald	Schools	Wayne-Union City merger, petition for
5/4/1957	Journal-Herald	Schools	Wayne-Union City merger, Wayne will vote Tuesday
3/5/1954	News	Schools	Wayne-Union City school boards set up consolidation resolution; to be called "Union City-Wayne School Corporation"
3/27/1957	News	Schools	Wayne-Union City school vote is May 7
11/8/1950	News	Schools	Wayne-White River consolidation blocked; Wayne 177-369; White River 410-442
9/6/1950	News	Schools	Wayne-White River consolidation sought
7/9/1946	Journal-Herald	Schools	West River and Nettle Creek consolidation plans
1/5/1950	Journal-Herald	Schools	West River and Nettle Creek consolidation plans for coming election
8/23/1899	Journal	Schools	West River Township teachers listed
9/4/1895	Journal	Schools	West River Township teachers listed: 1, 2, 3, 4, Huntsville, 8, Modoc, 10, 11, Carlos
11/19/1913	Journal	Schools	West River Township, Ashland No. 4 [sic] old to Rollie Harper and A. O. Haynes; No. 1 sold to Seward Gordon
11/27/1913	Democrat	Schools	West River Township, Ashland School sold to A. O. Haynes for $56; Rollie Harper purchased land for $97.50; Seward Gordon purchased No. 4 for $163
10/22/1913	Journal	Schools	West River Township, Ashland, No. 4 and No. 1 will be sold on November 13, 1913
11/28/1913	Herald	Schools	West River Township, Ashland, sold to A. O. Haynes for $56; land purchased by Rollie Harper for $97.50; Seward Gordon purchased building and ground of No. 4 for $163 [may be some problems with this]
3/29/1893	Journal	Schools	West River Township, Botkin School, West River Twp. No. 1 known as
10/9/1872	Journal	Schools	West River Township, Cabin Creek or Oren Schoolhouse exists

Date	Source	Category	Description
3/7/1888	Journal	Schools	West River Township, Clarence Johnson's Schoolhouse is near Martindale
1/1/1913	Journal	Schools	West River Township, College Corner and No. 10 schools sold on Friday
4/4/1894	Journal	Schools	West River Township, College Corner, West River No. 18
3/6/1878	Journal	Schools	West River Township, Hardscrabble School, West River No. 7
10/3/1888	Journal	Schools	West River Township, Harris Schoolhouse near Martindale
9/3/1890	Journal	Schools	West River Township, Harris Schoolhouse, Lewis Coffin will teach
8/11/1875	Journal	Schools	West River Township, Hugh M. Hunt's Schoolhouse, south of Unionport
11/30/1870	Journal	Schools	West River Township, list of teachers
9/5/1894	Journal	Schools	West River Township, no schools in districts 5, 6 and 9 [they were consolidated at Huntsville]
9/5/1894	Journal	Schools	West River Township, No. 1, Gertrude Farquhar, teacher; No. 2, L. J. Coffin; No. 3, Orpha Botkin; No. 4, Mary Gwin; No. 7 Blanche Carter; No. 8, Smith Lee; No. 11, John Hardwick, Angie Norman; Huntsville, Georgia Ladd, N. Kabel, Jared McGunnegill
10/22/1890	Herald	Schools	West River Township, No. 1, Shears' Schoolhouse [probably not correct]
3/15/1871	Journal	Schools	West River Township, No. 11, new building built by Osborn and Beard of Economy for $675
11/30/1870	Journal	Schools	West River Township, No. 2 is Buena Vista, No. 5 is Huntsville, No. 7 is Hardscrabble, and No. 8 is College Corner. There are twelve schools in the township.
7/17/1912	Journal	Schools	West River Township, No. 3 repaired
5/14/1919	Journal	Schools	West River Township, No. 3 to be sold on May 31; property was purchased on August 31, 1860 from Thomas and Rebecca Cox by Elisha P. Gaddis, trustee
12/25/1895	Herald	Schools	West River Township, No. 3, Ashland
7/24/1912	Journal	Schools	West River Township, No. 3, bids for repair
7/18/1912	Democrat	Schools	West River Township, No. 3, Section 17, bids for repair
5/26/1915	Journal	Schools	West River Township, No. 3., notice of sale of school land: nw 1/4 Section 17-18-13 on June 2, 1915

Date	Source	Category	Description
12/18/1912	Journal	Schools	West River Township, No. 5, frame building at Huntsville; No. 8, College Corner; and No. 10 to be sold on December 27, 1912
2/28/1877	Journal	Schools	West River Township, No. 7 damaged by fire on February 13 but saved
9/7/1870	Journal	Schools	West River Township, No. 8 known as College Corner
3/1/1876	Journal	Schools	West River Township, Oren's Schoolhouse in West River Township
8/21/1872	Journal	Schools	West River Township, Oren's Schoolhouse in West River Township
7/25/1942	Journal-Herald	Schools	West River Township, Pleasant Ridge school reunion
7/28/1942	Journal-Herald	Schools	West River Township, Pleasant Ridge school stands on Lee Gaddis farm
5/17/1871	Journal	Schools	West River Township, Pleasant Ridge Schoolhouse is 1.5 miles north of Huntsville
4/4/1894	Journal	Schools	West River Township, Pleasant Ridge, Wilson Hardwick, teacher
8/9/1922	Journal-Herald	Schools	West River Township, Section 10, T 18, R 13 to be sold on August 19
11/10/1859	Journal	Schools	West River Township, several schoolhouses built within the last year or two; there are eight or ten districts
9/8/1909	Journal	Schools	West River Township, Shears Schoolhouse, north of Huntsville
11/22/1866	Journal	Schools	West River Township, teachers listed
1/1/1913	Journal	Schools	West River Twp., C. R. Farquhar purchased College Corner School for $247; Bales Pugh purchased No. 10 for $96 last Friday
7/22/1938	Journal-Herald	Schools	White River "To White River Taxpayers" in support of new school
5/7/1958	News	Schools	White River again rejects merger with Winchester, 746-332
6/5/1958	Journal-Herald	Schools	White River and Lynn High Schools are granted first class commissions; Union City and Winchester already had them
8/17/1959	News	Schools	White River Elementary School [McKinley did not exist]
5/28/1970	News-Gazette	Schools	White River Elementary School, Glen Myers retires as principal
8/12/1970	News-Gazette	Schools	White River Elementary School, Ralph Fowler starts as principal
8/13/1976	News-Gazette	Schools	White River Elementary School, Ralph Fowler was principal from 1970-72
3/30/1983	News-Gazette	Schools	White River Elementary School, third grade students will return to Baker for 1983-84

Date	Source	Topic	Description
6/2/1956	Journal-Herald	Schools	White River School construction bids are acceptable until June 19
10/26/1955	News	Schools	White River School land case is venued to court at Richmond
6/14/1955	Journal-Herald	Schools	White River seeks appropriation of fifty acres near McKinley
1/16/1956	News	Schools	White River to build 14-room school
9/19/1894	Journal	Schools	White River Township has 22 schools
9/10/1908	Democrat	Schools	White River Township has schools 1 through 22 except 13, 16, and 19
6/27/1917	Journal	Schools	White River Township is investigating auto hack service
6/12/1918	Journal	Schools	White River Township Schools sold on Saturday: Sugar Creek brick schoolhouse to Asahel Martin for $50; Unionport sold for $105 to Herman McNees; petition for sale of Fidler; leaving only two schoolhouses
11/29/1866	Journal	Schools	White River Township schools: Clark's, Hagerman's, Irvin's, Coats, Butterworth, Pugh
9/12/1906	Journal	Schools	White River Township tax levy listed
8/28/1895	Journal	Schools	White River Township teachers listed
9/21/1881	Journal	Schools	White River Township teachers listed
9/23/1896	Journal	Schools	White River Township teachers listed
9/27/1893	Journal	Schools	White River Township teachers listed
9/30/1891	Journal	Schools	White River Township teachers listed
9/6/1899	Journal	Schools	White River Township teachers listed
9/17/1919	Journal	Schools	White River Township, Abbott Schoolhouse on Bosworth Pike sold to threshing ring for $302
6/19/1895	Journal	Schools	White River Township, Abbott, new schoolhouse will be built
11/5/1919	Journal	Schools	White River Township, Abbott, notice of sale of school property on November 22, 1919
8/29/1917	Journal	Schools	White River Township, auto hacks described
5/8/1863	Journal	Schools	White River Township, brick schoolhouse on Bear Creek Road, 2-3 miles west of Winchester
11/13/1863	Journal	Schools	White River Township, brick schoolhouse three miles west of Winchester
8/30/1905	Herald	Schools	White River Township, Brittie Pottle will teach at No. 22 [Orphans' Home]; Numbers 13 and 19 are closed

Date	Source	Topic	Description
1/12/1887	Journal	Schools	White River Township, Burnworth Schoolhouse is four miles east of Robert Sommerville's and south of Ward Howell's
1/2/1895	Journal	Schools	White River Township, Cerro Gordo, Mrs. Sam Newfarmer teaches at school 1.5 miles north of here [White River No. 22]
10/4/1922	Journal-Herald	Schools	White River Township, Dull School, White River No. 8, reunion
5/23/1877	Journal	Schools	White River Township, Edward Wright Schoolhouse mentioned
2/5/1873	Journal	Schools	White River Township, Fidler School is also known as Pleasant Grove
9/23/1914	Journal	Schools	White River Township, Fidler School will open Monday
12/16/1952	Journal-Herald	Schools	White River Township, Fidler Schoolhouse burned
3/27/1924	Democrat	Schools	White River Township, frame schoolhouses sold; No. 4 for $209 to H. E. McNees; was deeded to township in 1859 by Nathaniel Heaston; lot was expanded in 1883; No. 1 was sold to William H. Coddington for $230.50; called "Lost School" because it was surrounded a thick woods; No. 1 School will be converted into a dwelling
6/22/1898	Journal	Schools	White River Township, Green School, new schoolhouse will be built in Green District, west of Winchester; bids will be received on June 29
4/8/1903	Journal	Schools	White River Township, Green School, White River No. 15
6/28/1917	Democrat	Schools	White River Township, hacks, White River Township will buy motorized hacks
4/16/1873	Journal	Schools	White River Township, Halderman's Schoolhouse is No. 2 in White River
9/5/1900	Herald	Schools	White River Township, has 22 schools
6/5/1895	Journal	Schools	White River Township, Hawkins Schoolhouse is south of Maxville
1/11/1911	Journal	Schools	White River Township, Hiatt Schoolhouse, west of town
9/14/1881	Journal	Schools	White River Township, Hull Schoolhouse is 1.5 miles from Winchester on Lynn Pike
10/26/1904	Herald	Schools	White River Township, Hull, north of County Infirmary and Willis, No. 22, to be sold on November 12, 1904 at auction
1/21/1880	Journal	Schools	White River Township, Hull's Schoolhouse existed
10/1/1879	Journal	Schools	White River Township, Hull's Schoolhouse exists

Date	Source	Topic	Description
11/26/1879	Journal	Schools	White River Township, Hull's Schoolhouse exists
12/17/1902	Journal	Schools	White River Township, Kabel, old schoolhouse one mile north of Unionport
4/10/1924	Democrat	Schools	White River Township, last of the district schoolhouses sold; Lickskillet School was sold for $257.50 to Hugh Miller; all White River Township district schoolhouses have been sold except No. 7 (Moorman), which became the residence for Lincoln School's janitor when B. E. Hinshaw was trustee
6/12/1863	Journal	Schools	White River Township, letting of contracts for buildings in Districts 4, 5, and 10
9/4/1912	Journal	Schools	White River Township, Lickskillet School repaired
3/6/1924	Journal-Herald	Schools	White River Township, Lickskillet School sold on April 3, 1924
8/7/1912	Herald	Schools	White River Township, Lickskillet will keep school
11/3/1897	Journal	Schools	White River Township, Lickskillet, 54 pupils enrolled due to new truancy law
8/14/1912	Journal	Schools	White River Township, Lickskillet, bids for repair to be received on August 31, 1912
8/28/1912	Journal	Schools	White River Township, Lickskillet, bids on Saturday for repair
8/14/1912	Herald	Schools	White River Township, Lickskillet, building will be repaired
8/7/1912	Journal	Schools	White River Township, Lickskillet, Judge Engle orders school kept open
7/17/1912	Herald	Schools	White River Township, Lickskillet, lawsuit
7/3/1912	Herald	Schools	White River Township, Lickskillet, lawsuit over School No. 5; school has existed for 50 years; had 51 pupils
7/23/1919	Herald	Schools	White River Township, Lickskillet, No. 5, to be abandoned and sold, leaving only one district school in township
7/31/1912	Herald	Schools	White River Township, Lickskillet, order to replace or remodel school
4/10/1895	Herald	Schools	White River Township, Lickskillet, P. M. Lavin, teacher
7/17/1912	Journal	Schools	White River Township, Lickskillet, school case in taken under advisement
6/19/1912	Herald	Schools	White River Township, Lickskillet, School No. 5 condemned
12/11/1912	Journal	Schools	White River Township, Lickskillet, school opened with 40 scholars

Date	Source	Topic	Description
12/4/1912	Journal	Schools	White River Township, Lickskillet, school started Monday in the remodeled building
7/3/1912	Journal	Schools	White River Township, Lickskillet, suit to erect new school and petition to build a joint school for Districts 4 and 5, Abbott and Fiddler [sic, it should be Districts 3 and 4]
7/25/1972	News-Gazette	Schools	White River Township, log schoolhouse stands three miles south of Maxville on farm of Alva C. Miller
7/16/1913	Journal	Schools	White River Township, Lost School, bids for moving
7/23/1913	Journal	Schools	White River Township, Lost School, Stanley and Stanley get contract to move for $1673 + 112.50
6/10/1941	Journal-Herald	Schools	White River Township, Maxville No. 6 School photo; school stands one mile southeast of Maxville and is the residence of Arthur Howell
4/4/1883	Journal	Schools	White River Township, Maxville, J. W. Denney, teacher
6/8/1887	Herald	Schools	White River Township, Maxville, new school to be built
9/14/1887	Herald	Schools	White River Township, Maxville, schoolhouse remodeled; new roof on Hull Schoolhouse; new roof on Unionport Schoolhouse
2/16/1865	Journal	Schools	White River Township, Mt. Zion School is 4.5 miles southeast of Winchester
3/9/1865	Journal	Schools	White River Township, Mt. Zion School mentioned
2/9/1887	Journal	Schools	White River Township, Mull School, F. F. Canada, teacher
11/29/1882	Journal	Schools	White River Township, Mull, Ephraim Shaver, teacher; 16 pupils enrolled
2/13/1919	Democrat	Schools	White River Township, Mull, Harold Butts is school teacher
12/25/1907	Journal	Schools	White River Township, Mull, John Miller is building an addition to School No. 5; protection for the well
5/26/1880	Journal	Schools	White River Township, Mull, Joseph Bright was teacher last year
9/19/1894	Herald	Schools	White River Township, No. 1 and No. 14; new buildings
9/19/1894	Herald	Schools	White River Township, No. 1 is not completed; No. 14 is new school
11/5/1863	Journal	Schools	White River Township, No. 1 known as "Lost School"
3/5/1914	Democrat	Schools	White River Township, No. 1, Bernard Benson starts as teacher
10/6/1886	Journal	Schools	White River Township, No. 1, Democrats elect director, James Evans
4/6/1916	Democrat	Schools	White River Township, No. 1, is known as Mader School

Date	Source	Topic	Description
6/4/1913	Journal	Schools	White River Township, No. 1, Lost School, to be moved across the road; petition to move was granted by Lee L. Driver
11/6/1863	Journal	Schools	White River Township, No. 1, Lost Schoolhouse, close of school
8/24/1916	Democrat	Schools	White River Township, No. 1, patrons desire school abandoned
6/26/1913	Democrat	Schools	White River Township, No. 1, petition for appropriation of real estate from Christian Mader
9/18/1913	Democrat	Schools	White River Township, No. 1, school is being repaired
6/25/1913	Journal	Schools	White River Township, No. 1, suit against Mader Heirs to obtain school land
7/23/1919	Journal	Schools	White River Township, No. 1, trustee petitions to abandon school, leaving only Fidler in township
10/22/1913	Journal	Schools	White River Township, No. 1, will begin Monday; it was moved
8/14/1912	Journal	Schools	White River Township, No. 12 sold last Thursday for $125; will be used on the Gray Farm
12/8/1897	Journal	Schools	White River Township, No. 13 is brick schoolhouse on Union City Pike
7/18/1877	Journal	Schools	White River Township, No. 13, bids for frame schoolhouse to be received on August 1, 1877
7/31/1907	Journal	Schools	White River Township, No. 13, brick schoolhouse to be sold at auction on August 31 at 10 o'clock
7/31/1907	Herald	Schools	White River Township, No. 13, brick schoolhouse to be sold on August 31, 1907
2/27/1889	Journal	Schools	White River Township, No. 14 exists
9/7/1910	Journal	Schools	White River Township, No. 14 students sent to Lincoln
2/9/1916	Journal	Schools	White River Township, No. 14, better known as the Orphan's Home School; will sell reasonable [sic]
7/11/1894	Journal	Schools	White River Township, No. 14, new schoolhouse on Windsor Pike, one mile west of city is being built by Luther Shetterly
7/13/1898	Journal	Schools	White River Township, No. 15, foundation for new schoolhouse
7/24/1912	Herald	Schools	White River Township, No. 15, Green, sold for $150 to Poplar Run Monthly Meeting; No. 14, Orphan's Home, sold to Mrs. Peter Wasson for $590; No. 11, Round Top, sold building to Frank Thomas and ground to Earl Hinshaw for $175; and No. 10, White River, to Charles Hiatt for $75.

Date	Source	Category	Description
8/1/1912	Democrat	Schools	White River Township, No. 15, Green, sold to Poplar Run Monthly Meeting of Friends for $150; No. 14, Orphan's Home, sold to Mrs. Peter Wasson for $590; No. 11, Round Top, sold to Frank Thomas and Earl Hinshaw for $175; No. 10, White River, sold to Charles Hiatt for $75
5/8/1964	News	Schools	White River Township, No. 16 is still standing north of Unionport
9/28/1881	Journal	Schools	White River Township, No. 16, Jim Watson resigned as teacher; Jim Goodrich replaced him
5/28/1879	Journal	Schools	White River Township, No. 16, Kabel Schoolhouse will be sold on May 31, 1879
5/21/1879	Journal	Schools	White River Township, No. 16, new schoolhouse will be erected
12/24/1879	Journal	Schools	White River Township, No. 16, schoolhouse near Philip Kabel's is now used for a dwelling by Mr. Hurst
9/6/1899	Herald	Schools	White River Township, No. 17
2/11/1914	Journal	Schools	White River Township, No. 17 will be sold on February 19, 1914
8/12/1914	Journal	Schools	White River Township, No. 17, B. F. Willis moved the schoolhouse to his farm and made it into a house
4/6/1904	Journal	Schools	White River Township, No. 18 is Wright School
8/25/1861	Journal	Schools	White River Township, No. 19, new schoolhouse to be built by M. A. Reeder for $420; C. A. Avery will built new schoolhouse on North Main Street for $1264
9/26/1912	Democrat	Schools	White River Township, No. 2, Huffman School, suit to restore school
5/27/1914	Journal	Schools	White River Township, No. 2, notice of sale of school property; sw quarter of Section 3; will be sold on June 12, 1914
9/27/1965	News	Schools	White River Township, No. 2, photo printed, belonged to Mrs. Fred Speed
3/26/1919	Herald	Schools	White River Township, No. 20, frame schoolhouse to be sold on April 12, 1919
3/2/1892	Journal	Schools	White River Township, No. 21 built last year
3/10/1920	Journal	Schools	White River Township, No. 21 sold to Dock Thornburg for $505; he already owned the ground
2/11/1920	Journal	Schools	White River Township, No. 21, notice of sale of school property on March 6, 1920
10/8/1890	Journal	Schools	White River Township, No. 22 exists
4/19/1980	News-Gazette	Schools	White River Township, No. 22, photo

Date	Source	Category	Description
7/23/1919	Journal	Schools	White River Township, No. 3, notice of sale of school property on August 9, 1919 due to petition
8/27/1919	Journal	Schools	White River Township, No. 3, notice of sale of school property on September 13, 1919
3/19/1902	Journal	Schools	White River Township, No. 4 is known as Fiddler School
3/19/1873	Journal	Schools	White River Township, No. 4 known as Pleasant Grove
6/29/1914	Journal	Schools	White River Township, No. 4, Fiddler, notice of erection of schoolhouse
6/10/1914	Journal	Schools	White River Township, No. 4, Fiddler, notice of letting for repair on July 1, 1914
7/1/1914	Journal	Schools	White River Township, No. 4, Fidler, bid to build a new schoolhouse is awarded to James Stanley for $2133
6/25/1914	Democrat	Schools	White River Township, No. 4, notice of letting for rebuilding
8/29/1918	Democrat	Schools	White River Township, No. 4, school will be kept open
3/11/1896	Journal	Schools	White River Township, No. 4, W. S. Freeman, director
8/7/1918	Herald	Schools	White River Township, No. 4, Willard Harman sues to keep school open; last in township [Lickskillet was also still open]
7/24/1919	Democrat	Schools	White River Township, No. 5 closed due to small attendance; No. 1 closed by petition; leaves only No. 4 in township
6/20/1912	Democrat	Schools	White River Township, No. 5, Lickskillet, condemned
8/1/1912	Democrat	Schools	White River Township, No. 5, Lickskillet, judge orders new or remodeled school
7/4/1912	Democrat	Schools	White River Township, No. 5, Lickskillet, new school building desired
8/8/1912	Democrat	Schools	White River Township, No. 5, Lickskillet, patrons win in school fight to keep school open
7/11/1912	Democrat	Schools	White River Township, No. 5, Lickskillet, school troubles continue
9/19/1912	Democrat	Schools	White River Township, No. 5, opening delayed due to remodeling
12/3/1919	Journal	Schools	White River Township, No. 6 [sic], Abbott, was sold to Grant Wolford for $330 on Saturday
10/29/1919	Journal	Schools	White River Township, No. 6, Sec. 8, T 20, R 14, 2 miles northwest of Winchester, to be sold on November 22
3/23/1904	Journal	Schools	White River Township, No. 7 is Moorman School
12/7/1881	Journal	Schools	White River Township, No. 7, J. H. Williams replaces John Commons as teacher

Date	Source	Topic	Description
3/19/1902	Journal	Schools	White River Township, No. 8 is known as Williams School
9/6/1923	Journal-Herald	Schools	White River Township, No. 8 reunion, opened in 1881 with A. E. Ludy as teacher
8/30/1923	Democrat	Schools	White River Township, No. 8 was known as Dull School
4/29/1914	Journal	Schools	White River Township, No. 8, bids for sale on May 6, 1914
5/13/1914	Journal	Schools	White River Township, No. 8, sale to be delayed
4/30/1879	Journal	Schools	White River Township, No. 9 existed
9/25/1912	Herald	Schools	White River Township, No.2, Huffman; suit to reopen; existed 40 years and had 26 pupils
7/24/1912	Journal	Schools	White River Township, Nos. 10, 11, 14, and 15 sold on July 18, 1912; No. 12 to be sold on August 8, 1912
4/19/1911	Journal	Schools	White River Township, Nos. 10, 11, and 12; West River Township, Nos. 5 and 11; Jackson Township, No. 9 are condemned by the State Board of Health; six of the fifteen condemned were in Randolph County
9/2/1903	Herald	Schools	White River Township, Numbers 13, 16, 19, and 22 are closed; a new school is opened in the Orphans' Home; Lickskillet School is down to one room
8/27/1902	Herald	Schools	White River Township, Numbers 13, 19, and 22 are closed this year
3/10/1909	Journal	Schools	White River Township, petition filed to abandon four schools in eastern part
2/14/1912	Herald	Schools	White River Township, petition for new school at intersection of White River, Washington, and West River Townships
7/3/1912	Herald	Schools	White River Township, petition for school house 1.5 miles from No. 5
3/15/1911	Journal	Schools	White River Township, petition to abandon Schools 10, 11, and 12
10/26/1892	Journal	Schools	White River Township, Reynard School, No. 17 was damaged by fire last Sunday night
4/27/1881	Journal	Schools	White River Township, Reynard Schoolhouse exists
9/28/1870	Journal	Schools	White River Township, Round Top and Coddington's schools mentioned
10/26/1892	Herald	Schools	White River Township, Rynard Schoolhouse in southwest part of township damaged by fire on October 23, 1892
9/7/1870	Journal	Schools	White River Township, school enumeration; Districts 12 and 14 discontinued; 13 merged into Winchester

Date	Source	Category	Description
9/12/1917	Journal	Schools	White River Township, school hacks
8/28/1902	Democrat	Schools	White River Township, schools at Numbers 13, 19, and 22 are closed due to decreased attendance
9/9/1909	Democrat	Schools	White River Township, schools exist at Numbers 1, 2, 3, 4, 5, 8, 9, 10, 11, 12, 17, 18, 20, 21, 22
8/28/1907	Herald	Schools	White River Township, schools listed by name
3/28/1906	Journal	Schools	White River Township, Sparrow Creek School No 17 [White River] exists
3/25/1903	Journal	Schools	White River Township, Sugar Creek School, White River No. 18
3/10/1859	Journal	Schools	White River Township, Sugar Creek, "brick schoolhouse near Edward Wright's"
7/17/1918	Journal	Schools	White River Township, Sugar Creek, schoolhouse is being demolished
9/23/1914	Journal	Schools	White River Township, Sugar Creek, with nine students, is the smallest in the county
3/15/1871	Journal	Schools	White River Township, T. W. Kizer built 17 schoolhouses as township trustee
9/3/1903	Democrat	Schools	White River Township, teacher will be provided at Orphans Home; Numbers 13, 16, 19, and 22 are closed due to small attendance
10/5/1892	Journal	Schools	White River Township, teachers listed
9/8/1897	Herald	Schools	White River Township, teachers listed, 22 district schools
7/4/1917	Journal	Schools	White River Township, Trustee B. E. Hinshaw purchased two Studebaker auto hacks
9/24/1890	Journal	Schools	White River Township, Unionport School is No. 9
6/12/1918	Herald	Schools	White River Township, Unionport School sold for $105 to Herman McNees; Sugar Creek sold for $50 to Asahel Martin; petition to abandon Fidler; would leave only two district school buildings
6/20/1918	Democrat	Schools	White River Township, Unionport School sold for $105 to Herman McNees; Sugar Creek sold for $50 to Asahel Martin; petition to abandon No. 4
7/12/1876	Journal	Schools	White River Township, Unionport, contract for new school to Ira and Joseph Hiatt for $449.50; 25 x 35
8/9/1893	Journal	Schools	White River Township, Unionport, lumber sawed for new schoolhouse
7/12/1876	Journal	Schools	White River Township, Unionport, new schoolhouse to be built; 25 x 35, for $449.50 by Ira and Joseph Hiatt

Date	Source	Category	Description
9/6/1893	Journal	Schools	White River Township, Unionport, plasterers at work on new schoolhouse
5/15/1918	Journal	Schools	White River Township, Unionport, Section 5-19-13, and No. 18, brick Sugar Creek Schoolhouse, will be sold on June 5, 1918
12/31/1902	Journal	Schools	White River Township, Wright School, White River Twp. No 18
3/7/1957	Journal-Herald	Schools	White River will vote on merger
2/25/1957	News	Schools	White River, 4000 attend open house; school cost $300,000
10/29/1935	News-Democrat	Schools	White River, 600 signatures on petition against new consolidated high school
10/29/1935	Journal-Herald	Schools	White River, 90% of taxpayers petition against new school
10/11/1935	Journal-Herald	Schools	White River, advisory board authorizes bond issue for new White River School
10/26/1961	Journal-Herald	Schools	White River, bids for addition including gym, music room, administration offices, cafeteria, etc, connecting the two buildings
5/8/1956	Journal-Herald	Schools	White River, building of new school is termed "regrettable" by state officials
6/23/1956	Journal-Herald	Schools	White River, contracts let for new school, $251,913; 12 rooms
11/25/1958	Journal-Herald	Schools	White River, court order halts vote on reorganization as a metropolitan school district
11/15/1935	Journal-Herald	Schools	White River, hearing for new school to be held Monday
3/8/1958	Journal-Herald	Schools	White River, holding company to complete school; second wing ready by September at a cost of $250,000; third wing ready by fall of 1959 at a cost of $500,000
5/13/1908	Herald	Schools	White River, Lincoln, new four-room school is planned for western White River Township
5/27/1908	Herald	Schools	White River, Lincoln, new school five miles west of town to cost $12,000; Gettinger and Mangas have contract
10/8/1935	Journal-Herald	Schools	White River, new school planned
11/22/1935	Journal-Herald	Schools	White River, petition for new school is denied
4/2/1959	Journal-Herald	Schools	White River, petition seeks metropolitan school district in township
6/6/1938	Journal-Herald	Schools	White River, petition seeks new school west of Winchester
2/21/1912	Herald	Schools	White River, petitions granted for four-room addition to school [Lincoln]

422

Date	Source	Category	Description
11/1/1935	News-Democrat	Schools	White River, plans for a new school are Okd
10/14/1958	Journal-Herald	Schools	White River, plans for third unit
2/22/1957	News	Schools	White River, public is invited to open house for new school on February 24
7/6/1938	Journal-Herald	Schools	White River, remonstrance against new school
7/2/1938	Journal-Herald	Schools	White River, school bond issue will be contested
12/12/1958	News	Schools	White River, State Tax Board clears way for third unit
7/16/1955	Journal-Herald	Schools	White River, suit over purchase of land near McKinley
3/29/1958	Journal-Herald	Schools	White River, table of votes on school consolidation
9/14/1898	Herald	Schools	White River, township has 22 schools
9/19/1938	Journal-Herald	Schools	White River, will not construct new building to replace Lincoln and McKinley
5/18/1955	News	Schools	White River-Wayne consolidation defeated; Wayne Precinct 165 yes-117 no; Wilson Precinct 189 yes-275 no; White River 379 yes-173 no
9/23/1950	Journal-Herald	Schools	White River-Wayne consolidation proposed
4/4/1955	News	Schools	White River-Wayne consolidation proposed; would be "Randolph Central School Corporation"; new school would be built near McKinley
4/11/1955	News	Schools	White River-Wayne consolidation resolution
4/2/1955	Journal-Herald	Schools	White River-Wayne merger discussed
7/31/1956	Journal-Herald	Schools	White River-Wayne merger planned; to be called "Randolph Central"
2/19/1957	Journal-Herald	Schools	White River-Wayne merger proposed again as Randolph Central School Corporation
5/14/1955	Journal-Herald	Schools	White River-Wayne school vote is May 14; to be called "Randolph Central School Corporation"
4/12/1955	Journal-Herald	Schools	White River-Wayne school vote is May 3
10/30/1954	Journal-Herald	Schools	White River-Winchester anti-consolidation committee organizes
11/20/1954	Journal-Herald	Schools	White River-Winchester consolidation is defeated; White River 382-674; Winchester 1450-346
3/21/1950	Journal-Herald	Schools	White River-Winchester consolidation petitions in circulation
9/30/1954	Journal-Herald	Schools	White River-Winchester consolidation proposed
10/7/1954	Journal-Herald	Schools	White River-Winchester consolidation proposed

Date	Source	Category	Description
4/13/1950	Journal-Herald	Schools	White River-Winchester consolidation would be called "Winchester Public School Corporation"
3/11/1958	Journal-Herald	Schools	White River-Winchester, petitions for consolidation as "Winchester-White River School Corporation"
10/15/1954	News	Schools	White River-Winchester, plans for consolidation to be called "White River School Corporation"
11/4/1914	Journal	Schools	Wilson, a large number of people were before Lee L. Driver relative to the location of a consolidated school in the north part of Wayne Township; addition hearing on November 10
9/13/1916	Journal	Schools	Wilson, bids awarded for schoolhouse in Wayne Township on Shockney-Conklyn land
5/3/1916	Journal	Schools	Wilson, bids for school in Wayne Township
5/24/1916	Journal	Schools	Wilson, bids for school in Wayne Township were taken under advisement
5/17/1916	Journal	Schools	Wilson, bids on Saturday for a school in Wayne Township
6/7/1916	Journal	Schools	Wilson, building of delayed
7/24/1944	News	Schools	Wilson, consolidated with Wayne in 1939; plans to sell
9/14/1916	Democrat	Schools	Wilson, contract let for centralized school
9/13/1916	Journal	Schools	Wilson, contract to on Saturday to Charles Sanders for $16,557; plumbing to Tibbetts and Brown; heating and ventilating to W. H. Johnson and Son for $2,356; total is $18,764
10/21/1914	Journal	Schools	Wilson, fear of an addition at Wayne School has led to a movement to build a centralized school in the northern part of the township
12/9/1914	Journal	Schools	Wilson, Lee L. Driver ruled on site of school in northern Wayne Township
10/29/1914	Democrat	Schools	Wilson, new school site to combine No. 2 and No. 10
5/11/1916	Democrat	Schools	Wilson, new school will combine Districts 1, 2, 10, and part of Harrisville
10/28/1914	Herald	Schools	Wilson, plans for a new school site for Wayne No. 2 and No. 10
5/23/1917	Journal	Schools	Wilson, Wayne Township v. Norman Shockney for schoolhouse land condemnation; ruling for defendants
3/23/1904	Herald	Schools	Winchester and Union City High Schools will play a basketball game on March 25, 1904
11/29/1866	Journal	Schools	Winchester and White River teachers listed

Date	Source	Category	Description
12/3/1969	News-Gazette	Schools	Winchester Community adds wrestling; Union City and Union have had it for several years
4/15/1969	Journal-Herald	Schools	Winchester Community High School dedication Sunday
4/9/1969	Journal-Herald	Schools	Winchester Community High School will be dedicated Sunday by Dr. George F. Ostheimer, former superintendent of Indianapolis Public Schools, who began his teaching career in Ward Township; cost $2,848,839
12/16/1969	News-Gazette	Schools	Winchester Community High School, Girls Athletic Association organized
4/9/1980	News-Gazette	Schools	Winchester Community High School, Nyle O. Fox named principal
6/28/1976	News-Gazette	Schools	Winchester Community High School, Richard Valandingham starts as principal
5/21/1976	News-Gazette	Schools	Winchester Community High School, Robert G. Jones retires as principal; started at Huntsville in 1933; became principal in 1939; Greenfield (1956-57), Winchester (1957-76)
2/26/1974	News-Gazette	Schools	Winchester Fieldhouse takes on new look in 23rd year
6/12/1878	Journal	Schools	Winchester Friends Church, public primary grades taught there
4/19/1923	Journal-Herald	Schools	Winchester H. S. addition contract awarded to W. T. Roush, heating, plumbing, and electrical to H. F. Hobbick; total cost $100,000; 70 x 122
9/9/1923	Journal-Herald	Schools	Winchester H. S., addition planned
9/27/1952	Journal-Herald	Schools	Winchester had football in 1895
1/21/1857	Journal	Schools	Winchester had seminary and new district schoolhouse on South Meridian
4/12/1973	News-Gazette	Schools	Winchester High School being razed
4/20/1973	News-Gazette	Schools	Winchester High School being razed
2/12/1908	Herald	Schools	Winchester High School has girls' basketball team
9/26/1936	Daily News	Schools	Winchester High School new song, words to
1/31/1924	Journal-Herald	Schools	Winchester High School occupies new addition
5/15/1956	Journal-Herald	Schools	Winchester High School songs
6/14/1926	Daily News	Schools	Winchester High School, A. R. Williams is new principal
6/17/1926	Democrat	Schools	Winchester High School, A. R. Williams is new principal, lives north of Farmland
8/15/1900	Journal	Schools	Winchester High School, Amos Maple resigned as principal

Date	Source	Category	Description
4/28/1936	News-Democrat	Schools	Winchester High School, Buell E. Crum succeeds C. G. Lawler as principal
7/11/1883	Journal	Schools	Winchester High School, C. H. Wood is new principal
7/22/1885	Journal	Schools	Winchester High School, C. H. Wood resigns as principal
12/15/1969	News-Gazette	Schools	Winchester High School, contents sold at auction; class composites sold
4/3/1973	News-Gazette	Schools	Winchester High School, demolition
10/9/1901	Journal	Schools	Winchester High School, football games against Muncie and Richmond
6/27/1917	Herald	Schools	Winchester High School, Fred Shaw will succeed C. E. McKinney as principal
5/16/1883	Journal	Schools	Winchester High School, H. W. Bowers elected principal
1/27/1892	Journal	Schools	Winchester High School, H. W. Bowers is principal
6/6/1883	Journal	Schools	Winchester High School, H. W. Bowers resigned as principal to become county superintendent
7/14/1880	Journal	Schools	Winchester High School, Henry Bowers starts as principal
5/28/1903	Democrat	Schools	Winchester High School, history since 1867
1/22/1925	Democrat	Schools	Winchester High School, J. H. Eiler starts as principal
3/27/1863	Journal	Schools	Winchester High School, John Cooper, principal
7/17/1973	News-Gazette	Schools	Winchester High School, last of old building is being razed
8/29/1900	Journal	Schools	Winchester High School, Lee L. Driver promoted to principal
7/20/1898	Journal	Schools	Winchester High School, new building
9/24/1936	Daily News	Schools	Winchester High School, new song written by Beldon Leonard
8/22/1900	Journal	Schools	Winchester High School, school board has applications for principal's position from Massachusetts, Wisconsin, and Virginia
6/1/1898	Journal	Schools	Winchester High School, W. S. Kaufman will design new school
2/10/1937	Daily News	Schools	Winchester joined IHSAA in 1904; played in first tourney in 1920 at Muncie
7/9/1946	Journal-Herald	Schools	Winchester new school building planned
6/23/1875	Journal	Schools	Winchester School Board consists of Marion Way, W. E. Murray, and T. W. Kizer
8/12/1914	Herald	Schools	Winchester School Board consists of Philip Kabel, W. J. Purdy, and D. F. Hardman

6/12/1901	Journal	Schools	Winchester School Board is composed of T. A. Helms, T. F. Moorman, J. P. Goodrich
6/8/1904	Journal	Schools	Winchester School Board is comprised of Dr. Milligan, T. F. Moorman, and J. P. Goodrich
8/5/1914	Journal	Schools	Winchester School Board is comprised on Philip Kabel, W. J. Purdy, and D. F. Hardman
5/27/1874	Journal	Schools	Winchester School Board, A. J. Stakebake and Marion Way appointed school trustees; Way to replace A. R. Hiatt
3/26/1879	Journal	Schools	Winchester School Board, A. R. Hiatt replaces F. M. Way
6/5/1889	Herald	Schools	Winchester School Board, A. S. Hiatt replaces T. S. Gordon on school board
6/10/1914	Herald	Schools	Winchester School Board, C. E. Milligan's three-year term is expiring
6/24/1914	Herald	Schools	Winchester School Board, D. F. Hardman replaces C. E. Milligan
6/25/1914	Democrat	Schools	Winchester School Board, D. F. Hardman replaces C. E. Milligan
10/15/1884	Journal	Schools	Winchester School Board, Daniel Lesley appointed to replace J. L. Stakebake
6/23/1915	Herald	Schools	Winchester School Board, E. S. Goodrich replaces W. J. Purdy for three year term
4/23/1873	Journal	Schools	Winchester School Board, first board ever is comprised of T. W. Kizer, L. J. Monks, and J. M. Hodson
6/6/1907	Democrat	Schools	Winchester School Board, H. E. McNees succeeds James P. Goodrich
6/11/1925	Democrat	Schools	Winchester School Board, J. L. Turner is appointed to replace Charles H. Davis
11/14/1894	Herald	Schools	Winchester School Board, J. P. Goodrich elected to school board
6/13/1894	Herald	Schools	Winchester School Board, new school board consists of J. W. Bishop, A. O. Marsh, C. W. Diggs
6/11/1913	Journal	Schools	Winchester School Board, Philip Kabel is reelected to Winchester School Board for a three year term
6/8/1910	Herald	Schools	Winchester School Board, Philip Kabel replaces H. E. McNees on school board
6/14/1916	Herald	Schools	Winchester School Board, Phillip Kabel reelected
4/2/1879	Journal	Schools	Winchester School Board: A. R. Hiatt, William Moore, J. L. Stakebake
6/14/1899	Journal	Schools	Winchester School Board: C. W. Diggs, J. W. Bishop, J. P. Goodrich
6/12/1895	Journal	Schools	Winchester School Board: C. W. Diggs, T. S. Gordon, J. E. Goodrich

Date	Source	Category	Description
6/13/1894	Journal	Schools	Winchester School Board: Calvin Diggs elected
6/10/1896	Journal	Schools	Winchester School Board: Calvin W. Diggs, T. S. Gordon, J. P. Goodrich
6/27/1883	Journal	Schools	Winchester School Board: Dr. Chenoweth, C. E. Magee, J. L. Stakebake
6/20/1888	Journal	Schools	Winchester School Board: Dr. J. T. Chenoweth, T. S. Gordon, W. W. Canada
6/27/1877	Journal	Schools	Winchester School Board: J. L. Stakebake, F. M. Way, William Moore
6/8/1887	Journal	Schools	Winchester School Board: J. T. Chenoweth replaces W. W. Canada
6/15/1881	Journal	Schools	Winchester School Board: J. T. Chenoweth, J. L. Stakebake, William Moore
6/8/1898	Journal	Schools	Winchester School Board: J. W. Bishop, C. W. Diggs, and J. P. Goodrich
6/15/1892	Journal	Schools	Winchester School Board: J. W. Bishop, J. M. Carver, and C. W. Moore
1/11/1882	Journal	Schools	Winchester School Board: Jesse Bates replaces William Moore
6/9/1886	Journal	Schools	Winchester School Board: Thomas Gordon replaced C. E. Magee
6/13/1888	Journal	Schools	Winchester School Board: W. W. Canada replaces Dan Lesley
6/10/1885	Journal	Schools	Winchester School Board: W. W. Canada, Daniel Lesley, C. E. Magee
6/16/1886	Journal	Schools	Winchester School Board: W. W. Canada, Daniel Lesley, Thomas Gordon
6/11/1884	Journal	Schools	Winchester School Board: W. W. Canada, J. L. Stakebake, C. E. Magee
6/16/1886	Herald	Schools	Winchester School Board: W. W. Canada, T. S. Gordon, Daniel Lesley
6/12/1889	Journal	Schools	Winchester School Board: A. R. Hiatt replaces T. S. Gordon
9/5/1900	Journal	Schools	Winchester school boundaries described
1/18/1941	Daily News	Schools	Winchester Seminary and other schools remembered by George Keller
7/5/1917	Democrat	Schools	Winchester Seminary was founded in 1842 (obituary)
6/7/1911	Herald	Schools	Winchester Seminary, Catalogue for 1850 described
4/11/1877	Journal	Schools	Winchester Seminary, Charlie Price has deed trouble on Woolen Mills/Old Seminary
10/9/1968	Journal-Herald	Schools	Winchester Seminary, established before 1827; new building built in 1841 by George W. Moore for $2200

428

Date	Source	Category	Description
1/13/1865	Journal	Schools	Winchester Seminary, Oliver White, principal
9/24/1957	Journal-Herald	Schools	Winchester Seminary, photos; Philip Kabel
8/19/1858	Journal	Schools	Winchester Seminary, trustees listed
3/14/1861	Journal	Schools	Winchester South District, Amanda Way, teacher
7/28/1939	Journal-Herald	Schools	Winchester South Ward School razed 17 years ago
4/19/1882	Journal	Schools	Winchester teachers listed
5/14/1890	Journal	Schools	Winchester teachers listed
6/21/1899	Journal	Schools	Winchester teachers listed
6/3/1896	Journal	Schools	Winchester teachers listed
6/8/1898	Journal	Schools	Winchester teachers listed
6/9/1897	Journal	Schools	Winchester teachers listed
9/13/1899	Journal	Schools	Winchester teachers listed
12/21/1904	Journal	Schools	Winchester versus Union City high school basketball game on Thursday
1/12/1981	News-Gazette	Schools	Winchester won third straight county wrestling title
5/21/1966	Journal-Herald	Schools	Winchester, "end of an era," Winchester High School to be abandoned
8/28/1907	Journal	Schools	Winchester, "lot sale" around Willard School
4/14/1915	Herald	Schools	Winchester, 1885 bell from Central School moved to new high school building
9/10/1982	News-Gazette	Schools	Winchester, 1951, early football team
8/8/1900	Herald	Schools	Winchester, Amos Maple resigns as high school principal
9/22/1959	Journal-Herald	Schools	Winchester, Baker dedication; Lee Driver was main speaker
9/19/1959	Journal-Herald	Schools	Winchester, Baker School to be dedicated on September 20
9/18/1959	News	Schools	Winchester, Baker School will be dedicated Sunday; cost $241,071.56
9/23/1958	Journal-Herald	Schools	Winchester, Baker School will cost $245,071; 17,437 square feet
9/21/1959	News	Schools	Winchester, Baker, 1500 attend open house
4/17/1959	News	Schools	Winchester, Baker, construction
4/2/1970	News-Gazette	Schools	Winchester, Baker, Dale Braun retires as principal
5/20/1970	News-Gazette	Schools	Winchester, Baker, Eugene Richardson named principal
5/14/1958	News	Schools	Winchester, Baker, new school is to be named for Oscar R. Baker; construction will start in October
10/29/1958	News	Schools	Winchester, Baker, work progresses
8/4/1951	Journal-Herald	Schools	Winchester, Beck, Merritt named high school principal

Date	Source	Category	Description
8/2/1955	Journal-Herald	Schools	Winchester, Beck, Merritt named superintendent; Lee G. Glentzer named high school principal
7/21/1870	Journal	Schools	Winchester, bell, new bell purchased for schoolhouse, 400 pounds; $167
7/25/1950	Journal-Herald	Schools	Winchester, bids for gym construction
1/29/1890	Herald	Schools	Winchester, bids for new schoolhouse
4/4/1906	Journal	Schools	Winchester, bids taken for "west side" school [Willard]
6/28/1893	Journal	Schools	Winchester, Bowers is superintendent; Baker is principal
9/25/1984	News-Gazette	Schools	Winchester, boys county cross country champions
7/26/1951	Journal-Herald	Schools	Winchester, Braun, Dale H. named superintendent
4/5/1917	Democrat	Schools	Winchester, brick schoolhouse near city power house along Big 4 has been razed; was on Jaqua lot and will be replaced by a canning factory
8/31/1937	Journal-Herald	Schools	Winchester, Buell Crum resigns as high school principal
8/25/1861	Journal	Schools	Winchester, C. A. Avery got contract for new schoolhouse; cost $1264 and to be completed by December 1861
4/29/1891	Journal	Schools	Winchester, C. H. Wood resigned as superintendent; will be superintendent at New Harmony
3/10/1915	Journal	Schools	Winchester, Central School being razed
7/16/1914	Democrat	Schools	Winchester, Central School condemned
3/10/1915	Herald	Schools	Winchester, Central School is being razed; lodges are moved to the third floor of the Randolph County Bank
5/10/1916	Journal	Schools	Winchester, Central, bricks from school are used in new Morton School
2/23/1915	Journal	Schools	Winchester, Central, history of; to be razed to make room for public library
11/18/1885	Journal	Schools	Winchester, Central, new bell, 700 pounds
3/11/1915	Democrat	Schools	Winchester, Central, old school is being razed; school bell to high school building
9/14/1892	Journal	Schools	Winchester, Central, school is closed; bell is rung there; but there is no school
8/19/1914	Journal	Schools	Winchester, city school board purchased houses in the north part of the city to build school [Morton]
8/15/1861	Journal	Schools	Winchester, contract for brick schoolhouse, No. 9, in north part of Winchester, to be let
5/15/1984	News-Gazette	Schools	Winchester, county boys' and girls' track champions
5/3/1952	Journal-Herald	Schools	Winchester, county track champions

Date	Source	Category	Description
6/24/1941	Journal-Herald	Schools	Winchester, Dale Braun named principal of Winchester High School
4/13/1963	Journal-Herald	Schools	Winchester, Driver Junior High and White River Elementary; addition completed last fall at a cost of $412,605.43
4/20/1962	News	Schools	Winchester, Driver Junior High School, construction progresses
2/13/1962	Journal-Herald	Schools	Winchester, Driver Junior High, frame is up on addition
10/27/1959	Journal-Herald	Schools	Winchester, Driver Junior High; Blue Hawks will be mascot; colors are blue and white
9/17/1959	Journal-Herald	Schools	Winchester, Driver, Golden Falcons will be mascot; gold and white will be colors; other choices were dragons, golden dragons, and tigers
9/10/1959	Journal-Herald	Schools	Winchester, Driver, new school song
4/18/1877	Journal	Schools	Winchester, E. H. Butler, new superintendent; H. W. Bowers is in grammar school
4/27/1898	Journal	Schools	Winchester, East Ward, destroyed by fire
10/23/1889	Journal	Schools	Winchester, East Ward, new schoolhouse will be built on Quaker Hill; will have eight rooms; Wing and Mahaisin of Fort Wayne are architects; no work until spring
1/29/1890	Journal	Schools	Winchester, East Ward, notice to bidders
7/24/1889	Journal	Schools	Winchester, East Ward, plans for eight-room school in southeast part of town
2/18/1891	Journal	Schools	Winchester, East Ward, school opened in new schoolhouse last Monday
12/19/1940	Journal-Herald	Schools	Winchester, effective March 15, 1941, Philip M. Wesner succeeds Ellis H. Bell as superintendent
4/24/1936	News-Democrat	Schools	Winchester, Ellis Bell named superintendent to replace A. R. Williams, deceased
6/10/1891	Journal	Schools	Winchester, F. S. Caldwell promoted from principal to superintendent
12/5/1947	News	Schools	Winchester, Field House planned
9/6/1876	Journal	Schools	Winchester, Friends Church basement is fitted with school desks
1/30/1889	Journal	Schools	Winchester, Friends Church basement used for public school classes
4/11/1867	Journal	Schools	Winchester, graded school building to be completed
10/14/1914	Journal	Schools	Winchester, ground purchased for school earlier in year [Morton]
4/17/1924	Democrat	Schools	Winchester, growth of school system
6/17/1891	Journal	Schools	Winchester, H. W. Bowers named principal of high school

Date	Source	Category	Description
7/13/1892	Journal	Schools	Winchester, H. W. Bowers promoted from principal to superintendent
7/13/1892	Journal	Schools	Winchester, H. W. Bowers will succeed F. S. Caldwell as superintendent
6/16/1897	Journal	Schools	Winchester, Henry Peacock is here to replace Lee L. Driver, who was promoted
7/13/1892	Herald	Schools	Winchester, Henry W. Bowers elected superintendent of schools; was twice principal of high school
4/27/1898	Herald	Schools	Winchester, high school building burned Sunday morning
7/13/1946	Journal-Herald	Schools	Winchester, history of schools
6/9/1915	Herald	Schools	Winchester, history of schools
11/16/1887	Herald	Schools	Winchester, history of schools since 1870
5/8/1901	Journal	Schools	Winchester, Jesse Moorman has purchased the red schoolhouse on North Main Street; will make it into a dwelling
8/28/1952	Journal-Herald	Schools	Winchester, joins Mississinewa Valley Conference
7/4/1894	Journal	Schools	Winchester, list of teachers; Bowers, superintendent
10/22/1879	Journal	Schools	Winchester, list of teachers; E. H. Butler, superintendent
12/10/1859	Journal	Schools	Winchester, meeting held to advocate erection of new graded school
12/30/1915	Democrat	Schools	Winchester, Morton, "Oliver P. Morton" is name of new school
8/19/1914	Herald	Schools	Winchester, Morton, a new school will be build on Residence Street
8/3/1956	News	Schools	Winchester, Morton, addition at Morton will cost $140,000
1/15/1957	Journal-Herald	Schools	Winchester, Morton, addition contracts signed for $114,580.86
6/19/1956	Journal-Herald	Schools	Winchester, Morton, addition costing $125,000 planned at Morton
2/25/1915	Democrat	Schools	Winchester, Morton, begin work on school
5/10/1916	Journal	Schools	Winchester, Morton, brick from Central School used in Morton
5/27/1915	Democrat	Schools	Winchester, Morton, contract awarded for school [later canceled]
6/17/1915	Democrat	Schools	Winchester, Morton, contract for construction canceled
5/26/1915	Journal	Schools	Winchester, Morton, contracts awarded
5/26/1915	Herald	Schools	Winchester, Morton, contracts awarded; Shiel-Chapin Company, construction, for $24,470; Brush Co., heating and ventilating for $4200; Hobbick Company, plumbing and electrical for $2306
5/24/1916	Journal	Schools	Winchester, Morton, cornerstone was laid last week

1/3/1917	Journal	Schools	Winchester, Morton, first used on January 2; students transferred from North Ward and old Christian Church
1/5/1915	Journal	Schools	Winchester, Morton, is name of new school
8/26/1914	Herald	Schools	Winchester, Morton, J. P. Goodrich donates tract for playground
8/20/1914	Democrat	Schools	Winchester, Morton, James P. Goodrich donates playground
1/19/1973	News-Gazette	Schools	Winchester, Morton, John Kidder has been principal since 1954
5/24/1976	News-Gazette	Schools	Winchester, Morton, John Kidder retires as principal
5/15/1976	News-Gazette	Schools	Winchester, Morton, John Kidder was principal from 1938-48 and since 1954
8/22/1984	News-Gazette	Schools	Winchester, Morton, mascot is devil or red devil
1/5/1916	Journal	Schools	Winchester, Morton, new school will be "Oliver P. Morton"
5/12/1915	Journal	Schools	Winchester, Morton, notice to contractors
1/3/1917	Herald	Schools	Winchester, Morton, Oliver P. Morton School Building opened Monday
10/7/1957	News	Schools	Winchester, Morton, open house was held on October 6 for addition
6/9/1976	News-Gazette	Schools	Winchester, Morton, Phil Wray replaces John Kidder as principal
10/14/1914	Herald	Schools	Winchester, Morton, school board will sell houses to make room for new school
12/28/1916	Democrat	Schools	Winchester, Morton, school will open
5/4/1916	Democrat	Schools	Winchester, Morton, work on new building
1/22/1863	Journal	Schools	Winchester, New brick schoolhouse in north part of Winchester
1/21/1858	Journal	Schools	Winchester, new district schoolhouse recently seated by M. A. Reeder
10/12/1951	News	Schools	Winchester, new gym may be ready by January 1
2/14/1952	Journal-Herald	Schools	Winchester, new gym will be used for first time on Saturday; cost $270,000
10/13/1949	Journal-Herald	Schools	Winchester, new high school addition
11/8/1923	Democrat	Schools	Winchester, new high school addition is 75 x 122
4/19/1923	Democrat	Schools	Winchester, new high school addition is assured; auditorium and gymnasium will cost about $98,000
12/8/1921	Democrat	Schools	Winchester, new high school is being sought
9/20/1899	Herald	Schools	Winchester, new schoolhouse

Date	Source	Category	Description
11/5/1879	Journal	Schools	Winchester, new schoolhouse to be occupied on Monday, November 24 by grades 1-4; old building kept; Friends Church to no longer be used for school purposes
2/18/1891	Journal	Schools	Winchester, New schoolhouse was opened last Monday, housing grades 1, 5, 6, 7, 8
10/25/1882	Journal	Schools	Winchester, North Ward, brick work on new schoolhouse is nearly done
6/4/1914	Democrat	Schools	Winchester, North Ward, condemned
2/25/1920	Herald	Schools	Winchester, North Ward, converted into glove factor
12/5/1883	Journal	Schools	Winchester, North Ward, cost $4600
5/3/1882	Journal	Schools	Winchester, North Ward, new schoolhouse planned in northern part of Winchester
8/3/1956	News	Schools	Winchester, North Ward, photo and article
6/3/1914	Herald	Schools	Winchester, North Ward, school condemned
8/15/1883	Journal	Schools	Winchester, North Ward, schoolhouse is ready for use
6/28/1882	Journal	Schools	Winchester, North Ward, work on new school will begin soon
5/22/1895	Herald	Schools	Winchester, O. R. Baker replaces H. W. Bowers as superintendent
4/16/1954	News	Schools	Winchester, old gym will be remodeled into auditorium
12/20/1968	Journal-Herald	Schools	Winchester, old high school will be razed when new building is completed
5/8/1901	Herald	Schools	Winchester, old schoolhouse on North Main Street sold to J. T. Moorman; built in 1861 by Charles Avery; will be made into a house
6/5/1895	Journal	Schools	Winchester, Oscar Baker promoted to superintendent; Amos Maple promoted to high school principal
5/7/1931	Democrat	Schools	Winchester, Oscar Baker retires as superintendent; A. R. Williams replaces him
7/20/1892	Journal	Schools	Winchester, Oscar R. Baker, of Knightstown, will succeed Bowers as principal of Winchester High School
5/16/1883	Journal	Schools	Winchester, petition to teach German in the schools
5/19/1956	Journal-Herald	Schools	Winchester, Phillip Kabel gives history of schools
5/6/1896	Journal	Schools	Winchester, plan to purchase Lot 3, NW Square for school
2/11/1891	Herald	Schools	Winchester, primary classes moved from Friends Church to new school on Quaker Hill
6/4/1873	Journal	Schools	Winchester, Professor Cooper resigned and will take charge of Richmond Public Schools

Date	Publication	Category	Description
6/16/1886	Journal	Schools	Winchester, Professor Wood, superintendent
11/16/1972	News-Gazette	Schools	Winchester, razing old school is not cheap
5/3/1957	News	Schools	Winchester, Robert G. Jones replaces Lee Glentzer as principal
4/21/1915	Herald	Schools	Winchester, sale of northwest corner of outlot No. 3, NW Square, then east 50 then south 182 then west 50 feet
3/9/1973	News-Gazette	Schools	Winchester, school bell, history of
1/22/1958	News	Schools	Winchester, school board plans for new Central Elementary School [Baker] and new Willard Elementary School
9/5/1900	Herald	Schools	Winchester, school boundaries
9/12/1900	Herald	Schools	Winchester, school boundaries, revised
5/12/1880	Journal	Schools	Winchester, school officials listed
1/21/1858	Journal	Schools	Winchester, schools described: Seminary; Miss Way teaches at new district schoolhouse; Miss A. E. Brice teaches on South Meridian Street
9/11/1907	Herald	Schools	Winchester, sixth and seventh grades at Willard
6/3/1908	Herald	Schools	Winchester, South Ward School purchased by Goodrich Brothers to raze and use material for elevator repair
8/20/1879	Journal	Schools	Winchester, South Ward, brick work begins on new schoolhouse
8/11/1915	Journal	Schools	Winchester, South Ward, city will donate site to city for a park
5/18/1922	Democrat	Schools	Winchester, South Ward, lot is made into a park
11/5/1879	Journal	Schools	Winchester, South Ward, new schoolhouse is about completed; all students south of Franklin Street will go there; use of Friends Church as a schoolhouse will be discontinued
10/29/1879	Journal	Schools	Winchester, South Ward, new schoolhouse is enclosed
10/15/1879	Journal	Schools	Winchester, South Ward, new schoolhouse will soon be ready
10/1/1879	Journal	Schools	Winchester, South Ward, plastering
4/20/1881	Journal	Schools	Winchester, teachers for next year listed
5/22/1895	Journal	Schools	Winchester, teachers listed
6/6/1888	Journal	Schools	Winchester, teachers listed
8/24/1892	Journal	Schools	Winchester, teachers listed; discussion of new building

Date	Source	Category	Description
8/3/1881	Journal	Schools	Winchester, the schoolhouse that stood near the water station, west of town, has been moved to the corner of Phil Lykens' farm, on the Windsor Pike. Mr. Tripp intends to have a new house erected on Mrs. Goodrich's farm, one mile west of where this house formerly stood
7/24/1951	Journal-Herald	Schools	Winchester, Wesner, Philip M. resigns as superintendent
10/11/1971	News-Gazette	Schools	Winchester, Willard will be dedicated on October 17 by John I. Loughlin, State Superintendent of Public Instruction
4/5/1906	Democrat	Schools	Winchester, Willard, bids received on school building
8/15/1906	Herald	Schools	Winchester, Willard, building is nearing completion
5/10/1905	Journal	Schools	Winchester, Willard, city condemned land for school on west side of town
10/15/1969	Journal-Herald	Schools	Winchester, Willard, construction begins on new building
4/4/1906	Herald	Schools	Winchester, Willard, contract for school was not let
10/18/1971	News-Gazette	Schools	Winchester, Willard, dedication
9/22/1971	News-Gazette	Schools	Winchester, Willard, dedication planned for October 17
10/23/1969	Journal-Herald	Schools	Winchester, Willard, groundbreaking was October 22
1/31/1917	Journal	Schools	Winchester, Willard, John Stine resigns as principal
2/1/1917	Democrat	Schools	Winchester, Willard, John Stine, principal, resigns
4/6/1970	News-Gazette	Schools	Winchester, Willard, new building is "growing rapidly"
8/9/1906	Democrat	Schools	Winchester, Willard, new school is surrounded by a weed patch
6/1/1970	News-Gazette	Schools	Winchester, Willard, photos of old and new buildings
8/27/1969	Journal-Herald	Schools	Winchester, Willard, plans for new school building
2/8/1917	Democrat	Schools	Winchester, Willard, Ray Wright appointed principal
2/7/1917	Journal	Schools	Winchester, Willard, Ray Wright starts as principal
2/7/1906	Journal	Schools	Winchester, Willard, school board accepts plans for west side schoolhouse
6/7/1905	Journal	Schools	Winchester, Willard, school city purchased land on west side of town; new building will replace South Ward School
6/8/1905	Democrat	Schools	Winchester, Willard, school grounds purchased
5/24/1905	Journal	Schools	Winchester, Willard, school officials will look for new location in west part of city
1/30/1970	News-Gazette	Schools	Winchester, Willard, walls are up

Date	Source	Category	Description
4/11/1906	Journal	Schools	Winchester, Willard, west side school house contract is awarded to J. M. Steel of Union City for $20,300.
6/27/1906	Herald	Schools	Winchester, Willard, work is progressing on "west side school house"
5/31/1906	Democrat	Schools	Winchester, Willard, work progressing on school
9/15/1937	Journal-Herald	Schools	Winchester, William Kingsolver starts as high school principal
1/6/1865	Journal	Schools	Winchester, work to raise funds for new schoolhouse
11/19/1953	Journal-Herald	Schools	Winchester's first football team was in 1893
11/20/1936	Daily News	Schools	Winchester-Union City, record of basketball contests since 1924
5/3/1950	News	Schools	Winchester-White River consolidation defeated by township; city 521-314; township 1190-624
10/29/1946	Journal-Herald	Schools	Winchester-White River consolidation discussed
4/28/1950	News	Schools	Winchester-White River consolidation discussed
7/25/1946	Journal-Herald	Schools	Winchester-White River consolidation to be put to vote in November
7/9/1959	Journal-Herald	Schools	Winchester-White River Schools are named for Lee Driver
6/18/1959	Journal-Herald	Schools	Winchester-White River, Metropolitan School District of, formed
11/6/1946	News	Schools	Winchester-White River, township vote blocks consolidation
6/17/1959	News	Schools	Winchester-White River; suit planned to challenge consolidation law; White River 267-710; Winchester 992-419
2/7/1863	Journal	Schools	Winter schools described at Jericho, Union City, Number Eight
6/16/1915	Journal	Schools	Witter, bids to remodel will be let on July 3
11/21/1861	Journal	Schools	Woman teacher, concern over in a winter school
7/10/1872	Journal	Schools	Wood's Schoolhouse and Thornburg's Schoolhouse, near Neff, mentioned
8/27/1913	Journal	Schools	Work permit; school attendance laws described
6/26/1918	Journal	Schools	World War I, resolution at County Superintendents' Meeting in Indianapolis to drop the teaching of the German language; also to insert loyalty clause in teachers' contracts and that no person with conscientious scruples against war be employed
6/7/1961	News	Transportation	ABC Bus Service

Date	Source	Category	Description
7/30/1919	Journal	Transportation	Airplanes, Harry Lay of Ridgeville will be the first resident of Randolph County to own an aeroplane
3/23/1971	News-Gazette	Transportation	Airport, county plans to buy it [plan failed]
11/18/1968	Journal-Herald	Transportation	Airport, Everett Cox to sell
10/5/1961	Journal-Herald	Transportation	Airport, hard surface runway at Randolph County Airport
6/4/1962	News	Transportation	Airport, hard surface runway dedication
1/4/1983	News-Gazette	Transportation	Airport, Oxleys own Randolph County Airport
7/5/1984	News-Gazette	Transportation	Airport, plane crash near
7/2/1971	News-Gazette	Transportation	Airport, sold to Virgil Oxley
9/4/1948	Journal-Herald	Transportation	Airport, Winchester Airport dedication planned
9/21/1948	Journal-Herald	Transportation	Airport, Winchester Airport will be dedicated on September 26 by Ralph Harvey
11/30/1953	News	Transportation	Airports, history of airports and landing strips in county
9/7/1948	Journal-Herald	Transportation	Airports, Winchester, old airport was "northeast of Winchester on Greenville Pike"
3/18/1957	News	Transportation	Arba, photo of tollgate
7/30/1913	Journal	Transportation	Automobiles, new license numbers arriving
5/3/1893	Journal	Transportation	Bridges, Bear Creek Bridge near James M. Addington's washed out
3/30/1922	Democrat	Transportation	Bridges, Bear Creek Church bridge, bid for work
9/3/1873	Journal	Transportation	Bridges, Bear Creek, W. G. Bundy will build bridge over Bear Creek (Walnut Corner Items)
7/6/1881	Journal	Transportation	Bridges, bridge is being built over Bear Creek at New Dayton
8/4/1875	Journal	Transportation	Bridges, Deerfield Bridge washed out [it was not, September 1, 1875]
7/2/1879	Journal	Transportation	Bridges, iron bridge at Fairview is dangerous
11/9/1887	Journal	Transportation	Bridges, new bridge at Fairview
11/28/1883	Journal	Transportation	Bridges, new bridge at White River Friends Church
3/22/1899	Journal	Transportation	Bridges, new bridge planned at White River Friends Church
7/26/1871	Journal	Transportation	Bridges, New Dayton Bridge planned
2/15/1882	Journal	Transportation	Bridges, new iron bridge on Bear Creek Road
10/12/1904	Herald	Transportation	Bridges, new iron bridge over Bear Creek at Quaker Hill
7/14/1897	Herald	Transportation	Bridges, new iron bridge over White River south of Farmland
8/21/1878	Journal	Transportation	Bridges, new iron bridge planned at Ridgeville
5/3/1966	Journal-Herald	Transportation	Bridges, photo of old bridge over White River at Farmland

8/27/1959	Journal-Herald	Transportation	Bridges, Quaker Hill Bridge collapsed
5/9/1917	Journal	Transportation	Bridges, Quaker Hill Bridge, new plank put down
10/8/1959	Journal-Herald	Transportation	Bridges, Ridgeville, dedication of new bridge on October 10
4/2/1913	Herald	Transportation	Bridges, Wright Covered Bridge is in bad repair
8/27/1914	Democrat	Transportation	Buggy, Michael Aker brought the first buggy to Winchester many years ago; it was considered a wonder
6/7/1916	Journal	Transportation	Bundy Mill Road is also known as J. G. Johnson Road
4/16/1902	Herald	Transportation	Corduroy Road, found on North Main Street in Winchester
10/28/1937	Journal-Herald	Transportation	County Roads were named
12/23/1896	Journal	Transportation	Covered bridge south of Farmland replaced
4/21/1979	News-Gazette	Transportation	Covered Bridges featured in Saturday Extra
5/21/1884	Journal	Transportation	Covered Bridges, commissioners accept
6/2/1897	Journal	Transportation	Covered bridges, covered bridge south of Farmland is being torn down after thirty years
7/8/1972	News-Gazette	Transportation	Covered bridges, Emmettsville Covered Bridge
5/5/1973	News-Gazette	Transportation	Covered bridges, Emmettsville Covered Bridge burned
7/29/1963	News	Transportation	Covered bridges, Emmettsville Covered Bridge, repaired
6/26/1958	Journal-Herald	Transportation	Covered bridges, Emmettsville Covered Bridge, sheet metal placed on it
12/10/1960	Journal-Herald	Transportation	Covered bridges, history of in Randolph County
7/4/1883	Journal	Transportation	Covered Bridges, new bridge over White River southeast of Farmland is under construction
4/4/1867	Journal	Transportation	Covered Bridges, new covered bridge, 140 feet long, is being built south of Farmland by E. F. Halliday and R. C. Shaw
6/18/1941	Journal-Herald	Transportation	Covered bridges, Steubenville Covered Bridge to be replaced
10/13/1966	Journal-Herald	Transportation	Covered bridges, Wright Covered Bridge burned
11/2/1964	News	Transportation	Covered bridges, Wright Covered Bridge, siding placed on
2/9/1971	News-Gazette	Transportation	Fairview Bridge (photo), built in 1868 to be replaced; first iron bridge in Randolph County
12/4/1912	Herald	Transportation	Farmland has first mile of brick street

10/8/1919	Journal	Transportation	Grade separation, F. M. Hubbard et al petition Trustee Comer for a grade separation at Nigger Holler; went to Public Service Commission; dismissed; railroad will probably build it
3/4/1926	Journal-Herald	Transportation	Highway 21 [now 27] will move to east of railroad between Lynn and Fountain City
11/18/1917	Democrat	Transportation	Highways, Hub Highway is being organized from Chillicothe through Greenville, Union City, Muncie, and Frankfort, to Indianapolis
3/18/1972	News-Gazette	Transportation	Highways, Lynn Bypass opened on October 26, 1971
6/19/1967	News	Transportation	Highways, Lynn Bypass planned
4/25/1959	Journal-Herald	Transportation	Highways, Lynn Bypass planned for two years in future
7/26/1922	Journal-Herald	Transportation	Highways, Pike's Peak Highway will come through Randolph County
1/14/1920	Journal	Transportation	Highways, plans for state highways through Randolph County
8/16/1926	Daily News	Transportation	Highways, road numbers will be changed on state roads to conform to the federal system
1/21/1920	Journal	Transportation	Highways, State Highway Commission in Randolph County
2/25/1920	Journal	Transportation	Highways, State Highway Commission put Randolph County in the Greenfield District
1/6/1984	News-Gazette	Transportation	Highways, State Highway Department purchases building in Winchester
9/21/1984	News-Gazette	Transportation	Highways, State Highway Department purchases building on State Rd. 32 West in Winchester
9/30/1926	Daily News	Transportation	Highways, state highway numbers will change today
1/14/1932	Journal-Herald	Transportation	Highways, State Highways planned [now 1, 36, 28, and 227]
5/26/1932	Journal-Herald	Transportation	Highways, State Road 21 [now 35] contract let
8/27/1931	Journal-Herald	Transportation	Highways, State Road 28 [now 32] renumbered as State Road 36
10/16/1980	News-Gazette	Transportation	Highways, State Road 28 between Deerfield and Union City to reopen
3/26/1979	News-Gazette	Transportation	Highways, State Road 28 between Deerfield and Union City; rebuilding begins
4/14/1936	News-Democrat	Transportation	Highways, State Road 28 entrance to Union City on Columbia in place of Plum
6/3/1936	News-Democrat	Transportation	Highways, State Road 28 into Union City is rebuilt
10/23/1935	News-Democrat	Transportation	Highways, State Road 28 to be moved from Plum to Columbia Street in Union City

Date	Source	Category	Description
12/23/1926	Daily News	Transportation	Highways, State Road 28 to be paved from Union City to Muncie [this was State Road 32]
9/15/1936	Daily News	Transportation	Highways, State Road 32 is rerouted in Union City off of Columbia Street
10/2/1958	Journal-Herald	Transportation	Highways, Winchester Bypass being constructed
8/15/1961	Journal-Herald	Transportation	Highways, Winchester Bypass is nearly complete
9/21/1961	Journal-Herald	Transportation	Highways, Winchester Bypass opens on September 22
10/25/1911	Herald	Transportation	Interurban line planned from Richmond to Portland via Union City
12/7/1933	Democrat	Transportation	Interurban, Civil Works project is the removal of the interurban tracks
6/22/1904	Herald	Transportation	Interurban, Eastern Indiana Traction (Richmond to Muncie via Winchester) is dead
8/28/1901	Journal	Transportation	Interurban, electric traction line first planned through Randolph County
9/13/1917	Democrat	Transportation	Interurban, Farmland IUT store room and car house burned last week
5/8/1918	Journal	Transportation	Interurban, Farmland, new station opened on South Main Street
9/28/1904	Journal	Transportation	Interurban, first car
9/14/1904	Herald	Transportation	Interurban, first car ran last Thursday
8/9/1905	Herald	Transportation	Interurban, first traction car from Muncie to Winchester
11/30/1904	Journal	Transportation	Interurban, first traction car to Farmland
6/20/1917	Journal	Transportation	Interurban, Germany, a stop on the IUT east of Winchester, will have a new name
5/23/1978	News-Gazette	Transportation	Interurban, Hiatt Station photo; also W. J. Davisson
5/24/1981	News-Gazette	Transportation	Interurban, history and photos
2/28/1906	Herald	Transportation	Interurban, IUT depot at Green Road, west of town, is completed
1/30/1930	Democrat	Transportation	Interurban, IUT line to be abandoned
6/12/1907	Herald	Transportation	Interurban, IUT Station north of Harrisville built; called "Germany"
5/20/1914	Herald	Transportation	Interurban, new efforts to build north-south traction line
11/11/1903	Herald	Transportation	Interurban, plans for line from Winchester through Modoc to Indianapolis
4/29/1903	Herald	Transportation	Interurban, plans for line through Winchester from Richmond to Marion
9/11/1901	Herald	Transportation	Interurban, right of way for Richmond to Portland Traction line
8/26/1903	Herald	Transportation	Interurban, track began to be laid to Richmond for line to Marion
7/26/1905	Herald	Transportation	Interurban, Traction company rented room in Masonic Block for depot

Date	Source	Category	Description
7/23/1902	Herald	Transportation	Interurban, Union City, Winchester, and Muncie Traction Company incorporated
7/3/1930	Democrat	Transportation	Interurban, west traction station in Winchester to be converted into a filling station
12/24/1983	News-Gazette	Transportation	Interurban, Winchester Station pictured
6/20/1907	Democrat	Transportation	Interurban, Winchester, IUT office to be moved to W. Washington Street
2/1/1911	Herald	Transportation	Interurban, Winchester, IUT plans new brick depot on West Washington Street
3/1/1911	Herald	Transportation	Interurban, Winchester, IUT plans new depot
12/5/1906	Journal	Transportation	Interurban, Winchester, IUT will erect a two-story brick depot west of the Old Journal Building
10/27/1909	Herald	Transportation	Interurban, Winchester, new freight depot
2/22/1912	Democrat	Transportation	Interurban, Winchester, new station
2/21/1912	Herald	Transportation	Interurban, Winchester, new station will be built on West Washington in the spring
4/24/1907	Herald	Transportation	Interurban, Winchester, Old Harter Building on West Washington is old Traction Depot
5/10/1911	Herald	Transportation	Interurban, Winchester, plans for new IUT depot scrapped
7/15/1903	Journal	Transportation	Interurban, Winchester, powerhouse under construction
10/30/1902	Democrat	Transportation	Interurban, work begins on the line
4/24/1965	Journal-Herald	Transportation	Milligan's Curve, located on State Road 32 east of Winchester
10/8/1919	Journal	Transportation	Nigger Holler Crossing, petition for grade separation at
12/4/1965	Journal-Herald	Transportation	Old Keys Road
6/11/1913	Journal	Transportation	Pipeline, gas pipeline is being laid north of Martindale
5/4/1887	Journal	Transportation	Railroads, Bee Line water tanks
4/3/1901	Herald	Transportation	Railroads, Big 4 to be double tracked
6/26/1918	Herald	Transportation	Railroads, Big 4 to be double tracked
10/9/1901	Journal	Transportation	Railroads, Big 4, double track will be built from Union City to Muncie
6/29/1887	Journal	Transportation	Railroads, CH & D RR Surveyors were here (Richmond to Jonesboro)
7/21/1897	Herald	Transportation	Railroads, Crete Depot burned last Monday
3/1/1967	News	Transportation	Railroads, derailment at Farmland
5/3/1882	Journal	Transportation	Railroads, first train over IB & W derailed in Nettle Creek Township
6/5/1950	News	Transportation	Railroads, flashers and gates on New York Central in Winchester
2/25/1920	Herald	Transportation	Railroads, G R & I to become Panhandle Railroad

Date	Source	Category	Description
9/14/1881	Journal	Transportation	Railroads, I. B. & W. Railroad work started
2/7/1979	News-Gazette	Transportation	Railroads, IB & W history
5/3/1882	Journal	Transportation	Railroads, IB & W, stations will probably be established at Losantville, Boundary Road, Washington-West River Line, Lynn, and Arba Pike
7/8/1891	Journal	Transportation	Railroads, J. E. Hinshaw surveyed proposed railroad
7/3/1901	Journal	Transportation	Railroads, Lake Erie and Louisville Railroad bed (Lynn to Union City) may be used
3/1/1977	News-Gazette	Transportation	Railroads, line from New Castle to Lynn to be abandoned
2/7/1867	Journal	Transportation	Railroads, Logansport and Union Railroad is about to reach Ridgeville
3/21/1883	Journal	Transportation	Railroads, Losantville Depot will be built on pike south of town
3/28/1883	Journal	Transportation	Railroads, Losantville Depot, frame was completed Monday
2/4/1914	Journal	Transportation	Railroads, Losantville, C & O Depot burned last Thursday
3/28/1912	Democrat	Transportation	Railroads, Lynn Depot to move
11/29/1882	Journal	Transportation	Railroads, Lynn Union Depot is nearly completed
9/6/1882	Journal	Transportation	Railroads, Lynn, I B & W erecting depot
7/13/1956	News	Transportation	Railroads, Lynn, photos of depots
12/8/1955	Journal-Herald	Transportation	Railroads, Lynn, railroad water tank razed
4/15/1903	Herald	Transportation	Railroads, Lynn, Roundhouse under construction
7/30/1903	Democrat	Transportation	Railroads, Lynn, Roundhouse under construction
6/19/1912	Herald	Transportation	Railroads, Modoc, new brick Big 4 Depot
6/19/1912	Journal	Transportation	Railroads, Modoc, new stone and brick depot planned
11/12/1890	Journal	Transportation	Railroads, new Big Four water tanks, one at Harrisville and one west of town are discontinued
5/2/1888	Herald	Transportation	Railroads, new depot in Ridgeville
1/22/1896	Herald	Transportation	Railroads, new G R & I depot finished in Winchester
12/13/1871	Journal	Transportation	Railroads, new railroad completed
8/11/1870	Journal	Transportation	Railroads, new railroad reached Winchester on Tuesday last
12/11/1889	Herald	Transportation	Railroads, new union depot in Ridgeville
8/29/1964	Journal-Herald	Transportation	Railroads, New York Central tower in Winchester is removed
10/22/1958	News	Transportation	Railroads, New York Central will close freight stations at Farmland and Modoc
11/21/1883	Journal	Transportation	Railroads, Parker depot burned

12/29/1875	Journal	Transportation	Railroads, Parker has a new depot
1/24/1983	News-Gazette	Transportation	Railroads, Parker, depot
1/20/1892	Journal	Transportation	Railroads, Parker, new depot
8/31/1974	News-Gazette	Transportation	Railroads, Penn Central to abandon tracks from Richmond to Ridgeville; announcement of the abandonment of the Modoc-Lynn line was made in February
7/12/1976	News-Gazette	Transportation	Railroads, Penn Central, Lynn to Ridgeville will be abandoned effective July 29
10/5/1966	News	Transportation	Railroads, Pennsylvania and New York Central to merge
9/22/1973	News-Gazette	Transportation	Railroads, Pennsylvania station in Winchester razed; built in 1890s
6/25/1947	News	Transportation	Railroads, petition to discontinue passenger service on north-south railroad through Winchester
9/8/1973	News-Gazette	Transportation	Railroads, photo of Pennsylvania Railroad station in Winchester
6/6/1970	News-Gazette	Transportation	Railroads, photos; no passenger service in Randolph County
6/3/1891	Journal	Transportation	Railroads, plan for railroad from Union City to Huntington via Portland (Chicago, Union City, and Cincinnati Railroad)
7/7/1870	Journal	Transportation	Railroads, Railroad crossed county line from Richmond, will reach Lynn on Saturday
6/22/1887	Journal	Transportation	Railroads, railroad planned between Lynn and Union City (St. Marys to Cambridge City)
3/5/1890	Journal	Transportation	Railroads, Ridgeville Depot opened
3/26/1975	News-Gazette	Transportation	Railroads, Ridgeville to Richmond line will cease at end of year
1/8/1913	Herald	Transportation	Railroads, Ridgeville Union Depot opened on Tuesday (January 7, 1913)
1/28/1983	News-Gazette	Transportation	Railroads, Ridgeville, depot demolished
1/9/1913	Democrat	Transportation	Railroads, Ridgeville, new depot
1/8/1890	Journal	Transportation	Railroads, Ridgeville, new depot approaching completion
9/4/1912	Herald	Transportation	Railroads, Ridgeville, new Pennsylvania depot is nearly done
5/23/1912	Democrat	Transportation	Railroads, Ridgeville, new union depot
1/8/1913	Journal	Transportation	Railroads, Ridgeville, new union depot is ready for occupancy
5/29/1912	Herald	Transportation	Railroads, Ridgeville, new union depot planned
11/11/1885	Journal	Transportation	Railroads, Ridgeville, Panhandle Depot burned Sunday
5/15/1912	Journal	Transportation	Railroads, Ridgeville, plans for a union depot
11/4/1891	Journal	Transportation	Railroads, Saratoga has new depot

Date	Source	Category	Description
7/21/1911	Democrat	Transportation	Railroads, Saratoga has new railroad station
11/2/1910	Herald	Transportation	Railroads, Saratoga, depot moved across track
5/1/1913	Democrat	Transportation	Railroads, Stone Station, new depot planned
6/22/1881	Journal	Transportation	Railroads, surveying begins for I. B. & W. Railroad
8/24/1887	Journal	Transportation	Railroads, Union City to Cambridge City, boom for railroad is dead
8/1/1912	Democrat	Transportation	Railroads, Union City, new depot
11/7/1912	Democrat	Transportation	Railroads, Union City, new depot
5/28/1913	Herald	Transportation	Railroads, Union City, new Pennsylvania Depot opens this week
11/23/1910	Herald	Transportation	Railroads, Union City, new Pennsylvania depot planned
7/23/1890	Journal	Transportation	Railroads, Whitewater Valley Railroad may be extended from Hagerstown to Losantville
7/30/1890	Journal	Transportation	Railroads, Whitewater Valley Railroad, survey completed to Losantville
4/10/1907	Journal	Transportation	Railroads, Winchester has new depot
5/27/1903	Herald	Transportation	Railroads, Winchester, Big 4 Depot built 45 years ago; history of Big 4 Depots in Winchester
1/24/1906	Herald	Transportation	Railroads, Winchester, Big 4 will build new depot
7/4/1883	Journal	Transportation	Railroads, Winchester, CCC & I freight depot being razed
10/1/1884	Journal	Transportation	Railroads, Winchester, G. R. & I. Depot has been moved to east side of tracks
7/6/1881	Journal	Transportation	Railroads, Winchester, G. R. & I. Depot will be moved to east side of main tracks
9/10/1884	Journal	Transportation	Railroads, Winchester, G. R. & I. Depot will be moved to east side of main tracks
1/29/1896	Journal	Transportation	Railroads, Winchester, G. R. & I. Depot will soon be ready
8/28/1907	Herald	Transportation	Railroads, Winchester, new Big 4 Depot opened last Friday; old depot used for freight
8/13/1873	Journal	Transportation	Railroads, Winchester, new C. R. & Ft. W. R. R. depot opened yesterday
4/17/1902	Democrat	Transportation	Railroads, Winchester, new depot is planned east of the old one; Big 4 Railroad
11/15/1906	Democrat	Transportation	Railroads, Winchester, new depot is under construction
7/16/1873	Journal	Transportation	Railroads, Winchester, new depot of C. R. & Ft. W. R. R. erected in the last week
5/4/1910	Herald	Transportation	Railroads, Winchester, new freight depot

Date	Source	Category	Description
7/29/1909	Democrat	Transportation	Railroads, Winchester, new freight depot on East Street
2/26/1896	Herald	Transportation	Railroads, Winchester, new G R & I Depot
2/19/1896	Journal	Transportation	Railroads, Winchester, new GR & I Depot described
11/13/1895	Journal	Transportation	Railroads, Winchester, new GR & I Depot planned
7/3/1895	Journal	Transportation	Railroads, Winchester, new GR & I Depot planned
5/11/1910	Herald	Transportation	Railroads, Winchester, old freight depot razed
4/7/1859	Journal	Transportation	Railroads, Winchester, railroad depot to be moved
1/17/1900	Journal	Transportation	Railroads, Winchester's railroads described
12/7/1961	Journal-Herald	Transportation	Randolph County road signs [number roads] being installed
10/6/1907	Journal	Transportation	Road districts organized and described in White River Township
8/10/1881	Journal	Transportation	Roads, Bear Creek Road is being straightened through the farms of Albert Jessup and Frank Fudge; new bridge will be built there over White River
6/12/1863	Journal	Transportation	Roads, Bear Creek Road, improvements along
9/7/1887	Journal	Transportation	Roads, Buck Creek and Buckingham Turnpike abandoned
4/27/1892	Journal	Transportation	Roads, Bundy Pike is now free
3/10/1880	Journal	Transportation	Roads, Daniel Horn secured pike from Olive Branch to Ridgeville
5/12/1886	Journal	Transportation	Roads, efforts to make Stone Station-Olive Branch Pike free
11/12/1879	Journal	Transportation	Roads, Hog Back Road mentioned
7/30/1890	Journal	Transportation	Roads, Huntsville Pike in West River Township has been purchased by the township; only five miles of toll road remain in Randolph County
11/12/1879	Journal	Transportation	Roads, Huntsville Pike is completed
2/23/1887	Journal	Transportation	Roads, Lynn Pike is now free pike
4/9/1919	Journal	Transportation	Roads, new county road law mentioned
4/16/1902	Journal	Transportation	Roads, old corduroy road found on North Main Street in Winchester
6/22/1881	Journal	Transportation	Roads, petition to join Stone Station-Olive Branch Pike to Deerfield Pike
12/19/1883	Journal	Transportation	Roads, petition to vacate old Camden Road beyond the Bosworth Pike
7/27/1922	Democrat	Transportation	Roads, Pike's Peak Ocean to Ocean Highway proposed to run through Randolph County
1/19/1865	Journal	Transportation	Roads, plans to build turnpike from Union City to Winchester

Date	Source	Category	Description
6/9/1886	Journal	Transportation	Roads, Randolph County has 130 miles of free gravel road
6/7/1916	Journal	Transportation	Roads, Randolph County's first cement road is Bundy's Mill Pike, known as J. G. Johnson Road
6/7/1956	Journal-Herald	Transportation	Roads, Rural-Urban request approved by commissioners to name, number all roads
1/16/1907	Journal	Transportation	Roads, stone roads, petitions for are common
11/19/1879	Journal	Transportation	Roads, Stone Station-Olive Branch Pike is almost done; tollgate is up at west end
10/6/1886	Journal	Transportation	Roads, Stone Station-Olive Branch Pike is now free; some old tollhouses removed
10/17/1877	Journal	Transportation	Roads, Stone Station-Olive Branch Pike is under construction
6/2/1886	Journal	Transportation	Roads, Stone Station-Olive Branch Pike, petition to make free
9/2/1908	Journal	Transportation	Roads, Stoney Creek Township is the only township not taking advantage of the three mile limit law for gravel roads
2/20/1907	Journal	Transportation	Roads, three mile road law passed; allows commissioners to improve any three miles of road without an election
3/29/1951	Journal-Herald	Transportation	Roads, Tollgates remembered
9/25/1889	Journal	Transportation	Roads, turnpike law
10/22/1890	Journal	Transportation	Roads, Union City, old tollhouse in northeast part of Union City burned Friday
5/4/1887	Journal	Transportation	Roads, Union City-Winchester Pike in White River Township will be free
9/19/1888	Journal	Transportation	Roads, West River and Washington Township and Buena Vista, Unionport, and West River Turnpikes will be abandoned
10/17/1906	Journal	Transportation	Roads, Winchester, bricking of Main Street is completed
3/25/1903	Herald	Transportation	Roads, Winchester, plans to pave Main Street
5/4/1887	Journal	Transportation	Roads, Windsor Pike and Bundy Pike still charge tolls
12/4/1889	Journal	Transportation	Roads, Windsor Pike made free; only five toll roads left in Randolph County
10/27/1960	Journal-Herald	Transportation	Roads, Yield signs are installed at county intersections [county under Democrat rule]
11/16/1906	Herald	Transportation	Winchester now has about ten automobiles
6/28/1905	Herald	Transportation	Winchester to brick streets
5/3/1916	Herald	Transportation	Winchester, first car theft ever in Winchester
8/15/1917	Herald	World War I	World War I, dependent and physical exemptions listed

Date	Publication	War	Description
4/17/1918	Herald	World War I	World War I, Henry Middleton jailed for opposition to war
9/13/1917	Democrat	World War I	World War I, J. E. Hinshaw is elected county chairman for the Liberty Loan fund
11/27/1918	Herald	World War I	World War I, John P. Clark is federal food administrator for Randolph County
7/17/1918	Journal	World War I	World War I, largest call of soldiers from Randolph County; 73 called
9/18/1918	Herald	World War I	World War I, new conscription board appointed
1/2/1918	Journal	World War I	World War I, photo of Randolph County boys at Camp Taylor
7/17/1918	Herald	World War I	World War I, servicemen leave
7/5/1917	Democrat	World War I	World War I, U. N. Davisson resigns from Draft Board
8/19/1926	Daily News	World War I	World War I, vote to paint over sign that said, "Food Will Win the War" on the south side of the Post Office Building in Winchester
5/2/1917	Herald	World War I	Conscription Board appointed: Sheriff Davisson, Clerk Gard, F. C. Focht; registrars included Lewis J. Coffin, Ira E. Smithson, Russell Addington, et al
1/29/1941	Daily News	World War II	Conscientious objectors, 23 in Randolph County, names listed
4/3/1941	Journal-Herald	World War II	Draft, no COs
5/8/1945	Journal-Herald	World War II	German surrender noted
6/11/1942	Journal-Herald	World War II	Lumpkin, R. and L. at CPS Camp
6/27/1946	Journal-Herald	World War II	World War II, list of Randolph Countians KIA, etc.

www.ingramcontent.com/pod-product-compliance
Lightning Source LLC
Chambersburg PA
CBHW071222230426
43668CB00011B/1271